Culture

The William Carey Library Series on Applied Cultural Anthropology

William A. Smalley, Editor

Becoming Bilingual: A Guide to Language Learning by William A. Smalley and Donald N. Larson, 425 pages

Culture and Human Values: Christian Intervention in Anthropological Perspective edited by William A. Smalley, 464 pages

Customs and Cultures: Anthropology for Christian Missions by Eugene A. Nida, 320 pages

Manual of Articulatory Phonetics by William A. Smalley, 522 pages

Message and Mission: The Communication of the Christian Faith by Eugene A. Nida, 253 pages

Readings in Missionary Anthropology by William A. Smalley, 384 pages

Understanding Latin Americans with Special Reference to Religious Values and Movements by Eugene A. Nida, 164 pages

Culture and Human Values:
Christian Intervention in Anthropological Perspective

Selections From the Writings of Jacob A. Loewen

William Carey Library

533 HERMOSA STREET • SOUTH PASADENA, CALIF. 91030

In accord with some of the most recent thinking in the academic press, the William Carey Library is pleased to present this scholarly book which has been prepared from an author-edited and author-prepared camera-ready manuscript.

Library of Congress Cataloging in Publication Data

Loewen, Jacob Abram, 1922-
   Culture and human values.

   Papers originally appeared in Practical anthropology, 1961-1970.
   Includes bibliographical references.
   1. Missions--Addresses, essays, lectures.
2. Communication (Theology)--Addresses, essays, lectures. 3. Indians of South America--Missions--Addresses, essays, lectures. I. Practical anthropology. II. Title.
BV2070.L58   266   75-12653
ISBN 0-87808-722-2

Published by the William Carey Library
533 Hermosa Street
South Pasadena, Calif. 91030
Telephone 213-799-4559

PRINTED IN THE UNITED STATES OF AMERICA

Contents

CONTENTS

Original Order of Publication

The order in which the papers of this volume originally appeared is listed here, together with the original volume and number in *Practical Anthropology*. This may help readers keep the papers in historical perspective, and may facilitate finding in this volume the references to the original PA publication cited in the footnotes. The papers through 1965 were written at Tabor College, Hillsboro, Kansas. The remainder were written in Lima, Peru.

Preface

During a period of several years when I was editor of *Practical Anthropology* (PA), Jacob A. Loewen was one of the most insightful and stimulating (as well as prolific) of the authors who made major contributions to that modest journal. He had a way of coming to the human heart of questions of cross-cultural Christian communication, and of stating the issues of Christian witness in an intensely personal and intensely revealing way.

I have repeatedly received requests that Loewen's PA papers be published together in a book, but I hoped that Loewen might himself write a new book which would more fully integrate his insights in a single presentation. Since such a volume has not been forthcoming, here at last are Loewen's major papers from PA. They have been collected in this way as part of a project to make the best material from PA (now absorbed into *Missiology)* more readily available to missionaries and to others concerned about the missionary task of the church.

Jake Loewen has never tried to disentangle his roles as missionary and anthropologist. Born and reared in a minority community with a strong religious culture and a long history of persecution, this Russian-born, German-speaking, Canadian-reared Mennonite developed deep sensitivity to the complexity and workings of the spirit of man and the Spirit of God. On this he built professional training in linguistics and anthropology at the University of Washington, sharpened it by teaching at Tabor College in Hillsboro, Kansas, and honed it with his observant field work as a missionary with the Mennonite Brethren Board of Missions and Services, and as a Translation Consultant with the United Bible Societies. It is an interesting commentary on "free" American society, and more particularly on academic anthropology, that this Canadian Mennonite, whose family had come to the New World as refugees from the lack of religious freedom in Eastern Europe, could not take his degree in the Anthropology Department at Washington because he was a missionary. The Linguistics Department took him instead.

To Loewen, anthropological tools and insights are all-important resources for developing a more profound understanding of people — people as human beings, people as members of society, people as children of God. Loewen the anthropologist and

Loewen the missionary are one person: Loewen the catalyst, by whose probing questions, or articles, people understand themselves better so that they can destroy the barriers among them, and between them and God.

The title of this book was carefully chosen. A sense of "human values" pervades Loewen's work. Park of his gift is the faculty for helping people see what their real values, their motivating forces, are and face up to them. In this sense he is more missionary than anthropologist, because he spends no time in forming abstract theories and models of how disembodied societies work. But at the same time, Loewen is also more anthropologist than missionary because his understanding of human values is rooted in the recognition of the behavior-molding force of human culture. People do not have their values — there are no human values — in isolation. People share experiences; they interact in patterned ways; they carry with them rules of behavior, of outlook, of interpretation. That is, people are carriers of culture, and the roots of their values and motives draw from their culture as well as from the pan-human nature of man.

We are not republishing quite all of Loewen's PA articles here.[1] A few did not fit even into the elastic framework of this volume. They will be included, we hope, in another volume of reprints from PA. The papers we did include have been rearranged, out of the order in which they originally appeared, under different categories related to the theme of "culture and human values in the communication of the gospel." The Introduction was written by Loewen for this volume and outlines the integrating assumptions and themes. The original order of the articles and the original PA references are given following the Table of Contents.

We have made no effort to reedit, rewrite or update these papers in any way. They are reprinted as they originally appeared. Where their insights are valid they are timeless, and in the impact of their honesty they are still fresh. The disadvantages of mechanical inconsistencies resulting from this process of reproduction are greatly outweighed by the fact that it is possible to make the material available at a substantially lower price than would otherwise be possible.

William A. Smalley

1. Loewen has authored numerous articles which have appeared in publications other than PA, of course. However, for the period covered by this book (1961-1970) the major thrust of his writing had its outlet in that journal. An up-to-date bibliography of Loewen's publications (over 175 items, including many reviews and some Scripture translations, primers, etc.) may be obtained from the Translations Department, American Bible Society, 1865 Broadway, New York, N.Y. 10023, USA.

Introduction

"Every tribe and culture uses one or more of these . . . ." (as I was speaking, I was pointing to the blackboard on which a simplified listing of Wissler's cultural universals had been written)[1] ". . . as the heart, the most important center or hub of their way of life. It is like the axle of a wheel, which forms the center around which the whole wheel turns. You say that you have known the missionaries for about twenty years. Can you suggest one of the items in this list which you would consider to be the axle of the missionaries' way of life?"

"Money!" the group of teachers from a South American Indian tribe exclaimed unanimously and unhesitatingly.

"But do missionaries really teach about money?"

"No, they usually talk about God and religion, but money is still the most important thing in their way of life," the teachers — all Christians — affirmed with obvious conviction.

The missionaries present were beginning to fidget, and I noticed several of them shift towards the edge of their chairs as I continued.

"How can you be so sure that money is the axle of the missionaries' way of life?"

"Because . . ." and then with devastating accuracy the Indian Christians one after another recounted personal experiences that showed how money was the ultimate yardstick (value) in both the material and spiritual areas of the missionaries' life and culture.

I was deeply intrigued and so cautiously probed farther.

"Have you ever heard of communist Russia?"

"Yes, we have. We have received quite a few communist books here in our country already."

"Have you any idea what might be the axle in the communist way of life?"

After a moment's hesitation one of the group pointed to *political structure* on the blackboard, and another quickly added *economics*. After a brief discussion the group agreed unanimously that government and money-making formed the axle of the communist way of life.

By now I was profoundly impressed and so gambled for even higher stakes. "What about your fathers and grandfathers before the missionary and the white man came; what was the axle of their way of life?"

"War," was the prompt, laconic response.

"War!" I exclaimed incredulously. "Did your grandfathers really love to fight and kill other people?"

"They had to kill because that was the only way they could get spirit power."

No sooner had the Indians mentioned *spirit power* than something in my own "innermost" (pp. 135-155) clicked, and I realized we had arrived at the crucial question: "What would have been the axle in your grandfathers' lives if they had been Christians?"

Without as much as blinking, the teachers responded: "The Spirit of God, because he . . ." Just then an audible gasp by one of the missionaries caused the speaker to hesitate for a moment, but he continued: ". . . because the Spirit of God is the most powerful of all spirits."

"And now," I continued, "that all of you here are Christians, is the Spirit of God the axle of your Christian way of life, too?"

"No," they responded, obviously subdued, "our axle now is . . . is money."

"How come? Are you not children of your ancestors? If the axle of their Christian life would have been the Spirit of God, why is it not yours?"

"Money is our axle now because that is what we have learned from the missionaries."

Later I discovered the cause of the missionary's gasp. The missionaries from several missions working with the tribe had avoided the concept of the Holy Spirit in their teaching because the tribal language offers a whole series of words that can be translated as *soul* or *spirit*, and there was strong inter-mission and inter-missionary disagreement about which of these words, if any, could be used to designate the Spirit of God. So the missionaries had taught about God, God's love, God's Son, God's justice, etc., but not about His Spirit.

The preceding encounter with the Christian Indians in the jungles of South America in 1970 aptly illustrates the title for this volume of reprinted articles. Man — whether the alien missionary messenger or the home-grown catechumen receptor of the gospel message — is a creature of his own culture. Its values — spoken or unspoken — color what he sees and hears, and determine what he says and does. If the Gospel, brought by an alien missionary communicator, is to "scratch where it itches" (pp. 3-26), the missionary not only needs to be deeply aware of the cultural matrix from which he himself comes and speaks, but he must also be empathetically knowledgeable about the culture and the values of the receptors of his message. If he is not, tragedies like the watered-down Christianity of the Indians described above, or the Shiriana use of the teaching of prayer in order to kill some men and steal some women (p. 13), are inevitable.

The articles in this book were not at first written to be grouped together in this way. A few, such as the articles on socialization and confession and role, were written as a series, but most of them were intended to stand as independent treatises of their respective themes. As a result, there is considerable overlap — the same event is cited as a pertinent example in several papers — and there also are significant gaps. There is no mention of the fact that the first response of the Waunana (pp. 111-114) has not remained simply an interesting and tantalizing experiment; there today are at least half a dozen thriving Waunana churches under the umbrella of the *Iglesia Evangélica Unida* (the official name of the Chocó church). The son of one of the Waunana men who accompanied me to the Siguirisua River has translated the New Testament into his own language, and two of the sons of another are teachers and leaders in the church today.

Furthermore, the grouping of the articles under major section headings in this book is obviously an afterthought. The "fit" of some of the articles in their respective sections can only be seen by a certain stretch of the imagination.

Although the articles may be diverse in content and intent, however, they are all characterized by a number of important presuppositions which underlie them. These are:

1. *Anthropology is not only a useful tool; it is an absolute essential for the missionary who wants to make a relevant communication of the Gospel.* In the past — and even today by many missionaries — anthropology has been considered to be highly critical of, if not basically hostile to, the missionary and his task of communicating the good news. In the articles of this volume, however, anthropological insights are seen and used as tools par excellence to make the missionary witness relevant, effective and enduring.

2. *The indigenous culture is not an enemy of the Gospel.* It need not be totally eradicated before a person can be a Christian or before a Christian church can take root and flourish in that culture. The indigenous culture is seen and used as a pre-existing but essential framework which will give meaning, support and stability both to the individual convert and to the Christian community which will make up the indigenous church.

Some of the articles contain extensive ethnographic accounts because anthropological information is seen as essential to both the understanding of the situation and to the meaningful pre-programming of the missionary message. While not spelled out explicitly, the assumption is that you can have a truly vital indigenous church only when the ideals of the culture in which it is to grow are being fulfilled by the gospel in action. The thesis of Donald McGavran's book, *Bridges of God,*[2] that social structure is the foundation not only for discipling, but also for the subsequent deepening and developing of the indigenous church as an ongoing institution, is being demonstrated again and again in these papers.

3. *That Christianity and the church can take root and flourish in any and every culture.* No matter how different the modern-day receptor culture may be from the Mediterranean or Western culture through which most people have experienced Christianity, that culture can function as equally fertile soil for church growth. This also presupposes that the missionary's culture, Western or whatever, is not totally Christian, nor even especially ideal for Christian development. It is viewed as merely one of the many possible imperfect cultural wrappers into which the gospel can fit. Therefore, the Christian missionary must become aware of the limitations which his own culture will impose on his understanding, his faith and his Christian life. If the South American Indian evaluation of the Western missionaries' culture as cited above is in any way related to

reality, then the limitation of the Western missionaries' Christianity cannot be denied, for if "mammon" rather than the Spirit of God is the mainspring of our action, then how Christian are we missionaries really?

4. *That the missionary must be prepared to learn as much as he will teach.* Men in all cultures reflect some unique dimensions of the image of God, their creator: Thus the missionary messenger, entering a strange culture, must be humbly aware that the people he wants to evangelize and teach have a lot to teach him. I must honestly confess that Aureliano (the Empera), Chindia (the Waunana), José (the Chulupi), Nito (the Lengua), and many others have taught me much about life and faith in God. I feel deeply indebted to them for their patience, because I, too, first went abroad convinced that I had the truth, if not the whole truth.

5. *The Gospel and God's concern relates to the whole man.* The Gospel and the Christian church are seen as interested in the whole man, not only his soul; and in all of his life, not only his hereafter.

6. *The incarnation, "the Word became flesh," is seen as the great example and supreme model of all cross-cultural witness.* Only as the missionary, as a human being, is willing and able to accept his own cultural limitations and his human weaknesses will he be able to sympathetically accept his fellow human beings in another culture and be able to be of genuine help to them.

Human Values in Communication

The articles included in the first section of this volume are probably the most diverse in content. The first article looks at the way culture is designed to meet man's basic needs, and shows how a culture's failure to meet these needs adequately may be an open door for the gospel. This thesis is not only hypothetical, but is documented in the last article in this section, which describes the experience of the Chulupi in the Paraguayan Chaco. They tried revolution, but found the highest and best answer in making peace with God.

Several of the papers in this section focus on the missionary messenger, his attitudes and values. At least four major principles are highlighted:

1. *Reciprocity.* Only when the missionary messenger is willing to be known as a culture-bound human will it be easy for his receptor to reveal himself as less than perfect. Reciprocity is an early version of the "I'm OK, You're OK" philosophy.[3]

2. *Sponsorship.* Only when the missionary is willing to make himself vulnerable and dependent on the people whom he wants to serve can his message become truly good news. Many gospel messages fail to achieve their purpose because they come through as only propaganda.

3. *Self-exposure.* The missionary's willingness to show himself to be the "first sinner" provides a relatively risk-free invitation to the other person to become transparent about his problems, failures and sin. Because the would-be listener-priest is already "a sinner kneeling at the cross," there is little likelihood that he will be tempted to condemn the other penitent.

4. *Catalyst.* In God's economy his messengers often play only very incidental roles in

the action they are commissioned to precipitate. Jonah proclaimed the divine judgment on Nineveh, but it was the king who seized the initiative and brought the people to repentance. So frustrated was Jonah by the absence of a further meaningful role that he withdrew to mope under a juniper bush. Likewise, missionaries are frequently called upon merely to spark or to initiate a response to God, but the moment the response has been set into motion, the messenger who occasioned it becomes obsolete. This principle is clearly illustrated in the final article in this section, "The Way to First Class."

Two papers in this section look at the missionary's counterpart — the local leader or prophet, who, ideally, is really the one to carry the ball in the spread of the gospel and in the development of the indigenous church. Both papers deal with Aureliano, one of the several men from different cultures who have made me aware of and sensitive to many of the crucial ideas expressed in these reprinted papers. Among those men Aureliano stands out as one of my greatest teachers. It was he who played the decisive role in the birth and early development of the Chocó church. Currently he is undergoing a severe crisis because his two oldest sons, caught in the insecurities of rapid culture change, have failed to follow their father's example, and both have been expelled from secondary school because of their behavior. However, Aureliano's influence in the Empera branch of the Chocó church is still crucial, and one can only hope that the burden now weighing him down will eventually be lifted.

Cultural Setting of Communication

The second section describes the entrance and impact of the gospel in four different cultural settings — the Waunana and the Empera (Chocó) of Colombia and Panama, the Lengua of the Paraguayan Chaco, and the Toba of the Argentine Chaco.

The Waunana paper poses some tantalizing questions that are not answered in this volume. As mentioned earlier, the initial response to the Gospel is only the first part of a happy story. But the growth did not come in Colombia. The Waunana were uprooted from their homes by persecution and transplanted to Panama in migration. Here, under the influence of the Empera, they made a new start and a new commitment, and today they are carrying the major leadership in the developing Chocó church.

The two papers on the Chocó of Panama deal largely with the Empera branch of the Chocó. There is not indication in the two articles that the events described form part of a long-range attempt to follow a tribal society in its experience of change from a pre-Christian hunting-and-gathering economy to a church which is participating fully in the national society. This long-range program — a kind of Christian Vicos program[4] — has in part been described in the series of articles that appeared in *Practical Anthropology* and others that are now following in *Missiology*.[5]

The articles on the Lengua and the Chulupi of the Paraguayan Chaco in this section contain much more ethnographic information than interpretation, but they provide the basis for frequent references in the two succeeding sections dealing with the development of the church in those cultures. The Lengua church is especially interesting because the Mennonite immigrants, who have settled beside the Lengua, are providing a rather comprehensive religious, economic and educational model which the Lengua are copying zealously. The presence of this model has precipitated a much more comprehensive whole-man and all-of-life approach than the mission to the Lengua had originally visualized.

In contrast to the Lengua, who are borrowing so heavily from an outside model, the Toba in the Argentine Chaco have fallen back on the models of their own pre-Christian past. Many of these models contained ingredients harmful both to individual spiritual growth and to the general prosperity of the church. A second important contribution of the Toba paper is its illustration of the important role sympathetic and sensitive missionary catalysts can play in the development of a truly indigenous church like the Toba.

Communication for Stability and Change

The third section contains three articles that were originally written as a series. They attempt to discuss the implications of socialization and social control in the development of the indigenous church, both in the initial stages and in the succeeding generations. They stress the importance of the social context for the resocialization of the adult convert, but also the problems connected with Christian socialization of the believers' children, so that they too will become convinced and practising members of the church of their parents.

The last two articles in this section discuss the indigenous church in its multi-denominational and multi-racial milieu. Especially the last article points to a problem that is very crucial for the Americas: how can a Christian church, born in a specific and often small tribe, effectively relate to the national church of a different language and different culture?

Healing Through Communication

The next section contains four papers dealing with confession, forgiveness and healing. The papers begin by showing that many tribes in their pre-Christian state had mechanisms and practices to deal with problems of sin and illness, but then that under the influence of Western church practice many of these meaningful local practices have fallen into disuse, often leaving the penitent's (or patient's) deepest needs entirely unmet. The articles in this section contain extensive examples from church life of the Lengua and Chulupi in the Paraguayan Chaco as well as the Chocó tribes of Panama and Colombia.

Missionary Method and Role

The final section contains at least two broad focuses. The first highlights several aspects of missionary method. Two principles are worthy of special mention.

The first is the use of Bible stories to construct a frame of reference or matrix that will prevent detrimental restructuring. This principle was put into practice by the Methodist church in Chile which commissioned Dr. and Mrs. R. Valenzuela to produce a Spanish Bible study course entitled *Nueva Vida en Cristo*. The Chocó church in its outreach has greatly benefited from the first-year program of this course which has appeared in print.[6]

The second deals with literacy as an evangelistic and church-growth tool. The Chocó found that there was widespread interest among their people in learning to read. They capitalized on this and responded to many invitations to come and teach people on other rivers to read. Invariably questions were asked about "God's little Word," the matrix series of Bible stories. Thus the hosts not only learned to read, but invariably also responded to the gospel message.

The article on "Mission to Smaller Tribes" tries to make the idealistic missionary aware of his long-range responsibility. The joy of giving the Gospel to a people who have never heard it before must be matched by an equal acceptance of the responsibility for the results that the first contacts can produce. The missionary needs to be aware that the minor illnesses of his children can decimate newly contacted tribes long before the Gospel has effectively taken root.

The final three articles relate to the missionary role. The paper on role and self-image deals with the broader implications of role in the daily interaction of people, both in a given culture and across cultural boundaries. It points out that there are two dimensions to the role — the expectations from the outside, and the way the person sees himself in a given role, i.e. his self-image.

The review article on the book on the *School at Mopass* looks at the missionary role and its effects through the eyes of a hostile anthropologist. Like a lance that opens a boil, it hurts, but it does reveal a lot of unsoundness. However, even when the missionary role is looked at through the eyes of observant missionaries themselves, as in the final article of the section, it becomes readily apparent that not all is well.

A number of the papers contain critical evaluation of the missionary and his work, but the criticism is always made with a strong consciousness that I too am a missionary, and that while I am stepping on the toes of others, I am standing even harder on my own. This strong identification with the missionary family is one of the reasons why so many of the articles were written in the first person.

Another reason for the use of the first person was that my time for observation in a given setting was often very short, so I did not want to describe what I saw as absolute history, but wanted to leave room for other people's interpretations. In general, I have felt called to be descriptive and illustrative, rather than to generalize and to abstract impersonal, universal principles.

Both my wife and I feel that our own mission work has been enriched by the self-evaluation these papers represent, and as they are now launched in a book we hope that they will enrich the work of others and be instrumental in helping the development of strong, healthy, self-producing indigenous churches in many societies where the Gospel is being proclaimed.

Jacob A. Loewen

FOOTNOTES

1. Clark Wissler expounded his cultural universals in his book *Man and Culture*, New York: William Crowell, 1923. His list and the adjusted expressions used in the lecture are the following:

Wissler	Adjusted
1. language	how people talk and write
2. art	painting, carving, dancing, etc.
3. knowledge and education	school
4. social organization	family and relatives
5. economic organization	how people earn money and use it
6. political organization	how people get their chief and how he commands
7. religion	how people worship and pray to their god
8. material culture	houses, canoes, weapons, and other things people make
9. war	war

2. Donald A. McGavran, *The Bridges of God*. New York: Friendship Press, 1955.

3. Thomas A. Harris, *I'm OK, You're OK*. New York: Avon Books, 1969.

4. Allen R. Holmberg, "Changing Community Attitudes and Values in Peru, A case study in guided change," in Adams, et al., *Social Change in Latin America Today*. New York: Vintage Books, 1960; and Henry D. Dobyns and Mario C. Vasquez, *The Cornell-Peru Project: Bibliography and Personnel*. Ithaca: Cornell University, Department of Anthropology, Pamphlet No. 2, 1964.

5. Other articles relating specifically to the Chocó church are "Experiencia de alfabetizacióo con los Indios Chocoes" (with Nicasio A. Vargas), *América Indígena* 23 (1963):121-125; "Anatomy of unfinished culture crisis," Supplementary Article, *Revista del Ateneo Paraguayo* 2 (1966):231-234; "From nomadism to sedentary agriculture," *América Indígena* 26 (1966):27-42; "I want to be a human being too," *World Vision* (December 1967):10-12, 28; "Missions and the problems of cultural background," in A.J. Klassen, ed., *The Church in Mission*. Fresno, Calif.: Board of Christian Literature, Mennonite Brethren Church. 1967:286-318; "The Christian encounter with culture," *World Vision* (January 1967):13, 20, 28; (February):13, 26, 30; (March):11, 22, 30, (Also published in pamphlet form); "Relevant roles for overseas workers," *International Review of Missions* 57 (1968):233-244; "El cambio cultural entre los Chocó de Panama," *Patrimonio Historico* 1 (1971):61-72, (Also in *América Indígena* 32:159-168; "Leadership in the Chocó Church," *Missiology* 1.1 (1973):73-90.

6. Dorothy and Raymond Valenzuela, *New Life in Christ Course*. Concepción, Chile: Comisión Evangélica Latino-Americana de Educación Cristiana [CELADEC], 1968.

Human Values

in Communication

Religion, Drives,
and the Place Where It Itches

A GROUP of Lengua Indians was sitting around a fire outside one of the newly erected temporary shelters in a recently settled village in Paraguay. The group was in the process of changing its nomadic hunting way of life to one of sedentary agriculture.[1]

The author, sitting with them, was making an anthropological investigation of the situation, hoping to find ways and means to facilitate this difficult transition for the tribe. He had been entertaining the group with accounts of his early missionary experience among the Chocó Indians of Colombia. Among other things he had told them about some of the cultural errors he had made when he first tried to reach that tribe with the gospel. After exposing his own mistakes at some length, he suddenly stopped and asked, "Have the missionaries who brought you the message about Jesus Christ also made mistakes like this?"

A painful silence followed. It was finally broken by the host who felt obligated to answer, "It is very hard for Lengua Indians to say if

missionaries have or have not made mistakes." The visiting anthropologist well understood the truth of this assertion, for the Lengua concept of the "good innermost"[2] did make it very difficult to criticize others. However, not wanting to lose this excellent occasion for discovering some of the attitudes of the Lengua toward the existing missionary program, he continued to press: "Maybe you could mention at least one of the areas in which there have been mistakes." After another period of silence the host answered in the Low German vernacular highly influenced by Lengua syntax, *"Es krautze woa nich es yeiche,"* which freely translated said, "They are scratching where it doesn't itch."

I have been struck by the number of missionaries in South America who confess doubts about the relevance of their preaching to tribal societies. Anthropology seemingly has helped to make them aware of the *need* for a relevant message, but many of them feel that it has not helped them make their message relevant; it has not helped them to find the place where it itches. It is the purpose of this paper to present

[1] For more detail see Jacob A. Loewen, "Research Report on the Question of Settling Lengua and Chulupi Indians in the Paraguayan Chaco," a multilithed report published by the Mennonite Central Committee, Akron, Pennsylvania, 1964.

[2] Jacob A. Loewen, "Lengua Indians and Their 'Innermost'," PA, Vol. 13, No. 6 (Nov.-Dec. 1966), pp. 252-272.

several attempts to locate the itchy spots in South American Indian societies. This paper does not propose to provide *the* answer, but it hopes to point out at least one more way of finding areas of felt need in a tribal society. It is intentionally slanted toward tribal societies, but the same principle should be applicable to more complex societies. For this reason a section on Western society has been included as well.

I

In order to understand why the missionary message often has not scratched as the missionary intended it to, we must consider several predisposing factors.

Faith and religion

All too often the American-trained, evangelical missionary approaches Christianity from the point of right belief. The missionary task is thus seen as replacing a wrong belief with the right belief. The right faith is *the* answer to man's problems. "Faith," in its current North American connotations, has undergone some subtle changes from New Testament times. For many deeply evangelical people it essentially involves mental acceptance of a set of premises or doctrines as truth, and it frequently lacks the concomitant ingredients of commitment and obedience. This means that faith has largely been separated from life.

Such an attitude is very frequently reflected in translation. In a number of the South American tribal languages the words "to believe" and "to obey" come from the same root word. In trying to distinguish between these two concepts missionaries have then translated "to believe" as "to accept as true." This, however, translates only the "static" component of faith and leaves out the most important dynamic component of personal commitment which the Biblical use of the word emphasizes.

Religion and the totality of life

Frequently, and possibly as a consequence of faith being interpreted as right belief, religious experience has been so completely separated from the totality of life that people have developed a kind of remote "spiritual" interpretation of how God works in the lives of men. Dr. Eugene A. Nida has pointed out the fallacy of this view:

Some Christians tend to think of church growth almost entirely apart from the cultural contexts in which it has taken place, as though it were some special supernatural phenomenon involving only the struggle between the forces of God and the wiles of the devil. There is no doubt that church growth is directly related to the total plan and purposes of God; but at the same time it is equally true that God has evidently determined to work within the structures and patterns of human society, even as He works out His purposes for an individual's life in accordance with the physical and psychological principles He has created to govern it.[3]

Anthropologists like William Howells have underscored the fact that religion is not just another aspect of life which can be added or subtracted at will. Religion permeates and is an integral part of the totality of life in every society.

It is, instead, a question of what there is in man, or about him, which makes him religious .... There has in the past been brisk discussion of a religious emotion, or "instinct," as the one responsible factor, and such a thing has been accepted and sought for in other supposed emotions or derivations combinations of them: awe, love, fear, shame, conscience, as well as diverted sexual or social longings, and so forth and so on ... The quest for some such factor has not succeeded ... It is (instead) a matter of certain palpable facts about man and his past which tend to show that it is not one lone element within him, but rather his whole organism and life which predispose him to "religious" behavior – which cause him to produce religious ideas and then to respond so readily to them.[4]

This inseparable involvement of religion with the totality of life and culture is again stated by E. Adamson Hoebel:

Of all the manifestations of man's intellectual and social life, none is so elusive of definition as is religion. Yet none is more important. For religion, as an aspect of supernaturalism, consists of systems of belief, thought, and action that lie at the bottom of all primitive and civilized cultures. These systems of belief and actions work upward and outward throughout the cultural fabric. At points they thread so finely into the total pattern that it is impossible to say where the religious ends and the mundane begins. Religion presents so many aspects, intertwined with so many phases of culture, and is so variable, that it is difficult to delineate it in terms both broad enough to encompass the whole, and discriminating enough to isolate it for study.[5]

Conversion and culture change

Since religion is viewed by our missionary as involving only man's soul, conversion and its concomitant change of life is seen as a merely spiritual manifestation, without realization that such change of behavior at once involves a change of culture. "Whether missionaries are inclined to admit it or not, they are profes-

---

[3] Eugene A. Nida, "Culture and Church Growth" in Donald Anderson McGavran, Editor, *Church Growth and Christian Mission* (New York: Harper and Row Publishers, 1965), p. 87.

[4] William Howells, *The Heathens: Primitive Man and His Religions* (Garden City, New York: Doubleday and Company, Inc., 1948), p. 12.

[5] E. Adamson Hoebel, *Man in the Primitive World* (New York: McGraw-Hill Book Company, Inc., 1958), p. 525.

sional agents of culture change, for there is no other way of establishing, consolidating, and perpetuating the Church in a society than through its culture.[6]

However, it is not merely a change of outward form that the missionary seeks to establish, but a basic change of heart and fundamental values. Man is to become a new creature. Thus Luzbetak continues:

Especially in spiritual matters the transformation sought is meant to be more than the mere adoption of externals that might be accepted one day and discarded the next. The transformation sought is meant to be more than the recitation of a creed and a theoretical acknowledgement of certain articles of faith or the mere adoption of a ritual. "Conversion" means a "turning" away from old ways toward new ways, a basic reorientation in premises and goals, a wholehearted acceptance of a new set of values affecting the "convert" as well as his social group, day in and day out, twenty-four hours of the day and in practically every sphere of activity—economic, social, and religious. The changes effected must become *living* parts of the cultural "organism."[7]

Sacred and secular

Preliterate tribal societies usually

[6] Louis J. Luzbetak, *The Church and Cultures: An Applied Anthropology for the Religious Worker* (Techny, Illinois: Divine Word Publications, 1963), p. 6.

[7] Loc. cit.

do not divide their daily experience into secular and sacred categories such as characterize North American Christendom today. This view defines the nurse serving in a North American hospital as just earning a living and the nurse on the mission field as being "in full-time service for the Lord."

The oneness of daily life and religious experience was demonstrated in a fascinating way by the Chocó Christians. The short-term missionaries from North America were visiting in Pastor Aureliano's house helping to complete the church building and to prepare for the organization of the first Chocó church. The whole place was bustling with activity in anticipation of the coming festivities. As part of this total complex, in the yard outside there was a large pig tied to a tree by one leg. It was to be killed early the next morning to provide meat for the fellowship meal to be held in connection with the church celebration.

That afternoon as people from far and near began to arrive there were many inquiries concerning the visitors' families. Many regrets were expressed that these families could not be present at these wonderful celebrations, and it was decided that in compensation they should at least receive greetings from the leading people who were participating in the services. These greetings were duly recorded on tape for sending to the U.S.A. When Pastor Aureliano's turn come to speak to the author's wife, he took the microphone into his hands and spoke the following words with moving sincerity, "Ana, that squealing you hear outside is a big pig. We are going to kill it tomorow to the glory of God and then we will eat, drink, and celebrate. We are all going to be happy together here at our house." It is no overstatement that most North American Christians have not had any recent experiences of "killing a pig to the glory of God." For them pig-killing, even for a church celebration, would be a purely secular activity.

Change needs a "reason"

The willingness to change religion will often depend on how well the present religion meets the daily needs. Because religion is so thoroughly integrated into the total fabric of life, there will be motivation for change only when a system frustrates an individual or a whole society at some rather crucial point. Every culture tries to achieve harmony between its parts, but such harmony is never complete. Again, all cultures are changing and very frequently even minor changes can lead to changes in the completeness with which man's needs are met by the religious system of his culture.

If and when severe frustrations, imbalances, or conflicts arise, a man will not only be willing to consider change—he will actually be looking for relief. These areas of frustration in a culture can become open doors for the gospel, for they represent, as it were, "the places where it itches." Therefore, in order to ascertain those places which would readily predispose men to listen to the Good News, it is of utmost importance to investigate the fundamental needs of man and to find out how these needs are being met by the given system. In such an investigation, the mechanisms by which a religion fills needs and the efficiency with which they fill the needs must both be considered. At times the mechanism itself creates imbalances.

Failure to provide adequate drive

Missionaries have frequently been frustrated by the shallowness of the penetration of the Christian message into the life and thought of tribal believers. Could one of the reasons for this lack of depth of penetration be that the Christian experience was not linked to any fundamental drives or needs of such a society, and that therefore the new life lacked an "indigenous source of steam" which could provide the push for deeper development of the Christian life?

But not only in the individual experience has the drive been weak; there has also been a singular failure to provide a drive for the group to evangelize its own people. James Scherer in his book *Missionary Go Home* has effectively pointed out that one of the major failings of Christian missions has been an inability to pass on a zeal for witnessing to national Christians.

There is finally a spiritual failure. By his presence the missionary should bestow on his host church the precious gift— the passion for missions, the desire to go beyond itself, the yearning to live up to the best it has seen. Missionaries have labored faithfully and tirelessly. They have spent themselves in works of healing, teaching, and evangelism. Often, though, nothing of their labors has endured. They have not succeeded in enduing the church with the zest for being engaged in God's work or for loving its neighbors.[8]

II

Some human drives

If the missionary, therefore, would actually like to have the gospel "scratch where it itches" in a culture, it would seem to be of utmost importance to isolate some of the basic needs that provide "drive" for human behavior, and to see how these could be used as channels to further rather than hinder the gospel in its penetration of life and culture. In a more specific sense this would require the missionary to study the religious culture of the area of his service in order to find out how it provides satisfaction for these basic human needs.

The thesis of this paper is in a large part based on A. H. Maslow's "holistic-dynamic theory" of motivation involving drives and their gratification. The following quotation neatly summarizes this theory:

One main implication of this phrasing is that gratification becomes as important a concept as deprivation in motivation theory, for it releases the organism from the domination of a relatively more physiological need, permitting thereby the emergence of other more social goals. The physiological needs, along with their partial goals, when chronically gratified cease to exist as active determinants or organizers of behavior. They now exist only in a potential fashion in the sense that they may emerge again to dominate the organism if they are thwarted. But a want that is satisfied is no longer a want. *The organism is dominated and its behavior organized only by unsatisfied needs.*[9]

Maslow's list of needs and drives involved in the determination of motivation and behavior includes the following: physiological, safety, love and belongingness, esteem, self-actualization and esthetic needs.[10]

He further states that these drives operate in hierarchical fashion:

Obviously a good way to obscure the higher motivations, and to get a lopsided view of human capacities and human nature, is to make the organism extremely and chronically hungry or thirsty. Anyone who attempts to make an emergency picture into a typical one, and who will measure all of man's goals and desires by his behavior during

---

[8] James Scherer, *Missionary Go Home! A Reappraisal of the Christian World Mission* (Englewood Cliffs: Prentice Hall, 1964), pp. 72-73.

[9] A. H. Maslow, *Motivation and Personality* (New York: Harper and Row Publishers, 1954), p. 84. (Italics mine.)

[10] Ibid., especially chapters 4 and 5.

Drives	Needs
ESTHETIC ACTIVITY	SELF-EXPRESSION
MENTAL ACTIVITY	REASON TO BE
PHYSICAL ACTIVITY	PHYSICAL WELL-BEING
SOCIAL ACTIVITY (BELONGING)	TO LOVE AND TO BE LOVED
SEX	PROCREATION AND FAMILY
HUNGER	PHYSICAL SURVIVAL
THIRST	PHYSICAL SURVIVAL[13]

Table 1.

extreme physiological deprivation is certainly being blind to many things. It is quite true that man lives by bread alone —when there is no bread. But what happens to man's desires when there is plenty of bread and when his belly is chronically filled?

At once other (and higher) needs emerge and these, rather than physiological hungers, dominate the organism. And when these in turn are satisfied, again new (and still higher) needs emerge, and so on. This is what we mean by saying that the basic human needs are organized into a hierarchy of relative prepotency.[11]

In the light of the above fact, Dr. E. A. Nida has recommended that the following hierarchy of biological and psychological drives, and the needs to which they are linked, can provide a framework by means of which it is possible to analyze how well a culture provides satisfaction for its participants; and if not, at

11 Ibid., p. 83.

what points and to what degree it frustrates them. The proposed hierarchy may be seen in Table 1.[12]

This list of drives read from bottom to top constitutes an ascending scale of universal drives in the light of which any culture's performance can be measured. They are stacked in this way to suggest that the lower drive must be satisfied before the next higher drive can be successfully met. If a lower drive is frustrated, distortions in the fulfillment of a higher drive are almost inevitable. It is, of course, possible to frustrate a drive and still have a positive response. Psychology labels this sublimation. Thus a young woman, frustrated in finding a husband and being unable to raise a family of her own, may sublimate her sexual needs and her need to belong by starting an orphanage for homeless

12 Eugene A. Nida in a lecture series presented at the Mennonite Brethren College in March, 1966.

13 As the title of this section suggests, only some of the human drives appear in this list. There are others such as the elimination of body wastes, etc., which have not been included in this system.

children. Again, an individual may by circumstances be located far away from the person he loves and desires sexually, so he sublimates this drive and writes love lyrics.

Frequently, however, man regresses; if he is frustrated in a given drive he will seek satisfaction at the next lower level. For example, the "Don Juan" type of male is usually a very frustrated and insecure individual who has no real sense of belonging. In order to convince himself that he is somebody and that he does have deep relationships with others, he tries to capture sexually every female he meets. Sometimes, and especially in women, frustration in the area of sex is met by a tendency to eat too much.

Two poles of satisfaction

Before we proceed to study these drives and the related needs in specific cultures, we need to point out that there seem to be two poles in terms of seeking satisfaction for individual drives. These two are generally in tension with each other. The first and negative pole is a type of egocentricity (in a tribal sense it would be ethnocentricity) which demands that the drives be satisfied here and now and to the individual's full capacity.

The second and positive pole suggests that the fulfillment is supposed to have the highest possible meaning. It is here that religion enters. Its function is to relate man to ultimate purposes—in the case of the Christian to the will of God. This certainly would be in keeping with New Tes-

tament teaching, for, speaking of the greatest commandment Jesus said, "The first is, 'Hear, O Israel: the Lord your God is the only Lord; love the Lord your God with all your heart, with all your soul, with all your mind, and with all your strength'."[14]   In fact, one of the fundamental aspects of conversion is to change man from his natural self - centeredness to Christ-centeredness.   Thus Jesus asserted, "Anyone who wishes to be a follower of mine must leave self behind; he must take up his cross and come with me. Whoever cares for his own safety is lost; but if a man will let himself be lost for my sake and for the Gospel, that man is safe.   What does a man gain by winning the whole world at the cost of his true self?   What can he give to buy that self back?"[15]

Religion functions as a component in the highest fulfillment of each of the drives listed in the chart. However, religion does not only seek to provide ultimate meaning to the fulfillment of the drives; it also restricts this fulfillment to the moral and ethical requirements of the given religious system.   As Christians we would probably add that unless man's nature is changed, it is impossible for him to live according to God's highest requirements.   But to have the desire for the highest level and then not to be able to achieve it would be frustration par exellence.   It is here that the gospel becomes relevant.   It is God's good news about how men can be changed; how they

14 Mark 12:29-31, NEB.
15 Mark 8:34-36, NEB.

can become new creatures who truly want and can live the new life, fulfilling the highest and best for each one of the needs and drives in their lives. The application of this approach to mission would therefore mean that the missionary must study the local culture in order to ascertain how individual drives and the concomitant human needs are satisfied or frustrated. Once these facts are known, they can provide him with guidelines for presenting the gospel message in a way that will "scratch where it itches."

III

The Shiriana[16]

The Shiriana (Guaica), who inhabit an area in northern Brazil and southern Venezuela, are a tropical forest tribe numbering several thousand. They are a hunting-gathering people who live in autonomous bands of approximately fifty to seventy persons. Semi-nomadic, they live and hunt in an area until the game is exhausted and then move on. They do have incipient agriculture, but seldom stay in one area for more than a year or two. They may return periodically to harvest produce from their previous plantations, but only as a part of their general hunting-gathering pattern. Missionaries flying over the jungle areas inhabited by the Shiriana have located a sizeable number of these bands. They usually live a week or ten days' journey from each other. Some groups seem to have had very little contact with others. This separation has caused extensive dialect differentiation within the tribe. In an effort to retain an inter-dialect communication vehicle the Shiriana developed a type of ceremonial chanted speech which was employed between groups who could not understand each other's normal speech. Generally the shaman or one of the older men from each of the groups separated from the rest and communicated with the representative of the other band via this medium of chanted talk. However, it seems that today only older people still know this chanted talk. Very few missionaries have observed its use in more than a decade of work among the Shiriana.

When the missionaries were asked which of the drives in the above list they thought might be frustrated in the Shiriana culture, several suggested that it was the hunger drive, for whenever one meets a Shiriana Indian at home or on the trail he will aways follow his greeting with "I am hungry." In fact, even if a Shiriana had just been fed by one missionary, he would still greet the next missionary on arrival with the same word: "I am hungry." If he were unable to consume any more food he would still use the greeting and just take the surplus food with him. Nor is it only with the mis-

---

16 The Shiriana research was carried on by missionaries from Baptist Mid-missions and the Unevangelized Field Mission. Eugene A. Nida and the author spent some time with the Shiriana in January, 1966. For additional information see Johannes Wilbert, "Los Sanema" in *Indios de la Region Orinoco Ventuari* (Instituto Caribe de Antropologia y Sociologia, Monografia No. 8, Caracas: Fundacion La Salle de Ciencias Naturales, 1963), 263 pp.

sionaries that the Shiriana do this; it is standard behavior with tribe members.

On the surface this really looks like a good indication of a concern for food, but a few questions to the informants showed that this was not the case. It was the signal that some other drive was in trouble. When informants were asked, "Why would a person say, 'I am hungry,' to a stranger?" they answered, "How can you know if a person is your friend except if he is willing to give you something to eat?" It became apparent in this way that the Shiriana was asking for food not because he was hungry but because food was a way of measuring friendship. Thus the statement, "I am hungry," was not connected with the hunger drive but rather with the need for belonging, the desire to be loved. The question now arises, "Does this indicate that the drive to belong was frustrated in Shiriana society?"

Even a rather cursory review of the situation indicated that the drive to belong was indeed severely frustrated. The bands were not only widely separated from each other geographically, but they had developed social distance to a frightening degree. The ceremonial speech mentioned earlier was employed only by the older people, and many of the younger individuals did not even know it. This indicated that the Shiriana had been experiencing a marked decrease in the number of contacts between bands for ceremonial purposes. This separation

was intensified by aggression, for the missionaries had evidence on a whole series of killings between bands. On pursuing the question of intergroup killing, informants listed two reasons why people attacked other bands : to avenge a death supposedly caused by sorcery, and, more frequently, to steal wives. The first reason, of course, was related to the drive for physical well-being, the second to the sex drive.

How, then, do the Shiriana satisfy their sexual needs? Actually there were several well established patterns.

First of all, a group could kill some male members of another band and appropriate their wives. But this would often be followed with revenge by the stolen wife's people. Why did they steal wives—because they liked to steal or because they had to? Were there cultural reasons for having to steal wives? There were both cultural and physical reasons why many men could not get wives. The cultural reason rested upon the fact that the tribe practiced female infanticide and also had certain marriage restrictions. An individual was not permitted to marry any descendents of his father's blood line. Even the parallel relatives on the mother's side were taboo for the individual. Since the bands were small it very often happened that there was a very uneven distribution of sexes. Coupled with female infanticide this often left several men for every eligible female. Formerly this uneven distribution was "solved" through frequent ceremonial encounters at which several bands got together to celebrate. At such times acquaintances were made and inter-band marriage relationships established. Now, however, in the almost total absence of friendly contact and ceremonial get-togethers, peaceful exchange was well-nigh impossible. In their desperation men stole wives from other bands; but as one band raided another for wives, an endless cycle of killing and being killed was initiated.

The precariousness of this wife-getting situation was demonstrated by one of the experiences of the mission. After some members of the band at the mission had become Christians, the missionary pointed out that one of the women who had two official husbands should really have only one according to the Scriptures. He suggested that the older man keep the wife and that the younger man find himself a new mate. Under missionary guidance this separation was now effected. Shortly thereafter the younger man took two of his brothers and several other willing men and together they made a journey of some ten days to another band of Shiriana. On arriving they told this group that they had learned to talk to God and that they had come to teach them how to talk to God also. In order to talk to God one must close his eyes, fold his hands, and bow his head. When the hosts complied, the visiting "missionaries" decapitated several of the men. The rest fled, but three women were taken.

However, there was also a way within the tribe by which a man could satisfy his sexual needs without having his own wife. The Shiriana practiced the so-called *warima* relationship. The word *warima* basically means "asking;" i.e., a man could ask a woman to establish a casual relationship with him, and if she were willing the two would become *warimas*. Interestingly enough the *warima* relationship was closely linked to food. In order to prepare for a favorable answer to such a request, a man began to give food to the woman of his choice. Once the relationship had been established he nurtured it through further gifts of food. Thus food and the sex drive were closely linked in this case.

Today the food-reward pattern in the *warima* relationship is undergoing drastic change. Trade goods are now rapidly replacing food as a means of getting sexual favors. The mission practice of favoring professed believers with employment has exposed the latter to added temptation: since they are able to get more employment with the mission, they are also able to acquire more *warima* relationships. The survey of one group showed that the average sexually functioning woman had at least three *warima* relationships.

What happened when a woman's husband discovered that his wife had established a *warima* relationship with another man? The reaction would depend somewhat on the respective status of the individuals.

If the *warima* of the wife was a powerful individual, a weaker husband might just be quiet. If they were social equals, however, or if the husband considered himself stronger, he usually made a complaint and publicly accused the other. At such times all the blood relatives of the accused individual rushed to the latter's defense denying that such a thing would ever take place. This not only involved family loyalty but it also reflected the cultural practice that individuals never discussed their *warima* relationships with anyone they called father, mother, brother, or sister. Here the missionaries had unwittingly excluded themselves from all *warima* information because they had introduced the practice followed by some North American Christian groups of calling believers "brother" and "sister."

One of the missionaries reported that when he discovered that one of his leading converts was maintaining several *warima* relationships, he had asked him why he had never been open about this. In anguish the man said, "But I couldn't talk to you about it because you call me 'brother' and one cannot talk about these things to his brother."

In order to settle the intra-tribal tensions that grew out of the *warima* relationships, the tribe had developed a tension-relieving ritual. This had a mild form (chest beating) and a more serious form (head clubbing). If a husband became angry or bitter about his wife's *warima* relationship with another man, he could challenge the latter to a chest-beating duel. The two individuals each took a large rock into his hands and then began to pound each other on the chest. The accuser always extended his chest to receive the first three blows. After he had received his blows he in turn hit the accused three times. They kept on hitting each other in turn in this way until the accuser's anger was spent. Such a chest-beating ritual was supposed to remove all the rancor and bitterness in the offended husband.

One of the missionaries reported that recently she had observed a chest-beating encounter between an older man and several younger men. Since the younger men outnumbered the older man, the latter soon began complaining that he was getting tired. So the young men took one of their number and put him on the old man's side so that they could continue beating because their feelings were still bitter.

Clubbing—the more serious form—occurred when the accuser was very angry and felt that chest beating would not be enough to remove his feelings. He then challenged the accused to exchange blows with the flat side of the war club. The accuser again extended his head first and received a blow by the accused. Then the accused held out his head and received a blow in turn. Sometimes the angry feelings subsided after several blows. Occasionally if the accused had already been knocked out but the accuser was still angry, a blood relative of the accused took the fallen person's place. The clubbing continued until the accuser's rancor was spent, he was knocked out, or the group decided to call a halt to the clubbing.

These rituals were to remove intra-tribal tensions and bitterness. In actual fact they seldom removed all the bitterness, at least for long. In several cases this ritual slugging resulted in splintering the band even more. The decrease in the size of the band in turn not only increased the danger of outside attack, but also decreased the opportunity for them to get wives. As a result there was even greater pressure for establishing *warima* relationships and more temptation to kill men in other bands in order to steal their wives. So the cycle simply became more vicious.

For the Shiriana there are thus two drives that are severely frustrated and two basic needs that are not being met adequately by their socio-religious system. These are sex and the need to belong. The most frustrated of the two is sex, but the two are in a vicious circle relationship with each other. As men try to satisfy their individual sexual needs at the expense of another band, they increase the inter-group tension, thereby making it more difficult to get wives peacefully from other bands. Or, as men establish *warima* relationships within the group, they increase intra-group tension which can either splinter the group or leave the group with serious internal tensions.

Does the gospel have anything to say to such a situation? It is the author's contention that it does. Concerning the sex frustration the Creator said, "It is not good that the man should be alone; I will make him an help meet for him."[17] Jesus reaffirmed this principle when he said, "But from the beginning of the creation God made them male and female. For this cause shall a man leave his father and mother, and cleave to his wife; and they twain shall be one flesh: so then they are no more twain, but one flesh."[18] The Scripture thus reaffirms God's purpose that man have a wife and woman a husband.

Again, the atonement of Christ—according to the Scriptures—broke down the enmity between peoples[19] and established the church—the fellowship of the born-again who truly love each other. Thus the gospel brings men the good news that their guilt can be forgiven by both God and men and that peace can be established between groups who have a history of enmity. The church in turn can provide the context in which the people can get together for meaningful fellowship to establish greater group belonging and also to form the desired husband and wife relationships without the current built-in problems.

IV

The Chimane[20] are a jungle tribe

[17] Genesis 2 : 18, AV.
[18] Mark 10 : 6-8, AV.
[19] Ephesians 2 : 14, AV.
[20] Research on the Chimane was done by New Tribes missionaries. The author spent some time with the tribe in March, 1966, and was greatly helped by Eugene Calloway.

living in the Beni district of Bolivia. They number about five thousand. Their traditional habitat was close enough to the Andean Highlands so that they came under Quechua influence during the Inca empire. Following the Spanish conquest they became one of the first objects of Roman Catholic missions because they were generally considered a peace-loving tribe. Many of the old people living today can still recall their life on the mission compound with priests in charge. There is a dearth of detailed information about the Chimane past, but the old people speak rather wistfully about the times when things were better. These "better times" they define as the times when they lived in larger groups with chiefs and other officers who kept discipline and order in the tribe.[21]   Present-day Chimane are living scattered along the various rivers of the upper Beni area.   There are no villages proper, but occasionally one finds small clusters of houses of immediate relatives living together. If more than one immediate family lives together, the houses usually cluster by families with some distance between the clusters.

The Chimane became the object of evangelical mission work some fifteen years ago. The missionaries lived with them and learned their language. At first the efforts were

rewarded by fairly good response, but gradually the missionaries became aware that distance was developing between them and the Chimane and that the latter were becoming increasingly cool toward the gospel. Here and there individuals and isolated families proclaimed continued loyalty to the gospel, but by and large there was apathy, if not hostility. Finally the missionaries became convinced that they were not meeting the need of the people. This led to a brief study by the author. The burning question for the missionaries was, "Is there anything in our approach that antagonizes the Chimane? Is our message actually irrelevant to the Chimane?" This seemed like an ideal opportunity to test the drive hypothesis proposed earlier in this paper. The following are some of the findings.

Missionary concerns

To start the investigation the missionary and the anthropologist noted a number of anthropological and cultural traits that had arrested the attention of the mission workers.

First, the missionary reported that there seemed to be a real ambivalence about the language. While the Chimane spoke their language among themselves and with the missionary when alone, they seemed to be very hesitant to use it in the presence of Spanish-speaking people. Gospel Recordings, Inc., had prepared some records with gospel messages in the Chimane language; and while the Indians were quite willing to listen to them (in fact, many were

[21] Julian H. Steward, Editor, *Handbook of South American Indians* (Smithsonian Institution, Bureau of American Ethnology, Bulletin 143, Washington: U.S. Government Printing Office, 1946), Vol. 3, p. 527, states that in 1682 the Mositene averaged 166 persons per village.

buying them) they spoke of them depreciatingly. Frequently after having purchased a set of Chimane records they would return and ask for a set of Spanish records saying that they liked the latter much better than the Chimane. The missionary felt certain that it was not the content of the message nor the linguistic quality of the Chimane records. There seemed to be a confusing ambivalence about wanting to belong to both the Chimane and the Spanish cultures.

Another item that had attracted the missionary's attention was the inter-group tension. Even during the short years of his observation there was a steady increase of group splintering. Various and sundry quarrels and disagreements caused individuals and families to separate from the group clusters. Usually they built their new home in entire isolation. Whenever a quarrel developed between two individuals, both of them tried to intimidate the other by saying such things as, "I have a lot of relatives; I am not alone! You better not tangle with me; my family will help me!" Usually, however, there was no overt violence.

A deep concern of the missionary dealt with the quality of the Chimane conversions. As stated earlier, there had been excellent interest at the beginning and a number of the Chimane had made a profession of faith, but the number of the faithful was steadily dwindling In fact, the missionary expressed serious concern about the quality of the conversions of even the current professed believers, All of them manifested excessive concern about health and material protection, and very few showed any "spiritual concern or spiritual insight."

Another area of question involved the name for God. There seemed to be a generic word *jent* for a quartette of culture heroes which the Chimane equated with the Spanish word *Dios;* but since the individual culture heroes, who had personal names, exhibited behavior that was not at all commendable even by Chimane standards, the missionary expressed grave doubt as to whether or not the use of this generic word for God was advisable. The author sensed an unspoken question as to whether or not the use of *jent* as the name for God was undermining or at least limiting the quality of the Chimane conversions.

Investigation and results

Since the question about the name for God was indeed fundamental, and since it obviously would involve the Chimane mythology of the origin of the world and people, the discussions were begun at this point. There seemed to be no information on the origin of the world, but several myths recounted how the world had been destroyed a number of times. Who had destroyed it? Jent had done it. In searching out the reasons for the destruction of the world, the informants pointed out that it was because all the people had become sorcerers and they were shooting each other with magical arrows. When Jent saw that people were killing each other off, he decided to exterminate all of them through a flood. However, since many of the people had become very powerful sorcerers, they defied Jent and burrowed into the earth. Thus, even though the flood covered the whole earth, many of them escaped. Then Jent created a special animal that tunneled into the earth and there destroyed the sorcerous people.

Such cataclysmic destructions of the world have taken place four times—once through water, once through wind, once through fire, and once through darkness. Each time the destruction was precipitated by a proliferation of sorcerers among the people. This raised the important question, "Are there any sorcerers today?" The informants insisted that there were no known sorcerers today. There were many curers—shamans who heal—but there were no known sorcerers. But did people still die of sorcery? Yes, many people died of sorcery. How then did people know that individuals had died of sorcery if there were no known sorcerers today? The informants explained that one could identify death through sorcery by the fact that "something" would come out of the natural orifices of the victim's body. The most frequent of these "somethings" that came from the body of a person killed through sorcery were little "snakes." These snakes were described as being about as long as a human hand or a little bit longer and generally white in color. (To the author this seems very much like a description of ascaris worms. In his own observation in Colombia he has seen that when a person with a heavy infection of ascaris worms dies, very frequently worms come out through the nose, mouth, or anus)

The informants then went on to describe that once these objects of sorcery came out of the body, the relatives could identify and eliminate the killing sorcerer through a special ritual. They took the "object" and put it into a large bottle which contained a solution of chili peppers and fish poison. After shaking the bottle with the "little snake" and the other ingredients, it was tightly plugged with a wooden stopper. Then the thick end of the bottle was put into the fire until it exploded. Once it exploded the witchcraft returned to its origin, and within ten days or so the sending sorcerer died. It was almost startling to hear how many testimonials even the Christians could give concerning sorcerers who had died as a result of the "boomeranging" of their witchcraft.

On being asked whether the family of such a person who died within ten days would actually recognize that their relative was the sorcerer, the informants were not too certain. They admitted that the relatives sometimes denied that the person was guilty. Did such relatives ever do anything about such a killing? Oh yes, they often in turn proceeded to the bottle technique described above to get revenge. Obviously, this could soon result in a vicious cycle of magical revenge "killings."

What kinds of illnesses were usually caused by sorcery? The most common illnesses included measles, smallpox, whooping cough, tuberculosis, diphtheria, pneumonia, and others. The chief culprits in this list of sicknesses were the contagious diseases of Western society. The informants pointed out that when epidemics came, the people generally fled and moved away from the place where the people were sick.

Inquiries on how such sorceries "reached" the victim were met with the explanation that the wind carried the spells cast by the sorcerers. Any gust of wind would be suspect of being a carrier of disease spells. The spell carried by the wind then produced the death-bringing "something" in the human body.

One of the informants, a Christian, reported that he had recently moved because at the place where he had formerly lived there were a number of tall trees, and very frequently at night there was "whispering" in the top of the trees. His family had gotten sick very often and they had finally become so afraid that they had all moved to the current place of residence which was well sheltered from the wind. None of the Chimane houses were on the river bank. All of them were somewhat inland — sheltered by surrounding trees.

Did some people also die without sorcery? Yes, the informant admitted that there were some sicknesses which probably were not caused by sorcery, but there still was hesitation over whether the deaths actually were just "ordinary" deaths. But even the burial of people who had died a non-sorcery death required special handling. All the people of the area came to the funeral and each one was careful to throw at least a small amount of dirt on the body during the burial. While the informants were not able to explain the reason for this very clearly, it seems as if there must have been some fear of the dead person's soul. Angered souls often returned in the form of tigers which killed people; thus all the people tried to be equally "guilty" of the burial of this person so that the angry soul would not single out one of them as extra guilty and then do him harm.

Testimonies by Christians

During the evenings of the days of the investigation the missionary and the anthropologist shared in worship services with the Chimane believers. In each of the services there was extensive singing and also a period of testimony, discussion, or prayer. On the first evening the missionary asked people to relate what had moved them to accept Jesus Christ as their savior. All of the testimonies stated that they had accepted Jesus Christ as savior so that he would keep them from getting ill, that he would protect them when they were at work or were travelling, and that he would preserve the health of their growing children so that they would grow up. At the prayer meeting the various individuals were invited to express themselves in prayer to God, praying for needs and thanking God for the benefits he had bestowed. Each of the prayers of thanksgiving revolved around a cure from illness, and the petitions were exclusively directed toward protection from illness or harm.

At another service the question, "What do *you* want from God?" was raised. "What is the deep desire that you carry in your heart?" One of the foreigners led the way in sharing some of his personal, spiritual concerns. When the Chimane began to express their desires, the common request was for a miracle— something that would keep them well and safe.

Interpretation

Very obviously at least two of the basic drives are in serious trouble— the drive to belong and the drive for physical well-being. In fact, the two drives seem to be in a vicious cycle relationship of reciprocal aggravation. The lack of belonging fosters ever greater isolation and splintering. Greater isolation breeds more abundant suspicion. In the atmosphere of hyper-suspicion every death is interpreted as sorcery. Acts of sorcery call for "boomerang" magic both to identify and eliminate the offending sorcerer. Deaths following the bottle technique have led to a cycle of revenge, driving the people still farther apart and increasing the fear of each other.

The most serious frustration is obviously in the area of physical well-being. This is borne out by the testimonies and prayers of the Christians, and its universal importance is demonstrated in the mythological accounts detailing the destruction of the world because men were magically killing each other. The Chimane culture had provided a mechanism by means of which sorcerers could be identified and eliminated. However, even though the mechanism was efficient from the point of view of eliminating the alleged killer, it hardly resolved the conflict. It really only created a cycle of hostility which increased the social distance, frustrated even more the need to belong, and sowed the seeds for still greater suspicion in the area of sorcery and attacks on physical well-being.

Clearly, one of the first things that needs to be done to improve the Chimane situation is to break the vicious cycle frustrating the two drives mentioned above. Since so many of the diseases listed in terms of the sorcery classification were the contagious diseases for which immunization is available, an immunization campaign could possibly help break this cycle and could stop the treadmill, at least for a time.

Once the deaths through "sorcery" decline it may be possible to restore mutual confidence and to foster more contact and fellowship among the people. As men are born again and their old animosities and guilt are removed through a change of heart and life, the church can become the institution to provide the supporting social context the Chimane now feel lacking.

It would also seem that the mission should take very seriously the matter of physical well-being. Even if the current fear of sorcery could be broken, the Chimane still have an extensive world of evil spirits which is lurking about, ready to harm human beings. God's concern about man's physical well-being should form an integral part of the message. Surely the ministry of Jesus points to the fact that he was just as concerned about man's physical needs as he was about his spiritual needs.

V

The Chocó[22] situation is here discussed in retrospect, for the work was begun before the development of the thesis proposed in this paper. The general situation in the Chocó at the arrival of the missionaries and the response to the gospel has been described elsewhere.[23]

In 1960 Indian Aureliano, one of the first Chocó to learn to read, paid a visit to the United States. It was in the course of his experiences in the United States that he learned to understand the Christian message and Christianity not only through missionary explanation, but also through personal observation and participation in Christian living in another culture. In this cross-cultural setting Aureliano developed the basic premises for the Chocó outreach.

At the end of his visit to the United States the author, missionary Glenn Prunty, and Aureliano met and discussed the past and future of the Chocó work. Aureliano first enunciated the principles which he considered fundamental to the development of the church among the Chocó: (1) Chocó Indians need the church because they need an institution in which many people can be brought together for fellowship without any fear of being poisoned and where there will be no fighting or killing. (2) The Chocó need to know that if they will "give God the hand and walk on God's road" (just like the fathers gave their hand to the devil), then they will come under the protection of the power of God and will no longer be subject to the evil spirits of sorcery. (3) If the Chocó will "give God the hand," he will "clean up their eyes and thinking" so that they can learn to read and know. Once they know, they can also become first-class people in the world. (4) The people need to know that if they will "give God the hand and walk on God's road," they have clan members all over the world, for there are Christians everywhere. They need not be ashamed any longer of being only Indians.

Aureliano put these ideas into practice and instituted weekends of fellowship. To these gatherings the people brought food, and Aureliano

22 Research on the Chocó was done by the author during his years of missionary service to both Waunana and Epera groups of the Chocó.

23 Jacob A. Loewen, "The Church Among the Chocó," PA. Vol. 10, No. 3 (May-June, 1963), pp. 97-108; "Literacy: Bridge in Chocó Evangelism," PA. Vol. 12, No. 2 (March-April, 1965) pp. 76-89.

as host generally killed one or more pigs. At such occasions the people fellowshipped, had church services, conducted literacy lessons, and played games. Soon the church gathering became the functional substitute for a pagan drinking festival which had previously held an important place in the lives of the people. It became the social setting in which people talked things over and shared concerns without the negative influences of drunkenness and sorcery. Not only believers attended such fellowship gatherings. Unbelievers also come, and even during the services they were given attention and respect.

It has been interesting to observe the rise in self-esteem among the Chocó. As they have learned to read and have developed their own school system they have also gained the courage to evangelize their neighbors—Indian and non-Indian. In fact, they frequently testify to their non-Indian neighbors of the many "brothers and sisters" in the faith they have in other parts of the world. They invite their neighbors to share in the family of God in which all men become brothers. Thus, before the Chocó church was one year old it had firmly established itself as an important social unit within Chocó life.

In the Chocó situation the drives of physical well-being and the drive of belonging were in trouble. Men wanted to get together with others in the drinking festival, but if they did they might die because it was at these drinking festivals that much poisoning of enemies and other violence took place. The frequent poisonings and the sorcery interpretations drove people farther and farther apart socially. As seen in believers' testimonies, the church became the social institution in which believers and unbelievers alike could share without any fear of being killed. For believers the Spirit of God had become the great protector of people against the encroachments of the evil spirit world.

What is most fascinating for the thesis of this paper is that the solution to the frustrated drives has caused the Chocó to move up in the hierarchy of felt needs. Currently education and the struggle for a reason-to-be are matters of deep concern.

VI

Prisoners in concentration camps

This section is largely a summary of observations made by Bruno Bettelheim,[25] a psychoanalyst and educational psychologist, who himself was a prisoner at Dachau. It emphasizes the fact that man under extreme physiological deprivation moves down in his hierarchy of motivating values. Bettelheim begins by pointing out that when millions of people—many of them from the middle and upper classes—were herded into Nazi con-

[25] Bruno Bettelheim, *The Informed Heart —Autonomy in a Mass Age* (Glencoe, Illinois: The Free Press, 1960). Also discussed in Betty Friedan, *The Feminine Mystique* (New York: Dell Publishing Company, Inc., 1964), pp. 294-298.

centration camps, all were systematically dehumanized. The whole structure of the camps had been so set up that individuals were forced to give up their individuality and to merge into the amorphous mass of the camp population. It was a gradual process which occured in almost imperceptible stages, but which nevertheless systematically destroyed adult self-respect, and in the end the entire adult frame of reference. People became "walking corpses" who were reduced to the level of infants in terms of their motivations and drives.

When new prisoners arrived, they were often amazed that the prisoners who had been there for a longer period of time were completely oblivious to any reality outside of the camp.[26] They had ceased to think about the future and the world at large. They were concerned only about their personal survival in the present in this camp.

Bettelheim observed that the more adult prisoners gave up their individual human identity and contact with the "outside" world, the more they became preoccupied with their sexual potency and the basic animal needs. Even conversation, their only form of recreation, ceased to be intellectually stimulating and became focused on sex and food. The people no longer functioned as persons. They were physiological robots who willingly lined up to enter the gas

chamber.[27]

In the midst of this environment of human decay Bettelheim records one moving experience. An SS officer, having discovered that one of the female prisoners was a famous dancer, ordered the latter to dance for him. Even though the setting was most incongruous, something "happened" to the woman as she danced. She at once moved closer to the officer, grabbed his gun, and killed him. She was immediately shot down by the other guards, but Bettelheim is moved to ask, "Could it be that while she danced her old self was revived, and that as a person she had courage to avenge the affront on her human dignity even at the cost of her life?"[28]

American middle-class women

This section is largely a digest of the ideas expressed by Betty Friedan in her book *The Feminine Mystique*.[29]

Earlier generations, especially the pioneer and immigrant women, seemed to find meaning in life even

---

[26] Ibid., pp. 162-169.

[27] This moving down the scale of human values and drives has also been noted in connection with Korean prisoners of war. Army doctor Clarence Anderson, who was able to move around freely among the many American prisoners of war, was appalled by the mass deterioration of human character. The soldiers soon became inert and inactive until some thirty-eight percent of them died of what he calls "give-it-up-itis." See Eugene Kinkead, *In Every War But One* (New York, 1959).

[28] Bettelheim, op. cit., p. 265.

[29] Friedan, op. cit.

while they were struggling for survival in a new country. Under such circumstances a woman could express her creativity biologically in procreation, and socially in the resourcefulness with which she provided food, clothing, and education for her brood. To us her existence may seem harsh as she worked alongside her husband in the pioneer struggle for survival, but in it all she found a meaningful reason-to-be.

By contrast, the modern American middle-class married woman is frustrated by what Betty Friedan calls "the problem that has no name." The middle-class woman may have all the comforts of life, a compatible marriage, a healthy family, an adequate income, and a recognized standing in the community; but again and again in the quiet of the night she asks herself a burning question, "Is this all?"[30]

Theoretically, modern American women are the happiest housewives of all times because no other women have ever had such an easy way of life. Educators in particular and society in general have glorified the role of mother and wife. Women have been discouraged from being too "intellectual" because this would detract from their "femininity." Their female sexuality has been exalted as the "precious pearl" in life. Sales people have converged upon them with their sex-based sales talk. They have offered them more and more gadgets to provide freedom from drudgery and to make them happier and more "fulfilled" women.

Everything from toilet tissue to dishwashers have been "designed" to bring out more of their femininity.[31]

Betty Friedan then goes on to show that family planning has taken the challenge out of procreation, and the comforts of middle-class existence have removed the challenge of pioneer resourcefulness. But instead of increased satisfaction, women have experienced growing frustration. The answer seemed to be more sex. In the chapter "Sex Seekers" Betty Friedan discusses the pathos of women who drive themselves to live by sex,[32] and who, instead of satisfaction, are "reaping" frustration. They are learning the bitter lesson that "women cannot live by sex alone."

Some women have resigned themselves to "the comfortable concentration camp of the middle-class home" and are living in the world of things—food and sex. But the vast majority are restless. They want something more than a husband, a family, and a comfortable home.[33] Betty Friedan reports their testimonies: "I feel so empty and somehow useless as if I don't exist." Or, "I feel as if the world is going past my door while I just sit and watch."[34] While possibly overstating her case to make a point, Betty Friedan nevertheless does corroborate the thesis of this paper that as the lower needs in the hierarchy of drives are met, humans tend to move

---

30 Ibid., p. 11.

31 Ibid., pp. 197-223.

32 Ibid., p. 247ff.

33 Ibid., pp. 27 and 296.

34 Ibid., p 232

up the scale in their needs. Since middle-class women have all their lower physiological and social needs met, these drives, including sex, have lost their motivational potency. The women now want a higher reason-to-be. Nor are they satisfied with only a general reason-to-be; they want to make a unique personal contribution to the world in which they live. They need both a meaningful intellectual orientation and a channel to express this reason-to-be individually.

American college youth

During my years as a college professor I had occasion to observe and to get acquainted with many young people of college age. I must confess I often felt frustrated in my attempts to communicate with them because their values and premises seemed so different from my own. When I look back upon this experience with college youth in the light of the proposed hierarchy of drives, I can see that college students are frustrated at the level of intellectual activity and in their need for esthetic self-expression. They are desperately searching for truth and meaning in life, as well as for a way to express this personally. Students are manifesting very strong reactions against current American values. They consider these values "trashy, materialistic, and useless."[35] As the college generation rebels, the rest of society asks why. U. S. News and World

Report states, "The college youth are worried about what they call American hypocrisy—the difference between American creed and American action." In another connection the same essay continues, "Another new thing about college students today is a very serious, and often even desperate search for ethical, moral, or personal standards which might regulate...behavior...."[36]

"Existentialist philosophy has permitted the college youth to look upon his contemporary society as an outsider, and he has found it wanting, if not dishonest. Because of this he rebels against the status quo and seeks to find new ways to become a person. This drive to become an individual and to find self-expression takes several forms. There is the youth who goes abroad with the Peace Corps in order to "realize himself;" or there is the student who wants to experience the "enlarged self" by means of LSD and other hallucinogenic drugs."[37]

It seems to me that even though the frustration of college youth is different in detail, it is identical in essence to that of middle-class women. The lower physiological and social drives are being met adequately, and they have consequently lost their motivational value for behavior. Young people are frustrated intensely, however, at the level of intellectual and esthetic activity. It almost seems as if these two drives are developing a vicious cycle relationship with each other.

[35] "The Truth About Today's College Students," *U. S. News and World Report*, May 30, 1966, p. 47.

[36] Loc. cit.
[37] Loc. cit.

In the attempt to find self expression youth feel that they must reject the intellectual and moral values of their generation. I was personally impressed by the excitement of college students who discovered the translation of Mark 8:36 in the NEB: "What shall it profit a man if he gain the whole world at the cost of his *true self?*" (Italics mine.) I had learned to appreciate this verse translated as "and lose his own soul." For the college generation, however, "soul" was relatively meaningless, but the concept of the "true self" was exciting.

It seems to me that here again the New Testament message could be good news for the frustrated. New birth means the personal actualization of our membership in God's family and the beginning of a design for living that embraces the totality of man's existence. The concept of the personal will of God offers nothing less than self-expression in terms of the highest possible meaning. It puts a premium on man's individuality and calls for an expression of it that is significant not only for time, but also for eternity.

Reciprocity in Identification

The idea of reciprocity in identification was originally conceived during the author's first term of missionary experience in Colombia, but it was actually born experientially during the 1959 summer literacy testing program at the home of F. Glenn Prunty at Jaque, Panama. A number of the associated ideas advanced in this paper have grown out of the visit of the Choco Indian, Aureliano Sabugara, to the United States[1] and the return visits by the missionaries on the invitation of the believers in Panama. This Choco experience has highlighted at least three definite areas on which such reciprocity should manifest itself: the exchangeability of the participants' material facilities; a willingness on the part of both to know and to be known; and reciprocal recognition of and respect for individual worth and status.

THE varied facets of the problem of identification have led many concerned missionaries to ask themselves and others, "What is a realistic goal in the matter of identification? For what should I strive?"

I have tried to wrestle with these and other questions in my own experience and now want to propose that reciprocity can be a realistic and practicably attainable goal in any missionary-national identification.

False Identification

It has been adequately demonstrated by missionaries of Roman Catholic and Protestant faiths that "going native," the attempt of absolute identification in terms of standard of living, by no means guarantees inner identification. In fact, this kind of false identification may indeed close the doors for a reciprocal relationship with nationals who "misunderstand" — or who may actually understand too well — such behavior on the part of the foreigner. Nida effectively verbalizes the nationals' suspicion of missionaries going native. "If these Europeans know how to live better than we do, why don't they? We would if we could."[2]

On the other hand, remaining aloof from what the nationals eat, have, or do is equally objectionable.

While visiting Latin America, I had occasion to converse with a missionary

---

Jacob A. Loewen is Professor of Modern Languages, Anthropology, and Missions at Tabor College, Hillsboro, Kansas. This article is another in a series currently running in each issue of PA.

[1] Jacob A. Loewen, "A Choco Indian in Hillsboro, Kansas," PA, Vol. 9, No. 3 (May-June 1962), pp. 129-144.
[2] Eugene A. Nida, *Message and Mission* (New York: Harper and Bros., 1960), p. 62.

27

about the question of whether or not a foreign missionary should accept the only bed in a national home when circumstances forced him to stay with a national family. This person felt that the missionary should be humble enough and polite enough not to usurp such sleeping facilities and use alone a bed which would normally sleep all the family. As we continued our conversation, probing within ourselves in order to separate real reasons from rationalizations, it was interesting to observe how on further introspection we became convinced that the real motive was quite different from the one proposed. This professed politeness was really only rationalization. A more basic reason was that he did not really want to become that intimate with the nationals. By being polite when he was in their homes, he was trying to convince them that they ought to be polite and not expect to use his guest bedroom when they came to visit the mission residence.

All too often we have said there is feeling against the missionary because he lives in too nice a house. Actually T. Stanley Soltau comes much closer to reality, in my opinion, when he says that it is not nearly as important what kind of a building or property one has, but it is how one uses these facilities that is decisive.[3]

This idea is also documented rather effectively in the letter from Jane and Wendell Sprague who report how an African leader speaking to the missionaries said that their so-called wealth — nice homes, clothes, appliances, etc. — was no real problem to the Africans as long as the missionary's heart was right.[4]

And when the missionary's heart is right, staying in the guest bedroom of the missionary residence could be a very ego-building experience for a national who had often wondered about what it might feel like to sleep in a soft bed. The important point, in my estimation, is that the national's home, whatever it be, and the guest room in the missionary residence, however good or modest it be, should become exchangeable.

This matter of exchangeability of facilities has become a rather interesting outgrowth of the exchange visits by Aureliano Sabugara, the Choco Indian, and the American short-term missionaries. This reciprocity began to develop during the summer of 1959 when the missionaries, David Wirsche and Jacob Loewen, were testing the Epera literacy materials at Jaque. Both the missionaries and the Indians came to the home of F. Glenn Prunty. In order to give the missionaries more control over the working day it was decided that at least the noon meal should be eaten together. Thus every noon the missionary teachers and the literacy students shared in a fellowship meal, which consisted of both missionary and national food. While the lunch was being prepared after the morning classes, both missionaries and Indians would go out into the ocean, where the Indians tried to teach the foreigners how to ride the surf. At first the missionaries were very clumsy

---

[3] T. Stanley Soltau, *Missions at Crossroads* (Grand Rapids: Baker Book House, 1954), p. 118.

[4] Jane and Wendell Sprague, "Missionary Standard of Living," PA, Vol. 6, No. 1 (Jan.-Feb. 1959), p. 19.

at this, and it was a source of great amusement for the Indians to see how the missionaries were swamped by the waves again and again. But gradually as thy gained some efficiency, the nationals actually stood by and cheered, happy that they had been able to teach something to these foreign teachers. At the end of the school day the missionaries and the Indians again took off an hour during which they played volleyball, a new experience for the Indians; and it took some time for them to get acquainted with the sport and to learn to appreciate playing it. The rules had to be modified somewhat to get them to participate, but gradually they learned to play a very respectable game of volleyball.[5]

It was in this setting of cooperative playing that Aureliano, during a rest period, inquired about the cost of the missionary's trip to Panama. When he learned about the amount, he asked, "Does it cost the same amount for a person from Panama to go to your country?" The affirmative answer elicited the following comment from him, "Well, since I have given God the hand and am walking on God's road, and don't drink any more the way I used to, I can save enough money from my banana cuttings to come and visit you in the United States." And this is just what he did.[6]

---

[5] William A. Smalley reports how he and William D. Reyburn joined a group of Africans in a local game. Even though their performance was very crude, the nationals scemed happy about it. Later they reported that this was the first time a missionary had ever played with them. Foreign games taught by the missionary are sometimes viewed as "work."

[6] Loewen, "A Choco in Hillsboro," op. cit.

Exchanging of Facilities

During his stay at the missionary's home, where he occupied the guest room, he participated in all the activities of the American family. Whenever he needed to go to town to make some purchases, the author took him in his car. When his laundry needed washing, the author's wife washed his shirts and other things for him. He ate the food that was on the table with the rest of the family, even though there were some things, like salads, which he did not like. All in all he was a very congenial guest. His parting prayer — offered at the airport while waiting for the flight which was to take him back to his family in Panama — was most heartwarming. He asked God for the opportunity to have the missionary come to his house in Panama so that he and his wife could share their things with the missionary in the way the latter had now shared their things with him. And so in 1961, when the missionary went to Panama for the next summer program, he was really paying a return visit to the home of Aureliano, who had in the previous year visited him.

The reception of the missionaries at Aureliano's home was almost overwhelming. He helped string their hammocks, he set up substitute worktables for their work and he saw to it that they had water to wash and to shave in the house. While the missionaries pitched in by purchasing rice and some of the other commodities that were "store" items in the Indian household, Aureliano assumed the burden of the provisions for the whole period of their visit. His comment to local visitors about the guests in his home was that they were just like Indians who belonged to the family. It is reminiscent of Soltau's statement: "They eat our food with us, and we feel close to them."[7] This also parallels Reyburn's experience that to "empty a pan of caterpillars" is more convincing identification than many pious words and kind deeds. Certainly the highest tribute for a missionary is to be accepted by nationals as their equal: "White man Kaka is eating caterpillars. He really has a 'black heart.' "[8]

Another interesting incident, highlighting the reciprocity of services, took place one afternoon when the missionary went to the river to wash his own nylon shirts. As soon as Aureliano realized this, he rather excitedly and almost disappointedly called to the missionary saying, "When I was at your house, your wife washed my shirts, and when you are at my house, my wife will wash your shirts."

A similar scene took place when the missionary tried to pay him for the use of the canoe, in which they had been traveling. He said, "You never charged me for taking me around in your car when I was in your country; and certainly you don't expect me to charge you when you are at my house."

Already during our early contacts with the Choco in Colombia we had learned that whenever a visitor came

into their homes and if they received the visitor with respect and welcome, the lady of the house always gave the visitor some food. With the acceptance of this food the visitor indicated that he was putting himself under the protection of the head of the house. This was very significant, because as we realized later, poisoning and witchcraft were so rampant that people who did not partake of the offered food thereby indicated their suspicion of the host and by the same token laid themselves open to the suspicion that possibly they themselves were on an evil mission. For this reason we found it necessary to always stock candy or crackers, with which to treat the Indians who came to our home. Thus, whenever a group of people (no matter how large) came to our home, we would invite them into the house and my wife would give the oldest Indian sufficient crackers or pieces of candy for distribution among all those present.

The Willingness to Know and to be Known

One of the first qualities that a missionary needs is the continuing willingness to learn. This quest must be motivated by a genuine concern for and a deep appreciation of a way of life that is different from one's own. The cheap sentimental, romantic approach, which gushes over "native things" as if they were very quaint novelties, rather than to provide for reciprocity, will lead to psychological distance, for no one wants to be regarded lightly. The missionary will have to take both the national and the national way of life seriously,

7 T. Stanley Soltau, *Facing the Field* (Grand Rapids: Baker Book House, 1959), p. 30.

8 William D. Reyburn, "Identification in the Missionary Task," PA, Vol. 7, No. 1 (Jan.-Feb. 1960), p. 9.

regardless of how strange or exotic a practice may seem to him. A common substitute for the genuine willingness to learn and to know is a kind of smug paternalism, in which the missionaries speak familiarly in terms of "our people," "our Christians," and "our Indians." We need to remind ourselves that such statements are a reflection that the speaker is really building his own ego, and that he views himself or his mission as the center and the national people as a "nice flock of dependent satellites."[9]

A missionary in West Africa made it a regular practice during his itinerant evangelism to stop in a village for several days and evenings and to inquire concerning the local beliefs in God, before trying to deliver his message. After having explained their way to him, the elders invariably asked him to explain his faith. The missionary used this approach not only to elicit curiosity; he was convinced that in order to effectively tell the people about God, he would first have to understand their way of thinking.[10]

Earl Stevick provides a rather convincing example of the value of the "learner approach" in identification in his account of entering a store in Central Africa to hear the people talk. The proprietor's wife greeted him with a subservient, but aloof "Yes, boss?" However, when Stevick mustered his best Shona to say, "I have come to stand and to listen to the people talk, so that I can learn to speak Shona more correctly," the lady relaxed and asked him to come to the best place in the store, but no longer as a "boss-foreigner," but as a friend.[11]

Soltau also makes this same point when he says that when entering an unevangelized village, a foreigner must always be prepared to spend days or weeks before he can really enter into the lives of the people and before he can communicate the good news to them in terms of local idiom. By saying this, he does not in any way want to reflect on the missionary's lack of consecration, intelligence, or learning. He is simply underscoring the fact that the missionary is a foreigner and will remain such, and that he must constantly be a learner even though he already knows much about the language and the way of life of the people.[12] For the resident the point of concern in learning is not so much absolute mastery as progress. There are plenty examples on record of good learners who became stagnant and settled for getting by.[13] Genuine respect for the national way of life often coincides with good language learning. In fact I agree with Smalley that progress in language mastery and cultural understanding are often outward visible signs of inward identification.[14]

9 Soltau, *Missions at Crossroads*, op. cit., p. 118.

10 Eugene A. Nida, "The Relationship of Social Structure to the Problem of Evangelism in Latin America," PA, Vol. 5, No. 3 (May-June 1958), p. 119.

11 Told by Earl Stevick at Missionary Orientation Center, Stonypoint, N. Y., 1962.

12 Soltau, *Missions at Crossroads*, op. cit., p. 156.

13 Reyburn, "Don't Learn That Language," PA, Vol. 5, No. 4 (July-Aug. 1958), p. 177.

14 William A. Smalley, "Editorial Remarks: Respect and Ethnocentrism," PA, Vol. 5, No. 4 (Jan.-Feb. 1958), p. 191.

But there is another facet for the missionary to consider. There must be a willingness on his part to also be known. This will require willingness to sacrifice privacy. We of the West have developed a real obsession for privacy of life and person. We have well-developed social mores which keep us from asking a person how many suits of clothes he has. And, because the nationals may not always respect this personal privacy, the missionary feels that he must lock his barrels to assure at least some privacy. Again, we feel that it is not polite to ask the amount of monthly income a person receives, but revealing this may be precisely the price that we must be willing to pay if we as missionaries want to know and be known, if we want to establish a reciprocal relationship with individuals in the different culture in which we are trying to serve. As Eileen Lageer so aptly says, "In missionary work, at least in this part of the world, the gospel is always easy to give, but it is the *imparting of our souls that counts and hurts.*"[15] (Italics mine.)

To illustrate this, permit me to refer to Aureliano again. During his visit in the United States, he, of course, took the liberty to inquire of the missionary as to the type and the amount of income he had, the amount of money he paid for his house, whether he owned it, whether he rented it, how much it cost him to operate the car, and so on. In the course of these discussions the missionary took pains to be open and

honest about his income, the total amount of his expenditures, the amount he paid in tithes, etc. When the missionaries visited the Indian church in 1961 it was rather surprising for them to experience that on a Sunday afternoon after the communion service, Indian Aureliano used the wages of the two American visitors as his point of departure in an appeal for national volunteers to witness to people in other areas. After stating the wages of the workers, he outlined their monthly payments for house, for light, for car, for water (and here he added parenthetically, "You see Jake doesn't have a river by his house"), and for tithes; he concluded, "So you see he really doesn't have enough left over to come here. But when he does, he comes here not for fun but because he wants that we who are his friends should learn to know God, so that we too can walk on God's road and do what God wants us to do." As a result of this testimony one of the Indians got up and said, "If Tiger and Fox (Imama and Kuriwa, the intimate nicknames of the two visiting missionaries) are willing to make a sacrifice to come here to give God's message to us, I am ready and willing to be a missionary for other people also." To our great joy this man not only volunteered but actually left the next morning to take the message to a village several hours down river.

A Psychological Concern for Privacy

This concern for privacy in our culture is manifested in the vast number and variety of physical closures

---

15 Eileen Lageer, "Poured Out," *His* (May 1963), pp. 27-28.

which we have developed. We have separate rooms for children of different sexes; we close the door when we are changing clothes, we lock our doors, cars, and letter files. But all of these locks are really only cultural reflection of our great psychological concern for privacy.

I became aware of a new dimension of privacy during my learning to dress in a Waunana home. The Indian home has no walls; and in this large open area often three, four, or even more families may be living. The person who wants to undress in privacy generally walks into the middle of the floor, takes his dry clothes over the wet ones and drops the latter and then adjusts the dry ones. The first time I changed in the Indian home, I went to one of the outside edges of the house, turned my back toward the people and carefully began to undress. The people, of course, not recognizing my concern for privacy, wondered what I was trying to do by this secrecy, and so they all flocked around and leaned over me to see what might be different enough about my anatomy to make me so secretive. I learned quickly and thereafter I always enjoyed privacy by changing my clothes in the center of the house where no one paid any further attention to me. I think this capacity of respecting privacy — psychological privacy, if you will — is relatively foreign to us.

Because we have not learned this type of psychological privacy, we are very dependent on walls, doors, high fences, and locks to mark what we consider private. Everything not enclosed or locked thus tends to be viewed as public. In the Choco situation we who were working with the Indians were often embarrassed when others of our missionaries visited the Indian homes with us. Because there were no walls or curtains to hide a shaman's paraphernalia on the shelf, these visiting missionaries often went to these shelves and picked up objects and looked at them. This was a serious breech of privacy in the eyes of the Indians. They would never touch such items because in the first place they were afraid of the spirit powers associated with these objects and in the second place that shelf, like many other places in the absolutely open house without even an outside wall, was the private domain of the individual. Its being open did not in any way make it public from the Choco point of view.

Another problem that I have observed in this connection involves the use of a foreign language in the presence of the nationals who do not understand it. In the absence of physical walls, the missionaries attempted to provide privacy by employing their home language to say things the rest were not to hear. This, to my mind, is not only very impolite but also definitely harmful to the establishment of a relationship of reciprocal trust.

This willingness to know and to be known will definitely have to go beyond the mere externals or the outer shallow kind of identification which is so often characteristic of our Western social relationships. We greet our neighbor politely but we know possibly no more than his name. In the missionary-national relationship, if ours is a genuine concern to know and to be known and to develop a genuine reciprocal relationship, we must remember that no amount of externality will be sufficient. While we may overtly express real interest, if this is not the genuine attitude of our heart, we will be in serious difficulty.

Paramessage

Nida has recently added to his earlier statements on the SMR[16] (Source, Message, Receptor) in the structure of communication, a dotted M which stands for paramessage. The paramessage involves our inner attitudes — the prejudices and the values — which may substantiate, which may detract from, or may even vitiate completely the message that is being orally transmitted. In a recent meeting with psychiatrists, I was struck by the statement of one of them who said that children, schizophrenics, and primitives have not lost their sensitivity toward the paramessage of others. They are able to read the paramessage, the attitudes of a person, more readily than a normally acculturated person who through enculturation has learned to block out many of the cues.

An example of such reading of a paramessage which contradicted a spoken message we observed some years ago when a North American missionary lady, who had real difficulty in accepting nationals in the private sanctum of her missionary residence, made extra efforts to invite national believers to her home on Sunday afternoons to have a cup of

coffee with them. One day a group of these nationals were visiting in the author's home and began talking about this missionary lady. One of them said, "You know, we have never been able to enter that woman's home." Not understanding the impact of the statement fully, we corrected the speaker saying, "Surely you have been at her house a number of times, and you had coffee there with us together last Sunday." The national then responded, "Yes, we've been in her house, but she has never opened her home to us. That is closed for all nationals." In this case even the very solicitous entertaining of the missionary had not helped to block out the destructive and contradictory paramessage of her inner attitudes.

On another occasion a group of nationals were talking about a deceased missionary lady and one of them made the comment, "You know, she had some real problems in her life. She always felt that nationals were dirty. She always had to wipe off the chairs and the floor as soon as they left." While we as missionaries had been somewhat aware of this situation, we had never realized that her negative attitude had so clearly filtered through to the nationals.

Our willingness to know and to be known will have to be personal and individual. All too often we display a pious kind of humanitarianism, one which loves "all the natives" but which would definitely shrink from the identification with any individual person.[17] We will have to be willing

16 Nida, *Message and Mission,* op. cit., pp. 33-61.

17 Albert Camus, *The Rebel, An Essay on Man in Revolt* (New York: Vintage Books, 1956), pp. 18-19.

to take off our personal cultural masks and to let other individuals know who and what we are if we want to encounter the person with whom we are trying to establish identification, because only then will this person also be able to reveal who and what he is.

This type of a relationship will not be easy to establish. In fact, genuine sharing, transparency, or reciprocity is quite rare even in our evangelical testimony meetings. In place of transparency we as protestants have fallen prey to using what Nida calls "protestant Latin." This is a kind of spiritual jargon which is used to demonstrate the supposed warmth and genuineness of one's experience, but which in actual fact reveals nothing about the person or his experience. The Christian experience is an intensely personal one — man meeting God face to face. The prophets of old were conscious that God knew them by name. They spoke with the conviction of personal experience. I have been struck by the fact that in the book of Acts, Paul's conversion is told three times, and at two of the occasions, Paul's very life was at stake.[18]

Reciprocity in Communication

If we look at this willingness to know and to be known from the standpoint of communication, it becomes readily apparent that what we are trying to achieve is a bidirectional flow of communication. Under a paternalistic relationship the communication is unidirectional, downward from the superior to an inferior. It is very difficult for an inferior and a

---

[18] Acts, chapters 9, 22, and 26.

superior to maintain a reciprocal communication relationship. Since the missionary task revolves around the intelligible communication of the message, feedback from the recipient becomes the indispensable indicator for the source as to how his message is getting through. In our own culture, business firms frequently find it necessary to sample the opinion of the populace as a kind of social feedback to determine the community's reaction to their product. A sensitive missionary will likewise be concerned with feedback from his recipients in order to enable him to adjust his communication until it is being understood and is meeting the needs in the lives of the recipients.

The value of this kind of reciprocity was highlighted in an experience by David Wirsche in the summer of 1962. In the course of teaching some arithmetic to the Indians he tried to explain the concept of zero. He had spent a number of hours on several occasions trying to explain this illusive mathematical necessity before Aureliano finally grasped the concept. This happened just as they were called to lunch. When they got to the house and were about to have their regular prayer before the meal, Aureliano called the attention of all the people in the house and said, "God has spoken this morning. He has told us what zero is." Then he proceeded in his prayer to thank God for the insight that had now come to the people — that they now knew what zero was. After he had finished the prayer, he turned to Wirsche and said, "Now, Fox, if you ever want to explain this zero to other Choco people, you ought to explain it like this . . ." Here was a good example of reciprocity in communication. It shows how exchange can serve to sharpen the communication's focus of the message.[19]

The missionary who wants to communicate good news to the national will, therefore, have to spend time — often many hours of time — listening to the concerns, fears, and superstitions of his audience. At first this may seem a waste of time to him because he would so much like to deliver the important message of the love of God. However, once we recognize that effective communication is a dialogue — that, in fact, all genuine witnessing is really dialogue — we will realize how important the listening stage is in establishing a reciprocity with the people of other cultures.

In an earlier article[20] we have discussed some of the service styles that the Indian church has developed. For us it has been very instructive to observe how effective a feedback-oriented style of service has been in Choco evangelism. Such discussion took place between believers, both missionary and national, and between believers and unbelievers.

A further example can be seen in the encounter that took place at a communion service where the exchange extended from the missionary to believer to believer. One of the believers who could read Spanish got up and said that the service had been wonderful, but is represented only half the truth. When Jesus instituted communion he washed the disciples' feet.

All eyes now turned on the translator and several asked why this had not been included in the Choco translation. The translator explained that there were four Gospels, but that only Mark had been translated into their language. Could the missionary prove that the Gospel of John told about footwashing? A Spanish Bible had to be gotten. The passage was then read in the Gospel of John. An intense exchange between believers followed this presentation and ended in the concensus that since they now knew that Jesus had washed the disciples' feet, they might as well obey it already, even before it was translated into their language.

Such bidirectional communication also took place between the believers and unbelievers. A good example is seen in the account of the medicine man attending the communion service on whom Aureliano called for a word of advice. The medicine man's response was, "I have watched the proceedings of this day with real interest and I am convinced that the Word you are teaching is of God. But you know that I do not belong. You know my involvements with the evil spirits. I would like to get free, but I cannot." To this Aureliano responded, "Yes, we know your in-

---

[19] An interesting sidelight took place when several months later a group of visitors from the ministry of education came to Aureliano's home and asked him to demonstrate Indian teaching. In response he proceeded to explain the concept of zero in the Spanish language. The visitors were so impressed that they returned to the capital with the recommendation that Aureliano be appointed as a teacher to his own people in spite of the fact that he had never officially had any schooling.

[20] Jacob A. Loewen, "The Church Among the Choco of Panama," PA, Vol. 10, No. 3 (May-June 1963), pp. 97-108.

volvements and we will pray for you that you find a way to be delivered from the evil spirits. For God is stronger than all the evil spirits." And to everyone's joy, a year later this same medicine man belonged to the church.

Such reciprocity of communication often became quite personal. During a service in Jaque village a child was sent to invite some Indian relatives to the meeting. The child went to the wrong house and so brought a family of complete strangers to the service. Aureliano immediately stopped the meeting and asked the reader to read again the story of blind Bartimeus for the visitors. When the visitors said that they had not understood the story it was read for them two more times. Finally Aureliano asked the oldest man, "How many Indians on your river are walking on God's road?" The old man's negative response brought forth Aureliano's next question, "How do you as oldest man on the river expect to answer before God that no one has given God the hand?" When the old man brokenly said, "But we don't know. How can we?", Aureliano countered, "But we know and you could ask us to come and tell you." The result was an appointment for a visit and the conversion and baptism of a substantial number of people on that river.

The Recognition of Individual Worth and Status

A third and very fundamental lesson that I feel I have had to learn in my relationship with primitive people is the matter of respecting their ap-proach to reality and society as equally valid as my own. Maybe such mutuality could be extended even to our respective body odors. I remember how Aureliano one day asked me whether it would take long for him to smell like an Indian again once he got back to his people. "Now," he said, "I stink just like the rest of you Americans."

Smalley goes so far as to say that without this respect it will be impossible for the missionary to identify with others,[21] and we could add that the absence of respect will also mean that he in turn will not be respected by the nationals. Reciprocity and mutuality of respect are fundamental to reciprocity in identification.

For Aureliano the U.S. visit meant the enlargement of his concept of people. To witness this growth of his "people concept" was a most interesting experience for us. It was after an interracial prayer meeting which he had enjoyed very much that he confided, "I have been thinking. If we can pray together like this, then you and I are really more Epera [i.e. members of the same tribe] with each other than with Indians who do not walk on God's road." Just as Aureliano's concept of us had to grow until we changed from "white beings" to people, so we need to expand our concept of people and brethren so as to be able to accept as members of the family of God, men from all tribes, nations, and races. This is an important issue for us. Many of us who come for the first time to a preliterate society with our technological gadgetry are quite susceptible to the

21 "Editorial Remarks," op. cit., p. 49.

delusion that our way of life as a whole is superior. If we add to this our greater financial resources, our broader education experience, and our deeper awareness of history, it is so easy for us to ethnocentrically conclude that we are, indeed, superior. There is no little danger that we develop a kind of "boss" or "great white father" image of ourselves. Such an image permits the foreigner to feel that it is entirely just for him to demand immediate attention by the native government officials. This self image can easily cause the missionary to feel that the natives are disrespectful and that they are very grabby about authority and status. Soltau records a painful example of this ethnocentric self-satisfiedness and the accompanying downward slant approach toward nationals in the report of his travel with another missionary couple. While traveling on a launch from the dock to a ship anchored in mid-river a number of Chinese people were sitting on a bench enjoying the river scenery. Much to Soltau's chagrin, the senior missionary preemptorily ordered these people to move so that he could sit down. Such action, of course, is only possible if one's self image is grossly and ethnocentrically inflated.[22]

Soltau, however, also provides an example of a positive reciprocal attitude in the account of the missionary who visited a notoriously anti-Christian Confucianist, who was causing a lot of trouble and persecution for the local Christians. The Confucianist invited the missionary to come in and to sit on the ground. The missionary tried to get in a few words of greeting, but the man seemingly paid no further attention to him. For one and a half hours while the missionary was hoping to make a contact with the Confucianist scholar, the latter only discoursed with another visitor. When the missionary finally left, he felt himself to be an utter failure. To his amazement, the native Christians came to him next day saying, "Last night you really made a friend. The Confucianist scholar is going all about the village, saying that you are one of the most humble and polite individuals that he has ever seen, because he made you sit on the floor for a long time and you did not become angry."[23]

While this may be easier to do in societies that have more of a class structure, it is equally important also in preliterate folk societies where the chiefs may have a lot less external marks of status that we be the first to recognize and pay tribute to those who bear tribal responsibility. It will be very easy for the missionary to be misled in paying high tribute to the culturally marginal or the social outcast who is willing to pay court to the missionary and to neglect to pay respect to the leader of the community who has remained relatively aloof.

Wirsche reports a rather narrow escape from making just such a mistake. He was about to begin a literacy program at Lucas in the home of a believer who had invited him for that purpose. On a sudden inspiration he decided to call on the blind old chief, to ask him for permission to conduct the literacy work in the area, to seek his counsel as to how to set up the

---

[22] Soltau, *Facing the Field*, op. cit., p. 49.　　　[23] Ibid., p. 51.

program, and to get his advice on individuals who might make potential teachers for teaching others to read. The chief, who had expected the missionary to by-pass him, was overjoyed when the missionary called on him. He said, "If you want to cooperate with us, we are going to help you in whatever way we can." And so he assigned a home, provided for the necessities, and also appointed several individuals as potential teachers of others. He added, "If you would have worked with that other individual, who is not really walking on God's road as he says he is, we would not have cooperated with you."[24]

It was interesting for me to observe that in the service of the dedication of the first Choco church, Aureliano, the newly selected leader of the church, paid tribute even to the unbelieving shaman who attended this special service. The full account appears earlier under the feedback discussion. This wise request for counsel by the church leader went a long way to save the shaman's self-respect and to prepare the way for his becoming willing "to give God the hand." Again, the warmth and intensity of the prayer response by the congregation indicated the depth of their identification. Max Warren ably underscores this when he says that identification means "sympathetic entering into the life of another." Again, only a "deep mutuality" can save identification from the "purely romantic" and

"unreality. . . . The true dignity of the relationship demands the recognition of mutuality."[25]

Another example of this situation was reported at a recent Mennonite Central Committee meeting in Chicago. The Moros, a nomadic tribe of the Paraguayan Chaco who have killed a number of white men in recent years, have now decided to join the people in civilization. The chief of one of the bands attached himself to the head mayor of the Mennonite colonies in Paraguay and would not move from his vehicle. Though they had no common language, and no one knows how he had ascertained "the chief" of the white people, somehow the primitive Indian had discerned the leader and was now also seeking the same type of recognition on the part of the colony administrator.

Another aspect of the recognition of individual worth will be the treatment that individuals will receive in relationship to others. It would be very easy to assign a fellow missionary the spare bedroom and ask a national — who normally sleeps on the floor — to sleep on the floor of the porch. Of all the features in our relationship with the Choco Indians for which we are very thankful today are the numerous occasions we have been able to practice reciprocity in terms of the assignment of sleeping quarters.

During the 1956 visit researcher Loewen and Indian informant Diego slept together in the guest room of the Prunty home. They worked and

24 David Wirsche and Jacob A. Loewen, *Report on the Summer Program in Panama,* 1961. An unpublished report to the Board of Foreign Missions of the Mennonite Brethren Church.

25 Max Warren, "The Meaning of Identification," in Gerald Anderson, *The Theology of the Christian Mission* (New York: McGraw-Hill Book Co., Inc., 1961), pp. 229-238.

shared together. Every afternoon at four they went to swim together. These sessions of swimming together turned out to be some of the most fruitful informant sessions. Because of the relaxed atmosphere many insights into native thinking were gleaned as the two men walked and played together.

Search for Equal Status

Tremendous concern has been expressed by some Americans over the abuse of white women by Congolese after the independence of the Belgian Congo. To me these cases were evidences of the Congolese search for proof of their status as equals. White government officials on their state visits had been very willing to accept the bed partners offered by the tribes people. Now, when by the declaration of independence, the Congolese became first class citizens in this world and the Congo a country in its own right, it seemed only natural that they should seek to prove this status by taking liberties that white men were still failing to extend.

During our experience at Noanama, Colombia, we found that invitations to meals were an excellent way of paying our tribute to people's social status. The national people were well aware of the fact that we often enjoyed the company of other missionaries. They knew that at such times we put out the best china, the prettiest tablecloth and consumed quantities of choice food. Very often we and the visitors were embarrassed by the many Indian and Negro faces that were pressed against the screening of the porch to watch these entertain-

ment proceedings. My wife and I decided to do something about this embarrassment. We decided to invite local villagers to similar banquets. And so in the course of time we invited not only missionary families, but also local families: white, mestizo, Negro, and Indian. The only difference that we made at such occasions was that when we invited people who were not used to using cutlery at the table, the setting included only spoons. We used the same china and similar menus were served to all the visitors.

During our later years in Cali, where we received many night guests into our home, we often ran short of beds. These circumstances pushed us into an additional way of expressing recognition of status or equality. It involved paying additional tribute to the person whose position was most precarious. As a result a "pecking order" was established. If there was a shortage of beds and it involved a missionary and a national, the missionary would sleep on the floor. If it involved a white and a Negro, the Negro would sleep on the bed. It came to a sort of climax during our last night in Colombia when so many nationals came to our home that all the beds (and much of the floor space) were taken. This meant that all our missionary co-workers had to sleep on the floor in a neighboring apartment.

One of the antecedents that led to the development of this pecking order, is still a painful memory for my wife. A good friend, a Negro, was looking for work in the city and daily came to sleep at our house, until one morning another missionary arrived to claim her room and bed. My wife offered her a bed on the floor, but that night she did not return and as far as my wife remembers she never asked for night lodging at our house again.

William Reyburn makes the point that the African wants to be treated as a self-respecting person. He says, "He does not want to be the only first class citizen, but he certainly wants to also be included in this category."[26] And we do well to recognize that the need on mission fields today is not for fathers, people who will be paternal in their attitudes towards the members of the younger churches, but for brothers, who will be willing to treat as equals those who will obey the gospel message.

Probably one of the most unsettling experiences that I remember of my own missionary career was in the connection with drunken Indians. Since drinking was such a prevalent vice among them, I wanted to make sure to dissociate myself from it. Whenever a drunken Indian tried to stay at our place for the night, I refused him lodging; or, if they got drunk after they had arrived at our place, I would march them off the yard. One night at midnight, a drunken Indian stumbled into our porch. I got up to lead the man off the yard. As we went, he was hanging heavily on me because his legs could scarcely carry him any more. As I walked him across the bridge that separated the compound from the village, this Indian turned and said to me, "Jaco, today you are hurting me very much. When I am sober, then I know what I am doing. But when I am drunk, I do not know what I am doing; and then I need you as a friend. You only want to be a friend to me when I am sober." I have never again had the nerve to march a drunken Indian off my yard, realizing that he needed me as a brother and friend at that time possibly more than at any other.

A missionary co-worker reported from their experience on the field that one day one of the leading families of the community suffered a very humiliating embarrassment. Their eldest daughter, who had been attending Bible School in preparation for entering nurses' training, was found to be pregnant by a good-for-nothing transient who had come to the community. The parents were socially very embarrassed before all the people in the community and especially so before the missionaries who had helped them in getting education for the girl. This great embarrassment drove them into hiding. When the missionaries sent them a message saying that as their friends they wanted to share their burden with them, the grieved parents were able to come to the missionaries' house and to pour out their heart. Together missionaries and parents asked God for guidance in this experience which was so very painful for all of them. The missionaries reported how this family became one of their most loyal supporters in the community.

In a paper on self-exposure,[27] I have detailed the experience of my encounter with Aureliano on the shore

---

26 Reyburn, "Practical Problems: The Missionary in Human Relationships," PA, Vol. 5, No. 2 (Mar.-Apr. 1958), pp. 88-89.

27 Loewen, "Self-Exposure in Missionary National Fellowship," to be published.

of the Pacific Ocean where we discussed some of our mutual job temptations. This insight into the missionary's temptations was such a tremendous encouragement to him that he later slapped David Wirsche on the back saying, "David, I know I am a Christian. Tiger and I have the same kinds of temptation."

There is a sequel to this story. Recently tension has been building up between Aureliano and another potential leader in the tribe. As a part of this struggle for power the incumbent accused leader Aureliano of having made improper advances to a woman. Of course, this report also reached our ears. Since we were far away, there was little we could do about this matter at that moment. Then F. Glenn Prunty visited El Mamey and had occasion to discuss this matter with Aureliano. As a result they made a tape recording in which Aureliano relayed a message to the author in Hillsboro. In this message the Indian Aureliano reminded the writer of their sitting together on the log on the shore of the Pacific Ocean and making a commitment to serve God regardless of what the cost might be. Suddenly the voice on the recording became louder as the speaker moved closer to the microphone. Then he said, "Tiger, did you mean what you said when we sat on that log and together pledged that we would be faithful to God? Well, I want you to know I meant it just as much as you did. People may accuse me of having done things.... I know that I made a mistake in walking together with those women, but I know too that I did not make the approach they speak of. If you want to believe their accusation, you can go ahead and believe it. But I want to tell you as man to man that I am still just as serious in my commitment to God as you were when we sat on the log together."

Not only is such mutuality highly desirable, we have to recognize that without it many a national Christian will be seriously hurt. Oscar Lewis' account of Pedro's becoming a Christian and subsequent backsliding as a result of the discrimination and the rejection he experienced is certainly a pointed warning.[28] One of the most prevalent manifestations of inequality attitudes in missionaries that I have observed in Latin American mission fields is the hesitance to turn over to nationals the authority to baptize and to administer communion — both highly essential attributes of the indigenous church.

Nida adds another interesting dimension to the missionary's position in the native setting when he says that the missionary should never enter the arena of cultural change as one of the litigants, but rather as a "friend of the court,"[29] as one who respects the society's wisdom and responsibility to choose what will be best for the society. As the friend of the court he can best demonstrate that he accepts the national Christians as joint-heirs of the Kingdom and equally recipients of the Spirit of God.

[28] Oscar Lewis, "The Backsliding of Pedro Martínez," PA, Vol. 10, No. 3 (May-June 1963), pp. 137-138, reprinted from Five Families: Mexican Case Studies in the Culture of Poverty (New York: Basic Books, Inc., 1959).
[29] Nida, Message and Mission, op. cit., p. 56.

Sponsorship:
The Difference between
Good News and Propaganda

FOR THE last six months of 1963 I was engaged in a study of the culture and of the problems resulting from the contact between two Indian tribes living with some ten thousand Mennonites who have settled in the Chaco of Paraguay since 1929. The Mennonite settlers had developed missions and, more recently, a colonization program for both of the Indian tribes. Now an anthropologist had been brought in to study and to interpret these groups to each other: Mennonites to Indians and Indians to Mennonites. One of the major problem spots was a Chulupi Indian group that had remained marginal to the mission program and that had recently been the seat of an ugly rebellion against the white settlers. Though no human blood had been shed, the feelings were still running high on both sides. Could I as an absolute stranger and another Mennonite find a key to these Indian hearts so they would share their problems from their point of view and thus provide under-standing that could lead to establishing peace?

In the hour of my need I turned to sponsorship. I located two Indian Christians who had relatives in the problem group. These two men had become my friends during my study in their community. They now served as my guides and sponsors for this assignment.

I parked the jeep which was at my disposal and the two Indians hitched their horses to a borrowed buggy and drove me thirty-five kilometers through the hot Chaco sun to the problem camp. En route I shared my concerns with them very openly and asked them to go ahead to the Indian camp to tell the people about me and my assignment. I then stopped off for several hours to interview the Mennonites in a village nearby. At the appointed hour my two friends called for me and took me to the Chulupi camp. They introduced me to their relatives who provided us with our night's lodging. The relatives in turn presented all the people of the camp to me. All the people, even the children, came to shake my hand. Some of the women brought out sheep skins and beckoned me to sit down. Then all the villagers sat down around me. When all were seated I said to them,

Jacob A. Loewen is Professor of Modern Languages, Anthropology, and Missions at Tabor College, Hillsboro, Kansas. This article is one of a series he is currently writing for PA.

43

"The men who have brought me have already told you who I am and why I came. I am ready now to listen to what you have to tell me."

For the next two hours I wrote furiously while my two companions translated for me the accounts of the grievances and hurts that poured from the pent up hearts of the Indians. After they finished I suggested that we eat and think for a while. Maybe we could talk more later. As soon as it became dark I realized that the villagers were preparing for a second assembly. They asked me to speak to them. Using one of my sponsors as interpreter, I explained the ideals of the settlement program to the assembled Indians. To my pleasant surprise the only baptized Indian of the camp and leader of the meeting got up and responded for the group. "We are not ready to accept land and implements for settlement. These things are given by God's people and we have too much blackness and too many wrongs in our hearts. We must first confess our evil and be cleaned up by God before we can work any land under his blessing."

While one of my sponsors faithfully interpreted into my astonished ear, I witnessed how Indian after Indian got up and confessed concerning the sweet potatoes, the manioc, the chickens, and other things they had stolen from the Mennonites. Others confessed that they had killed and eaten Mennonite cattle. I was overwhelmed. What seemed impossible had happened. The two men who had taken me with their horses and buggy had provided a bridge of confidence between a researcher and a supposedly treacherous and bad group of Indians who were meeting for the first time.

If there was any secret of success, to me it lay in the use of local sponsorship, locally recognized individuals who served as hosts, guides, and sponsors of one who was to bring a message.

My wife and I must confess that not all our mission work has been done according to the sponsorship principle. We will thus first describe some of our earlier approaches to mission work and then point out some of the frustrations that prepared us for the ideals of sponsorship which are presented here.

Our Early Independence

When my wife and I in our most introspective moments survey our early mission work, there arises in us a certain haunting awareness that, even though it was done innocently and with the best of intentions, much of our work must be rightly labeled *"foreign missions."* This is so not only from the perspective of the homeland which we had left, but also from the point of view of the country of our mission. As persons, in our life, outlook, and message, we remained independent of and foreign to the people to whom we had been sent. Our modest "country-club" style missionary station[1] outside the local village and the later "embassy-like" compound within the city have gotten

[1] I believe I first heard this striking label from William A. Smalley. The label *"convento protestante"* in Latin America is equally indicting. (Eugene A. Nida, "The Ugly Missionary," PA, Vol. 7, No. 2 (Mar.-Apr. 1960), p. 75.)

adequate criticism within the last few years. For us the isolation of the residence was really only one of a larger bundle of related problems. We feel that it might have been relatively easy to get rid of the stations — as has happened through some of the independence movements in other fields — but still not lose the foreign outlook.

In the course of this self-analysis of our "bundle" we think we have been able to identify at least several determining clusters of attitudes and behavior patterns. Two of these, sometimes separately and other times interacting with each other, seemed to have been major sources of our isolation.

The first cluster of attitudes appeared to center around a theological confusion in our lives. As missionaries we had indentified ourselves very deeply with the divine message we had come to proclaim. Our deep awareness of its supernatural origin, in so strange a cultural environment, led us to consider our feeble approximation of living according to the will of God as the universal ideal of godly living. This confusion manifested itself in at least two distinguishable behavior complexes.

The first was a kind of retreat from reality in which we deceived ourselves into believing that the national people around us were unaware of our carefully masked weaknesses so that in their presence we could act as if we actually were living up to, or at least very close to, the ideal we were preaching.[2] Our inner awareness that this was hypocritical, of course, made the inward withdrawal from the "na-

tives" all the more obligatory since the fear of our real selves being discovered behind the pious mask now reared its ugly head every time individual nationals attempted to come close to us.[3]

The second behavior complex involved a kind of "deaf-blindness" based on the previously mentioned identification of our kind of spiritual life and worship with the very expression of divine intent. Fortifying this confusion was the suspicion that most, if not all, of the strange local ways were evil and therefore to be eliminated. When even converted nationals ardently defended some of these strange practices, our now extended suspicion of the genuineness, or at least of the depth of their conversion served to short-circuit our perception of the still, small voice of the Spirit of God in them. Now, left stranded as an island of holiness in the midst of a perverse people, we quickly yielded to the urge to transplant *in toto* the hallowed and very familiar home-church service patterns. Because we were the sole authorities and also the only efficient practitioners in this procedure of church and worship, we felt quite sufficient to proceed entirely independent of the counsel of the leaders of the local community. And besides, by this time we were so busy with scheduled meetings and

2 See William A. Smalley, "Culture Shock, Language Shock, and the Shock of Self-Discovery," PA, Vol. 10, No. 2 (Mar.-Apr. 1963), pp. 49-56.

3 Opposite to this attitude of retreat from intimate contact with the national believers see Jacob A. Loewen, "Self Exposure in Missionary National Identification," to be published in PA.

administrative responsibilities that we had little time to notice our serious lack of contact with the grass roots of the local situation. We did notice the growing opposition of the local leadership, but opposition was to be expected, wasn't it?

Lest someone get the feeling that we weren't working for an indigenous church, let me hasten to say that we certainly were — in principle. But our experience was convincing us that this would take time. The older generation was too steeped in superstition, immorality, and ignorance to meet the divine standard. It might take generations to educate the children and to train workers who could carry on the indigenous church that we had set up on paper at the last missionary council meeting.

Too Much Money

The second cluster of attitudes — in a way it almost seems absurd to suggest it — centered around the fact that we had too much money.[4] Our financial resources (private support or mission budget) permitted us too much independence. We could simply be too self-sufficient. Away from home we could afford the privacy of a cheap hotel rather than seek lodging with some obliging homeowner or join the traveling multitude in a crowded hostel. (Health considerations and need of rest provided us with the conscience salving rationalization.)

[4] In John Ritchie, *Indigenous Church Principles in Theory and Practice* (New York: Fleming H. Revell Company, 1946), p. 96, we find the striking indictment that many missionaries view "money as an instrument of missionary propaganda."

Our finances permitted us the luxury of having our private transportation: cars, boats, in some cases even planes. These permitted us to go quickly and directly from one point to another without becoming dependent on local unscheduled bus transportation with its hours of delay or the erratic narrow gauge trains loaded with everything from pots and pets to people and their parasites. ("The King of kings' business requires haste" was an adequate rationale.) Like everyone in America we missionaries operated on a tight schedule. We hurried from engagement to engagement, and that without the assistance of a booking agent. But could this also have meant that our schedule did not allow for the seemingly unscheduled witness to a blind Bartimeus by the wayside, a Samaritan woman by the well, an Ethiopian in his lonely chariot, or a Zaccheus in a tree?

Money also permitted us to hurry up the evangelism by renting buildings for scheduling services, without being dependent on the development of readiness in some believer or sympathizer to open his home to give local validity to the message. Our North American high pressure evangelistic and publicity techniques, which we had learned in business, school, and church, urged us to buy and to freely distribute Gospels, Testaments, and tracts in house-to-house saturation campaigns. ("God's word will not return void" was a good biblical conscience cushion, and statistics in thousands were not to be mocked.)

The budget allotment also permitted us to give free medical aid. Since it was the Lord's money that paid for the medicine, we arranged for the patients to listen to the Lord's word before they received help. Those who came too late for the message one day had to wait until the next for their medical attention.

Looking back now, it all seems so plain — a captive audience at the dispensary, lots of free and often unwanted literature, a blaring public address system in the market and strange preaching by a foreigner in locales rented with foreign money — our message was propaganda, just plain propaganda and not the good news.[5] Because people viewed it as propaganda by someone "selling an angle" (which at the moment they might not yet have identified), the culturally marginal and the gold-digger were the ones who came to the meetings and who responded to the altar call. The culturally marginal neurotic could strike a blow at his own society and at the same time bask in the attention of the solicitous foreigner. Now we can understand why the gold-digger at the altar interrupted in the middle of our prayer to ask for his handout, preferably in greenbacks. In fact, we now see that we led many converts and sympathizers into a very unpleasant situation of duplicity through providing employment for "believers,"[6] who in

some cases now paid lip service to us and to our message in order to remain on the payroll and then had to spend a large percentage of their wages on liquor etc. in order to convince their friends and the community that they were not evangelicals.[7]

Even our former long range educational goals withered under fire in recent frank conversations with non-Christian parents in Ecuador concerning a mission's educational program.[8] Their strong feelings helped us to understand why even our school program did not help us to win more friends for the gospel. To be sure we graciously provided underprivileged people with the opportunity to get the much desired education for their children, and this (by our own evaluation) in the ideal setting of an evangelical school. Many non-Christians sent their children to the school, but we learned that we had deluded ourselves in thinking that they loved us

---

[5] John Howard Yoder of the Mennonite Board of Missions and Charities recently pointed out in a chapel talk at Tabor College that according to 1 Peter 3:15, the effective message will be the solicited one. Possibly our emphasis on the unsolicited message has dulled the impact of our witness.

[6] Luis Chicaiza, an Ecuadorean evangelist, told the author recently that missionaries often

violated the friendship of casual acquaintances by asking to use their homes as preaching centers. He felt that a premature request and an affirmative answer would force the sympathizer into disowning the missionary and his message before his friends, thereby closing the door for further obedience to the word.

[7] William D. and Marie F. Reyburn, *Picalqui: Retrospect and Prospect,* a mimeographed report, August 1955, p. 15.

[8] The indictment came at least on two counts. First, the mission undermined the authority of the parents; and second, by giving scholarships to single young men to attend secondary school they were undermining morals. In order not to lose the scholarship for their child, parents could not force marriage on the discovery of his involvement in sex relations, as is the local Quechua pattern. They thus blamed the mission for promoting promiscuity among their children.

for it. The truth was, they had had to compromise.[9] Their poverty gave them no choice in the face of a free (or relatively so) education. In their hearts they blamed the mission for forcing them to compromise and every change in their children under the gospel's influence actually heightened these uncomplimentary emotions. As the children became Christians and educated beyond their parents, naturally there came rebellion, rebellion which we often justified because we interpreted parental reaction as persecution from unbelieving parents. Today, I believe, we can understand something we never understood on the field — the basis for the readiness of the people to hang the label "communist propaganda" on evangelical mission work. It, too, was part of the price of our independence.

An Alternative

If you have found the preceding lengthy confession on missionary aloofness disturbing, we want to tell you that it is even more disturbing to make it. But we believe that it is an honest and fitting background against which to highlight the thesis of this paper: sponsorship can make the difference between propaganda and good news.

We feel that the proposal concerning sponsorship has a solid foundation in the teaching of Christ himself, and that it has many precedents in the experience of missionaries both past and present. It is being written with the hope that it will stimulate more concern wih an even wider application of the principle of sponsorship in the outreach of the church.

In both accounts of the sending of the Twelve,[10] as well as in the commissioning of the Seventy,[11] the Lord of the harvest saw fit to stress to his missionaries that it was absolutely necessary to be dependent and to be sponsored. In regards to the former he warned against carrying any extra outfit, all excess baggage, even food and money. On entering a community they were to find a worthy person who would receive them in peace. They were to eat what the host put before them and they were to stay with this sponsor until they left the community. And the biblical record provides evidence that this method produced results.

A look at the ministry of the great missionary, Paul, reveals several interesting sidelights that point to the fact that he operated on this principle. When he obeyed the vision to go to Macedonia, he found Lydia, whose heart God opened. After she had been baptized, the Scriptures tell us that "she besought us saying, 'If ye have judged me to be faithful to the Lord, come into my house, and abide there.' "[12] And so the newly converted seller of purple became the sponsor to the first missionary enterprise in Europe.

At Thessalonica we find that Paul was sponsored by Jason, for the accusers of the missionaries complained

---

[9] I recently read of a Mohammedan who joined a mission church and then educated his seven children in a mission school. When they had all graduated he again left the evangelical church.

[10] Matthew 10:5-15 and Mark 6:7-13.

[11] Luke 10:1-11.

[12] Acts 16:14-15.

to the city elders, "These that have turned the world upside down are come hither also: whom Jason hath received."[13] Neither the accusers nor the elders of the community attacked Paul and Silas, but rather called to account Jason, their sponsor.

For the early part of his stay at Corinth, when Paul ministered to the Jewish people, he was sponsored by Aquila and Priscilla. They were tentmakers; and while Paul stayed with them, he shared in tentmaking to maintain the household. Once the Jews became rebellious and obstinate, Paul went to the house of Justus, who, with his home near the synagogue, now became the sponsor of a ministry directed to the Gentiles.[14]

Even as a prisoner in Rome, Paul sent for the elders of the Jews to enlist their sponsorship for his witness in the capital of the empire.[15]

Modern Examples

An outstanding missionary in Peru, John Ritchie, who was instrumental in establishing more than two hundred congregations among the Quechua Indians, made it a rule to never go into a village except by invitation. He then went to the home of the villager who had invited him, and he remained there during the days of his visit. He never went unannounced or unexpected into an Indian community to evangelize. He felt that as a missionary and a foreigner he needed to be sponsored by someone belonging to the local village. His host might not necessarily be a Christian,

but he must be someone who was sufficiently interested in the gospel to invite the missionary to come to his home as a personal guest. Such an approach also meant that there was little or no danger that other villagers would organize an attack to drive the missionary from the community, for he was a guest of a member of the face-to-face community and thus relatively immune from overt opposition from hostile elements in the community. However, the primary purpose of this invited approach is not self-protection but increased effectiveness of the communication. Nor was this the end. Once the missionary had established a friendly relationship and the people had learned that he would not impose himself like a campaigning politician, former hosts would encourage their friends and relatives in other villages to invite the missionary. Especially many of the leading men who desired to have a contact with the gospel, invited the missionary to their homes and thus not only heard the gospel personally, but also validated it for the many people of the community who looked to such leaders for guidance.[16]

Eugene A. Nida also reports that a similar approach is being followed by a mission doing very successful work among people of Indian descent in Mexico. Either a Mexican evangelist or sometimes the American missionary goes into one of the new villages or suburbs and establishes

---

13 Acts 17:5-9.
14 Acts 18:1-11.
15 Acts 28:17.

16 Eugene A. Nida, "The Relationship of Social Structure to the Problems of Evangelism in Latin America," PA, Vol. 5, No. 3 (May-June 1958), p. 119.

friendship with some leading person. Once the relationship has been established, he is likely to be invited into the home of this leading person. This means that he will have access not only to one home but also to a large number of families related to one another by birth, marriage, or the extensive godfather system.[17]

In his account of the entrance of the gospel to the Meo, G. Linwood Barney points out that while the Khmu Christian, Nai Kheng, was the carrier of the gospel message, a well-known Meo shaman actually deserved the credit as the innovator; for he became the sponsor of the young Khmu missionary. Being a recognized man in the Meo communities, his request for the meetings and his personal presence and testimony added validity to the good news that rapidly found roots in the Meo society.[18]

Witness to the Choco

Sponsorship has played a vital part in the witness to the Choco of Panama. Several specific situations should be pointed out.

When David Wirsche first came to the village of Lucas in order to start a literacy campaign, he visited the chief and showed him the readers and explained to him the method and the purpose of the approach which was to teach a few key Indians to read, who then would become responsible to teach the others to read. The chief, who had been expecting the mission-

ary to use one of the local converts as a contact, thereby by-passing his authority, said to Wirsche, "If you want to accept us as your authority, that is good. We will help you. We will give you a home where you can stay. We will tell you which people will be good teachers in our community and we will help you to get the program started." And the chief then appointed two of his key helpers, who were considered individuals .apt to teach, to be the first pupils.[19] This successful cooperation led not only to a large group of readers, but also to the establishment of a vigorous church of which one of the chief's earlier reading appointees has become a leader.

Sponsorship played a major role in the founding of the church in El Mamey. In 1960 an Indian, Aureliano Sabugara, came to visit the missionary in the United States.[20] He enjoyed the hospitality of the missionary's home and before he returned he invited the missionary to come to Panama for a return visit to his home. In 1961 the missionaries, Wirsche and Loewen, accepted this invitation and became guests in Aureliano's home. It was very interesting for the missionaries to observe the effect of this guest status. Aureliano assumed full responsibility for them. He helped sling their hammocks, provided their

---

17 Eugene A. Nida, *Message and Mission* (New York: Harper and Bros., 1960), p. 111.

18 G. Linwood Barney, "The Meo — An Incipient Church," PA, 1960 Supplement, p. 48.

19 William A. Smalley, "The Bridges of God," PA, Vol. 5, No. 1 (Jan.-Feb. 1958), pp. 22-26, points out how much more convincing a chief's approval will be than that of some marginal nonentity that is seeking personal gain by becoming a Christian.

20 Jacob A. Loewen, "A Choco Indian in Hillsboro, Kansas," PA, Vol. 9, No. 3 (May-June 1962), pp. 129-133.

food, and arranged for their transportation to visit other homes and areas. While the missionaries chipped in to provide for the necessities for the family, he assumed that just as he had eaten in the missionary's home they would now eat at his home. In fact, Aureliano felt so keenly responsible for the missionaries that when one of the latter tried to wash his nylon shirts in the river, he came running from his house rather excitedly saying, "When I was in your house, your wife washed my shirts; so when you are in my house, my wife is going to wash your shirts."

In the evenings he would invite the community — friends, relatives, and others — to come in. He would make some kind of an introduction in which he would refer to something he had learned while he had worked with the missionary on the translation of the Gospel of Mark in the United States. Then he would turn to the missionary and ask him to expound upon the given point which he felt was worthwhile for the people to know. The resulting discussions and Scripture readings often lasted till two o'clock in the morning.

What was even more astounding to us was the fact that while unlearned in all indigenous church principles, the young church at El Mamey immediately proceeded to use sponsorship to extend its own witness among the Choco. At least three separate incidents can be underscored.

First, the use of relatives as sponsors in new areas. In planning its outreach the newly organized church took inventory of the many relatives that individual believers had on other rivers who could become the contacts and sponsors for the witness in those areas.

Second, a similar approach was observed when the El Mamey church reached into the Waunana-speaking population on the Chado River. They located a Waunana Indian (married to an Epera woman) who had some relatives among the more recent Waunana immigrants from Colombia. With this man as contact and interpreter and the resident relatives as sponsors, they took the message to the Waunana and established a church among them that by 1963 had more than forty members.

Possibly even more dramatic is the third example. During a Choco service in the town of Jaque, several Indians who had never previously heard the gospel walked into the meeting. Aureliano stopped the service at once and asked that the Scripture story be read again for their benefit. This done, he enquired of the oldest man in the group as to whether he had understood. He had not. So he had the story read again. Finally he asked the old man, "Do the Indians on your river walk on God's road?" To the visitor's negative response, Aureliano said, "How do you, as the oldest man on the river, expect to answer before God, if your people are not walking on God's road?" This almost reduced the old man to tears and he stammered out, "But we don't know. How can we?"

"You could invite us to tell you! We have learned how to give our hand to God and walk on his road and would be happy to teach you." And immediately a visit was arranged that led to the baptism of more than a dozen people on that river.

Sponsorship in Western Society[21]

Especially[22] during the past two years the German department at HCJB ... has experienced a phenomenal increase in mail response from listeners. ... It has been thrilling to read heart-stirring letters from more than fifty countries of the world where German-speaking listeners hear the gospel message. ... But it wasn't until I had the privilege of paying a personal visit to areas in Brazil, Argentina, Uruguay, and Paraguay, where our listeners are most heavily concentrated, that the real effectiveness of radio was forcefully brought home to me. ... Radio has a very unique way of breaking down barriers which seem to thwart every other method of gospel propagation, and of penetrating hearts of people. ... The following experiences excerpted from my recent visit to the above mentioned countries will bear out this fact very clearly.

As the Brazilian aircraft headed over the northern section of the state of Parana toward M—, a booming city which mushroomed into existence only fifteen years ago, I had no inkling of what to expect from the German-speaking population in that area. We had contacted a listener by mail some time ago asking him whether it would be possible to arrange for a radio rally to be held there. He had

21 Nida, *Message and Mission*, op. cit., p. 112, says, "In the United States the rural 'missionary' may be able to get the backing of the richest farmer in the region where he works."

22 This section is excerpted from an unpublished report on radio evangelism by David Nightingale from the German department at HCJB, the international radio station in Quito, Ecuador, and is here reproduced with his permission.

replied promptly that his son-in-law was pastor of a certain church and would no doubt be willing to make the facilities available for the desired meeting. Now, as the plane landed at the little airport in M—, not only the listener who had been our contact man but also the pastor and his wife were there to meet me. They were most cordial as they took me to the home of the listener. ... By starting time the place was literally packed and outside people crowded around the open door and the windows. This was all very encouraging, to be sure, but there was something much more amazing. Here I was in the pulpit of a denominational church. ... I was presenting the challenge of the cause of missions in this rather formal church. ... The response to the invitation was remarkable. ... The following day, while one of the listeners was taking me to his home on a coffee plantation, I heard the detailed story of what had transpired behind the scene before my visit to M—. The pastor, in whose church we had just held this successful rally, had not at all been willing to permit his church to be used for this purpose when he had first been approached regarding the matter. His wife had declared that she would refuse to be seen with a representative of the missionary radio station from Quito. However, one of the members of this congregation had told the pastor, "If you don't permit this man to hold the meeting in our church, you may strike my name from your membership list.". ...

In another large town in Brazil, there had been a similar situation about which we knew nothing until after the meeting had been held. This again was a denominational church. Here, again, we had a listener as a contact man and he was a member of this church. The acting pastor had been very opposed to anything of this nature taking place in his church. Through the overwhelming influence of other listeners who were members of his church, he was pursuaded to give his consent.

I believe this informally written report, while not pretending to be so, is actually an eloquent and practical demonstration of the use of sponsorship among people of European descent.

In conclusion I want to underscore that sponsorship is no cure-all. One of its major limitations is the fact that it may require more time. First of all, it will require some preparatory work to build a sponsorship base. Even when sponsorship has been established, it may still take more time to get the job under way, because the missionary has now tied himself to local people who will most likely not be as time conscious as he is.

Secondly, it will demand a certain amount of sacrifice of personal independence on the part of the missionary in such matters as transportation, housing, food, and method of work. Under sponsorship these will be more or less completely out of the missionary's control.

But if one is willing to accept these and other limitations, sponsorship also provides some wonderful compensations. As demonstrated in Nightingale's writing, it will provide entrance into places that seem entirely impregnable via the standard independent approach. Again, the message given under local sponsorship will be subject to much less suspicion and resistance. This will mean that it will have much greater "good news" value for the prior local approval permits immediate positive response.

Finally, as the message takes root, it will be doing so according to local forms and under local leadership, which means that we have taken several big steps toward the establishing of a truly indigenous church.

Self-Exposure:
Bridge to Fellowship

"THEN you can't do anything about native morality," solemnly opined a veteran missionary who had just heard the author's account of the developing church among the Choco of Panama,[1] highlighting the fact that this group was operating without resident missionaries.

"But we do!" was the response. "We have been using self-exposure." The following experience is here presented as a "definition by example" of this self-exposure approach.

During the summer program of 1961[2] we faced a serious problem. There were reports from a number of sources that a leader of the Choco church had committed adultery. From others we heard that he himself had denied it. When we inquired about it of several leading Indians, they just shrugged their shoulders and said, "Who knows?" Weeks had gone by

[1] Jacob A. Loewen, "The Church Among the Choco of Panama," PA, Vol. 10, No. 3 (May-June 1963), pp. 97-108.

[2] Ibid., p. 102.

Jacob A. Loewen, formerly Professor of Modern Languages, Anthropology, and Missions at Tabor College, Hillsboro, Kansas, is now a Translations Consultant for the Bible Societies in South America. This article and his other article in this issue are part of a series he is currently writing for PA. 315 S. Wilson, Hillsboro, Kansas, U.S.A.

and we hadn't done anything about it; but we felt rather uneasy, fearing that such a scandal would not only undermine his witness, but could actually destroy the church that had just been established. When several of the leaders accompanied the missionaries to a meeting with mission executives to be held in the city, we hoped that possibly during this time together there would be opportunity to talk face to face with the leader in question and thus maybe deal with this problem, but no suitable occasion presented itself.

The mission executives left. The missionaries stayed to see off the national brethren who were returning to their homes by boat; then they themselves were leaving for another assignment. But the morning the Indians were to leave, the boat in which they were scheduled to travel broke down. When this happened for four successive mornings, the missionaries began to feel that there was some reason for it. They became convinced that it was this unsettled problem of the alleged adultery. What could be done? After prayer and heart-searching, they decided to call a prayer meeting with the three national brethren. At this prayer meeting the missionaries opened their own hearts and lives. They revealed to the Indian brethren that they undergo sex tension when they are away from their families for the summer. They confessed that on numerous occasions there had been tension between husband and wife because of sex. They admitted to the nationals how, as Peter says, their prayers had been hindered when they as husbands did not live with their wives in wisdom.[3] Then they asked the Choco brethren whether Indians had this kind of problem in their lives, too. Before much else could be said, the leader under suspicion burst out, "I got involved with one of my former wives."

In trying to respond to this confession, one of the missionaries asked him, "Do you think that we can now 'throw stones' at you as the Pharisees in the story of the public woman wanted to?"

"No," he replied, "for I know that you men have sex problems, too."

"Well, if the three of us have similar problems, would it not be best. if we would all kneel down and ask God to forgive us and help us maintain victory?" The Indian readily agreed to this.

We were just going to kneel down, when the other two national brethren said, "But are you the only ones that are going to get forgiveness? Can we not get it also?" We had to delay our prayers of repentance while these men pointed out some of the tensions that had arisen in their homes and which were straining the husband-wife relationships. As climax of this experience the missionaries together with the three national brethren knelt down and asked God to forgive them individually and collectively for their

---
[3] 1 Peter 3: 7.

many common shortcomings in the area of sex.

Missionary self-exposure thus became a bridge across the moat that separated the foreign missionary from the national brother.

Underlying the main thesis of this paper are the following premises:

1. That just as there is a gulf between God and man, so also there are barriers, gulfs, and walls of separation between man and his fellows.

2. That all men by nature as partakers of human culture are trained to wear a variety of masks to cover their true identity.

3. That missionaries, like other men, have learned to live with masks which will stand as a barrier between them and the nationals whom they want to serve.

4. That God in the incarnation of Christ has demonstrated that man needs a "human" sympathetic priest, one who has experienced and is willing to admit the pull of temptation and the limitations of the human flesh and nature.

5. That effective witness to others, especially to people in a different culture, will require an honest differentiation between the reality in one's daily life and the ideal of one's profession.

6. That the honest facing and admission of the reality in one's life can often serve as a catalyst for a redemptive response in the life of one's brother.

Social Distance

Sociologists and psychologists of our Western culture have noted the increase of social distance that is accompanying rapid urbanization. The familiarity of the rural areas is left behind when men and women move to the large urban centers. They often feel lost and alone in this new impersonal context, but they mask their insecurities with an aloof conventional smile, not realizing that the one at whom they flash this smile also wears a mask and is suffering from the same insecurities.

Paul Tournier has illustrated this encounter of the "masked" so vividly in his book, *The Meaning of Person,* in which he relates the account of the man who

> had just come from a house of a friend who represents his country in the United Nations organization. A brilliant reception was in progress there, and the house was thronging with all important international figures of Geneva. Behind tht bowing and the smiles, behind the friendly words and the witticisms, the empty phrases and even their silences and their aloofness — all were playing a cautious game. Each sought to dissemble his own real thoughts — his secret intentions — while trying to unmask those of his neighbor.[4]

Not only in the game of international politics is there social distance. It is found between ordinary people, people living even in the same apartment building. In her book, *Woman to Woman,* Eugenia Price cites the example of Mrs. Woodrum, a widow of fifty-five, who jumped to her death early one morning from the twelfth floor of her apartment building on the north side of Chicago. Just before she jumped she saw the janitor working on the balcony of the same floor

in the next wing of the building. Mrs. Woodrum waved to him from across the thirty-foot court and smiled, and he smiled and waved back; but when he turned his back she jumped to her death. On her orderly desk, Mrs. Woodrum left this note, "I can't stand one more day of this loneliness. No sound from my telephone. No mail in my box. No friends!" On the sixth floor of the same large city apartment building lived Mrs. Jenkins, another widow. Mrs. Jenkins told reporters, "I wish I had known she was lonely; I could have called on her. We could have been friends."[5]

In my own counseling experience with college students I have frequently observed that a student will poke his head into the office door, asking with a broad smile, "Are you very busy?" When I then say, "No, not especially. Would you care to come in?," still smiling, he enters. As he steps in, I suggest, "Would you want to kick that door a bit?" He pushes the door and watches the fall of the latch. The moment he sees the door lock, he drops his mask. In the four steps from the door to the chair beside my desk, he has changed from smiling to bitter weeping.

I have been even more startled to learn at what an early age our youngsters have already learned to use their mask. Recently our community was shocked by the death of a young father in a tractor accident. His son was in the same room as our first-grade son, who, because he knew the other first-grader so well, was very faithful in

---

[4] Paul Tournier, *The Meaning of Person* (New York: Harper and Row, 1957), p. 28.

[5] Eugenia Price, *Woman to Woman* (Grand Rapids: Zondervan Publishing House, 1959), p. 159.

daily praying for him. One week we, as a family, made an attempt to be "extra sensitive" to the Spirit about witnessing and sharing our lives with others. Billy, the first grader, also tried. One night he could hardly outwait the finish of the table prayer to share his experience. He was walking down the stairs after school with the boy who had lost his father. He had decided to witness to the boy and so he asked, "How are you getting along?" The boy smiled and said, "Fine, just fine!" Then Billy continued, "Do you know I have been praying for you every day since your Daddy got killed?" No sooner had he said this than the other little fellow grabbed his hand and took him behind the school building. "That was a lie when I said things are going fine," he said. "They are not fine. We are having trouble with the cows and with the machines. My mother often doesn't know what to do. But I didn't know that you were praying for me."

Religious Distance

We also practice religious distance. Tournier speaks of the calculated effect in our relationship.[6] *The New Testament in Modern English* renders the description of the Pharisees as men who ordered their lives "with an eye to the effect."[7] However, we must be honest and admit that not only the Pharisees, the hypocrites of bygone tradition, but also modern people, of every stripe in theological background, are deeply involved in social and religious distance and calculated effect. Very often this invades

our testimony meetings, where, instead of giving a transparent witness of our experience with God, we use cliches, pious jargon, "Protestant Latin,"[8] to impress people. Another avenue to religious distance is to institutionalize or professionalize our witness. We can witness when we are in front of a Sunday school class, a congregation, or some organized group. We can read the Bible and pray at our family altar; but beyond these formal and scheduled settings we are unable to talk transparently about our Christian experience.

This was burned into my consciousness recently at a retreat of high school young people in which we attempted to analyze our spiritual condition by discovering the differences between the ideal we professed and the reality which we were living. I made a startling discovery, a discovery which has deeply affected also my own home life. In the course of the discussion of "knowing and becoming known," we had to face the problems of our homes, and these young people firmly asserted that their parents never spoke to them about the word of God except during family devotions or while meting out discipline. I was convinced this was a glaring overstatement until I polled my college faculty colleagues and found that many of them could recall no instances in which their parents had spoken to them about the gospel outside of formal settings such as devotions or disciplinary encounters.

---

6 Op. cit., p. 137.
7 Matthew 23:5 (J. B. Phillips).

8 Eugene A. Nida, *Commission, Conflict, Commitment* (Urbana: Intervarsity Press, 1961), p. 191; and S. M. Shoemaker, "Lingo," *His* (May 1962), pp. 6-7.

This led us to check on the use of the Scriptures in our own home, and to our shame we found the indictment was far more true than we dared to admit; we also were using the Bible as a "whip" for our own teenagers.

The way of the mask, of course, is the way of compartmentalization, where we have a church life and an everyday life, a life of reality at home and the way of the facade in public, of which a youngster's passionate plea to his missionary mother — "Mother, why can't you be at home, the way you are among people?" — is an illustration.

But this matter of masking, of hypocrisy, can even invade our intimate experiences with God. In the retreat with young people mentioned earlier, we were trying to share some of our common difficulties in living our faith. A high school senior confessed, "I have not been a Christian very long, and I have trouble with my temper on the basketball floor. Sometimes I say things that I ought not to say." Moments later, when one of the girls burst out in tears and cried, "I get so angry that I swear at my mother," this senior blurted out, "That is exactly what I meant — I *swear* on the basketball floor." Until it is "socially acceptable," we do not want to admit that we are away from our ideal, and so we mask the truth in the very act of confessing to God.

Nor is the mask a modern phenomenon; when God looked for Adam and Eve after they had disobeyed his command, he found them making aprons of fig leaves — a first mask of human experience. Cain hid behind ambiguity when God asked

him, "Where is thy brother?" and he countered, "Am I my brother's keeper?"[9]

Festo Kivengere speaks about Jacob coming in Esau's name, dressed in Esau's clothes, and covered with goatskins to get the blessing. He points out that it took twenty years before Jacob actually got that blessing. In order to get it he had to unmask. Twenty years later he had to face the same question, "What is your name?" and now he admitted that he was Jacob, the deceiver, not Esau. Once he "owned" this reality, God changed the deceiver's name to Israel, he who strives with God."[10]

Missionary Distance

Since we grow up in an environment where walls of social distance and barriers of religious distance are current, we will need to remember that even when we go to foreign lands as missionaries, we carry this practice with us. Only in the mission situation there will be an additional barrier, the difference in cultures.

This difference is accentuated by ethnocentrism on both sides. While we missionaries from America feel ourselves to be technologically and educationally superior, the nationals in their own ethnocentrism likewise feel superior. When the Waunana looked at us and at themselves they said, "We are Waunana, *people*; but you are not people — you are *white beings*." This ethnocentrism in ourselves and in others builds a wall

9 Genesis 4: 9.
10 Festo Kivengere, "Personal Revival," *Commission, Conflict, Commitment* (Chicago: Intervarsity Press, 1962), pp. 27-46.

around us and leads us to suspect the person from the differing culture.

There are superficial cultural differences which are so strange to us, such as the seeming hyper-frequent shaking of hands in France, that William A. Smalley mentioned.[11] How queer can people become!

I remember how my wife used to do our laundry in a salvaged gasoline washer which had no lid. When this washing machine was started early Monday morning, all the Indian women, some from several days' journey away, came to see the spectacle. They would crowd into the little laundry room and watch as she dumped the clothes into the foaming water. They would cup their hands under their tummies which were hanging over their wrap-around skirts and chuckle with laughter. Finally one of them became brave enough to ask, "Why do you wash like that? Don't you know that intelligent women wash in the river?" When my wife said that this was in keeping with our culture, they stopped laughing even though their interest in the affair did not subside.

To this we add our Western mania for privacy — privacy for dressing, privacy for talking, privacy for eating, privacy for personal belongings — evidenced by the many locked cases and barrels that contain the "poor" missionary's outfit, and are so suggestive of wealth. Perhaps most persistent is the use of the missionaries'

own native language when talking to fellow missionaries in the presence of nationals who are not supposed to understand it.

Our privacy concerns and our facility with the mask very often have led missionaries to deceive themselves in regards to what the people around them know about foreigners. All too often the faults that we have carefully masked and feel are completely secret, are the talk of the informal gatherings of the native community.

A short-term worker in Africa who had lived in an African village instead of on a mission compound could entertain the college crowd for hours by telling "inside information" on the missionaries' relationships to one another, their tempers, and their weaknesses. One story that I vividly remember involved the house-boy whose "mama-boss" always lost her temper over his mistakes. After serious discussion the group concluded that since she always got "mad as the devil" she probably was not a Christian.

In my own experience I remember a group of national teachers discussing the marital adjustment of a missionary couple that was having trouble. It was a top secret in the missionary family and only three mission officers knew about it. I was shaken to the core to realize that it was common knowledge among the nationals. All too often, we are like Moses trying to help his people after he had buried the dead Egyptian in the sand. We have, of course, sealed the grave where the dead Egyptian lies, but still there is a gnawing uncertainty.

---

11 William A. Smalley, "Culture Shock, Language Shock, and the Shock of Self-Discovery,'" PA, Vol. 10, No. 2 (Mar.-Apr. 1963), p. 49.

As missionaries we want so much to live up to the ideals and standards of the doctrines we preach. However, we need to remind ourselves that the sins we have learned to recognize in our own culture are limited. Some things are too bad even to mention, and toward other things our own culture has blinded us. In what we do recognize, the awareness of our own falling short of the ideal, the growing suspicion that our mask may not be fooling the people of the new culture, and, for that matter, our conscience activated by the Spirit who is trying to lead us into "all truth," often cause us to retreat into a cloak of artificial piety.

Festo Kivengere forcefully illustrated this in an account of a missionary-native encounter in his own country. The missionary pleaded with the national brother that he should be open with him so that they could pray togther about the latter's problems. The national replied, "Brother, my box is open, but your box is not only closed but locked."[12] While there is a great preoccupation in our Western church with sins of sex, we often are not nearly as conscious of the sins of temper which in many cultures are far more seriously weighed than sex.

Eugene A. Nida has recently developed the concept of the "para-message" which communicates our attitudes, our feelings alongside our spoken message.[13] Very often nation-als, like the children in our own homes, read the "para-message" before they listen to the spoken message.

The Divine Example in the Incarnation

"And the Word was made flesh and dwelt among us, (and we beheld his glory, the glory as of the only begotten of the Father) full of grace and truth."[14] In these unassuming but pregnant words, John the apostle begins his witness concerning the identification of God with men. But before we reach the end of John's account of "the Christ in human flesh," we learn that this incarnation is only a beginning, a pattern and an example of a chain of becoming flesh. "As my Father hath sent me, even so send I you."[15] If the Christ crossed the infinite-finite barrier to translate the truth of God into a form intelligible to men, Christ's disciples are sent to translate this truth across the many cultural and social barriers that separate men. If God had to become man to become intelligible to the human race, it stands to reason that finite men will have to "become men" in other cultures if their experience of God is to become intelligible in such different cultures.

The possibility of such a cross-cultural identification was demonstrated when Christ Jesus was born of a woman; and the basis for it was provided by the death of Christ. Writing to the Ephesians Paul says, "But now, through the blood of Christ, you who were once outside of the pale are with us inside of the

---

12 Festo Kivengere, "An African's Point of View," *Commission, Conflict, Commitment* (Chicago: Intervarsity Press, 1962), pp. 27-46.

13 Eugene A. Nida, Lectures on Communications at Drew University, July 1962.

14 John 1: 14.
15 John 20: 21.

circle of God's love and purpose. For Christ is our living peace. He has made a unity of the conflicting elements of Jew and Gentile by breaking down the barrier which lay between us. By his sacrifice he removed the hostility of the law with all its commandments and rules and made himself out of two, Jew and Gentile, one new man, thus producing peace. And he reconciled both to God by the sacrifice of one body on the cross, and by this act made utterly irrelevant the antagonism between them."[16]

To the Colossians, speaking about this new man, he says, "In this new man of God's design there is no distinction between Greek and Hebrew, Jew or Gentile, foreigner or savage, slave or free man: Christ is all that matters, for Christ lives in them all."[17]

Ever since and all the while man has tried to hide himself from God. God has been trying to reveal himself to man. Finally, in the incarnation God entered the human setting, he accepted human limitations so that he could "feel" with men and become their sympathetic high priest. One of the valuable features of the Bible is that it accepts man in his weaknesses and speaks of the men of God not as perfect, but as those being perfected. It recounts their shortcomings and their sins as faithfully as their victories and accomplishments. Paul was so deeply aware of his past as a persecutor, a blasphemer, and a reviler, that he accepted his accomplishments entirely as the grace of God working in him. James puts forth the passionate plea that men should be open with one another, for in openness lies growing wholeness. "Confess your faults one to another, and pray for each other that you may be healed."[18]

Self-Exposure in the Man-to-Man Encounter

If we really want to enter into any intimate relationship with other human beings, there is a way: the way of self-exposure. We will have to be willing to be known, if we want to know. Self-exposure will be of utmost importance for the missionary, for it will reveal in real life his encounter with the doctrines he is teaching. Values are always best taught in the drama of life, not in preaching. Then, as he will practice self-exposure, he will also become aware of the work of God in other men who are willing to be known, as is recorded in the example of Peter and Cornelius. Finally, self-exposure will help us to operate on the principle of the "heart of flesh" rather than the "heart of stone" — like God in Christ, we can become sympathetic "priests." It will prevent us from casting the first stone at the person caught in shortcoming, because we will already be kneeling at the cross in repentance for our own weaknesses.

Self-Exposure on the American Scene

Probably one of the most revealing experiences was the previously mentioned encounter with the young people in the camp where we attempted to discuss the discrepancies between the real and the ideal of our lives. In our first group meeting (nine

---

16 Ephesians 2: 13-16 (J. B. Phillips).
17 Colossians 3: 11 (J. B. Phillips).

18 James 5: 16 (J. B. Phillips).

high school students and the counselor) we just attempted to establish a communication relationship by praying for each other in a circle. In the second encounter we tried to share some of our ideals and at least one area in which we were still struggling short of our mark. The discussion was to last thirty minutes, but the first of six such meetings broke up after one and a half hours. As community became more real and actual, not only the socially acceptable "sins" were mentioned, but again and again one would interrupt, saying, "That's exactly my problem. I thought I was alone; you all appeared so holy."

This "holy" appearance which seems to be such a popular halo, to my mind is an indictment rather than a credit. This conviction came to me through an encounter with two young men at a missionary conference. The first public meeting of the conference was a dedication service at which Evangelist Billy Graham called 5400 young people to voluntarily "put their lives on the altar for God." Many hundreds of them responded to this appeal.

After this service there were group prayer meetings in all the residence halls. The group of about thirteen in which I shared had some four or five of the newly "dedicated." These dominated the prayer service literally "gushing" dedication. "Once and for all we have turned over our lives to God."

Knowing my own battles with the imperfections of my complete dedication, I began to share some scenes from the mision field in which some co-worker's foible had undone my

consecration. In fact, I admitted that right at that moment patience with students and especially with my own children was a weak spot in my consecration. It was an attempt on my part to introduce a little realism into a situation soaring high in ideals, but I felt I had failed, for instead of others joining me in confession, the group retreated behind the pious mask and prayed for my victory.

Feeling my failure rather keenly, I tried to step out quickly to go to my room, but two fellows who had not prayed grabbed me by the sleeve and pulled me into their room. One locked the door, the other paced the floor in great agitation. He took out a cigarette, lit it, took a few puffs, threw it down and stamped it out fiercely, "I get so fed up with all this damned Protestant jargon! I got up in response to the appeal tonight to 'dedicate' my life. What have I actually done?"

"Nothing that you do not know about."

"Did I deal with my sin?"

"Not unless you consciously turned it over to God."

Then the young man dropped into a chair and in tears cried, "Where can I finally go to deal with my sinful habits? I have already joined the church, but it didn't help. So I entered the priesthood and it only makes you hide your evil even more. Now I thought, 'The evangelicals find forgiveness and peace. I'll go there and get it too.' This is what I tried to do when I got up after Graham's appeal. But when we got into that prayer meeting and those dedicated people spouted piety, I felt utterly nauseated. I don't want to be hollow like them. You seemed a little less 'holy' and so I thought maybe I could talk to you about my sin."

Several hours of confession followed that night and several private sessions that followed I was able to watch a "real sinner" find the real Savior.

I have also had to learn that a one-time recognition of my humanity is not enough. I quickly reach for my pious mask again and so become insensitive and unapproachable. A good lesson came to me during a series of pre-Easter services. Until Wednesday night the response had been very good. I had been trying to be extra sensitive to the needs of others in counseling and in the method of presenting my message. That evening I began my message with enthusiasm, but somehow the words seemed to bounce back at me from the open rafters. The more I struggled, the more my words seemed to bounce.

Finally at the end of the service I slipped out of the church through the side door without taking leave of anyone and began to walk toward my lodging rather than to phone for the car as had been prearranged. I walked the streets for quite some time, trying to search my heart for the reason why. Unable to discern any apparent cause, I finally began to walk homeward dejectedly.

As I walked by a lighted window, I became aware of a "still small voice" which told me to enter and speak to the individual who lived there. The person was well-known to me as one who had been marginal to the church for many years and who was publicly criticized often and seriously. I felt that I just couldn't enter in the state of mind in which I found myself. I walked another block, but then retraced my steps and went in. The individual was alone. Without any polite introduction I said to him, "I don't know why I'm here; I just had the feeling I should come in." Then I went on to tell him what had happened in my church experience. I told him that I felt completely defeated and that maybe he was the one who could tell me what my trouble was.

I had not yet finished when he broke in, "For thirteen years I have been bearing some very bitter burdens, always wishing that somewhere I would meet someone with whom I could share these concerns, but everybody appeared so whole, so complete, so holy that I never dared reveal my imperfection." After that three-hour session I realized that God had answered my prayer. He had tried to make me sensitive and that required another losing of my "mask of perfection."

Nor do I believe that this is entirely an expression of my own idiosyncrasy. During my college teaching career I observed how one young man tried to witness to another one, who seemed to be under a real burden. After a number of attempts the first young man was ready to give up, saying to himself that he just did not know how to witness. Then he remembered the statement, "Sometimes it is necessary to be the first sinner." So he impulsively revealed to the "closed" young man the problem that was causing him deep concern in his life, saying that he needed his friend's prayer support. On hearing this the other burst out, "I didn't know that you had this problem; that is exactly what my problem is." I then observed how these two young men met in my office every day for a whole semester, praying with and for each other, winning the victory over their common problems.

Possibly one of the most dramatic examples of self-exposure took place in a jail service in one of the towns not too far from the college where I teach. I was accompanying a group of college students, and en route we discussed the matter of how to approach men who had already been branded as guilty by society. We decided there would be very little use of speaking about the sinners inside the bars, for those men were all parading under the mask of innocence. It might be best to speak about the experiences of the sinners outside of the bars. A college sophomore with a radiant smile had been asked to give her testimony. When she got up in front of the jail group, she grasped the bars with both hands and with a voice choked with deep emotion revealed to the prisoners that her father, a prominent minister, had committed suicide and that this had caused some very intense conflicts in her life. She admitted that in her darker moments, she hated her father for what he had done to her reputation. Then again she realized in those very thoughts the depravity of her own heart and could only say that she was deeply grateful that she knew that God still cared for her, was concerned about her, and wanted her to find peace, joy, and meaning in life.

One of the prisoners was so deeply shaken by the girl's unmasking that after the group left he called the jailor and confessed that he was not an orphan from Chicago as he had previously affirmed, but rather a runaway from a wealthy Canadian family. He said, "I don't know why that girl had to be so honest; I am the one who is dishonest. She had no business taking off her mask like that. She wasn't that bad; not as bad as I." The result was that this young man was reunited with his family, and even the impersonal county in which he was condemned to a prison sentence was moved to suspend the sentence because they witnessed the transformation that had taken place in his life.

Self-Exposure in the Witness to the Choco

Aureliano, the Indian from Panama who visited Hillsboro,[20] and his missionary hosts had developed a very transparent relationship. In fact, the missionaries tried to be very open with all the Choco about their wages, their property holdings, and their experiences. In the evenings as the groups would sit around the smoking lamps and discuss some Scripture verses or personal experiences, the missionaries shared with the Choco Indians some of the battles of their own spiritual development. At one occasion one of the missionaries told how he as a young man during the depression had walked from Saskatchewan to Alberta, slept with the bums

---

[20] Jacob A. Loewen, "A Choco Indian in Hillsboro, Kansas," PA, Vol. 9, No. 3 (May-June 1962), pp. 129-133.

beside the road, begged for some of his food while he was searching for work, and how there had been a real struggle in his life at that time wondering whether God was really concerned about him.

The Choco Christians responded with testimonies about their encounters with evil spirits. In these sessions of face-to-face fellowship, intimate and practical concern for each other was established. Often the meetings would end with the principals who had shared experiences, exchanging their concerns and personal burdens and praying for each other. In this way an interesting feeling of responsibility for the other was developed. Soon Indians were asking missionaries, "How are you getting along with your concern; are you finding an answer?"

It was this atmosphere of intimacy and mutual concern that led to the self-exposure experience related at the beginning of this paper.

In 1962, when the missionaries visited the Choco churches, which had grown to three by this time, they noticed that over the leader there rested sort of a cloud. We did not believe that there had been any offense, and yet we could not ascertain what it really might be. When the time came for us to leave, I personally felt so burdened about this matter that I walked along the shore of the Pacific pleading with God, "There is a burden resting on my brother,. God. Make me sensitive to his burden. If it is necessary to open an area of my life to him in order to make it easy for him to say whatever is burdening him, I am willing." As I sat on a log beside the ocean and watched the tide come in, I tried to search my heart. The only thing that I could think of was that I had recently turned down a job at one of the larger universities that could have more than doubled the pay that I was getting in the church college, involved about half the work load, and promised quantities of research money. But this didn't seem to make sense to me because the Indian no longer had any income. The money he used to earn from bananas was no more, for the banana industry had collapsed. Yet I could think of nothing else. As I walked back to the house, all the while praying that God should reveal the real thing that I should open up to my brother, I could find nothing else.

Finally, taking the brother along the same way that I had walked along the ocean, and sitting down on the same log, I prayed once more, "God, if within the next few minutes you will not reveal anything different to me, I will say this to him." When nothing came, I told him. The result was that he just threw his arm around me and tears began to fill his eyes. He said, "Brother, you and I have the same temptation." Then he told me how recently he had been offered the job as foreman on a construction program that was taking place not too far from his home, a job which would have paid him five hundred dollars (U.S.) a month in wages. But he had turned it down. Then another job offer had come which would have paid three hundred dollars a month, and it turned that down, too.

Now he was wondering whether he

had been plain stupid. "At other moments I wonder," he said. "If I am tempted by money, maybe I am no Christian at all. The missionaries don't seem to worry about money. Then I knew that on all these jobs there would be liquor. I don't know whether I am strong enough to resist drinking when liquor will be passed out. Secondly, even if I should be strong enough, I know that as foreman I would have to hand out the liquor to the other men. Knowing what liquor did to my home, I don't know how I as a Christian could hand it out to others. And thirdly, haven't I said to God that I would help him build the church?" When the missionary and Indian returned to the house and met the other missionary, the Indian slapped him on the back and said, "Kuriwa (David Wirsche), I know that I am a Christian, because Imama (the author) and I have the same kind of temptations."

Self-Exposure in the Altiplano

Self-exposure has very often been a useful approach in interviewing while seeking answers to specific problems. In order to start the discussion I would tell informants about certain segments of our own culture and ask them, "How does this work in your way of life?" Most people are then willing to reciprocate, and tell you about their culture. A good example of this type of self-exposure took place in the Altiplano in Ecuador, where a mission wanted help in discovering some of the underlying causes for a large number of pregnancies that had been discovered among the un-

married girls in their church membership. A secondary question revolved around the obvious unwillingness of the national church leaders to be involved in the problem.

We visited the home of one of the older men who was considered an open individual and one who also knew the community well. We began an animated conversation in the course of which I mentioned to him the problem of heavy petting that we were facing in many of our churches in America. Then I branched out into the premarital sex problems among the Choco and concluded with the question, "I have read in books that in the olden days the Quechua had trial marriage. How is it today? Do the Indians here have any problems with sex at that time too?"

My question unleased a torrent of words fraught with real deep emotion. "Before the missionaries came, we used to be able to manage sex. Young people would get together sexually when they found individuals whom they liked, but this always took place in the homes. As soon as parents discovered this, they would have these young people publicly declared as being in trial marriage. But now, since the mission has come and the young men are getting scholarships to go to secondary school, the parents can no longer do this because the mission won't support students with wives. This means that when the young men who go to school get involved with girls again and again, their parents just have to be quiet and tolerate it. They have to act as if they don't see it. The mission first teaches the children to disrespect parental authority in school and then makes our children promiscuous by their rules for scholarships."

Equally important can be the catalytic effect of self-exposure. When I was introduced to one of the congregations in the Altiplano as an anthropologist, I was sure that most of the Indians who were present did not know what the word "anthropologist" meant. (One of the people present had heard about physical anthropology, and he wondered what I would say about skeletons.) Preceding my talk there had been a Bible study about the public woman who washed Jesus' feet with her tears and dried them with her hair. Instead of saying some of the things that I had intended to say, I took off from this story and told them a little bit about myself. Among other things I recounted the frustrating preaching experience that was described in detail earlier, and also pointed out several other experiences in my life, in which God had to deal with me in a special way. I ended up saying that I was very grateful that God had had so much patience with me, but that I was sure God was just as good to Indians. I was now wondering, since I was a stranger in their midst, whether they might want to share with me some of the things that God was doing in their lives.

A man got up and asked me what I would do if I had quarreled with my brother-in-law. Not knowing whether this was a real or a hypothetical situation, I said, "Now you must recognize me as a foreigner. I do not know what to do in your culture, but let's ask the people here what you should do if you quarrel with your brother-in-law." The people willingly gave all kinds of counsel — they should be reconciled, they should love again. But I asked, "How can they love, if the heart is full of anger?" Some said, "Well, if the heart is full of anger, you have to confess it. You have to tell it to the person."

As this conversation about reconciliation unfolded, I didn't realize that I was witnessing a very real drama, that this little group was split by a very deep rift of quarreling and tension, and that the major protagonists were actually present in the meeting. This was no hypothetical situation; it was real life. After the discussion had clarified the main points, I turned to the Indian brother sitting beside me and said, "It seems to me that we have an answer here — one ought to do according to what our friends have said." The man beside me got up, walked across the room, and embraced a man who was sitting there and said, "Brother-in-law, I am sorry that I went to denounce you before the law. I want to ask you to forgive me and to love me again. I have hated you in my heart and I know that you have had to hate me." Then he went to the man's wife who was his sister, and said, "Sister, I have been very mean; I am sorry." The three of them embraced and cried in front of the congregation and settled a feud of long standing.

Before the group broke up that evening several more problems were confessed and settled, and in the atmosphere that was generated, the catalytic self-exposure of the foreigner was all but forgotten.

A Chocó Indian
in Hillsboro, Kansas

Antecedents

During 1956, 1958, and 1959 I was engaged in language research and Bible translation work with the Chocó Indians living in the Darién province of southern Panama. The work was conducted on the field in the Chocó setting so I could learn to appreciate the Chocó culture and world view.

During the 1958 and 1959 assignments I made acquaintance with Aureliano (Hombría) Sabúgara, a Chocó Indian, living on the Jaqué river close to the Panama-Colombia border. Aureliano had initially heard the Word of God when the Rev. Glenn Prunty of the New Tribes Mission read to the Indians a series of Bible stories. These Bible stories had first been translated into a Colombian Chocó dialect, and subsequently they had been "desk edited" for the Chocó dialect spoken in Panama on the basis of my 1956 field notes. Aureliano was one of several scores of Indians who in response to this good news "gave God the hand" and then began "to walk on God's road."

Aureliano, officially listed as 43 years

Jacob A. Loewen is Professor of Modern Languages, Anthropology, and Missions at Tabor College, Hillsboro, Kansas. He is author of "Good News for the Waunana," which appeared in PA, Vol. 8, No. 6 (Nov.-Dec. 1961).

old (actually probably between 35 and 40), is a progressive farmer. He cultivates about 17 acres of bananas which provide him with the princely income of seventy to one hundred dollars every two weeks. Socially he is a leader who enjoys having others around him. This had formerly led him to spend most of his take at each banana cutting on liquor for social consumption.

In 1959 Aureliano took part in an adult two-language literacy experiment in which ten bilingual (Chocó-Spanish) adults learned to read the Chocó language (transcribed as far as possible into Spanish orthography). After two months of Chocó reading study, these new literates were confronted with simple Spanish readers, and much to the encouragement of the experimenters, David Wirsche and the writer, they demonstrated nearly equal ability in reading both languages.

It was during this reading program that Aureliano suddenly received an inspiration to visit the United States. He reasoned that since he had been converted and had gained the victory over his liquor habit, he had some surplus income. This money he would save and invest in a trip to get acquainted with the brethren in North America. We tried to impress him with the ideals of Christian stewardship, saying that before a Christian invested so much for pleasure, he ought to inquire what the Lord would have him do, both with respect to his time and his money. As a result Aureliano decided to come to the United States during a time when the author would be free to work on the translation of Scriptures for the Chocoes. Aureliano would pay his way to the United States and would give his service without any remuneration for two months. The Mennonite Brethren Board of Foreign Missions would provide room and board in the United States and would pay his return trip to Panama. The Rev. and Mrs. Glenn Prunty helped Aureliano to secure the needed travel documents.

On March 20, 1960, the Pruntys and Aureliano boarded a Pan-American clipper at Tocumen, Panama, bound for Portland, Oregon. From Oregon, Aureliano accompanied the Prunty family on a deputation trip through the mid-western states. He arrived in Hillsboro on May 22. On July 11 after six weeks of translation work he boarded a Braniff Airlines plane and returned to Tocumen and Jaqué unaccompanied.

Aureliano's Reaction to Western Culture

A revealing incident took place on the Portland-bound clipper. The experience is here told in Mrs. Prunty's words:

My husband, Hombría and I were seated in the large four-engine plane that was to take us to that magical land called America. Hombría was seated by the window, his dark eyes alive and shiny with excitement. His nose was pressed flat against the window pane as he watched the last minute flurry of our take-off. Beads of perspiration began to form on his forehead, brought on, no doubt, by the unaccustomed attire of a suit complete with a bright red necktie. The engines began to roar in the process of the warm-up; then we began to move; and soon we were going up, up, up. I relaxed and reached for my book. Hombría was chattering like a magpie in wondrous amazement as he watched houses and land become smaller and smaller as we gained altitude. I became absorbed in my book. Several minutes passed before I realized that our friend by the window had become very quiet. I stole a glance and saw that his head was lowered and his hands were firmly clutched to the arm rests of the seat. I quietly called, "Hombría." With a start he turned to face me and immediately a smile replaced the soberness upon his face. I asked, "You aren't afraid, are you?" I leaned over to have a look outside. Only blue skies and fleecy white clouds were visible. Then I knew that Hombría had become frightened the moment houses and the land had disappeared from view. "Don't be scared," I said. "We are in the Lord's hands and he will care for us up here just as much as he does when we are on the ground." His smile broadened; he leaned back in his seat, folded his hands on his lap and said, "No, I'm not afraid, but I was just thinking that if any other member of my tribe had been here, he would have been scared to death."

Missionaries have often been afraid of exposing natives to the American comforts of life, fearing that they would become spoiled for their own more primitive culture. We were, therefore, alert to spot any symptoms of such falling in love with American gadgetry. But instead of finding our way of life as ideal or at least as superior to his own, we often found Aureliano making negative value judgments on our conveniences. After several months of tub bathing, we took him to a local lake for a swim. On the return trip he confided that he would be able to go at least a day or two without a bath now because the swim in the cool lake water had cleansed and refreshed him so thoroughly. "For," he then added about the bathtub, "I can bathe three, four, and five times a day in your 'pig hole,' and yet I cannot feel satisfied."

One day our IBM electric typewriter broke down, and our translation work had to be interrupted by a trip to Wichita, some fifty miles away. The Indian informant enjoyed the trip, but found the loss of translation time annoying, and commented: "You white people have too many things in your homes that are too big for you. We Epera (Indians) never have anything in our house that we cannot fix ourselves."

American food also was a problem for him. The month of deputation had led him from home to home on the standard entertainment diet of meat and potatoes. When Mrs. Loewen served him rice and lentil soup on his arrival in Hillsboro, he really gorged himself, offering as excuse that for a month he had not been able to eat well because he had received only "dry food." Gradually he learned to enjoy many American dishes, but to the end he refused to eat raw vegetable salads saying that grass was for the rabbits and that he was a human being. When once a tornado warning drove all of us into a storm cellar in the middle of the night, he sarcastically reminded us that this must also be rabbit country where everyone dives into his hole when the whistle blows. In the light of this he could also understand why we needed to eat rabbit food.

Enlargement of Aureliano's World View

Almost daily we observed how his experience in North America influenced his philosophy of life and his view of the universe. Of these changes three impressed us greatly. They were: (1) the knowledge that the world was a sphere, (2) the awareness of a world-wide brotherhood of man, and (3) the experience of fellowship of the saints within the church.

Already when we checked the translation of the expression "to the end of the earth" from the Great Commission, we felt that there was something amiss with the Chocó translation, but found no way to isolate the problem. For this reason we carefully explained the concept of world evangelism as a background for a translation of "unto the uttermost part of the world" in Acts 1: 8. Again, he translated: "to the last earth." This time we read the Spanish source again and pointed out: "You translated wrongly; it is to the remotest 'orilla' (Spanish, edge) of the earth, not to the 'last earth.'" He countered with: "Your explanation, however, said 'all the people.' What about those who live beyond this 'orilla'? Aren't there seven seas?"

"Well," I allowed, "we generally speak of five oceans but you can divide them into seven or more if you like." As our conversation progressed, it was very obvious that we were talking past each other. But where? What was wrong?

On a sudden inspiration I went to the geography room and wheeled a large globe into my study. I pointed out Panama, the United States, and the route of his travels. Next, I pointed out the five oceans and also traced the course of the destructive tidal wave that struck far-off Japan after the earthquake in Chile. He was dumbfounded, constantly looking at and turning the globe. My attempt to continue our work failed. He was too deeply engrossed. I began re-writing some of the translated verses, but he continued as if glued to the globe.

Finally he said: "So the earth is not land, but one big ocean and many islands." I countered: "No, do you see these different shades of blue in the ocean; they indicate the depth. Under the water is a 'land' bottom, so the earth is still land with big oceans." He continued in his contemplation for a while; then suddenly he arose, went to the blackboard, and drew a sketch, saying: "I knew the world was round, and I always thought that Panama and the United States were in the center of the world. Around this round land, I thought there was a 'ring' of water which was the first sea. Then followed successive rings of land and water until there were seven seas and seven lands. The last land is frozen to the sky, so what you wanted me to translate just does not make sense. There are no people on the last earth, because it is too cold."

Intimately linked with the new world concept was the recognition that the whole world has "people." Viewed from the basis of his indigenous culture only the Epera are "people." All the rest are "beings." Already some time previously his view of people had been enlarged to include the white Americans. However, the Negroes still came from across the ocean from the land of the "colored beings," and to him they were illegitimate descendants of black devils. But now he saw Negro Christians worshiping together with white and oriental believers. They even prayed together. He heard their testimonies and became convinced that they also were "people" and that they also could become sons of God through the sacrifice of Christ on the cross. "My people will also have to learn this," was his comment on this interracial fellowship experience.

However, the new insight Aureliano himself talked about most was the experience of brotherly love and fellowship within the church context. In regard to this experience Mrs. Prunty writes:

Everywhere we went people were captivated by Aureliano's radiant smile and glowing personality. His Spirit-directed testimony, so spontaneously given, did much to encourage and edify the people. When asked what his greatest impression of the United States and its people was, he would invariably answer that the love of the brethren had all but overwhelmed him.

Of course there was also a cultural reason to account for the depth of this impression. The social organization of the Chocoes has seriously disintegrated under the influence of the Western world so that there is little redress for the individual through the channels of the society. Redress has become revenge and that is now the prerogative of the individual; and magic is the great weapon. A man's isolation from, if not actual opposition to, his fellows is felt so keenly that in some areas every household includes a shaman. The more remote origin of a person, the greater the suspicion as to his intent. For this reason, when Aureliano, contrary to his expectation, found himself received in love by all the brethren here in remote North America, and when he saw how they also loved and trusted each other, he was profoundly impressed.

Evaluation

Looking back upon the experience of bringing the Indian to Hillsboro for translation work, we can evaluate its effects both from what was observed in the United States and from observation in his native setting.

On the negative side we observed that the sexual tensions due to being separated from his family were severe for Aureliano. Should a similar occasion develop, we would endorse Aureliano's recommendation that next time he come, he bring his wife with him.

We can also report several very positive values:

1. The initiative taken by an Indian believer to give money and time removed the translation project out of the realm of propaganda. It also caused Aureliano to be very much concerned about progress of the translation. If visitors interrupted the work, he would soon tell the translator to stop visiting, because there was work to do

2. The personal investment by Aureliano also stimulated a long-range vision in his heart to help build the church in the Jaqué area and to take the Word of God out to other areas so that the ultimate purposes of God could be fulfilled. Reports of his active evangelism after returning to Jaqué provide a living evidence of his vision.

3. The experience of a new culture by the informant gave added dimensions to his insight into the message of God and into the problem of translating the Word accurately. This greatly facilitated the work of translation.

The author later visited in Panama for three months and had the occasion to evaluate Aureliano's experience within the native setting. The almost unanimous evaluation of his fellow Indians and his Spanish-speaking neighbors was that he had returned unspoiled and with a real vision of bringing the message of God to his people. The author was able to witness the organization, under Aureliano's leadership, of a Chocó church whose spirit and warmth was reminiscent of the first chapters of Acts.

Jacob A. Loewen and F. Glenn Prunty

Aureliano:
Profile of a Prophet

WHEN[1] the first church among the Choco of Panama came into being during July of 1961 at El Mamey,[2] the missionary observers present were puzzled by the fact that the Christian Indian community never even entertained the question of whether or not it would be necessary to elect or to appoint Aureliano (Hombría) Sabugara as the leader of the church. In fact, the foreign missionaries' cautious inquiry about what method would be best for the Indian church to use in its choice of a leader met with universal and unfeigned surprise. "Why, we don't need to look for any leader! Aureliano is our leader!" When the unconvinced missionaries asked the individual heads of families about how they knew that this man was their leader, they invariably answered, "Because he led us to know the Lord Jesus," or "Because he taught us God's way."

Then, as the missionaries reflected they realized that it was Aureliano who had received them into his home. It was he who had initiated the erection of the church building, and who was even now inviting the people for the dedication services. In fact, he was actually assuming full responsibility for the various aspects of the program, including the food for all the visitors.

On the dedication Sunday morning the still doubting missionaries—who felt uncomfortable since there had been no democratic election—had to satisfy their consciences and ask whether their observation that all the people wanted Aureliano to be their leader was correct. The Indian word *mae* (Meaning "yes, indeed!") resounded enthusiastically from all quarters of the congregation.

As the dedication Sunday program progressed, the missionaries saw this leader ask several men to screen all the previously baptized Indians before their names were entered on the church roll. Only those who were currently "walking on God's road" could have their names written in the church book. Again, it was Aureliano who took the initiative in arranging for the examination of the candidates for baptism. Finally, it was a challenge he voiced at the afternoon communion service that led to the volunteering of the first Choco missionary.[3]

---

[1] Much of the material in this paper was gathered by F. Glenn Prunty. The writing, however, was done by J. A. Loewen, who must assume responsibility for the emphases as well as any misinterpretations.

[2] Jacob A. Loewen, "The Church among the Choco of Panama," PA, Vol. 10, No. 3 (May-June 1963), pp. 97-108.

Jacob A. Loewen is Translations Consultant for the American Bible Society in South America. Apdo. 5764, Lima, Peru. F. Glenn Prunty is a missionary of the New Tribes Mission.

[3] Ibid., pp. 105-106.

The agent

But not only on that first Sunday did Aureliano take the initiative; we must today in retrospect say that in almost every aspect of the phenomenal spread of the gospel among the Choco and beyond their boundaries, Aureliano was either at the head of the movement, or was the immediate agent that set the advance in motion. During the brief span of time from July, 1961 till June, 1964, the original church at El Mamey, with Aureliano as its pilot, had started two more Epera Christian concentrations (Corobal is still unorganized, but Lucas has its own church) on the Jaque River, and had planted another church among the Epera on the Tuquesa River. This latter group was reported to have spawned several subsidiary nuclei of believers on neighboring tributaries.

Next, following Aureliano's persuasive example, the Epera conquered their fear of the culturally similar, but linguistically separate Waunana Indian immigrants from Colombia and brought them the good news. The first group was baptized on the Chado River, a Jaque River tributary. More recently two more Waunana concentrations on the Chitola and Maje Rivers have been visited, and especially at Chitola another church is developing.

Finally, since Pastor Aureliano employed several families of non-Indians on his banana farm, he was also able to lead a number of these people to the Lord. He was a real innovator when he baptized the first non-Indians professing conversion, but it opened the door for him to win to the Lord and to baptize at least twenty more. This outreach to the non-Indians led to the founding of a dynamic Spanish-speaking church in the village of Jaque at the mouth of the river by the same name. Since members of this latter church had relatives in Colombia, they, together with Aureliano and other Epera believers made several trips across the border with the gospel message. Thus today, in the Colombian Choco, there are three nuclei of baptized believers and sympathizers among the non-Indians and two among Epera Indians speaking the Baudo dialect.

This summary of Aureliano Sabugara's involvement and influence in the growth of the church among the Choco corroborates and specifically illustrates within the realm of the church, a contention that Margaret Mead makes for successful people's movements in general: A viable people's movement requires a "prophet" as one of the basic essentials for success.[4]

If this postulate is indeed a universal one and if successful group movements—both positive and negative—must have such prophet leaders, missions and missionaries would do well to take a rather close look at them and the dynamics of their development and operation. This paper proposes to take a step in that direction by presenting a biographic portrait and some scenes illustrating

[4] Margaret Mead, *New Lines for Old: Cultural Transformation—Manus, 1928-1953* (New York: William Morrow, 1956). Mead lists the following prerequisites for a "conversion" type social change: (1) A universal awareness and dissatisfaction with some cultural disequilibrium. (2) Awareness of alternatives to the current problems. (3) A prophet to formulate the discontent and to propose a new way. (4) Some internal cultural "value" basis on which such a change can be justified. (5) Sufficient time for diffusion until the group can reach a consensus for action. In it all, the prophet is basic.

Aureliano Sabugara's role as leader of the church among the Choco. It is written with the hope that other missionaries will be led to study Mead's thesis and then be stimulated to review the leading personalities of group movements in their areas.

Such studies could provide the basic data needed for isolating the essential personal and leadership qualities of actual and potential prophets. For actual, recognized prophets, such a study would help to make the missionary more understanding and sympathetic, and to that degree also make it possible for him to relate more constructively to any movement the prophet may lead. In regard to potential prophets an early recognition could prevent the missionary from stifling or frustrating such a prophet in his development. Not only is it possible, but it is highly probable that conflict between missionaries and emerging prophets will arise. Nor is it enough to admit that such conflict can and has occurred; we must actually admit the fact that many splinter groups and nativistic movements are anti-missionary today because their developing leaders were frustrated or rejected by some unappreciative missionary.[5] Even where a movement and its leaders manifest negative leanings, sympathetic understanding of the dynamics of continuing group and leadership development could provide clues and insights for possible involvement in re-directing such movements toward more ideal goals. Certainly sympathetic involvement in the lives and experiences of

such leaders ought to make one more sensitive toward and appreciative of the role of the prophet in any group movement.

A biographical sketch

Aureliano's citizen's registration states that he was born on the Jaque River on February 18, 1925; but this represents merely a guess by some political registration officer, for his birth was never registered, nor are many details known about it. His father, Camilio Sabugara, came from the Puricha River in Colombia as a young man who was "getting to know the world," as the Choco call the wanderings from river to river by teen-age boys looking over the girls in search for a wife. At Lucas, brightly painted-up Camilio became amorously involved with a daughter of a famous shaman family.[6]

Because young Camilio married into such a powerful clan, he was never able to take his bride home to his people. Usually the young man stays with his in-laws only until after the

---

[5] Maybe missions should take a lesson from the political scene. Most of the leaders of new Asian and African nations spent time in colonial jails. Could a parallel be true of prophets in the indigenous church too?

[6] Even today among the Christians on the Jaque River such names as Primitivo Dobiaza, Felix Cabrera and Rutilio Cabrera make people pause in awe to retell some great accomplishment of these medicine men. During the interview for this paper even Aureliano got involved in telling about Uncle Rutilio, the great shaman who had more than sixty curing canes (the Choco recognize a full-fledged practitioner when he has eight canes). "He was so powerful," recounted Aureliano in all seriousness, "that every night at sundown a single-file train of poisonous snakes would climb up the pillars of the house and make their way to the shelf with his canes." These snakes were the "disguised" familiar spirits subservient to witch-doctor Rutilio. "I used to lie quietly at night and watch that endless procession of spirits. He was a powerful man, my Uncle Rutilio."

birth of the first child, when he announces that he must now show the new grandchild to his father. The "visit" generally marks the permanent change of residence to the environment of the husband's family. Since his own family had no powerful shaman protectors, young Camilio never dared brave his wife's family's wrath to take his bride to his own home. So he stayed on the Jaque River until his death. This circumstance is largely responsible for the fact that Aureliano today knows little more about his father's family than his grandfather's name.

Aureliano was born as the sixth and last child, and he was still only an infant when his father was killed by poison at one of the Lucas drinking festivals. Why? Aureliano surmised that his father might have been unhappy that he could not take his wife to his own river and that as a result he may have shown too much resentment against his wife's family.

For Aureliano life changed little even with his father's death. He and the other children continued living with their mother, Celia, who was from the Rengifo family. He was approaching puberty when his mother suddenly passed away. This broke up the home and Aureliano went to live with his oldest sister who had recently married and was living near the present El Mamey. He did not like living with his brother-in-law, and so he soon set out "to know the world." He did not travel far, for already on the first river (the Jurado) in Colombia he became the husband of a "big, pretty" girl, Aldeana Marmolejo. Like his father before him, orphan Aureliano

did not have the prestige to declare his liberty and to take his wife to the Jaque River after their first child was born. "I could not even say 'I have received word that my father wants me to show him his grandchild.'" To complicate matters even more, the first three children all died within a year of their birth. So he continued working with his brothers-in-law gathering natural rubber in the Choco jungle. By his own reckoning Aureliano stayed there nine years, but possibly six would be a more realistic figure. By that time his maturing self-image found life with the in-laws more difficult. A son, the fourth child, was born, and he seems to have been a strong child. Once again Aureliano tried to convince his wife "to go and visit his people," but she refused. "So when Luis was about six months old (he is a young man of about twenty now), I left Aldeana and went back to my people alone."

Again he did not stay long with his sister. He found a job as dishwasher on a fishing boat and so left the Indian environment. Soon, however, the cook was fired because of drunkenness, and Aureliano became the head of the kitchen. The captain noted that he had a fine eye for both river and ocean travel, and considered appointing him seaman and pilot; but, since he was quite young, the chief mechanic convinced the captain to make him the mechanic's mate instead. According to Aureliano's reckoning he served on this boat for three years, but again the figure seems inflated.[7] He was serving as

[7] This lack of time consciousness seems to be characteristic of Hombría. Recently he reminded the author of an event that happened a year ago, but he referred to it as having happened more than two years ago.

mechanic's assistant, when a Canal Zone machine shop operator made his acquaintance and offered him a job as motor maintenance man. He was exceedingly happy with his new position and resolved to work hard to become a first class mechanic. But then Pearl Harbor threw the United States into the war. Shortly after America declared war, Aureliano's older brother, who was also working in the Canal Zone, came to him excitedly one night and told him that the Japanese were on the way to bomb the Canal. He urged Aureliano to flee back to his people with him. That night then, both of them left for the Jaque River without even stopping to claim their pay for the days they had worked.

But the war had come also to Jaque. An emergency landing strip was being built near the mouth of the river. Gradually the appeal of the greenbacks overcame the fear of bombs, and Aureliano joined the work crew engaged in building the runway.

Immediately after his return from the Canal Zone, Aureliano cleared some land at El Mamey and planted a thousand plantain shoots—he had decided to establish a home. Possibly while still working on the runway he took Natalia Cabrera, a distant cousin of his, as wife. He was still living with his in-laws when the banana market in the Jaque area opened up. Eager to cash in on this bonanza, Aureliano bought several hundred banana shoots. "They were very scarce in those days, but I took good care of them and transplanted all the new shoots until I had a hectare of bananas." Since the market demand for the banana was strong, Aureliano was able to increase his farm by a thousand or two of new plants every year. He hired men by contract to do clearing and planting, and gradually drifted mainly into the manager function. In this way he built up a plantation of some 17,000 banana plants and several thousand plantains. This made him one of the most prominent Indian farmers in the Jaque area. However, with success he also fell prey to the appetite for hard liquor which he had acquired during his tour of duty on the fishing boat.

The cultural milieu

The development of the banana industry had some very far reaching effects on Choco society. Indian participation in the raising and selling of bananas introduced surplus cash, something their economy had never known before. But what was more important still, it permitted the development of disparaties of income. No longer were men more or less equal; some were becoming wealthy and others found themselves serving as day laborers for the rich. This laid an axe at one of the principal roots of Choco society, which held that all men were equal.

The expanding banana market also made the Jaque River—hitherto largely an Indian territory—very desirable for non-Indians. At first the Indians in their desire for social acceptance with the non-Indians were quite ready to let outsiders "use" lands the Indians claimed as their own, but it did not take long until they began to feel the effects of this infiltration. First of all, it greatly weakened Indian cohesion, because everywhere non-Indian neighbors were nesting between them. Often as not these infiltrators used gossip to drive wedges between Indian families so that they could broaden their land holdings. Next, they became the means of teaching the Indian that he was socially inferior, for these non-Indians soon took possession of most of the best accessible lands and forced the Indians to retreat to the smaller tributaries.

The money economy made possible the purchase of guns and other luxuries which soon began to attract Indians from Colombia, where fire-arms, even for hunting, were not on the market. The Epera of the Jaque found ready use for these Indian immigrants as workers on their banana holdings. These strangers from Colombia, speaking unintelligible Choco languages and dialects, were very much afraid in this strange environment; so they sought protection in witchcraft. This led to an influx of Colombian shamans who sold "insurance" to Indians who were outside of their home territories. As these "foreign" Indians began to ogle local females and eventually also began to marry them, the inter-tribal tension increased rather than decreased. Deaths of non-local sons-in-law, like Aureliano's father, became quite common.

Affluence permitted local Indians much more free time—laborers now did much of the hard work. It permitted them to have more frequent drinking festivals with cane wine or maize *chicha*. This increase in the number of drinking festivals can be viewed as an attempt on the part of the society to stem the growing tide of breakdown in their face-to-face relationships. But instead of strengthening social bonds, the introduction of vengeance by poison administered in liquor actually drove people further apart. They no longer trusted each other; but no one dared to admit this overtly, for that would bring him under suspicion as a potential poison dispenser. Thus as social drinking increased, so also did the deaths through poisoning. Aureliano stated that the majority of his male relatives from his mother's side were killed by poisoning.

The arrival of the non-Indians had another rather tragic result. It introduced communicable diseases which annually killed large numbers of Choco children. Not understanding these epidemics of measles, small pox, whooping cough and diphtheria, the people reached for spirit and witchcraft explanations—some sorcerer was killing their children. This provided further reason for poisoning at their drinking sprees. Of this period Aureliano sadly said, "I don't know whether it was because we were so afraid of the evil spirits and because we believed so many evil things, that our children always got sick and died. Why, I did not have children (that is, living and growing) during those years. My oldest boy (with Natalia) drowned as a three year old while we were at a drinking festival, and the other three got sick and died while they were small. It seems to me that my children have prospered only after I found and began to walk on God's way. Look at José (now about twelve years of age) and my other three children. They hardly ever are sick now.[8] God gives his people health now."

Affluence also permitted the Indians to purchase commercial hard liquor, and this really became their undoing. First of all, the physical effects were

---

[8] The answer, of course, is in large part the preventative medicine that the Christian Medical Association of the Canal Zone has brought to the area.

far more detrimental than those of cane wine or *chicha*. Secondly, they became drunk away from home, and involvements with other women and quarrels became more frequent. The non-Indians of course found this very useful. To offer to drink with an Indian whom he had abused made the Indian feel better. Soon the Indian was paying for all the liquor; and as he got drunk, his non-Indian "friend" extracted promises of sale of land, canoes, cane fields and whatever the Indian had. When the Indian came to and denied such sale, he was hauled before the law—still other non-Indians —and forced to comply. Not being able to venge himself on the non-Indians, the Indian often turned on his own people and agression became commonplace even in the formerly peaceful (by older Indians' evaluation) drinking festivals.

As the Indians' personal worth was crumbling and their social cohesion disintegrating, individual Indians grasped for acceptance with the non-Indians all the more eagerly. Rather than solve their problems however, this often became the occasion for their complete destitution.

Another approach to redeem one's self-image was to become "civilized"— to build a house in Jaque village and to send one's children to school. Especially several chief men among the Indians tried this approach. It too failed, for when Indian children entered school they became the object of ridicule and scorn—"Look at this *cholo* (a derisive term for Indian); he thinks he can learn." Since the Indian children were weak in spoken Spanish, and psychologically cowed by the treatment as inferiors, they seldom learned to read and write. As a result the local prejudice could write off an Indian as uneducable with the words, "They are brute." Gradually the Indians came to parrot this themselves, for on being asked in 1958 why they did not learn to read Spanish, they said, "It's because we are so 'brute' stupid."

The good news of the new way

Into this unhappy and unhealthy cultural "mess" came the good news of God's way. The details of the arrival and the Choco acceptance of the gospel have already been told in an earlier paper.[9] Even though Aureliano was among the first to hear the message, it was not until a year and a half later that he actually made his decision to follow the way. Here is his firsthand account.

I heard Francisco (F. Glenn Prunty) talk about God in the very beginning, but I did not want to listen to his words. I was a slave of hard liquor. Every banana cutting I would get my money, and then I would begin to buy liquor for my friends. Soon I lost awareness. I do not know what actually happened, but when I became sober I was entirely penniless. Did I actually drink it all? Did someone steal it? I do not know. Often even the new clothes I had bought before beginning to drink were in the hands of others. My wife got no food. I did not buy her what she needed. True, I did not kill any of my children like Gabriel, who in a drunken fit beat his eleven-year-old daughter until she died, but I am nevertheless ashamed of those days. I was such a fighter.

9 See footnote No. 2

I abused many of my Indian neighbors and became involved with their women. Many people hated me, and with reason. Sometimes I was afraid that someone would poison me at one of the drinking parties. But Nata always watched very closely whenever I was drinking with Indians. Then I began to get sick. I was just drinking too much. There was much "fire" in my body.[10] I was getting worried. One day I said to Nata, "Wife, I wish I could stop drinking." She immediately said, "That's good. Let's go and see Francisco and then you can 'give your hand to God' and he will take away your desire to drink." I did not want to go. It took several weeks until I finally agreed to visit the Bible studies. Then one day we all went to the meeting.

Of this service F. Glenn Prunty recalls, "There were many people at the service, but this was not unusual. First we had a literacy lesson reading Choco syllables, and then I taught the Indians a Bible lesson. As soon as I finished talking Aureliano got up and said, 'I have decided to give God the hand and want to walk on God's road.' As soon as I began to pray with Aureliano it seemed as if the whole clan was also beginning to pray. There were many decisions that day."

However, giving God the hand was not the whole answer to the liquor problem, for time after time Aureliano

got drunk again. But each time he sobered up he was determined that this must stop. He claims, "God finally changed my stomach so that I could no longer take liquor. It began to make me sick. If I did not stop with the first drink, I had to vomit."[11]

Aureliano had been a believer for only six months when he became a student in the 1959 literacy experiment. He had long harbored an intense desire to learn to read, but had always considered it out of his reach. Once he saw that he, an Indian, could also master the printed page, he applied himself with total dedication. Soon he was one of the best readers. When he received his first folklore reader on completion of the primer course, he spent the whole night reading the book by candlelight and came to class the next day with bloodshot eyes. David Wirsche, his literacy teacher, reported the following concerning Aureliano. "He was the second-best reader in the group... The man has good leadership qualities—spiritually and socially. He did much independent reading."

Little did the missionaries at this time realize what reading would do to Aureliano's—and for that matter to the whole Choco tribe's—self-image. Once he was able to read the book of Bible stories which served as final reader in the literacy program, he counselled another Indian who was debating whether he should attempt to learn to read, "Once you can read you can receive the message directly from God, and you don't have to depend on what others say that he said."

---

[10] Choco Indians believe that sex relations and liquor leave "fire" in the body. When too much fire has been accumulated the person gets sick. Saline purges are frequently taken to get rid of excess fire.

[11] It is interesting that the genuineness of a man's conversion is popularly evaluated by whether or not his stomach tolerates liquor. A truly converted person will vomit as soon as he starts drinking, the Chocos say.

During the weeks of the literacy program an atmosphere of easy fellowship and familiarity developed between Aureliano and his teachers. So one day he asked them, "How much does a plane ticket to your country cost?"

"About $200.00."

"Is that all? Why, then I can come and visit you. Now that I don't drink anymore I can easily save that much money." And he did. During the summer of 1960 Aureliano spent a number of weeks in Hillsboro, Kansas with author Loewen translating Mark and Acts into the Choco language. Some of his reactions and changes in worldview experienced during this visit have already been described in a separate paper.[12] For purposes of this paper we underscore at least two of the mentioned changes: (1) the awareness that all men are "people" and that the new birth brings men into a brotherhood that supercedes race, language and national boundaries, (2) that the church is a fellowship of believers who love and help each other. Both of these insights became fundamentals in the message Aureliano delivered to his people on his return from abroad.

At least two more of his experiences in the United States should be recounted, for both add dimensions to our understanding of Aureliano as a person and as a leader.

Soon after his arrival in Hillsboro the author took him to a rescue mission in the slums of Wichita. This was an attempt to show him that there are also whites who are "down and out." On his first visit the condition of these men did not seem to register at all. However, after the expansion of his view of people and the experiences of Christian fellowship had taken place, the author took him to the same mission for a repeat visit. This time he grasped the situation and instead of a sermon, he shared with the men a personal testimony of his involvement with liquor and of his victory on the Jesus road. His transparent witness moved the men in the benches. When several of them came to the altar for prayer, he experienced the first joy of a successful soul winner. On the way home he reasoned, "If God can bless my testimony to white men and cause them to decide for Christ, should I not be able to preach to my own people?"

Just before he returned to Panama the Board of Missions had a reception for him. Though he was an "Indian from the jungle" he surprised everyone including the author with the speech he delivered on that occasion. He had been asked to say something about his people and the gospel. His speech actually detailed a plan to establish the Choco church on his return.

After the reception he spoke in private to some of the board members, "When Imama and Kuriwa (nicknames of the author and David Wirsche, respectively) come to visit us next summer we will be meeting in a church at El Mamey just like God's people do here in the United States."

Armed with his changed world view and the conviction that the Christian message was just the good news his people needed, Aureliano returned to Panama. The news of his return brought many curious people to his house and provided a propitious setting

---

12 Jacob A. Loewen, "A Choco Indian in Hillsboro Kansas," PA, Vol. 9, No. 3 (May-June 1962), pp. 129-144.

for Aureliano to step into the role of witness and prophet. His capacity to present the truths that spoke to the immediate needs of the people moved the Epera of the Jaque River. They not only began to gather for meetings, but Aureliano inspired them to join him in building a meeting house. Thus when David Wirsche and the author came to Panama in June of 1961, they found a chapel almost completed and a church (although unorganized by our standards) meeting in Aureliano's house. The dedication of this meeting house and the installation of Aureliano as leader have already been detailed in the introduction.

Discussing these events once more in June of 1964, the author asked Aureliano for his personal opinion on why the people had chosen him to be the leader of the church. Without hesitation he supplied two reasons. "It was because of my manner of thinking." "I somehow had the knack of earning a good living."[13]

The prophet in action

Instead of continuing a chronological account of Aureliano's leadership activity in the Choco church, it seems best to spell out in detail a number of specific areas of activity and to try to isolate from these experiences some of the qualities that seem to have been crucial for success or failure.

The drinking festival had been the main Choco social activity, but it had become contaminated. Instead of

---

[13] Aureliano's severest testings seemingly have come in the economic sphere. The collapse of the banana industry, the slaughter of his pigs, etc., have tried his endurance again and again. It is only recently that he is again making more economic headway.

fellowship and belonging, the repeated poisonings had reduced it to a source of fear and death. The Choco definitely needed a social fellowship institution, and Aureliano decided that the church was made to measure for this purpose. It is hard to say how much design and how much chance there was operative in the development of the service pattern, but when the missionaries arrived at El Mamey in June of 1961 they found that the church had established periodic two- or three-day gatherings which generally involved Friday, Saturday and Sunday. The missionaries' inquiry for the reason of the extended gatherings was met by, "We always used to gather for several days at a time to drink (the actual duration was generally determined by the supply of wine and *chicha*), so why should we have church meetings only on Sunday? And besides, we need to teach reading and other things, and Sunday is not enough."

What greatly interested the visitors in 1961 was the fact that Aureliano was willing to invest pigs and produce in order to provide a suitable table for the fellowship periods. His own explanation was, "If the teacher wants to teach the people something, he must be convinced enough to be willing to invest something. The people must have an opportunity to learn that here at the church even the unbelievers can come, eat, and fellowship without fear of being poisoned or killed."

A second feature—a real innovation for the Jaque—that Aureliano had introduced in 1961 was the practice of working bees. The believers went from farm to farm and collectively worked for each other. The author had seen a similar pattern among the Choco Indians living in the Rio Verde area of Colombia, but in Panama this was entirely new. The program got off to a very successful start. The believers manifested real enthusiasm for the fellowship approach to work. However, with the collapse of the banana market the working bee seems to have perished also. It has not been observed during more recent visits in connection with rice which, in a measure, is now replacing bananas.

Watching Aureliano's leadership in the meetings proper was very instructive. Never at any time did he feel it necessary to consult the missionaries about whether or not to have services, but once he had called a meeting he would not hesitate to ask the missionaries to fulfill special roles. For example, he might ask F. Glenn Prunty to teach the people the melody to some Spanish song Aureliano had heard. The author frequently was asked to explain to the people something he had discussed with Aureliano in Hillsboro in the course of the translation of Mark and Acts. Aureliano followed up each discourse with questions and applications, always encouraging a free discussion of the new ideas presented.

The teacher

Aureliano's own approach to teaching was most fascinating. He had a wonderful capacity to explain and drive home a truth once he grasped it. Not that he was always the first to grasp it, but once he did, he was outstanding in passing it on to others.

David Wirsche reports a revealing episode in connection with a hygiene lesson on the housefly as an agent in the spread of disease. The lesson inclu-

ded pictures of the fly's leg greatly magnified to show disease germs stuck to the cilia of the leg. The lesson was not quite finished when the call to lunch interrupted the class. Before eating, Aureliano, as usual, stood up to lead the group in a hymn and prayer, but this time he called all the people present to the rear of the house which overlooked the cesspool into which all garbage, banana peels and slop-water were thrown. Then he solemnly said, "God has spoken this morning. He has told us that flies carry disease and that he does not want his children to be sick. Do you see all those flies in the cesspool ? They are hatching and growing there, and that is also where they pick up the disease. Then they walk over our food and make us sick."

He paused and turned to his wife, "Nata, fetch a basket !" She did. "Nata, now fetch an earthen vessel !" She did that too. Then he commanded, "From now on in our house banana peels will be thrown into the basket and all garbage water into the earthen pot. Both shall be emptied into the river for God does not want his children to be sick any longer."

Wirsche also reports some interesting details on Aureliano's difficulty to grasp new truth. "In the course of teaching the essentials of arithmetic to adults in preparation for entrance into the government adult education program in Panama City, I ran into trouble trying to explain the concept and the function of zero. Several days passed and Aureliano had still not grasped this elusive mathematical entity. Finally one morning the light dawned and he grasped it. Then he at once interrupted me and began to tell me how I ought to teach zero if I wanted Indians to understand it. I just stood there almost dumbfounded at the masterful way in which he could explain it, now that he had grasped it."[14]

On the other hand one must say that Aureliano was generally very quick to extract meaning from experiences and very adept at making the applications. This trait can be readily seen in another experience reported by Wirsche in 1963.

I was teaching the multiplication table to a group of adults. Aureliano was also in the group, but neither he nor the other adults seemed to grasp the basic principles. When all my attempts failed to produce the desired results, I decided that I needed time to pray and to think; so I called a recess for the rest of the day. By next morning I had new inspiration and it worked. The whole group grasped the principle. Several days later when the church met, pastor Aureliano stood up and said, "Do you know what Kuriwa does when he gets stuck and doesn't know what to do? He stops his work and talks to God. After God tells him how to do it he goes back to work. I want all of you to learn that we must not fret, get angry or worried when we are stymied. We must learn to stop and to talk with God just like Kuriwa did. God will teach us too!"

His respect for the tribal leadership patterns in public meetings also needs to be underscored. For example, the first communion service, celebrated on the dedication Sunday, attracted many visitors. Among these was also one of the local shamans. After a number of believers had given testimony of their experiences in "the way" leader Aureliano suddenly interrupted and said, "We have a guest in our meeting today. There is neighbor so-and-so from upriver; maybe he has a word of counsel for us at this time." Slowly and with dignity the shaman arose and said, "All of you know that I do not belong. You all know that I am involved with the spirit world and that I do not know a way out." After the medicine man sat down, Aureliano thanked him for his words and asked the believers to pray that their neighbor could find an exit. An impromptu prayer session for the shaman followed.[15]

The same meeting was also attended by a very successful Indian farmer who was every bit as successful as Hombría himself. Aureliano also called on him for a word, even though he was an unbeliever at the time. This man expressed his satisfaction over the fine time of fellowship he had been able to enjoy. "I know I do not belong to the way, but I do know that all the things you have said about God are true." Leader Aureliano immediately launched into one of his picturesque responses. "That is the way I like to hear my people talk. When you know that something is a dog, don't call it a cat."

---

[14] An interesting sequel took place when the ministry of education sent a delegation to investigate Choco educational advances. The ministry representative asked Aureliano to show how he taught the people. Aureliano immediately launched into an explanation of zero that was so masterful that the commission recommended he be appointed in spite of his lack of formal education.

[15] As a sequel to this we can point out that a year later this shaman had accepted Christ and was a baptized member of the church.

Use of Choco leadership patterns

His use of Choco leadership patterns as tools in witnessing was equally impressive. In Jaque village he sent a child to invite some relatives who were from a different river but who had also come to town to sell bananas, to come to a meeting. The child made a mistake and invited strangers from a completely different tributary. When this extended family group of twelve to fifteen Indians entered, the service was already in progress. Aureliano immediately stopped the meeting, however, and began over for the benefit of the visitors. In it all he never addressed himself to the group as a whole but rather spoke to the elderly man—the patriarch of the visiting group.

His personal approach reached a climax during the Bible reading which involved the story of the blind beggar Bartimaeus. After the first reading of the story Aureliano asked the old man whether he had understood it. Upon hearing the old man's negative response he ordered the passage to be re-read. This scene was repeated two times. When the old man still answered negatively, he made the application. "As you can see, God has not cleaned up your eyesight; that is why you cannot understand. You are just like the blind man begging by the road. You have to take the explanations and things other people give you, for you cannot read with your own eyes what God has said."

Then he abruptly switched. "How many people on your river have given God the hand and walk on God's road?" When the old man again had to admit that there were none, Aureliano continued to press the point. "How do you as the oldest man on the river expect to answer to God if none of your people are walking on God's road?" The old man was almost reduced to tears and countered, "But we do not know how to give God the hand, and how can we walk on God's road?" Now Aureliano clinched the point. "But we know and we have God's message, and still you have not invited us to come and tell you about it." Before the meeting ended the old man had extended an invitation to the El Mamey church to come to their river with a literacy-evangelistic campaign.

While he seemed to use his authority quite bluntly in the preceding scene, one cannot say that Aureliano clung to power. He was generally willing to share it and certainly he was a master at delegating it. An excellent example took place during the 1963 literacy-evangelistic campaign to the Tuquesa River. Together with a team of five or six other believers Aureliano was bringing the good news to a new area. The results were phenomenal. In the three-week campaign several scores of people learned to read, and about two dozen were baptized on the confession of their faith.

At the conclusion of this campaign the members of the evangelistic team prepared a tape-recorded report for the author. During the course of his speaking, leader Aureliano told of the enthusiastic response and of the great possibilities in the Tuquesa area, but then went on to say that he had not actually kept on teaching to the very end of the campaign because he had suddenly realized that once the team left, it might be a long time before anyone could return. If this group of Christians was to grow in strength and in number, it would have to function as a church. "I suddenly realized that they would need power (his way of describing authority to baptize, administer communion and lead church services) if they were to grow. So I began to look around among the converts and found among them an older man who was a good teacher and who knew how to lead people. Thus, instead of teaching more new people, I spent the last four days together with this man instructing him how to baptize and do all manner of church work. In fact, the last group of converts on this river were already baptized by this new leader. Now this church has power so that it can work and grow just like ours on the Jaque River."

There are several workers in the expanding church movement today who began as members of a team doing literacy - evangelism. Then Aureliano assigned specific tasks to them, and through these experiences they gained confidence so that today they are recognized as leaders in their own right. An example is the teacher-leader among the Waunana, who accompanied Aureliano and the team on their first visit to Chitola. Since he served as teacher, interpreter and preacher under Aureliano's leadership, he was so inspired that he just stayed on to continue the teaching ministry among his own people when the rest of the team left.

The prophet between
the church and the world

This section is focused on Aureliano's relationships with the non - Indian unbeliever and especially the civil and police authorities.

While conversion and the acceptance of the way solved many intratribal problems, it also introduced a series of new problems and tensions in the Indians' relationship to the world around them. One of the earliest problems especially acute in 1961 involved the Jaque saloons. For the duration of the banana marketing era the Indians had provided a constant source of income – possibly close to 70% of the Indians' receipts—for the saloonkeepers. With the advent of the church and the development of a taboo against drinking both in Indian drinking parties and in the saloons, there was a sudden and drastic drop in the consumption of commercial liquor. This was a severe economic threat to the liquor interests. These at once launched an intensive campaign to regain their clientele. At first they distributed bottles of free liquor to their customers of long standing, and as a result were able to get them drunk again. Even more effective was the non-Indians' attack on the Indians' self-image. Saloonkeepers and their cronies invited Indians in for a chat and then served them a friendly glass. When the Indian hedged or refused they called his friendship into question, often insinuating that the Indian wasn't polite or civilized. Because Indians were still very desirous of the non-Indians' good will and supposed friendship, they often took the drink and once having tasted liquor, they usually got solidly drunk.

In the course of these attacks by the saloonkeepers, Aureliano of course, was singled out as a chief object of attack, especially since his return from the United States and because of his obviously growing authority. Although

Aureliano personally was trapped a number of times, he became a rallying pillar within the Indian community to stand firm under the temptation. Having himself fallen, Aureliano seemed to have a deep understanding for and an almost inexhaustible patience with his fellows who were still being caught. His personal confessions and testimony must be credited as the key to victory for many believing Indians. (Currently only two saloons are left in the struggle for survival; five of the seven have already gone out of business.)

Another very important factor was the rise in the Indian's self-image as a result of the successful literacy campaigns. As Indians learned to read not only the Indian language but also the Spanish, and that often in record time, their self-confidence increased. This made them less dependent on the approval of the non-Indians. Again the decrease in drinking made them more independent also of the credit that saloonkeepers had formerly extended to them for supplies after all the Indians' income had been spent on liquor.

However, not only liquor interests were frightened by the newly found self-confidence of the Indian. The exploiting community in general was severely shaken. As a result rather widespread harrassing tactics developed. For example, when the collapse of the banana industry led to an extensive shift to rice, the many pigs which always scrounged in the banana orchards became a problem and the source of a lot of Indian abuse. The local oral law permitted a person whose crop of rice or corn was being violated by hogs, to dispose of the offending animals, if the owner had not heeded two warnings. Now non-Indian unbelievers seized upon this law to inflict hurt upon Indian believers. In fact, they generally did so without any warning whatsoever. Often the Indian owner did not learn of the shooting until he searched for his missing pigs and came upon their decaying carcasses near some neighbor's field. During the 1962-63 rice harvest, leader Aureliano without any warning lost fifty pigs in this way near a rice field of whose existence he did not know. This of course, broke the man financially, and he disposed of the few remaining animals at a sacrifice price. On the other hand the non-Christian neighbors turned their pigs loose to damage the rice fields of Indian believers.

Here is how Aureliano and the church handled this problem. In 1962 when David Wirsche arrived at El Mamey, he noticed that there were no meetings of the church. On his inquiry Aureliano told him that the church had decided that believers should no longer kill their neighbors' pigs even after repeated warnings failed to make the owner watch them. Instead they discontinued the weekly meetings so that the families could daily police their ripening rice fields and protect them from the non-Indians' pigs. They had decided that for the witness of the church the watching of their fields in a non-violent way was more important than worship services coupled with killing of the offending hogs.

Ever since the founding of the church, it has had to face an even knottier problem; and this one has probably also been handled less successfully. Every year the Indians from upriver have provided the main source of labor to clean up Jaque village for its patron saint festival on July 20. Since this matter was partly civic and partly religious it presented a very thorny issue for the Christian Indian community. Should the believers participate in the clean-up for a festival of a religion to which they did not belong. Wasn't the clean-up a prelude to the annual visit of the priest? The national guard sergeant who ordered the clean-up claimed that it was a purely civil affair (though the religious linkage was obvious), while Aureliano viewed it as an overwhelmingly religious affair. It might not have become serious had not the whole urban community been worried about the rising Indian self-image. This issue thus provided them with a legal weapon to humiliate the "cocky" Indians.

Aureliano, however, was aware of bigger officials beyond, so he responded to this attack in kind. He went over the heads of the local authorities and made a trip to the capital to obtain a hearing with higher officials. And he found willing ears, but he did not realize that they were politicians from the opposition party who felt that here was an issue that could provide them with votes. The Indians were commended for their stand, and all types of oral promises were made about correcting this abuse. Actually the Indians had only angered local authorities and put themselves into a bad light with the government in power. The issue was still not settled in 1964. Leader Aureliano admitted in private conversations with the missionaries that he had made a mistake, but he found it very hard to think that he alone—the sergeant obviously would not admit his abuse of power—would have to assume the guilt and make an apology.

However, maybe the "burning of his fingers" with the politicians also had some benefits. In the recent elections in which Indians were wooed and threatened by three candidates, the leadership confided to the missionaries that they had decided to split their vote about equally for the three parties feeling that in this way they would make the least enemies for themselves.

The prophet and the foreign missionary

Unlike leaders of some other people's movements, Aureliano seldom has manifested frustration in respect to missionaries. Already in his conversion experience F. Glenn Prunty's sympathy and personal experience with enslavement to liquor provided a basis for a concept of equality with the missionary. The 1959 literacy experiment, in which he as an adult passed from the "brute" stage to literacy in both the Epera and the Spanish languages, became a definite support for a rising self-image. While local elements—as seen in the previous section—tried to demean the Indian, the missionary became identified with the Indian's acceptance as a first-class person in the larger world. In 1959 there was the dinner with Christian businessmen and an encounter with the Canal Zone governor. This was followed by his visit to the United States in 1960. The respectful treatment by American Christians and the openness of his missionary hosts became additional support for his claim of being of equal worth with the missionary.

Since there was continued local attack on his self-image, Aureliano clung tenaciously to this concept of equality with the missionary. For example, when he foolishly accompanied some women, one of whom was running away from her husband, he exposed himself to all sorts of gossip and blame. When the various rumors reached the author in the United States, he sent a tape recording to Aureliano inquiring about the facts of the situation. On the return tape made by Aureliano, he forthrightly explained his behavior and admitted his mistake. Then suddenly—as he became more eager—he moved closer to the microphone and said, "Imama, when you and I prayed together on the beach, did you mean it when you said that you wanted to belong to God and wanted to obey him? Well, I want you to know that I meant my words just as much as you did yours."

In fact, for his interracial witness he often uses his equality with the missionaries as proof of the wider brotherhood of man and the equality of the members of the body of Christ.

During an evangelistic trip to Colombia in 1963, Aureliano used an outboard motor belonging to co-author F. Glenn Prunty. They had some trouble with the motor and while trying to repair it in a small coastal town, they carelessly let the tide carry away the boat and all the belongings. Aureliano immediately sent a telegram to the missionaries in Panama telling of his problem. The officer in charge of the Colombian garrison asked him what he hoped to accomplish with the telegram. Aureliano explained that the Americans to whom he was sending the telegram were his brethren in the faith and they would most likely come for him with a plane. The officer found this to be utterly naive, if not ridiculous and asked, "If you *cholo* (a derogatory expression for Indian) believe that some *gringo* will hire a plane to come and look for you, you are absolutely crazy."

Next morning at about nine o'clock the officer met Hombría again and maliciously asked, "Have your brethren answered already?" "Yes," said the Indian, and handed the unbelieving officer a telegram—"ARRIVING CESSNA 180 TOMORROW MORNING." "I expect them tomorrow morning." They were still talking, however, when a Cessna 180 came in for a beach landing. The telegram had been sent the day before, and the Indian had not looked at the sending date. The officer could not get over his amazement and wanted to know more detail. "Then," as Aureliano explained later, "I told him how we believers from all languages and tribes become brethren and sisters when we give God the hand and walk on his road; and brethren always help each other." On his return to Panama this episode became the basis for a sermon by Aureliano on the brotherhood of believers in the Spanish-speaking church at Jaque.

Having become aware of their strategic involvement with the leader's self-image, the missionaries have attempted to use this channel wisely to further the growth and maturation of the church leadership. This has been possible at several levels.

In an effort to prevent the leader from becoming smug, the missionaries have always approached the leadership as "becoming ones." Annually there have been sessions in which missionaries shared with the leading brethren some personal accounts of shortcoming, repentance and growth during the past year. After their own self exposure they would

then ask the Indian brethren to reciprocate. Such periods of sharing have
permitted Aureliano to confess many
personal problems. Each time missionaries and nationals then wound up
the encounter by a joint dedication for
the coming year. The dedication previously referred to by Aureliano involved
one such encounter. These self-exposure
sharing sessions have been discussed
more fully in a different paper.[16]

A second area in which the missionary could contribute in leadership
growth and possibly also in the direction
of the group movement has been the
selective planting of new information.

---

[16] Jacob A. Loewen, "Self-exposure: Bridge
to Fellowship," PA, Vol. 12, No. 2 (March-
April 1965), pp. 49-62.

On every short term visit the missionaries
have tried to identify the current needs
of the church through national eyes.
Once these had been located, attempts
were made to provide some answers,
or at least some suggestions for solutions.
However, rather than give such information to the group as a whole, it has
been found that if such answers or alternatives were shared with one or two
leaders in private, the presentation of
such new information by the leader to
the congregation as a whole, helped to
build the leader's image before the
people. Rather than resenting missionary
questions as intrusions, the leaders
generally have welcomed them because
out of such discussion has come much
of their teaching and many of their
sermon ideas.

The Way to First Class: Revolution or Conversion?

"ONE wants to become a human being. . . ." The suspended intonation pattern indicated that the statement was still incomplete, but the words uttered by the Chulupi Indian speaker were pronounced with such intensity and vehemence that the author, an anthropologist engaged in research among the Indians of the Paraguayan Chaco,[1] was almost startled. All he had really asked the group was, "What is the most important desire that you carry in your 'innermost?'"

"One wants to become a person. . . ." Deliberately the anthropologist looked from one face to another of the Chulupi men gathered around the small fire of oil-rich palo santo wood that was actually giving more light than warmth. As if being polled individually, several men solemnly reiterated, "Yes, one wants to become a human being." Nor were these the only Indians that voiced such feelings, for group after group visited by the anthropologist made similar confessions. Obviously something was

threatening the status of this tribe of former hunting and gathering warrior nomads. That this threat was tribe-wide in its scope could be seen in the universality of the response, and the vehemence with which the statements were uttered rendered eloquent testimony to the depth with which the Indians were feeling it.

This paper proposes to describe some of the factors that have brought the Chulupi self-image under attack and to recount some pertinent aspects of two alternative courses of action that the Chulupi have tried in their drive to redeem their self-image. It will raise the questions, "How universal is this struggle for first-class identity in our modern world?" and "How far is our missionary witness geared to its demand?" Lastly it will underscore that the gospel does have some specific good news for this intense and widespread human concern about personal worth.

Before the Arrival of the Colonists

The Chulupi, called Ashluslay by Nordenskiold,[2] inhabited the area north and east of the Pilcomayo River in the Chaco of Paraguay. They were

[1] The research was carried on under the auspices of the Mennonite Central Committee and the Indian Settlement Board during July to December 1963.

Jacob A. Loewen is Translations Consultant for the Bible Societies in South America. 315 South Wilson, Hillsboro, Kans., U.S.A.

[2] Erland Nordenskiold, *Indianerleben El Gran Chaco* (Leipzig: 1912).

nomadic hunters and gatherers. The Tobas and Matacos, who inhabited the Argentine Chaco south and west of the Pilcomayo, were their traditional enemies. Chulupi folk tales and folk history tell of many daring exploits against these Indian enemies, against the Spanish conquistadores, and most recently also against the Bolivians, whom they seem to hate very intensely.[3]

Gradually, however, national armies, especially during the Chaco War between Paraguay and Bolivia (1932-34), defeated the Chulupi so decisively that they lost their will to resist and became afraid of being massacred by the soldiers. Their first major peaceful contacts with civilization seem to have been with the sugar cane growers of the Argentine Chaco, who employed Indians for five or six months of each year to harvest their crops. The sugar industry had wisely made its agreements with the chiefs, to whom the employers gave retainer wages. The chiefs did not actually work, but they made the agreements and settled any problems between employers and labor that arose during the contract period. The sugar concerns gave the Indian employee only fifty percent of his wages each month during the employment period, but when the season ended the worker received the other half in a lump sum. This was to provide for the Indian during the slack season. Actually, the off months

corresponded to the *algorrobo* season in the Chaco. So, armed with some cash and supplied with an abundance of easy food and drink through the extensive *algorrobo* forests now in season, the Indians spent several months feasting and celebrating.

The excursions into Argentina, however, introduced the Indians to commercial hard liquor and to prostitution. Both of these vices gave the tribal leadership grave concern. When during the latter thirties the messianic movement to Pentecostal Christianity that swept through the Toba tribe[4] also reached the Chulupi Indians, the latter decided to discontinue their work in the cane harvests and to seek their fortune with the Mennonite colonists who had just then settled in the Paraguayan Chaco,[5] roughly to the north and east of Chulupi territory. Thus during the latter 1930's groups of Chulupi Indians began to appear in the Mennonite colonies, especially on the southwestern rim of Fernheim colony.

The white settlers generally welcomed the arrival of the Chulupi because they were much more extroverted than the Lengua Indians whom the colonists already knew. Eventually the Chulupi became as-

---

[3] During the Chaco War both Paraguay and Bolivia tried to use Indians as spies, but neither side really trusted them. As a result they were often shot by both sides, but the Chulupi carry their strongest resentment against the Bolivian army.

[4] See William D. Reyburn, *The Toba Indians of the Argentine Chaco: An Interpretive Report* (Elkhart: Mennonite Board of Missions and Charities, 1954).

[5] In 1928-30 several thousand conservative Mennonites from Canada moved to the Chaco of Paraguay to escape compulsory education, which they considered a threat to the spiritual life of the church. They were joined by Mennonite refugees in 1930-31 and in 1947-48. In all they have established three colonies in the Chaco.

sociated with several of the colonies and, since different relationships developed in the different colonies, at least two of these need to be traced separately.

Animals and Fences

In the northeastern area the Chulupi moved out of their traditional wandering territory and formed satellite villages near the existing European settlements on which they found employment. The Chulupi were practicing limited animal husbandry, so with them came a menagerie of sheep, goats, cows, horses, and innumerable dogs. Since fencing wire was at a premium during the pioneer years and many of the settlers' plantings were quite inadequately protected by fences, the animals of the Indians often did extensive damage. This soon became a source of severe tension between the Indians and the whites. Even where no great damage was inflicted, the roaming animals of the Indians were a general nuisance. A number of the white villages solved this problem at least partially, by building a fence around a plot of land assigned to the Indian village. This action greatly eased the mounting tension, but even then pressures of various types gradually led the Chulupi to dispose of almost all of their domestic animals except their dogs.

Since a mission to the Lengua Indians was already well established when the Chulupi arrived, a new mission was now opened for the latter. This gave the Chulupi interpreter-protectors, for whenever problems between colonists and Indians arose, the colony authorities generally called on the missionary and asked him to intervene. This was a most fortunate arrangement, for the missionary's understanding of Chulupi culture and his fluency in the language generally permitted adequate explanation in both directions. Ultimately it led to a quasi-official pattern which made the tribal leadership responsible for any breaches of discipline by Chulupi both on the mission and in the colonies.

Women's Loss of Authority

Possibly the most devastating cultural upset that resulted from the Chulupi contact with the Mennonite settlers was the loss of authority and responsibility suffered by Chulupi women. The tribe had traditionally been strongly female-oriented. It was the female who chose her sex partners and finally her marriage partner. In the hunting and gathering life she was assigned certain fixed responsibilities by the sexual division of labor. Husbands brought home the game and sighted wild honey. Women prepared the game for food and the hides for clothing or bedding. Women also brought home the wild honey the men had located. While husbands did the hunting, wives did the gathering; they picked forest fruits and dug up varieties of edible roots which the forest produced. Being nomadic, the Chulupi moved frequently. The decision of when to move and where to go was generally made by the women. Once the move was effected, the wives also built the new home.

In the area of child training women were supreme, for they alone built the "human soul" in the new-born child. Mother's milk was the great food of the soul and on it the child was to be ·fed for four to five years, while maternal love, care, and constant presence were to provide an atmosphere propitious for the child's development. From the mother the child was also to receive most of its instruction and training, except sex education, which was the responsibility of the maternal grandparent who continued the child's education after the mother weaned it. Mother and grandparents were also the child's disciplinarians. With the move to the colonies, the whole range of the female division of labor and indeed the very foundation of the female's reason to be was unintentionally but irrevocably undermined.

Since the Indians now lived more or less permanently in one location, there was no further need for decision on when or where to move; and since they did not move there were no more houses to build. Nor were there any hides to tan, for husbands no longer went hunting. There were no roots to gather, for due to their permanent residence, the native supply of edible roots was exhausted. It became physically impossible for the woman to fulfill her former responsibility.

On the active side, the white settlers made arrangements with and hired Chulupi husbands; wives were not even consulted. To add insult to injury, the employers fed their male Indian employees three meals a day, for they wanted the Indians to be able to do a solid day's work. During the early contacts when Indians worked largely for food and clothing, the employer had often provided food for the whole family. Then the wages

graduated to yard goods, and when this became unwieldy, money became the medium of payment. Under the money economy, the settlers, instead of giving food for the family, often had the Indian plant a garden for himself and his family. Now the husband was made responsible for something that was formerly the woman's domain.

Last but not least, money belonged to the Indian category of private property. This category of property was entirely individual, so individual that it had to be buried on the owner's death. It was not only undesirable, but absolutely dangerous for all non-owners to handle someone else's private property. In the Chulupi situation, the introduction of money led to serious complications, for money became the weapon by means of which men could enforce their new position of exclusive authority. A practical example of the use of the money weapon can be seen in the following illustration of the change in the husband-wife relationship.

The culture did not permit a woman to have sex relations during the entire period of lactation which, as stated earlier, ideally lasted four to five years. For the nursing period the husband joined the unmarried and satisfied his sexual needs there. When male missionaries — early missionary wives did not learn the language — brought Christianity to the Chulupi and the men became Christians, they were also taught Christian morality insisting on fidelity to their one wife. Husbands now wanted to live with their wives even during the nursing period. Wives, however, resisted their husband's sexual approaches because they were under strong taboo — sex relations damage the child's soul and consequently cripple the body. But now husbands subverted their wives and forced them into sexual submission, using their newly gained money weapon as the tool.[6] Men did not feed or clothe their wives until they submitted to their sexual advances. By this means the women were finally humbled into submission to the husbands. While women may have also blamed their husbands, the major resentment was directed against the white settlers whose contact had precipitated this drastic change in husbands. The Chulupi woman held white man's culture as the culprit in her loss of reason to be and for her fall from status and authority.

At first the settlers accepted the Argentine pattern of chiefs negotiating for the whole clan, but as the Indian's awareness of the return in wages increased and the chief also began to function as collective bargainer for better conditions for Indian labor, the settlers resented his function and began to seek ways and means to undercut the chief's authority. They no longer acknowledged him as the sole voice of the clan and began to bargain with individuals. Only in the cases of misdemeanor was the chief's authority universally recognized and used. In Filadelfia, where Paramount Chief Manuel was the leader, such sidestepping of authority did not pass unnoticed, and Manuel finally began

to look for outside sources to bolster his prestige.

Overtly the settlers were able to negotiate successfully with individuals. Covertly, however, the Indians were dissatisfied and the feeling that they were being exploited became common. The chief, of course, encouraged such attitudes. Occasionally Indians helped themselves to the settlers' property to equalize the return. This was patterned after their former arrangement of exchange in which the giver and not the taker was responsible for getting a just return. The giver was entitled to take from the receiver whatever he felt was his due.

While the wage situation permitted the individual to feel cheated, another factor elevated the accompanying resentment to a tribal scope. Since 1947 Lengua Indians had been participating in an agricultural program begun by the mission. By 1959 there were a number of Lengua agricultural villages, but no Chulupi Indians had participated in such a program because the Chulupi were satellites to the "urban" centers. This inequality in the mission programs gradually brought about a Chulupi group reaction. They complained that the settlers were biased toward the Lengua and that they were being discriminated against in the program of agricultural settlement. Rapidly mounting pressure led to the founding of the Indian Settlement Board which sponsored the anthropological research on which this paper is based. By 1962, when the Chulupi rebellion began, there were twelve Lengua villages to one village of Chulupis. This inequality was one of the conditions that triggered the

6 Jacob A. Loewen, "Paraguayan Mennonite Missions and Crisis in Chulupi Culture Change," to be published in *Mennonite Quarterly Review*.

reaction that will be described later.

Land Disputes

The second situation was probably unique to two villages in the most recently settled of the three white colonies. These villages were located on land the Indians claimed as their own. Thus immediately with the first harvest by the colonists, several Chulupi chiefs came to collect a tribute of watermelons or cloth for the use of "their" land. The settlers, not wanting to tangle with Indians whose language they did not understand and who they had heard were dangerous, simply paid the small rental fees the Indians demanded. Later, when the Indians began to work for the colonists, the demands for fees gradually disappeared.

These white villages were settled by displaced peoples who had undergone some very trying experiences during the last European war and who as a result had acquired a decidedly "watch out for yourself only" attitude. They sponsored no mission program for the Indians and no one really learned to speak the Chulupi language. As in the first situation described, the Indian menagerie soon became uncomfortable. Here, however, individuals just reached for their firearms and disposed of the offending animals — intending to teach the Indians a lesson through it. In the face of such drastic action, the Indians quickly discontinued raising domestic animals, but not without feelings of deep bitterness which were fermenting dangerously in their innermosts.

In the other colonies the white settlers had generally enclosed some land which the Indians could claim for their village. In an area of the two villages under discussion, however, the struggle for personal survival was so absorbing that nothing like this was undertaken. In fact just the reverse happened. As the European settlers expanded their acreage, Indians were forced to vacate several sites, because they were claimed as private property by individual settlers. Thus it was not until about 1959 that the Indian village actually received a plot of land and a fence. But even that seemed to be under question again in 1963, for a white farmer claimed that this land was actually his by colony assignment, and that it was only by the goodness of his heart that the Indians were permitted to continue living there.

Another acute problem that accompanied the absence of an allotment for an Indian village was the lack of a well for drinking water. The wells were very deep and water was scarce. Even the settlers had to draw water from a common well for many years. This, of course, meant that the Indians also began to use this well. This sharing of the well caused much tension. The whites did not like "filthy" Indians dipping water with them, but rather than dig a separate well for the Indians, they permitted their children to harass the Indians who frequented the colony well. Only in 1959 did the white settlers help the newly fenced Indian village get its own well.

Since the Indians, who had learned Spanish in Argentina, resented and resisted learning the colonists' vernacular (Low German) and no colonist learned Chulupi, a very unsatisfactory communications situation developed. Inability to understand each other led to mutual suspicion, much of it justified. Whites suspected the Indians of stealing and Indians felt they were being robbed by the low wages the settlers paid them. When theft was discovered, there was little chance of communication and of identifying the culprit. The frustrated local villagers then just seized some Indians at random and beat them roundly, advising them this was a lesson for both the guilty and the innocent. There was to be no stealing.

The suspicion of the Indians was heightened by the variability of settler reaction. During the cotton harvest, when the pressure on the colonists to reap their crop was great, Indians were coddled and pampered; but as soon as this need was past, their actions toward the Indians changed. Instead of receiving a welcome and gifts, the poor Indian who came begging for help was sent away empty, even driven off the yard. To the Indians this was an indication that basically the whites hated them; they only tolerated them for personal gain.

This second area faced another complication in that the Indian group was led by a sub-chief who was very insecure and consequently moved his people to various places, at none of which they achieved any at-homeness.

The Rebellious Outburst

The second half of 1962 brought a very severe drought to the entire Chaco. As always in such times of calamity, the white settlers, faced with scarcity, retrenched in order to conserve their resources. They laid off all their Indian laborers and began to ration their food to see themselves through the period of drought. For the Indians, to be laid off was nothing short of disaster. They had become entirely dependent on food provided by the Mennonites. They had no resources of their own, and, in fact, they were even forgetting the techniques of survival of their hunting and gathering days. The problem was aggravated by the increased number of mouths to feed, for under mission influence the Chulupi were discontinuing the practice of infanticide. To the Indians, the settlers' move to conserve their resources seemed completely irresponsible and heartless. Did not good people always share resources, especially in time of need? Had not the Indians helped raise the food the Mennonites were now hoarding for themselves? Did not much of the hoarded food actually represent wages due to the Indians?

Thus, at a time when Indian-settler relations were already extremely bad, for the settlers held all the land and the Indians did not have gardens of their own, the situation immediately became desperate. The Chulupi of this area repressed their dignity and tried the only avenue they knew — they appealed to whites' pity by coming daily and begging, especially with those people in whose employ they had stood. At first there was a fair response on the part of the settlers, but gradually, as the burden became greater, they began to give less and less in quantity and definitely less and less willingly. The colonies appealed to the Mennonite Central Committee[7] for emergency aid for the Indians; and the relief agency was able to channel some supplies from Food for Peace reserves to the area. But the amount was so limited that it had to be designated only for children, pregnant females, the sick, and the aged. Able-bodied persons were expected to hunt, work, or find their food on their own.

When the Food for Peace supplies arrived at the Chulupi village, the colony mayor and the missionary brought along an Indian teacher. Overtly he was to conduct a school for the children (for a part of the supplies had been designated for school lunches), but covertly he was to supervise the distribution of the supplies. Having been humiliated again and again by unwilling white villagers to whom they had appealed for help, the Chulupi interpreted this as just one more insult, this time from the highest official of the colony and the mission. The local chief, of course, also saw in the teacher a puppet chief who must be defied at all costs. As a result the group ostracized the teacher and forbade all the Indians to accept any handout from him. To feed themselves the Indians began widespread stealing from their colonist employers: sweet potatoes, grains, chickens, pigs, even cattle. They justified the action as just taking things the settlers had been withholding from them. Of course they feared the results. What if the immigrants should call in the troops? Especially for rustling cattle,

punishments were extremely severe in the Chaco.

The teacher observed what was happening, and even though he was being ostracized, he tried to plead with his fellows. This only angered them more and they threatened to kill him as a traitor. Meanwhile, night after night and all through the night, war councils were being held. Parties were sent out to raid and bring back food. Should they also do away with some of the chief white offenders? Fear of the soldiers deterred them at first; then came a messenger from Chief Manuel. The chief had gone to federal authorities and they were promising help. This raised the hopes again and stayed the intended vengeance. A second messenger arrived saying that the Indians would get land to settle.

This changed their tactics. Instead of doing away with the offending settlers and thus becoming liable to punishment, the Indians decided that all would leave the colony, settle on their own land and so let the Mennonite economy — which they felt was based almost exclusively on Indian labor — deteriorate and collapse. So appealing was this alternative that the group packed up to leave even before final word on the land grant arrived. They rejoiced that now white settlers would become destitute and starve, and Indians would become independent. Thus all of the more than two hundred Chulupi came to Filadelfia and squatted beside the mission near a large water hole.

Meanwhile in Filadelfia the general Indian populace was much more relaxed when the drought began. Many did have gardens on their employers'

---

[7] Mennonite Central Committee is the relief and welfare arm of the churches of Mennonite faith.

property and there usually was some work around the city so that survival was not nearly as precarious. There were also, however, some Indians who had arrived more recently and who had no patron relationship with any settlers. Their condition was not so good.

As already mentioned, Chief Manuel was very busy seeking ways to assert his authority and to avenge the slights inflicted by the white leaders. To complicate the situation, just prior to the uprising the Chulupi-speaking missionary was out of the country on vacation. Since all the Indians were largely unemployed, there was much time to talk. All real and imagined hurts were aired publicly and tension was beginning to build up. Then came Chief Manuel's first message — independence, official help, and their own land, just around the corner. That sent a wave of excitement through the tribe. Then Manuel came in person with the confirmation: "Yes, we will receive official help. We will not be dependent on the Mennonites any more. The trucks bringing our outfits are to arrive any day."

Promises of Independence

Manuel had full confidence that help was on the way, and he played the role of savior and prophet with real satisfaction. One missionary reports hearing him address the excited populace at night as follows: "My people, the day in which we must beg is past. Each family will have land, equipment, and much food. Your children will no longer hunger. You will put food on the table and call your children to eat. When their bellies are full, you will send them out to play. Everybody will have what he needs and all my people will be happy and independent."[8]

In referring to the wonderful future ahead, Manuel was able to remind the people, especially the women, that their former independence was soon to return. This spoke a very potent language to the women, whose current subjugated and humiliating position was a source of much repressed tension. Manuel realized that the women would now be his strongest supporters and he lost no time in capitalizing on this fact.

A teacher in the bilingual school reports how the wife of a Chulupi student came back from a visit to Filadelfia where Manuel had talked to her. Three days after her return the husband suddenly announced that he was following his wife to join Manuel. Yes, he still wanted to study, but his wife wanted him to come and so he was going.

So desirous was Manuel of getting the loyalty of all the people that in his nightly talks he frequently slipped in accusations of what the whites were doing to the Chulupi working for them. Among other things, he "leaked" the secret that the Mennonites were putting poison on the bread they gave their employees so that the latter would not become people of worth.

Into this already charged atmosphere the arrival of the two hundred rebels from the southwest brought new fuel for rebellion against the whites. Each day the tension was

---

8 Reported by Gerhard Hein, missionary to the Chulupi.

mounting visibly. To trigger the actual uprising in Filadelfia a young man stole some money at a local store. The owner called the deputies, who apprehended the suspect and went with him to get Manuel. The deputies, the suspect, and the chief were sitting in the jeep in front of the cooperative store waiting for the mayor's arrival. By the time he arrived a vast crowd of excited observers, both Indians and whites, had gathered. When the mayor noticed the large excited mob, he decided to move the interrogation to the courtyard of the store and directed the jeep to go there.

But this was also where the local jail was located, and the Indians interpreted the order as meaning that both Manuel and the suspect would be jailed. Before the mayor himself reached the enclosure it was swarming with angry Indians, mainly women, armed with sticks, knives, stones, etc. The mayor, immediately realizing how volatile the situation was, dismissed both the suspect and the chief with the excuse that in the absence of the missionary interpreter there was little value in talking and that he would call Manuel concerning the problem later, when it was more convenient.

While violence was prevented at the moment, this experience had raised the Indian temper to the boiling point. Lengua-speaking missionaries and colony church leaders tried to calm the Chulupi and to dissuade them from any drastic action, but their appeals were drowned out by the mob's shouting: "Our ears burn, our ears burn." (Meaning, "We are tired of your continual lying and we won't listen to you any longer.")

Then came the news that the promised official help was not forthcoming. This was a severe blow to all the Indian hopes. Finally the message was modified so that at least a certain "camp" (a grassy plain) would be given to the Indians for settlement, but no food and implements would be supplied. The Indians debated and finally it became apparent that they were intended to move to this camp. To the white settlers this was sheer folly. The camp was far away — no one knew the exact location. There were no wells there and this was at the height of the drought.

A well-meaning rancher whose extensive land holdings lay in the direct path of the proposed destination decided to personally intervene to stop the Indians from moving. He went to the Indians to notify them that when they crossed his land he would have to forbid them access to all water because it was needed to keep his cattle alive. Instead of the reaction for which he had hoped, the Indians responded with violence and only a hurried exit by jeep saved him from being dismembered by the angry Chulupi, who interpreted this as another attempt to block their way to independence.

Then the water hole near Filadelfia dried up. Horses were dying for want of water and food. There seemed to be no alternative — the Indians had to pack up and leave. By this time the Chulupi-speaking missionary had returned but restraint was now impossible. The group, now numbering over seven hundred, moved several kilometers to another water hole. Obviously their draft animals were no longer capable of making the proposed long trek. Then this water hole went dry, too. Now there seemed to be no alternative but to set out for the promised camp. At the missionary's urging, the colony provided tractors and trailers to move the Indians to the proposed land grant. When they arrived there, they found the place to be very sandy, unfit really for agriculture.

Their first efforts (with some white help) were to dig wells. Sweet water was essential for survival. But attempt after attempt failed. Observers recount that when it appeared evident that no potable water would be found, Manuel left the group and spent the night in the open, alone. He himself said he had spent the night appealing to his ancestral spirits and praying to God to give water so that his people would be saved and vindicated. But no water was found. To stay there any longer was impossible. About half of the group returned to the colonies. The others, led by Manuel, set out on foot for Guachalla on the Pilcomayo River, several hundred kilometers away.[9]

Even though a year had passed when the researcher arrived, it was still a very sensitive issue. Tension was still apparent. For this reason the colony leaders asked for a special study of the rebellion and the events

_____

[9] The question has been raised as to whether this was not a rebellion against the mission. This researcher feels it was not. For at the height of the crisis a member of another mission appealed to the Chulupi Indians to come to their mission. They would give them help there. Observers say the Indians angrily turned him down, saying: "We don't want to go to a different mission — we want to become independent people." This conclusion has been questioned, however.

that produced it. The data presented in this paper are a part of the findings.

Facing Conversion

In the course of the investigation the anthropologist visited the area where the episode with the Food for Peace took place. In view of unfortunate missionary involvement in the event the researcher decided that it was essential to go there independent of the missionaries. In an effort to identify with the Indians, however, he reached for Indian sponsorship. He located two bilingual (Chulupi-Spanish) Indians, both of whom had relatives in the area in question. He explained his assignment to them and appealed for their help in seeking a way which would lead these Indians "to become people."

To strengthen his dependence on the two Indians, he parked his jeep and let them take him to the tribe by horse and buggy. To facilitate identification, the researcher shared some of his personal struggles for self-identity with his guides. Having gone to Canada as an immigrant, and having received all his education in that country, he had often found himself at odds with the prevailing "old country" world view of his community and church. After his ordination to the ministry, he courageously began to share some of his concerns in messages, only to be "rapped on the head" by the older brethren. "No, what you said was not wrong, but you are too young to say it." Or, "We don't mention such things from the pulpit in our church."

All of this increased the frustration of the young rebel. For a while he channeled his rebellion against some of the men who were supposedly not letting him be a man in his own right. But this produced guilt. Finally through the counsel of a sympathetic older man, he recognized that if he were in God's will he would channel his rebellious energy against issues rather than people. God had a purpose for him that was uniquely his alone. In obedience to God, he had found personal first-class status.

Did his experience in any way parallel the Indian-colonist struggle? Did Indians feel that the whites were holding them down? Had the 1962 revolt brought guilt to the Indians? Should they (the two Indians and the researcher) be older brothers to the rebel Indians and point out ways of action that would lead to first-class citizenship without the accompanying guilt that the rebellion had brought them? The two Indians were most responsive and cooperative. They offered to prepare the way for the anthropologist by explaining to the Indians who he was and why he had come. While the two went to the Indian village, the researcher visited the white colonist villages, talking with the people and gathering data from their point of view.

In the middle of the afternoon the two guides called for the anthropologist and took him to the Indian village. The welcome he received there was overwhelming. Every man, woman, and child came to shake his hand. Sheepskins, three deep for the visitor, were piled on the ground. All sat down. When the visitor then said, "My two Chulupi friends have already explained why I have come. What do

you think I should know in order to be able to help you?" the Indians immediately opened up.

For the next two hours the Indians, sometimes five or six persons talking at the same time, poured out the hurts and slights suffered at the hands of the colonists. The two interpreters had been instructed to not miss a single complaint. While the people spoke the visiting researcher wrote down just enough detail to nail down each separate event. For two hours words poured forth like a river swollen by a tropical cloudburst; then the flow slackened to only an occasional addition, until finally they said, "Now there is no more."

The researcher was moved by the account of human suffering and said, "The people who did this to you are my people. My innermost is pained to its depth. I must go aside now to think." He really needed time to think of what to do next. Before he was ready, however, the people forced his hand by calling an evening meeting. He went and joined the group, sitting down on the sand with some of the men. Soon, however, the leader called him and asked him to sit on the bench, again draped with sheepskins. He was to be the speaker of the evening. His first impulse was to refuse, but then he leaned over to his interpreter and asked him whether he should repeat to this group the story of his personal struggles for self-identity and the finding of the status he now enjoyed as a child of God in the will of God. The interpreter thought that a splendid idea, and so the researcher repeated what he had told the two Indians in the buggy. Then the interpreter proceeded to make a local application.

When the message was finished the supposedly only Christian in the village got up and said, "Yes, we all want to become people like God wants us to be; but let us remember, even if we do get plows, horses, land, etc., we are dirty inside. We can never enjoy the blessings of God in our present condition. We have spent two hours telling what white people did to us, but what about all we did to them?"

When he sat down another two-hour period of spontaneous confession followed. Indian after Indian got up and owned his own wrongdoings against the settlers. The two interpreters faithfully relayed the burden of the confessions to the researcher. Finally, when the confessions ceased, the lone Christian again arose and said, "It's only proper that we admit what we did; but do you know all the while we did it God was watching? What about him? Nobody has mentioned him." Then a number of older men were delegated to lead the whole community in prayers of repentance before God. Somehow the scene reminded the amazed author of the verse of Scripture that was so meaningful at the time of his own conversion, "Him that cometh to me, I will in no wise cast out."[10]

Search for Self-Identity

The author has already referred to his own personal struggle for identity and first-class status within a church made up of immigrants from another country and culture. Now that he has

---

10 John 6: 37.

become a father and is trying to raise his own children in American culture, he is finding that the children, even as natives in their own culture, are not immune to this struggle. The teenagers especially seem to experience intense lostness. In fact, sometimes the intensity of this need of belonging and self-identity becomes almost alarming. Possibly it is the rapidly advancing technology, the increasing social distance that accompanies urbanization, and the almost frightening new vistas opened by education that lie at the root of such insecurity. At any rate it has become necessary to have monthly family sessions to help the children "find themselves."

That this is not the problem of just one family, the author learned during his years of service as professor in a denominational liberal arts college. Especially for the college student, education often leads to disillusionment with the world view he has inherited by tradition. As more and more items of his home-town faith come under fire, insecurity and rebellion often result.

Certainly foreign students, especially those from animistic backgrounds, often experience major personal crises as many of their cherished traditions wither under the fierce heat of scientific inquiry. But cutting loose from a binding tradition does not necessarily make men free, it may only lead them to lostness in human values, to a sense of lack of belonging, and the lack of direction in behavior. Detribalization and urbanization in Africa, Asia, and South America have produced many lost people who are desperately searching for first-class status.

William Reyburn writes concerning the situation in West Africa: "The African wants above all other things to be treated as a self-respecting person sharing in the spiritual and material rewards of modern life. He does not demand that he become the only one entitled to first-class citizenship, but he does demand to be included in that category."[11]

In fact, the whole drive for national independence that is bursting at the seams of African and Asian status quo, and which is producing such a motley array of new nations (many of whom hardly seem viable) must really be considered a part of a worldwide drive for personal and national first-class status. To understand this "epidemic" we need to recognize that personal self-definition is in large part related to the clarity of definition of a person's status in a given culture. Whenever this culture enters a period of rapid change, especially in the areas of world view or social structure, the felt need for self-location will generally become quite acute.

A quick survey of the world situation reveals that a very high percentage of tribal cultures find themselves in such periods of rapid social change today. Their contact with Western culture and its science and technology has disillusioned them with their own traditional animistic world view and has dazzled them with a Utopia of instant equality in status and material wealth along with the most advanced nations. Their current

feverish struggle to reach El Dorado
[11] William D. Reyburn, "The Missionary and Human Relations," PA, Vol. 5, No. 2 (Mar.-Apr. 1958), p. 88.

is often quite unintelligible to the observer, because all too frequently their old world view still provides the basic premises for their values, judgments, and actions.

After the independence of the Republic of Congo in 1960, some of the missionary refugees told of what to them was a most puzzling experience. As they were traveling toward Angola, they were met by an angry mob of Congolese who wanted to know if the fleeing missionaries were taking the church records with them. Once the mob was convinced that the missionaries had left the church membership records in the Congo, they let them pass without further objections.

Now after their most recent (1964) evacuation from the Congo, these same missionaries were able to interpret that earlier experience. The young rebels were openly accusing them of making slaves of the Congolese. "Of course," they said, "physical slavery — capturing people and transporting them bodily — is no longer in style. The practice of slavery has been refined to a spiritual form. You missionaries now come and write the names (souls) of black Africans into your church records. This, instead of enslaving the body, harnesses African soul power, which America needs and uses to operate its industry."

The rebelling youth groups, capitalizing on this commonly accepted myth, were correctly telling the people that the four years of independence had not raised the Congo to a first-class nation. Was this not a clear indication that Congolese soul power was tied up? And how did they propose to liberate this enslaved soul power?

"We will drive the white men, especially the missionaries, from the Congo, destroy all their property, and wipe away every vestige of their influence. Once we are free, we will give all the people new names and with these new names new soul power; and so fortified the Congo will quickly rise to wealth and prestige."

Situations like the Congo illustrate at least one more pertinent consideration. The drive for status by one person or group will often serve as an attack upon the status of another. Minorities will often be ruthlessly destroyed or driven out as refugees. All of this underscores the sad truth that the quest for status can become a vicious cycle of attack and counter-attack.

Benjamin Colby has pointed out this fact for the Latin American scene. The destruction of the face-to-face relationships of the aboriginal people through conquest or subsequent hispanization has resulted in very serious and very deeprooted interpersonal tensions. As tribal social structures were weakened or destroyed and as people were no longer able to define themselves in terms of the group, they turned to individual self-assertion and this generally at the expense of some of their fellows.[12]

Individual and Group Drive for First Class

The sensitive observer in modern Latin America can everywhere — from the Highland Indians numbering

12 Benjamin N. Colby, "Mesoamerican Psychological Orientation," to be published in *Handbook of Middle American Indians*, Vol. 9.

in the millions to the nomadic Chaco bands which number only several hundred or several thousand at the most — see evidence of this growing individual and group drive for first-class status.

Several years ago the author had a very instructive experience with some Highland Quichua. They were *huasipungeros* 'debt servants' who belonged to the land in perpetuity. For centuries they had worked five days a week for their patron, allowing only two days a week in which they could work for themselves. Usually they spent these two days in town drinking cheap alcohol. Whether one observed them at work or drunk in town, one could not help but receive the impression that they were docile and apathetic. They had pretty well lost their self-consciousness.

One day a number of them learned that the author was born in Russia. This rather insignificant discovery on their part led to an eye opening for the author. The Indians at once surrounded him and eagerly asked whether he would be willing to come and talk to them about Russia and communism. An evening was designated. As soon as the author stood up before the assembled group, he realized that he was not facing docile and apathetic Indians. Here were desperate seekers after first-class status. From everywhere came questions like: "Will we get land when the Russians come? Will they actually help us get rid of the white patrons? Will we all become independent people like the patrons and foremen are now?"

Realizing their onesided exposure to communist propaganda, the author tried to treat both the ideals of communism as well as some of its negative practices. At this point the group divided. Some of those present identified the speaker with the patron class, a smooth talker who was determined to keep the Indian under. Others wanted to continue the discussion, for "this man knows many Indians and maybe he knows ways other than killing the patron for us to get land and independence."

Interestingly enough a rather parallel situation developed during the research in the Paraguayan Chaco with the hunting and gathering Chulupi. They were demanding settlement land from the white settlers for whom they now worked. When the author tried to point out that there were other alternatives like ranching or day labor in industry through which the Indians could become people, the Chulupi angrily accused him, "Now you are talking just like the rest of the Mennonites who do not want us to become people."

The Gospel and Man's Need for First-Class Identity

Many missionary readers will be able to supply examples of the struggle for first-class human status from their own area of experience, pointing out vividly the almost universal distribution of this human need. This leads us to two questions. If the struggle for first-class identity is so widespread, does the gospel, the missionary's message, have any good news for the lost of this kind? And if it does, to what extent is our current missionary approach geared to meet this need?

In regards to the first question, the writer of the fourth Gospel affirms that God has designed a way to first class, to become sons of God: "And the Word was made flesh, and dwelt among us .... But as many as received him, to them gave he power to become the sons of God."[13]

Paul, the first great missionary, also stressed this *new* first-class status of men in Christ: "In this new man of God's design there is no distinction between Greek and Hebrew, Jew or Gentile, foreigner or savage, slave or free man."[14]

Finally, it seems to boil down to the ultimate question of whether modern missionaries, like the Son of God,[15] can be sympathetic and empathetic priests to a lost world needing identity and belonging. All too often missionaries may find themselves condemning nationalism and the rebellion against colonialism, rather than identifying with the aspirations of the people. True, the expressed goals of such movements are often in direct opposition to those of the church, but cannot the missionary as a sympathetic listener and questioner serve such people both as a goal-clarifying mirror and a source of alternatives for more ideal ways of reaching the goal?[16] This certainly seems to have been the function of Jesus with his disciples who wanted to reestablish the Jewish kingdom rather than build the Kingdom of God.

---

13 John 1: 14a, 12.

14 Colossians 3: 11, J. B. Phillips.

15 Hebrews 2: 14-18; 4: 15-16.

16 For a fuller discussion of this principle see Jacob A. Loewen, "The Church: Indigenous and Ecumenical," Vol. 11, No. 6 (Nov.-Dec. 1964), pp. 241-258.

Finally, the author would like to testify that at least in his personal experience the finding of self-identity (in his case already as a married man) meant a redirection in life that was as far-reaching as his teen-age conversion experience. This is the kind of new birth the church needs and claims to preach, but in actual fact we must accept V. Gordon Childe's indictment that religion, once it becomes organized, very readily becomes wary of progress and change and certainly the opponent of the identity seeker who dares to challenge the status quo.[17] Is rebellion really the only recourse for the seeker of identity either inside or outside the church? The Chulupi Indians tried both rebellion and conversion. They recommend conversion.

17 V. Gordon Childe, *Man Makes Himself*, (New York: Mentor Books, 1951).

Cultural Setting
of Communication

Good News for the Waunana

If the church of Christ is to take root and grow indigenously, it is indispensable that the gospel be presented in a manner relevant to this indigenous environment and world view. Recognizing this, the ambassadors to the Waunana tried to find in the Waunana world view some indigenous points of departure on which to anchor the message. The following is a brief résumé of the historical, geographical, and cultural setting which provided the framework within which the gospel message to the Waunana was delivered. As will be seen, contact with the Waunana was brief and inconclusive. Many questions are tantalizingly unanswered. What created the feeling of guilt which gave rise to the beseeching ceremony? What elements in the missionary message struck such a responsive chord? Nevertheless this account is presented with hope that it will stimulate search for the most effective methods of presenting God's good news.

The Historico-Geographical Context

In the San Juan River basin in north-western Colombia there live some 2500 Indians who call themselves *Waunana* 'the people.' Like their ancestors they dwell in circular houses, the floor of which is raised some six to ten feet from the ground to escape some of the humidity produced by the 400 or more inches of annual rainfall this area receives.[1]

However forbidding the climate, the country is rich in gold and platinum,[2] objects of real interest for *conquistadores*.

The lust for gold on the part of the Spaniard has led to an antithetic reaction on the part of the Indians. Thus today gold for the Waunana is the object of great abhorrence. Being unable to force the Indian to work in gold mines, the Spaniards introduced the Negro slave. The latter succeeded, at least in part, in making the Indian his slave. The result was and is very intense hatred for the Spanish-speaking world in general and the Negro in particular.

The Roman Catholics of colonial times early attempted to evangelize the Waunana[3] but they were frustrated by the stubborn apathy on the part of the Indians. This apathy called into action a local inquisition through which the Indians' own religious faith was driven underground.

[1] *Geografía Económica: Chocó* (Controloría General de la República), Vol. VI (1943), p. 45.

[2] Mining figures for 1940 were: 640,000 ounces of gold and 35,859 ounces of platinum. Ibid., pp. 390-391.

[3] The missions began in 1629 according to Lorenzo Hervas y Panduro, *Catálogo de las lenguas de las naciones conocidas, y numeración, división, y clases de éstas según la diversidad de sus idiomas y dialectos* (Madrid: Administración del Real Arbitro de Beneficencia, 1800-1805), Vol. I, p. 218.

Jacob A. Loewen is Professor of Modern Languages, Anthropology and Missions at Tabor College, Hillsboro, Kansas. He worked previously as a missionary translator in northwestern Colombia and southern Panama.

This was so thorough that it took almost four years before the Indians admitted to the missionary investigator the presence of an indigenous mythology. That the Indians should have adopted at least some features of the new religion is to be expected, but it is striking to note that they did not incorporate into their mythology any motifs that are distinctly Catholic.

Summary of Pertinent Mythology

The Waunana creation is said to have taken place on the Pacific coast a little north of their present habitat. God (Ewandama) and his unnamed son were the creators. Having finished the world, the little son became lonesome for playmates. Thus at his father's command he attempted to make people, first of dark-colored palm wood, and then of light-colored balsa wood; but in each case, having made but two dolls, he cut his hand. In his third attempt he was able to cover the whole beach with dolls made of clay. These his father animated. From the dark pair came the black magic spirits and their human counterpart, the Negroes; from the light pair proceeded the white magic spirits and their human counterpart, White men.[4] The clay dolls became Indians, but much to the young man's dismay, all were women. Half of these were then anatomically modified by use of some local fruits, and transformed into men.

The Indians, the myth continues, enjoyed Edenic conditions. Each morning their food was at eating maturity, and Ewandama was teaching the Indians all things. One day, however, while Ewan-

dama was away, the trickster and devil came and with artful sales talk caused the Indians to buy axes and machetes. This occasioned Ewandama's statement: "Indians don't trust me any more, so I will withdraw from the world."

Knowing that illness would now come to the Indians, Ewandama promised to return soon to instruct the Indians in the art of healing the sick. While he delayed, the trickster-devil came along and sold the Indians their present demon-centered curing ceremony. However, he exacted a "hand-giving" contract which put Indians under his jurisdiction. This, they say, caused Ewandama to withdraw completely from human affairs.

In the course of Ewandama's instruction he had also tried to teach them the art of sex relations. Already early, the Indians failed to follow his instructions. This failure gave rise to marital infidelity. But even worse, some time after Ewandama had withdrawn, a brother and sister committed incest. The result was a great flood sent to cleanse the earth, and in this flood Ewandama allowed all the people to drown. Only a few little children were rescued by Ewandama from the flood waters as they were carried down river in a gourd dish.

Today when Indians die, a myth continues, their skulls split in an invisible manner to permit the exit of the soul. This soul must turn right immediately and thereby enter the road that leads to Ewandama's present abode; straight forward or a left turn lead into the "land behind the sun," which is equivalent to hell.

Waunana Ceremonials

At the heart of modern Waunana ceremonial activities is the so-called curing ritual. In this ceremony the shaman, with the aid of eight subservient spirits, effects some

---

[4] There is another version which leaves the Negroes and Whites out of the original creation and has them appear later as they crawl out of a hole in the ground which the Indians had dug.

magic results. Most often this is curative, and then the disease bearing "foreign" spirits (often in the physical form of tobacco fibre or a fishbone) are extracted from the body by charms and by sucking. It can also be preventative or divinatory. In the former, friendly protective spirits are "injected," while in the latter, information about cause of death, identity of a thief or some other question is gathered from the spirit world.

The ritual includes hours of chanting by the shaman over eight dishes of liquor — one for each of the eight subservient spirits — and often continual dancing by friends of the patient or the shaman. Such a ceremony can be conducted in any house that has been ceremonially prepared. To begin the ceremony there is fastened to each of the four main pillars of the house a plaque on which are drawn two spirit figures. The resulting total of eight spirit figures equals the eight spirits a full-fledged shaman controls. Such rituals are generally conducted during the night.

Over against this magic spirit-centered ceremony is beseeching, which is directed towards Ewandama. This ceremony is conducted in utter Indian privacy. The presence of a foreigner is said to rob it of its efficacy. Any Spanish spoken would at once attract the devil.[5] In this ceremony a canoe-drum is suspended in the center of a house that has roof of "god's roofing." Ordinary roofing would identify it as prayer to the trickster-devil. The oldest woman of the house beats this canoe-drum while the men blow pan-pipes of assorted pitches. Beseeching is conducted from sun-up till sun-down. During this time a complete fast is observed, even by little babies. Beseeching appears to relate itself to communal and family dangers, while the curing ritual is often more highly personal.

The First Message

It was in December 1952 that a fellow missionary, David Wirsche, and the author were invited by the Waunana to participate in such a beseeching ceremony. We were told that this was the first time in history that a white man was permitted to attend. The occasion for the ceremony was a series of visions that had shaken the whole tribe. The visions all foretold a great flood — far greater than the one that followed the first incest — that was to sweep away all the people, because they had become so wicked. The specific sins were incest, sex relations with Negroes, and beating children. The meetings were to last a whole month with daily fasting during all the daylight hours.

While witnessing these daily beseeching sessions, the missionaries — in spite of their weak command of the language — felt constrained to give the Waunana the first gospel message in their own language. The following is a brief summary of a half-hour message there given.

"Your fathers told you that God made the people. That is correct. They told you that he made people of clay. That is correct. They told you that in the beginning God provided everything for the people. That is correct. They told you how one day the people listened to the voice of the devil rather than the voice of God. That is correct. They told you that God then left the people, but that is not correct. The people, because of their guilty hearts, went away from God." (Here an illustration of error due to word of mouth transmis-

5 A drunken and thus uninhibited Indian once told the missionary: "You are very stupid to preach about Ewandama in Spanish. Spanish is the language of the devil, and our Ewandama knows our Indian language perfectly."

sion was inserted. It concerned a recent event which had been completely distorted as it was orally spread from river to river.) "But how do we know what God really said? We know it definitely because we have God's book, the Bible. The Bible says that after the people had done evil, God still loved them and so he decided to buy them out of the devil's hand. This he did through his Son[6] whom he sent into the world to die for the people and to teach them how to walk with God once they have been redeemed. Thus with his own death the Son of God paid for all the sin of men. Today he is pleading with all the people: 'Your fathers listened to the devil and gave him their hands. You yourself have often listened to the devil. Will you listen to me now and give me your hand and then walk with me on my road?'

"You are told that when you die, your soul must turn right to get to God's house. That is not what the Bible says. It states that if we give God the hand during our life, God will hold our hand even when we die, and he will take our souls to his abode."

The message then concluded with an appeal: "Will you listen to God today? Will you give him your hand?"

The Response to a First Message

It was a genuine thrill to have the thirty people who heard this message to talk and reason and finally decide: "If we want to give God the hand (the concept of faith and commitment) and walk on God's road, we must get rid of our curing ceremony." This ceremony had not been specifically mentioned except in the idiom of "giving the hand." It was wonderful to observe

how the Holy Spirit was applying even this first message of God's Word to their own situation and need.

However, the surprise was to come. The missionaries had to return home to meet other schedules, to attend council meetings, and conduct services. Then one day weeks later, five Indians from the Siguirusua River came to the missionaries' house. Following a token meal and formal greetings, they entered the study, and here they delivered their news: "Chief Enrique sends you word that all the Indians on his river have decided to give God the hand and to walk on God's road."

At this point the missionary interrupted to remind them that there were only thirty people in the house where God's message had been given and that there were at least forty houses with more than four hundred people on the river who did not know.

Impatiently the Indians said: "But they do know. After you left we waited for three days till the chief returned from his trip. We told him what you had told us, and he said this was exactly what his people needed. Then he took us to the house nearest the headwaters of the river, and we had to tell them the story. Thus, we went from house to house till all the people knew. And now all the people have decided to give God the hand and to walk on God's road."

Epilogue

On January 29, 1953, just one month after the delivery of the first message, the Colombian Government and the Vatican signed a new concordat valid for twenty-five years, in which this Indian territory like many others was made a mission field of the state church. Missionary Wirsche made one more brief trip into the area in the fall of 1953, but since then it has not been possible to follow up the work.

---

6 The name Jesus was avoided at this point, because 'esú, the Indian equivalent of that name, carries negative connotations.

The Church Among the Choco of Panama

Both missionaries and mission executives have been heard to express con-cern that the articles being written about the application of anthropology to the missionary enterprise are largely negative in nature; they seem to be directed more at exposing missionary errors than at providing principles for preventing or correcting them. At other times, where "anthropology" has tried to formulate principles and has ventured to suggest programs, these have often been met with a certain amount of skepticism and sus-picion. There appear to exist at least traces of feeling that anthropology can be applied only at the expense of spiritual or Biblical principles. This article, which is largely a documented report of an anthropologically conscious approach to a mission situation, was written to serve as a posi-tive example of anthropology applied in missions; and to stimulate both thought and action which will advance the witness of the gospel to all nations.

First Contacts

Choco Indians (numbering up to twenty-five thousand in some estimates) live scattered among many lesser rivers in northwestern Colombia and south-east-ern Panama. Though separated from each other by a variety of natural barriers, they exhibit a surprisingly uniform cul-ture. Linguistically, however, they have developed at least ten distinct dialect areas.[1] Of these dialect areas, the Darien of Panama is probably the largest, with some four or five thousand speakers.

One of their earliest contacts with the gospel of which the author has knowledge took place in 1953 when a representative of Gospel Recordings together with a missionary of the Foursquare Mission in

Panama came to the Darien and prepared four records of Bible stories. The Choco informant on this occasion was a bilingual Indian who had been won to Christ through the witness of the Foursquare Mission in the Spanish language. Stimu-lated by this contact, Vinton Johnson of the Foursquare Mission spent several months with the Indians during which he recorded several hundred Choco expres-sions.

In 1956, as part of a larger program to study all the Choco dialects for Bible translating purposes, the writer, a mis-sionary with the Mennonite Brethren Mis-sion, came to the Darien to study the dialect of the Choco living there. Mis-sionaries Vinton Johnson of the Four-square Mission and F. Glenn Prunty of the New Tribes Mission graciously co-operated in the research undertaking. Mr. Prunty carried with him a tape recorder

---

[1] Jacob A. Loewen, "Dialectología de la Fa-milia Lingüística Chocó," *Revista Colombiana de Antropología*, Vol. 9, pp. 9-22.

and a recording of the Bible stories prepared by Gospel Recordings. The stories had been put on tape without any introduction or intervening explanations so that the Indians tended to conceive of them as one long message from an "extra-human" source. Probably since there was so little context for the message, the Indians restructured it. The result was a tremendous emotional upheaval and a rather desperate inquiry about what they might do to forestall the end of the world.

Since the Mennonite Brethren intended to concentrate their work with the Choco of Colombia, they shared with the Foursquare and New Tribes Missions the resulting sketch of the grammar and the preliminary dictionary of the Choco language. The latter two missions divided the Choco field in Panama between themselves and began to plan a ministry. In August of 1957, the Mennonite Brethren Mission also shared with both missions a copy of the suggested translation of twenty-five Bible stories for the nine northern Choco dialects. F. Glenn Prunty received his copy in September, and while on a trip during the month of November he was able to read them to the Indians for the first time. He describes the result in a letter dated January 10, 1958, as follows:

> Now for the big news! The test Bible stories are beginning to bear real fruit for Christ in the Jaque area. I had just finished a literacy class among 45 students at Lucas when a

Jacob A. Loewen is Professor of Modern Languages, Anthropology, and Missions at Tabor College, Hillsboro, Kansas. Previous articles in PA include "A Chocó Indian in Hillsboro, Kansas," Vol. 9, No. 3 (May-June 1962), which provides an interesting bit of background for this paper.

former witch doctor told me that he wanted to talk to me. He told me that because of the Bible stories, his people had understood the gospel for the first time. He said that he, along with others, was ready to give his heart to Christ so that he might clean it up and make them new creatures in Christ. Some thirty-five adults and young people came forward to grasp my hands saying they wanted to be saved.

All in all more than a hundred and fifty Choco Indians in the Jaque area were baptized upon their profession of faith.

Literacy Efforts

In the meantime, F. Glenn Prunty began a literacy program in the Jaque area using a mimeographed syllable chart, but the success was limited. To strengthen this effort the Mennonite Brethren Mission authorized two of their workers to prepare a complete series of primers to teach the Choco to read their own language. In the course of the preparation of these primers, it was decided to employ the orthography of the Spanish for transcribing the Choco language, hoping that this would also facilitate their learning to read Spanish, the official language of the country. The experiment was successful, and of the ten Indians who entered the initial reading program in the summer of 1959 two progressed to read not only the Indian language, but Spanish as well.

It was during this reading campaign that one of the advanced readers, Aureliano Sabugara, suggested that he visit the United States.[2] This visit took place during the summer of 1960. In the course of the weeks spent translating Mark and

---

[2] This visit is described in Jacob A. Loewen, "A Chocó Indian in Hillsboro, Kansas," PA, Vol. 9, No. 3 (May-June 1962), pp. 129-133.

Acts, especially during the work on the latter, a great deal of discussion about the church, its structure, and its obligation in the world took place. Worship services, prayer meetings, and other types of Christian association in the United States provided the Indian with a personal experience of warm Christian fellowship. This was novel and profoundly meaningful to one who came from a people who lived in perpetual fear of sorcery and black magic. Christian fellowship provided possibly the most outstanding impression of the United States for Aureliano. During this time he also met with executives of missions and shared with them his aspirations for a church among the Choco. With impressive enthusiasm he spoke of organizing a church. He even detailed plans on how a chapel could be built. He put feet to his words on returning to his people and began an effective witnessing program.

The First Choco Church

The summer of 1961 David Wirsche and Jacob A. Loewen of the Mennonite Brethren staff returned to Panama in order to follow up the earlier reading experiment. Together with F. Glenn Prunty they witnessed the completion of a chapel which Aureliano and other believers had begun to build at El Mamey. On July 2, 1961, they shared in the dedication of this building as the sanctuary of the first local church among the Choco.

The dedication Sunday was a memorable day. But possibly even more important was the following Monday, when this little group of thirty-three believers sent one of their members as their first missionary ambassador to Lucas, another Choco village about two hours down river from El Mamey. (The foreign mission-

aries had intended to make Lucas their next center of activity, but because of this development they decided to move their work to a different point, so as not to interfere with the outreach of the young church.) Between July of 1961 and January of 1962, this worker taught some forty people to read at Lucas. He introduced regular worship services, helped select and train two local leaders, sparked the beginning of a church building program, and in general laid the foundation for the second Choco church. This was organized on May 11, 1962. Before the dedication of this chapel, the Indians inquired whether they should delay the dedication until the return of the missionaries in the summer; but when encouraged to go ahead independently, the believers at Lucas together with the El Mamey church proceeded to dedicate the chapel and to organize their church.

Outreach Beyond the Tribe

During October and November of 1961, the believers from the church at El Mamey went to two other river areas with the gospel. Outstanding was the success of their witness among the linguistically related Waunana Indians, who have recently migrated to Panama from Colombia. They were able to communicate the message so effectively that some fifteen Waunana "gave God their hand" and were baptized during the evangelistic efforts on this river. On a second visit in May of 1962, nineteen more Waunana "decided to walk on God's road" and were baptized.

In addition, representatives of the church at El Mamey have been able to share their Christian experience with a number of Spanish-speaking individuals. To date more than a dozen of these *ladinos* have been baptized by the Indian

church. The example of the Indian believers has become the source of a new
inspiration to the Spanish-speaking people
of the area and they are now organizing
their own church.

Even though it was not completely
planned this way, it is readily apparent
that the work has developed largely according to the four principles set forth
in Eugene Nida's *Message and Mission*
as the best approach to people living in
a face-to-face society:

> However, once we have recognized
> the fundamental structure of such
> societies, we can see that the ap-
> proaches which have proved to be
> most successful in them are the ones
> that made optimum use of the na-
> tural flow of communication. The
> basic principles in such an approach
> are four: (1) effective communica-
> tion must be based upon personal
> friendship, (2) the initial approach
> should be to those who can effective-
> ly pass on communication within
> their family grouping, (3) time must
> be allowed for the internal diffusion
> of new ideas, and (4) the challenge
> for any change of belief or action
> must be addressed to persons or
> groups socially capable of making
> such decisions.[3]

Communication on Friendship Basis

From the very beginning of the work
informant Diego and researcher Loewen
shared the guest bedroom of the Prunty
residence. Later Glenn Prunty spent
periods of time in the Indian homes,
while the Indians in turn spent two or
three days at the Prunty home when they
came down river to sell bananas. This

reciprocal friendship situation was reinforced when Aureliano came to the
United States in 1960 as guest of the
Loewen family. Before leaving, Aureliano
invited his host to pay him a return visit.
Thus the following summer the missionary
was not only a messenger sent by the
stateside church; he was also an invited
guest at Aureliano's home and received
Aureliano's sponsorship. It was Aureliano
who assumed the initiative for calling
meetings. It was he who asked the visitor
to give the message, thus lifting the gospel
witness out of the realm of foreign propaganda. He would often recall discussions
or observations he had made in the United
States and ask the visiting men to explain
them to his people because they were
"things his people both needed and
wanted to know." In fact, when missionary Loewen tried to wash his nylon
shirts, Aureliano indignantly said: "Didn't
your wife wash my shirts? Now my wife
washes yours!"

When placed on a friendship basis, the
communication of the message provides
for feedback. The communication becomes
reciprocal. There will be feedback between the missionary and the local situation; however, this will also have to be
present between the Christian and the
unbelievers of his society. For this reason
the workers found it imperative to encourage worship patterns which would provide
for feedback.

The present Choco pattern of worship
involves two days a week, Saturday and
Sunday. This group worship is generally
supplemented in the home by a hymn and
a prayer before all meals and by a kind
of family service in the evenings during
which they read Bible stories and sing.
This may last until midnight. As for the
Saturday-Sunday worship, the Indians
explained: "The American people in the

---

[3] Eugene A. Nida, *Message and Mission:
The Communication of the Christian Faith*
(New York: Harper and Bros., 1960), p. 110.

Canal Zone do not work on Saturday either, and besides we need an extra day for teaching and playing."

Much has been written about substituting positive elements for negative traits in a culture. Here was a beautiful example of such a substitution. The Indian drinking festivals, the only kind of get-togethers they used to have, usually lasted two or three days. Now the church had substituted a two-day service pattern for the former drinking orgies. The program itself was instructive. As early as Saturday morning people came to El Mamey for breakfast. There was singing and some instruction in reading, and at mid-morning games began. After a noon meal there was more reading and more recreation while some of the men were sent out to hunt game to provide meat for the meals. In the evening there was more singing and Bible reading. The Sunday meeting began with the service of singing, Bible reading, testimonies, and prayer. The afternoon was spent in games. The evening brought another service very similar to the morning, only much longer.

Indigenous Worship Patterns

Because this involves an area so vital to the life of the church, the visiting missionaries spent considerable time at El Mamey discussing patterns of worship that would follow indigenous ideals and could be carried on by the Choco without hesitation even after the visitors had left. The question, "Can the Indians do this without further training?" was the chief criterion for evaluating service patterns. The following types seemed to find immediate acclaim:

Sharing meetings in which both missionaries and Choco told of their conversion or of other experiences such as testings, trials, defeats, and the lessons which had been learned from them. Such "self-exposure" revealed how "one" all peoples are as sinners and how "one" they can be in their receiving of forgiveness through Christ. Some of the testimonies were most touching:

An old man testified: "I was a drunkard and I beat my wife and children whenever I was under the influence of liquor. In fact, two years ago I beat my eleven-year-old daughter so hard that she died as a result. I was very much ashamed, but I could not help myself. Then I gave myself to Jesus, and today I am free from liquor and I have money to buy things for my family."

A woman known as a terrible fighter: "When I was not a Christian I would get drunk and look for fights. I loved to grab other women by the hair and beat them. Even when I was not drunk I would taunt other women that they could not match me in fighting. I have dragged most of the women here tonight by the hair and have beaten them. And now I am ashamed because I did that. But today there is peace in my heart. When people taunt me, there is enough peace in my heart to quietly turn my face the other way and go by. I have peace with God and with my neighbors."

The man elected church treasurer: "A few nights ago we had a real testing in our house. A Colombian witch doctor came to visit a relative who lives in my house. I used to be very afraid of devils, and so when this witch doctor was going to 'sing demons' at night, I was worried that I would again become afraid. So before going to sleep I told God about the things that I was afraid of. I told him: 'You have bought me from the devil's hand, you have taken my fear away. Don't let me or my family become afraid this night.' It was after midnight

when I was suddenly awakened by someone's loud talking. When I listened I
heard the witch doctor say, 'Who has
been praying? My devils won't come tonight.' I was so happy to know and to
see again that God is stronger than all
the devils. When God watches my house,
the devils can't even come there."[4]

Much to our surprise even the uncommitted people were encouraged to speak
in the services. We witnessed an example
of such a reciprocal communication situation between believer and unbeliever on
dedication Sunday. Aureliano asked a
man who was known to be "riding
the fence," to tell how he felt. When
the man admitted he believed that the
gospel was the truth and that he was
convinced he would have to commit himself to God, Aureliano told him approv-
ingly that such frank speaking befits a
man. "When you know something is a
dog, don't call it a cat."

A notorious witch doctor who was also
attending the meeting was asked to speak.
He said, "I know that I do not belong
with you, but I am convinced that the
gospel is true. You all know the involvements [with the spirits] which keep me
from following God's way. I want to
follow God's way." Aureliano then
answered, "Yes, we know, brother, and
we will pray that God will help you
find the way."

In meetings with smaller groups, especially with the leaders, the visitors tried
to demonstrate spiritual openness before
God and man. They removed the ideal-

istic masks of their outward appearance
and revealed to their Indian brethren
some of the areas of inner struggle in
their lives. In one such meeting the visitors
shared some of the sex tensions and
temptations which they faced during the
months they were away from home and
from their families. One of the brethren
also related how tension in the area of
sex between husband and wife had hindered prayers in their home. It was at
this occasion that Aureliano was able to
confess a sin that would have ultimately
ruined his testimony. His confession then
opened the way for several of the leading
Indian men to admit areas of unresolved
problems in their lives. The meeting climaxed with visitors and Indians kneeling
together asking forgiveness for the common burden of sin which they had been
able to admit and confess. Some of the
sins had previously been denied. Now
under the prompting of the Holy Spirit
they were confessed spontaneously. This
helped to strengthen the teaching that
men are responsible to God when they
sin, not to a foreign missionary.

Scripture reading. During the evening
several of the Indians able to read took
turns reading Bible stories. But even the
reading of a Bible story would be interrupted by the reader to ask questions
of the hearers. This often led to discussions between the Choco leaders and congregation or between believers and unbelievers.

When new people were present it was
very interesting to observe the approach
the Indian believers used towards them.
Rather than taking refuge behind general
exhortations, as we are prone to do, they
would single out the head of the group
and impress him with his responsibility
before God towards the members of his
family.

---

[4] This consciousness of spirit powers inherited from their animistic past has some very
interesting spiritual implications. Just as they
were conscious of evil spirits before, once
"walking on God's road," they seem to have
the same strong consciousness of the presence
of God and of the Holy Spirit.

It was on just such an occasion that Aureliano asked the oldest man of a group of Indians who were hearing the gospel for the first time what was being done on his river to teach people "to walk on God's road." When the man said, "Nothing," Aureliano pointed out to him that he as the oldest was responsible before God for all these people. This almost reduced the Indian to tears and he said, "But we don't know. Where can we learn?" Out of this grew an invitation for the Indian Christians to visit that river. They did this and the result was the conversion and baptism of thirty-four adults.

Prayer meetings. On our arrival we noticed that praying was confined to a few individuals who prayed often and long. For this reason conversational sentence prayers were introduced. This was an immediate success. Some of the simple statements which were the first audible prayers of many of the Indians were touching. Such prayer services became the occasion for many to pray in public. In fact, even the normally shy women began to pray in the meetings.

Prayer for one another was also very well received. Sitting in a circle each one prayed for a need his neighbor had presented. This more than anything else showed that the "fear" of one another due to witchcraft had been overcome by faith in Christ.

Communion. During the reading of the book of Acts in preparation for the church organization, communion services mentioned in it were discussed. It was at this occasion that Aureliano, who had shared in communion services in the United States, told the visitors that the Choco Christians had already discussed communion and that they had decided to practice it, as soon as their church build-

ing was finished. At this meeting the problem connected with the absence of grapes and wine was considered. Much to the joy of the visiting missionaries, the nationals suggested cane juice as a good substitute, for it is locally available at all times. And so they celebrated their first communion service using unfermented sugar cane juice.

At the communion service one of the believers who could read some Spanish got up and said that what they had just shared was wonderful, but that it was only a part of the whole; for when Jesus had celebrated communion with the disciples, he had washed the latters' feet. All eyes turned on the translator asking: "Is that true?" They accepted the explanation that in the Gospel of John which was not yet translated into their language, there is the record of the footwashing; however, in Mark, which was translated, there is not. The ensuing discussion resulted in the decision to wash feet in conjunction with the communion in the future, pointing out poignantly the simplicity of their obedience to the Word of God.

Allowing Time for Diffusion

Periods of time allowing for the diffusion of new ideas have come into the Choco work largely unintentionally. Since the visiting missionaries were regularly employed during the United States school year, their visits with the Indians were limited to the months of June, July, and August. This resulted in a pattern of three months of thrust, during which new ideas were introduced, and a period of nine months for the assimilation and diffusion of these ideas. The original fear that the discontinuities of such a program would obligate the workers to a perpetual repetition of the previous summer's beginnings, turned out to be entirely un-founded. On the contrary, the interrup-tion of the thrust provided for a period to sift the materials that had been pre-sented. False thrusts just died a natural death and the pertinent approaches were assimilated and developed. For example, last summer David Wirsche saw himself obligated to depart radically from the program planned at home because the development during the nine-month in-terim had taken a direction quite different from the one the workers had anticipated. For the missionaries concerned these ex-periences have highlighted the relevance of the caution that Nida expresses in *Message and Mission*:

> Whereas in our own churches we often think in terms of high-pressure, dynamic programs intended to reap results overnight, the approach to face-to-face societies must be of quite a different order. Traditionalists liv-ing within the comfortable emotional security of their "extended family," which maintains itself primarily by resistance to ideas from the outside world, cannot be pushed into making quick decisions. Such people, con-fronted by a "crash program," will be inclined to reject it at once. . . .
> At this point, an acute problem arises, for the missionary's tendency is to encourage some especially re-sponsive persons to step out, repu-diate the traditions of their tribe, and declare themselves for Christ. Such a procedure often causes the people as a whole to reject the mes-sage. . . . By far the most effective work among folk societies has been done by those sensitive to the "tim-ing" of the first converts.[5]

Perhaps of greatest importance, these periods of diffusion have helped to develop

indigenous leadership. Anthropologists have long been aware of the fact that the leaders in a face-to-face society are in a large measure influenced by the group they lead. Thus, leaders in people's move-ments will generally not move too far ahead of their people. If the leaders take the initiative and align themselves with a new thrust, a period of diffusion that permits the congregation also to accept these ideals must follow. This gives the leadership the solid backing essential to maintain their position in their society.[6]

Appeal to the Responsible Individuals

Here we combine two of Nida's prin-ciples, that the communication should be directed toward those who are capable of passing the information on to their fellows and that appeal for change must be pre-sented to those persons in the culture who are responsible for making such decisions.

The Choco Christians were operating on these principles, at least in part, as illustrated earlier in the discussion on reciprocity and feedback. Especially when new people were present in the meetings or at the Bible readings, the leading Christians would single out the leader or the oldest person of the visiting group. They would face him with such ques-

---

5 Op. cit., pp. 113-114.

6 I observed while working among the Ne-groes in Colombia some sad examples of Co-lombian workers who were pushed so far ahead of their people through Bible school training that they were alienated and reached for se-curity and place among the missionary circle. Not finding acceptance there, they lapsed into sins of such serious proportions that they shocked their own people. To my mind it was but an attempt to be again integrated into the society from which they had become sepa-rated, even if at the lowest level.

tions: "How can you answer to God if your people do not learn to read and do not follow God?" Such individuals would invariably ask for prayer and for help, saying that they wanted to follow God, but that they were so ignorant. It often resulted in an invitation for the Christians to come to a new area to bring the message.

We found that for us the first step involved a recognition of and a respect for the existing patterns of authority. These patterns should, if rightly approached, further rather than hinder the work of the gospel. Some of the practical implications of this principle in the area of literacy are detailed by David Wirsche as follows:

> We stopped over at the chief's house at Lucas. We approached the chief saying that we had heard that his people had a desire to learn to read and we were at his orders to teach those individuals whom he would appoint to be taught. This attitude pleased the chief greatly.... He showed every possible cooperation towards initiating a reading program. He said that he himself was turning blind, but that he wanted his people to learn to read.[7]

Such working under national authority may call for real discipline on the part of the foreign worker. But if it has limitations, on the other hand, it is also an answer to his needs. David Wirsche thus continues:

> This was a new experience of teaching in an Indian home. We approached this method with the awareness of its limitation, but deemed it

advisable from the point of view of making the program indigenous and coming to the Indians as their helpers. At the beginning this program was frustrating to an American-trained teacher who is used to work according to a schedule. Sometimes there was reading during the day, sometimes there was reading only during the evening or afternoons. Again, at times . . . the Indians would practice reading until midnight . . . and the results of this unscheduled and apparently disorganized literacy program was that in eight days twenty-four individuals were taught to read. Of these, six attained the Bible story reading level.[8]

Selection of Leaders

Possibly an even more delicate step was that of developing a spiritual leadership within the church. This aspect of the assignment was approached with a certain amount of fear, for the missionary, who generally does not know the intimate life of the nationals well enough, may all too easily be misled by outward appearances. For this reason the visitors told the Indians that their stay with them was much too short and that they were too ignorant of the situation to choose wisely. They insisted that it was the national brethren's responsibility to choose a leader from their midst, for they knew the individuals who had leadership qualities, who were living in accordance with the Word, and in whom the group could have confidence. Private conversations with the heads of several Christian families invariably produced the response: "I was won to the Lord through Aureliano. He is our leader already." And, indeed, his home was the site of the weekly meetings, and his

---

[7] David Wirsche and Jacob A. Loewen, "Report on the Summer Program in Panama, 1961," an unpublished report to the Board of Foreign Missions of the Mennonite Brethren Church.

[8] Ibid.

initiative the foundation of the church building effort. Thus when on dedication Sunday the church was faced with the question: "Is it true that you choose this man to be the leader of the church?" There was a resounding *mae* 'yes' from all parts of the congregation. On the strength of this community decision, the missionaries set Aureliano apart as pastor of the church.

For this occasion translated passages from Paul's epistle to Timothy were read.[9] When these qualifications for the leader of the church and the responsibilities of the church toward its leaders were read, both Aureliano (and his wife) and the whole congregation publicly pledged themselves to obey this teaching in God's Word.

However, it may be instructive to point out that there was another individual in the village, a man of Spanish-Indian descent called J, who was also a Christian and who demonstrated leadership ability too — for that matter, he had an even better education than Aureliano. It soon became apparent that this individual would become jealous if Aureliano were selected. A partial answer to the problem was found in spending time with both individuals separately, helping them see their own strengths and problems and assisting them to discover their individual place in the program of God. But the real solution was provided when on dedication Sunday under the guidance of the Holy Spirit the church recognized J as their most qualified "teacher" and then commissioned him as their first missionary to Lucas, a small village two hours downriver from El Mamey. His assignment was to conduct literacy classes and to encourage the believers there to establish

a church. The results have already been reported.

To be honest, we must also point out how close we came to making a mistake in regards to leadership at Lucas. The best reader in the 1959 literacy program came from Lucas and he had invited the team to Lucas for a reading campaign. The workers knew that he had difficulties in his spiritual life, but he assured them that everything had been settled. True, questions to other Indians about him met with little response, but no one opposed our expressed intention of working with him. Nevertheless, we became uneasy about the situation. When we confided this to the chief at Lucas and asked for his counsel, he said, "Oh, if you want to work with us, fine — we will help you. But if you want to work with C, we don't want any part of it. C is not *andando con Dios* "walking with God'." We were afraid this might be mere jealousy, but three days later C took a group of young Indians to another river to a promiscuous drinking festival, thereby revealing his true attitude.

Stifling Initiative

This experience called into focus at least two very subtle problems that all too often subvert the divine program for raising up leadership in the emerging national church: the stifling of indigenous initiative by the missionary and the limitations of many of our leadership training programs.

We have experienced some of the sharpest correction from the Lord precisely in the area of stifling indigenous initiative. We found that for us this danger was at its peak when we were experiencing exceptional success in a given program. We tended to be so "spiritually" elated at such times that the Lord had

---

[9] 1 Timothy 3: 1-7; 4: 12-16.

to take drastic measures to get our attention.

David Wirsche reports this temptation in the teaching of reading. There was real satisfaction in quickly and efficiently bringing people to a reading knowledge of the Bible. But again and again he had to check himself, realizing he must find an Indian to teach the new learners. Knowing the brevity of the summer, and recognizing the Indian might be less efficient, it often was hard to obey, but for the development of the church it was imperative that Indians learn to teach others.

Jacob A. Loewen had a similar experience in the establishment of family worship services. After the wonderful experiences in this respect in Aureliano's home, he decided to go from house to house among the believers. The meeting at a nearby house next evening was wonderful; but while he was evaluating the experience, the Spirit of God pointed out his error. He was usurping the responsibility of the national pastor. The missionary may instruct the pastor how to do something, but then he must stay in the background while the pastor teaches it to the heads of family of his parish. It was a lesson the short-term workers had to learn time and time again during a summer's experience. For the resident missionary, who is not as conscious of the necessity for the church's independence, the temptation to do too much himself will be even stronger.

Of utmost importance is the careful evaluation of our current leadership training programs for the younger churches. At the Inter-Varsity missionary conference at Urbana in 1961, Eugene A. Nida said, "If we are honest we will admit that in most cases we are guilty of training nationals for followership rather than for leadership." Paul's principle "to teach others to teach others"[10] can hardly be overemphasized. In the development of the Choco church this principle has received high priority. As soon as an Indian could read Book I, he was given the responsibility for teaching it to another person who wanted to learn to read. In fact, we are convinced that this teaching others to read, indirectly provided training for person-to-person witnessing about "God's way."

Reviewing the various experiences and lessons that we learned in connection with the development of leadership for the Choco church, we feel that several guide lines are becoming apparent. These are:

That leaders must be chosen by the group and not by the foreigner. Leaders must find their authority in the group and to it they must be responsible. The missionary can serve as a "catalyst" and Biblical counselor in such situations, but never as the source of authority.

That, as the Scriptures teach, God has given to his church all the gifts it needs for healthy functioning.

That even the young national church will have spiritual insight to discern their leaders, if its vision is not distorted by outside intervention.

That the local church can solve its problems of support if the church structure grows out of the local situation rather than being imposed from without.

Standards for Church Membership

We found it imperative to recognize the authority, under God, of the local community of believers in determining the qualifications for baptism and for

---

10 2 Timothy 2: 2.

church membership. We can have confidence that the same Holy Spirit who
came to the Gentiles[11] will guide these
new children of God into all truth. This
especially applies in the areas of church
standards, discipline, meeting times, and
service patterns. If nationals feel the missionaries do not fully trust them and
therefore police them, they will much
more easily be tempted to live a double
life.

What standards should a new church
set up? When we discussed the attributes
of Christians with the Choco believers,
they pointed out to us that not all people
who live like Christians are necessarily
Christian. They knew people who had
none of the vices but who still had not
been *entregados* 'having given themselves',
to the Lord. On the other hand, Aureliano
also pointed out that none of their people
were "finished Christians." They had a
lot to learn, but he was confident as they
learned more of the Scriptures they would
obey the teachings.

Implicit obedience to the written word
was not limited to the Scriptures. After
reading in a book on health that garbage
around the house attracts flies and flies
carry disease, Aureliano announced to
his wife that from now on there would
be a box in the house to collect garbage
and no more was to be thrown behind
the house.

A readiness to accept and obey the
Bible seemed to be almost universal. When
an old man on the Bayano river heard
that the Word of God had arrived at
Chepo, he came to David Wirsche and

asked to be taught to read because he
wanted to know God's Word. The son
of a chief from the same river on learning
to read the Scriptures remarked: "I never
knew God said all these things. We are
really going to have to pay attention to
do what he says."

Trying to analyze the results of our
experience in connection with church
membership and standards of church conduct, the following principles seem to be
significant:

That the missionary teach the standards
set forth in the Bible, but that he leave
all the examination of candidates and the
decision on qualifications of membership
to the national leaders.

That, rather than posing a long list of
prerequisites for membership, the right
attitude toward the teachings of the Scriptures be stressed. As Aureliano said, "We
are not complete, but whatever the Word
teaches, we will do."

That we teach all rules of conduct in
the context of the Scriptures and not in
a separate book of rules or doctrine. This
would also be in harmony with a face-
to-face society's practice of teaching in
context, never in isolation. In such a case
only those aspects of conduct would be
considered that are contained in the portion of Scripture already translated into
their language.

That by emphasizing the indigenous
responsibility of decision we demonstrate
that we accept them equally as "heirs of
the Kingdom" and equally led by the
Holy Spirit. Thus, the responsibility of
the church, or of the individual believer,
is to God and not to the missionary or
a mission.

---

[11] Acts 10.

The Choco and their Spirit World

Loewen's article deals with the spirit world of the Choco and its effect on the thinking of Christian converts about spirits and the Holy Spirit. The implications which he draws reach far wider than the Choco, however. They call into question the ability of secularized Western missionaries to understand the way in which the Holy Spirit works in such a community as the Choco, and the hindrance which such missionaries can be. This article is one of a series written by Loewen now running in PA. These articles draw pointed, significant conclusions from missionary anthropological work among Indians of Latin America.

MISSIONARIES — at least from the time of Saint Boniface, the apostle to the Germanic tribes of northern Europe, who sought to demonstrate the superiority of the Christian God by cutting down the sacred tree of the Teutonic people's pagan deity — have often yielded to the temptation to demonstrate the absurdity of the animists' fear of spirits. By word and deed they have sought to liberate benighted people from their pagan superstition. And by and large they have been extremely successful. Many a returned missionary has awed the home audience with a personal testimony of having destroyed some object of superstition to demonstrate to frightened devotees the impotence, if not the non-existence, of the

spirits they feared. There have been a few voices of protest and warning, such as Johannes Warneck, who warns new missionaries against destroying native shrines and fetishes:

> It is not wise to disturb the sacred festivals or cut down the sacred trees where the soil of heathenism has not been prepared. Europeans do not thereby prove the impotence of their idols, but they only wound the religious feelings and increase their fear.[1]

More recently Donald H. Bouma has cautiously pointed out the negative effects of the debunking of native spirits as manifested in the so-called "dirty Christian villages" in Africa. These people believed that spirits were watching to see whether the women kept things clean around their houses. Everyone "knew" that if this taboo were broken, serious consequences would follow, not only for

Jacob A. Loewen is Professor of Modern Languages, Anthropology, and Missions at Tabor College, Hillsboro, Kansas. Previous articles in PA include "The Church Among the Choco of Panama," Vol. 10, No. 3 (May-June 1963), and "Bible Stories: Message and Matrix," Vol. 11, No. 2 (Mar.-Apr. 1964).

[1] Johannes Warneck, *The Living Christ and Dying Heathenism* (Grand Rapids: Baker Book House, 1954), p. 204.

127

the person involved but also for the whole society. Once the spirits had been debunked by the missionary, the meta-physical and social incentives for keeping the village clean were gone; and so — without a new motivation to take its place — the villages of the Christians became dirty.[2]

On the other hand, if we look at some of the dynamic and spontaneously grow-ing, truly indigenous churches in Latin America today, we find that most of them place heavy emphasis on the Spirit.[3] The following testimony of a Choco believer is a vivid illustration of this "Spirit consciousness."

> I am so glad for the powerful Spirit of God who keeps those who have given God the hand and walk on God's road. A few nights ago we had a real testing in our house. A Colom-bian witch doctor came to visit a relative who lives in my house. I used to be very afraid of devils, and so when this witch doctor was going to "sing demons" at night, I became worried that I would again become afraid. So before going to sleep I told God about the things that were on my heart. I told him, "You have bought me from the devil's hand; you have taken my fear away. Don't let me or my family become afraid this night." It was after midnight when I suddenly awoke hearing someone talking loudly. When I listened, I heard the witch doctor say, "Who has been praying? My hai won't come tonight." I was so happy to know and to see again that God is stronger than all the devils. When the Spirit

of God watches my house, the devils can't even come there.

Something very similar can be said of the revival movement among the Otomi Indians in the Mesquital area of Mexico, of the Pentecostal Church in Chile, of the Toba Indians of the Argentine Chaco,[4] and others.

If we look a little bit more closely at the Tobas, who were a very heavily spirit-oriented, face-to-face society, we find that the conversion movement among them was not begun by missionaries who came to them, learned their language, and brought them the message, but rather by Toba Indians having an experience with Pen-tecostal cultists outside of their envi-ronment and then bringing their testimony back as a relevant message to their Toba tribes people. Reyburn characterizes the Toba movement as an "international pen-tecostal" movement, which he defines as having "a strong emphasis on gospel preaching and the visible manifestations of the Holy Spirit."[5]

The accounts of these indigenous evan-gelistic movements bear a striking similar-ity to the story of the early church in Acts, in which the working of the Holy Spirit was central and paramount. This leads us to several serious questions. If sensitivity to the Holy Spirit was one of the important characteristics of the early church and is now operative in these new spirit-oriented, truly indigenous churches, did their primitive consciousness of the evil spirit world serve as the basis for their consciousness of and sensitivity to the Holy Spirit? Could the premature loss of faith in their native spirit world

[2] Donald H. Bouma, Anthropology and Missions (Grand Rapids: International Pub-lications, 1957), p. 10.

[3] Eugene A. Nida, "The Indigenous Churches of Latin America," PA, Vol. 8, No. 3 (May-June 1961), pp. 97-105.

[4] William D. Reyburn, The Toba Indians of the Argentine Chaco: An Interpretative Report (Elkhart, Indiana: Mennonite Board of Mis-sions and Charities, 1954).

[5] Ibid., p. 45.

also make such people insensitive toward the Spirit of God? Could our scientific disbelief in or doubts concerning the reality of the evil spirit world possibly be the reason why the traditional Western churches experience so little of the Spirit's manifestations? And because we as missionaries have had so little home experience with the work of the Holy Spirit, could this be a reason why it is so hard for us to recognize where, when, and how the Spirit is working?[6] These questions are asked with the concern that the following account of the Choco and their spirit world will stimulate thinking, questions, and research that may in turn clear the channels for a freer operation of the Spirit of God in all the programs of the church.

Animists and the Spirit World

Like other animists,[7] the Choco visualize themselves as facing not only a hostile and seemingly perverse physical world, but also a vast, powerful and dangerous world of spirits. In true animist fashion they see no watertight distinction between animals and humans or the animate and the inanimate. Animals may become men and men change into animals, trees, or other objects. They see no distinct cleavage between the physical and the metaphysical, the material and the spiritual. At the very least these realms are experienced as interacting; and, more likely than not, they are merely superficially differing manifestations of the same realities.

William D. Reyburn illustrates this unity-of-nature view very graphically in his account of the unsuccessful African bushfire hunt.[8] The participating missionary explained the lack of success in terms of the weather — a physical condition. The non-Christian Africans knew that something had gone wrong in the carefully executed procedure, which in part consisted of taboos kept by the wives at home. Since the hunters had carefully done their part, no success meant that the careless wife had been noisy or had swept around the house and thereby awakened the dormant spirits of former hunting quarry. The aroused spirits of these previously killed animal had warned the living of the impending danger, and these had then escaped out of the circle, possibly even in spirit form. The Christian natives who had participated in the hunt also knew that something was amiss, but they were extremely frustrated. They could not beat their wives — the mission would not understand. But why then hadn't God answered their prayers? Was God really as sympathetic as claimed? These unspoken questions are apparent in the disgusted outburst of one of them, "Sometimes one gets the feeling that God doesn't have any stomach!"

Or take the missionary in Colombia who, trying to prove to his converts from animism that disease is caused by germs rather than evil spirits, introduced his

---

6 Bishop Lesslie Newbigin, in "Bringing our Missionary Methods under the Word of God," *Occasional Bulletin,* from Missionary Research Library, Vol. XIII, Nov. 1962, p. 7, testifies that it took years of missionary service before he finally learned that his duty was not just to launch a mission *program* in a new situation, but that he must first listen to ascertain where the Spirit is already working and then take this work of the Spirit as the core and foundation for that which is to follow.

7 Eugene A. Nida and William A. Smalley, *Introducing Animism* (New York: Friendship Press, 1959).

8 William D. Reyburn, "The Missionary and Cultural Diffusion — I," PA, Vol. 5, No. 3 (May-June 1958), p. 141.

awed disciples to the microscope and to a series of slides showing the malaria parasites having invaded red corpuscles. To the Western mind this proved the disease to be caused by something physical, a germ. But the unconvinced Indian only responded, "I never knew that those spirits looked like that and that they were so small."

Besides the animists' conception of the basic unity of nature illustrated above, there are at least two other considerations that need to be stressed for this paper. First, spirit power is basically non-moral. It can be used by and for both good and evil. Second, it is possible to develop at least some control over the spirit world. The two main channels are by manipulation through the use of magic and by supplication or other forms of religious appeasement. The shaman and the priest are the specialists who know how to deal with the supernatural.

The Choco Spirit World

The Choco call the general amoral spirit powers *hai*. *Hai* are generally viewed as sexless amorphous spirits which may or may not be harmful. They are the carriers of witchcraft but also the tools of the shaman for both good and evil. They are usually not personified.

Besides *hai* there are also many personified spirit powers. Two of these stand in an antithetic relationship to each other: *ewandama* (ākhōre) as the good god and *tiauru* (dosiäta) as trickster, the mischievous (and often evil) opponent, who tries to undermine or at least neutralize the good work of the creator. Souls of men are slated to become spirits in the land "where *ewandama* is," but should a soul fail to turn right as soon as it leaves the invisibly split skull after death, it will end up in the place "where it is dark,"

a portion of the underworld that is described as exceedingly treacherous.

There are at least three unpardonable "sins" that will "damage" one's blood and predestinate one to become a harmful spirit. These three are incest, sex relations with Negroes, and beating one's children. Souls of damaged blood become harmful spirits known as *aribamia* and *aripada*. Both are of human origin as "souls of death," the former having escaped from the body after burial and the latter after death, but before burial.

Modern Choco are rather unconcerned about *ewandama* since he is benevolent and is actually considered as having retreated from the world. There is one great fear, however, that abnormalities in sex or other behavior are now abounding so much that *ewandama* will be forced to remove the iniquity from this world with another deluge. Day to day, however, man's chief concern is with the spirit beings that are associated with *tiauru* and which are bent on doing harm to men. Man's protection is largely dependent on the keeping of taboos and the sucessful manipulation of the *hai*.

There has been a marked increase of shamanism in recent decades. This increase seems to parallel the breakdown of tribal social control under increasing national governmental influence. In some areas every home has at least an aspiring "learner," if not a full-fledged *hai* practitioner. This condition renders poignant testimony to the facts that the Choco consider even the most everyday activities as fraught with spirit encounters and the accompanying fear, and that their web of social relations has degenerated so as to cause each one to mistrust and to fear all people beyond the immediate household.

A Choco Tale of a Spirit Encounter

A man was walking into the forest. When he arrived deep in the forest, far from home, he found a monkey. He shot it. Having killed it, he was bringing it along the trail. As he was walking along, he found a turkey. He shot it too. Having killed it, he continued along the trail carrying the monkey together with the turkey. He stopped to pull out a vine to tie them together. He had just finished tying them together and was about to put them on his shoulder when he heard a shout. He stopped and reflected, "Who could be coming here deep in the forest? I didn't meet any footprints either. Who in the world could it be? I will wait and see whether it will shout again." Then he heard the shout again. He said to himself, "I will wait and see if it is a friend in order to walk with him. I want to find out what person is going to appear." Then it shouted again. As soon as this happened, he felt goose pimples all over his body. Then he knew that this was no human. He began to run wildly. He did not remember when he began running. He forgot whether or not he had picked up the turkey. He was just running back and forth and falling down and getting up. Then he knew that he was out of breath (that his soul had stayed behind), so he rested.

Having caught his breath (soul) again, he started running again. This time he ran along the trail. Now it was close behind. He dropped the turkey and continued running. The demon (*tiauru*) stopped to devour the turkey. Then he dropped the monkey. He continued running. Then he cut a stick and made a puzzle. He could hear *tiauru* eating. He hung the puzzle in the trail. Then *tiauru* came to where the puzzle was hanging. He tried to take the puzzle apart, but it was getting late. Then *tiauru* said, "If I continue doing this, I will not eat this man. I had better leave it alone. I will run after him." Then *tiauru* came running. He came to the place where there were four puzzles hanging. He tried to take them apart. Finally said, "If I can take these puzzles apart, I will eat the man; but if I cannot take them apart, I will not follow him any more. I will keep this puzzle for myself. And when they are with fever, I will confound them with it; for I myself have become crazed."[9]

Commentary on the Tale

The name of the tale *kiranemamia* refers to the magic puzzle the hunter made to escape from the pursuing ogre. The puzzle is made from a green stick which has a rather hard shell and a pulpy interior. It consists of four interlocked units skillfully carved out of one stick. It can be opened to form a foursided figure. The individual sides can be moved back and forth, but since the ends are closed, they cannot be taken apart without breaking the ends. The informant made them quite efficiently and was thus able to make four of these puzzles during the two hours this tale was discussed. The *kiranemamia*, literally translated, means "crazy-making being." The suffix *mia* implies spirit power.

The hunter recognizes the true nature of the voice when he feels the "goose pimples all over his body." Goose pimples always indicate tension in one's own spirit and, especially in isolation, will be inter-

[9] For the Choco language version of this story see Jacob A. Loewen, "A Choco Miraculous Escape Tale," *America Indigena*, Vol. 20, pp. 207-215.

preted as an indication of the proximity of spirit forces dangerous to one's soul.

The effect of the consciousness of the ogre's nearness is immediate and violent. The hunter runs for his life. He leaves trail and reason and just charges wildly into the jungle. The auxiliary verbs used graphically emphasize the disorientation the hunter feels as he madly runs back and forth and falls down and gets up again. However, this senseless activity only exhausts him and leads to "soul" loss.

The Choco conceive of man as having four souls: (1) the soul of the sun and (2) the soul of the moon are evidenced by the shadow during the day and night respectively; (3) the wandering soul, which leaves the body when one dreams, is exhausted, or becomes the victim of soul-stealing; and (4) the soul of death, which leaves the body after death and which will become a harmful or useful spirit being. Thus the hunter, after his mad and useless running, had to "catch his soul" before he was able to cope with the supernatural opponent.

The pursuing spirit being is identified as *tiauru*, the trickster, who always opposes the good god of creation. For the conclusion of the tale this identification could be appropriate; but when one considers the "ogre" qualities that are stressed in the eating of the dead game and the pursuit of the hunter, the use of *tiauru* is somewhat anomalous.

The strategy of the hunter, whom the raconteur identified as a *haipana* 'shaman,' warrants comment. After he "gains his soul," his first step is to locate the trail. The reasoning, according to the informant, was that while the man made little headway in the dense jungle, *tiauru* was not so limited. Once back on the trail, the hunter begins to drop his game as obstacles to delay the pursuing ogre. The delay is only brief, but long enough to permit the making and introduction of the first magic *kiranemamia*. The "little" magic of the first puzzle then provides the substantial delay which permits the preparation of the four puzzles which ultimately facilitate his escape.

The conclusion of the tale contributes at least two important considerations. First, it provides the Indians with an explanation for the origin and mechanics of delirium. This fact could be viewed as a justification for the telling of the tale. The hunter becomes representative of the Indian race, and *tiauru* becomes the generalized symbol of the spirit forces which oppose man. Second, it expresses the defeatist philosophy which most observers have noticed in present-day Choco. Two aspects of this attitude are here revealed: (1) The Indian only wins "rounds" in his struggles against outside people and spirits, and in the end he will still remain the vanquished victim of other races and spirit beings. The other aspect of this philosophy revealed here is in connection with the belief that one can be harmed by witchcraft performed on personal possessions. Thus (2), in the very process of winning, the Indian has left with the enemy spirit a puzzle of his making, or, in the case of a lawsuit, his signature or thumb print, which then becomes the avenue through which he is finally overcome.

The Choco Convert and the Spirit World

The Choco view their present condition of isolation from *ewandama* as the direct result of having learned *hai* curing ceremony from *tiauru*, who caused them to "give him their hand" as seal of the contract.[10] The Choco's fear of the spirit world was indelibly impressed on us one day when an Indian who was working for us tragically died of a lung hemorrhage. The Indians' consultation with the diviner "revealed" that "the spirits that make the blood run were loose at Jake's house." In a flash all the Indians including our informant fled. Three weeks we waited in vain for our teacher to return. Then one day at noon he poked his head into the door, his face ashen with fear and his voice choking with emotion and the hurry, and said, "Jaco, I've come to tell you that the spirits that make the blood run are loose at your house and they are dangerous not only to Indians, but also to white people." We realized that he could not come in, so I accompanied him to his canoe parked downriver. Here sat his wife crying because of the risk her husband was taking, but to all her objections he had only one answer: "Jaco is my friend and I must go and warn him." Once far enough away from my house we sat down and I tried to reason with him that God is stronger than the evil spirits. Suddenly as if exasperated with my arguments he cried out, "Jaco, you are not as stupid as all that. You know that our fathers gave their hand to *tiauru* and that we now belong to him."

That the burden of this yoke of fear is keenly felt even by the shamans who are supposed to be "owners" and manipulators of the *hai* is evidenced in the following scene that took place at the first Choco communion service when the leader asked a notorious shaman, a non-Christian, if he had a word for the people. The old shaman arose and in a voice deeply affected by emotion said, "I know I do not belong to the church, but I am convinced that the message is from God. You all know my involvements (with the *hai* spirits) which do not let me follow God's road." In a voice equally charged with emotion the leader of the church said, "Yes, we know, but we will pray and God will free you from their power."

Conversion is thus viewed as man's release from the bondage of the evil spirits and from the perpetual fear that accompanies this. At one of the church services a woman gave the following testimony:

I always used to hear noises at night which made me very much afraid. There were so many demons around us. Even at daytime I was afraid to be alone in the forest. But now Jesus has taken my fear away and I have peace. Even when I sleep at night, I don't have to think of evil spirits any more because God watches our house.

The release from fear is a very popular point of appeal to the uncommitted. And with what appears to be almost endless patience, witnessing Christians permit such uncommitted people to tell of the gruesome experiences and of narrow escapes in the spirit encounters of their past. The answer of the Choco Christians to such confessions is a personal testimony of the experience of the power of God's Spirit over the fear of spirits in their own lives.

Witness to a Personal Dilemma

When I first began to read an early draft of the translation of the Gospel of Mark to the Choco Christians in 1961, little did I realize that I would experience

---

[10] Jacob A. Loewen, "Good News for the Waunana," PA, Vol. 8, No. 6 (Nov.-Dec. 1961), pp. 275-278.

what T. S. Soltau so succinctly states, that Bible reading in an area where witchcraft is practiced can be a revealing experience.[11] As in paragraph after paragraph the *mia* (spirit-being indicator) suffix for all diseases and the names of many spirits, caused the Choco enthusiasm over the wonderful power of God to grow, I began to realize that they were appreciating something about the gospel narrative that I could not, or at least did not, to the same degree as they. I thought my own discomfort was successfully masked. In fact, when the pastor's wife came down with fever (Choco: fever-spirits), I suggested the laying on of hands and prayer. When she suffered a relapse next day, I noticed the Choco Christians praying for her again, but this time without me. My cautious inquiry as to why I was not included brought the ego-deflating answer, "Because you don't believe." And I had to admit that to me germs under a microscope did prove the material origin of sickness.[12] And I did not know at what point spirit and matter meet and interact to heal. I had to learn that my "primitive, animistic" brethren could appreciate a dimension that I could not honestly claim. Indeed, I have had to conclude that since they had been so very conscious of the evil spirit forces as non-Christians, these new converts were now equally conscious of the presence of the Spirit of God.

---

[11] T. S. Soltau, *Facing the Field* (Grand Rapids: Baker Book House, 1959), pp. 24-25.

[12] J. W. C. Dougall, "African Separatist Churches," *The International Review of Missions*, Vol. 45, No. 7 (July 1956), p. 261, says that for many Africans, Western medicine deals only with the physical aspects of disease, and for this reason they seek additional "spirit cure."

Proposals for Consideration

The following conclusions are an attempt to clarify my own thinking in regard to these experiences. I am not sure that they are all final. Maybe they should be treated more as proposals for consideration with the hope that they will stimulate serious concern and study which in turn will lead to the formulation of answers that are dictated by the Spirit of God.

1. If, as we have often been told about communism, we cannot overcome the enemy until we take him seriously, and if we want to leave our converts from animism sensitive to the Holy Spirit who can liberate them from their spirit fears, we shall need to accept the reality of the evil spirit world and show some respect for the native experience with and fear of it.

2. That we will need to accept the modern "Gentiles" from animistic societies as equally heirs to the Kingdom and as equally potential for Spirit-filling and Spirit-guidance. If the animists seem fixated at the "spirit" end of the concept of supernatural power in the universe, maybe the Western Christian is equally extreme in his "person" orientation to the Holy Spirit.

3. That we, who come from the so-called traditional Western Christianity with very little experience of the manifestation of the Holy Spirit in our midst, must recognize that we cannot deceive the people in a face-to-face society by talking and acting "as if we believed" in the presence and work of the Holy Spirit, when the experience is foreign to us.

4. That more of us missionaries will need to learn to listen, to identify where the Spirit of God is already working, before we launch any kind of program.

Lengua Indians and Their "Innermost"

"THESE people will simply *'poijh'* us to death," stated one of the white immigrant settlers concerning the Lengua Indians who work on the settlers' farms as peones. "We've lived with them here in the Paraguayan Chaco for more than thirty years now, but I still find this habit of theirs most exasperating. You know for a fact that they want *something*, but they just stand there impassively and keep on repeating *'poijh'* 'nothing.' There have been times," he continued in all seriousness, "that I felt convinced that they didn't actually know what they wanted; but, lo and behold, when you least expected it, they did express their wish. When I then asked, 'Did you know what you wanted when you arrived?' they would answer in the affirmative. If you then reprimand them and say, 'Why didn't you tell me this as soon as you arrived?' they will again assume that impassive facial expression, or at the most shrug their shoulders, but say no more."[1]

"They are just plain ignorant and basically dishonest," said another settler.

"You can't trust these Indians nohow, not even the converted ones. Their heathen lying habit is so deeply ingrained in their nature that they cannot possibly tell the truth."

Both of the speakers were Mennonites[2] who with several thousand of their fellow believers had settled in the Chaco and who were now struggling to wrest a livelihood from its harsh environment. As non-conformists of Anabaptist heritage they had retreated to the Chaco in order to find an environment in which they would be permitted to practise their faith without contamination from the civilized world. They were a God-fearing people who believed the Bible and were convinced that all lies were from "the evil one."

Both of the men quoted were talking about some 5000 Lengua Indians, who in their own language call themselves "the people." The Lengua had been a nomadic hunting-gathering tribe until contact with Paraguayan civilization,

[1] This paper represents a part of the anthropological findings that grew out of the research program described in "Chaco Missionaries and Anthropologists Cooperate in Research," PA, Vol. 12, No. 4 (July-August 1965), pp. 158-190. An adapted version of this paper appeared in the *Mennonite Quarterly Review*, January 1965, pp. 40-67, under the title of "A Mennonite Encounter with the 'Innermost' of the Lengua Indians."

[2] The white settlers who figure very frequently in this paper are Mennonites, an Anabaptist group which had its roots in the left wing of the Protestant Reformation. The first group came to the Chaco from Canada in 1928 for religious reasons. The second group came from Europe in 1930 mainly as refugees from communist Russia. The third group arrived in 1948 and included mainly displaced peoples of Mennonite faith from Eastern Europe, who needed a new home.

missions (Anglican, New Tribes and Mennonite), and particularly the Mennonite colonies launched them in great cycle of change. Sweeping changes in their overt culture have already taken place, especially since they have adopted so many material traits from the immigrant settlers. Furthermore, the majority have also accepted the Christian faith!

This paper, however, will describe not so much the overt culture of the Lengua, nor the culture change, but rather the covert, the "inner," or the "psychic" nature of man as the Lengua Indians used to, and as they even now, see it. It proposes to present an ethnographic description of man's "inner life" as seen through the eyes of the Lengua Indians who represent a worldview which at many points differs radically from our own—which we, of course, consider to be the right one. It will illustrate by examples from everyday experience how the mutual lack of understanding of the respective covert worldviews can lead to prejudice, frustration and even crime for members of the cultures in contact. [3] It will point out some of the advantages that an understanding of the Lengua concepts of the "innermost" can have both in the evangelistic efforts of the missionary and also for the everyday

[3] There is a half-secret wish in the "innermost" of the writer that, even though not all of the readers of PA may have experienced contact with "exotic" cultures, the "dailiness" of the experiences recounted may make possible flashbacks of personal encounters with "impossible" people even in the home culture. Maybe there will even be awakened a strong enough feeling of guilt about these negative encounters, that the individuals will be stimulated to become inquisitive about the covert factors that were the real basis of the misunderstanding.

dealings between the settler and his Indian employees. Its purpose is to whet the appetite of all the readers to develop sensitivity to and ever-increasing appreciation for the worldview (and its unspoken value hierarchies) of all the people who, in the economy of God, become our neighbors.

The Lengua innermost

The Lengua distinguish at least four foci in a man's inner life. (1) The -valhoc (the hyphen before a Lengua noun indicates that such a stem can never stand without a possessor, generally a possessive pronominal prefix) is translated as the 'innermost.' It serves as the mainspring of behavior in a man's life. (2) The -vanmongcama, which is most frequently translated 'soul,' 'dream,' or 'shadow,' has very little to do with behavior; it is really the core of a man's life or existence. Should it be lost, stolen, or ill, a man will surely die. (3) The -nenyic, translated 'chest,' can refer both to the chest anatomy and to its psychic functions. It carries with it the implications of deep involvement of the entire inner make-up of man. (4) The -jangauc, translated as 'soul of the dead,' is the disembodied inner existence that is "born" from man's total inner being at the moment of his death. Most frequently it is treated as the dead man's counterpart to a living person's 'soul,' but in actual function it seems to include also the functions of the 'innermost' and the 'chest.'

If we look at these foci in terms of their locus, their habitat within the body, we notice that the latter, the 'soul of the dead' is the total spiritual counterpart of the person, including his recognizable appearance. However, it may also be used occasionally in a limited sense as the "soul" or essential core of the dead person. The chest includes the whole thorax from the navel up. As already indicated earlier it is frequently used to refer to the sum total of the living man's inner being. The 'soul' resides either in the upper part of the chest or in the brain, possibly both. The 'innermost' is located in the lower part of man's chest, or in the upper part of his abdomen, possibly in his stomach.

Linguistic idioms. From the abundance of -*valhoc* 'innermost' based idioms in the Lengua language we can conclude that it definitely is the seat of the emotions. The following is a list of expressions[4] that proceed from and involve man's innermost (in each pair the idiomatic English translation is followed by a literal translation of the Lengua expression): to love, the innermost dissolves; to hate, the innermost does not dissolve; to be happy, the innermost spreads out; to think or thank, the innermost mentions; to meditate, the innermost searches; to be afraid, the innermost falls down; to excite, become excited, the innermost labors, works hard; to worry, the innermost keeps on mentioning it with concern; to hope, the innermost waits; to be greedy, the innermost demands; to be kind, the innermost receives, accepts; to frighten, be frightened, the innermost jumps up high; to cry with fear, the innermost trembles.

To be sympathetic, the innermost is

not locked up; to be proud, the innermost praises (mentions) itself; to be humble, the innermost does not praise itself; to be obedient, the innermost is soft or gentle; to be upset, the innermost is wavy (turbulent); to be calm, the innermost is clean; to be sick, the innermost is unclean, or bad; to be sickly, the innermost is rotten; to be sick (sorcery), the innermost is judged, or known; to be sick (sympathetic magic), the innermost is under a spell; to become well, the innermost is restored; to be converted is to change one's innermost; to comfort is to refresh the innermost. There are many other such expressions.

In addition to the emotions or states of the innermost there are the following emotions or conditions of the chest: to grieve, the chest goes away; to be alive and healthy, the chest is strong; to breathe is to drive breath out of the chest; to die, the chest remains without breath, or the core of the chest tears off; to sigh deeply, the core of the chest flees; to desire intensely, the core of the chest dies.

All of the expressions in this latter group seem to carry overtones of something very intense and possibly more inclusive than the states of the innermost. This agrees with the former statement that at times the 'chest' expressions frequently refer to the totality of man's inner life.

The function of the innermost. In some respects the -*valhoc* compares very favorably with the conscience of our Western inner life, for like the latter it can distinguish between good and evil; but it can also *be* basically good or evil in character. Thus conversion is very often spoken of as the exchanging of a

---

[4] This list was collected almost exclusively by missionary Dietrich Lepp from Laguna Pora Mission.

bad innermost for a good one. The idiom is drawn from a Lengua folktale about a very bad man, who, through the change of his innermost, became a very kind and good man.

But we must here immediately point out that the Lengua term 'innermost' also carries a much more physiological connotation than the metaphorical usage of English "heart." This contrast can be demonstrated in connection with the Lengua expression 'changing or exchanging one's innermost' when used to translate the Christian concept of conversion.

Missionary D. Lepp, as a new missionary zealous to eradicate shamanism and magic, forbade all medicine men to practice their art at his mission station. As soon as he heard their chanting— day or night—he went and ordered them to desist or to vacate the premises. After about three months of consistent interference by the missionary all the chanting had apparently ceased. When shortly thereafter a number of women came to 'exchange their innermosts,' he was delighted. His firmness was now paying dividends in conversions. When however, more and more groups began coming to 'change their innermosts,' he began to be suspicious.

"Why did they want to change their innermost?"

"Because the missionary was telling them that God wanted them to do this."

"But why do it now and so many together?"

After some hesitation someone finally volunteered: "You see, you told all the medicine men to stop singing—well, some of them are still singing softly. Since

they do not seem to be afraid of you or of your God, we are beginning to fear that their medicine and magic may be stronger than we thought. We are becoming very much afraid of them. However, we want to remain your friends, so we have decided we would ask you to give us *Lenco*[5] innermosts so that we can become immune to the medicine man's magic." This request reveals that the Lengua expected far more than only a "psychic" change of heart.

It is probably correct that the *-valhoc* has both physiological and psychic function. Consider the interesting distinction made in the case of hemorrhages. The Lengua identify two kinds of chest hemorrhages. In the first, the bleeding is organic and proceeds from the actual organs of the chest; in the second, it is the 'innermost' that is bleeding. Tubercular hemorrhages, for example, are classified not as bleeding of the organs, but as bleeding issuing from the innermost. The informants identified great fear as the major cause of bleeding of the innermost. In like manner other ailments, especially those of the thorax, will be classified on the one hand as being physiological or organic, or on the other as emotional, resulting from conditions of the innermost.

At other times during the research it seemed as if the innermost could to a large extent be equated with the Western concept of personality, especially since it develops in the social context, rather than through mother's milk, as in the case of the soul. As such,

---

[5] *Lenco* is the Lengua form of the word *gringo*. It is used by Lengua to label the Mennonite settlers.

the innermost is also responsible for making decisions, for "thinking" is one of its main functions. However, "feeling" runs a close second.

Nor are human beings the only ones possessing an innermost. Everything has - *valhoc*, but people are more concerned about those of certain objects. The camera, for example, is said to have a diviner's innermost, for it can put on paper the things it sees and thus "reveal" them long after it is no longer possible to see the scenes with the human eye. This parallels their experience with the shaman whose soul can identify the thief of a stolen object, or the place where something was lost. Like the camera which produces a photograph, the soul of the shaman retains its observations of a world invisible to the natural eye in which it wanders when the medicine man has visions. At a later date, he can thus graphically describe this "universe" to the other members of the tribe.

Like the soul, the innermost can leave the body of the person. Informants were able to list at least four common reasons: (1) to accompany the soul when the latter wanders about during dreams or visions; (2) when it is stolen, or lost, either together with or separately from the soul; (3) if a person is suddenly and violently frightened; and (4) at death, when it ceases to exist entirely, or rather is absorbed together with the rest of man's inner being into the soul of the dead. This overlap with the soul of the dead will be treated more specifically under the discussion of innermost-linked property. The fourth cause for separation of the innermost from the body, of course,

was permanent. Loss or stealing can involve absences extending up to several weeks in length. During dreams, visions, etc., it will be separated for only shorter periods, while in the case of fright it will be absent only momentarily.

It will not be necessary at this point to discuss fully the function of the soul. Its origin will be discussed in the next section and further remarks about it will be made in connection with death. We only underscore that the soul is essentially the bearer of life. If the soul is lost or stolen, death is sure to follow in due time, while its return to the body means a return of health and life. For this reason dreaming and visions can be dangerous in at least two ways. They leave the thorax empty and open for the entry of one of several kinds of unattached spirits or souls of whom the universe is filled. Then, too, the wandering soul is much more vulnerable to capture and "getting lost" than when it is "at home."

When a person finally dies, his living soul, (together with the other inner aspects of man's existence) is transformed into his soul of the dead. This soul of the dead is one of the greatest sources of fear for Lengua Indians. It also will be described in more detail in connection with property and death. A detailed discussion is being prepared in a separate paper.[6]

The origin and development of man's inner life

Lengua informants tended to be very vague about the origin of the soul.

---

[6] Jacob A. Loewen. "The Spirit World of Chaco Lengua," in preparation.

However, in several group and also private informant sessions the concensus was that the "seed" for the soul comes from the father. For this reason a father is charged with taboos at the time of childbirth. He abstains from certain foods, does not perform hard physical labor or bathe in cold water at least until the umbilicus has healed. Some fathers do not bathe in cold water until the mother stops bleeding. However, even though a child has the "seed" for a soul at birth, it is not viewed as having either a developed soul or an innermost. And because neither the soul (life) nor the innermost (personality) are functional at birth infanticide is not viewed as killing. Thus the question of whether or not a newborn child should live was an open option. The decision of life or death was based on other values than that this meant killing a living person. Should a mother die at child-birth, infanticide was considered obligatory for the soul of the dead mother (-*jangane*) would be greatly angered if she were deprived of her infant.

Soul food. Mother's milk was viewed as the great food of the soul. In order to assure that full development of the soul the Lengua viewed three or four years of breast feeding as imperative. Because mother's milk plays such an important part in the development of the soul, the Lengua have found bottle feeding with other milk than mother's milk to be very barbarous. A few of the Lengua babies raised this way by missionary nurses are, even today as grownups, being called "animal babies." Their full humanity is still in question.

Just how the innermost developed and was nurtured informants did not seem to be able to answer. The Chulupi, who have a very similar outlook, explain that man's innermost develops through breast feeding and attention (love and instruction) from the mother. We can thus suggest that breast feeding builds the soul ; and mother's attention, love and instruction nurture the innermost. In both cultures fathers have very little responsibility beyond the taboos at birth.

Becoming human. When a child was eight days old it underwent the first of a series of festivals.[7] This celebration involved the piercing of the child's earlobe with a cactus thorn. This marked its entrance into the human race. From now on it was considered to have both an innermost and a soul. To kill a child after the piercing of the earlobe was considered murder. Once the child's earlobe had been pierced it was also accorded the respect of a complete person. Mothers tried as much as possible to do what the "person" wanted. Out of respect for the innermost of her child a mother would not force it to take medicine when it resisted. She would try to persuade the child, but if it would not accede, she would not use force. The missionary's threat, "If you don't give the child medicine it will die, "would be met by a shrug and possibly the slowly spoken words, "But he/she wants to die." This certainly does not mean a lack of maternal concern for the child, for mothers have been known to plead in tears with their children, but they would not resort to force.

[7] Jacob A. Loewen, " Lengua Festivities," a paper describing an extensive festival cycle is now in preparation.

Growing up. To encourage the developing innermost (self-consciousness) both boys and girls become the object of a second festival somewhere between eight and ten years of age. This festival follows the first adult deed of the youngster, such as the first killing of game or the performing of a difficult errand all by one's self. At this time the whole community recognizes the emerging personality and the chief gives the child a pep-talk to continue in this way, for then he or she will become a person of great worth and respect.

There is another "growing-up" feature for girls, the female puberty ceremony. At the climax the celebrated girl is dragged by a group of youths until she faints. When she is revived with cold water, everyone rejoices that "the girl has died and a woman has been born."

Ideals concerning the innermost

Simply stated the Lengua ideal holds that the good person will have a stable innermost and he will exercise great respect for the innermosts of his fellows. He will not talk or act when his own innermost is "wavy" (unsettled). Negatively stated, he will avoid those things in speech and action that will disturb his neighbor's innermost. Positively stated, he will say or do those things that will pacify it or keep it calm.

Poijh and the innermost. This philosophy lies at the base of the use of *poijh* 'nothing' discussed at the beginning of this paper. If one asks a Lengua Indian who has obviously come for something, "What do you want?" he will, indeed, say "*poijh*" at least two times for his own benefit. He is testing his own innermost to see whether it is at peace and whether he will be able to utter his request without losing his inner even keel. But he generally says *poijh* more than twice, often more than four times.

After having checked out the condition at his own innermost he may continue to say *poijh*, first, if he feels that his own innermost is not at rest. He must not express his purpose when excited. Secondly, he may also be checking the condition of the innermost of the person to whom he is speaking. If the third and fourth utterance of *poijh* already elicit impatience in the hearer, he knows that he had better not state the purpose of his coming for fear of agitating his hearer's innermost even more. While certainly the ideal of respect plays an important part, one must not overlook the fact that fear is also a major motivation. Should he disturb his neighbor's innermost during daytime, there is much more possibility that the neighbor's angered soul will come to do him harm when it wanders about at night.

If we again look at the use of *poijh* as a test of one's own innermost, there is an instructive experience reported by one of the Chaco missionaries.

The Yalvo Sanga Mission herds were being decimated by a tiger that was killing both sheep and calves. Something needed to be done. The carcass of a sheep was poisoned with strychnine, and an Indian, who was called "Father-of-Tiger" because he had single-handedly killed seven of them, was delegated to hunt down the marauding beast. Early next morning the hunter shouldered his old muzzle-loader and set out.

Shortly after noon the hunter returned.

His clothes were in shreds, his one arm and leg were caked with blood from some deep gashes that were visible on them, and the butt end of his gun was chewed up. Obviously something serious had happened. The missionary hurried out and asked him, "What happened?" But the Indian only answered with an unemotional "*poijh*" He kept on repeating "*poijh*" so many times that the exasperated missionary finally left him. A full four hours later, when the hunter's innermost found its even keel again, he finally recounted his experience:

> I went to the poisoned sheep and found that the tiger had been there. So I followed his tracks. Not too far away in the bush in a little clearing I found the tiger lying down. Since one never knows if there is a deceased shaman's soul living in the tiger, one must always speak to him before killing. So I said, "Father Tiger, you have become bad, very bad. You kill sheep. You kill calves. If you only killed to eat, we would not be angry, we know that you too get hungry. But you have become bad, you kill many more animals than you eat. You have become a killer. So I must now kill you.
>
> I pointed my gun at him while I was still talking, but it wouldn't go off. Then I noticed the tiger was becoming restless, so I said, "Father Tiger, lie still, my gun is old. It will not go off. But I must kill you." I tried to adjust the gun, but it still would not fire. Then the tiger jumped. I threw myself down and the tiger jumped over me. The tiger turned, jumped, and missed again.

> The third time he knocked the gun out of my hand and tore my clothes and clawed my arm and my leg. Then growling he began to chew the butt of my gun. I then said to him, "Father Tiger, I must get my gun and kill you." I reached out slowly, slowly until finally I was able to grab the barrel of the gun. Then I pulled the gun out of the tiger's mouth, aimed it and fired. This time it went off. I had blinded the tiger. Then I jumped on his back and finished him off with my knife.

The incredulous missionary immediately went to investigate and found the scene just as described — the marks of the tiger's jumping in the sand, the pieces of wood gnawed from the gun butt and the dead beast. The account illustrates dramatically that while his innermost was perturbed and excited, the old hunter did not talk. He was a great hero, who knew how to control his innermost both in and away from danger.

The "wavy" innermost. Regardless of what the circumstances may be, the ideal adult should not lose his even keel. One missionary related a very humbling experience with a Lengua in connection with an Indian's horse that was always grazing on the missionary's pasture and garden. The missionary had spoken to the owner of the offending animal a number of times and had explained that he did not want the horse there. This was his own private property. But every day the offending horse was there again.

After several weeks of this the missionary was exceedingly exasperated and felt that other methods were now legitimate. He got a club and rather unceremoniously beat the animal as he drove it from his property. To be sure the horse did not return next day, but one of his Indian friends came and spoke to him about his deed. "You did not live like a man: you beat a horse that did not know better. You were angry. It is not good for a missionary to be angry." The missionary realized that in Lengua eyes he had acted very unwisely. After serious inner battles he finally went to the owner of the horse and apologized. The Indian's face lit up and he said, "It is good. You are a man."

Our own culture also stresses emotional equilibrium, but certainly not to the degree the Lengua do. We do believe there are legitimate occasions for a person "to blow off steam." This difference is reflected in the following experience of pioneer missionary to the Lengua, W.B. Grubb, who reports that he became very irritated one night when after a difficult day of trekking, many mosquitos and sandflies made life very miserable. As soon as he began to take out his ill-will on the Indians, they wanted to know the reason for his irritation. When he told them that obviously he was annoyed because of the mosquitos and sandflies, they were greatly amused. Some asked him whether he could talk mosquito language. If so, he should really bawl them out and tell them to leave Indians alone also. Then they added that he should remember that shouting at Indians did not bring relief from biting mosquitos.[8]

---

[8] W. Barbrooke Grubb, *An Unknown People in an Unknown Land* (London: Seeley Service and Co., Ltd., 1925), p. 198.

Truth or lies?

Mennonites, too, believe in "righteous wrath" and that this was a constant source of frustration and problem for the Lengua was evident in the universality and the frequency with which Indians made mention of this situation during the anthropological investigation. One of the Lengua bitterly remarked that it was impossible to keep the Mennonite innermost calm. "You tell them the truth and they get angry. So you tell them the opposite—a lie—and they still get angry. What shall you finally say to them?" If we take another look at this use of *poijh* or of silence as a protection for the perturbed innermost of the neighbor, we find some additional and rather interesting ramifications in regard to truth and lies. Consider the experience recounted by one of the colony leaders, who for a time was administrator of the mission ranch. It was during the pioneer years and barbed wire was still very scarce. Only three sides of the mission pasture had a barbed wire fence. The fourth side was closed off by a barrier of brush, but this was now all dried up and for that reason cattle often broke through it. Once out on the open range, the cattle quickly disappeared because of rustlers. During some busy season the administrator had completely forgotten about the cattle. When he finally did remember them, he became quite worried that the cattle might have broken out and if they had, that they would have been stolen. He at once dispatched a Lengua to check. When the scout returned, the administrator hurried to meet him and asked, "Has something happened to the cattle?" The Indian's answer was *"poijh."*

"Have any of the cattle broken out?"

"*poijh.*"

"Was the brush fence damaged anywhere?"

"*poijh.*"

Deeply relieved the manager walked toward his house. About half an hour later an older man came to tell him confidentially that the cattle had broken out and that they had all strayed from the pasture. The administrator contradicted him saying that he had just finished sending an Indian to check and this man had reported that nothing of the kind had happened. Then the old man gently insisted, "But the man you sent to look, now sends me to tell you that the cows are all gone." Angrily the administrator retorted, "But why did he lie to me before?" Then the old man answered, "When he came back you were so excited that he was afraid that you would 'blow a gasket' or something. He was hoping your innermost would be able to take it now. That's why he sent me." [9]

It is not too difficult to believe that in their desire to keep the Mennonites' innermosts from becoming upset the Lengua told lies. In fact, in discussing this during the ethnographic research, the Indians confided that it was very difficult to live with the Mennonites because of their unstable innermosts. "You can tell them a lie to try and keep them calm, but they get angry. So next time you tell them the truth, but they still get angry. They even get angry when you are quiet and don't say anything."

---

[9] A personal communication from Fernheim Colony Mayor H. Duerksen.

The missionaries reported how at one of the early mission baptisms a Lengua girl raised as an orphan in a Mennonite home was being examined for baptism by an assembly of Mennonite ministers. Since she spoke German, and knew the appropriate expressions, all were deeply impressed with the "wonderful work of God's grace" and decided to baptize her without consulting the Indian leaders. Three weeks after the baptism it became apparent that she, though still unmarried, was pregnant. She had been living with several men in a most profligate manner even at the time of her baptism. When the Mennonite ministers scolded the Lengua leaders, who had known the truth, for not telling them, they answered, "How could we say anything like that? Your 'innermosts were spread out widely' as you listened to her testimony and you would have become very unhappy with the truth. And besides, you didn't ask us."

In the current trend of culture change and with the introduction of schools, the demand for respect for the other's innermost is giving rise to some serious problems. As the younger generation begins to develop insecurity and rebellion, the older, the teachers, are in a serious dilemma. The foreign pedagogy they have learned instructs them to discipline with the rod — but what about the respect for the child's innermost?

The length to which Lengua will carry this respect for the innermost of others is quite amazing. The missionary at Loma Plata reported an interesting lesson he had learned from the Indians on his station. Saturday, when all the men were home from work, had been designated as the improvement day for the village. All the residents of the mission village were to share in building fences, drainage ditches, schools, etc. There was, however, one able-bodied character who for many months contrived to be "unavailable" every Saturday. The missionary noticed this with growing concern and finally decided that the time for action had come. He summoned some of the village leaders and shared his concern with them. All agreed completely to the fact that this man was shirking his duty. However, when the missionary proposed economic sanctions, he was faced with silence. Finally after having listened to several expositions of the missionary's plan, one of the braver men spoke up and said, "Yes, that is the way you Lencos do it, but it is not the Lengua way. Maybe that man should work; but if it does not come out of the desires of his own innermost, he will only be unhappy if we make him participate Maybe it is better that we do the work for him and wait. Who knows, one of these days his innermost will think and realize the path of duty. When this happens he will come and be happy to share in the work. Maybe it is better that we wait for him until his innermost knows his duty."

One certainly cannot say that the reasoning of these Lengua leaders was immature. Possibly their way was more in accordance with Mennonite peace principles than that proposed by their spiritual mentor.

Hurting the innermost

Whenever the innermost of a person is not respected, hurt results. Although every phase of Lengua existence is associated with the innermost and therefore it can be hurt at almost any point, informants were able to single out at least four major areas in which hurts were most frequent. These are gossip, embarrassment, disapproval of action and disregard of person. Each of these areas will now be discussed in some detail.

Gossip. Gossip appeared to be by far the most common source of hurt. Interestingly enough Christianity has helped increase both the incidence of gossip and the potential for hurt. The former resulted from the catalogue of specific sins that the missionary work has introduced. These now serve as a ready yardstick to measure short-coming and provide "gossip material" on the behavior of one's fellow. The potential for hurt was increased through the downgrading of spirit fear. Formerly fear was the most powerful emotion. It drove people to stick together closely. This was seen most clearly in their village layout. When a village was subject to excessive fear, people always built their houses in a circle, house against house, and then at night they huddled around the common fire trying to draw courage in togetherness. As the settlers raised doubts about the validity of these spirit fears, and faith in the gospel brought about certain release from former fears, the hurts of the innermost began to climb in the value hierarchy. Paralleling the weakening of fear was the disintegration of clan togetherness. More and more Lengua were beginning to live with their employers. This introduced social distance, personal insecurity, and interpersonal rivalry. So that one must conclude that the culture change has greatly fortified both incidence and degree of hurt to the innermost.

Illustrating this fact is the experience with the first settlement of Lengua Christians. The village was laid out with a central street and a row of houses on either side. The individual lots were 25 meters wide. This distance was actually much greater than in the circular villages the Lengua had used during the Chaco War, and yet the program had to be discontinued because the villagers constantly complained that they could hear all the remarks their neighbors were making about them and this caused too much pain in their innermosts. In fact some of the Lengua settlers became so deeply hurt that they left the village for periods of several months to regain the equilibrium of their innermost somewhere removed from the scene of the problem.

When the question of the village pattern and the issue of private versus communal work were aired, the settlement director of Yalve Sanga reported that the Indians rejected a communal long-house with separate family rooms on the grounds that this would bring them into even closer proximity and therefore increase the potential for hurt. The Indians then chose the same village pattern they had had, only the width of the lots was increased from 25 meters to 100 or 125 meters.

One of the Indian "failures" as settler by the administrator's evaluation, (he has never yet delivered even a single kilo of cash crop) answered the question on whether he was happy as a settler with a confident affirmative. "Yes, I am very happy now. Formerly on the 25 meter lot I could always hear the neighbors say I was lazy. This made much hurt. Now on the 100 meter lot I can never hear them and I am very happy."

Embarrassment. As a source of hurt, embarrassment could of course be closely related with gossip, but it also goes beyond. Take the young man who was observed by a missionary when he left the sleeping quarters of a girl to whom he was not married. He was immediately deeply embarrassed and though no word was spoken the young man immediately left the community for a number of months.

On other occasions parents, embarrassed by some negative behavior on the part of their children, have disappeared from the community. Especially if siblings quarrel or resort to physical aggression, parental embarrassment becomes acute.

In the case of marital infidelity, it was generally the "innocent" partner that was embarrassed and who at once left the community. A missionary illustrates this well in the following account of an experience with his informant and early convert.

At the end of a day of working on translation with the missionary, the informant went home. This day he came home a little earlier than usual and surprised another man having relations with his wife. Right after the informant's departure the missionary decided to take a walk to the Indian camp some 100 meters away from his residence. When he arrived in the Lengua village he noticed his informant was just leaving with a small bundle of his belongings over his shoulder. The missionary hurried and overtook him.

"Are you leaving?"

"Yes, I am leaving."

"Have I hurt you in some way?"

"No, you are not responsible. I am leaving now and I will never return." With this the Indian began walking resolutely down the trail.

The missionary walked after him and pleaded for the reason. Suddenly the Indian stopped and said, "It is of no concern for you. When I came from your house I surprised another man with my wife. This man is a shaman. I am now leaving. I will not return."

The missionary tried to reason with him, but no avail. The man continued walking away. There was nothing left but to follow. Occasionally, the missionary called his name, but the man just kept on walking and repeating, "I cannot come back." Finally the missionary offered, "If you cannot go back to your own home, come and live at my house. I will be your brother." Gradually the Indian slackened his pace. Then he turned and said, "Yes, I will come to your house."

However, the missionary noticed how inwardly torn the man was, so he suggested prayer to God. Together they knelt down. The missionary prayed first in his own language. Then to the missionary's surprise the Lengua who had never prayed before, poured out his heart to God about the hurt of his innermost. He asked for strength to be calm. After a few days of living with the missionary, he appeared one day with his former wife and announced that he was returning her to her people.

After that he himself returned and continued to work with the missionary.

Such embarrassment was often associated with amorous affairs. A girl rejected by the man whose belt she took during an evening dance might immediately leave the community because of the resulting embarrassment

Informants also cited Lengua marriage customs as a source of embarrassment. Generally at the festivals, when a young man and a girl were seen to spend consecutive nights together, relatives would suddenly grab them and set them down together in public proclaiming them husband and wife. Where this was premature, marriages were frequently broken up because of the embarrassment that resulted. Generally the youth would be first to leave the community.

Interestingly enough, even death was viewed as a source of embarrassment. The sudden death of a member in the family showed that it lacked power. This was embarrassing. The bereaved family might avoid the public, occasionally certain members actually left the area, embarrassed by this public revelation of their collective lack of power.

Disapproval of behavior. Ritualized disapproval of behavior could also be linked to embarrassment, but it generally involves the "confession" of wrong behavior (not one's own) at some public gathering. Missionaries have found this aspect of Lengua culture somewhat objectionable. Either during an evening gathering around the fire, or at a scheduled public meeting, a person will begin to confess the shortcomings of his child, marriage partner, or relatives. While this certainly is not ideal, by our standards, it seems to be an accepted pattern of overt confrontation for the Lengua. Because of the mutual respect for the innermost, parents and children, husband and wife, and relatives seldom air their differences in a face to face encounter. If a problem is brought into the open, it is almost always in a public setting. But we need to point out that in such a public airing, the audience serves both as witnesses and as checks against violent manifestations. If "confessions" are made, it is generally done without any overt display of emotion. If one compares this with the violent face to face encounters between husband and wife in the Spanish environment, the Lengua institution has many advantages. However, because it goes against their theological grain the missionaries are generally discouraging it.

One of the missionaries reported how recently a husband had recounted his wife's shortcomings at a church service. As soon as he sat down the wife got up and said that she had been completely unaware of what she was doing to her husband and that she regretted this. In this case the matter was resolved at once.

On another occasion, however, a husband "confessed" his wife's intimacies with another man. There was no immediate repentance, and as a result all three persons eventually left the community. First, the man who had been the initiator in this illicit affair left, because of the public disapproval of his deed. Then the wife was overcome by embarrassment and she left. Finally the innocent husband who had "confessed" this offense also felt guilty over his lack of control over his inner-

most as revealed in the public confession he had made and so he also left.

Similarly when a church group disciplines one of its members, he generally disappears for a period from three to six months. Once he has found himself he returns to make amends to the church. There is a record of a case of wife stealing in which the culprit returned to face the church after a period of six months of absence. The church listened to his statement, but did not find "his innermost genuinely changed." This man immediately left the village for another extended period. His next appearance in the community led to his restoration to fellowship. He was today a very respected member of the believing community.

Retreat from the community is not the only exit, however. Missionary Grubb reports the case of attempted suicide following a reprimand by the missionary.[10] There is also a recent record of a suicide by a young woman who was rejected in an amorous approach.

Possibly the most serious reprimand for a Lengua does not involve sexual lapses (as in the missionary's value hierarchy), but stinginess in regards to food. Since immigrant settlers do not share their edibles as the Lengua culture demands they are classified as stingy. One of the meanest modern insults for a Lengua is: "You are as stingy as a Lenco."

Disregard of person. The fourth major source of hurt could actually include all the others already discussed. It is

---

[10] W. Barbrooke Grubb, *The Church in the Wilds* (London: Seeley Service and Co., Ltd., 1914), p. 154.

here used in a more specific sense of the Indian-white relationship, especially as employees and employers.

The European immigrants were used to differential treatment—to each according to desert. With the Lengua they found that approach did not work. They could not show favoritism or give differential wages. If one Indian who did especially fine work was singled out for special reward he generally refused it. If he did accept under pressure, two types of problems generally developed. First, the employees not so rewarded were hurt and frequently left this employer. Secondly, even the rewarded person might leave if he did not receive the same reward at the end of the following week. To give special reward only occasionally involved reflections on the person's worth. The settlers had to learn that additional reward for better individuals could not be used as an incentive for better production It generally resulted in the loss of all the employees. Today, under growing individualism, this trait is beginning to show signs of change.

Should a wife and mother want to hurt her husband, she could do so by mistreating their children. Husbands will be deeply hurt by wives who do not respect the personalities of their children. Such husbands will generally leave the community. This is one mechanism women can use to drive away unwanted husbands.

Mechanisms for handling hurts. As already indicated repeatedly, the major mechanism in resolving a hurt innermost is personal retreat from the scene. It appears that with culture change such extended withdrawals are becoming increasingly burdensome and possibly also less frequent. Going away at the first appearance of the hurt before the community sanctions became operative, was definitely considered as an ideal type of control of one's innermost.

The public revelation of some one else's shortcoming was not ranked as the most ideal behavior. At least up to a point it showed both lack of control over one's own innermost as revealed in the very act of talking; and it showed a certain disregard of person, for the confession was bound to upset the person who was concerned. Its survival in the face of missionary disapproval is interesting. Possibly to the Indian mind it is more closely related to the ideals of Christian confession than missionaries have realized. It could also be that growing social distance and individualism are increasing interpersonal tensions and thus in the absence of other face-to-face avenues to resolve them, the public confession serves as the most reasonable alternative. Again, absenting oneself from the community is becoming increasingly more difficult with the advance of sedentary agriculture, so there is a real need for an alternative mechanism to settle these differences.

An avenue that appears to be gaining rapidly in popularity today has probably grown out of missionary mediation like that mentioned in the earlier incident of the husband who surprised his wife in infidelity. Increasingly Lengua are taking their hurts to an extra-cultural source—the missionary, the settlement officer, the colony official, or just any white settler, who then functions as a mediator to bring about reconciliation. Settlement officers found themselves spending considerable time dealing with damages done by neighbor's horses, and complaints that "my neighbor does not want me to use the (shared) plow."

The intent of the innermost

Technically speaking, dreams and visions are experiences of the soul, but practically it is often very difficult to separate the innermost from the soul in this respect. The dream of sexual intimacies with a given woman is taken to indicate the intent of the innermost to behave this way. Once a man has been involved sexually with a woman in a dream, the actual physical union is viewed as secondary. That intent is primary over act is well illustrated in an experience related by Grubb.

One day a Lengua arrived from a village about 150 miles away and demanded compensation for some pumpkin that Grubb was said to have stolen from the Indian's garden. At first the missionary thought this was a joke and explained to the man that he had never even been near to the village in question. To Grubb's satisfaction, the Indian agreed that the missionary had never been there in person, but he still in all seriousness demanded payment for the stolen items. The bewildered foreigner then learned that the man had seen the missionary take three pumpkins from his garden in a dream. For these he now wanted compensation. To Grubb's repeated avowal that he had not been there and that he had not taken any pumpkins, the old man answered, "But if you had been there, you would have taken them, because that's what your soul (sic) wanted to do." By Indian reasoning it was obvious that Grubb's innermost intended to appropriate the pumpkins and thus he was liable to be charged for them, even though he had not actually taken them.[11]

Grubb records another interesting experience that illustrates the primacy Lengua place on intent in the account of the attempted murder by Poit. Poit was Grubb's travelling companion. In the course of their associations, Poit had frequently pilfered the missionary's properties and as a result must have accumulated serious guilt. Most recently he was anxious to appropriate a new gun Grubb had acquired. Then one night Poit dreamed that the foreigner was pursuing him with this new gun, because he somehow had become aware of Poit's stealing designs This dream had serious implications for Poit. The dream revealed that Grubb knew his intentions. He himself knew he was guilty. The dream also revealed that the missionary intended to punish him. As a result he arranged to get Grubb alone on the trail. There he fired an arrow into his back, and left, thinking he had killed the missionary. Even though the missionary survived, the tribe still treated Poit as a bonafide murderer. Poit's pleas that the dream indicated Grubb's intentions seems to have been disregarded. Poit was judged guilty in spite of the fact that he had not actually killed Grubb. His tribesmen told him that the fact that Grubb survived was an accident. Poit had intended to kill the missionary and this intent made him guilty. They then drugged him and then clubbed him to death according to Lengua oral law.[12]

---

[11] Grubb, 1925, op. cit., pp. 127-129.

[12] Ibid., pp. 119, 169, 271.

This intent of the innermost is also at the base of most marital infidelity. When a person's "innermost caves in" and becomes attached to a member of the opposite sex, the adultery or infidelity has been committed; the presence or absence of the act is judged as secondary. Often the dream of a sexual encounter becomes the guide to the conduct of the individual. He seeks to fulfill the desire of the innermost as revealed in the dream. The body in a sense is then viewed merely as the vehicle to carry out the intents of the innermost.

The innermost and the future

As in the above example, dreams can also serve as warnings as to the intent of another person. Related to this is the function of premonition of events. This is quite evident in the recent death of a blue baby from the Anglican mission. This blue baby had survived a number of years, but it was becoming evident that without surgery it would not live much longer. The mother permitted it to be taken to Asuncion where an examination indicated a 90% possibility of success and recovery. However, the child died unexpectedly during the operation. When the mission sent a radio message next morning, the mother met the bearer of the news at the door and said: "The child is dead. I knew this before you came, for during the night the soul of the dead child appeared at the window and knocked." Because she had sent the child against the wishes of the other members of the family, the mother was now embarrassed and left the community.

An unfavorable dream prior to childbirth previously always meant that the child would be disposed of at birth.

As already stated, it is the soul that leaves the body and has experiences abroad. At times the innermost also seems to be involved. Consider the story related by Grubb concerning his encounter with a very agitated Indian. On inquiry the Lengua admitted he had just had a bad dream. He dreamed that his soul had left his body and just outside of the house it observed several soul-stealing evil spirits, going toward the body the soul had just vacated. He then observed how they entered and began to drag away his soul (innermost?). Near the forest, however, the soul escaped and returned to the body, so the dreaming soul also quickly returned. His present agitation was the result of this experience.[13]

The innermost and property

The Lengua culture distinguishes two kinds of property: communal and private. To the communal category belong food, products of the garden, game and gathered items. These are shared with all men alike. The insult "stingy" discussed earlier would imply that a person would not share communal items. So strong is the sharing ideal in the area of the communal that Indians frequently find that they have had to use their stored "seed" to feed some unexpected visitor or relative.

Private property, however, is private indeed. It is intimately linked with one's innermost. Because of this people generally give a living person's private property wide berth; and after his death all of it is destroyed or buried

---

[13] Ibid., p. 134.

with the corpse in the grave. Should any survivor as much as dare to touch such property the soul of the dead would immediately attack the offender. Accounts of the dire results for people who tried to violate a dead man's private property abound. Consider the following eye-witness account of a white colonist.

We had not been in the Chaco very long. There were several Lengua families working for us. They lived on our yard. Once an old woman died at our place. She had just purchased a large cast-iron pot. It was brand new. When they buried her all her other property was buried with her. Her dogs were shot and burned. Only this new pot stayed out. Somehow it seemed too new to bury. It lay there for about three years. One day a new Indian family came to work for us. The man liked that pot, but was told its history. After many days of looking at it from a distance, this man finally went and picked it up to look at it closely. Immediately he screamed and ran to the bush, straight into the nearest prickly cactus plant. He rolled himself against the cactus thorns until the blood flowed. Then he ran to the next cactus…and the next. Finally he came running toward the house at full speed, but already in the garden he fell down, screamed very loud and then passed out. The family members rushed up and began wailing. They said, 'He has lost his soul.' They wailed for a long time. When the man finally came to he told us, 'As soon as I lifted the pot, the soul of the dead owner appeared to me and was going to kill me.' He had rolled in the cactus to get the soul of the dead caught on the thorns, but he had not been successful. Finally running toward the house his fear was so great that he had lost his soul, but luckily it had escaped the avenging soul of the dead. 'Now I will never even look at that pot again'[14]

The innermost and exchange. While studying Lengua property values and methods of property exchange, the investigator created the following setting. He shared his need of a horse to visit all the Indian villages, but added that he would like to acquire it like a good Lengua. Since he did not know how, he wanted the informant to teach him how to do it in the Lengua way.

"First," the Indian said, "You must look until you find a horse your innermost wants. Then you go to the owner and talk with him about the horse and frequently look at it. Then the owner will see that your innermost is attaching itself to his horse. If you also say three times that you would like to have that horse, the owner will give it to you."

"Why would he give it?"

"Well, he knows that if your innermost links itself to the horse, then when you dream at night, your innermost will accompany the soul to see the horse. If he were not willing to give it, then your soul-innermost would get angry and wait until his soul left the body in a dream and then it would

---

[14] A personal communication from Missionary Henry Toews.

enter and tear him all up inside and make him sick."

"What about price?"

"One does not talk about price. The owner just gives the horse, but this is 'non-thank' giving. That means once the former owner's innermost has found its equilibrium after the loss of his horse, he will visit you. He will see what good things you have. If you have sheep, he may say, 'Those are nice sheep, I'd like three of them.' Then you would give them to him."

"How long can such a former owner come to get things?"

"As long as the horse lives, he may come and get things from you."

At La Esperanza the workers reported the following curious episode which illustrates innermost-property linkage very effectively.

An Indian wanted a horse, so he began to save money to buy one from a Paraguayan rancher. One day out hunting he killed a tiger and collected 3,200.00 Guarani (Paraguayan currency) bounty from the colony administration. Then he did day work until finally he had 5,000.00 Guarani. He entrusted the money to his son-in-law whom he delegated to buy the horse. After several weeks the son-in-law returned with the newly-purchased horse. Soon thereafter the man came and asked the missionary for work to earn money to buy a horse. The missionary pointed out that he had just bought a horse. No, that horse belonged to the son-in-law.

"But wasn't it your money that the son-in-law had used to buy the horse?"

"Yes, it was, but since the son-in-law bought it and rode it, his innermost has linked itself to the horse and so I still do not have one."

Problems from innermost-property linkage. This innermost linking has led to all sorts of misunderstanding between Indians and settlers. A settler hires a Lengua to chop firewood. Later he notices that the Indian takes home some of this firewood. This annoys the white colonist who feels that he is paying for the work and so the firewood is his. But this doesn't register with the Indian who explains that it was he, and not the colonist, who cut the wood, and so the wood is linked with his innermost and not really with the colonist's.

In a way one can say that this type of property concept and exchange system serves as a damper on "material progress." Asked why he did not buy four bars of soap in a package because there was a savings, the Indian replied, "It does not help for me to buy more soap than I am using now. Visitors come; they see the extra soap. They keep looking at it until their innermost gets linked to it and so one has to give them a cake."

This concept has also spelled problems for the Indian settlement program. It was reasoned that since white colonists had begun in the Chaco sharing plows and draft animals, the Indian who had never known any better should surely be able to share the implements, especially if everything was already being given to him. Thus when the equipment was distributed, each family received one horse and harness. Every two families together received a plow. Their two horses together now made up a team to pull the jointly-owned plow. Thus when the rains came and with this also the time for plowing (Chaco farmers can plow only within 24 to 48 hours after a rain), the settlement administrator felt het Indians would be eagerly plowing. To his great disappointment he found no one plowing. Neither explanation nor scolding could move them. Exasperated the administrator caught the one man's horse and harnessed it. Then he harnessed the neighbor's. He hitched the two of them to the plow and began plowing. Once he had made a start he ordered the Indian to continue. The administrator then went to the next pair of Indian settlers. He was just beginning to plow there, when he noticed that the first man was already unhitching.

" Why ? "

Well, hadn't the settlement officer dropped the plow on the neighbor's yard? Now the neighbor's innermost had linked itself to that plow. He just could not bring himself to plow when his neighbor's unhappy innermost was "dragging along" with the plow. "Why, this will not only ruin this harvest, it may even damage the fertility of the land for days to come." Lengua belief in soul-linked property automatically eliminates shared equipment.

At Loma Polaina it was interesting to note that all Lengua farmers invested their first year's harvest (the land had been plowed with a tractor belonging to the mission) in redeeming the half of a plow and buying a second horse and harness. This was a minimum requirement for success among all the Lengua settlers. Jointly owned property was inconceivable for them.

One missionary reported that a woman died the day after she collected her pay for work in the cotton harvest. She had earned a 30-yard bolt of good quality cotton. She received the cloth on Friday morning and Friday night she suddenly died. Twice the missionary picked the bolt of cloth out of the grave and gave it to the people, but each time they threw it back into the grave. When he picked it up for the third time, a relative took the bolt and threw it at the missionary's feet. Finally the missionary himself threw it into the grave and it was buried. Fear of revenge by the soul of the dead appears to be the motive in the great aversion to touch the private property of others. Of course, the soul of the dead is even feared in itself. To this fact the burning of the village, the shaving of the widow's head, and the painting with charcoal of all close relatives render eloquent testimony.

The innermost and Christianity

As the reader will already have noticed, there are a good number of Lengua beliefs concerning the innermost that show rather striking similarity to some very fundamental Christian ideals. In fact one must almost conclude that the very central thrust of Lengua innermost ideals stands in harmony with the highest New Testament ideals on Christian character and godly living. For this reason these similarities do not only have the value of points of contact for the introduction of Christian teaching, but they actually provide both foundation and support for behavior "worthy of sons of God" taught in the gospels and the epistles. This is not the place for a detailed discussion of similarities, but it may be instructive to conclude with a few of the most obvious parallels.

(1) The Lengua emphasis on intent as primary over deed, finds reecho at many places in the New Testament such as Christ's emphasis on the spirit of the law as being more important than some outward form of obedience.[15]   Related is Jesus' assertion that "evil deeds" are "born" in man's heart even before they become overt.[16]

(2) The Lengua ideals of the mature innermost and its respect for the "self" of others lines up with Jesus' dictum that "to love one's neighbor as oneself" is equal to the greatest of commandments.[17]   It parallels Paul's instructions about avoiding behavior which will harm the faith of a brother.[18]   In its application to self control, especially in one's speech, the Lengua emphasis is reminiscent of the book of James and its teachings on the control of the tongue.[19]

(3) While far from being consistent or universal, one notes Lengua emphases on the avoidance of force, argument and personal advantage that would be worthy of some of the highest ideals in Anabaptist peace principles. The author was even tempted to think that possibly Lengua methods of child training were actually more effective in inculcating respect for the worth of man, and for the peace position than our own Mennonite training.

(4) The Lengua also exhibit some rather interesting "koinonia" concepts and practices. Most obvious here is the unlimited sharing of the necessities of life; but the submission to group discipline is worthy of note. Maybe in this respect missionaries will need to learn from Lengua rather than teach them.

---

[15] Matthew 5-7, 23.

[16] Matthew 15 : 17 - 20, Mark 7 : 17 - 23.

[17] Luke 10 : 27.

[18] I Corinthians 8 - 9.

[19] James 3.

Lengua Festivals
and Functional Substitutes

A LENGUA war party is returning. None of its members were injured. Four Lenguas have taken scalps. The raid has been a success... or has it? The four heroes are sleeping apart from the rest of the war party surrounded by a circle of fire fueled by red quebracho wood (a hard and dense wood from which tannic acid is extracted) which throws off flares of sparks in all directions when it burns. The heroes are sleeping in their "fortress of fire" because they are afraid of the -*jangaoc*, the 'souls of the dead' of the slain enemies. They fear that these 'souls' are even now pursuing them. How will these men ever regain peace of mind and their -*valhoc*, their 'innermost?'[1] The answer is one month away. Then the band will have a festival to purify the heroes and to reinstate them as "clean" members of the group again. Then the four will be free of fear once more.

Why are some people frantically cutting off the hair of a group of men, women, and children? Why is everybody hurriedly grabbing his belongings as if to run away? Why are they putting all their houses to the torch?

Someone has died. The relatives must be disguised by haircutting and by painting with charcoal, and everyone must flee from the place of the death to escape the wrath of the soul of the recently deceased. Will these relatives ever be able to shed their disguise? Will the group ever become free of its fear? Yes, after one or two moons in their new place of residence they will celebrate a 'feast of the dead,' the *yocsac*. Then the relatives will be cleansed and become part of the community again. Then everything will become normal once more.

Here is a Lengua band of nomads who through some freak of fate has lost much of its manpower. There is a whole series of pubescent girls but there are no young men. No one is worried, however, because the festival season is just around the corner, and there these girls will "catch" husbands. This will replenish the band's manpower.

Why is that Lengua woman working so hard stripping cactus fibres and weaving more baskets when she already has more than she can comfortably carry for her nomadic existence? Doesn't she know that the tribe will soon move and that then she will have to carry all these new baskets in addition to existing family chattels? Yes, she is well aware of this. But a large festival has been announced for the next week near Lagoon X, and she is preparing some

[1] For a fuller discussion of the Lengua innermost see: "Lengua Indians and Their Innermost," PA, Vol. 13, No. 6 (Nov.-Dec. 1966), pp. 252-272; or "A Mennonite Encounter with the Innermost of the Lengua Indians," *The Mennonite Quarterly Review*, (January 1965), pp. 40-67.

goods for trading.

The old medicine man of the band near Lagoon Y is dead. He died of a bleeding 'innermost' (generally tuberculosis). Who will now check with the "spirit owners" of the area whether the group will be permitted to camp there? Who will now ward off the evil disease-bearing *quilyicjama,* 'evil spirits'? Who will heal the sick? Obviously this band is in trouble, but not for long. Already the group is preparing for a festival in which they will help one of the men of their band to 'get power from the stars.' This will speed him on to become their medicine-man-protector.

A Lengua band is on the move again. The mother is loaded down with all the family chattels, and besides all these she is carrying a sick baby. It is almost a year old but still is only the size of a six-week-old infant. If the Lengua are so free with infanticide, why does not this mother dispose of the sick child? If you should suggest it, she would react with horror. Impossible! Absolutely impossible! Why, this child has undergone an earlobe-piercing festival; it is now a person. To kill such a child is murder.

Lengua festivals, known by the generic name *caya,* were a very central feature in Lengua culture. The preceding illustrations are a sample of the many different types of situations and needs which could be met only by the celebration of a specific kind of festival. This paper proposes:

1. To describe Lengua festivals in order to show (a) how almost all aspects of Lengua culture became involved in one way or another in the festive cycle; (b) what a central motivation the ideals of the innermost formed in Lengua festive life.[2]

2. To point out the factors that led to an almost complete disruption of this cycle as a basis for (a) calling attention to the current personal, cultural, and ideational conflicts the Lengua are experiencing, and (b) raising the question: Does a mission have any responsibility to provide functional substitutes in the face of the breakdown of this festive cycle?

I

One of the important functions which Lengua festivals served was that of defining social status and role. The Lengua ideal of living with a calm innermost necessitated that all social relationships be rather clearly defined. Thus the Lengua developed a series of festivals to mark the differing statuses and accompanying roles for the various states of a man's life. The descriptions of the individual festivals by the informants did not always provide a clear-cut series. There was some overlap between the functions of the various festivals, but this "confusion" may actually represent regional differences of practice. At least eight specific festivals marking different stages in life can be singled out.

Festivals of early life

Tayjaycoc. This was the festival of the puncturing of the child's earlobe. When a child was eight days of age, the parents and relatives called a special festival. A lot of food was gathered and many people were invited to participate. At least half a day was spent in eating and drinking. If the child was a male,

[2] Ibid.

the men danced one night employing the *chai*—the men's dance. If the initiate was a girl, only the women danced. At the appropriate moment in the festival the mother brought the child. Then one of the shamans present, using a cactus pricker, punctured (literally "shot") the child's earlobes. The performing shaman usually got a string of beads in reward for his services. This ritual signified that the child was now considered a human being and as having a soul. It could no longer be killed with impunity as was the case with a new-born child.

Pomsiclha. The next festival was also celebrated either for a boy or a girl and generally took place between the ages of eight and ten years. It was very frequently celebrated in connection with a pumpkin festival (described below). There was no fermented liquor at this festival. It was a feast of joy at which the parents and the community expressed happiness over the way the child had grown up to this point. Usually it celebrated some significant act of the child. For a boy, for example, this act might involve his having run a first difficult errand alone or having brought home his first piece of game.[3] The girl might have successfully woven her first basket or constructed her first skin garment alone. The individual being celebrated generally sat in the middle of the group, while the celebrants danced around him.

This festival was definitely pre-puberty and thus there was no fear connected with it for the children. For boys the festival sometimes also involved races, especially if several boys were being celebrated at the same time. They would run a race of several kilometers with each other. At an appropriate moment the chief would make a speech to the child (or children) and encourage him to continue in such deeds as had just been accomplished. This festival generally lasted two days and two nights. It marked the fact that the individual was becoming a useful member of the community; for girls it usually signaled the readiness to engage in premarital sex.

Puberty festivals

Natenmaicam.[4] This is the boys' puberty festival called *wainkya* by Grubb[5] and *guainka* by Alarcón and Pittini.[6] Actually *wainkya* is the name for the drums that were used at this festival— the wet deerskin stretched over clay pots containing varying amounts of water in order to produce different sounds. Like the girls' puberty festival, it often lasted a month or more and was gen-

---

[3] When informants were asked what might be a reasonable substitute for a notable deed for a boy today where there is little or no hunting, the informant suggested that it might be the breaking in of a wild horse. One of the missionaries from the Anglican Mission suggested it seemed to him that in the southern area cattle stealing had for a period become the substitute, for at the height of the cattle stealing trouble some twelve years ago, unmarried teen-agers had been the principle offenders.

[4] Several of the informants called the boys' puberty ceremony *yamsiclha*, which was really the ceremony of the dedication of the shaman. Possibly since it was not an obligatory festival, this was the first step of a young man in the direction of becoming a shaman or chief.

[5] W. Barbrooke Grubb, *An Unknown People in an Unknown Land* (London: Seeley, Service and Co., 1925), p. 157.

[6] José de Alarcón y Canedo and Riccardo Pittini, *El Chaco Paraguayo y sus tribus. . .* (Turin: Ajam Canale, 1924) p. 157.

erally celebrated during the algarrobo season (described below). The boy celebrated usually was twelve or thirteen years old and should be sexually mature. Sometimes the festival was delayed until the boy was older than this.

It was not an obligatory festival, but most fathers tried to have their sons go through this experience. The father was responsible to sponsor such a festival. In preparation for it the father, his relatives, and friends accumulated vast quantities of food. The algarrobo (a tree with large edible pods) was the major source of both food and drink. A separate festival was celebrated for each boy. Any young man who aspired to become chief or shaman would of necessity have to go through the *natenmaicam* puberty ceremony. Because of the length of this festival a wide variety of dances and activity took place. Heavy drinking and sex also played important parts in this ceremony.

Alarcón and Pittini point out that there are several ordeals connected with this initiation ceremony.[7] Informants mentioned various ones such as splashing with cold water, scratching two bloody lines from the shoulder to the abdomen, the piercing of the tongue with a sharp heated instrument, and the drinking of a concoction made of fermented poisonous manioc.

This latter beverage was to represent some of the harmful aspects of the universe to which the young man was to be made immune. It was imbibed first by several shaman who then vomited the material back into the container.

[7] Ibid., p. 57.

Their vomit was thought to contain some blood. Of this regurgitated drink the young man was to consume one liter. After drinking it the young man usually fainted away and he was said to have died. The shamans then revived the young man by singing. It was to symbolize the death of the child and the birth of the man. Once the ordeals were past, the dancing was carried on for one more night and the festival was concluded.

Yanmana.[8] The girls' puberty festival was the greatest festival of Lengua culture. Like the boys' ceremony it could last from a month to seven or more weeks, depending on the amount of food that was available. But it definitely outranked the boys' puberty ceremony in importance. It was obli-

[8] The informants listed the following functions of the *yanmana* festival: (1) The continued running until she fainted was to strengthen the endurance of the woman so that she would be able to meet all the physical demands that would be placed upon her as a woman. (2) The men impersonating the evil spirits symbolized the close involvement of the menstruous female with the spirit world. Her survival through the dragging by the spirits symbolized the fact that she had now developed a "resistance" to the spirit world and thus was fit to become a wife and a mother. (3) The ceremony was the parents' way of expressing that the girl was now ready for marriage. It should not be forgotten that this was also a period of intensive instruction for the girl in the art of her marriage responsibilities. (4) Finally, the *yanmana* was a happy community festival. Men celebrated the event that another female had been prepared for marriage and child bearing. A tribe could have continuity. This emphasis on the continuity of the race is interesting in the light of the fact that many more females than males were strangled at birth by the Lengua.

gatory that all girls go through the ceremony. As soon as possible after the girl had experienced her first menses, messengers were sent to all the outlying villages announcing the coming *yanmana* festival. Parents, relatives, and friends helped to provide great quantities of food. Goats, sheep, and cattle were killed in large numbers. But again the algarrobo was the main source of food and drink. For this reason the festival usually took place during the algarrobo season.

Once the festival began the drums would beat incessantly, day and night, although the dancing and drinking was carried on only during the evening and night. During the first part of the festival the girl in whose honor the celebration took place was kept in seclusion. A special hut was built for her on the margin of the village where she stayed with several female attendants. She was not permitted to circulate freely among the people, although she was not actually kept in total isolation.

During this time of restricted movement the girl received instruction from one of the chiefs or shamans who spoke to her about her duties as a woman. From some older females the girl also received instruction concerning housekeeping, the planting of crops, and her marriage obligations.

As at the boys' puberty festival, the whole range of Lengua dances took place in the course of the celebration. However, the most important dance was a special woman's dance called *maning*. In this dance a woman, generally an older woman, with a gourd rattle stood in the middle of a circle of women each of whom held a pole to which deer-

hoofs or ostrich claw rattles had been tied. As they danced, they stamped in rhythmic fashion, not only with their feet but also with the poles with their hoofs or claw rattles. In addition to rattling her gourd and beating time the woman in the middle engaged in grotesque bodily contortions which were to stimulate the dancers in the outer circle.

Occasionally male dancers wearing brass bells which were to indicate the great joy they were experiencing in the festivity, joined the women in their dancing. The men formed a larger circle around the dancing women, rattling gourds and brass rattles, rhythmically stomping their feet. As already alluded to previously this festival was one of greatest sexual liberty, and also the time when most of the weddings took place.

As the food supply was nearing its end, the festival was finally brought to a climax. For the last great event several young men were selected. These retired into the forest where they were painted and dressed up and masked with bags covered with ostrich feathers. The disguise and ornamentation was to give them the appearance of the spider called *sovalac*. This name denotes not only the spider but also a type of malignant spirit whom the young men were to impersonate in the ceremony.

After these young men had been properly disguised in the forest they came back into the camp, mingling with the crowd, crying very shrilly, and frightening the people with their impersonations of evil spirits. Bit by bit they wormed their way into the vicinity of the celebrated girl, chanting "now we will take her, now we will take her."

Then suddenly two of them rushed forward, grabbed the girl by both arms, and dragged her out onto the dancing area in front of the house. All the disguised men in pairs followed the two who were dragging the girl.

As they ran over the dancing area all the women and children ran after the spider spirits with sticks and shouted loudly as if trying to drive them away. When the two young men tired, another pair of masked youths came from behind to take their places, continually dragging the girl by her arms until she became utterly exhausted and finally fainted away.[9] As soon as the girl lost consciousness she was laid under a tree in the shade. The shaman stepped forward and began to call to the young woman. He then threw some cold water into her face until she was revived. As this happened the crowd sighed with relief, for the girl had died and a woman had been resurrected.

Men's festivals

Apyinaycaoc anmin. This festival, as all the others to follow, was a man's festival connected with the person's entrance into the drinking fraternity. It was celebrated when a man was twenty or more years old and symbolized his arrival at full manhood. Generally this experience came to a man who distinguished himself in hunting or war, and he was now received as a drinker among fellow drinkers. About half a day was spent in eating and drinking. During

the night there was chanting but no dancing. All the men sat around troughs hollowed from the bottle tree, drinking until the morning. It was another step for a man in the direction of status and leadership in the society. It was required for both chiefs and shamans.

Canjeapyova or the 'festival of the power of the stars.' The aim of this festival was to select a star as a source of supernatural strength for the individual. The person celebrated was to become like "the people from above." Once a person had thus been invested with the power of the stars he had been fortified to become a partaker of the power of this world. His immunity to negative power was symbolized by the eating of raw poisonous snakes, and the acquisition of positive power was symbolized by the drinking of a concoction to get power from every type of matter. This concoction was an "extract, distilled" from all material things that could be found: broken metal objects, nails, pieces of wood, leaves, rope, leather, cloth, glass, bones, etc. In more recent times money, pages of the Bible or hymnbook, or Catholic medals have also been added.

Drinking of this type of extract seems to have occurred in connection with several festivals, but in its most meaningful form it occurred free from any celebration when an individual fasted in the forest and drank quantities of this extract for five days. If the drinker was able to retain the material without vomiting, he was thought to have absorbed the power of the material world around him. This event could again be celebrated by a festival, but at this festival only the celebrity danced, shook

---

[9] One of the informants suggested that the young women became unconscious through psychological suggestion on the part of the men who were dragging her. They were desirous of ending the *yanmana* festival and did not want to frighten the girl any more.

his gourd rattle and chanted.

Yamsiclha was the festival of the dedication of the shaman. It is sometimes also popularly called the festival of chanting. It could be conducted under at least the following two circumstances. One of these was the initiation of a new shaman. At this festival a known shaman sang to "send away" the soul of a new initiate so that the latter could "go into the sky" to learn power songs. During this festival there would be public singing, but the main emphasis was on songs learned by celebrated individuals during the time of their trance. They were private songs. The incumbent shaman had to be a married man. The ceremony usually lasted one day with singing and drinking. The liquor for this festival generally consisted of gourds of honey wine which had been prepared by the chief or shaman in charge of the activities. There was no dancing at this festival, but very very heavy drinking, for any man who aspired to this type of leadership also had to be a great drinker. Great drinking capacity was always associated with distinguished leadership.

The second condition under which this ceremony could be celebrated involved the practising shaman who was seeking to increase his healing powers. Such a festival was generally organized by the shaman himself and often did not include the involvement of any outside shaman.

Yocsac or the 'festival of the dead,' was designed to help the surviving relatives over their fear and bereavement, and to integrate them into the community circle once more. Since immediate relatives always were the most vulnera-

ble to the soul of the deceased, the bereaved were partially isolated during the period of mourning, and it was for them a time of dread fear. The *yocsac* festival was designed to decontaminate the bereaved and to rid them of their great fear.

During the festival friends and neighbors helped the bereaved relatives to wash off the black paint with which they had disguised themselves from the pursuing soul of the dead. The now cleansed relatives joined the rest of the community to spend the night in eating, drinking, and making merry. Meanwhile everyone spoke words of encouragement, assuring them that the soul of the departed was no longer in the vicinity. It had now left the area for good.

To help them forget their fear, masked boys disguised as dragon flies performed silly antics to cause all the people to laugh. Especially during the advanced stages of drinking, a pipe of tobacco was passed from mouth to mouth to infuse unity and strength to all. At last, under the influence of great quantities of liquor and heavy tobacco smoking, the people finally became drowsy (if not drunk) and fell asleep. When they awoke the sun was high in the sky and the whole community including the bereaved, freed from fear, went about their ordinary way of life which, among other things, permitted the bereaved to again eat from the common pot which had been forbidden during the mourning period.

Ticyowam ajangaoc was the feast preparatory to war. Its purpose was to stimulate the men to perform valiant acts on behalf of their tribe.[10] At this

[10] Grubb, *An Unknown People*, op. cit., pp. 177-179

festival contests of strength and skill played a prominent part, but probably the most important feature, as implied by the name 'the hardening of the innermost for battle,' was to arouse the men to perform dangerous and courageous deeds. As a climax those going to battle placed themselves as targets while men shot arrows close to them and women threw firebrands at them to see "if they still showed fear." At other times the would-be-warriors were pummelled and beaten with sticks or with thorny branches.

Each of the preceding celebrations established the celebrated individual's status and role and also defined in a large measure the responses of the members of the community to such a person. Both aspects were very essential for man to live according to the ideals of the innermost.

Breaking the monotony of existence

Anyone who has become acquainted with the Chaco and has looked at it from the standpoint of living in it as a nomad can well imagine what a long, difficult, monotonous struggle for survival life must be. The festive cycle thus introduced pleasant breaks in this perennial struggle. Every occasion which could be celebrated, especially when coupled with the availability of surplus food, became an excuse for a festival.

In its simplest form the evening young people's dance, *juengquenetin,* served as social mixer for the unmarried. In this dance the youths (and also all married men whose wives were nursing babies) formed a circle around a group of drummers who beat the rhythm for the dance. The dance tempo was slow at first, but gradually as the twilight deepened the rhythm became faster and the antics more pronounced. As soon as the youths began to dance all the unattached young women gathered around to watch. As the dusk deepened and the tempo accelerated, the girls, too, became animated and were gradually drawn into the dance. One by one they advanced to take their place behind the partner of their choice. At first they only danced behind this partner, then gradually becoming bolder they touched his waistband or laid a hand upon his hip or his shoulders. A very popular male might have several young women dancing behind him, each trying to outdo the other with attention. The dance was basically a prelude to sex contact. The invitation to spend the night with the girl was formalized when she snatched away a garment or an ornament from the male. When he later went to retrieve his possession he usually stayed for the night.

When these young people's dances took place during the festive cycle near the algarroba forests, young men from various bands danced together. On these occasions, quality of the performances and endurance became important added features of the dance.

Strengthening togetherness

The requirements of their nomadic existence did not permit the Lengua to live together in large bands. Among the Lengua, as in human settings in general, such separation introduced social distance, mutual suspicion, and intergroup tension. The annual festive cycle thus provided an occasion for the people to get together to break down developing distance and to settle many inter-group rivalries and tensions.

Most weddings took place during the algarrobo harvest, when bands from various areas came together to exploit these strategic resources. Since the festival cycle lasted several months it provided extended contact between young people of the various groups. Naturally many of the amorous liaisons formed between young people developed into permanent marriages. Each intermarriage between groups in turn provided another link in the chain of their togetherness.

Even at the band level local festive activities served as a bond to strengthen their belonging. This function is most obvious at such festivals as the feast of the dead.

A rather similar demonstration of group solidarity can be seen in the so-called "scalping festival." This festival was celebrated when a man returned from war having taken a scalp. The express purpose of the festival was to honor the war hero. However, in actual fact the festival seemed to be much more designed to help this supposed hero overcome his fear of the pursuing soul and to once more integrate the "unclean" individual into the community.

During the festival the scalp of the enemy was carefully combed and painted, mounted on a stick, and carried around like a flag. Meanwhile all the observers made light of their dead enemy. One of the major elements of this festival was the undressing of all the "pretty" women. Every evening as the festival resumed, the hero commanded the women to undress for one hour. The woman who was least embarrassed

was rewarded by the hero with some trinket, usually a string of beads he had received as tribute from his tribesmen. The informant stated that the reason for the undressing was to distract the mind of the hero—he was to forget the soul of the dead enemy. The naked bodies of pretty women were to get his mind on sex.

While Christian informants hesitated to say this, there is strong indication that the woman who was rewarded with the beads also became his bed partner. This is borne out by one of the informants who added that he had heard that men were eager to have the victor sleep with their wives because they thereby hoped to gain some of the power which he had exhibited in slaying the enemy.

It is interesting to note that common effort even accompanied the development of leadership, for the emergence of a leader was not a matter of individual aggrandizement but rather a case of the group working for its common good through an individual. This is quite obvious in the festival of the worship of stars. While the calling of the festival was an overt declaration of the person's intention of becoming a shaman, the group participation stressed the fact that not he as an individual acquired power from the stars, but that the participant group helped him acquire it.

Release from repression and tension

Not only was physical life in the Chaco difficult. Lengua psychic life was equally demanding. The ideals of the good innermost demanded that people repress many of their emotions. This meant that one should not speak when his innermost was excited, or when one's message was bound to upset the receptor's innermost. This often made it very difficult to find a suitable occasion for sharing difficult messages. Here, again, the festival season served as a great tension reliever. As people ate, drank, and celebrated together, there came uninhibited moments during which these bits of unpleasant information could be shared. It was at such times that the "confessions" of obnoxious behavior on the part of other persons was made. In this way many of the divisive and tension-producing situations were aired.

In spite of the high ideals of the calm innermost, the Lengua had a certain competitive spirit. The festive cycle provided the setting in which such competition could be exercised under proper controls. This was especially true at the puberty ceremonies, which lasted many weeks. At these times there were football matches, hockey matches, wrestling, archery contests and bola throwing competitions. Thus much of the inter-group tension and rivalry could be released at the festivals in the course of competitive sports.

Again, every culture that has many taboos and regulations is bound to develop a certain amount of tension against the status quo. Interestingly enough, a festival cycle also provided for release from many taboos. This was particularly evident in a variant form of the woman's *maning* dance in which married men and women alternated in a circle, each putting his hand around the waist of the partner on either side. The group then began to stamp out a rhythm. As the tempo increased, the bodily movements were accentuated, thus providing a great amount of bodily contact between the partners in the circle. It was usually a prelude to new sex contact between married people.

Establishing wider leadership

The festivals celebrating the different statuses in a man's life were usually held by a local band. This limited the individual's status and leadership more or less to that group. However, the extensive festive cycle which brought together many bands with their respective leaders provided an occasion for the development of a "pecking order" among the leaders of the various bands.

II

In addition to the functions of delineating social status and role so far described, Lengua festivals also served an important function in the economic realm. Lengua culture distinguishes two types of property: communal or shared property and private property. To the communal or shared property belongs land and all it produces, be that the product of the hunt or produce from the garden. Communal property is shared freely with relative and stranger alike.

Private property, however, is private indeed. It is viewed as linked with the innermost of a person. No non-owner dared even as much as touch such property without exposing himself to serious danger of harm. For this reason Lengua traditionally did not borrow. They only gave.

Two types of giving

Lengua distinguished between two types of giving, which in turn corresponded with the two types of property. These are currently labelled in western categories as "thank-you-giving" and "non-thank-you-giving." In the case of thank-you-giving, involving shared products, the transaction is finished as soon as the person expresses his gratitude in the culturally acceptable form. Non-thank-you-giving, on the other hand, involves private property. It is not complete after the initial transaction. It can be best illustrated by citing an example.

A Lengua is visiting in another village. His fancy is captured by one of the villager's horses. So he looks at the horse again and again. On several occasions he remarks to the owner, "That is a very nice horse. I would so much like to have a horse like that." If the owner has a good innermost (by Lengua definition) he will at once notice that the innermost of the visitor is linking itself to his horse. He will, therefore, out of the "goodness" of his innermost give this horse to the visitor. But in this case it is a non-thank-you transaction.

To the outside observer possibly it is not so much the goodness of the owner's innermost that causes him to "give" as the fear of what the innermost of the visitor will do to him if he should not give; for once another person's innermost links itself in this way to some piece of property, the non-giving owner exposes himself to mortal danger. At night the "inner part" of man is known to wander. White people call this "dreams." When the innermost strongly desires an object, it is bound to come to "visit" during a dream in order to see the highly desired object again. Being deprived of it because its owner is "stingy," the visiting innermost is bound to become angry. And in its anger it will invade the chest of the "stingy"

owner and there take its revenge. At best the result will mean serious illness; at its worst it could mean death. For this reason the owner generally gives to the visitor when the latter's innermost desires one of his possessions.

After the innermost of the giving individual has found its even keel again following the loss of his possession, he will find an occasion to visit the recipient. Here the former giver will now observe the property of the former taker until something strikes his fancy. Then the giving process will be reversed. The former giver will now make some comments about a sheep or any other item of property, and after several such comments the recipient of the horse will reciprocate and give his visitor the desired possession. How long can the former horse-owner keep on collecting? As long as the original horse lives.

These two property concepts were intimately linked to the Lengua festive cycle. In fact, to the outsider it looks as if the festive cycle was almost a must if the Lengua were to live up to their ideals of the innermost. We shall now look at festivals in their relation to these two types of property.

Festivals and shared property

During the rainy season Chaco nomadic bands could find water and food in many places. True, there was not too much game in any one place, and for this reason the bands had to be small; but usually such small bands could find water, game, and other natural food resources in fair abundance as they moved from place to place. This situation changed radically once the dry season arrived, especially when the dry season became quite extended, as was (and still is) very frequent in the Chaco. In such cases the water in all the smaller lagoons dried up and only the larger lagoons in the lowlands contained this prime necessity for survival.

These lowlands were also the habitat of the extensive algarrobo forests which seem to thrive best on land that is under water at least a part of the year. The algarrobo pod harvest corresponded to the dry season or the season of greatest food shortage. This meant that all the bands were now forced to seek survival by the lagoons and the accompanying algarrobo forests. If individual groups should lay claim to a given lagoon and the surrounding algarrobos, this could easily disturb the innermosts of another group that would thereby be deprived of food and water. In order to keep all innermosts on an even keel, such resources had to be communally exploited. For this reason the dry season, during which the algarrobo pod was the main staple for both food and drink, was also the time when the Lengua festival cycle reached its annual climax. As bands from all over came together at strategic lagoons to share the algarrobo pods, the water, and also the lung fish that became available as the lagoons began to dry up, the Lengua began feasting. Thus the annual festive cycle became the excuse for the group to get together to jointly exploit the only available food resources.

On a smaller scale the same principle was operative also within smaller groups. Should a lagoon in a given area dry up and many lung fish become available, for example, the group closest to the lagoon would calculate the amount of

food available and would accordingly invite neighboring bands to share in the exploitation of the fish resources. Similarly, should a band of hunters be able to surprise a whole herd of wild pigs and be able to kill a large number—more than the group could comfortably consume—Lengua etiquette dictated that the lucky group call a festival instead of smoking the meat or drying it for future use.

However, even planned surplus food could be exploited in this way. If a man had an abundant harvest of pumpkin, watermelon, sweet potatoes, or even had just discovered a grove of palm cabbage, he called a festival. Such planned surplus as garden produce would frequently be the occasion for celebrating a festival of the puncturing of a child's earlobe.

Any abundance of food could thus give rise to a spontaneous festival. Into this category of spontaneous festivals would also fall the seasonal festivals which Grubb[11] describes. If such a festival was held in spring, it represented the anticipation of the new food supply that was to come. In summer it took the form of thanksgiving for the algarrobo harvest. In the autumn it celebrated the ingathering of the main crops, such as pumpkin, maize, watermelon, and sweet potatoes. This latter celebration is also described by Susnik as the festival of the ripening fruits, and is called *yoscama caya*.[12]

One festival of this type deserves to be singled out and described specifically. This is the festival of the gathering of

----

[11] Ibid., p. 178.

[12] Branka Susnik, Mimeographed notes on Chaco Indian tribes, p. 63.

the pumpkin. On this occasion large amounts of firewood were collected and a large fire was built. Much food was prepared, especially great quantities of pumpkin baked by these fires. When the food was ready, all the men gathered around the pumpkins piled in an open space in the center. After the men had performed the *chai* dance for fifteen minutes, the women laid out large quantities of baked pumpkin and the men began to gorge themselves. After half an hour of eating, smoking, and drinking *yerba mate*, the men danced for another short period of time. Then followed more eating, drinking, and smoking. This pumpkin festival was often held by full moon in order to have better light for dancing at night. Although weddings usually took place at the major festivals, they could also be celebrated with a pumpkin festival.

While the pumpkin gave its name to the festival, similar celebration could be connected with any of the fruits harvested—sweet potatoes, watermelons, etc.

Festivals and private property

Equally as basic as the belief that private property was soul-linked was the Lengua concept that all men are equal. This, of course, meant that there should be no great disparities of property among men. While their nomadic existence and their wanderings in many distant places were hardly amenable to much easy accumulation of property, it at the same time prevented any exchange of the property they did have. For this reason the annual festive cycle had an important trading function, not only for the actual exchanges that took place, but also because they initiated the basis

for visits that would have to be made after the festive cycle by givers in non-thank-you transactions who needed to get their return "gift."

In the first place, the congregating of many different bands in the larger algarrobo forests provided an ideal setting for *seeing* the possessions of others. Again, the length of time that the people were together permitted the innermosts of people to become attached to objects belonging to others. Finally, the owners, in the spirit of the festive occasion, readily responded in non-thank-you giving when their property was desired. In fact, before the festive cycle ended many of the transactions had passed on into the second stage where the non-thank-you giver had already received something in return from the recipient. However, most of the transactions were left incomplete at the end of the celebrating. This meant that during the year these individuals would have a legitimate occasion to call on the band of the recipient in order to look over the property and then in turn to receive a gift in exchange for the non-thank-you debt incurred at the festival.

The festive spirit also encouraged the Lengua in one of their special pastimes—gambling. This could take a number of forms. A favorite gambling game was called *jastava*.[13] One person would throw a possession of his on the ground and dare someone to match it. Frequently the first individual threw down a much more expensive item than the one who matched him, but nevertheless the spirit of gambling was so strong that

[13] W. Barbrooke Grubb, *The Church in the Wilds* (London: Seeley, Service and Co., 1914), p. 151.

people continued to play this game in spite of unequal exchanges. Another form of gambling was betting on the outcome of games and other competitions.

The outside observer can, of course, see that all this was just a way of exchanging surplus property. People who had specialties (such as making baskets, bows, good arrows, or spears) had an occasion to dispose of their surplus property either in gambling or in non-thank-you giving. The festival provided the convenient context for such exchanges.[14]

III

The third major function of Lengua festivals was to provide an occasion for communal ritual communication with the supernatural. Since the supernatural was greatly concerned with the proper exploitation of the resources of the world, every act of sharing, especially the sharing of the surplus at the festivals, was a means of obtaining the favor of the supernatural forces. Even the most local festivals dealing with unplanned surplus and the product of their garden plots must be viewed as celebrations in thanksgiving for the food yielded to man by the non-material forces which inhabited and "owned" all areas and their resources.

There was one festival which appears to have had the express aim of receiving communication from the celestial supernatural. The people danced and chanted while they waited for the *ingyapam*, the ancestral father or god, to send a communication. This message to come in the form of a paper with writing that floated down from the sky. As soon as the paper arrived from "above" the people attached it to a pole and planted the pole in the center of the village. All the people then danced around this pole to receive strength and encouragement from this visible demonstration of supernatural concern for men.

Interestingly enough, some of the informants felt that this was a Christian festival; others seemed very hesitant to discuss it. The idea of a Christian origin may not be so wrong. Paper and writing are hardly aboriginal features. This practise may point to the fact that the Lengua also had some contacts with the Jesuit missionaries who dominated early Paraguayan mission history.

Beyond the above communal communication, all the other festive efforts of the Lengua seem to have been directed toward helping individuals establish a proper relationship with the supernatural. These individuals were then to use these supernatural powers for the benefit of the whole.

---

[14] Nomadic cultures such as the Lengua have little or no specialization in storing or merchandising surplus. They tend to avoid surplus wherever possible. First of all, if a person or a group kept more food than it needed, the neighbor's innermost would become angry and envious. Such envious souls or innermosts would surely come at night in dreams and do them harm. Again, the spirit owners of each area carefully watched for any waste of game or produce. Infractions invariably resulted in tragic castigations by the supernatural; so that the best way of preventing harm from coming to a community that was blessed by surplus food was to share it with others in a festival. In other words, a festival not only gave an opportunity for the joint exploitation of food resources and the resulting inter-personal and inter-community good will, but it also purchased the good will of the spirit owner of the area.

Group effort toward individual contact with the supernatural

While the whole series of rites of passage had the general function of making contact with the supernatural, certain festivals reveal a very focused effort in this direction. The first of these was the alternate form of the *pomsiclha*, the "strengthening of the chest and the eyes" of the young person. A strong chest equals good health, strength, and life. It was especially performed on boys so that they could progress on the path toward leadership. Another step in developing supernaturally fortified individuals was the festival connected with the power of the stars which has been described above. This group effort to harness power for individuals reached its peak in the festival of the dedication of the shaman which has also been discussed above.

We should remember, however, that the Lengua did not consider this enduement with power as a personal achievement or something to be exploited for personal benefit. Any abuse of this power, especially its use for personal benefit, incurred the wrath of the supernatural. Abuse of power was dangerous not only to the individual but also to the entire group. For this reason the empowered individual was expected to put his resources to work for the welfare of the community. If he became selfish, it was the community's responsibility to eliminate such a shaman.

Major functions of the shaman

One of the duties of the shaman was the acquiring of spirit consent for the group to camp in a given area and to exploit the food resources extant there. Since each area was viewed as having a spirit owner, such spirit owners had to be consulted and their permission was a prerequisite to any exploitation of the resources. It was the duty of the shaman during the first night that the group camped at a given place to make this spirit contact and to get the permission or receive the denial of privileges.

Furthermore, it was the shaman's responsibility to be alert to any lurking harmful spirits. Such spirits came either of their own accord or they were sent by enemy shamans. When any such spirits threatened the group it was the shaman's task to sing and "disarm" the spirits, for shamanistic power songs always "tamed" and "charmed" fierce evil spirits. Since, however, they did not want to be "charmed" to the point of being identified, the spirits generally fled as soon as they had lost their "ferocity." Under certain circumstances it was necessary also to purify the people and the environment. Thus once the shaman had ascertained that evil spirits were indeed in the environment, he could arrange for the fumigation of the village either through the burning of *palo santo* wood (an oil-bearing wood which gives off a very pungent odor when burned) and letting smoke pass over the entire village, or by having all the individuals wash themselves in a *palo santo* solution. This removed from the individual the susceptibility to the attacking *quilyicjama* and served as a type of immunization.

In case some malignant spirit had already brought illness to a member of the group, it was the shaman's responsibility to help restore the individual to health. In cases of serious illness very frequently shamans from several groups banded together around the sick individual to effect the cure. This participation in curing in other bands is interesting, for it not only served as an augmentation of spirit power, but it was also a public affirmation that their band was not the one guilty of sending the harmful spirits.

Possibly the most dramatic function of the shaman came in the case of an epidemic or in the case of severe drought. These crisis experiences were the great tests of the shaman's power, for at such times the threat rested on the whole group. The shaman was expected to throw all his resources into play to stem the tide of the epidemic or to end the drought by the production of rain.

The rain-making ceremony might take place in an individual band or could take place during the extensive festival season near the algarrobo forests where many bands had gathered. Since the algarrobo harvest corresponded with the dry season, the shamans from a number of bands participated. The shaman (or shamans) and the group of "laymen" danced and chanted until the shaman had partaken of enough liquor to "lighten" his soul. He then "sent" his soul to the "sea of the north" where the "souls of the birds of myth age" were viewed as lying. Present-day birds do not have souls. It was the duty of these bird souls to bring the rains. Each bird had several gourds which it filled with water and put under its wings. Then it flew two days to the south to deposit its rain in the Chaco. Occasionally these birds fell asleep. It was then the duty of the shaman to sing and to awaken them.

Far more serious, however, was the condition when some enemy *quilyicjama* spirits had laid seige on the bird-souls to prevent them from bringing rain. In such cases the lightened shaman soul had to first identify the source of the trouble ; then sing a different song which was to charm the enemy spirit forces so that they would become "tame." Once robbed of their "ferocity" the spirits generally fled because they did not want to be lulled into being identified (and being caught).

Group effort toward individual or family decontamination

Over and beyond the spirit sources from the outside were the conditions of individuals within the group who had to be decontaminated. The most common source of threat to group health was the menstruous woman, for nothing angered water spirits as much as the smell of menstrual blood. For this reason every menstruating woman had to abstain from getting water from the water holes. In fact, she had to observe a whole range of taboos, such as abstaining from meat; for should she eat meat not only would the weapon that killed the animal become useless for future hunting, but the very animal resources might become sterile and unable to reproduce.

The pinnacle of such decontamination activity was the girl's puberty ceremony. The masked men who entered the camp and dragged her demonstrated very vividly that the menstrous woman held a sinister attraction to the alien and harmful spirits. But the group effort saved the woman and drove off the spirit forces. Thus as soon as the girl fainted (died), the spirits left and a new decontaminated woman was resurrected. She was now fit to become a wife and a mother. True, she had to keep certain menstrual taboos even after the puberty ceremony. Nevertheless, in a way one must say that the active participation of the whole tribe in the girl's puberty ceremony was a ritual attempt to reinforce their cleansing by a form of immunization against the susceptibility to the evil spirit world.

In a lesser sense the decontamination motif is also seen in connection with the festival of the scalp and the festival of the dead. In both cases it was the danger from the soul of the dead which was a threat to the living. Once the individual had successfully completed the prescribed mourning period in which the danger was greatest, the group helped to decontaminate and re-establish the infected person as a functioning member of the community. This was ritually dramatized in the washing away of the paint disguise with a warm *palo santo*-flavored solution. As assurance to the individual (or the family) that he was no longer dangerous he was again permitted to eat from the communal pot from which he had been isolated during the mourning period.

IV

Today the cycle of Lengua festivals has been lost almost in its entirety. Only individual motifs, such as earlobe piercing, seem to have persisted universally, and these without their original festive trappings. The girls' puberty ceremony was the longest to persist. An entry in the diary of the central station of the Anglican Mission reads: "The last *Yanmana* festival permitted took place on Sept. 19, 1936. After this the mission no longer permitted its celebration at any of its stations." Hack, the Dutch anthropologist, states that the last *yanmana* in Fernheim colony took place in 1952.[15] However, missionaries reported that some of the smaller groups on ranches have maintained at least aspects of the festival even until today.

The earlier part of the paper has shown the strategic significance of the festivals in the Lengua way of life, and for this reason several questions automatically arise: If this whole series of activities has been lost, what precipitated their loss? What substitutes, if any, have been developed? What are some of the results of the loss or the resulting vacuums? Does the Christian mission have any responsibility in this regard? What can the church offer to fill some of the existing voids?

Precipitation of loss

We can list three major factors as operative in the loss of the Lengua festive cycle: the arrival of the Mennonite colonists, the evangelistic efforts of the Christian missions, and the expansion of ranching and settlement in the Chaco.

Since much of the evangelistic effort was an outgrowth of the concerns that the Mennonites developed once they became better acquainted with the Lengua way of life, the arrival of the Mennonite colonists in the Chaco must be credited as a factor of prime impor-

[15] H. Hack, *Die Kolonization der Mennoniten im Paraguayischen Chaco* (Amsterdam: The Royal Tropical Institute, 1958) p. 266.

tance. The Mennonite arrival in the Chaco came at a very strategic time as far as the Lengua were concerned. No sooner had the Mennonites arrived than the Paraguayan - Bolivian war erupted. Both countries tried to use the Lengua Indians as spies, but also shot them at sight. Seemingly their only place of refuge was in the Mennonite colonies. Once having found refuge, the Indians were quite willing to work for the Mennonites clearing land and performing other agricultural tasks.

At first the farmers found that it was necessary to deal with the leader (chief or shaman) of a group who would then bring out his whole band to work at a given task. As long as the employer had an adequate amount of food, the Indians asked for no more. This procedure had several problems for the settlers. First of all, it was often difficult to feed such a large horde of people ; secondly, the average farmer preferred to have a few people helping him over a longer period of time than many people for several days.

The Mennonites' effort to persuade individual families to work for them led to the introduction of the wage motif—at first items of clothing and trinkets, and finally money. Gradually the employment periods became longer and longer until now most Indians can find work for at least nine months of the year. In fact, many of them work year round with their Mennonite employers.

Having once committed themselves to work for the Mennonites, it was rather difficult for the Indians to take off the amount of time that the festive life required. The employers definitely frowned upon this practice; then, too, the loss of the hunting pattern removed the possibility of spontaneous celebrations following an abundant kill. The Mennonite practice of providing food for the Indian and his family eliminated even the small Lengua agricultural efforts to raise pumpkin, corn, and watermelon, which had also supplied food for smaller festivities.

Furthermore, as the Indians associated more with the colonists the latter learned more about the Indians' concepts of disease, healing, and power. The questions that the settlers raised soon began to undermine the Indians' own faith in these practices. Thus the loss of the old way of life and the questions about many of their beliefs and practices all worked together to undermine the extensive festive cycle. On top of this, the money economy also undermined the value of native arts and crafts, for no longer was it necessary to trade goods with each other. They could now buy store goods with the money they earned.

This still left the dry season when employment was at its lowest and when the algarrobo was at its peak. This coincided with the season for the girls' puberty festivals. The discontinuation of this festival must be attributed largely to the conversion of the Indians and the efforts of the Christian missionaries. Missionaries universally agreed that the participation of the believers in the girls' puberty festival was one of the most frequent causes of backsliding in the early years. The mission had four major objections to the festivals: the universal drunkenness, the extensive sex activities, the gambling, and finally the waste of weeks and weeks of time. But it wasn't until after the first Indian believers settled as agriculturalists in 1942 that the Indians themselves actually made serious attempts to avoid further involvement in the festival.

The third major factor contributing to the breakdown of the festivals was the general development of the Chaco. Recent decades, especially after the Chaco war, have led to wide-scale development of ranching programs. As ranchers built fences to protect their cattle from predators, the Indians found large scale nomadic hunting more and more difficult. Many of the best hunting areas had now become private property. Then, too, many of the ranchers employed Indians. Usually the ranchers were able to employ a whole clan or several clans. This prevented the group breakup that characterized the situation in the Mennonite colonies. And while ranchers generally did not discourage native festivities for moral reasons, many of them found it necessary to curb the festivities for economic reasons. All too often their ranch hands were disloyal to their work because of a festival.

So gradually the ranches forbade the holding of extensive festivals except once or twice a year. As a kind of appeasement the ranchers provided commercial liquor for these periods of permitted celebration. Both the artificial curtailing of the festivals and the introduction of commercial liquor have greatly adulterated the function of the festivals, and on ranches they have degenerated into drunken brawls.

Substitutes for the Festivals

As culture changes it would, of course, be understandable that the festive cycle would change. It is not surprising that changing conditions would necessitate changes in ritual activity, but usually the changed activity would also be more rewarding for the new circumstances. This can hardly be said of the Lengua festive cycle.

As already explained, the ranche limited the Indian celebrations to such times as fitted into the ranchers' program, and at those times the rancher also provided the commercial liquor. This practice robbed the festive cycle of most of its useful functions and introduced instead several rather negative ones.

The most extensive series of substitutes are found within the missionary program. The aboriginal dancing and music have been replaced by the singing of the Christian church. But this singing is generally unaccompanied by bodily movement and without instrumental accompaniment. A recent addition to the singing has been the introduction of western harmony. This means that every Lengua congregation will have at least one choir. These choirs, of course, have been patterned after the models observed in the Mennonite churches.

Church services have in a large measure replaced the festival celebrations. While these get-togethers have fulfilled some of the need of togetherness and have even, at least in part, made possible the confession of problems and sin between members of a community, they have on the whole left much to be desired in terms of the type of involvement that the group had in the former festive cycle. Since Mennonites do practice several special services a year in which the members of the congregation share a meal together, this aspect has also been introduced into Lengua church life. It has functioned as a minimal replacement for some of the fellowship in food of the earlier festive life.

The annual Christian harvest thanksgiving festival practised by the colonists has also been accepted by the Indians. It can be viewed as a replacement of some of the seasonal festivals that the Indians celebrated in order to insure the growth of their food crops.

Of the extensive cycle of rites of passage the only seeming replacements are baptism, marriage, and funeral services in the church. The ritual within their Christian practice, however, except for baptism, is expressed almost entirely in verbal symbols. This has been a weak substitute for an activity oriented people.

Gambling has been largely discontinued. It seemingly has survived only in one furtive form—gambling at the Sunday afternoon soccer games which the mission has permitted.

Possibly the area of health is the one that has undergone the most extensive secularization. It is no longer necessary to have specialists with supernatural power to ward off disease or to cure it when it strikes; this is now done by the dispensary and the local store, which serve as sources of medical help.

Pressures resulting from the loss of festivals

One of the most visible pressures arising from the breakdown of the festive cycle has been the greatly weakened feeling of group and intergroup unity. Even though the settlement program has organized twenty or more families into village units, they have not yet become mutually supporting communities, but are rather a series of juxtaposed families separated from each other by surprisingly extensive walls of social distance. Settlement authorities have tried to foster community action, but they have not been able to compensate for the greatly weakened capacity for developing consensus and organizing group effort.

The distance between families is nurtured by the absence of spontaneous invitations to share surplus which their earlier hunting and gathering life made so easy. Settlement authorities have had great influence in cutting down spontaneous sharing of planned surplus by pushing the Indian to "save for the rainy day."

This growing distance between people has been most harmful in the area of the innermost. Each manifestation of social distance resulted in a hurt innermost on the part of the goal, and guilt on the part of the source. So far, repression has seemed to be the only "Christian" answer to deal with these innermost hurts now that the loss of the festival has robbed them of the opportunity to experience release from their pent-up feelings. In fact, some missionaries expressed concern about the occasions at which Lengua began to bare the hurts of their innermost in church services. The missionaries viewed this as confessing the sins of other people—and they felt that Christians should confess only their own sins. Actually, since church meetings are quite preaching-centered, there is little opportunity to develop the emotional atmosphere in which individuals would feel comfortable in sharing their repressed feelings.

The medical workers among the Lengua have expressed concern about the Lengua capacity to simulate illness. The missionary nurse was probably right in saying that the patient had no real physical symptoms, but she was wrong in saying he was not sick—the Lengua was suffering from a sick innermost.

Self-definition is another major area of problem. Formerly self was defined in terms of the group. In fact, the group worked to help the individual past the various crisis stages of his life. The discontinuation of the festival cycle not only left the individual to fend for himself, but it failed to provide him and his fellows with a clear definition of their respective statuses and roles. In his attempt to find a niche for himself the person often seriously hurt his fellows, who in turn hurt him by their own search for identity and status. Several burning questions were uncovered during the research. How does a person know what his status really is? How must one act toward his neighbor? How should one expect his neighbor to act toward him? Obviously Lengua are finding it very difficult to live with a calm innermost when everyone is at sea with regard to everyone else.

Serious problems have also arisen with regard to the former metaphysical function of festivals. Under missionary influence illness and medicine have been largely secularized and "de-spiritized." Missionary medicine has been singularly effective in many cases, but it has been just as singularly impotent in what seems to be the most strategic area—epidemics. During the time the author was in the Chaco a whooping cough epidemic broke out in one area and claimed the lives of twenty or more Lengua infants. As the "cough" became serious Lengua parents hurried their children to the hospital, only to be told that there was no medicine and that the doctor was unable to help them. This shook even the most stalwart of the believers. What kind of an illness was it? How come there was no medicine for it? The author was bombarbed with questions. Did he think it was just a bad, ordinary sickness or could this be a *quilyicjama*-produced epidemic?

A very similar reaction accompanied the extended drought. When rains failed to come month after month, some Lengua Christians "backslid" and went into the forest to drink and chant in order to send a shaman's soul to the sea of the north to release or awaken the rain-birds. Others asked the author what he thought they should do. Should they continue to pray? Or would it be wise to join the group at the rain-making ceremony?

In the area of the metaphysical there are also remnants of fear of the soul of the dead. True, the Christians conduct a funeral service immediately following the death, but somehow this has not eliminated fear in the bereaved. During the months of Chaco research, several cases of reversion to pagan practice—attempts to frighten away the souls of the dead—were reported. Obviously the bereaved have been left alone to fend for themselves against the pursuing souls.

What could the mission do?

Speaking specifically of the Lengua, the author feels that there are a number of concrete possibilities for the mission to fill the void created by the loss of the festivals.

In the area of epidemics and the accompanying intense fear, the mission could initiate a universal immunization program. This would eliminate most epidemics and also the accompanying fear.

Regarding the repressing of problems in the innermost, the church could work toward special "sharing" meetings at which the pent-up feelings of the innermost could be bared and even the "sins" of others brought into the open. If missionaries and Lengua church leaders faced this need squarely and developed such confession sessions, it would give the church a very important soul-healing function. At the same time much personal guilt would be uncovered and many people provided with a context in which to receive forgiveness.

In the area of self-definition and individual status and role, I believe both church and school could provide recognition and community context for experiences that were formerly celebrated as rites of passage. Thus the church could dedicate the new-born infant. The school and Sunday school could provide recognition for individual achievement. Instruction for baptism, church membership, and marriage could deal with the puberty crisis. For adults, greater recognition could be given to pastors, choir directors, and teachers at special dedication services. At convenient periods the length of service could again be recognized to further define the person's advancing status. This would not only clarify the status of many people but it would also define the appropriate reactions of the general public toward these people It would mean emotional security and more peaceful innermosts for most of the people concerned.

With regard to the bereaved and their fear, the church might assign certain persons to stand by the bereaved family in a special way, especially during the first month after the decease. This period could be ended by special recognition of the bereaved in a church service in which the family would offer prayers of thanks for the knowledge that their loved one was with God. Such a public expression would then serve as a ritual marker for the end of mourning.

Application to non-Lengua

As the title indicates, this paper is limited exclusively to the Lengua situation. However, the author has written it because he feels that there are many peoples who have undergone similar losses in their festive life with the advent of civilization and missions. For many of these people serious and harmful voids have remained. It is hoped that this paper will make missionaries more aware of the kinds of problems that can develop through changes in this area of culture, and that this will indirectly help deprived tribal peoples to find satisfactory answers to their needs.

Jacob A. Loewen, Albert Buckwalter, and James Kratz

Shamanism, Illness, and Power in Toba Church Life

IN December 1963 author Loewen spent a week with co-authors Buckwalter and Kratz, Mennonite missionaries to the Toba Indians of the Argentine Chaco. The three men visited two indigenous churches, where they shared in three services with the Toba believers. On arriving at the Miraflores church for a weekend visit, they learned that the pastor had suddenly and unexpectedly withdrawn from the church two weeks earlier. Not only had he resigned his pastoral responsibilities, he seemed to have completely severed his relationship with the church. Cautious inquiries as to the reasons for the pastor's drastic action were met with blank faces and shrugged shoulders — one did not know why the man was behaving thus. Finally one brave soul ventured, "Wouldn't he automatically disqualify from the leadership of the church if

Jacob A. Loewen is Translations Consultant for the American Bible Society in South America. 315 S. Wilson, Hillsboro, Kansas. Albert Buckwalter has worked among the Toba Indians of northern Argentina since 1951. He is author of "A Toba Anthology," PA, Vol. 4, No. 2 (Mar.-Apr. 1957), pp. 92-95. James Kratz is a missionary with the Mennonite Church under the Board of Missions and Charities (Elkhart, Indiana). He has served as a colleague of Albert Buckwalter for four years.

he were *empty?*" Later someone else stated emphatically that a pastor who was sick had no choice but to resign, for how did he intend to keep the flock well if he did not have enough power to keep himself well?

It was obvious at once that the phenomena in question were not inherent in the Christian faith, but were elements of the traditional Toba culture still operative in the church. Convinced that information on Toba power concepts could provide clues for interpreting the fuller meaning of the questions and statements that had been made in connection with the pastor's withdrawal, the resident missionaries and the visiting anthropologist invested a number of sessions with a Toba minister and informant, Francisco Rodriguez. The data presented in this paper are a part of the valuable information gleaned during these sessions.

As more and more details of Toba thought and practice came to light, and especially as the relationships between and the organizational patterning of the individual items of cultural detail became apparent, the investigators felt that they were discovering a new validation for the work of the missionary in a truly indigenous church.

Each time it became apparent that another model of pre-Christian Toba social and religious life was currently operative in the Toba church, there arose more questions about our current indigenous church philosophy, which seems to hold that the church that works out its own patterns and practices quite apart from the missionary and the practices of the church from which he comes must truly be a Spirit-led church. By a "truly indigenous church" do we mean that it will be limited more or less exclusively to the models of its past experience? From where do we expect an indigenous church to actually draw its models? How will such a church develop new models to express the new life in the Christian faith? Will too great dependence on indigenous models that are alien or even hostile to the spirit of the Christian faith not weaken the church or even undermine it? Will a truly indigenous church not be the first to need some missionary ambassador as a sounding board to help test its current models and to serve as a source of alternatives in those areas where new models need to be considered?

There are a number of factors that make the Toba situation an ideal setting in which to investigate some of these issues. As shown in the writings of William D. Reyburn,[1] Eugene A. Nida,[2] and Albert Buckwalter,[3] Christianity among the Toba developed quite spontaneously with a minimum of outside missionary influence. To be sure, they received their initial impetus to accept Christianity through contact with Pentecostal witness, but Pentecostal ministers and churches have consistently refused a more than casual involvement with what they considered a highly paganized expression of the Christian faith. Again the Mennonite missionaries, whose early mission work was rejected by the Toba community because their rigid pietistic practices were too foreign to Toba needs and experience, have made some interesting adaptations in their missionary approach. They have accepted the Toba expression of Christianity as equally valid with their own and are trying to serve as loyal friends to the Toba church, which today has a completely independent organizational structure called the Iglesia Evangélica Unida (United Evangelical Church).

The approach of this study will be to present, first, a summarized description of Toba shamanistic activity and power concepts as they were known among the Toba in their pre-Christian state. Next, there will follow some observations on the Toba church in action. Finally there are listed in digest form some of the reflections of former Toba models in the current practices of the church. (Some of these last should be considered as only suggestions of possibility.) On

---

[1] William D. Reyburn, The Toba Indians of the Argentine Chaco: An Interpretive Report (Elkhart, Indiana: Mennonite Board of Missions and Charities, 1954).

[2] Eugene A. Nida, "Report on Toba Program" (an unpublished report, March 1960).

[3] Albert Buckwalter, "Victory Toba Day," PA, Vol. 2, No. 3 (May-June 1954), pp. 136-137; "Anthropology and Mission Work," PA, Vol. 3, No. 3 (May-June 1955), p. 102; and "A Toba Analogy," PA, Vol. 4, No. 2 (Mar.-Apr. 1956), pp. 92-95.

the basis of the data presented, the study will conclude with the assertion that the truly indigenous church, especially, needs missionary help to develop patterns and practices that will further the life of the church, and will help it to grow toward Christian maturity.[4]

I

Shamanism and Illness in Toba Culture

Toba shamans were of three classes. The first was the *pi'oxonaq* or the doctor who had learned to heal. Next, the *natannaxanaq* was the healer who is called *curandero* in Spanish. He is a person who has been endued with healing power. Both of the names may be used for the medical doctor of civilization, but the latter is the most frequent. Most potent, however, was the *napinshaxaic,* who had the power of spirits. This kind of shaman could harm or heal. He had the ability to "see" the cause of illness. He was also able to send his soul in search of a lost soul, for he was able to communicate freely with the supernatural. Usually the shaman was also the chief, because his prowess as shaman led him to become a political power as well.

To become a shaman a man needed a sponsor, either human or supernatural. Most frequently the power

was passed from father to son. A shaman-chief father put a "thing" into his son during his own lifetime. This thing became a source of power in the son, especially after the father's death. A person could also go to a shaman of repute and ask to be empowered by him. If the latter so desired, he would then for payment give the apprentice one of his spirits — the spirit of serpent, tiger, or some other spirit being. Such a spirit deposit functioned as leaven which started the apprentice on his way to develop his own power. Interestingly enough, the giving shaman was not viewed as having been weakened through the power transfer, but was considered to have as much power as before.

A related way to become a shaman grew out of childhood illness. A child that was very sickly was taken to the shaman who would examine it and then pronounce its present soul as incurable. He would then proceed to put a "power object" into the child. This object was to "recharge" the soul, if not entirely replace it. Should such a charged child suffer a relapse, the shaman would check the inserted object for condition and position. Generally it had "fallen over" and needed only to be set upright again. Normally such an object was removed before puberty. If it remained till after the person was eighteen years of age, it automatically led him into becoming a shaman. Some very powerful shamans resulted from living on a power object since their childhood.

A further dimension of the shaman's power to "put in" was reported in connection with female infertility.

---

[4] This statement must not be taken in isolation, but must be considered in the light of the specific functions proposed for the missionary in the conclusion. The missionary who would effectively discharge such a ministry to an indigenous church will need a high degree of sensitivity both to the Holy Spirit and to the needs of the culture which he would serve.

If a woman did not conceive, she could go to the shaman and have him see the cause of her trouble in a vision. Once he located the problem he would let her choose between a male and female object, which he then proceeded to plant in her womb where it grew into a male or female child according to the mother's selection. Another version says that the shaman sees the *nqui'i* 'soul' enter the woman, whereupon he pronounces her successful. He can inform her whether the fetus is male or female.

Possibly the contradictory reaction to injections that nurses report among the Toba stems from this putting in model. Those fearing a harmful object will oppose an injection to the utmost, while those believing it to be good want nothing but injections whenever they need medical help. They are eager to have power put into them.

Equally important is the converse of the preceding, the matter of taking out harmful objects. Thus one of the Indians defending hospitalization for operations affirmed that medical doctors could remove stones and other objects from the abdomen, because he remembered how his grandfather, a shaman, had removed stones, pieces of wild animal bones, fish bones, and other calcified objects from the stomachs of people. Where an object is suspected to be the cause of illness, the removal through surgery is quite acceptable.

Sponsorship for shamans could also come through a number of spirit beings. With these beings the person himself could not take the initiative, for they revealed themselves only to such as they liked or chose.

The first of these spirit beings was the *no'ouet,* the owner of an area. All areas were visualized as being owned by one of these spirit beings. Generally they were male in sex and belonged to one of three varieties: those of the grassland, those of the forest, and those of the waterholes or lagoons. If one met a spirit owner of the area and the latter stopped to talk with him, such an individual was in luck and would receive power to cure. Since women too could meet them, there were also women shamans among the Toba.

However, such an owner could also cause sickness and he could even kill. This was especially so if the shaman-chief had not consulted with him at night on behalf of the clan to solicit his permission to take honey, game, etc., from the owner's domain. If he was not willing to give, the group had to move on at once or someone in the camp would die. Especially if the meat of game was wasted or animals were maltreated, this owner became very angry. A shaman spoke to the owner only at night when the latter was abroad in his domain, but for power he appeared to people by day.

A second class of spirit being that could bring power was *huashi,* a female figure, small in stature. She appeared in both young or old forms. The *huashi* could be met only at daytime in the forest. They have not been known to perform any evil to mankind.

Thirdly, there was *qasoxonaxa,* another female figure, who could also appear in the form of a giant elephant, a bear, or a mountain.[5] This spirit is the source of very great power. When angered she takes the form of lightning and strikes the ground. She can be called to strike by a shaman whom she has empowered, but she also strikes on her own. Quarrels among the people, and especially critical remarks about the weather, are the two major causes of her wrath. Alfredo Métraux reports that she also punishes women's quarrels by fog, rain, and thunder.[6] The *qasoxonaxa* was especially partial to women, and some of the most famous women healers owed their power to her. Women endowed with her power were also able to pass power on to other women. One of the most renowned female shamans met her in the form of a giant bear and gained her favor by building a fire by whose smoke *qasoxonaxa* was able to rise into her upper realms again. Unique to women shamans was the power over *choit* (a kind of owl), a bird that could be sent to get food leftovers for performing sorcery. Shamans who gained their power from *qasoxonaxa* were able to wield lightning as a weapon against their adversaries.

The informant reported that this spirit was also a source of power for warriors. His grandfather was one of the famous warrior chiefs who

had been given immunity to weapons and lightning by *qasoxonaxa*. He could stand in one place under fire — even white man's gunfire — but would not be hit. He became a famous chief who could fearlessly lead his people into battle and bring them victory over their enemies. But such warrior chiefs have been rare. Most chiefs reached their position through shamanistic power.

The Toba tell the tale of a man who lost all his property through gambling and as a result was promptly thrown out by his wife. All he now had was a fishhook and line. He went to the lagoon, threw his line in three times, and called, "If you want to talk to me, come!" A giant cayman appeared and offered to take him to the underwater world. Holding to the back of the cayman, he arrived at the underwater city where the spirit owner of the place received him. The spirit owner allowed him to make a petition for power. He asked to become an invincible warrior, and his request was granted. When he returned, no arrow or bullet was able to do him harm.

Maintaining and Increasing Shamanistic Power

Once a man had been launched as a shaman by one source or other, his whole life seems to have been a constant struggle to increase his own power and decrease the power of other shamans around him. The way to increase one's power was to overcome some other shaman and appropriate his power. The battleground was always some innocent tribesman whom one shaman was trying to kill and

---

[5] It is interesting to note that the elephant, which is not a native animal and which is known to the Tobas only through pictures, is being interpreted as a representation of this spirit being. It seems as if any large object, even a mountain, can be interpreted as being *qasoxonaxa*.

[6] Alfredo Métraux, *Myths of the Toba and Pilaga Indians of the Gran Chaco* (Philadelphia: American Folklore Society, 1946), p. 51.

the other was trying to cure. The winner gained the power of the loser, and the loser correspondingly was weakened. The battle for power could take place with each of the manners of inflicting hurt upon people that were within the scope of a shaman's power. We will discuss this power more fully later. In one such battle between two medicine men, the informant reported that two whole villages were annihilated by smallpox which each of the competing shamans sent to hurt the other's village.

Nor was the battle always merely shaman against shaman. The informant recalled a recent death of a healer when four shamans joined resources to empty and destroy the fifth.

If we now look at their powers to hurt, we find that the most common attack was to send (literally 'to shoot') objects into the victim. The object might be a frog, a serpent, or a piece of wood, glass, or metal. Such objects penetrated the victim's body, generally the chest, and always resulted in illness. The protecting shaman had several counter weapons at his disposal. He could fill a gourd with various objects that had spirit power and place the gourd near the patient so that it was located between him and the sending source. The sent objects would then strike against the gourd with sharp clicks. Each click assured the patient that another harmful object had been stopped. If, however, objects had already penetrated the victim's body, the shaman could remove the foreign objects. The removal technique included spitting, rubbing, and sucking, especially on the chest, in which the *lauel*, the heart or the seat of the soul, was located.[7]

When a shaman was able to extract the foreign element, the patient got well. But the sending shaman had thereby been robbed of that amount of power because his *lauel* was viewed as intimately connected with the objects he sent. Thus the one shaman had gained a piece of the other's soul and had correspondingly increased his own power. In order to demonstrate this addition to his powers, the shaman would take into his hand the object he had removed by sucking, spit on it, and press it into his chest near the arm pit, whereupon his interior absorbed the power object. It is interesting to note that what functioned as a harmful, malignant element in the layman meant power and prestige for the overcoming shaman.

Another interesting feature was reported by Elmer Miller, who pointed out that once this power object has been sent it will accomplish its original good or evil purpose irrespective of the source's possible change of mind.

A mother in Miraflores accidentally killed her own son. She was intending to kill the boy's uncle, but inadvertently bewitched a watermelon seed spit out by her son instead of one spit out by the uncle. Even though the mother realized the error and deeply regretted the mistake when her son became ill, she could not undo the harm. Shortly before the son died he pointed out his mother as the one who had killed him. Apparently no

---

[7] Literally translated, *lauel* is 'his living interior.' Like the Lengua Indians of the Paraguayan Chaco, the Toba have many idioms associated with the *lauel*, which functions as the seat of emotions.

retaliation was taken since it was considered an accident.[8]

The informant was able to point out some of the important features of such object removal. In the case of snakebite, the shaman began by removing the food of the snake (frogs, lizards, or small birds); then he removed the poison, next the fangs, and finally the whole snake. The informant observed that it was important to kill the offending snake, but that this must be done in such a way that the body of the snake remained intact. If the snake was torn, it was almost impossible for the shaman to remove it completely. For the outsider this involves a paradox for the snake may be "in" the person it bit and at the same time escape through the underbrush.

Soul Stealing

A second type of harm could come from soul stealing. A medicine man sent his own soul to the victim at night. Here the shaman's soul waited until the victim's soul left the body in a dream. The shaman's interior would then grab the victim's interior and carry it off captive. The aim was to take the soul to a far away place and lock it up. Once a soul was locked up, death was almost inevitable for the victim; but if the soul loss was discovered before it could be locked up, another shaman could pursue the soul thief, fight him, and recover the stolen interior. Soul stealing and locking up is now attributed even to God, who is said to send his angels to catch the interior of sinners. God then locks

up the captured interiors and the sinners die as a result.

The soul stealer usually rode on the spirit of a winged dog, but some shamans used the spirit of a horse or a tiger as a means of rapid transportation. The pursuer also mounted whatever spirit vehicle he could command; and once he overtook the soul thief, the battle was on. During the struggle the stolen soul stood by while the souls of the two shamans struggled with each other. If the former won, the soul was carried away and locked up and the patient died. If the latter won, the soul was returned to its owner and he became well.

There is an interesting related issue with small children. If a child got seriously ill, it was taken to a seeing shaman, who during the night seance ascertained whether the soul of the sick child was absent. One of the common reasons for soul loss in children was excessive beating by fathers. Such a child's soul became extremely sad and finally left of its own accord. If the shaman could locate the soul and induce it to return, there was comfort and life.

When a Toba shaman needed to consult his familiar spirit cohorts, he crawled under a blanket, shook his power rattle, and muttered or chanted an appropriate incantation. After a while he would tremble and jerk under the blanket. Sometimes he would start with a violent jerk, almost as if given a powerful electric shock. This was unmistakable evidence that the spirit had come to him. Then the soul of the shaman and the spirit consultant began a dialogue. The latter answered in a very shrill and often unintelligible

---

[8] Elmer Miller, missionary to the Toba for four years, in a letter dated March 1, 1964.

voice. When the shaman emerged, he interpreted the spirit message to those concerned.

A further service of familiar spirits was that of guardian angel. The informant told of how his shaman grandfather had sent his spirits to accompany him when he went on a lonely or difficult errand. The informant, now a Christian, commented, "And do you know, I really felt those spirits walking along beside me."

A third form of harm was the entrance of a shaman's own soul into the body of a victim. The presence of this soul in a person caused immediate serious illness and its departure produced sudden improvement. This type of possession was used to explain the periodic illnesses and improvements that some patients exhibit. A seeing shaman had power to diagnose the presence of such an intruding shaman's soul. Often the victim himself, when close to death, would point out the aggressor whose soul was causing his death. Once a patient admitted that he was possessed by a shaman's soul, every effort would be made to kill the intruding soul and thereby also its shaman owner. There were five methods known to the informant to accomplish this end.

The first three were types of poisoning. Relatives might persuade a nonrelative — for relatives have too much sympathy — to administer poison to a dying person. This would kill not only the sick person but also the intruding soul and the shaman, the owner of the soul.

A second method involved the administration of a potion made of poisonous snakes or certain poisonous frogs. The effect was that of the previously described poison.

The next manner was also listed as poisoning but it included a secondary effect of sympathetic magic. Bottle tree bark was boiled and the poisonous potion was administered to the possessed person. The offending shaman's body would then bloat up like the bottle tree until it burst and the shaman died.

A fourth method was to plunge a new knife that had been heated until it was red hot into the dying person's chest. If there was a gurgling sound (possibly due to the collapse of the lung), one knew that the soul of the possessing shaman had been mortally struck and that his death was now inevitable.

Yet another method of nullifying a sorcerer's power was to tie up the legs and arms of the possessed person with a certain vine until the body was completely immobilized. Since the shaman's spirit was within the victim, the power of the shaman was neutralized, and in this immobilized state he was now vulnerable to sorcery and death.

The informant, however, felt that such destruction of offenders was not becoming to a Christian and went on to tell how a believer recently passed away after being possessed by the soul of a sorcerer. On his death bed he said he knew the aggressor's identity but as a Christian he did not want to have the man killed, and so he died without revealing his name.

This matter of the sorcerer's soul has still another dimension. If the bite by a sent snake was serious, such a bite became virulent and usually fatal if the sorcerer's soul was possessing the snake at the time of the bite. The informant interpreted the previously mentioned battle between two shamans in the case of the smallpox epidemic that was fatal to two whole villages as having taken such malignant form due to the presence of the souls of the respective shamans in the smallpox agents.

However, sorcery could also be performed on objects which had been in contact with the body. This involved nail clippings and hair but more often the remnants of food such as peels, pits, and bones. Persons fearing sorcery would avoid eating this type of food in an unfriendly environment; but such abstinence not only revealed their fear, it also made them suspect as agents of revenge sorcery.

Illness Through Non-Shaman Sources

But not all illness or loss of power was due to the invasion of forces sent by shamans. The Tobas recognized two more types of illness: sickness and loss of power due to the violation of menstrual taboos and sickness that comes of its own accord or at least is not caused by any known agent. The menstruous female was greatly feared. In fact one must say that the menstruous woman not only lacks positive power, she is actually charged with a negative power which neutralizes all positive power it contacts until the victim is debilitated to the point of illness. Since some menstruous females will be found in almost every situation, they were objects of constant and intense fear. For this

reason etiquette demanded that every menstruous woman identify her condition as soon as she approached another person, especially a man. She indicated her dangerous condition by responding to all greetings with "I am hungering," that is, "I am on a menstrual diet."

Illness and harm due to violation of menstrual taboos could affect both the woman herself and also the persons that came into contact with her. For example if a man touched her or even came too close to her, he immediately lost his hunting power and possibly his physical strength as well. If the woman touched a hunting weapon or ate some meat accidentally or secretly, the weapon that had felled the game immediately lost its power. In fact, the informant felt that such contact might even affect adversely the fertility of the animal family from which the meat came. To restore the gun to power the woman had to confess and both she and the gun had to be cleansed through a ceremony. If the woman kept the thing secret, the remedy lay in catching a live poisonous snake and passing it through the barrel of the gun. This restored power to the gun and caused the offending female to die of a violent hemorrhage soon afterward.

Again, if a female approached a water hole during her bleeding time, the water dragon would be offended by the odor of blood and would cause the earth to quake.

Should a person lose his power to find honey through a menstruous female, he could recover it by taking the remains of an extra large bees' nest found by someone else, set it on fire and purify himself with the smoke. To be efficacious the smoke had to envelope his whole body.

Finally, there was illness that comes of its own accord. This includes what we might call "illness from natural causes," usually by invasion of the body by spirits who came unsent by any shaman, entirely of their own accord. The spirits most feared in this respect were the souls of the dead which were viewed as resident in the graves. If someone stepped on a grave, even accidentally, the souls of the dead became angry. Their anger could be recognized by noise in the cemetery. If angered during the day, the spirits came at night to take possession of the offending person and the person became insane. A shaman could often get such spirits to leave by talking kindly to them and by asking their permission to have them leave. If they left, the person again became sane. If a person suspected that the spirits of the dead had been angered, he could protect himself by building a fire of *palo santo* wood and having its smoke pass over his body, his house, and the whole village. Similar protection could come to a person drinking a tea of boiled *palo santo* either alone or mixed with *yerba mate*.

Since the souls of the dead were the most frequent offenders in "voluntary" invasion of the body, much care was exercised to keep them at peace. If a corpse of one recently deceased was heavy, the soul had been offended and the pallbearers put it down at once. All who suspected that they might have offended the deceased knelt and asked forgiveness. Once such a dead soul was appeased, the corpse

became very light. Likewise, approaching the cemetery for a new burial, an older person leading the way would speak gently to the souls in the graves and address them as "grandfathers." He would announce the arrival of another "grandchild." Should a person have to be buried away from his relatives, he would be reburied near his family once the "bones were dry." This reburial was imperative, for souls of the dead are at peace only among their own. Both for the opening of the grave and at the reburial, soothing talk would be carried on continually.

But soft talk was not enough. Once a person had died, all his belongings had to be buried in a swamp so that their use by the living would not arouse the anger of the dead. In addition, the family might leave the immediate area for a number of months. These factors closely match the behavior of the Lengua and Chulupi Indians of the Paraguayan Chaco who cut their hair to deceive the souls of the dead. However, for the Toba, hair cutting was not a disguise to mislead the soul of the dead; it was a genuine sign of mourning.

Nor was the cemetery the only place where the souls of the dead were feared. In a recent prayer service in memory of a murdered Toba the victim's name was never mentioned. Those present explained to the missionary that the old people believed that the soul would be angered if its name were mentioned. They did this in spite of the fact that the victim in question was buried at least fifty miles away.

A further protection against the

dangerous soul of the dead was the disposal of the house where the dead individual had lived. Formerly, like other Chaco Indians, the Toba burned their houses. In fact, very frequently whole villages were destroyed after the death of a single individual. Today, however, the houses are merely dismantled when the bereaved relatives return to their homes after a period of absence. The house is rebuilt a few meters away from the former site. Occasionally, merely the doors and windows are changed and moved to different places in the same house. This prevents the soul of the dead from recognizing his former place of residence. At other times the house is just abandoned and wind and rain destroy it.

Among the negative spirits feared by the Toba there was also *sataxanaqyi*. His function was that of the devil, or better, of the god of this world. This was a dual role. In the first place, it put him over against the god of the supernatural as the master of the natural or material. In the second place, he was also owner and commander-in-chief of the spirit world, especially the spirits associated with the material world. For this reason, before going on a trip beyond the authority of the spirit owner in whose domain the individual was currently residing, the Toba always sought to calm this god of the material world. To do this a shaman spoke to him somewhat like one spoke to souls of the dead when they were to be quieted.

Because the whole area of illness and death were, for the Toba, connected either with loss of power or with being overpowered by some shaman or some spirit being, no sick shaman could remain chief and leader. His illness was the sign that he had lost his power to protect himself and therefore also his capacity to protect and to heal others.

Even highly acculturated Toba are not yet ready to replace the object entry explanation for the germs of medical science. They will rather refer to them as complementary explanations. This probably means that disease has both a physical aspect and a spiritual aspect, much like the belief of animists of Africa.[9] The scientific explanation would be received as acceptable for the physical aspects of disease but not for the spiritual aspects. This also explains the belief that the medical doctor and his medicine are acceptable when you intend to deal with the physical aspects of disease, but many types of disease also require a spiritual ritual if the illness is to be dealt with completely.

There is also an interesting relationship between age and power. Children are viewed as being without power and subject to fear, while older people are considered as more powerful and less fearful. For this reason it is an older person who administers poison to kill a dying person containing a shaman's soul. It is also an older person who leads the way to the cemetery and converses with the soul of the dead at the time of the burial. In fact, young people generally do not even participate in a burial ceremony.

---

9 J. W. C. Dougall, "African Separatist Churches," *The International Review of Missions,* Vol. 45, No. 7 (July 1956), p. 261.

The Shaman's Reward

Toba shamans received their power most often as a gift from a spirit owner and therefore they were to use their power for the well-being of their people. No shaman was to put a price on his service. On the other hand, people of respect would be grateful for the shared power and would of their own volition make gifts to the healer. Besides a copious supply of food and drink that was provided when the shaman or college of shamans was active at a healing, the relatives or the patients gave their first donation when some improvement in the condition of the patient was registered. This payment was generally in the form of sheep or goats. When a patient was fully recovered, an even more substantial gift was made.

However, it is not difficult to understand that this ideal was not maintained in practice. Shamans did demand and receive payment. Especially since spirit power led to political power and chieftainship, they often extracted tribute, over and above payment for service rendered. The informant stated with a certain degree of sadness that regardless of when and what a shaman demands, everyone gives. If one refuses, he exposes himself to sorcery and death. In his own words, "Everyone gives because he is afraid." For the informant the decline of the Toba during the past decades was the direct result of the breakdown of shaman morality. The spirit owners who gave power had become upset by the selfishness of shamans and for that reason had been limiting their power. This resulted in more people becoming ill and fewer people being cured.

The result was a double accusation for shamans. For one thing, they were misusing their free gift of power for personal advantage. They were extracting reward where they had no reward coming. In the second place, when the reward was not adequate by the shaman's estimation, even though it was all that the sick individual could give, the shaman neglected to apply his full strength. Reaction against the shaman developed and the people demanded that he perform his duty and use the full extent of his power to heal each sick person. If a shaman failed to bring healing or if he could not retrieve a stolen soul, he had to provide a very good alibi lest he be suspected of negligence. To fail without a valid reason was to confess lack of concern and that was considered synonymous with intent to murder. A shaman suspected of murder was secretly judged by his clansmen and then killed by some three to five individuals appointed by the rest as executioners. This led to a further compromise in the manifestation of Toba power resources. For more often than not, the spirit owner who had endowed the shaman that was thus killed was even unhappier with the disposal of his protegé than with the selfishness of the latter.

II

Dancing, Singing and Visions in the Toba Quest for Power

The Toba informant used in this research was quite insistent that dancing was not a native element of local Toba culture. He would not even allow that it had been practiced by the ancients. Only when dance was linked with the northern sub-groups of the Toba, especially with the Pilaga, who lived near the Pilcomayo River, did he accept that dancing had played a prominent part in their culture. There could be two reasons for this reticence. He might have been very strongly influenced by Christian morality and for that reason did not want it to be true. Or it could be that the Toba near Sáenz Peña were already so acculturated by the time the informant reached puberty that he never actually experienced the dancing milieu.[10]

The first kind of dance mentioned by the informant was indulged in mainly by women. He called it the dance of unexpected joy. When a woman saw a long lost relative or heard some very good news, she would break out into a spontaneous dance of joy during which she jumped and chanted. This kind of dance could also take place when the husband returned from an extra successful hunt or when the warrior returned from some expedition with an enemy scalp.

Another kind of dance was also mainly a woman's dance. The women would gather in a circle, stamping

their feet in rhythm. Each woman held in her hand a long pole with ostrich claw rattles tied to the top. With this pole she would also stamp the ground. Very frequently an older woman would be stationed in the center of the circle as a sort of chorus director. She would set a rhythm by stamping her feet and her stick rattle. This was copied by the others. She would also chant loudly, much louder than the other women in the circle. Unlike the rest of the women she would perform contortions with her body which were to stimulate the tempo of the rest of the dancers. If men joined in this dance, they generally formed a ring or circle around the women and stamped their feet in silence. The informant could not give any special occasion or reason for this type of dance. In the neighboring cultures, this type of female dancing with rattles was associated especially with female puberty festivals and with the festival of scalping. Basically, it was a festival of joy.

Métraux mentions that dancing was one of the principal recreations of the young people among the Toba.[11] Young people of both sexes participated. The circle was made by alternating men and women in a continuous chain, with each person putting his arm around the person on either side. Together they would dance in rhythmic motions. In the center there was generally a drum which beat the pace. At first the tempo of the dance was slow but gradually the drum began to beat faster and the tempo increased. As the body motions in the dance became more accentuated,

---

[10] In direct contradiction to the informant's statement on the absence of dancing in the Sáenz Peña area, Miller writes that preachers had confessed to him that in their pre-Christian days they had often danced during the evenings in order to be chosen as sex partners for the night by the young women. According to these confessions even married folks took part in this type of dancing. In a number of cases this had become the occasion for wife changing.

[11] Métraux, op. cit., p. 15.

body contact increased. The informant classed this dance as having definite sexual basis.

If we look at this dance among some of the neighbors of the Toba, like the Choroti or the Chulupi, we can find a little more pertinent detail. The dance could take several forms. A favorite Chulupi form began with a circle of young men who danced in an open area near the village at sundown. As the dusk settled, girls would gather around to watch. With the deepening dusk and the increase of the tempo of the dancing, gradually the girls became excited and would draw nearer. Before long some of the more daring girls had selected a male favorite and were dancing behind him. As the excitement increased, the girl or woman would grab hold of the young man's belt or waist. Popular fellows often had several girls or women holding their belts. The bravest of these girls would suddenly snatch the dancer's shirt or some object of clothing. This was the signal that he had been selected as a sex partner and was to retrieve the object during the night. It was and still is the popular nightly recreation and sexual mixer of the Chulupi.[12]

In another Chulupi variant the women joined the male dancers but instead of dancing behind the partners of their choice, they would gradually enter into the ring of dancers, women interspersing between the men. The partners would be embraced from either side just as described for the northern Toba. Married people took part in both of these forms of dancing

only at special festival occasions when many of the moral barriers were relaxed and even then generally only when they were at a village other than their own. Once married folks participated, they would be selected as sex partners just as any single person.

For the Lengua of the Paraguayan Chaco, the female puberty festival was an occasion at which married men and women danced and made new sexual contacts. Bodily contact of some type or other was usually a prelude to sexual contact. A favorite Lengua expression for being touched sensually by a woman is "she tasted me."

Finally, there was the dance of the shaman with his gourd rattle which contained power objects. This dance was almost always associated with magical power. It either was to strengthen or to encourage the shaman's familiar spirit forces. At other times it might be to frighten away some of the attacking spirit forces by a noisy display of power objects in the gourd rattles, or again dancing with the gourd rattle was a vehicle by which a shaman's soul got into the proper state to perform investigations of a certain illness or to look for a lost or stolen soul. This type of dancing was also indulged in by the novice who wanted to acquire power.

Especially at the dances of mixed sexes, drums provided the rhythmic beat that the dancers followed. While there often was singing or chanting during these dances, songs were more often associated with the dance of the shaman or the person who had just received power as the result of a vision. Chanting with drums generally

---

[12] Nordenskiöld, *Indianerleben, El Gran Chaco* (Leipzig: Albert Bonnier Verlag, 1912).

revolved around nonsense syllables. Songs learned during a vision were full of power. Shamans used them to charm or exorcise the evil spirit forces. Songs could also serve as a protection against invading evil spirits. Thus a person awaking from a bad dream would break out into a monotonous rhythmic chant or, if he had a song, into his power song. Such chanting was generally accompanied with the shaking of gourd rattles.

If a person was not able to acquire a song through a vision, he could purchase a song from a shaman or an individual who had several. For a price the owner would transfer the song and its power to the interested individual. This song could function just like a song received supernaturally. Métraux emphasizes that the rattle was an important means to add power to a song. He mentions two other occasions for the use of the rattle with chanting: one when a young man wanted to charm a girl and gain her favor; the other when a hunter wanted to gain power and luck for hunting.[13] Among the Lengua the rattle was also used to "herd" game into the area in which the hunter was intending to hunt the next day.

III

The Toba Church in Action

Reyburn characterizes the Christianization of the Toba as follows:

While it is not an ideal movement to many, the overwhelming fact remains that it is a "movement" and has proclaimed the gospel in a prodigious fashion. The international Pentecostal movement is dominated by no ec-clesiastical authority laying its plans in a systematic step by step procedure. It is characterized by a strong emphasis on gospel preaching and the visible manifestations of the Holy Spirit. These manifestations are not everywhere the same, a common point of dissension among these churches. It is largely unconcerned with the relationship of Christianity to culture. It places strong emphasis on healing the sick by prayer and anointing with oil. It likewise uses what musical mediums are available as an integral part of the worship services. Such is the Toba. It did not come by Pentethe form of Christianity that came to tecostal missionaries going and living with the Tobas and learning their language. Rather the Tobas went to live in the cities along the Parana River. They heard the gospel preached and experienced the Pentecostal *cultus*. Those who heard began to preach it among their own people. The result: Pentecostalism soon sounded a new key for the lives of several thousand Toba Indians.[14]

After the movement had led to the establishment of churches — which must be registered to have official recognition by the Argentine government — the Toba groups sought affiliation with denominations having registration. Attempts were made with some of the Pentecostal groups from whom the initial impetus had come, but these found it difficult to accept this "pagan" Christianity and withdrew from association with it. As the Indians described it, "They became offended and went away." At the time when the group movement to Christianity swept the Toba tribe, the Mennonite (Old) Church was

---

13 Métraux, op. cit., p. 17.

14 Reyburn, op. cit., p. 45.

developing a missions program in the area. Their concern about this nativistic manifestation led to a study of the situation by William D. Reyburn.[15] On the strength of the findings of this study, the Mennonites decided to discontinue their standard missionary program and instead have their missionaries serve as friends and advisers to the indigenous Toba churches. To prevent forcing the Toba churches into a Mennonite mold, the missionaries helped them to acquire their own registration with the Argentine government under the name of Iglesia Evangélica Unida. At the time of registration some twenty-four churches joined the organization as charter members. Today it has grown to more than forty churches.

To comply with government requirements, one of the Toba church leaders had to sign as the executive officer of the organization. In actual fact, however, the leaders of all the churches form a council of equals. They have an annual convention which is controlled completely by the Tobas, although Mennonite missionaries attend the sessions. While the latter do not carry actual responsibility, their presence does add cohesion to the program. As Reyburn indicates, there are considerable regional differences in the "manifestations of the Spirit," and these differences have produced serious tensions and some divisions.[16] Missionary presence and meditation have often served to bridge the gaps both between individuals and between churches. While the Mennonite missionaries are not the only ones that

visit the Toba, they are probably the ones who are doing so in the most continuous and systematic manner.

A Toba Church Service

First, this description must be taken as typical of only the area near Miraflores where these observations were made. There are other areas where dancing is a rare phenomenon. Second, not all of the events described in this service were witnessed in one service, but as a whole this account offers a fairly typical picture of the range of activities that do take place in a Toba worship service in the area described.

Sunday morning at daybreak while the visitors were still under their mosquito nets, the first people were already arriving at the church. About the time of sunrise several of the song leaders (one of the three kinds of officers operative in the Toba church) drifted into the church and began singing. About ten people were standing on the stage behind a table singing. There were a few people in the benches below.

One young couple sitting near the left front facing the stage was singing loudly. Shortly thereafter, the young man got up and began to stamp his feet rhythmically. He punctuated the stamping with rhythmic, raucous exhaling. About fifteen minutes later the young woman also arose and stood there shivering slightly waiting for "power to take hold." When nothing happened, she raised her hands several times, sighing deeply. She shook herself some more and finally sat down with her eyes closed.

Meanwhile, more people were arriving and the only benches in the build-

15 Ibid.
16 Ibid.

ing, on the left side facing the stage, were filling with women and children. In the open area on the right a few men stood leaning against the wall. Most of the men mounted the stage and shook hands with all who were there before taking a place. Occasionally the song leaders alternated with each other in introducing songs. The anthropologist, a few guests, and the dignitaries of the church sat on chairs on the stage or in the right hand corner near it. Gradually this area filled and some men stood in the rear of the chapel. Most of the men and women entered the church wearing a small cloth bag in which they carried a black Bible. Some appeared to have only a Testament, for their bags were quite small.

Suddenly the singing was punctuated by the loud cries of an older woman. She got up, came into the open area, and tied the Bible in a vertical position firmly to her right side by means of two strings attached to the bag. Then she began to chant and dance. A while later a second older woman joined her. Sometimes side by side, sometimes facing each other, they danced. During the next song a man suddenly let out a yodel-like whoop on the stage as he and another man began dancing. Each had his arms draped over the other man's shoulders. Their heads were bowed as they rhythmically stamped their feet and exhaled loudly. Occasionally the song leaders stopped to discuss what song to sing next, but the dancing continued without interruption.

As the dancing progressed, the tempo and the bodily movements increased continually. As the dancers moved beside or in front of sitting people, they would often point a finger at one of these and make a hissing sound. At other times the dancers touched the chest or the temples of a person sitting. Some did not react, others began to whine. One woman began to tremble. Then she got up and began to dance also. The informant identified this touching as an attempt to pass a "leaven of power" on to another person. Once the person danced, he did so on his own personal power, but he could be started on the power of someone else.

With the next song, entitled "Holy Spirit, Power Divine" (which marks prayer as the next item on the program), a larger number of people began dancing, often emitting loud cries. When prayer was called, all began to pray at the top of their voices. Several of the individuals were shouting the name of Jesus loudly and repeatedly. Others knelt down and beat their foreheads on the ground as they prayed. All through the prayer period the dancing continued unabated. Some dancers were exhaling loudly in rhythm and others were chanting loudly.

After the prayer session the preaching began. The first of the three visitors was called upon to speak. In the rear of the church a circle of men and women mixed indiscriminately had been formed. Each was holding the other person by the waist and all were moving in rhythm. The speaker could only be understood by those who were very close to him, for the general noise was very great. His talk was followed by a song. Gradually some of the dancers began falling out until when the anthropologist got up as the third speaker only two men were still dancing, and they had stepped off the stage and moved to the back of the church. Early in the course of the anthropologist's talk these men also stopped dancing. After each of the speakers had finished, those on the stage and near the platform came forward to shake the speaker's hand. Each talk was followed by another song.

Confession of Sin

After the three visitors had spoken, several local men were called on for a word. One of them called forward another man with whom he had enmity and they confessed their sin and settled their differences in front of all. This was a joyous moment in the church service, and several of the women broke out into chanting and dancing again. With the next song several men joined the women in dancing. Like the preceding dancers, they were all careful to tie the bag with the Bible firmly against their right side. Toward the end of the service the pastor who had unceremoniously quit two weeks earlier got up to apologize for his action and to suggest the selection of a younger man as his successor. He proposed that the criteria for the choice of this person should be the ability to speak in public and the ability to read the Bible fluently, for he felt that many were preaching without being able to study the Bible. During this part of the service a man and a woman were dancing together, holding hands. The woman was local, but the man was a

visitor from a village some twenty-five kilometers away. Since the visiting anthropologist had no further part in the program and the people were moving around rather freely, he too moved from place to place in order to observe the dancing, speaking in tongues, and other activities that were going on during the service.

The missionaries, who had often attended such services, added that occasionally a dancer or one speaking in tongues would faint away. This did not happen during the services observed. A person is permitted to remain unconscious for a while in order to experience the "vision" but soon the people begin to work on him to make him come to again. Some will dance holding their hands over the person; others will rub his chest, touch his temples, exhale loudly at the person, or even try to lift him.

The informant interpreted this as having a double meaning. First, it is not good for the soul to stay away too long from the body; and second, everyone is anxious to share in the joy of a new manifestation of power as the one who has experienced the vision begins to dance again. Frequently, the dancer will also sing a new song "learned" during his vision experience. As soon as a woman falls to the ground in a tongues or vision experience and begins to roll, some other female quickly rises and ties her skirt into a knot between her legs to prevent indecent exposure. At times when dancers were in danger of falling over a bench or bumping into a post, others guided them past the danger or protected them from hurt.

Conspicuously, only older people

were engaged actively in dancing in the service. In fact, teenagers often laughed and hurried from the sanctuary when one of the dancers acted strangely. Just outside the door a whole group of teenagers was laughing at the dancing and the antics of those speaking in tongues. Missionary Miller, who read a preliminary draft of this paper, states that this is not entirely typical and that there have been services at which teenagers were among the most active dancers. He reports that one evening service that began at 8:30 p.m. could not be closed until 2:30 a.m. because of two dancing teenage girls. The leaders felt that they should not stop the meeting as long as there was "joy."[17]

Toward the conclusion of the service, another song marked the beginning of the healing service. This song, "The Great Physician," began another period of prayer for health and healing. Though no sick individuals were brought forward for healing, people were praying for the healing of the sick and for their own health. The missionaries added that when the sick are brought forward, they are quickly surrounded by the older people who then touch them, rub their chests, and pray for them. If there is any major moving of power during the healing period, the dancing increases volubly. Often the benches are removed for the terminal part of the service, and those dancing may continue for some time even after the service has been officially closed. This happened at the Sunday morning service under description. When the anthropologist stepped out of the

auditorium it was after 11:00 a.m. The service had lasted more than four and a half hours.

A number of interpretive comments were made by the informant on aspects of Toba church life. The majority of these comments were made during the discussion of the Toba church services and the retreat of the pastor at Miraflores.

Illness and Health

Physical healing is obviously a very central concern for the Toba. The informant felt that many Toba Christians date their conversion as following an experience of healing. The preoccupation to stay healthy is equally strong. Since illness is always viewed as an absence of power, those having power are responsible to keep themselves and their fellows well. But not only the personal power of select healers is of concern, the collective power of all adults in the group is important. For this reason, even the relatives of a person who dies may suffer shame. Their home or their family stands indicted as not having had sufficient power to protect the one who died.

It follows then that a pastor who is physically ill is automatically disqualified from the task of keeping the flock, for how can he preserve others when he does not have the power to keep himself well? This was also the basis of the retreat of the pastor of the Miraflores church that was described in the introduction. The fact that he was "empty" became evident through his kidney ailment; and as an ailing man, he could not serve as

---

[17] Miller, op. cit.

shepherd of the flock. But how had he become empty? The informant suggested that he had either sinned and lost his power or else he had been emptied by someone. The retreating pastor's attitude toward one of the men in the church indicated that he considered the latter to be the cause of his loss of power.

In reviewing this pastor's history, the informant pointed out that some five years prior, when the pastor first went to Miraflores to help in the church, he immediately became ill. He came back at once saying that witchcraft was still deeply entrenched in the community. He stayed away for some months until he had recovered, and then went there again, this time with his whole family. Shortly after their arrival, the wife got ill; and so the family retreated from the community for a whole year before going back once more. He was then chosen as the pastor of the church and had served in this capacity until his current loss of power caused him to retreat from the church completely.[18]

Both the missionaries and the Toba minister-informant pointed out that it is common practice for ministers to refer to their own and their family's health as evidence of their right relationship to the Spirit of God and of their participation in divine power. Again the informant underscored the fact that church members usually refer to illness and death as temptation or shame. Families experiencing the

death of one of their members will often stay away from church meetings for several months. They return only after they have overcome their shame.

Even going to the hospital is frowned upon. It is permissible to take a child to the hospital, for children have no faith — they are too young to believe — but adults should never go there, for they ought to have faith and power. Going to the hospital is nothing less than a confession of emptiness and powerlessness. Another reason for shunning the hospital is the isolation. No longer does the family and the church gather around for prayer. Even where this would be physically possible, the fear of being contaminated by the lack of faith and the "backsliding" of the patient keeps others from going to him. They seem to regard the "faithless" person, like a menstruous female, as taboo and dangerous. Furthermore, relatives of the sick person oppose his going to the hospital because this also reflects on them. Their environment is indicated as not having enough power to bring healing to the infirm. Possibly because this indictment is hard for relatives to accept, there is much hesitation on the part of kin even to come and to bury the member of their family who has died in the hospital.

Other believers have tried to rationalize and to regard the hospital as employing the power of God. Informant Francisco reported, however, that recently an Indian tuberculosis patient had hurriedly left the hospital when an Indian in one of the other wards died. His reason: "There is no power to heal left in this hospital

---

18 He has now been installed as pastor again. The retreat seems to be part of a continuing struggle for power between the chief and the preacher.

any more." On another occasion a chief entered the hospital with an acute abdominal infection. Several days after his arrival, someone died; and he immediately left the hospital and went home. Here he had some medicine and prayers performed. His abdominal abscess opened, drained, and finally healed. Since his healing, his wife has been a persistent dancer in all the church services.

Even drugstore medicines are not free from the taint of unbelief. Where they must be used, they are generally taken in connection with a faith formula. The person holds the pill in his hand and then says, "In the name of the Lord" before swallowing it.

Since so many believers are still illiterate, the Bible has remained merely a power object for them. This makes syncretism very easy. Thus, where the cause of illness is unknown, even believers have been known to burn pages of the Scriptures to create smoke to disinfect a patient and to serve as an antidote against disease.

The discussion of Christian healing brought out the following details. The people who feel that they are filled with spirit power surround the sick one in an effort to focus their power on him. They rub the patient's chest to demonstrate visually the entrance of power. Each participant tries to transfer power from himself to the patient who is without power. As the group sings and power becomes more manifest, dancing frequently breaks out. Former shamans are usually among those persons most likely to begin dancing, both in the church services and in the private home healing meetings. The informant felt very

strongly that former shamans had been among the originators of dancing in the church services, and now were among the most persistent in carrying it on.

Nor is the dance the only remnant of former shamanistic practices still found in the church. In the church at Miraflores, where many of the observations recorded in this paper were made, a missionary reports having witnessed the following incident. A well-known elderly Toba woman had a severe soreness on the back of her hand. During the service one of the older men danced around her, blowing and sucking over the affected area, while the woman herself chanted and prayed. After he finished sucking and she had returned to her seat, he put his hand over his mouth as if depositing something in it. He then placed this hand inside his shirt on the left side of his chest. He repeated this operation several times, spitting objects into his hand, then reaching into his shirt and pressing the objects into the left side of his chest.[19]

When informant Francisco was asked about his pessimism over former shamans becoming true Christians, he asserted, "No shaman who expects to live can ever cease to practice shamanism. First of all, if he quits, he becomes vulnerable to others who will certainly still have grudges against him from the past; but also when he stops practicing, he will gradually lose his power, and with his power, personal prestige." Francisco cited the example of one shaman who brought all of his paraphernalia to the missionary for burning in a

---

19 Miller, op. cit.

public meeting. However, in a few weeks the same man was busy again rebuilding his inventory. Fear and shame drove him back into shamanism.

Francisco felt that there was only one remedy to this situation — as he called it, the remedy of Elijah. All known shamans should be liquidated just as Elijah disposed of the prophets of Baal on Mount Carmel.[20] This was said in all seriousness and dramatically points out how deeply entrenched the Toba themselves feel the roots of shamanism and power to be.

Leadership

There are three kinds of officers in the Toba church: preachers, song leaders, and doormen. There appears to be little competition among doormen, more among song leaders, and serious competition among the preachers. It is most acute in the scramble to be the executive officer of the Iglesia Evangélica Unida, but even among the pastors in general there is a constant jockeying for power and advantage. Several factors encourage this. The government of Argentina has chosen to downgrade traditional chiefs and to encourage the development of new individuals as social and political leaders. The church is not entirely above this issue. These new leaders, including those in the church, often are insecure and seek to strengthen their position by stepping on others. Each wants to buttress his own authority and prestige by having access to church funds. Thus church offerings become a vital part of the ministerial struggle for power. The

one who has acted for the group as executive officer in the past feels that a share of all offerings should be sent to the central office of the church, that is, to him. Others resent this and say that he is no more than anyone else and that he is trying to take away power from other people. In fact, some have even tried to get a missionary to become the chief executive of the Iglesia Evangélica Unida. This could mean that they want to get a leader who is above the current struggle for power, and there might also be some prestige involved in having a foreign leader in the church, since acculturation is a highly desired goal for many of the Toba.

As to this man who has been acting as the organizational head of the church, one is struck by his almost parasitic attitude. He goes from church to church, often uninvited, and announces evangelistic campaigns. People who stay away will definitely suffer in the estimate of their spirituality. He expects each church to support him and his numerous family in good style during the two weeks or month of the campaign. His pitch to the constituency is, "If the churches don't support their pastors, there won't be any blessing ('power') of God." Francisco, in very obvious criticism, added, "And what is he doing for the church? He is doing little or nothing to make the church grow and develop. He just lives off the church. He isn't even ashamed to demand things in return for his preaching."

The informant expressed concern that the "you owe me support" attitude of some of the ministers could

---

[20] 1 Kings 18.

lead to the same type of decline in the church that he had described for the Toba past when the shamans began to demand undue tribute and thereby impaired not only their own healing powers but, in fact, the whole power structure of the tribe.

Singing and Dancing

The song was always a visible demonstration of having acquired power. The vision or dream was the general setting for receiving a song, for during this experience the living "interior" was able to have intercourse with spirit powers. The daytime encounters with spirit beings were another occasion for acquiring songs. With this background it is interesting to see the emphasis on singing in the Toba church. About half the service time is spent in singing. The song leader is an important man in the meeting. The informant highlighted this by pointing out that the Tobas' favorite Spanish translation for the shaman is *encantador* 'enchanter,' and the singer in the church is called *cantador* 'chanter.' The missionaries, however, point out that for the more acculturated, the song leader is now called *cancionista* 'singer.'

The songs of the past were highly individual and could be used only by their owners. Some informants claimed that in ancient times there were songs that were sung by all, but gradually this fell into disuse until more recently songs were all privately owned. In fact, when a folklorist taped one Toba's song as an example of Toba singing, others were incensed that one man's song should be considered the song of the people. In light

of this it is noteworthy that individual song leaders carried pieces of paper on which they had copied the words of a song not contained in the two Spanish songbooks that were in general use. Certain song leaders had gained a degree of distinction as ones that often taught the people new songs.

During the review of the dancing that had been observed in the Miraflores church, the informant was asked to rate the individual manifestations as positive or negative, and if negative, to suggest why he graded them so. He explained that the women who had danced when the two men made up their differences had been dancing for joy. This was a wholesome dance. He felt that there could also be a dance of sadness when people are moved by a revelation of sin or a word of rebuke. It, too, would be good.

The dance of the two men who embraced was classified as good. These men were supporting each other in their quest for power.

The mixed group dancing in which all embraced their neighbors in a circle was questionable. The informant felt that it had a sexual basis and that the participating men and women "tasted" each other by bodily contact and this usually led to moral problems. The dance of the man and the woman holding hands was definitely classified as sexual and negative. This was the first example actually discussed, and the anthropologist had primed the informant by saying, "If this had happened among the Choco in Panama, I would have said it means s-e-x." The informant looked at the speaker, then at the missionaries present, and blurted out rather sheepishly, "I guess that's exactly what it means among us, too." Then he listed a series of cases in which people had become morally involved after having bodily contact during such dancing.

At this point one of the missionaries described a dance he had witnessed in which two women bent over backwards. This had been performed in front of the platform where all the men were standing. The informant without hesitation said, "Good women don't do it. This type of dance calls for sex."

In another dance a man and a woman danced facing each other and carried on what sounded almost like a conversation. Both were speaking in tongues, but they spoke alternately. The informant classified this dance as bad. He viewed it as seeking sexual contact, but as being afraid to touch. He considered the intent to be as bad as the act.

The dance of the shaman's wife after her husband's healing was characterized as good, a dance of joy and gratitude.

Origin of Dancing

Somewhere in the discussion the informant raised the question whether Indians in other countries also danced in their churches. When he was told that not all Indians danced, he said, "Some of us have often wondered whether we should dance." This led into a discussion of the origin of dancing in the Toba church. The informant insisted that dancing had not been a major item at the outset of the Toba conversion movement. He then named several people who

introduced the dance and spread it as a part of their evangelism. Two of these people came from the northern area where dancing was also more prevalent in the pre-Christian state. The first man received his instructions for dancing after an encounter with a spirit owner in the forest. His instructions were that if the people wanted God's power, they should dance.

This man started a group of churches in the Formosa area which now bear the title *Corona* 'crown.' However, he has also visited numerous churches in the area of the Iglesia Evangélica Unida. He and most of his people were illiterate, but they faithfully carried a black Bible. When an epidemic ravaged the population in the area of these churches some time after dancing had been firmly established, the brother of the innovator warned the people that this calamity had come because people were using the Bible as a power object or a fetish. He warned them not to burn pages from the Bible any more for fumigation purposes, but rather to learn to read and obey it.

A second person connected with the origin of dance was also a preacher. He actually referred to himself as a prophet. He could read, but seldom did. He claimed that his authority for dancing came to him during a time of serious illness. A female approached him one night on his sick bed — he suspected that it might have been the Virgin Mary — and told him that he would get well and that he should teach all the people to dance for power.

Francisco said that the prophet had

both good and bad points. "Maybe it was because a woman appeared to him that he always liked to dance with females." And then he mentioned the names of several concubines this man has left in Toba territory during his evangelistic tours. When reproached by other Indians, he is supposed to have said, "Where the nanny goat leads, the billy goat follows."

The missionaries added that during the height of this prophet's influence audible preaching by others was impossible. He would often dance and chant loudly right in front of the pulpit, drowning out all the preacher was trying to say. Francisco claimed that he inspired some very extreme behavior like jumping off trees, burning money in bills, and undressing while dancing. Frequently the prophet and his dancing disciples would point to the Bible, to their feet, or to the palms of their hands. This Francisco felt, was all fetish. Pointing to the hands and feet was to represent the wounds of the crucified.[21]

There is, however, another aspect that must be considered before condemning the dancing as bad. Much of the dancing needs to be looked at in the light of the "taking out, putting in" pattern discussed earlier. Thus Kratz, coauthor of this article, reports that during a recent visit to League 17, an area where dancing is not widely practiced, a young Toba

asked him about the meaning of the church dancing at Miraflores. Kratz passed the question to the other members of the group. Several of them defended the dancing and insisted that it was essential for people to get "it" out. This "it" which is most frequently referred to as *gozo* 'joy,' has a very wide range of meaning, certainly much wider than its Spanish usage.

These scenes from a recent Miraflores weekend of services illustrate the function of *gozo* in dancing. At one of the meetings a group of teenage girls from a neighboring area where heretofore the gospel had had little influence, danced rather violently until they fell into trances. Older people worked over them, rubbing their chests and praying. In the next service this group of teenagers came to the altar to dedicate themselves to the Lord.

The explanation given was that "something" had to come out of them before they could belong to God. This something is also referred to as *gozo*, but certainly it was not joy. It seems to be related to the life of sin and the conviction of the Lord that comes upon sinners. Once this *gozo* gets hold of a sinner he dances until he faints, then it is supposed to have come out.[22] The minister supported

---

[21] That some of the churches, at least, express their disapproval of this evangelist's message and conduct was demonstrated recently when the evangelist tried to visit the churches in the southern area. He was given no offerings or support and because of this he had to abandon his plans.

[22] It is interesting that this negative *gozo* (that must come out) was so strongly felt by teenage girls. One wonders whether this is related to the pre-Christian model which demanded that the pubescent girl must dance until she fainted so that she would become a good wife. This in turn seems to find validation in the myth about the *vagina dentata*: early women became human and fit mates for men only after they had been freed through strenuous dancing.

this idea strongly, asserting that people could not give themselves to God without first having the negative *gozo* taken out. He felt that this current group was definitely converted and that they would be baptized soon. For this reason Toba ministers find it very hard to close a service when someone is still dancing with this kind of *gozo*.

There is a second kind of *gozo* which can come after such a conversion experience. This one seems to be related to the idea of filling (putting in) with the Holy Spirit. It is quite obvious that dancing both to get out negative *gozo* and to demonstrate the presence of positive *gozo* would be classified as good.

About dancing and visions in general the minister believed that all people want more power and at best secret power. Once a person faints and has a vision he can learn secrets. This, however, can also be very dangerous for the novice. For this reason one does not leave a fainted person in that state very long but tries to revive him and to make him dance in demonstration of the power he has received.

IV

Reflections of the Pre-Christian Models in Toba Church Life

This ·list of reflections is not intended to be exhaustive, nor is it asserted that all are fully documented and fully operative in Toba church life. They are here listed because there seems to be evidence that these models or parallels to them are functioning in at least some areas. This listing

does not imply that all the models contained in it are entirely bad. Some, in fact, may be desirable; but there are those that appear to be inconsistent with, or even diametrically opposed to, the ideals of the Christian faith the Tobas profess. More observation, investigation, and exchange between missionaries and Tobas will be necessary to evaluate the positive and negative roles of these models.

Models Associated with Power

1. *The function of the power object*: In pre-Christian days power objects appeared in the gourd rattle, the thing the shaman shot into a person to harm him, and the object-soul replacement for the infirm child. It is today reflected in the use of the Bible as the protective fetish that every believer must carry.

2. *The position of the power object*: In the child whose weak soul had to be replaced by a power object, the latter had to stand upright. Should it fall over, the child would suffer a relapse into its weakness. In the current use of the Bible it is tied into a firm upright position during power dancing.

3. *The use of incense, fumigant, or disinfectant*: *Palo santo* smoke purified and disinfected a person or a village against the soul of the dead. It also appeared as a cure for the loss of honey-gathering power. *Palo santo* tea could also be substituted for smoke in the case of disinfection against the soul of the dead. Even today *palo santo* is used for disinfecting purposes. Missionaries report that Indians eagerly take all pieces of *palo santo* wood that they have found.

A Christian parallel would be the burning of pages of the Bible in the case of illness of unknown origin.

4. *Visions*: Visions served as a source of getting power and also of seeing in the shaman's diagnosis of illness or soul loss. Related also could be the encounters with the spirit beings that gave power. In the church both dancing and healing can lead to fainting and visions. Spirit filling is a reflection of power through spirit encounter.

5. *Communication with the spirit world*: This occurred during the encounter with the spirit owners in the seances of the seeing shaman, and in the wanderings of the soul. It is today operative in the vision and tongues experiences in the Christian church.

6. *Incantations, magic formula, and power songs*: In the shaman's life these came as gifts from spirit beings or were learned during the wanderings of his soul in the spirit world. In the church the ritual use of songs like "Holy Spirit, Fire Divine" or the "Divine Physician" are examples. An example of a magic formula is "In the name of the Lord," which is used when taking drugstore medicine.

7. *The passing of power from one person to another*: This is seen in the shaman's taking of power objects from his own interior and introducing them into the soul of the patient or the budding shaman. It was practiced between a shaman-father and his son, or between a shaman and a patient. It could also happen when a shaman gave a song to a layman. Perhaps spirit beings giving power to their favorites should be added to this category. In the church it is seen in the healing practice where older and stronger people touch the sick one while praying. It is seen in the breathing at and touching of sitting persons by one dancing. Also pertinent are the laying on of hands for spirit filling and tongues, and the touching of the body of the person who has fainted in a vision.

8. *Old people are more powerful than the young*: Old people perform burials and have the courage and the power to calm the ghosts of the deceased. Today, children may be sent to the hospital because they are too young to believe, but older people should not go. Again, old people surround the sick person and touch him at the church healing ceremony. Usually it is also the older people who dance and who have the tongues experiences in the church.

9. *The loss of power*: The unclean person loses power, but he is not only powerless, he is also dangerous to others who have power. In the old life this was most marked in the fear of menstruating women. People who came in contact with such women lost their hunting power, their power to find honey, and certainly their power to heal. An individual who had hurt or insulted a person was vulnerable to attack by the soul of the dead after the death of this person. For this reason people apologized to a heavy dead body. Toba Christians believe sin to be one of the great reasons for power loss. Unclean persons are shunned. In the Christian experience the faithless believer who enters the hospital is shunned by relatives. They do not visit him and show

great hesitation even to bury him if he dies there. It is also reflected in the ostracism of the emptied ministers whose condition is revealed when they become ill.

10. *Jockeying for power and mutual attempts to empty rivals*: The great struggle between shamans to overcome each other and to appropriate the opponent's power is the classic example. In the church, it is evident in such cases as the pastor's angry retreat when illness declared him empty of power, and also in the accusation of the minister that others were undermining him with sorcery. However, it is also evident in the belief in soul stealing, which is still a current explanation for illness and death. Even God is believed to steal the sinner's soul in order to punish him with death. A further reflection of it is seen in the fear that people have to assume authority. This will single them out as targets of sorcery and they do not trust their capacity to withstand.

**Models Associated
with Illness and Dancing**

11. *The great preoccupation with phyisical well-being and healing*: This is seen in the elaborate system of explanations about disease and spirits, in the prestige awarded the shaman, in the extensive curing ritual, and in the multiplicity of the men engaged in the healing profession. In Christian times it is reflected in their choice of Pentecostal healing over the pietistic approach of other missions, in the emphasis given to healing in the services, in the dogged persistence of shamanism, and in the frequent boasting by the well concerning their health and power.

12. *Illness and death as sources of embarrassment*: Formerly, each clan with its shaman leader and protector was viewed as having power to prevent illness among its people. If illness or sorcery penetrated the tribe, the shaman healer identified and corrected the situation. If he failed, all were embarrassed and humiliated. They destroyed the village and fled to a different area. Today with the breakdown of the clan and the acceptance of Christianity, not only the pastor but also the head of the house or of the extended family is to be such a reservoir of power. Illness, especially of this person, demonstrates the enfeeblement of this protector head, and also points up the emptiness of all the adult Christians in the group. It causes people to stay away from the church for several months both during and after an illness, and especially after death.

13. *The dance of joy*: Just like the happy wife of the successful hunter or the woman seeing a long lost friend who breaks out into a dance of spontaneous joy, so the people of the church can today erupt into dance as the joy of the Lord comes over them during a service. The dance of the women after the reconciliation of estranged brethren is a good example. The dancing of the wife of the shaman who was healed of his abdominal abscess could be considered another example.

14. *The dance of mixed sexes*: Mixed sexes always danced at the major festivals. On summer evenings

the young people especially used the dance as a sexual mixer. This mixed dance was, first of all, a courtship device for the young. Married indulged in it only at special festivals and usually when away from the home village. The circle dance of mixed sexes and holding hands between dancers in the church seemed to be vehicles of new sexual contacts. Certain dances by females assuming suggestive postures in front of men appear to reflect the original sexual initiative of the female who chose her partner during the dance.

15. *Bodily contact as the last step in seduction*: The greatest seductive device was bodily contact. In the mixed dance the female grasped the waist of the male and danced behind him. Or, in the case of the circle dance, they embraced each other as they stood side by side, or a woman might just touch a man casually in passing. Especially the latter was denominated "tasting." Such bodily contact was a definite prelude to sexual contact. For church dancing the informant felt that all contact between sexes, whether in the circle dance or in the holding of hands between people of mixed sexes, was the prelude to sexual involvements.[23]

16. *New sexual contacts of married men*: These usually took place when people were at villages and festivals away from home. The dance of the visiting man and the Miraflores woman holding hands could be representative of the present-day church

example. The informant claimed that male church members generally only held hands with women when they were away from home.

17. *The dance of people seeking or demonstrating power*: The shaman, the war hero, the new initiate, or the person who was the special object of a festival danced both when he sought power and when he demonstrated received power. The dancers seeking a tongues experience or a vision in the church would be an example of the former, and the dance after a vision experience would parallel the latter.

18. *Singing and power*: Songs of the shaman, continual chanting at a festival, and chanting beside sick persons were always associated with the manifestation of power. Singing was a way to lull the malignant spirit forces. The extensive use of singing and the importance of song leaders, and the impact of such songs as the "Great Physician" or "Holy Spirit, Fire Divine" seem to show a definite similarity to the function of the power song of the past.

19. *Confession as a means of cleansing impurity*: The female who had violated a menstrual taboo could be saved only through confession. People who felt that they had offended a dead person (recognized by the heavy corpse) could be released from their guilt and consequent attack by the soul of the dead, if they confessed their guilt before the corpse. Since sin is considered the great destroyer of personal and collective power, its confession becomes a very important element in the prevention of disaster for the whole church. This is evi-

---

[23] Missionaries express doubt whether the rubbing on the chest of a fainted individual by persons of the opposite sex should be considered as an attempt at sexual contact.

denced by the frequency and the detail of confessions in the church.

20. *Giving evidence of harboring no negative intents toward or suspicions of a person*: The absence of suspicion could be demonstrated by the eating of food that involved leftovers which could potentially be used for sorcery. The absence of negative intent was to be proven by one's attendance at festivals given in honor of individuals. In the Christian life this motive is manifested in extensive handshaking when a visitor arrives and in the conspicuous handshake with the preacher who has just delivered a message to the congregation.

V

The Missionary and the Indigenous Church[24]

It is the conclusion of this research that the Toba church as an indigenous church desires and needs missionary involvement. Their questioning on whether or not they ought to dance is an indication of their awareness of the need of evaluation. Toba Christians feel very keenly the times they have been rejected by Pentecostal groups as still being pagan. They are very self-conscious about the occasions on which they have been humiliated by preachers who stamped out of their churches when dancing and other unacceptable forms of behavior were manifested. At the same time they are deeply appreciative of the Mennonite missionaries who have helped them achieve their own church

___

24 This conclusion has been written by Loewen who alone must accept responsibility for the positions taken.

organization and have remained their friends in spite of everything that has happened in the churches. As one expressed it, "These missionaries are not as delicate as the Pentecostals." This complete acceptance in spite of all their shortcomings the Toba have appreciated greatly. Another individual spoke warmly of the almost unlimited patience the missionaries have had with the Toba church even at a time when there were so many things that the church still needed to learn, if not change.

When one looks at the history of the annual conventions, it is obvious that the missionary has served as the main cohesive force. Because he checked where and when such a convention was going to be held and because he consistently kept his promise to be present, conventions were not only held regularly, but they have also gradually grown to play an important part in the life of the Toba church. The constant visits by the missionaries to individual churches, many of which were unexpected and unannounced, have exercised great catalytic influence.

The visit to the Miraflores in which the anthropologist participated was an excellent example. The church was stunned by the retreat of the empty leader. There was dissension, and it appeared as if several families would withdraw permanently from the church. Then the missionaries unexpectedly appeared on the scene. They called on the chief who, while not being a leader in the church, was a major force in the community. They talked with the retreating leader of the church and with the church members who had been accused of hurting and trying to empty the leader of power. Their conversation and questions brought about rethinking. Their inquiry of whether they would meet each of the principals in the church services resulted in all of the people attending. The reconciliation of the two brethren, the resolution of the pastoral problem, and the apology by the retreating pastor all were the results of the missionaries' catalytic presence.

As one considers the numerous reflections of the pre-Christian models in the current church life, one is led to conclude that the church needs to do some serious evaluating and in this the missionary can have at least two important functions, namely that of a mirror against which the church can perform such an evaluation and as a source of alternatives as the church seeks for new models by which to express its new life in Christ.

In 1954, at the time of the Reyburn study, the mission realistically faced the existing situation and decided that the mission-centered approach was not in the interest of the Toba church. The missionaries embarked on a new approach which (a) accepted Toba Christianity as valid and (b) was committed to helping the Indian church

establish its independence. Today this independence has been more or less achieved. Today the missionary has been accepted in the role of fraternal counselor. This should make it possible that in 1965 the missionary accept a new or expanded role in this counseling relationship — that he function as a mirror. He can do this by asking questions about various church practices. Obviously such inquiries will stimulate evaluation and questioning by the Tobas themselves.

Once the church reaches the conclusion that change is necessary, the missionary with his wider Christian experience can become the source of alternatives.[25]

To the outsider many of the pre-Christian models seem to be incompatible with Christianity. They seem like weights that hinder the church in its spiritual race.[26] Helping such an indigenous church to recognize the hindrances and assisting it to find ways of victory stand forth as bold challenges to the missionary in the Toba situation as well as in many similar situations across the world.

---

[25] Jacob A. Loewen, "The Church: Indigenous and Ecumenical," PA, Vol. 11, No. 6 (Nov.-Dec. 1964), pp. 241-258.

[26] Hebrews 12: 1-2.

Communication for

Stability and Change

Socialization and Social Control: A Resume of Processes

RECENTLY in an Andean Quechua community a young Indian—a rebel against his home and community—killed a fellow Indian. His cultural and linguistic identification with "civilization" had earned him some white friends who were willing to use their influence on his behalf. Thus when the law tried to call him to account for his crime, he was found to be "immune" by reason of this support in high places. He came home from his arrest with bold arrogance: "With the help of my white friends it was easy."

But that was before the community began to set into motion the wheels of its own tribal justice. Informal gossip began to spread spontaneously but relentlessly until it had blanketed the entire community. The young man soon began to feel its subtle, constricting pressure—a pressure from which his non-Indian friends could not deliver him. When shortly thereafter the seasonal rains failed to come and the crops withered and died within weeks of sprouting, the gossip wondered about the possible connection between the unsettled crime and this supernatural judgment on the Indian community. Before long the gossip began to speculate whether the supernatural might not all at once begin to focus its avenging wrath on the culprit, since he was obviously failing to heed the general message

to society. Then suddenly, without any overt punitive action, the young man broke down, confessed his crime, and made restitution according to local custom. Social isolation and fear of personal punishment by the supernatural wrought a change of heart and behavior that far exceeded any rehabilitation our Western, civilized penal apparatus usually hopes to achieve.

On an Indian reservation in northern Canada a married man in his late forties violated a fourteen-year-old girl. Community feelings strongly condemned this anti-social act, and as a result both of the culprits came to the missionary before long seeking forgiveness from God and the church. The missionary, however, knew that a minor had been violated and a Canadian law had been broken, so he notified the Royal Canadian Mounted Police. The police investigator arrived. He interrogated the alleged rapist, the girl victim, her father, the chief, and finally the Indian elders of the church, but everywhere he drew a blank—there must be some big mistake in the white man's paper world since none of them had any knowledge of such an offense ever having been committed.

In Central American Indian society young people were permitted a certain amount of pre-marital sexual

211

liberty while they selected their life's mate. However, this liberty was severely curtailed by the fact that families lived in separate dwellings which were usually a considerable distance from each other. The reason for the presence of a strange young man near a home with a sexually mature daughter was readily understood by all, and only if the parents were agreed was it possible for the young people to make contact.

Then came the gospel, and a group conversion brought several thousand members of this tribe into the church within a matter of months. In order to facilitate daily worship services with the believers and also to be able to operate a school for the believers' children, a "Christian village" was organized around the missionary's residence. This sudden juxta-position of residences robbed the parents of their control over the young people's trysts, and a wave of teen-age promiscuity followed. The missionary thundered judgment from the pulpit, punished promiscuous girls, banished wayward boys, excommunicated "careless" parents, and finally tried a fenced and guarded dormitory for all unmarried girls eight years and older, but all without success. So severe did the frustration of the parents become that many left the "Christian village" and the gospel in an effort to save their children's morals.

These incidents, drawn from three widely scattered and very different groups of people, highlight a number of interesting facets of society's capacity to socialize and to socially control its members. In each of the examples the subtle social pressures of face-to-face society stand in forceful contrast to the overtly coercive practices of Western civilization. The success of the tribal society in the examples cited must not be viewed merely as luck or as biased selection, for the "batting average" in successful control in more cohesive societies is decidedly higher than that in our own fragmented urban society. Each of the events recounted also contains a warning that the missionary and his program can easily—although often unwittingly—interfere with a society's processes, thereby seriously disrupting the latter's capacity for socialization and social control.

In order to strengthen missionary awareness of these socializing functions, this paper proposes to summarize some of the insights anthropology offers us into the processes of socialization and social control, drawing particularly from *The Analysis of Social Systems* by Bredemeier and Stephenson.[1]

Socialization

Socialization, or enculturation as it is sometimes called in anthropological writings, is the process by which individuals are taught to function as members of a given society. The completely socialized or enculturated individual will carry within himself the knowledge, feelings, wishes, and values of the culture system. Ralph Linton, with a bit of characteristic humor, has called it the process by which "barbarian invaders [new-born

---

[1] Harry C. Bredemeier and Richard M. Stephenson, *The Analysis of Social Systems* (New York: Holt, Rinehart and Winston, Inc., 1962), pp. 60-176.

infants] of each generation are turned from uncivilized, ignorant animals into human members of the social system."[2]

By the same process green freshmen are turned into mature college graduates, civilians are turned into soldiers, immigrants into citizens, and, for our purposes, converted "heathen" learn to live like Christians. The process of socialization is actually an interaction between two kinds of persons: *socializees* (infants, raw recruits, immigrants, freshmen, apprentices, converts, etc.) and the *socializing agents* (parents, sergeants, natives, upper classmen, senior tradesmen, teachers, etc.) Inasmuch as the individual must learn to function properly in many new social contexts during the course of his life, socialization is a continuous process that begins at birth and carries on throughout life.

Motives for being socialized

Unlike members of termite societies who are biologically compelled to perform their adaptive and intergrative functions, man must *learn* to do so. Initially a child's motivation is purely biological. Bredemeier and Stephenson say: "The infant has only one motive for doing anything: pleasure."[3] But he soon learns that in order to obtain satisfaction for his biological needs, he must fulfill certain cultural requirements.

We could thus say that the process of socialization begins when the in-

dividual learns that the gratification of his biological needs is conditional upon his conformity to the requirements of the social system. Gradually the socializee learns to value social approval more than biological gratification. In other words, he discovers that if he wants to avoid shame and social disapproval he may sometimes have to forego certain biological satisfactions. Social disapproval is often expressed by some type of punishment, so the fear of punishment becomes one of the controlling motives for avoiding socially disapproved behavior. Once a child has been thus sensitized to the approval of others, he actually has been socialized to conform beyond the motives of his intrinsic biological gratification and has entered the world of social motivation.

There is, however, a further degree of socialization. At this final level, self approval is a stronger motivation for conformity to the society's mores than the desire either to avoid the censure or receive the praise of others. At this level the socializee has so internalized the standards that he can assess or censor his own behavior. He no longer needs to ask: What would my father, my mother, or my big brother do in this situation? By means of an "internal dialogue" he can, as it were, take a look at himself and the situation and make judgments and evaluations which he uses as the basis for action. In this way the individual is not only able to obtain the approval of others, but is also rewarded with his own self-approval. Piaget calls this the "autonomous stage" for the standards are

---

[2] Ralph Linton, *The Tree of Culture* (New York: Alfred A. Knopf, 1955).

[3] Bredemeier and Stephenson, op cit., p. 62.

now felt to be part of oneself and one's own will.[4]

At the autonomous stage the individual is back again to only two kinds of reward — pleasure and usefulness; but obviously these differ greatly from the child's biological definition of pleasure and utility. The autonomous individual's conception of pleasure and efficiency are cultural conceptions. His pleasure, for example, may be in his family's success, in discovering the cure for cancer, etc.

Bredemeier and Stephenson call attention to an interesting prerequisite for consistency in autonomous behavior: in order for a person to be true to his internalized values even in diverse cultural settings, he will of necessity have had to be exposed to contradictory norms some time during the process of his socialization. Uncontested (where the person has no option) standards, even when internalized, usually represent mere outward conformity. In such cases the value learned is not the behavior pattern itself, but conformity. A person so trained will sooner conform to the expectations of a new reference group than risk group disapproval by standing alone in his inherited behavior pattern.

Since social systems are structured, such internalized definitions of right and wrong will be ordered into hierarchies — some patterns of behavior will be more highly valued than others. For example, a child must learn that obedience to his father will take pre-

[4] Jean Piaget, *The Moral Judgment of the Child* (New York: Harcourt, Brace and World, Inc., 1932).

cedence over obedience to his playmates, and that occupational skills are more important than recreational skills. This hierarchy, of course, is never absolute, but is determined by each social system.

Inconsistencies in standards within the larger society

In most societies it is in the family that the individual receives his basic socialization. To the extent to which the values of the family are equal to those of the society at large, the two systems will reinforce each other. In face-to-face societies with little division of labor there generally is great cultural homogeneity and therefore much reinforcement. However, in larger societies with extensive division of labor, and in societies in contact with other social systems, there are bound to be contradictions between the sub-systems within the society or between the separate systems of the cultures in contact. In societies like our own in which a person interacts not only with his age group and family, but also with people at the church, the school, and the job, and is exposed to mass media such as radio, television, books, and magazines, the possibility of exposure to inconsistencies will be greatly multiplied.

In most initial socializing situations family members tend to sift and to screen the stimuli that impinge upon the socializee. Wherever possible they will shield the socializee from sources of deviant values. Where this is impossible they will "interpret or rationalize" unacceptable perceptions. The effort is designed to help the socializee become firmly integrated into the given "consistent" system. However, as the individual matures he will of necessity have to participate in conflicting systems. Here standards already internalized may need to be modified or rearranged in their value hierarchy. Thus most adults participate in several systems or sub-systems, each with somewhat differing standards. The mark of the mature individual is the capacity to move in and out of given systems without undue insecurity or reaction.

Initial Socialization versus resocialization

As has already been stated, socialization is a continuous process that begins at birth and continues throughout a man's life. However, for practical purposes we can speak of two kinds of socialization: initial socialization, by means of which a child learns to participate in the social system of his birth; and resocialization, the socialization of adults who in the course of their lifetime must enter new systems — either sub-systems of their own society or new systems altogether. There is a difference between these two, because in the latter type the individual does not enter the socializing situation with a "clean slate" like the child, nor will he be just a passive receptacle into which new behavior patterns can be poured. His former socialization may cause him to resist the efforts of resocialization or to modify the expected behavior pattern so as not to conflict too seriously with his earlier socialization. In other words, resocialization seldom erases completely all vestiges of earlier socialization.

Both types of socialization pose important implications for the indigenous church. Initial socialization is important for the enculturation of second, third, etc. generation Christians, i. e., for bringing the children of believing parents into the church.[5] Resocialization, on the other hand, is important in the case of adult converts, for when we speak of the indigenous church, we are usually thinking of individuals who have grown up in a tribal social system and who, as a consequence of their conversion to Christianity, must be resocialized in accordance with Christian values and behavior patterns.[6] (For the missionary, awareness of the initial socialization patterns of a society will be prerequisite to a sympathetic understanding of the problems which adult converts experience when they become Christians.)

Modifying earlier socialization

Like socialization, the resocialization of adults is a universal phenomenon. Frequently such socialization to new groups or new statuses does not involve any great amount of change. Sometimes, however, the definitions that have already been internalized need to undergo extensive changes in both content and valuation. In order for further socialization to take place, therefore, the person

---

5 The application of initial socialization to the indigenous church will be pursued in a separate paper: "The Indigenous Church and Socialization" to be published in PA.

6 The application of resocialization to the indigenous church will be pursued in a separate paper: "The Indigenous Church and Resocialization" to be published in PA.

will have to be motivated to give up or to modify his old definitions and to accept new ones. It may be worth underscoring that even at this stage the basic motivations are identical to those of initial socialization: the person will act in a given way if he will find it intrinsically pleasurable, or if such behavior will ultimately lead to intrinsic pleasure, or if it will earn for him the approval of others, or if it will raise his self-approval.

However, since resocialization involves a choice of either continuing in the old way or learning the new, there will have to be incentives that will tip the balance in favor of the new. These incentives usually involve either reducing the rewards for the present behavior (which would be the same as reducing the cost of changing), or increasing the estimate of the reward that will be received from the new behavior.

Reducing rewards for old behavior

We can predict that if the rewards for continuing to conform to old expectations are consistently withheld, socialization in the new will be facilitated. In fact, there is reason to believe that consistent denial of reward for old behavior is more important than consistent granting of rewards for the new. What ultimately counts is that the socializee does not obtain reward apart from the successful performance of his new status expectations.

Since a person's present self-conception may stand as a barrier to further socialization, the suppression of former statuses upon which this estimation is based may sometimes

be a necessary prerequisite for change. Sanford M. Dornbusch has provided an excellent illustration of purposeful suppression of former status in the training of cadets at the United States Coast Guard Academy:

> The assignment of low status encourages the cadet to place a high value on successfully completing the steps in an Academy career, and requires that there be a loss of identity based on pre-existing statuses. This clean break with the past must be achieved in a relatively short period. For two months, therefore, the swab is not allowed to leave the base or to engage in social intercourse with non-cadets. This complete isolation helps to produce a unified group of swabs, rather than a heterogeneous collection of persons of high and low status. Uniforms are issued on the first day, and discussions of wealth and family background are taboo. Although the pay of the cadet is very low, he is not permitted to receive money from home. The role of the cadet must supersede other roles the individual has been accustomed to play.[7]

Sometimes status transition can be facilitated by reducing the feelings of guilt that the socializee experiences as a result of the new behavior. We can again draw an example from military indoctrination. The army must change civilians — who have been taught to respect other people's

---

[7] Sanford M. Dornbusch, "The Military Academy as an Assimilating Institution," *Social Forces*, Vol. 33, (1955), pp. 316-321.

property, not to kill, not to destroy—into fighting men who will kill and destroy efficiently and without guilt. In fact, the very respect for life and property of the civilian is rationalized into a positive reason for killing and destroying. The recruit is taught that his action is "a war to end war," or "a fight to make the world safe for democracy."

Bredemeier and Stephenson list five ways of reducing the rewards of old behavior: (1) separating the socializee from his former associates and the environment in which the old values were recognized; (2) supplying peer group support in suppressing old statuses and old behavior patterns, thus linking self-approval to the lack of resistance to change; (3) emphasizing the consistency between the old and the new, which at the same time is de-emphasizing the discontinuity; (4) down-grading the earlier sources of gratification such as occur when a student moves from the home community to a distant college campus: as his old group ties become disfunctional their approval becomes less and less important; (5) de-grouping, i.e., shifting the relative value of associations so as to diminish the authority and power of the old. The latter can be illustrated in part by Western marriage on the basis of romantic love. Falling in love causes the young person to relinquish the ties to his home in favor of the new association with his marriage partner.

Increasing the rewards for new behavior

Because statuses in each society are generally structured in a hierar-chy, it is often possible to increase the reward for new behavior by means of anticipatory socialization. We can describe anticipatory socialization as a kind of role rehearsal by means of which the person learns to conform to part or all of the behavioral expectations characteristic of the new group while still a member of the old. Usually peer group attitudes support the socializee, because belonging to the new group is seen as advantageous by them. Engagement and the associated rituals of showers and farewell-to-single-life parties are examples of anticipatory socialization with peer group support.

It is possible, of course, especially in "earned" statuses, that the socializee conform to new group expectations even in spite of his peers' negative evaluation of the new status. In this case the new behavior serves as a demonstration of the socializee's readiness or of his capacity for the new status. An example would be the North American reservation Indian who, in spite of community pressures and peer group (especially school drop-out) ridicule, continues his education to become a teacher.

Sometimes such a shift merely represents the choice of a new reference group. This can be seen in the case of the missionary who was very closely identified with the nationals of the country of his service. A sudden shift in the mission's power structure made it apparent that he could become eligible for an administrative post. He at once began to violate the confidences of his earlier friendship with the nationals in order to demonstrate both his loyalty to the views held by the administration and his readiness to function in an administrative capacity.

The socializee's progressive movement up the status ladder can come in two ways. There are graded statuses, such as the age-grading found in many tribal societies, where each step carries more or less equal prestige. There are also ranked statuses, where each progressive step carries a higher value. We see the latter in Western society where individuals are ranked by prestige of occupation or by the size of their income.

Usually the successive stages in the status ladder have considerable continuity in expectations, but occasionally the discontinuity is sharp. In a tribal society an "ordinary" Indian might fall heir to the shaman role through the unexpected death of his shaman uncle. In our own society a poor homesteader is suddenly discovered to be the only surviving heir of some millionaire relative.

Discontinuities spell social insecurity. For this reason, it is often necessary to employ the concept of delayed rewards to fortify the socializee during the trauma of transition. Kimball Young, himself a descendant of founder Brigham Young, points out the way in which the Mormon prophet, Joseph Smith, used the concept of contingent rewards to help bridge the severe discontinuity which resulted from the introduction of the practice of polygyny. Smith linked the "new" practice to the earlier religious dogma that granted males the status rights of priesthood, and assured women who married priests and bore them children that they would share their husband's status in life and after death. The new dogma thus helped provide a degree of status consistency for the female, for now her statuses as a woman, wife, and mother all fitted together and were supported by a system of delayed supernatural rewards which could only be obtained with the full acceptance of polygyny.[8]

A further way of increasing the estimate of future reward can be found in the very structure of the socializee's reference group. The degree of deprivation or satisfaction which a person feels will depend not on the objective situation alone, but will also be related to the reference group which is used as the basis for the comparison. Thus if "all swabs are in the same boat" their feeling of deprivation will be neutralized and their common suffering will actually be a validation of their membership in the new group. Their frustration and deprivation can be redefined as "tests to prove their actual worth" and as "legitimate obstacles which they must overcome to prove themselves worthy of the new status."

Conditions influencing socialization

Bredemeier and Stephenson list ten functional conditions in the socializing situation which will either facilitate or retard the socialization process. These include: (1) clearly and con-

[8] Kimball Young, "Variations in Personality Manifestations in Mormon Polygynous Families," in Quinn McNemar and Maud A. Sherill, eds., *Studies in Personality Contribution in Honor of Lewis M. Terman* (New York: McGraw-Hill Book Company, Inc., 1942).

sistently defined statuses, (2) socializing agents who hold out consistent expectations, (3) consistency among statuses learned simultaneously, (4) consistency in status sequences, (5) clearly defined status transitions, (6) adequate mechanisms for managing tension, (7) a degree of permissiveness during socialization, (8) the possibility of role rehearsal, (9) the availability of models, and (10) gearing expectations to the capacities of and the physical facilities available to the socializee.

An example of the absence of status clarity and consistency we find in the teenager-adult transition in North America. For driver's license an individual is considered adult at the age of sixteen, but automobile insurance companies will give him adult rates only after twenty-five. He is allowed to enter a bar at the age of eighteen, but can vote only at the age of twenty-one.

The consistency in the expectations of socializers involves both the consistency of any one socializer in all circumstances and the agreement between the various socializers with whom the socializee interacts. Thus, for example, a father and mother coming from two different cultural or church backgrounds may differ in their expectations. In the same way immigrant parents and school peers will often differ greatly in their expectations. Inconsistency in expectations tends to retard socialization.

Since each person occupies several statuses simultaneously, the expectations within his status set should be consistent if they are to reinforce each other. The coed will be hindered in her socialization if the expectations as a daughter of the home, as a girl friend to a classmate, and as a student majoring in physics conflict with each other. Mirra Kamarovsky has pointed out that many undergraduate women confess that they play dumb with their classmates and throw games in favor of their dates in order to be accepted socially. But many of them suffer acute anxiety because "they are letting their parents down."[9]

Consistency in the status sequence can be readily illustrated with the Western educational system. A child begins in kindergarten, proceeds to elementary school, continues in high school, and finally moves on to university. Each step in the educational ladder is a preparation for the next.

In our Western society the clarity of status transition between the teenager and the adult is quite indistinct, and many anthropologists and sociologists feel that this is the reason for much teen-age confusion and reaction. In many societies transition rituals have been highly developed; the Lengua of the Paraguayan Chaco had a series of five or six such transition rituals in a man's life.[10] In our own society the behavior connected with marriage illustrates a clearly defined transition. A period of going steady culminates in engagement; the bride-to-be receives

[9] Mirra Komarovsky, *Women in the Modern World* (Boston: Little, Brown and Company, 1953), pp. 69ff.

[10] Jacob A. Loewen, "Lengua Festivities and Cultural Substitutes," PA, Vol. 14, No. 1 (Jan.-Feb. 1967), pp. 15-36.

showers and recognition of her approaching marriage by her peers; a bachelor party reminds the young man that his days of single liberty are about to end; and finally the wedding ceremony with its exchange of vows is solemnized with the support of both religious ritual and the authority of the state.

The presence or absence of appropriate models during socialization bears a close relationship to both the efficiency and the effectiveness with which the expected behavior patterns are internalized. Such models supply the symbolic as well as the concrete reference points for the behavior in the new status. The effectiveness of the model seems to hinge upon at least two points: the extent to which the socializee identifies with it, and the position which the model occupies in the social hierarchy. It has been suggested that the greater problem of the American male teenager stems from the fact that his models are much less visible than those of his female counterpart.

Finally, the socializee should have at his disposal the facilities necessary to fulfill the expectations. This includes both biological maturity and the necessary physical or social facilities. Serious strain may develop if the expectations are set either too high or too low. Mirra Komarovsky, whom we quoted earlier, has pointed out that as many as forty percent of undergraduate women, in order to buy social favor, do not work up to capacity. She also notes that many of them develop severe frustration because underachieving undermines their self-respect.[11]

The lack of necessary physical and social facilities for easy socialization can be illustrated by the experience of children from two cultural backgrounds who are being educated in one school system—Spanish-American children in the southern United States, for example, or the Indians in any national school system in Latin America. Because the children of immigrants or of the aborigines do not have the same economic, linguistic, or social background as national children, they are often severely handicapped in school systems geared to children of higher status.

Social control mechanisms

Social control can be defined as "arranging the circumstances so that deviance from expected behavior cannot be engaged in even if it were motivated." Bredemeier and Stephenson list five different kinds of social control mechanisms: (1) those which forestall the development of strain so that potential strain will not be actualized, (2) those which drain off or canalize the responses into socially accepted patterns if and when strain does arise, (3) those which make it very costly to express socially disapproved responses, (4) those by means of which—in the event all else fails—the deviant can be removed from the social system through banishment, execution, or imprisonment, and (5) those which attempt to resocialize the individual through special therapy, such as psychotherapy.

The forestalling of strain may be accomplished by segregating a person's statuses. Thus the man who

---

11 Komarovsky op. cit.

is a father, a husband, a golf enthusiast, a Christian, and a lawyer functions in his occupational status from nine to five, his father status from six to nine, his husband status from nine to eleven; on Sundays he occupies his religious status, on Monday through Friday his lawyer status, and on Saturday morning his recreational status. Strain can be introduced if any of these roles are allowed to overlap, as, for example, when the wife asks the father to take a small child with him on a round of golf with his business associates, or when the wife and children drop in at the office on a busy day.

In the above example, statuses are separated by allocating them to different times. They may also be separated by allocating them to different places; thus the college student may have a different type of behavior in the library, in the parked car with his date, in the dormitory bull session with his friends, and in church.

Separation may also be accomplished by segregating role partners. Certain polygynous societies handle the potential conflict between plural wives in this way. Each wife lives in a separate dwelling and the husband cohabits with each in rotation.

Another mechanism in forestalling strain has been called *insulation*, which is really a symbolic segregation of times, occasions, or partners. The so-called avoidance relationship among certain kinsmen in many societies, in which a husband may approach his wife's mother or his son's wife only with marked reserve, is an example of insulation. In the case of

the army, the differential rights and obligations of officers and enlisted men are elaborate mechanisms of insulation at points where segregation is impossible. In rigidly structured societies the linguistic forms of address, special honorifics, etc., insulate the interaction of people at points of potential tension.

A third institutional device for preventing status conflict is the establishment of status priorities. Under American law, for example, the role of wife has priority over her role as citizen, and she is exempted from testifying against her husband in a court of law. But the role of citizen takes priority over the status of friend in that same court. Of course, not all statuses are arranged according to priority, and this constitutes a source of potential strain. This type of strain is often seen in missionary wives for whom the relative priority of their statuses as wife, mother, and missionary has not been clearly defined.

Mechanisms for discharging tensions

If and when tension does result many societies attempt to provide mechanisms for releasing it harmlessly. American housewives often release the frustration built up in their housewife-mother status by means of political, religious, or social activities. The worker on the assembly line maintains a workshop in his home to compensate for the obsolescence of skill at his job. In many societies the so-called joking relationships between potential sexual intimates represent a highly ritualized type of tension-relieving mechanism in areas where tension frequently does develop.

Besides these accepted mechanisms there are others that are only tolerated, such as gambling and drinking to intoxication which may be suffered in college youth — "the boys will be boys." In fact, many societies have festivals of annual license in which pent-up tensions can be vented. Our own Halloween seems to have this function.

Raising the cost of deviance

Where it is not possible to prevent strain and where the society is unable to eliminate the motivation to deviate, it often develops mechanisms which make deviation difficult or costly. People are made to conform "in spite of themselves." Bredemeier and Stephenson point out that in the American voting practice election boards generally consist of both Republicans and Democrats rather than impartial watchdogs. The self-interest of the two contending parties is a mechanism to block deviance. Withholding taxes is another expedient to make deviance (non-payment) more difficult.

When other roadblocks to deviance fail, the society may try to deter deviant behavior by placing a high cost on it. Fines and imprisonment have this function. Recently a closed community "raised the cost of deviance" for .an aberrant church member by denying him economic privileges in the communal cooperative. By keeping him from buying and selling, the church community tried to force him to repent of his "sinful behavior."

In our impersonal technological societies the raised cost of deviance is usually punitive, but punishment is effective as a deterrent to behavior only if it meets the following conditions: (1) it must be severe enough to throw the balance in favor of conformity; (2) it must be immediate enough so as to be directly linked to the deviant behavior; (3) it must be applied uniformly to all persons engaging in the particular kind of deviance; and (4) its application must be relatively certain.

Application

The indigenous church as an institution must for practical purposes be viewed as a sub-culture within the larger cultural milieu. If such a church is to be viable as a social organism, it will need "mechanisms" for resocializing adult converts and socializing the succeeding generations according to the values and standards of the believing community, and for controlling deviance within its ranks. Each of these mechanisms will be further elucidated in separate paper also to be published in *Practical Anthropology*.[12]

12 See footnotes 5 and 6 for respective titles.

The Indigenous Church
and Resocialization

AN earlier paper[1] tried to define and illustrate the basic principles and practices of socialization and social control. The immediate relevance of these processes to missions, especially to the development of the indigenous church, is fairly obvious, for basically the missionary's message is a call to conversion, and conversion implies a change both in a man's value system and in the patterns of his overt behavior.

The commonly professed ideal for socialization as Christians is a conversion experience that so transforms the individual's inner nature that the convert henceforth under the guidance of the Spirit of God fulfills all the behavioral standards laid down in the Word of God. In actual experience, however, converts in every society, including our own, usually need a context which will help them actualize the Christian ideals they profess. Such expressions as "to grow in grace," "to gain victory over evil habits," and "to learn to demonstrate the fruits of the Spirit" indicate the need for Christian socialization even beyond conversion.

If we accept the fact that converts will need further growth or resocialization, we must also face such

questions as: Who is to effect this resocialization? What context will be most propitious for converts in internalizing these new values and behavior patterns? What will keep them from deviating or "backsliding"? Usually the "Pauls" feel very responsible for their "Timothies;" but if the examples cited in the previous paper teach us anything, it is that the outside socializing agency — missionary, mission society, international church organization, or alien (even national) government—has all the odds stacked against it. However, if the missionary is not supposed to "teach them to keep all things," who finally is?

It is the thesis of this paper that both the socialization of converts and the general control of church member behavior are the domain of the indigenous church. Mission history, however, shows that more frequently than not, expatriates have actually occupied the role of socializing agent. In order to demonstrate why the indigenous church rather than the missionary should be the socializing agency, we will review the essential conditions of socialization and social control, and try to point out the relative merits of the indigenous church versus the foreign missionary in these functions.

Before we can effectively compare

1 Jacob A. Loewen, "Socialization and Social Control: A Resume of Processes," PA, Vol. 15, No. 4 (July-Aug. 1968), pp. 145 - 156.

223

these two agencies of socialization, however, it will be necessary to look at the manner in which the indigenous church came into existence—through a group movement or through individual conversion — for these different means of development have far-reaching implications for the church's capacity for socialization and social control.

Group movement or individual conversion

In face-to-face societies where group decision is the normal pattern, we are most likely to find group conversion and the establishment of a church through a group movement. A group movement means that the tribe as a whole or some major segment of it decides to abandon certain old ways and to adopt new Christian ways. In such a setting "Christian" socialization will continue through the same agents and by means of the same mechanisms as all earlier tribal socialization. In other words, the enculturative mechanisms of the society will have remained relatively undisturbed; only some of the norms and the expectations will have been changed.

Under such circumstances any changes introduced by socializing agents will find relatively universal acceptance. In fact, the involvement of the whole group will mean that the convert may not even be exposed to conflicting reference groups. Thus, when the Manus Islanders under Paliau's leadership decided to get rid of the Sir ghosts — something all former missionary effort had failed to achieve—the whole group marched to the seaside and threw the skulls into

the deep. The change was universal and complete; but it was not executed until the entire group had reached agreement on the course of action. Under group conditions the discontinuity between the old and the new will be relatively painless because everybody is in the same boat. In fact, if any social disapproval is expressed, it will be directed toward those who might want to persist in the old ways that have been rejected.

The situation is notably different in the case of individual conversion. The individual convert usually has to step out of his normal socializing context. Even if there already is a functioning church which can provide a new social context, there frequently is marked discontinuity between the old and the new; and as pointed out earlier, discontinuity usually engenders insecurity. The earliest converts of a mission program are often completely deprived of any indigenous socializing contexts because years may pass before the converts are organized into a functioning church. This really means that during the time when they most need social support, converts are deprived of it.

Possibly it is because missionaries have sensed the lone convert's need for a socializing agent and a supporting context that they have so readily yielded to the temptation to fill these needs. However, in many missions analagous situations have continued to persist even after a church has been organized—converts must pass long periods of proving themselves before they are permitted to join the church. This means that the neophytes learn to see the church not as a source of socialization nor as a supporting context for change, but rather as an elite tribunal to judge the quality of their behavior. They will be permitted to join "the elect" only when they have reached the required stage of "perfection."

Moreover, even the organized church does not always assure new converts the badly needed context of social support for mastering the expectations of their newly found faith. If the church consists of a group of "individually" converted persons, it may have failed to establish the "community" necessary to function as a socializing context. This danger is especially acute in cases where the organizational structure of the church is foreign in model and origin. Such a church is merely a collection of individuals held together by an alien structure and is seldom able to provide the support or social pressure necessary to help the new convert overcome the pull of conflicting reference groups. If the church group is also small, the pull of the unbelieving majority will be a constant source of temptation for the lone, if not lonely, convert.

Is it then possible for a minority group to function successfully as a reference group and as a socializing agency? The answer is *yes*. Teenage gangs in North American society show that one can become socialized according to the expectations of a minority even when the standards of that group are in direct conflict with the values of the majority. In fact, the very disapproval of the majority may be viewed as a favorable sign of one's belonging to the exclusive group.

Similar evidence can be drawn from prison communities. Ostensibly, law breakers are isolated from society for purposes of rehabilitation; but often their incarceration merely confirms them in the expectations of the criminal minority. Usually, the elite in the prison community are not those who cooperate with the guards and the rehabilitating agents—who are really members of the outside society—but the "toughs" who defy prison authority and bait and harrass the guards. A contributing factor, of course, is the social distance that authorities enforce between the staff and the inmates. This distance seems necessary to prevent laxness on the part of the staff, but it often also helps push the lonely inmate to seek belonging in the anti-society in-group of confirmed convicts.[2]

The above examples call attention to the fact that where a small group of believers establishes community within the larger society, rebellion against the majority and its values can become a common motivation. Benson Saler has already highlighted rebellion as a motive for conversion,[3] but we must add that it hardly is a commendable one. If we look at "rebel converts" from the point of view of establishing a socializing context, we have to admit that such a group seldom is able to establish an ongoing socializing organism.

[2] The missionary, too, is separated from the indigenous convert by social distance which can seriously limit his influence.

[3] Benson Saler, "Religious Conversion and Self-Aggrandizement: A Guatemalan Case," PA, Vol. 12, No. 3 (May-June 1965), pp. 107-114.

In fairness we need to underscore the fact that group conversion is not "all good," nor is individual conversion "all wrong," for socialization purposes. Group conversion, because it does not involve a choice between alternatives for all the individuals concerned—many just conform to the majority—can often result in only very shallow penetration of Christian values and behavior. Seldom, except for some of the prophet-leaders, does one find group conversion leading directly to the autonomous stage of socialization.

By contrast, individual conversion always involves a choice between alternatives—the person can remain with the status quo or he can step out in favor of new principles he sees as right. If the experience of the individually converted involves a rather comprehensive range of alternatives, and if he has the inner resources to stand against the majority group pressures, then individual decision can produce highly motivated Christians.[4]

People who can actually function all by themselves, however, are few, and most converts have difficulty in standing alone against a majority group, even when they are convinced of the rightness of their own principles. Insecure converts are often in real danger of developing a double standard of behavior—one while under the missionary's observation and another when away from him. Such an ambivalent commitment to Christianity

will not only cheapen the gospel in the eyes of the convert and in the eyes of the community at large, but it will almost always also cheapen the convert in his own eyes. There is little doubt that the average convert will need both a Christian context and Christian socializing agents to help him "put away" those values and behavior patterns which are not in accordance with his professed faith, and to teach him to "put on the whole armor of God."

Socializing agent: indigenous or expatriate ?

On the basis of the principles reviewed in the previous paper we can now postulate the conditions required for proper socialization and effective control of converts within the indigenous church. Under each of the stated conditions the relative merits of the above sources of socialization will be compared.

Adequate socialization requires clearly and consistently defined expectations. It has been pointed out frequently already that the expatriate does not bring a pure gospel—his message always comes imbedded in his own culture and is accompanied by the behavioral expectations of that culture.[5] In fact, it is most difficult even for the best of expatriates to avoid projecting his own cultural expectations upon the indigenous scene. Such foreign expectations, however meaningful to the missionary, will usually be only partially understood by the converts, and often they will be conspicuously

---

[4] For an example of such an individual conversion under difficult circumstances, see C. H. Hwang, "Conversion in the Perspective of Three Generations," *The Ecumenical Review*, Vol. 19, No. 3 (July 1967), pp. 285-290.

[5] James A. Scherer, *Missionary Go Home: A Re-appraisal of the Christian World Mission.* (Englewood Cliffs: Prentice Hall, Inc., 1964), p. 158.

inconsistent with the general orientation of the convert's culture. Such incongruous values will be very difficult for the convert to internalize to the point of becoming autonomous. The expatriate needs to become aware not only of the danger of projecting his own values, but also of the inevitable limitations of his identification with the culture in which he is trying to minister. He will have to accept the fact that these limitations will prevent him from ever fully participating in the national's feelings of congruity and incongruity of expectations.

For example, when a missionary insisted that the polyandrous relationship of a Shiriana woman with two husbands be broken up and that the younger of the two husbands find himself a different wife, he introduced expectations that were incongruent with the convert's culture as a whole. When the young man left the woman, he was operating in accordance with the new expectations; but when he organized a war party and killed several members of another band in order to appropriate a wife for himself, he had shifted back to indigenous expectations and a pre-Christian pattern of behavior.

If, however, the indigenous church and its leaders define the new standards of behavior, such expectations should not only be congruent with the rest of the culture, but they should also meet felt needs in the society. The leaders of the Toba tribe in the Argentine Chaco had become seriously concerned about drunkenness and cattle stealing in which their people were engaging. When the Christian group movement swept the tribe, both of these behavior patterns were branded as sinful and as incongruent with their newly found faith. The new expectations brought the people not only release from personal guilt, but also eased the tension between the Toba and their Argentine neighbors, thus meeting a felt need of high priority.

For consistent socialization, expectations must be comprehensive, dealing with the whole man for all of life. Tribal culture is a comprehensive way of life, but very frequently, especially as a result of individual conversion, converts decide to turn their back on the "tribal way" and become "civilized" Christians. However, missionary preaching will seldom present a comprehensive whole; in fact, it is usually highly focused on the soul and on the hereafter. No convert can appropriate the whole of the missionary's way of life; for this reason the disconnected expectations upon which the missionary insists will leave the converts with many voids which they must fill with patterns drawn from the old life. The result will be a patchwork of inconsistencies. Serious conflicts frequently arise as a result of overlap in such a patched-up way of life.

Such incongruency often results from missionary medical practices. Since Western medical practice is almost completely materially oriented, it disregards the spiritual aspects of disease which preoccupy most of the animistic tribal societies. These tribal societies usually do not resist our materially oriented medicine, but it leaves them without a "cure" for the spiritual aspects of disease. When a group of Lengua found that their children had developed whooping cough, they hurried to the missionary doctor for medicine. The doctor had to inform them that he could prevent whooping cough with an appropriate vaccination, but he could not cure it once the children had caught it. This admission of limitation on the part of the doctor opened the flood-gates of repressed fear of spirit-caused disease. Many Christians were severely tempted to get shamanistic help for their coughing children. In fact, the rapid revival of shamanism that has accompanied independence in many African countries renders testimony to the limitation which Africans have felt in Western medicine.[6]

New role expectations need to be properly integrated into the culture's system of priorities if serious conflict is to be prevented. Conversion to Christianity often introduces drastic changes in a person's role set. When the new Christian behavior patterns are not adequately integrated into the indigenous system of priorities, the convert is bound to experience serious difficulties. Consider the conflict of the believer in a hunting—and—gathering society who hears the church bells calling him to a service just as word arrives that a herd of wild pigs has been sighted near the village. Should he feed the soul or the stomach?.

Often the missionary, who is not dependent on hunting for his survival, has a hard time appreciating the convert's decision to hunt instead of coming to church. If, however, the indigenous church is in control, one can expect that there will be great flexibility, and frequently hunting—and—gathering may take precedence even over scheduled church services. We observed this in Panama when unbelievers began to harrass the Choco believers by turning loose their pigs into the latter's ripening rice fields. Local law permitted the Christians to kill the offending animals, but instead the Choco church suspended its services until after the rice harvest so that the people could protect their crops without antagonizing their neighbors.[7]

Another area in which expatriates have often introduced role conflict is leadership. Most societies have developed fairly fixed status sequences that culminate in leadership. The general mission practice of establishing Bible school-trained young men as leaders of the church often stands in direct conflict to the indigenous status sequence.

Thorough socialization will require sufficient time for and adequate support during the learning (rehearsal) of new behavior patterns. Few converts will be able to break with all the bad habits of their past instantaneously. Patient encouragement within the socializing context and support by the socializing agents can be crucial in the convert's mastery of the new expectations. The indigenous socializing sources usually tend

[6] J. W. C. Dougall, "African Separatist Churches," *The International Review of Missions*, Vol. 45, No. 7 (July 1956), p. 261.

[7] For more detail, see Jacob A. Loewen and F. Glenn Prunty, "Aureliano: Profile of a Prophet," PA, Vol. 13, No. 4 (July-Aug. 1966), p. 111.

to be quite permissive at the learning stage. We became aware of the contrast between expatriate and indigenous tolerance in our relationship with the Choco church in Panama. The expatriates became disturbed over the backsliding of believers who got drunk in the market town, but the indigenous leadership cautioned us: "You (expatriates) have never been victims of strong drink; but we have, and we recommend patience."

This need for adequate time and occasion for mastering the Christian behavioral ideals is not limited to converts in mission areas. I remember how discourage I used to become while trying to help Christian college students in the States gain victory over long lists of problems they had confessed. Often within hours of confessing their problem inventory, they had already yielded to temptation again in one or other of the areas. It was necessary to learn that merely listening to the confession and praying for forgiveness was not enough—the counsellor had to help the person develop a context in which he could actually master his problems.

After many trials and errors we finally discovered a technique: Let the person make a list of all the problems he wants to overcome; and let him select the one problem that seems most urgent to him. Then begin to plot a strategy for victory with him. The person is not responsible for victory over the whole list, only for the one item under treatment. It came as quite a revelation that after we had won victory separately in two or three of the problem areas, the "socializee" suddenly announced: "I have victory over it all!" To inquiries about the sudden capacity for overcoming the whole list, the person confidently answered: "I had been to the altar for conversion and dedication so often without actually overcoming my problems, that I found it impossible to believe either in God's help or in my own worth. But now, after experiencing one victory after another, I have gained confidence to trust God for victory over all my known problems."

In the resume of principles it was pointed out that role rehearsal is greatly facilitated when readily visible models are available to the socializee. In the case of a child, the parents usually furnish the earliest models; and by analogy it would seem that the missionaries—the spiritual parents of the convert—should become the models. Without doubt this is what happens, at least to an extent, but it is rather sobering to realize that even as a model the missionary leaves something to be desired. More often than not, he is not a "good" example for imitation in role behavior.[8]

In contrast to the expatriate, indigenous models—Christian parents, older Christians, church leaders, etc. —will not only "fit" congruently into the culture, but will be unencumbered by detracting alien cultural foibles. Again, their full functional integration into the indigenous culture will provide them with both the "visibility"

8 The limitations highlighted here deal specifically with role bahavior and not with character. One would certainly hope that in character the missionary would be a model Christian worthy of emulation.

necessary for easy socializee identification and with a valuation positive enough to make their approval highly rewarding to the socializee.

Closely akin to the model is the reference group. We all measure our deprivation and gratification in terms of some group. In the believing community is a positively valued group, it will be able to supply the convert with extensive support; but if the church is made up of a collection of cultural marginals and rebels, their impact will be "scattered" and their reference value greatly weakened.

Socialization will be seriously hindered if the socializee does not have at his disposal adequate facilities for meeting the expectations. This principle is all too often forgotten by expatriates. For example, when missionaries insisted that Chulupi discontinue infanticide and practice marital fidelity, they created a double problem. In the first place, their hunting-and-gathering life could not provide them with sufficient food to feed the large family they now raised; and, secondly, the Chulupi cultural requirement, demanding that a mother dedicate herself for four or five years to building a soul in the child so that it would become a complete adult, was made impossible by new pregnancies. This has resulted in bitter frustrations which Chulupi Christian mothers have not been able to solve.

It is, of course, possible that an indigenous church introduce new expectations without prerequisite facilities, but it certainly is not very likely that they would be generally upheld for very long.

Social control will be greatly facilitated if adequate mechanisms for discharging tensions are available. No social system is perfect and tensions do arise, but when foreign expectations have been introduced into the cultural system, tensions usually are much more intense. Believers caught between their traditional expectations and those of the expatriate will often build up acute frustration. Since some tensions are almost inevitable, mechanisms for discharging them are of utmost importance, but tension-discharge facilities have seldom received adequate attention in mission programs.

Earlier we alluded to the new expectation for Chulupi men to be faithful to their wives during the lactation period. The tensions between husband and wife that arise out of this new behavior pattern are exceedingly severe. Missionaries have not been able to remove the cause, but since they have become aware of the problem, they at least have tried to provide a listening ear and a sympathetic heart to all Chulupi couples who develop difficulties. This opportunity to talk off some of their burdens has served to prevent many from going astray and leaving the church.[9]

In their pre-Christian days the Lengua of the Paraguayan Chaco, with their ideal of the peaceful innermost, had developed the mechanism of leaving the community whenever their innermost became greatly disturbed.

[9] For more detail see Jacob A. Loewen, "The Way to First Class: Revolution or Conversion?" PA, Vol. 12, No. 5 (Sept.-Oct. 1965), pp. 195-197.

They returned only after they had recovered their inner equilibrium, generally five or six months later.[10] Again, when wives were unfaithful to their husbands, the latter merely returned them to their families. Now, however, as Christians and as sedentary agriculturalists living in permanent villages, these earlier tension relieving mechanisms are no longer feasible. In response to the deeply felt need for tension release, the Christians initiated a kind of public "confession" in which a frustrated person brings into the open the behavior of his neighbor (wife or child) which is creating innermost conflict for him. The missionaries have seriously opposed this practice because it violates their criterion of confession—one may confess his own sins, but not his neighbor's.

In stratified societies with major class distinctions such as are seen in some areas of South America, lower class groups often try to alleviate their repressed frustrations in days of drinking, orgiastic festivities, or political riots. This raises a tantalizing question about whether the widespread response to Pentecostal type worship among the lower classes in South American cities is serving as one of these tension relieving mechanisms—the limitations of lower class existence are transcended, at least temporarily, through an intense religious experience.

Adequate control over deviance is prerequisite if high-level conformity is to be maintained. As pointed out

earlier, observability and subtle social pressures are two of the very important mechanisms of social control in face-to-face societies. Since everybody knows everything about everybody else, there is little privacy or even little concern for privacy. The expatriate socializing agent needs to realize that he can never have "enough eyes" to compete with the universal observation provided by the folk society. It is too easy to go behind his back to cheat.

Again, the missionary usually has had very little experience with the subtle social pressures of the folk context.[11] His experience and approach are usually much more directly coercive. Many Christians seem to operate on the philosophy that if you do it for the other person's good, you have the license to interfere in other people's affairs. When his interference encounters resistance, or when people try to escape it, the missionary is in danger of raising the pressure or of resorting to strong-arm methods like punitive discipline and excommunication. We need to remind ourselves that authoritarian methods are usually effective on a short-term basis only— they seldom lead to the quality of internalization that will help the person live up to the expectations when outside of the controlled setting.

One recent example of strong-arm indoctrination methods is the brainwashing of American soldiers by Chinese Communists during the Korean War. While Communists were

---

10 For more detail see Jacob A. Loewen, "Lengua Indians and their Innermost," PA, Vol. 13, No. 6, (Nov.-Dec. 1966) pp. 262-266.

11 The subtle pressure devices of folk societies include gossip, jokes, riddles, animal stories, and withdrawal. I was impressed in Africa with the clever animal stories that were used to put obnoxious people in their places.

able to socialize an unexpectedly high percentage of American soldiers under prison camp conditions, all but two or three have now forsaken the Communist gospel. The example of the effective social pressures of the Andean Quechua community on the rebel murderer cited at the beginning of the previous paper shows how much more subtle but more comprehensive and effective the gossip approach of folk society actually is. In fact, we can say that for folk societies in general, withdrawal from a person is the ultimate in sanction or punishment; and when this is done on a communal scale, individuals just collapse—they cannot stand alone.

Limitations of the indigenous church as a socializing agency

In spite of all the advantages that have been pointed out in the previous paragraphs, it is important to note that if the indigenous church assumes the function of socializing agent, the socialization of converts is subject to certain limitations.

First of all, we need to recognize that the indigenous church will teach and enforce only those values and behavior patterns which the group as a whole has accepted. This is one of the lessons missionaries to the Choco had to learn when the church was first organized. Choco leadership resisted adopting the catalogue of rules suggested by the missionary's church, and insisted on teaching only those things that were contained in the few Scripture portions that had been translated into their language. Leader Aureliano's reason is instructive:

I know that Imama (the author) knows many things he has not yet told me, but I don't want him to tell me any more now. In fact, I have not yet told the people many of the things which he already told me in Hillsboro, because the people must first learn to obey the things they already know. Indians are strange people. If they do not have it in their hearts to obey, just to command them is not enough. They go around the bend of the river where no one can see them and do it there. Next summer (referring to the next short-term summer program) maybe we will be ready to learn more.[12]

The slowness of new converts to conform to the "whole counsel of God" is frequently cited by missions as the reason for the long-time lapse between the profession of faith and baptism-church membership. But does such a delay and missionary socialization actually make "better" Christians? Lanternari insists that expatriate socializing agents have often been greatly deceived as to the degree to which their imported standards have actually been internalized. He reports that when German Lutheran missionaries in New Guinea were interned by the Australians during the last war, tribal religious practice at once sprang forth with amazing vitality, revealing that it had been clandestinely nurtured during the years of

---

[12] Jacob A. Loewen, "The Church Among the Choco of Panama," PA, Vol. 10, No. 3 (May-June 1963), p. 107; and "Field, Term, and Timing in Missionary Method," PA, Vol. 12, No. 1 (Jan.-Feb. 1965), p. 13.

missionary domination. The people themselves confessed: "If the missionaries asked us who made our crops grow we told them it was as they said—God, who lived above, made them come up. But we knew it was not God. It was the magic we had performed that made the yams grow big. Food does not come up on its own, and if we stopped these things we would have nothing. We hid them and knew our gardens would be well"[13]

Another of the limitations will be the persistence of many indigenous patterns of behavior which to the mind of the expatriate are not commensurate with Christian ideals. Examples of this are the dancing that occurs in Toba churches in the Argentine Chaco, and the total sharing of the Lengua Christians in the Paraguayan Chaco which prevents them from making much progress as sedentary agriculturalists. In our own experience we have noted the resistance of the Choco church to eliminate premarital sex as a legitimate means of finding satisfactory marriage partners.

Special limitations of the missionary as socializing agent

One of the most serious problems of the expatriate socializing agent is his personal involvement with the converts to be socialized. This generally results in overprotection. Because he wants to prevent the believer from being hurt by mistakes, he tries to shield him from sources

[13] Vittorio Lanternari, *The Religions of the Oppressed. A Study of Modern Messianic Cults* (New York: The New American Library, 1965.) p. 252.

of values that deviate from his interpretation of what is good for the convert. We need to point out, however, that while the mechanism of censorship has certain values in the initial socialization of a child, it generally is of very little value in the socialization of an adult, because for positive internalization of a given value, the adult socializee must be in a position to choose between alternatives. Only if he chooses in the face of other alternatives will it be possible for him to develop strong enough inner motivation to guide his behavior when he is alone in his own society's "world."

Some time ago a missionary friend of ours grew very unhappy with one of his fellow missionaries because the latter had permitted several of the former's converts to work for a farmer who had offered them some liquor. Even though the Indian Christians had internalized the value of abstention from liquor to the extent that they refused to drink, nevertheless the first missionary raked the second over the coals for permitting his converts to be exposed to such temptation.

The second problem is related to the social distance between the expatriate and the national. Whether we like it or not, such practices as furloughs, sending agencies, etc., keep the expatriate-national distinction and social distance between them alive. Because of this distance, missionary socialization is usually felt as unwarranted interference. An even more serious result of this distance is the temptation for the convert to manipulate the missionary for purposes of personal gain.

In the paper on principles of socialization it was pointed out that at the beginning stages the socializer has most of the advantage, but gradually the child-socializee gains certain bargaining power. Bredemeier and Stephenson point out that in the case of the spoiled child the socializee is actually able to control the socializer's action and attitudes without conforming to his expectations.[14] The missionary, likewise, is in danger of being manipulated by the converts and of becoming to the believing community what Pavlov is facetiously said to

have been to his dogs, one of whom is supposed to have said to a canine peer belonging to a different master: "I've got my man so trained that every time I ring the bell he feeds me."

If the ultimate goal of missionary effort is a church operating independently under the guidance of the Holy Spirit, then we must launch it in such a way that from the very beginning it will look to the Spirit of God rather than to the missionary or his sending church when seeking guidance in establishing the standards of Christian behavior for its membership. If Christ is permitted to be the "head" of the church He will not only nurture the "body," but help it develop to spiritual adulthood.

[14] Harry C. Bredemeir and Richard M. Stephenson, *The Analysis of Social Systems* (New York: Holt, Rinehart and Winston, Inc., 1962.) p. 65.

Socialization and Conversion in the Ongoing Church

"SURE, sure, I'm a church member, but what a laugh! I'm no more a Christian than this .... dog. Believe me, I've gone through all the motions. I prayed since before I could actually utter words, I memorized the catechism and recited the creed. In fact, as a kid I always lived like a Christian— of course, I had good reason to — if I didn't, my parents beat the hell out of me. Yeah! I was converted too. I must have been about eight or nine when some heap-big chief-scalp hunter preached fire and brimstone in our church. He upset my tender psyche and scared me to the altar. Big deal! I've gone through the whole ..... rigamarole, but it doesn't mean a ..... thing."[1]

Religion is first of all a response and a response is to something experienced. The religious response is a response to the ultimate and the sacred which are grasped as relevant to human life and its fundamental significance.... It is its constitutive element and out of it proceeds the process of the elaboration and standardization of religious institutions. Since such institutionalization involves the symbolic and organizational embodiment of the experience of the ultimate in less-than-ultimate forms and the concomitant embodiment of the sacred in profane structures, it involves in its very core a basic antinomy that gives rise to severe functional problems for the religious institution.... Moreover, since the religious experience is spontaneous and creative and since institutionalization means precisely reducing these unpredictable elements to established and routine forms, the dilemma is one of great significance for the religious movement....

In other words, religion both needs most and suffers most from institutionalization. The subtle, the unusual, the charismatic, the supra-empirical must be given expression in tangible, ordinary and empirical social forms....

...It is also characteristic of changes in the composition of the membership with the passing of the charismatic movement and the founding generation. The passing of the founding generation means that the religious body now contains people who have not had the original conversion

[1] An adapted version of a college student's statement made during a counselling session. During his years of teaching at a church-related college, the author heard other similar statements by disillusioned sons and daughters from Christian homes of various denominational backgrounds.

235

experience. Many are born members and their proportion increases with the years. The selection process which voluntary conversion represented often kept out of the organization precisely the kinds of persons who are now brought up within it.[2]

The preceding quotations—the first, the testimonial of a skeptic youth in his early twenties, and the second, an excerpt from an essay by an American scholar on the institutionalization of religion—both highlight the dilemma which forms the central concern of this paper: What happens to the succeeding generations in a church? Do they become "live" members of a "living" church? How? How many of them?

The approach will be to elucidate the issues and problems by: (1) defining some of the basic concerns of socialization and conversion, (2) presenting an analysis of a North American church illustrating the problem, (3) discussing some limited observations on the current practices of developing churches in various South American social settings, and (4) suggesting some important questions and considerations to missionaries and church leaders in regard to the socialization of succeeding generations in the church.

Christian Socialization

In the paper summarizing the principles of socialization and social control[3] it was pointed out that even though socialization is a continuous process throughout a person's life, it can for practical purposes be divided into two phases: initial socialization — the process by which a child is trained to function as a member of its social milieu—and later socialization, often called resocialization—the process by which the person's earlier socialization is modified to meet new requirements in his social setting. Both phases have immediate implications for the development of the indigenous church, the latter for adults converted to Christianity[4] and the former for the children raised in the homes of Christian parents. In this paper we are, of course, addressing ourselves primarily to the concerns of initial socialization, and specifically, as they apply to the children born into and raised in Christian homes.

One expects, of course, that Christian parents will socialize their children not according to their former pre-Christian patterns of behavior, but according to the ideals of their "new life in Christ." When we look at different evangelical churches from the point of view of how they add succeeding generations to the church, we find some striking differences.

Some churches see "Christian socialization" as a gradual process by which the child in the Christian home and church affirms for himself the

---

[2] Thomas F. O'Dea, "Five Dilemmas in the Institutionalization of Religion," *Journal for the Scientific Study of Religion*, Vol. I, (1961), pp. 31-33.

[3] Jacob A. Loewen, "Socialization and Social Control—A Resume of Processes," PA, Vol. 15, No. 4 (July-Aug. 1968), pp. 145-156.

[4] Jacob A. Loewen, "The Indigenous Church and Resocialization," PA, Vol. 15, No. 5 (Sept.-Oct. 1968), pp. 193-204.

premises upon which his parents and his church community are socializing him. These churches usually practise infant baptism and confirmation (or affirmation, as it is called in some circles). Under these circumstances infant baptism marks the parental commitment to train the child in the faith and to provide it with visible models of Christian commitment by means of their own life and behavior. Confirmation later provides the occasion for the socializee to affirm his personal acceptance of the beliefs, values, and patterns of behavior which his church and his family consider proper for a believer and member of the church.

Other churches — this includes not only many of the recognized denominations, but most of the so-called faith missions as well — affirm that a crisis conversion is the one and only means of becoming a member of a believers' church. The author's own branch of the Mennonite Church belongs to the conversion-emphasizing group. His own church experience has no doubt sensitized him to certain problems that this emphasis engenders; and in a certain sense his personal experience forms part of the motivation for writing this paper.

Initial Socialization

Social scientists stress the necessity of at least two preconditions to initial socialization: (1) the child must have the prerequisite biological and emotional inheritance (human nature) to make socialization possible;[5] and (2) there must be an ongoing society.[6] The latter condition is also most significant for "Christian socializa-

tion." Unless there is an "ongoing church" there can be no adequate Christian socialization. By an "ongoing church" we mean not only an institution that will persist over a period of time, but a church that has been able to establish the "community" necessary for socialization and social control to function.

Socialization, of course, begins within the family setting. Here the child learns the language, observes and participates in a variety of activities, and unconsciously absorbs the attitudes, values, and worldview of its parents.[7] The socializee's parents, older siblings, and family friends provide the early models for his socialization. The various social institutions in which the family participates will also play an important part. Once the child goes to school (or in societies stratified by age — once he enters the young people's society), however, the teacher and especially the socializee's peers will begin to play an increasingly important role in his socialization. Peer group influence usually loosens the child's dependence on his parents and permits him to develop his own per-

5 For "Christian socialization" the new nature resulting from new birth could likewise be considered a prerequisite without which the socialization (Christian growth) would be impossible.

6 Frederick Elkin, *The Child and Society: The Process of Socialization* (New York: Random House, 1960), p. 7.

7 R. F. Fortune, *Manus Religion* (Lincoln: University of Nebraska Press, 1934), pp. 1-8ff illustrates that tribal societies take belief and faith for granted and make no effort at inculcation. This appears to be a fairly universal tribal practice.

sonality in an atmosphere of equality, or at least near equality.

Even though the child's learning of these behavior patterns and the internalizing of the appropriate values and feelings is a continuing process, it is often convenient to think of it as involving a series of successive stages. The child learns and internalizes a part of the culture and establishes a temporary equilibrium at this level. Then new elements are introduced; this leads to new adjustments and possibly to new temporary equilibria.[8] In some societies the entrance into new adjustment cycles is marked by a transitional rite. The socializee is formally launched into the new phase.[9] In other societies no special stages or transitions are officially recognized.

This "successive-stages" approach certainly also has experiential validity for "Christian socialization." Most people looking back upon their Christian development can point to a number of stages[10] in which their commitment was deepened and extended. Even conversion-preaching groups find that a certain percentage of their membership cannot point to a definite time and a definite place of conversion, but rather to a series of affirmations matching their emotional and intellectual maturation. Thus Billy Graham points out that

his wife can remember no specific conversion date but rather a process of growth in the faith.[11]

The diachronic continuity of socialization can for all practical purposes be said to have begun even before the socializee's entrance into the social milieu, for in order to appreciate the present situation, he must also be made aware of the past in which this way of life developed. In fact, if he wants to be a "whole" person, he must affirm this past as also being his.[12]

We must underscore, however, that as the socializee grows older it will not be enough for him to be told by his superiors what things are permitted, prohibited, or demanded. Even the example of others is not always enough. In order for a person to internalize adequately certain patterns and values as normative for life and behavior, there must be a deep-seated conviction in both the socializer and the socializee that such behavioral demands are of ultimate and abiding value.[13] What is here stated as a general principle of culture, is usually true of Christian behavior. If the parent's commitment to the Christian faith is merely a useful profession which is not backed up by daily living,

---

[8] Jacob A. Loewen, "Lengua Festivals and Functional Substitutes," PA, Vol. 14, No. 1 (Jan.-Feb. 1967), pp. 15-36.

[9] Elkin, op. cit., p. 21.

[10] Such expressions as conversion, dedication, rededication, second work of grace, entire sanctification, etc., point to the recognition of stages in practical Christian experience.

[11] Billy Graham, "Conversion: A Personal Revolution," Ecumenical Review, Vol. XIX, No. 3, (July 1967), p. 279.

[12] Delbert Wiens, New Wineskins for Old Wine (Hillsboro: Mennonite Brethren Publishing House, 1965), p. 3. (Can be purchased from Mennonite Brethren Publishing House, Box L, Hillsboro, Kansas, 67063.)

[13] Erik H. Erikson, Childhood and Society (New York: W. W. Norton and Company, Inc., Second edition, 1963), pp. 249-250.

the children will be socialized not according to the professed "eternal values," but according to those values which actually are normative in their parents' lives.

The Dilemma of Conversion

As already stated earlier, for a large segment of the Christian church, conversion is the process by which a sinner and a member of the anti-God world becomes a child of God and thus a member of the church. This conversion (new birth) experience is usually viewed as a dramatic change in the values and behavior resulting from a transformation of heart and nature wrought in man by the Spirit of God. Allowance is made for progressive experiences such as Mrs. Graham's,[14] but progressive experiences without an initial or later validating crisis are definitely exceptions to the normal rule. In fact, the proponents of this position would insist that not even the most cataclysmic conversion can be viewed as terminal — the all-important crisic experience actually begins a life of sanctification. That is why the Scriptures urge the newly converted "to grow in grace," "to put off the old nature," etc.

Joining the church from without as a result of a personal crisis-encounter with God appears to work well as long as we are dealing with mature adults; however, when we look at children growing up in Christian homes, we are faced with some rather knotty problems. Once the parents guide their own lives according to the standards they consider Christian, they will not be content to be merely

models for their children to imitate, they will usually also try to discipline their children to live according to this Christian way. Speaking of such Christian training in the home, Delbert Wiens says:

Each child comes into the world believing himself to be the center of the universe, the sovereign lord of all that he surveys. The meaning of the training we give to a child is that we are removing him from such a total selfishness. We must civilize him, teaching him that we are all centers of the universe and that we must therefore respect each other's rights. The training in a Christian home goes even farther. It is designed to show the child that, finally, none of us are centers of the universe; only God can take that place.[15]

We can thus foresee that successful socialization in a Christian home will mean that children will learn "Christian" behavior quite apart from a conversion experience. This introduces the dilemma highlighted by the young skeptic's testimonial cited earlier. The basic premise of conversion theology is that every person by nature and behavior is outside of the church and can become a member of a believers' church only as a result of a crisic change in his life. Does this imply that a child raised "inside the church" must indulge in worldly behavior and be identified with the ungodly world before he can function as a member of the church? Let us first look at the experience of a North

---

14 Graham, *op. cit.*, p. 279.

15 Wiens, *op cit.*, p. 22.

American church which illustrates the dilemma that was synthesized by O'Dea and has been discussed in the preceding paragraphs.

The Mennonite Brethren Church

The following analysis of Christian socialization and conversion in the Mennonite Brethren Church has been largely drawn from a paper by Delbert Wiens entitled *New Wineskins for Old Wine.*[16]

Mennonite Brethren beginnings. In 1860 in South Russia a group of mature men whose average age was in the early thirties were converted. They had been living as nominal members of the Mennonite church when through the reading of God's Word they suddenly discovered that things were not right in their lives. As the awareness of their "lostness" grew, they developed a deep conviction of sin and an intense desire to be saved. Wiens describes a typical conversion experience as follows:

> For two weeks (three weeks, four weeks) I struggled with God. I could not eat or sleep. I felt that hell was swallowing me up. Then one day I could not stand in any longer. I stopped the horses and threw myself beside the plow and gave myself to God. Then, oh, the peace that came over me when my sins rolled away.[17]

Even though these men had been nominal members of the church, they suddenly saw themselves as outside God's family and as living in the

16 Wiens, *op. cit.*, 28 pp.
17 *Ibid.*, p. 4.

"world." Their continued study of God's Word convinced them that only through a radical change in their lives could they become a part of God's family. On the basis of their own experience they became convinced that the body of Christ is made up only of persons who have undergone such a personal transforming encounter with God. Since the existing Mennonite church contained many who had not undergone this experience, they decided to separate from the parent Mennonite church and to establish the Mennonite Brethren Church.

Even before their formal separation these converted adults began to meet together to study the Bible and to share their personal experiences with God. As they compared notes on these experiences they discovered that their highly individual conversions still contained many common elements. First of all, they had all felt lost, empty, and dissatisfied. Secondly, they had begun to seek for God, usually by reading the Bible; but as they read the Word, the awareness of their sin and guilt increased until they despaired of life. Thirdly, there came a violent struggle with self which often lasted for weeks. In the fourth place, after a long struggle they finally yielded to God. Then followed the fifth stage in which the peace of God flooded their hearts. Having thus identified the common elements of the individual conversion experiences, they now searched the Scriptures and found corroboration in its pages. As far as they were concerned, they had found *the way* to new life in Christ. Therefore they established this form of conversion as the cornerstone of Mennonite Brethren belief and preaching

During the first decades the church grew largely by more conversions from among the nominal members of the parent Mennonite body. This strengthened the conviction that all people must join the church from without. Since conversion was viewed as an adult experience, the children of believing homes were brought up in the general Mennonite pattern, and so they too joined the church from "without" when they became old enough.

The effects of closed and open communities. Before very long, however, exclusively Mennonite Brethren communities arose. Under these conditions it became necessary to develop a "controlled detour into the world" in order for the child raised in a Mennonite Brethren home to be able to join the church from without. This meant that in his middle teens a young man would furtively smoke behind the haystack or get drunk in a neighboring "wordly" village a few times until sufficient guilt had been built up for him to undergo a crisic conversion experience. For several generations—at least as long as the church people continued to live in communities closed off from the rest of the world—this "detour into the world" produced an effect very much like that of the conversion experience of the grandfathers. Then came the move to North America and the gradual but growing breakdown of Mennonite isolation.

In the first place, the contact with the general evangelical movement in America brought Sunday school into the Mennonite Brethren churches. Quite unintentionally it developed that adequate teaching in Sunday school could duplicate the very steps of conversion in younger children. A child of six could be taught to follow what looked like the same guilt-release sequence which his great-grandfather experienced at thirty-six. But as Wiens says:

We do not need to deny that this experience may be sincere. But it seems to me to be nonsense to assert that the experience at six has the same meaning that it had to another at thirty-six—even if the subjective form is similar... For the great-grandfather this had a quite specific meaning. He was a mature person with a formed character. But this was a self-centered, and therefore sinful, character. He had probably frequented the saloons, gambled, cheated in one way or another. Conversion meant a new way of life, a turning around. He ceased to live one kind of life and began another.

Our six-year-old also says he has been *converted*. But what does it mean to him? Basically he has affirmed, at whatever level is possible for him, that he has placed himself in the only way of life that he has ever really known. He also knows that he has sinned, that he has not always lived up to the expectations of our Mennonite Brethren-Christian way. And so the other meaning of his conversion and subsequent baptism is that his lapses have been forgiven. Unlike his great-grandfather, he has never really known a different way of life.[18]

However, the breakdown of isolation had another effect. Not all the young people could now be "socially controlled" to follow the detour back into the church. Some of them remained on the detour. Others even made a commitment and had a conversion experience, but, when they left the church community to work or study, they found that they lacked the inward controls to follow home-church behavior, and as a result they soon "lost" their original experience. But what may be still more telling is that even some of the staid adult members of the church were beginning to have some doubts about whether all the behavior patterns that were being taught as forming an integral part of the God-given package were really ultimate in meaning. And, as stated earlier, once the socializer begins to doubt the ultimate and abiding worth of his beliefs, it will be impossible for him to socialize the next generation convincingly.

The first centennial. By 1960, just one century after the founding of the church, it became apparent that all was not well. College students and people who had been members of the church for many years were questioning openly whether they had been basically changed when they were converted at the age of six, eight, or nine. Others, realizing the tremendous discrepancy between the

[18] *Ibid.*, p. 5.

ideal they professed and the actual level at which they lived, expressed severe disillusionment. Some were as cynical as the young man quoted earlier; others seemed to blame themselves in words like: "I guess my conversion experience just didn't grow." In an effort to bring about the change which they felt they had not achieved, many sincere young people had gone to the altar repeatedly, but without effect. One student cynically described the young people of her church as follows:

There's a set pattern for the high school graduates. The girls go to college for at least a year to catch a man if for no other purpose, while the boys with a career in mind go to college, and those without go to Denver. In either case, the girls end up in trouble and the boys end up with hangovers. I'm making a rash generalization for there are exceptions, but our church is rapidly deteriorating...I think our young people have been kept too caged up within a special environment. They are preached to for eighteen years, then released into a worldly society. With all the sudden freedom, they make a good attempt at drowning themselves. Some survive, some don't. They need to become acquainted with different social practices while they are growing up, not thrust into a strange society where they are asked to prove themselves. Remaining in the inner Mennonite circle, their faith is never questioned. Their religion grows stale and dies out of neglect and lack of practice. I believe it's a severe mistake for parents to protect their children from the world and its follies.[19]

Wiens goes on to show that for most third and fourth-generation Mennonite Brethren the conversion experience had been not so much a personal encounter with God that totally changed a man's value system, as an affirmation of dogma—the organized doctrines which the church had distilled from its earlier experiences. Thus Wiens continues:

By now it is clear that something is wrong with our actual practice. What we are more reluctant to admit is that something may also be wrong with our doctrine. We have abstracted from the experience of our grandfathers, an experience that was quite limited, however genuine it may have been. The problem for the grandfathers was to make it a highly visible, dramatic change of life. Of course, there was growth afterward. But the point of conversion itself was in the once-in-a-lifetime wrenching that guaranteed their new status. They had indeed placed themselves on a new road. They had turned around. They had been converted.

The pattern of their experience will repeat itself wherever adult pagans are confronted by the Gospel...

To apply the methods which are appropriate for adult pagans to half-formed children is to run the risk of doing them irreparable harm. To force them to repeat the patterns appropriate for adult pagans is to distort the genuine relationship with God that the child is experiencing. For I believe that God meets us in appropriate ways throughout our lives.[20]

Churches in Tribal Societies

The observations in this section are limited to churches in Latin America in which the author has had experience. They are also limited in their scope and deal only with individual situations. For this reason they should be taken as food for thought rather than as definitive statements of universal validity.

Because of the difference of social environment, however, it may be helpful to divide the churches into three types: those located in smaller tribes, those in the folk societies of the Andean Highlands and those in the various national societies. We look at the tribal societies first.

The Toba of the Argentine Chaco are a tribal society which became Christian through a group movement that began in the latter 1940's.[21] Even though more or less whole areas of the tribe were added to the believing community, only adults were actually baptized and considered members of the church. Thus for at least the first two decades of its life the Toba church *(Iglesia Evangélica*

19 *Ibid.*, p. 12.

20 *Ibid.*, p. 6.

21 William D. Reyburn, *The Toba Indians of the Argentine Chaco: An Interpretive Report* (Elkhart, Indiana: Mennonite Board of Missions and Charities, 1954).

Unida) seems to have followed the usual tribal pattern of socialization which makes no organized attempt to inculcate religion in its offspring.[22] Like other tribal societies, the Toba seem to assume that the children who have freely observed and who have participated at least in part in the religious experience of their parents, will become functioning members of the religion of their parents when they reach adult status. In fact, the very initiation into adulthood represents a personal affirmation of tribal religious values.

In pre-Christian times puberty rites were possibly the most dramatic religious and social experiences of Toba tribal life. It is not surprising therefore that teen-age conversion became the cultural substitute for the earlier puberty ceremony. The fact of this cultural substitution has already been mentioned previously,[23] but it warrants further description.

A typical Toba young people's group conversion can be described in the following paraphrased summary of a missionary observer's account: On Saturday night about 5:30 p.m. a large group of teen-age girls and boys from a village some distance away from M— came to the service. Before long they began dancing, at first timidly, but increasingly more violently. They continued to dance until they fainted away individually. The last member of the group did not faint until about 2:30 a.m. Sunday

morning. As soon as a young person fainted, older believers rushed to his side, rubbed his chest, shook him, and prayed over him. This continued until he regained consciousness. On Sunday morning at 6 a.m. the regular Sunday morning service began. All the youthful dancers of the previous night again came to the service. At prayer time they all went to the altar where they knelt in prayer for some time until they were "seized" by the Spirit and began to dance again.

The missionary witnessing these scenes reports that he was able to discuss the events with the Toba leaders that same Sunday afternoon. When he asked them whether he had observed correctly — all the young people who danced until they fainted the previous night had been "converted" in the morning — the elders assured him in the affirmative. When he asked whether this was good or bad, they emphatically stated: "It is very good." To his continued inquiry they explained that the young people were growing up and, since they had done wrong things, their hearts were filled with bad *gozo* (the Toba use the Spanish word *gozo* to describe the movement of the Holy Spirit, and in its negative sense it would mean the conviction of sin). When the young people danced on Saturday night, they danced until they fainted, and in this way they "died" to the bad *gozo* which was filling them. On Sunday morning they went to the altar to "give themselves to God" so that He could fill them with good *gozo*. The filling with good *gozo* was demonstrated by the seizure of the Spirit and the following ecstatic

---

[22] Fortune, *op. cit.*, pp. 5-6.

[23] Jacob A. Loewen, Albert Buckwalter, and James Kratz, "Shamanism, Illness and Power in Toba Church Life," PA, Vol. 12, No. 6 (Nov.-Dec. 1965), pp. 250-280.

dancing. After such a conversion experience the Toba young people are ready for baptism and full-fledged church membership.[24]

The Trios of Surinam. Missionaries working among the Trios report a similar teen-age transition-type conversion pattern. The Trio tribe numbering about four hundred has been "totally" evangelized. However, only adults have been baptized and are considered members of the church. Children participate freely in public meetings and observe all church functions including the disciplining of errant members by means of the ritual talk. (The ritual talk is highly stylized with the alleged culprit and the admonishing elder sitting somewhat apart and not looking at each other. They talk in turns using a ritual form of their language. Such ritual talk was formerly used in solving differences between hostile groups. It is today still used for bringing a person bad information such as the death of a relative.)

Like the Toba, the Trios appear to do very little about preparing their children to become members of the church. Apparently no effort is made to relate the children to the church until as young people they get sexually involved with members of their own age group. Usually the youth have their earliest sex experience with older females who, as it were, teach them the art of sexual cohabitation. The church makes no attempt to discipline either the young men—for whom this is seen as a necessary

step for becoming a mature male—nor the older woman, unless she begins to make a habit of seducing boys.[25] However, before long the young man begins to look for a girl his own age and becomes the object of church discipline which is basically designed to bring him into the church as a functioning adult believer. The admission of intimacy usually comes from the girl. As soon as it becomes public, the elders in turn deal with the young people, especially with the young man. They exhort him through ritual talk. Usually the young man resists for some time, but gradually he acknowledges his sin of having been intimate with the girl without the benefits of marriage. Such an exhortation by the elder usually takes several hours and may be repeated by other elders or by the same elder at intervals. Once the young man acknowledges his guilt, the emphasis shifts from urging confession to the deepening of his change of heart. The elders tell that they don't want him to admit his sin if his heart hasn't really changed. Only if he has really and truly changed his thinking, should he make a commitment to serve God and become a member of the church. In cases of doubt, the elders may recommend that a young man leave the community for several weeks to "clarify his thinking." After the elders are assured of a sincere change of heart in the young person, they announce this to the congregation and

---

[24] Personal communication from James Kratz, missionary to the Toba with the Mennonite Board of Missions and Charities.

[25] Recently one older woman had been known to initiate some ten boys in rapid succession. The church leaders reprimanded her publicly and suggested that no boys should carry firewood or water for her. This sanction brought immediate change in the woman's behavior.

the youth makes good his commitment by being baptized and becoming a member of the church.

Children of tribal believers. That the indigenous churches of tribal origin do not have any "native" feeling of obligation to inculcate the Christian faith in their children, was brought home to us in two separate incidents. In one case a Lengua and a Chulupi Indian were in our home in Lima for purposes of translation checking. As a part of our family devotions we all took a turn at telling about our conversion. When our children told about their childhood commitments, both the visiting Indians expressed surprise that even children could experience conversion.

The second event took place in Panama where our family spent some time in the home of Aureliano, the Choco pastor. Even though Aureliano had made no advance request, I warned our family that he would probably ask each one of them to say something during the Sunday service. When two of the children recounted their conversion experience and another told of an answer to prayer, Pastor Aureliano used the rest of the service to talk about children becoming Christians. He told the congregation that before this he had never thought about children making a commitment to Christ, but he realized now that the church would have to do something so that the children would also make decisions and become members of the church.

On the basis of these and other scattered observations it seems correct to assert that South American tribes have associated the conversion of succeeding generations with their transition from childhood to adulthood; and in a good number of cases like the Toba example, they have substituted conversion for the traditional puberty ceremony.

Churches in Folk Societies

The general attitude toward religious training in the folk societies of the Andean Highlands with which the author is acquainted is very similar to that of the tribal societies just discussed. Usually no conscious effort is made to indoctrinate the children. True, the parents may have their children baptized in their infancy, but often the social significance of the event outweighs its religious implications. This same attitude has been carried over into the indigenous evangelical church. Except where missionary effort has introduced Sunday school and the early appeal for commitment, these folk societies seem to expect that commitment to the church will follow automatically when the person reaches adulthood. When it doesn't take place, the older generation is often severely frustrated. It usually ascribes the failure to the influence of current social conditions.

For one area of southern Peru missionaries estimate that less than half of the children from the homes of believing parents actually join the church. Children leaving the rural folk communities for advanced education almost always are lost to the church for reasons similar to those to be discussed in the section under the national church. Those who do join the church seem to fall into two major categories: those who make a decision as teenagers, and those who are converted individually as mature adults. The latter often show little or no difference from new converts from nonevangelical homes. The former seem to be an example of peer group decision—a group of young people making a commitment to Christ together. Such decisions usually take place during a major church convention at which groups come forward to publicly express their commitment to the church. Such group action[26] may have its origin in several causes: the age groupings of earlier Inca times, the collective puberty ceremonies celebrated once a year under Inca rule,[27] or again, it may just be a matter of teen-age group decision. Generally speaking, the small percentage of children from Christian homes who join the church is felt to be one of the major reasons for slow growth of the church in the Andean Highlands.

Churches in National Societies

(The following observations in the evangelical church in South American national societies are not based on statistics, but rather on informal conversations with church leaders in various places. They should be taken as suggestive of trends rather than as an actual description of the situation.) At the national church level it again seems necessary to subdivide into at least three types of churches:

churches practising infant baptism and confirmation, churches preaching "adult" conversion and adult baptism, and churches of Pentecostal orientation.

Infant baptism and confirmation. This first type usually involves the denominational churches in urban centers, and in several instances of the author's observation, they also represent a somewhat higher stratum of society than the evangelical church at large. Such churches usually add to their church rolls a fair percentage of the children born into church homes. But very frequently the active participation in the church is weak, and the actual functioning membership tends to remain fairly small and relatively static. Often it seems that the most active and zealous individuals are not those who have grown up in the homes of the church members, but the new converts. Of course, there are some outstanding examples of leadership that have come from the second and third generation evangelical Christians, but these have been more exceptions than the rule.

Adult baptism. If we look at the segment of the national evangelical community which preaches conversion and adult baptism, we find severe complaints about the failure to bring the children from believers' homes into the church.[28] Two general factors are often cited by missionaries and church leaders as being the major causes of succeeding generation loss — social climbing and education. By

---

26 Julian H. Steward, *Handbook of South American Indians* (Washington: U.S. Government Printing Office, Smithsonian Institution Bureau of American Ethnology Bulletin 143, Vol. 5, 1949), p. 300.

27 *Ibid.*, Vol. 2, p. 283.

28 K. G. Case, *An Examination and Appraisal of the Work of the EUSA in Peru.* (An unpublished paper written in 1963 and duplicated in 1965.)

and large the evangelical community has had its origins in the humbler strata of national society, and conversion often serves as an inspiration and a new hope to improve one's social condition. In many of the larger cities the evangelical church is growing especially from the ranks of trades and professional people, thus producing a new middle class. (This middle class is not to be taken as synonymous with the middle class in North American society.) Because these people are usually living above the social level at which they feel secure, they tend to be quite reserved about witnessing. This lack of parental witness seems to speak very loudly to their children. Again, since rise in social class demands better education for the children, believing parents are doing their utmost to provide an education for them. Here the predominance of schools lined up with the state religion often becomes a problem. Very frequently severe pressure is applied on students from evangelical homes. (We saw this in the experience of the girl who works in our house and who attends a government night school. The teachers went out of their way to humiliate her before her class mates because of her evangelical faith.) As stated in the introduction, the school period is characterized by a loosening of parental ties and a strengthening of the peer group ties. Evangelical young people often find it hard to own their faith in the face of peer group ridicule. Especially girls in secondary education seem to go through school without as much as admitting their evangelical origin.

This, of course, means that they are often called to participate in activities that will produce guilt for them; thus having compromised their convictions over a long period of time, they find the "cost" of returning to the church too steep. Again, feeling the status rise that accompanies education, they are hesitant to identify with a church which is forever receiving new converts from those strata from which they are trying to dissociate themselves.

For practical purposes we could divide the churches in this group into those who have a strong Sunday school tradition with early calls for commitment, and those who have reservations about appealing to children to make a commitment. The former group often "immunizes" the children to the "call of God" by premature decisions. Unless special nurture [29] is provided, such child-converts tend to drop out of the church as teenagers and to conform to the majority society at school or at work. (It is interesting to note, however, that some of them will renew their commitment to the church as adults. Only long-range statistics could help us evaluate what effect these early appeals have in the long run.)

The second group usually has much less backsliding, but it also fails to reach a major portion of its youth

---

[29] Our four children all made early childhood decisions under circumstances beyond our control. We have found it necessary to nurture their experience by (1) frequent discussions of the experience, and (2) encouragement to include new "areas" as the growing child faced some previously unknown aspects of his unregenerate nature.

which becomes established in the life outside of the church. In general, missionaries teaching teen-age baptismal classes are often appalled at the lack of knowledge of Christian basics which children of believers exhibit.

A further percentage of junior teen commitments are invalidated at the time of marriage. Since religion for Latin America in general is largely a concern of women and priests, evangelical youths also easily forsake their church to please their wives-to-be of other faiths. The overall result is that many of the churches are growing mainly through the addition of adult converts. The children added to the church merely balance out with those who pass off the scene through death.

Pentecostal-type churches also preach adult conversion and baptism; but this group appears to be growing both through new converts and by adding a large percentage of the children from homes of believers. This is especially true where the church is not located in the lowest strata of urban society. In the case of converts from the very low levels of society, social climbing, mentioned earlier, often causes considerable falling away among the succeeding generations. The author has not had occasion to study in detail the reason for the larger number of children added to churches of Pentecostal origin, but it seems that the greater liberty for spontaneous, personal ecstatic expression of religious emotions communicates a paramessage of relevance to the growing generation, similar to that experienced by children in animistic tribal settings, who are confirmed believers by the time they are initiated into adulthood without having made a specific decision. Nor is it hard to understand that for many adults ecstatic experience is a meaningful mechanism to rise above the difficult mundane existence of lower-class urban life

Usually individuals and movements building heavily on emotions are also subject to greater entropy — cooling off. (The cultural revolution of Communist China is interesting in this respect. Mao Tse Tung seemingly felt that the new generation could not remain orthodox revolutionary without the personal experience of revolution. Thus the recent upheaval in China appears to have been a device to head off entropy — or revisionism, as it is known in Chinese jargon.) At least two factors seem to be operative in sustaining the Pentecostal momentum. One is personal involvement. Many people are able to share their ecstatic experience with others. This frequent involvement in passing on the ecstatic experience to others helps keep the personal experience alive. The other mechanism for forestalling entropy is schism. As the fire (or *calor* as it is called in Spanish) decreases in a group, the segment seeking to maintain the fervor splits from the parent body, thus enjoying a new spurt of life. Competition between the parent and the separated group can spur even the parent body to raise its spiritual temparature.

While it is true that the cases cited in this paper have been drawn from a rather limited area, it is hoped that the descriptions are realistic enough to suggest relevance to other areas. In order to stimulate further thought and concern, we add a series of leading questions. In fact, the author hopes that the questions will not only be pondered, but that they may lead to some serious investigation of the issues involved.

Questions

(1) Is it possible for an indigenous church to maintain a stable socialization structure and still practice crisis-conversion without sacrificing the spirit of the experience? Are process conversions like Mrs. Graham's inevitable in a stable system that is "Christian" in its orientation?

(2) Will it be possible for the home and the church to establish adequate socialization patterns in our day of rapid culture change? If so, what types of adjustment mechanisms will the social system need in order to retain relevance?

(3) Is it logically and practically obligatory for succeeding generations to live "outside" the church's standard of behavior in order to be able to be converted — "to turn from idols and to serve the true and living God?"

(4) Is the loss of the spirit and the retention of mere form inevitable in all great movements of change? Is this what prompted Mao Tse Tung to permit personal revolutionary experience for the "new" generation that had neither experienced nor seen the original Chinese revolution?

(5) Is standardization of doctrine and practice in the indigenous church desirable? Will a written statement of doctrine and practice impede adjustment to new situations? Tribal societies usually operate on oral law which is continually being adapted to new circumstances by common consent. Does this mean that orally transmitted principles are more adaptable than those transmitted in written form?

(6) What are the implications of increased contact between cultures for the younger generation? What kind of help can one give an indigenous tribal church to facilitate its intercourse with (and sometimes ultimate absorption into) the national church?

(7) Is the loss of succeeding generations in "social climbing" contexts inevitable? Is the disorientation of the younger generation due to the absence of relevant models? Or does their problem rest in the fact that they are caught between two cultures (or subcultures), experiencing the problems of both, but not participating adequately in the rewards of either?

(8) With increasing urbanization, will the church's role in socialization and social control increase or decrease? What implications does this have for the influence of the church in shaping behavior in the future?

(9) Closed societies such as the Toba, Trio, (or the Mennonite Brethren in the past) seem to develop patterns for achieving conformity in the next generation as long as they can continue to function in relative isolation. What kind of patterns will be necessary under conditions which do not permit isolation?

(10) Does the missionary have any responsibility in helping indigenous churches in tribal contexts to develop patterns for integrating the next generation into the church? What should one's attitude be toward the patterns developed by the Toba, Trio, etc.?

(11) Is Wiens correct in calling for a change in "theology" not only a change in practice for conversion-preaching churches like the Mennonite Brethren?

(12) If there are childhood conversions (and they can often not be avoided), what can the home and the church do to deepen and to extend the commitment so that it will eventually have the same transforming and motivating effect of a first-generation adult conversion?

The Church: Indigenous and Ecumenical

The words "indigenous" and "ecumenical" have become increasingly frequent in church writings during recent years. The word "indigenous," found almost exclusively in the context of missions and the development of younger churches, carries overtones of the local, the independent, the distinctive, the unique, and the separatist. The word "ecumenical," used most frequently but not exclusively so in connection with the older Western churches and denominations, emphasizes the broader, the more inclusive, the loss of distinctives (and often identity), and increasing cooperation and organizational mergers. It is readily evident that there is a difference in polarity in these two terms. Possibly for this reason some within the evangelical community have viewed these terms as being almost mutually exclusive. When the Holy Spirit can occupy a central position in the life of the church, there will be a balance in the expression of "indigenicity" and ecumenicity within the church. It will be difficult for the missionary and for the established church from which he comes to permit the spontaneous development of both the indigenous and ecumenical expressions in the national church because the missionary will reflect the patterns that have been developed in the experience of his own home church and in the parent denomination. Both the individual missionary and the sending institution will need to seek to develop special discernment and sensitivity to distinguish accepted tradition from direction by the Holy Spirit.

FIVE years ago when Choco Indian Aureliano made his early encounter with the Christian faith, he affirmed resolutely that he would never share this message with the people who lived on the other tributaries for they did not belong to his (extended) family. If we follow the rapid spread of the Christian message among the Choco, we find that it was not confined to Aureliano's family or even his tribesmen; it soon jumped tribal and racial boundaries.

Among the believers in the mother church at El Mamey there was an acculturated Waunana who lived among the Epera since his childhood and had married an Epera woman. This Waunana "foreigner" had an uncle among the Waunana who had immigrated from Colombia into Panama within the past three years. Now

252

the Epera church, using the acculturated Waunana as their excuse, took the latter to visit his uncle among the immigrant Indians. Then using this uncle as their sponsor within the tribe, they brought the good news to the Waunana. In two such visits over thirty were converted and baptized.

Meanwhile, Aureliano, who was then a sucessful banana farmer, had a Spanish-speaking Negro laborer. This man often stayed in Aureliano's house and so heard the gospel message. Before long he had accepted the Lord. His baptism sparked a feeling of responsibility toward the Spanish-speaking people of the area which has today culminated in the founding of a Spanish-speaking church in the village of Jaque, of whose membership some eighteen have been converted and baptized by the Indians from El Mamey church.

When I was able to witness these developments during my visit to the Jaque River in July of 1963, the concern of this paper was born.

On the Definition of "Indigenous"

In his paper discussing the churches in Latin America, Eugene A. Nida has ably demonstrated that the so-called indigenous church can take a variety of shapes. He classifies the churches he has observed into four categories: (1) the mission-directed church in which there is no pretense of being indigenous or of being under local leadership; (2) the national-front church, which is really mission-directed, but which has local persons as figurehead leaders; (3) the indigenized churches with varying degrees of mission leverage still in operation; and (4) the fully indigenous churches, concerning whom he makes the remark that very often they are "one spiritual generation removed" from missionary influence.[1]

In a recent paper Daniel J. Ebert sharpens the focus on indigenous versus indigenized churches by calling attention to several pertinent issues. By indigenous churches do we mean that every cluster of people shall become an isolated and distinct church island? Can a foreign missionary ever start a truly indigenous church? Ebert implies that truly indigenous churches are really splits from regular mission churches and sees the cause for such splits in missionary stereotypes which seemingly cannot permit the development of a really indigenous church.[2]

William A. Smalley had already shown that even a national pastor paid with national money is no sure sign of indigenous self-government. This pastor may have been trained in an entirely Western setting to perform a non-indigenous program based on principles and following practices that are intrinsically foreign. The converse can also be true. A missionary could be the pastor of a truly indigenous church. Nor do the presence of foreign funds preclude a church from being indigenous. The question is, are such foreign funds being used to manipulate and control the national church? Even an all-

---

[1] Eugene A. Nida, "The Indigenous Churches in Latin America," PA, Vol. 8, No. 2 (Mar.-Apr. 1961), pp. 99-105.

[2] Daniel J. Ebert III, "Establishing Indigenous Churches among Aboriginal People," PA, Vol. 10, No. 1 (Jan.-Feb. 1963), p. 35 ff.

native-funds church can be manipulated.[3] Smalley adds the extremely important but so sorely neglected feature that a truly indigenous church must have some normal, currently functional, and operating processes of enculturation as a part of church growth.[4]

James A. Scherer's rather penetrating criticism of the "three selfs" — self-supporting, self-governing, self-propagating — should be weighed. He feels that their contribution, when they were first introduced a hundred years ago, was to awaken the church to the 19th century fashion of missionary paternalism. For Scherer the three selfs define the relationship of the young church to the parent church, rather than their relationship to God. For this reason he terms them secondary or derivative qualities. To Scherer "any church any where, any time, that lives in obedience to Christ as Lord, keeps God's word and his sacraments, and preaches the gospel in the power of the Spirit, is an indigenous church." He feels that slavish obedience to the three selfs can actually amount to nothing more than ecclesiastical engineering. Where this happens, he says, we are "being dictated to by the world," where current fashion is replacing colonial paternalism with self-determination.[5]

---

[3] William A. Smalley, "Cultural Implications of an Indigenous Church," PA, Vol. 5, No. 2 (Mar.-Apr. 1958), p. 51.

[4] William A. Smalley, "Practical Problems, A Problem of Individual Sensitivity," PA, Vol. 5, No. 2 (Mar.-Apr. 1958), p. 85.

[5] James A. Scherer, "The Service of Theology to World Mission Today," Occasional Bulletin, Missionary Research Library, Vol. 14, No. 2 (Feb. 1963), pp. 1-11.

The Missionary's Place

The missionary's place in the indigenous church is not nearly as central as has often been assumed. While the past several decades have been marked by an increasing frequency of speaking about planting indigenous churches, we have all too frequently not seen a concomitant amount of doing in everyday missionary practice. As missionaries to the Choco we feel that we can today isolate at least five specific functions that we have been able to fulfill profitably in our relationship to the church among the Choco of Panama. These are: (1) to deliver a relevant message; (2) to discover the deep-felt needs, "the places where the Spirit is already at work," as a source of "native steam" for development and change; (3) to serve as a catalyst in such development and culture change; (4) to function as a source of alternatives;[6] and (5) to be a friend of the court. It becomes readily apparent that all of these functions place the missionary either marginal to the conflict or make him only temporarily necessary.

Many eloquent words have been spoken about the tremendous material and social sacrifice that is made by the missionary who leaves his homeland for foreign service. For me a recent statement, that the mission-

---

[6] Eugene A. Nida, who read a preliminary draft of this paper, correctly observes that the function as catalyst actually includes also the previously discussed function, the source of alternatives. However, since they emphasize two distinct aspects of catalytic function, they are treated as separate in this paper.

ary's sacrifice will not be leaving the homeland as much as a careful and even painful re-examining of his own cultural assumptions so that he and his message can be made intelligible to a people of a different culture, points to a far more essential kind of self-denial. If a missionary has developed an awareness of the dictates of his own culture and has been able to develop an appreciation for those of the target culture, solid foundations for identification have been laid. Let this be underscored: The purpose of this identification is not to provide the missionary with a feeling of at-homeness, but rather to create a setting for communication, or a communion, if you will, in which the missionary message can be shared as good news for the hearers. A relevant message will be one that will meet the specific and urgent needs of the culture.

In the Choco setting where social disintegration had lead to a cancerous multiplication of aggressive acts by individuals against their fellows, even a new missionary could soon sense the deep insecurities and the burden of guilt that violence, poison, and witchcraft were spawning. Good news from God should therefore include a "recipe" for the removal of personal and group guilt. It should provide an antidote for their paralyzing fear of the supernatural. And it should provide a basis on which it would be possible to re-establish community with one's tribal fellows. God's word contains all this and more. We feel that the witness to the Choco has shown that once the message was delivered in a relevant form, positive

individual and group responses followed almost immediately.[7]

However, we need to point out that mere relevance of the message alone does not always predicate that it is the very message of God. Because of the fear of the supernatural world, the prevalence of disease, the frequency of death, and the increase of the shaman activity among the Choco, physical healing had become a very central concern. One of the Choco groups became exposed to a distorted "faith healing" message. The excited heavy breathing of the healer was viewed as extraordinary soul power. No doubt this message had relevance, and nearly two thousand "decisions" were registered from January 1957 to August 1958. However, this message met only one aspect of the need in the Indians' lives. It left an imbalance that led to serious disillusionment and to a retreat into shamanism for most of the converts.

This points out the dimension that the truly relevant message speaks not only to an immediate need, but to a range of basic problems. As a true message from God it will provide a new or renewed reason to be for both individual and society. This becomes quite understandable if we accept (a) the theoretical position of Ruth Benedict's book[8] which stresses

7 Jacob A. Loewen, "Good News for the Waunana," PA, Vol. 8, No. 6 (Nov.-Dec. 1961), pp. 275-279; and "A Choco Indian in Hillsboro, Kansas," PA, Vol. 9, No. 3 (May-June 1962), pp. 129-133.

8 Ruth Benedict, Patterns of Culture (New York: Houghton Mifflin Co., 1934); also in paperback (New York: Mentor Books, The New American Library of World Literature, 1946).

that cultures are integrated around a central core of values and (b) that this pattern can be changed as seen in the practical example described by Margaret Mead.[9] She shows how a message relevant to a setting of cultural disintegration sparked an indigenous thrust that reintegrated and reoriented a total society but in a secular way. In the case of Manus, it included a deliverance from the fear of the *sir* ghosts that was paralyzing the whole tribe. Generally such a fundamental reorientation will be spearheaded by key individuals who serve as apostles of such a new way.[10] In the case of the Manus it was *Paliau*, and in the case of the Epera it has been Aureliano.

A Fountain of "Indigenous Steam"

This point is closely related to the issue of felt need and the search for an answer to it. Bishop Lesslie Newbigin makes a very pertinent appeal to missionaries when he testifies that he personally has learned that a missionary must listen, observe, and become sensitive to the moving of the Holy Spirit that has already begun in the individual, in the tribe, or both.[11]

This working of the Holy Spirit actually antedates the coming of the message. In each diffused and confused sense of need we must be alert for the work of the Spirit which is preparing readiness or receptivity for the good news. Once the relevant message has been delivered, the Spirit of God germinates the latent faith and faith leads to new life.

In connection with this new life the Holy Spirit often will occasion the reintegration around a new core or main spring for the life of the indigenous church. This will provide direction and thrust that will result in church growth. The deeply felt spiritual need met by the message of God can provide both impetus and direction for church growth and that without much foreign scaffolding.

Among the Choco of Panama the great satisfactions derived from the gospel have been the removal of fear of the spirit world[12] and the re-establishment of fellowship as manifested in the strengthened family,[13] lineage, and other group ties. This now finds practical demonstration in meaningful worship and fellowship, and in communal working bees on each others' farms; and a new sense of communication with and direction from God.[14]

---

[9] Margaret Mead, *New Lives for Old* (New York: William Morrow and Co., Inc., 1956); also in paperback (New York: Mentor Books, the New American Library of World Literature, 1961). See also Claude E. Stipe, review of *New Lives for Old*, PA, Vol. 5, Nos. 5 and 6 (Sept.-Dec. 1958), pp. 238-239.

[10] William A. Smalley, "Planting the Church in a Disintegrating Society," PA, Vol. 5, Nos. 5 and 6 (Sept.-Dec. 1958), p. 231.

[11] Lesslie Newbigin, "Bringing Our Missionary Methods Under the Word of God," *Occasional Bulletin, Missionary Research Library*, Vol. 13 (Nov. 1962), p. 7.

[12] William A. Smalley, "Planting the Church," op. cit., p. 233. See also Jacob A. Loewen, "The Choco and Their Spirit World," PA, Vol. 11, No. 3 (May-June 1964), pp. 97-104.

[13] William A. Smalley, "The Missionary and Culture Change," PA, Vol. 6, No. 4 (July-Aug. 1957), p. 233.

[14] When after three days of struggling, David Wirsche was able to explain the concept of zero to the Epera, Aureliano called the people together and thanked God that he had revealed this concept to them.

The Missionary a Source of Alternatives

This leads us to the third contribution of the missionary. The narrow ethnocentric cultural frame and very limited experience of a native people in certain areas may provide only very limited avenues for the working of the Holy Spirit. The missionary can thus serve as the source of alternatives.[15] By this we mean that his wider experience in church and church life and his observations of answers found by church groups in other places and in other cultures can provide a resource of alternatives. The actual choice, of course, will be made by the young church under the guidance of the Holy Spirit. Several Choco examples serve to illustrate this point. The first occurred in connection with the education of the believers' children.

As soon as the church was organized in 1961, the newly literate believers requested help to send some children to a Christian day school in Panama City. The missionaries did not believe that this was the answer but felt that they must cooperate and wait for readiness for other alternatives. They offered to match such funds as the parents and the church could raise for the purpose. Two children selected by the church were sent to school in Panama City. Money and other troubles abounded and so when the missionaries returned for the summer of 1962 there was obvious readiness to look for other answers. At this occasion the missionaries

faced the Choco group with a number of alternatives. The Choco could continue in the way they had begun. This would mean taking the children away from their parents for ten years until they finished secondary training before they could return to become teachers among their people. This led to the questions whether the children would still be Epera when they returned and whether they would still listen to and submit to the present leaders of the people and the church. Other alternatives were to hire a national teacher with mission and church funds; to ask the government to open a day school with non-Indian teachers; or to encourage the leading adults to study and acquire the necessary education to become the teachers of their own children, thereby retaining an enculturation vehicle even during the period of rapid culture change. It took only very little discussion for the Indians to realize the implications and Aureliano said, "I have never seen it that way before. We do not want detribalization and loss of adult authority that the first alternative offers. Nor do we want poor paternalistic non-Indian teachers (who would be the only ones willing to come to such primitive conditions). God is speaking. We 'oldsters' will just have to get busy and learn."

By this writing the first Choco church member has already completed his adult primary education and has been named teacher for grades one to three for the Indians on the Jaque River by the Ministry of Education in Panama.

Another example of serving as a source of alternatives came in regard

15 William A. Smalley, "Cultural Implications," op. cit., p. 58.

to service patterns. In the summer of 1961 David Wirsche, Glenn Prunty, and the author demonstrated a wide variety of approaches to prayer meetings, testimonies, discussions, etc., at informal evening gatherings, with the understanding that the Indians who led the official meetings would choose some of the patterns or would modify them until they could be used practically by the Choco church. At several occasions the missionaries were asked to perform certain aspects in official meetings, but these were always under the direction of Indian leadership.

A third example took place in connection with the communion service. While Aureliano was in the U.S. he partook of communion and in the course of translation of Mark and Acts the celebration of the communion was discussed in some detail. The missionary pointed out to him that churches differ in their practices as to whether they use fermented wine or unfermented grape juice. In 1961, preparing for the church dedication, the missionaries inquired whether the Indians had made any preparations for celebrating communion. Oh yes, they had decided that they would celebrate their first communion together with their church dedication. But how? At this point Aureliano reminded the missionary that churches differed as to their use of sweet or fermented grape juice. "Well," he said, "we have sugar cane juice, and that is just like grapes. You can press it and drink it sweet as *guarapo,* or you can let it stand and it will become fermented and turn to wine. Since all of us used to get drunk with fermented *guarapo* before, we have

decided it will be better for us to use unfermented juice for the communion service."

The purpose of the presentation of alternatives is not to dictate a pattern or even a choice among several avenues to the national church. It is rather to provide a multiplicity of possible ideas which in turn may stimulate or lead into still different possibilities under the guidance of the Spirit of God, who alone can lead the church to those insights and understanding that it needs to make the best choices for the indigenous situation.[16]

As Nida points out in a personal letter, a major value of the alternatives is the consciousness that the resulting action is really their own. Even where this decision is wrong or not the best, they have been learning in the process. All too often we as missionaries have been willing to allow the church to run independently — the way we have taught it to run.[17]

A Catalyst

The missionary can also serve as a catalyst — the agent that initiates the chain of action, but who, by the very inception of a national response, will already have become obsolete or at least marginal to the process. As T. Stanley Soltau said, the missionary's main thrust should be always to

[16] The need for this presentation-of-alternatives approach in terms of Scripture interpretation has already been stressed by Albert Buckwalter in "A Toba Analogy," PA, 1960 Supplement, p. 103.

[17] William A. Smalley, "Respect and Ethnocentrism," PA, Vol. 5, No. 4 (July-Aug. 1958), p. 194.

make himself unnecessary.[18] The function of a catalyst can often develop when the missionary, under the direction of the Holy Spirit, senses that the indigenous Christian or group of Christians faces a problem. He may then cautiously precipitate an airing of the matter.[19]

In the Choco church the missionaries precipitated a crisis. They gave so much money in the offering taken for the payment of lumber that they were sure there would be more than needed to cover the debt. This immediately led to the question, "What do we do? We have too much money. Shall we return it?" When the Choco leaders appealed to the missionaries, the latter became the source of alternatives. They underscored a number of possibilities. It could be returned, but to whom? Had the people not given it to God and his work? It could be used to finance outreach beyond the tribe, for any outreach involves expenses and maybe God was already answering before they had faced the need? Maybe this was money to make some further improvements in the church?

The ensuing discussion resulted in the decision that the money should be kept for outreach. But this decision immediately triggered another problem in which the missionaries again became the source of alternatives. Who should keep the money? The pastor? Inquiry about practices in other lands among other people led to a discussion of the diversity of gifts in the church. This led to the establishment of the office of treasurer apart from the ministry. The man chosen, however, did not have a suitcase with a lock. This problem was solved when the local merchant offered to let the man keep the money in his strong box.

The fifth contribution of the missionary has already been suggested by Nida. The missionary must continually serve as a friend of the court.[20] In the arena of cultural change that has begun through the coming of the gospel, the missionary is never to be a litigant. He remains an interested friend. All too often missionaries have stepped into the role of "center forward" and have begun to call the plays — generally, of course, along the lines of their previous experience or according to objectives that were laid down in advance.[21] But as soon as the missionary does this, he steps out of the role of the neutral friend of the court, who will be consulted, who can be counted on for sympathetic but neutral comment. If he dares to dictate, he disqualifies himself from further usefulness.

A negative example of such a situation occurred in the Choco setting when a missionary began to gather the believers out of their world of

---

18 T. Stanley Soltau, *Missions at Crossroads* (Grand Rapids: Baker Book House, 1959), p. 110.

19 John Beekman's campfireside questions and the resulting discussions are an excellent illustration of the missionary functioning as a catalyst. "Minimizing Religious Syncretism Among the Chols," PA, Vol. 6, No. 6 (Nov.-Dec. 1959), p. 245.

20 Eugene A Nida, *Message and Mission* (New York: Harper and Bros., 1960), p. 210.

21 Benjamin D. Paul, "Respect for Cultural Differences," PA, Vol. 7, No. 5 (Sept.-Oct. 1960), p. 210.

isolated houses along the river and began to build a Christian village in which he could shepherd them. The missionary residence, which also doubled as the church, was the hub of this Christian village. It has been painful to watch how a national, but not Indian, pastor has been waging a losing battle to create a Christian community. Instead of raising the moral standard of living, the village has become the occasion for license.

Traditionally, the Chocos live in houses scattered along the rivers. Courtship by young people is generally focused on premarital sex relations, but the limited contact between sexes, and the absence of privacy when contact takes place, serve as a strict check. Whenever a painted young man approaches a strange house that has an eligible daughter, the purpose of his visit is very apparent to all. The isolation of residence has in the past been a bulwark against promiscuity. But now, living in a village and going to a mixed school with girls and boys who were well within the Choco marrying age, a new pattern of promiscuity developed. The author, coming to the school building unnoticed, had occasion to overhear the making of trysts between the young men and the girls in the school classroom in the Indian language which the Spanish-speaking teacher did not understand. When this problem was finally opened in a discussion with the pastor of the church, the only solution that the latter could offer was a plan to erect a separate building surrounded by a high wall in which to intern all the girls that were within marrying age and thereby to protect them from the nightly visits by the young men. Shoul such a house be built, the missionary or the pastor at this point would become the hated policer of morals.

In discussing this with some of the village people, the observers quickly noted that the group was very seriously disgruntled about this decay of morals in their midst. On being asked about the many who had once belonged to the church and who were no longer attending, they said that these people had become unhappy and had left because they did not want their children to become morally contaminated by living in the village. Those that were living in the village and were putting up with the situation, said they were doing so only because the government was putting so much pressure on them to send their children to school. Thy thought that this evangelical school was a better school for their children, because in the regular government school Indians had to be in competition with the children of mestizos.

This position as friend of the court also carries with it another dimension. The indigenous group is bound to make some mistakes. The friend of the court will here be distinguished from the paternal lord in the attitude he takes toward these mistakes. The friend of the court can be counted upon for a sympathetic ear to hear the problem without any word of recrimination: "I told you so."

The Function of the Church in the Indigenous Setting

The following emphasis on the primacy of the local group is not meant to imply that there should be an absence of group or intergroup organization. The church is a body and it must function as such. It is to the church that certain prerogatives have been given. It is the church as a body that disciplines and it is the church that has the sacraments.

Certain evangelical missions have emphasized the meeting together in services, but have not been quick to establish churches. Services are good, but as Luis Chicaiza, an Ecuadorean evangelist, said, "The church needs power" — power to baptize, power to administer communion, and power to install its leaders. Until these are in the hands of national believers, the church is not equipped to function indigenously.

How highly this is prized by the Choco believers can be seen in the incident of training a leader for the new group of believers on the Chucunaque River reported under self-government. In the following paragraphs we present a few scenes from the Choco church in action.

First of all we look at its self-government. Being a folk society, there is no formal class distinction and little hereditary leadership. Most leaders are also shamans of sorts. Aureliano was a popular and up-and-coming young man before his conversion. His home was the scene of frequent drinking orgies; he himself was a real fighter when drunk. He had several women to his credit even as a young man, but gradually liquor drained off some of his success and he lost several of his wives. When finally his drinking became intolerable, his last and remaining wife urged

him to try the gospel. His conversion came in stages, but once he learned to read he progressed very rapidly. His trip to the United States and the insights it provided not only added certain stature but also lent greater depth to his words. His witness and his initiative in the church automatically prepared him for leadership. The manner of his installation was reported earlier in the story of the Choco church.[22]

The Choco awareness of the necessity of this power and leadership is apparent in the report on the latest evangelistic expedition of the Jaque River churches to the Chucunaque area, of which Aureliano reported on a tape recording: "I did not teach and preach any more during the last few days because I found a man who was a capable leader for the church. I spent the last three days teaching him how to baptize, how to administer communion, and how to lead the meetings, so that this church would be equipped with everything that it needs to grow. For how can a church grow if it doesn't have power?"

Equally interesting has been the observation on how the church has handled several knotty discipline problems. Liquor has been the great curse and the church has placed a strong emphasis on abstinence. In fact, several of the testimonies given by the Indians to the church witnessed to the fact that when they did drink after they had been converted, their insides just revolted and they had to vomit.

22 Jacob A. Loewen, "The Church Among the Choco of Panama," PA, Vol. 10, No. 3 (May-June 1963), pp. 97-108.

Again, one of the leaders at Lucas showed excessive tendency towards independence and so the group disciplined him for a number of months by not permitting him to lead in the services. Recently, however, we observed that he had been reinstated into his office in the church and was doing very effective work.

After the unsuccessful experiences in the earlier work in Colombia among the Choco Indians, where Indian children were taken to boarding school and trained to become later leaders of the church, the decision of the parents in Panama to learn and to become the teachers of their own children, was a source of real joy to the missionaries. This provided the church group with a firm parental leadership from the beginning and assured that the children would not as easily be trained to rebel against "ignorant" parents as is the case so often in missions. This point is crucial for both self-government and for self-propagation.

Self-Propagation

In the area of self-propagation we have been able to observe an interesting sequence of developments. On the very day of dedication the appeal by pastor Aureliano precipitated the volunteering of their first missionary. This missionary left the home base next morning and in less than ten months was able to invite his brethren from El Mamey to join in the dedication of a church at Lucas. Forty people had learned to read, others had been baptized, leaders had been trained, a building had been erected as a meeting house, and they were now ready to dedicate both house and leaders. They asked the missionary in the United States, "Shall we wait until you, the missionaries, return the coming summer?" The missionaries answered, "Since you have done the work and built the church, there is no need to wait for us." And so on May 10, 1962, the second Choco church was dedicated. During this same year several separate evangelistic excursions were undertaken by believers from the El Mamey church to witness on other rivers for shorter periods of time. In this way groups of believers have been formed on a number of the tributaries of the Jaque.

In the spring of 1963, upon the invitation of the New Tribes Mission, an evangelistic outreach had several interesting dimensions to it. For several years the missionaries in this area had been trying to reach the Choco Indians living there. They had literacy materials and Scripture portions at their disposal. And yet there had been little or no response among the Indians. Now they invited the believers from the Jaque churches to come and strengthen the witness. During the several weeks that the team of five Indians worked in this area they taught some fifty people to read, they baptized twenty-three individuals, and trained a leader for the group. The inviting missionary reported to the author by tape recording that he had asked these newly converted and baptized Indians, "Haven't we been telling you the same message as these Indians are giving to you now?" To this the Indians had answered, "Yes, I believe you did mention it."

When we look a little closer at how they began, we find that some Jaque believers had relatives in the Chucunaque area and these had again provided the group with local welcome and sponsorship. In fact, the normal channel for outreach within the Choco group has been the family. Relatives were contacted by other relatives. Each time a new area was visited an attempt was made to locate some kind of a relative as sponsor.[23] The interesting account of how they bridged the gap between the Epera group and the linguistically related Waunana who have migrated from Colombia to Panama in recent years has already been told at the beginning of this paper.

In regards to self-support of the church and the support of its workers, we have observed several interesting phenomena. First is the cultural pattern of hospitality which demands that every person who is received into the home will also be fed, even if the person is staying for several days. Persons staying longer generally pitch in and share in some of the urgent work or share in the hunting which supplies the meat. This has been one of the major sources of support for their first missionary. The people of the community he served simply fed him as long as he was with them.

A second factor became apparent when the sending church at El Mamey also shared in his support in that a working bee did some communal work on this missionary's farming plot. A third interesting item that we have noticed is the raising of communal crops for church purposes. Rice is the most frequent commodity. Cash offerings for support have been less frequent, but they have been observed on several occasions such as the retirement of the debt on lumber at the dedication of the El Mamey church mentioned earlier. At the local level all the workers of the church are self-supporting. They are lay people in the sense that they earn their living just like all the other members of the church.

Pre-eminence of the Holy Spirit

Even a superficial reading of the book of Acts — the early history of the church — will reveal the centrality of the Holy Spirit. The ascending Christ had said that power for the disciples' witness would come with the advent of the Spirit of God. And with the outpouring of the Spirit began the great Jewish conversion movement. Paul's sensitivity to the Holy Spirit is again and again pointed out in the story of his missionary journeys. Bishop Newbigin has well laid his finger on a place of need when he calls for more obedience to the Spirit of God on the part of missionaries. His plea for listening and listening long enough to discern the current movement of the Holy Spirit,[24] is one that all will need to heed carefully.

The warning by Claude Stipe deserves a hearing. There is no value for a missionary to teach the presence

23 Jacob A. Loewen, "Sponsorship: the Difference Between Good News and Propaganda," PA, Vol. 11, No. 5 (Sept.-Oct. 1964), pp. 193-203.

24 Lesslie Newbigin, op. cit., p. 7.

and ministry of the Holy Spirit if he overrules as much as one national decision made under the guidance of the Spirit.[25] I have stated my concern in this area in "The Choco and their Spirit World."[26] I feel very keenly that one of my greatest needs as a missionary is developing more sensitivity to the moving of the Spirit of God. One of the indelible experiences at El Mamey was in this connection.

As a missionary I had been overwhelmed by the success of a type of family devotions meeting — Bible story reading, asking of questions, praying for each other — which had taken hold in the house of the Indian pastor Aureliano. When the other missionaries, Prunty and Wirsche, left to begin a literacy campaign in a new area, the author decided to stay on and to teach this type of service in a number of key homes in the community.

One afternoon he went to another house and sparked such a service. Overwhelmed by success, he asked God for direction as to any improvements, but instead he became convinced that he was out of God's will and out of harmony with the moving of the Spirit, for he was doing the Indian pastor's work and was therefore stifling indigenous initiative. His confession next morning did not produce, "Oh, you must not feel that way, it wasn't as bad as all that," a comment of our Western politeness, but instead the humbling acknowledgement, "Now the Spirit of God is talking to him"!

Coming from an established church with a tradition and having studied the science of missions in school, the missionary, even with high indigenous ideals, runs another great risk. He will be tempted to transpose his own church or school answer in the form of a rule for living. This, as Dean Fredrickson and Dale Kietzman point out, will often amount to nothing less than making "the law an idol that displaces the Spirit of God."[27] For anything — even the rules or practices of a church — that stands between God and the church is an idol.

An illustration of this in the Choco experience can be found in the organization of the church. The missionaries were well aware that their church had a statement of faith and a roster of church requirements that were basic to church membership even for the indigenous church. The missionaries, however, felt led to deviate from the established practice which required promising to obey these rules and instead to have the nationals establish their own requirements. In order to clear this with mission authorities, a meeting was arranged between representatives of the mission board and the leaders of the Choco church in Panama City in 1961. To the missionaries' pleasant surprise the national leaders did not resent the questions from the mission but said, "We know that we are not complete. We know there are many parts of the word of God that aren't even in

---

[25] Claude E. Stipe, op. cit., p. 239.

[26] Jacob A. Loewen, "The Choco and their Spirit World," op. cit.

[27] Dean Fredrickson, "The Problem of Formalism and Missions," PA, Vol. 4, No. 6 (Nov.-Dec. 1957), pp. 220-223; and Dale Kietzman, "Conversion and Culture Change," PA, Vol. 5, Nos. 5 and 6 (Sept.-Dec. 1958), p. 206.

our language yet. But we are trying to obey those things which we know." When it came to the "dos and don'ts" the Indian said, "Our people are very queer. You tell them not to do a certain thing, but if they don't want to obey they just go around the bend of the river and there do what they please. How do you make people obey these rules in America?"

The meeting ended when the leader of the mission delegation agreed that it was of utmost importance for both the church in America and the church in Panama to remain obedient to the Spirit of God as he spoke through the word. The indigenous church owes obedience only to the word of God and to the Holy Spirit, not to the missionary or the organization he represents. Where a missionary or a mission precipitates change that is not the result of the Holy Spirit's work, a void will be created in the native culture. Many nativistic movements have been the results of such voids. Maybe Ebert's statement, that truly indigenous churches are splits, finds its roots in this type of hindrance to the working of the Holy Spirit.

Towards a Definition of "Ecumenical"

Ours is the day of ecumenism — an ecumenical spirit seems to be manifesting itself in all areas of Christendom — ecumenical conferences between major and formerly opposing camps of the Christian church and many mergers between denominations and churches with loss of many cherished identities. But as Smalley has well said, ecumenically united groups may still be at odds in spirit and non-united groups may often actually experience oneness.[28] For purpoes of this paper the emphasis in the definition of ecumenicity is going to be on unity of fellowship with much less concern about the organizational unity. This is not because I am opposed to mergers, or because I am not pained by the fragmentation of the church today, but because I have seen how organizational "unity" can be forced upon churches that could hardly be called indigenous, because the parent bodies in some foreign context were undergoing such an organizational experience.

If we want to look at the ecumenical experience of the church among the Choco we need first to look at the "human" geography of this group. The Choco of Panama, who call themselves Epera, generally live towards the headwaters of the rivers in the Darien area. Lower down these rivers are populated by Negroes and relatively white mestizos. Both of these groups speak mainly Spanish. More recently several hundred Waunana Indians have migrated from the area of the San Juan River in Colombia and have come to live in the Darien of Panama.

At first, when only a few individuals came, they were generally absorbed into some Epera family by marriage. Now, when whole groups of men and women have come, they have tended to segregate; both because they and the Epera are afraid of each other and also because they

---

[28] William A. Smalley, "A Case of Unity, If Not Ecumenicity," PA, Vol. 9, No. 4 (July-Aug. 1962), p. 185.

must communicate with each other via the Spanish language. Though their languages are related, they are mutually unintelligible.

The Spanish-speaking population of the non-Indian town of Jaque has undergone evangelism by a series of foreign missionaries and national converts of these. The major groups are the Foursquare Church, which still maintains a few believers in Jaque; the Church of God, which has left no type of group consciousness; the New Tribes Mission, which has had workers living in the town of Jaque but who were mainly interested in the Choco; and F. Glenn Prunty, now an independent missionary of Baptist background.

As a mission field, the Choco tribe in Panama has been divided between two major groups: the New Tribes Mission, now concentrated in the Yavisa area, and the Foursquare Mission, now concentrated in the Sambu-Sabalo area. The first major effort to study the Indian language resulted when the author, then with the Mennonite Brethren Mission in Colombia, came to Panama and worked together with Prunty of the New Tribes Mission and Johnson of the Foursquare Church. Since the Mennonite Brethren had to abandon their work with the Choco in Colombia in 1957, they have begun a program of assistance to the existing mission groups during the summer vacation months when the two Mennonite Brethren workers, Wirsche and Loewen, are free for some twelve weeks to work in Panama.[29] Beyond these groups there are a number of English-speaking churches in the Canal Zone which have taken a vital interest in the work among the Choco and have periodically visited and rendered assistance to the existing work.

Ecumenicity within the National Context

When we look at the account in the book of Acts we see how the Christian faith was at first narrowly interpreted as a Jewish prerogative. Only later were the Samaritans and the Gentiles drawn in. In fact God's Spirit records for us a very dramatic object lesson which came to Peter, who considered himself the apostle to the Jews, in order to prepare him for witnessing to the Gentile people at the house of Cornelius.[30]

The Choco situation offers some interesting parallels to this account in Acts. Five years ago, at the very beginning of his encounter with the Christian faith, Aureliano said that he would never teach the gospel to any of the people who lived on the other tributaries. He would only speak to people who lived in his immediate vicinity and who all were really members of his extended family. Today he stands as the leader of the movement of change among the Choco and a dynamic witness to other groups.

Aureliano's world view underwent some dramatic changes during his visit to the United States. The pertinent part here was the change in the area of meaning of the word

---

[29] Jacob A. Loewen, "Short-term Summer Programs Focus Attention on Time and Timing in Missions," to be published.

[30] Acts 10.

epera, 'people' or 'Indians.'[31] At first he assumed that all the people in the United States were Christians. It took at least two visits to Skid Row in Wichita before he comprehended something of the seamier side of life in our own society.

An interracial prayer meeting with several college students from other races made a very deep impression upon him. Each of the individuals prayed in his own national language, and yet all felt that there was a deep bond of kinship, a spiritual oneness. After this experience, he soliloquized, "Maybe fellow believers with whom one prays are really more *epera* to God's children than unbelievers of one's own racial background."

This enlargement of his view of people produced interesting results in his own homeland. For the dedication Sunday he had invited mestizo and Negro believers, that had been won to the Lord through his own witness since his return from the United States. At the whole service on dedication Sunday there was little Spanish except for the singing of hymns. After the communion service several of the visitors who were Christians were asked to give their testimonies, of course in Spanish.

Later came the diglot Scripture materials with Spanish on one side and Choco on the other. These early readers often read both sides rather than reading only the Indian and skipping the Spanish side. So when Spanish-speaking people entered their houses they were able to witness to them from the same book. This diglot book became one of the interesting foundations for their witness beyond their narrow ethnocentric limits; or we could say, for their ecumenical witness. Several of the non-Indian people who visited the dedication of the church in 1961 were so impressed that they invited the believers from the El Mamey church to share something of their Christian experience with others of their friends. Through this witness a number of additional believers among the Spanish-speaking people were won to the Lord and to date about nineteen of them have been baptized by the Indians, and a prosperous church has resulted in Jaque.[32]

So keenly has the Indians' sense of responsibility grown upon them in respect to witnessing beyond their narrow cultural confines, that when David Wirsche returned to Panama in 1962 the church requested that rather than teach them more in the Indian language, he should teach them more Spanish. They felt that they needed to know more Spanish to be able to witness more effectively to the Spanish people. Leader Aureliano said, "There are Spanish people coming to our services all the time and we must give them to eat."

That even the Epera community was divided by several deep-seated community rivalries was already apparent in Aureliano's early statement. From this standpoint it is interesting that the first Choco missionary went to one of the larger rival communities at Lucas. When the people at Lucas responded to the gospel, the believers at the El Mamey church, their former

---

31 Jacob A. Loewen, "A Choco Indian," op. cit., pp. 129-133.

32 This church in turn, via relatives, has started a church in Cuevita, Colombia.

rivals, then joined them in the dedication of the church, thus relieving some tensions of very long standing.

In 1961, after finishing the campaign at El Mamey and having moved from the Lucas situation where the first Choco missionary took over, Wirsche made an attempt to reach some of the immigrant Waunana for whom also a literacy course and Bible material had been prepared. The Waunana are old enemies of the Epera. There are large bodies of folktales describing the bloody encounters of the past. The lone Waunana living among the Epera usually lives in mortal fear. And so it was with the Indian who became Wirsche's first student. This Waunana had been employed by a Negro in the community, but was now unemployed. Wirsche encouraged him to join the reading campaign. However, this meant that by living near the missionary he also had to come into contact with the Epera, of whom he was afraid and who were also afraid of him. The missionary, serving as catalyst, tried to interpret the Waunana to the Epera and vice versa. Finally, after a prayer meeting, he was able to stimulate the Christian Epera to take the initiative to make a friendly approach to this fearful Waunana, and soon the Epera young men and the Waunana student were walking down the trail arm in arm, and one of the Epera remarked, "I never knew that the Waunana were so kind." This eventually led to the earlier mentioned evangelistic trips to the Waunana area, during which thirty-four individuals were baptized upon the confession of their faith.

On dedication Sunday at El Mamey, the North American missionaries delivered greetings to the believers at El Mamey from their respective home churches in the United States and Canada and from some of the other churches who were especially interested in the Choco church. Since Aureliano had visited some of these churches and knew the pastor or other people in the church by first name, this was a very moving experience for him; and he launched into a discourse to the church about the fact that the Indians were no longer alone in the world. "Why," he said, "we have brothers and sisters all around the world. Everywhere there are people who are walking with us on God's road."

Ecumenicity Among Mission and Church Groups

There was an attempt in 1958 to establish a cooperative missionary thrust between the Foursquare, Mennonite Brethren, and the New Tribes Missions in Panama. However, this paper agreement never materialized and instead the Mennonite Brethren workers have come to minister to the Choco as a people with the permission of the two missions who shared the control of the field. This has led to a number of interesting ecumenical ventures.

The earliest of these was the 1956 language research in which F. Glenn Prunty of the New Tribes Mission, Vinton Johnson of the Foursquare Mission, and the author from the Mennonite Brethren Mission jointly went to the Sambu area to begin study of the language. In 1959 during the testing of the Epera primers in the New Tribes area the Mennonite Brethren missionaries were also invited to visit the Foursquare area for a similar testing of materials. During the 1961 reading program, campaigns were held not only on the Jaque River, but also at the Foursquare Mission at Sabalo on the Sambu River, and at Chepo, the headquarters of the New Tribes Mission. In 1963 the Choco church was invited by the missionaries from the New Tribes field at Yavisa.

Such widespread cooperation has prevented the attaching of a denominational label on the Choco church and this in turn has permitted much wider cooperation by Christians from the Canal Zone. Thus the Balboa Union Church, the Margarita Union Church, the Corundu Protestant Church, the Christian Medical Association of the Canal Zone, and others have cooperated and have shared in building the church among the Choco. The Christian doctors have provided medical assistance. The church women provided typing help in the preparation of materials, Christmas bundles, and building supplies. One group supplied the roof for the school at El Mamey. Another group sent a representative to share in the dedication of the Lucas church.

In some ways the situation for the church among the Choco has been unique. The weakness, if not the complete absence of denominational emphasis, the long absences of the missionaries who were there only for several months of the year, and an awareness on the part of the missionaries that the brevity of their stay demanded utmost sensitivity so as not to disobey, to hinder, or to quench the Holy Spirit, have worked together to create a favorable climate. It has encouraged the development of indigenous expressions of their faith and the free association with other linguistic, cultural, and church groups, culminating in their current rather ecumenical outlook and practice.

From Tribal Society
to National Church

"For sheer and pervasive fervor, the love of nationhood has no equal among contemporary political passions. Independence is the fetish, fad, and totem of our times. Everybody who can muster a quorum in a colony wants Freedom Now—and such is the temper of the age that they can usually have it. Roughly one third of the world, some one billion people, have run up their own flags in the great dismantlement of empires since World War II, creating sixty new nations over the face of the earth. In the process they have also created, for themselves and for the world, a congeries of unstable and uneasy entities that are usually kept alive only by economic aid and stand constantly on the verge of erupting into turmoil. Nationhood is not an easy art to master as Ghana, Nigeria, and Indonesia have painfully learned in recent weeks."[1]

THIS "contemporary political passion" has also influenced the work of Christian missions in a variety of ways. The newly independent nations have often reacted against the "foreignness" of missions and have seriously curtailed their work. Such impediments have ranged from mere difficulties of paperwork in connection with entry and exit of missionary personnel to out-right confiscation of schools and the expulsion of the organization.

The national churches, too, have not escaped infection with the "bug of independence." Sometimes national believers were merely carried away with the enthusiasm of political self-determination which had permeated the whole nation. Not wanting to

be labelled anti-patriotic, they had to give evidence of anti-foreign sentiment. At times, however, such anti-missionary feelings went far deeper than momentary enthusiasm for national autonomy. In Latin American countries which have enjoyed independence for many decades, the feelings against missionaries have been equally strong. In fact, in several cases national church leaders have pressed for the complete withdrawal of all missionary personnel, because they felt that in one way or another their presence inhibited the national church in its indigenous development.

Even missions and missionaries have not escaped this "contemporary passion." For several decades now all missions considered up-to-date have lifted high the banner of the

1 "The Passions and Perils of Nationhood," *Time*, March 11, 1966, p. 26.

indigenous (self-governing, self-propagating, self-supporting) church. This raises some questions about whether missions merely "succumbed to the spirit of the times," or whether they were actually striking out courageously in a new direction under the Spirit's guidance.

It is worthwhile to note that the ideals of an indigenous church were first conceived of and implemented within the context of the peasant (folk) societies of Asia, noteably Korea and India. However, the "indigenous church" slogan soon became universal. Missions advocated it for all societies regardless of size or circumstance. It may also be worth noting that in the areas where indigenous church ideals first arose, they are now rapidly being overshadowed by concern for a world-wide brotherhood of believers. In smaller tribal societies, however, (at least in Latin America) the "gospel of the indigenous church" is still on the upswing in popularity. It needs to be underscored that in the latter case it is generally being advocated by the missionary and not by the Christians from the tribes.

The resulting situation raises a number of very serious questions for missionary policy: Is there danger that the term "indigenous church" is becoming a convenient umbrella for religious individualism and separatism? Do we really want every small linguistic or cultural group to become a religious "island?" How viable is the indigenous church in a small tribal society in the face of increased culture contact?

The purpose of this essay is not to question the validity of the indigenous church philosophy. The author is firmly convinced that "God is no respecter of language or culture, but in every cultural environment those who fear Him are acceptable to Him." On the other hand, however, the essay does want to suggest that missions and missionaries to smaller tribal societies[2] take a rather serious look at their responsibility and their program in the light of rapidly increasing culture contact. It is obvious that the cultural isolation of the past centuries is rapidly dissipating in the face of extensive national development programs and the rising expectations of minority societies everywhere. But along with this rapid social change, many societies have been unable to cope with the new circumstances and have collapsed, causing countless casualties.

As a member of the Mennonite Church which has undergone both the experience of cultural and religious isolation and the subsequent trauma of "modernization," the author has deep concern that missions not become partners in helping small, indigenous societies develop isolation[3] from the world of their day. Obviously missions and missionaries want to be part of the "answer" and not part of the "problem" for tribal societies. For this reason they must be prepared to rethink both their pro-

---

2 Paul R. Turner, "Part Societies," PA, Vol. 14, No. 3 (May-June 1967), pp. 110-113.

3 *Isolation* as used in this context is not a denial of *separation from the world*. In his prayer (John 17) Christ asked that the believers who were *in* the world should not be taken *from* the world, but rather that they be sent *into* the world as witnesses.

gram and their responsibility.

Culture contact with and the integration of smaller societies into the larger national whole is not only inevitable, but in many cases to be desired. For this reason missionaries need to be prepared to serve as bridgebuilders or mediators, or culture brokers between the societies in contact, especially in the case of the many smaller, animistic tribal groups now living under the national society "umbrellas." [4]

Tribal and National Church Relations

In order to understand the problems and the potentials of tribal-national rapprochement, we need to look honestly at the situation as it exists today. There are a limited number of examples of excellent cooperative relationships. One such example is the Presbyterian church in the market town of Ostuncalco, Guatemala, which consists of a handful of Spanish-speaking people and some four hundred Mam-speaking Indians. The Mam Indians spend the majority of their time in outlying communities in their own tribal chapels, but they are an official part of the church in the market town, and most of them attend the weekly services there when they make trips into town. [5]

An equally propitious situation exists in the Amuzgo country in Mexico with the local Presbyterian church. Even though the Amuzgos are still largely monolingual, those who do know Spanish attend the Presbyterian church whenever they are in town. Although not officially members of the church, they are received unofficially as full-fledged participants without discrimination. [6]

The Choco church on the Jaque River in Panama and the Spanish-speaking congregation in the village of Jaque at the mouth of the river by the same name, present an interesting example of what might be called a spiritual symbiotic relationship. [7] Many of the members of the Spanish-speaking national church have been led to faith in Christ and baptized by Choco believers. Thus when Choco believers come to the market town to sell their produce, or when nationals spend time on their upriver farms, they always attend each other's services as full-fledged participants. In the case of the Choco church which habitually conducts its services in its tribal language, the presence of Spanish monolinguals requires them to conduct at least part of the service in the national language. Likewise when Choco believers are present in the Jaque village church, they are usually called upon to share some

---

[4] Because of the author's limited experience, this essay will be illustrated largely with examples from Latin America. However the problem is not limited to that area, nor even to the smaller tribes. See David P. Ausubel, *Maori Youth: A Psychological Study of Cultural Deprivation.* (New York: Holt, Rinehart and Winston, Inc., 1965.)

[5] William L. Wonderly, "Indian Work and Church-Mission Integration," PA, Vol. 8, No. 5 (Sept-Oct. 1961), p. 194.

[6] William L. Wonderly in a personal communication.

[7] Anthropologists speak of a symbiotic relationship when two societies integrate their economic or social organization so as to become interdependent. The Congo Pygmies supply game and forest fruit to their Bantu neighbors, while the Bantu provide agricultural products to the nomadic Pygmies.

spiritual experience, and Choco church leaders are usually called on to deliver the message to the Spanish congregation. This interchange is possible, of course, because the Choco of that area are highly bilingual.

Eugene A. Nida has already called attention to the fact that the participation of tribal people in the services of national churches is greatest in churches of Pentecostal origin. He points out that in Pentecostal churches fellowship usually outweighs class distinction.[8] This, of course, is aided by the informal worship pattern and the emphasis on the Holy Spirit's guidance, which not only stimulate a personal religious experience but also have a levelling effect on the social differences within the church. Again, for tribal believers the intimate fellowship of the Pentecostal church often most closely duplicates the face-to-face fellowship of their tribal setting.

By and large, the situation is not nearly as fortuitous, however, and churches are separated from the tribal national church by a rather wide gulf. Even where there may be interest on the part of the tribal church to participate in national church life, there seldom is real encouragement because of the very evident orientation of superiority in the national church. In some cases, of course, this paternalism is a carry-over from the patron-peon relationships of the past.[9] In other situations this distance seems to arise merely from the strong class-consciousness which characterizes Latin American social organization.

That even the evangelical churches have not escaped such attitudes of social distinction is no secret. Dow F. Robinson has pointed out how mestizo pastors often speak lightly of Indian languages as "dialects" and of how they often ridicule tribal culture and indigenous ways of thinking as immature, if not childish. Any defense of their way of life on the part of the aborigines is viewed as evidence of the fact that they are wayward, stubborn "children." In fact, Robinson reports that mestizo pastors have even been known to forbid tribal preachers to conduct any services unless a pastor from the national church were present.[10]

However, if missions and missionaries will be honest, they will have to admit that they too have had a part in building this gap between tribal societies and the national church. In some cases this has resulted from the fact that the mission specialized in working with tribal societies and therefore it was both remote to and suspicious of the national society and national church. However, even denominational missions working with both national and tribal societies have often let separation between the two creep in. In our own earlier missionary experience, those of us working with the Waunana Indians found it necessary again and again to stress how different the requirements of that work were from

---

[8] Eugene A. Nida, "The Indigenous Churches of Latin America," PA, Vol. 8, No. 3 (May-June 1961), pp. 97-105.

[9] Wonderly, "Indian Work. . ." op. cit., p. 194.

[10] Dow F. Robinson, The Indian Church in a Sponsor-Oriented Society," PA, Vol. 9, No. 2 (Mar.-Apr. 1962), pp. 90-93.

those of the national church. This difference in requirements gradually led to an almost complete separation between the two areas of work.

Isolation[11] and the tribal church

The ideal missionary approach to any people, of course, will involve presenting the message in its own language and in terms of its own culture and values. One would hardly expect a people to heed a foreign message from God "who did not even speak their language."

Again, where there are a strong group identity and good communication channels (gossip channels in anthropological jargon) the Christianization of the whole tribe is usually more feasible and much more likely.[12] Cultural homogeneity and the face-to-face relationship usually are prerequisite to group conversion. However, Christianization by means of a group movement is by no means the perfect answer to the evangelization of a tribe.

For one thing, a really "indigenous" message may serve to reinforce existing tribal ethnocentrism. One need only consider the experience of Jewish Christians as recorded in Acts to see this phenomenon. Ethnocentrism mixed with the gospel very readily gives rise to the "chosen people" complex.

"Separation from the ungodly world" is always so easily confused with isolation from people who are different. Especially where the cultural and the church group boundaries are coterminous, there is danger that the culturally different out-group be equated with the ungodly. The in-group then will function as sort of a mutual admiration society.

A people's culture, furthermore, will of necessity limit their conception of the gospel; and unless there is adequate exchange with people from other "limited" views, a partial or warped view of the gospel may be propagated as the whole truth. Every group needs outside contact to serve as mirrors to make apparent the limitations and weaknesses of which the group itself is unaware.

A further problem relates to entropy. Anthony Wallace and Eugene A. Nida have already pointed out that group movements based on limited "information" (in the communication theory sense) will soon run out of "steam" unless more new information can be infused.[13]

For a large, heterogeneous group such "new" information often comes from other segments of the same linguistic or cultural group. For smaller tribal societies it must usually come from the outside. Obviously education is an ideal way of insuring both the introduction and the diffusion of new

---

[11] The North American Indian, in addition to social isolation, experiences the physical isolation of the reservations, which have not only become enclaves of acute poverty but also have robbed the Indian of his self-respect.

[12] The opposite can be equally true. A tribe can reject the gospel en masse. There are several societies in South America where after an initial favorable response, the whole group turned against the missionary and the gospel.

[13] Anthony F. C. Wallace, "Revitalization Movements, *American Anthropologist*, Vol. 58, pp. 264-281; also Eugene A. Nida, *Message and Mission* (New York: Harper and Brothers, Publishers, 1960), pp. 150-157.

information. However, here we need to recognize that limitations of both finances and personnel often greatly circumscribe the educational possibilities within the smaller tribe. The easier way, of course, is to send selected individuals across cultural boundaries into the larger, usually national church, environment to acquire the needed education.

However, as one African pointed out, when young Africans went through mission schools in trade languages and were finally ordained, they came back to their people not as members of the tribe but as "imitation Europeans." In other words, the person educated outside of his cultural environment very frequently is not able to find a meaningful niche in his own society when he returns.[14] It is the rare individual who is able to fit back into the tribal setting in a constructive way. Prophets of group movements are usually people who have been able to absorb information outside of their society and interpret it meaningfully to their own people. Paliau among the Manus Islanders and Aureliano among the Choco are good examples of this.

Another danger for small tribal groups of believers relates itself to the fact that it will be difficult for them to evaluate adequately new information that comes to them. As a result various types of sects and self-appointed prophets of heresy can cause serious havoc in young tribal churches. The Choco church in Panama recently underwent such an experience when an aberrant but highly evangelistic sect swept a number of the Choco churches into its fold. Even though the Choco have recovered their balance and rejected the aberrant teachings, their church is still suffering (after two years) from the effects of their original credulity. In some cases missionaries have tried to protect such societies from negative outside influences. This has seldom been successful. All too often people within the group rebel against such paternal protection and as a result reject the gospel itself.

Finally, there is the fact that the already small "islands" of tribal believers often broken up into even smaller units by separate denominations and mission societies. It is not uncommon in South America to have a tribe of three or four thousand people divided between three or four different denominations, often with little communication between them.[15] At a recent conference on missions to Canadian Indians, the Indian representatives present stressed denominational divisions as one of the biggest obstacles to the growth of the church among native peoples.

The barriers to integration

We need to remind ourselves that integrating smaller societies into the national society and national church is much easier said than done. The barriers that tend to impede such

---

[14] For a Bolivian example of a Bible school-trained leader who could not "fit" back into his cultural setting, see Monroe and Betty Jane Grams, "No More Lost Lorenzos," *The Pentecostal Evangel*, (July 19, 1967), pp. 16-17.

[15] For an appeal on the need for more interchurch statesmanship, see Ralph D. Winter, "The First Evangelical Indian Congress," PA, Vol. 9, No. 2 (Mar.-Apr. 1962), p. 89.

integration come from at least four sources.

The national church and society. Since the national societies of both North and South America in large part have their origin in Europe, they have the common heritage of the paternalistic and colonial attitudes which the European immigrants brought with them when they came to the new world. These earlier European attitudes have been slow in dying. They have generally given rise to the philosophy that the superior ought to "do good to the Indian." This "good," of course, was determined not by the tribal people in need, but by the national "superior." Speaking of this philosophy on the North American scene, James E. Officer says: "In order to remove the Indian youngsters from the influence of their families and tribal communities, the federal government placed them in boarding schools often located miles from their homes. Here they were subjected to rigid discipline and were prohibited the use of their tribal dress and tribal language."[16]

South America also has its history of forced assimilation and Christianization. Since the conquest was usually achieved only at the cost of a lot European blood, the conquerors often felt justified in using the conquered as a source of labor. This was abetted by the philosophy that the unbaptized Indian did not have a soul and therefore was considered to be on the level of the beast. Even

[16] James E. Officer, "The Role of the United States Government in Indian Acculturation and Assimilation," *Anuario Indigenista,* Vol. 25 (Dec. 1965), p. 77.

though the Spanish crown under church pressures abolished Indian slavery and substituted negro slavery instead, the *encomienda* system with *patron* and *peon* represented little or no improvement over the former slave status of the Indians. In Ecuador the remnants of the debt-servitude system are still extant.

The attitude of superiority on the part of nationals toward Indians is reflected in an interesting linguistic error which we frequently heard in Colombia. Instead of using the word *nacional* 'national' over against the word *indígena* 'Indian,' the rural nationals generally spoke of themselves as *racional* 'rational' over against Indian, thereby emphasizing the supposed savage and irrational qualities of the latter.

As the earlier quote from *Time* indicates, World War II marked the end of the colonial period for all practical purposes, but national independence has done little to change the attitude of national peoples toward the tribal societies found within their boundaries. The national evangelical church in Latin America by and large reflects the same attitude of class distinctions as the society at large. There are at least two factors that have kept the evangelical church from rising above these class distinctions.

In the first place, there is the strong heritage of class distinction in which all Latin Americans have been raised. There is little question about the fact that missionaries, too, have been and still are paternalistic, but very frequently local paternalism out-distances even the missionary variety.[17] Since the roots of the low-status evaluation of the tribal populations are spread through religion, politics, education, economics, etc., such attitudes will continue to present a very formidable barrier to Christian equality.

The second factor rests on the fact that while many of the members of the evangelical church in Latin America are converts from the humbler levels of society, in many cases the evangelical church has helped them to better their social condition. In fact, in the cities the growth of the church is often related to the growth of a new "middle" class. Since most of these converts are still quite insecure in their new higher status, they find it difficult to accept Indians as their equals. Often the presence of the Indian in the church functions is an unconscious assurance to the national believers that they are of higher status.

The tribal society. Barriers to integration also come from the tribal society itself and from its culture. Probably the foremost element is the linguistic barrier. As long as tribal peoples do not control the national language it will be very difficult for them to understand and appreciate the national culture. This linguistic barrier often outlives even cultural differences. In the Highland communities of South America there is, for the most part, very little cultural difference between people of Indian origin and the Latin or the person of mixed ancestry who considers himself a member of the national

culture. But even the person of part. Indian ancestry will emphasize the gulf that exists between him and the Indian; the feeling of "having arrived" is most often linked to mastery of the national language.[18]

Another strong cultural deterrant to the integration of the tribal society into national society is the strong group orientation which characterizes both the smaller face-to-face tribal societies and the larger folk societies. Even though the Quechua and Aymara of the Andean Highlands number many millions, there is very strong regional and community loyalty. In such closeknit social units self-definition is largely in terms of the group. Even decisions are hard for the individual to make. He always looks to the group for direction.

Where tribal individuals brave the "outside" world, they often receive severe psychic and cultural shock. Without the warm group context they feel lost, and in the face of social class distinctions they often feel deeply hurt. Thus even when students from the tribes receive scholarships from governments and other sources they often drop out of school and return to the security of the tribal environ-

---

17 Wonderly, "Indian Work..." op. cit., p. 197.

18 Allen R. Holmberg, "Changing Community Attitudes and Values in Peru: A Case Study in Guided Change," pp. 63-107; and Richard W. Patch, "Bolivia: U.S. Assistance in a Revolutionary Setting," pp. 108-176, in Richard N. Adams, and others, *Social Change in Latin America Today* (New York: Harper and Brothers, Publishers, 1960.) Both essays point out that since the "race" problem of South America rests not on skin color, but on language and culture, integration seems much more feasible, than in The United States, once the psychological barriers can be overcome.

ment. In fact, North American Indians have reported that drop-outs from the national educational system who have returned to the reserve are one of the major reservoirs of opposition to integration with the national society.

Another barrier to integration, especially within the context of the national church, comes from the nature of conversion in many tribal societies. Where people were swept into the church through a group movement that blanketed the whole tribe, individuals have often not learned to live in a heterogeneous society with more than one reference group. When such tribal converts move into a national society where the church is a minority group, they frequently become problem members because they are prone to use non-church models in learning new behavior. Again, where they were evangelized by individual conversion, their social climbing motivation often limits the depth of their religious experience and their commitment to the church remains tenuous.

Past experience. Probably the real problem lies not so much in the fact that the tribal and the national society have different cultures and different languages, but in the fact that the two have had bitter experiences with each other in the past. Such bad encounters usually leave deep-seated feelings on both sides.[19]

In the populous Highland areas where Indians have been near slaves for centuries, feelings against the nat-

ional society are often so deep-seated that periodic violence almost seems to be a necessity. An example of a spontaneous outburst of pent-up violence occurred in the three-day rampage in Bogotá in 1948 when the Liberal political leader Gaitán, who was of Indian origin, was killed. Indians burned and looted for three days. One wonders whether to a certain extent the atmosphere of readiness for revolution in Latin America does not stem from the pent-up bitterness of the oppressed tribal people.

Smaller tribes have likewise had their history of difficulty. The encounters of the Chulupi of the Paraguayan Chaco with Bolivian ranchers have been so traumatic in nature that even after thirty years of living in a different environment, the word "Bolivian" still raises the emotional temperature of every Chulupi male.

However, the majority society also has its grievances. Mennonite settlers in the Paraguayan Chaco experienced a number of deaths at the hands of the Moro (Ayoreo) Indians. Even though the number of settler deaths was small, the fear of the Indians and the attitudes toward them grew so strong that when in 1963 a group of Moros attempted to make peaceful contact with the settlers, the latter refused to have anything to do with the Indians. When the Indians refused to be discouraged by the settlers' impoliteness, the latter finally asked the army to haul the Indians away.

Believers, too, have had their "negative encounters." In one Mexican situation where Indian believers made tentative contact with one of the

---

[19] Ausubel, op. cit., pp. 96-109.

established denominational churches, the Indians were so angered by the domineering attitudes of the national believers that they withdrew completely from contact with the national church.

The missionary. The fourth obstacle to tribal-national church integration, sad to say, is often the missionary and his program. Especially in missions dedicated exclusively to tribal work, there is real danger that the missionary develop romantic attachment to the Indian and to his "primitive" way of life. This type of identification can easily become an obstacle.

In one area a nomadic tribe of several hundred accepted Christianity in a group movement and then established residence around the mission station. Today the missionary is the barrier between the Indians and the national society. The men of this tribe traditionally wore braids, but after some of them had contact with the outside world and saw that men wore cut hair, a number of the young men became interested in cutting their hair. The missionary intervened and in collusion with the tribal church leadership was able to forbid haircutting. The missionary is also imposing "exit restrictions" on people who want to leave the tribal area. Only those having "legitimate" business may leave the station. The fear on the part of the missionary may, of course, be well founded. Many of the Indians, because of their group conversion, have not internalized Christian values, and therefore will not be able to withstand the temptations of several reference groups in the divided society of civilization.

A second kind of missionary-based problem arises from the fact that the missionary is a foreigner to both the national and the tribal society. Since his work is often exclusively with the tribal society, he may master this language, but not the national language. Then, observing some of the national patron-peon abuses, the missionary readily identifies with the Indian society against members of the national society. This type of identification usually makes the missionary a serious obstacle to the tribal society in its transition to national culture.

Finally, there are the missions with limited or specialized objectives—social, medical, translational, etc. Such groups very frequently have only tenuous church connections, and therefore also rather weakly-defined church objectives. They initiate culture change (whether they intend to or not) through their programs, but often do not assume responsibility for the direction nor for the ultimate results of the change cycle. Such organizations seldom are in a position to build bridges between the tribal church and the national church society.

The problems of integration

The Christian church proclaims universal brotherhood: the new man in Christ is above class, race, or language distinctions. But in actual fact this ideal is seldom even approximated. Thus, even with the best of intentions the attempt to integrate a tribal society into the national society is fraught with difficulties. Only in isolated cases has such integration been accomplished without developing a two-class church. The national element usually dominates. Behind the profession of equality there stands the reality that tribal people are second-class members of the church, and as such they are used to doing the "dirty work." In one "integrated" church building program tribal believers on the average put in three times the amount of free labor on the church building project; and one of the national believers laughingly said: "They want to belong; let them prove it with work."

A further problem arises from the fact that in most cases tribal members enter the national society not as groups but as individuals. This means that often they are no longer psychologically or sociologically "whole." Their attempt to make an individual adjustment is often accompanied by a wholesale condemnation and repudiation of their tribal past and an over-identification with the present.

Richards tells of the tribal person who was wearing a thick woolen suit, woolen stockings, and two shirts while the national wore bermuda shorts, a sport shirt, and sandals. When the latter asked, "Aren't you uncomfortable with so many clothes on?" the former said, "You could go naked and the people would still know that you have clothes in your wardrobe. But if I don't wear my clothes, the people would say that I am an uneducated fellow who has no more than a pair of shorts." [20]

Because their self-definition is so precarious, such individuals often are highly explosive. [21]

One of the tragic manifestations of such status insecurity is the use of sex to secure belonging. Women in such a condition frequently buy belonging by promiscuous relations with non-tribal men, while the Indian man who would otherwise be loyal to his wife and family, finds a national mistress to be a useful status symbol. This problem has presented itself in the bilingual education program in Latin America. As Indian teachers progressed in their training, their status rose. To demonstrate this rise, some succumbed to the temptation of taking Spanish mistresses.

The missionary as culture broker

The preceding catalogue of obstacles and problems makes obvious the fact that mere contact between two societies is not enough to prepare them for cooperation or for smooth integration. Since both tend to view the problems exclusively from their own point of view, they often need a third party, a mediating agent from outside their two respective cultures (a culture broker), [22] to help them in mutual understanding and to assist them in their integrative efforts at bridge building. [23]

---

[20] Audrey Richards, *Lands, Labor and Diet in Northern Rhodesia*. An Economic Study of the Bemba Tribe (London: Oxford University Press for the International African Institute, 1939), p. 217.

[21] William A. Smalley, "Reply: Planting the Church in a Disintegrating Society," PA, Vol. 5, Nos. 5 and 6 (Sept.- Dec. 1958), p. 228-233.

[22] This term has been suggested by Eric R. Wolf, "Aspects of Group Relations in a Complex Society: Mexico," *American Anthropologist*, Vol. 58, No. 6 (Dec. 1956), pp. 1075-1076.

[23] The term "bridge-building" has been drawn from John Melling, *Right to a Future: The Native Peoples of Canada* (Toronto: The Anglican Church of Canada and The United Church of Canada, 1967), pp. 7, 92-103, 135-136.

Interpreting the societies to each other. Both societies will need help if they are to understand each other adeqately. The national society, because of its superior and paternalistic attitudes, very frequently does not even realize the necessity of trying to understand the "why" of tribal behavior. On the other hand, because of the very limited world view his culture imposes on him, the tribal person will generally interpret what he sees in the national society in terms of his own narrow cultural background. The national society, usually, a more heterogeneous society, exhibits a wide variety of behavior ranging from the universally accepted to the aberrant or even the forbidden. Here tribal people will need help in distinguishing what is acceptable and what is not. For example, a group of tribal men being educated in a bilingual school system had to be transported long distances by plane at great expense. For this reason it was impossible for them to bring their wives and families. The school program demanded that they stay away from their homes for periods of six months or more.

No one had ever thought to explain the prostitution pattern of the national society to them. Before the school administration became aware of the problem, more than seventy five percent of the Indian teachers-in-training had become infected with venereal disease at a prostitution center that developed within a few miles of the bilingual school. When the situation was finally uncovered, several of the tribal "culprits" innocently explained: "We thought it was very nice. You

could just pay a little and have a woman whenever you were too far away from your wife. We thought that this was what all civilized people did." They had not distinguished between the acceptable, the tolerated, and the disapproved in the national society.

On the other hand, it is of equal importance to interpret the tribal society to the national culture. The "glasses of superiority" which most of the members of the national society wear toward the aborigines are adjusted to see their behavior as queer, savage, uncivilized, and irrational. They need to be helped to understand that the tribal culture has values and motivations just as their own. In my own experience it was necessary to spend considerable time with the European colonists in the Paraguayan Chaco interpreting the Indian cultures to them. Since the colonists were serving as models for the Indians who wanted to settle, it was crucial that they as representatives of the "model culture" understand the motivations and problems of the tribal society. An example of serious misinterpretation of tribal behavior has been reported in my paper on the Lengua innermost.[24] The settlers thought that the Indian use of *poijh* was lying or stupidity. They didn't recognize that it was a mechanism to control the innermost.

Establishing bidirectional communication channels. If mutual understanding is to be facilitated, the importance of bidirectional communication cannot

24 Jacob A. Loewen, "Lengua Indians and Their Innermost," PA, Vol. 13, No. 6 (Nov.-Dec. 1966), pp. 252-272.

be overemphasized. Most tribal and folk societies have had long and unpleasant experiences with unidirectional harangues by government officials and persons in authority from the national society.[25] They have learned to nod in polite agreement to whatever is said during such harangues, but to interpret them in terms of para-message rather than message.

Bidirectional communication is exceedingly important if tribal members are to learn not only what to do, but why to do it. This became very apparent in the Indian settlement program in Paraguay. When asked in what way the white colonists could best help them, several Indians said: "We want them to talk with us. We know how, to plant cotton and we know when to do it, but we don't know why we ought to do it then..." Such bidirectional exchange is imperative if the felt needs of the tribal society are to be met. The danger for both societies is to accept their own behavior as universally understood and right and therefore to miss many opportunities for meaningful exchange.

Preparing societies for integration. This preparation will involve both the members of the tribal society and the members of the national society and national church. Often it is not enough for the mediating agent to interpret the national society in general to the tribal individual. He will actually have to anticipate many of the problems which the tribal person will encounter in his adjustment to national society. Such anticipation of problems will range all the way from the intimacies of sex to the nuances of etiquette in different eating places.

When we took the first Choco Indians to the Canal Zone and took them to eat in an American cafeteria, we had not adequately explained to the Indians the etiquette of standing in line. A lady whom one of the Indians was crowding stepped on his new shoes with her spike heels, severely lacerating his toe. Not knowing how to get the lady to remove her foot, he suffered the pain until she moved, but was then so "hurt" psychologically that he refused to eat. It was hours later when we finally discovered what had actually happened.

Also of great importance will be the broadening of the value base of the tribal person. It is very easy for him to learn or to adopt the practices of the national society, but unless this is matched with the proper world view and values, the long-range effect can be quite detrimental. The Vicos project in Peru, for example, has shown that it is not enough to provide the Indians with economic and political know-how; it may only help them to produce bigger and better fiestas, thus accentuating rather than solving some of their major social problems.

One of the very important preparations involves the development of proper attitudes toward language—his own as well as the national language. Frequently the tribal language has become linked with low status.

---

[25] Arthur H. Niehoff, Ed., *A Casebook of Social Change.* (Chicago: Aldine Publishing Co., 1966), p. 16.

The tribal person needs to understand that his language is in no way inferior to the national language. In fact, where the status linkage can be changed to one of situational usage, many of the worries and concerns of the tribal person will be alleviated.[26]

Education is another important element in the preparation of the tribal person for meaningful participation in national society life. However, here we need to remind ourselves that the education required is not only that of children, but that of adults. The Vicos project, mentioned earlier, has demonstrated that it was not so much the elementary education program for children that helped the community to make the necessary adjustment, but the effective adult education program.[27]

An interesting program of adult education is being developed in Guatemala. It is designed to train recognized adult community leaders in their home context rather than moving them to a school context outside of their society. The program will ultimately offer elementary, secondary, Bible school, and seminary level education through programmed textbooks and individual tutorship. Such an education program will not only permit the leadership to remain in the

societal context, but new information absorbed by the leader students will at the moment of its psychological impact also find its way into the community gossip channels and thus change or influence the whole community, not only the adult in training.

Education as a preparation for transition to national society is exceedingly important, because without it the tribal person is usually obliged to enter the national society at the very lowest level, and therefore will find himself in competition with the nationals of lowest status. Since the tribal person often is an economic or social threat to nationals at this level, the latter will obviously do all in their power to assert their superiority over the emerging tribal individual. If the tribal person can enter the national society with some education or with a trade, he will usually be able to sidestep the lowest levels and enter the society at a (higher) level where he will no longer be a challenge to the status of the people. It was interesting to observe that Canadian Indians attending city churches peopled largely by middle class professionals were much more regular in church attendance and also found their church life much more satisfying than those who attended mission churches in the inner city where they were in direct competitions with the lowest strata of Canadian society.

It has already been stated that persons in transition will need models for the change. If the tribal leadership is of such calibre that the leaders will be able to make a contribution not only to their own society, but also to the national society at large, such

---

26 Jacob A. Loewen, "Why Minority Languages Persist or Die," PA, Vol. 15, No. 1 (Jan.-Feb. 1968), pp. 8-15. Delivered as a lecture at the Congress of Americanists, Mar del Plata, Argentina, September 3-11, 1966, under the title: "Motivations for the Loss or Retention of Native Languages."

27 Holmberg, op. cit., p. 90ff. See also Harry F. Wolcott, *A Kwakiutl Village and School.* (New York: Holt, Rinehart and Winston, Inc., 1967).

leaders can function as useful models for emulation to the members of the tribal society in transition.

While it is true that the tribal society will in most instances make the major adjustments for integration, it is also important that the national society be prepared for change The national society must become aware of and rid itself of its paternalistic attitudes which the tribal individual seeking integration interprets as rejection.

William L. Wonderly has suggested that one of the ways of helping the national church to accept tribal church members is to provide the national church leaders with adequate anthropological information.[28] In my own experience as cultural broker between the European settlers and the Indians of the Paraguayan Chaco I found that such anthropological information was deeply appreciated; for time and again after a lecture explaining some of the Indian philosophy, individual settlers came to express their gratitude saying: "I had never realized that this is what these things meant. I am certainly going to try and be more understanding next time something like this happens."

Providing support during the transition. An interesting experiment is being conducted in some of the Canadian cities by so-called Indian Friendship Centers. At the Center an Indian coming from the reservation will receive orientation toward city and national society life, help in finding

suitable living quarters and work, counsel in acquiring the necessary skills for better-quality employment, and also contact with others in the process of making adjustment to the national society. Once a tribal person has been located in a job, the Center staff continues its mediating function by talking both with the employer and the employee to solve any difficulties that may arise.[29]

Wesley J. Culshaw reports that such assistance in transition need not be limited to the cultural outsiders. A minor government clerk, a native of one of the outlying islands, living at Fort Morseby, New Guinea, has established a veritable adjustment center for the people from his island. As they came into the city he took them into his home and helped them to learn the Neo-Melanesian language and interpreted the ways of urban society to them. After they had made their initial adjustment and had found employment, he remained a constant source of encouragement to the individuals in transition. As time went on, this group gradually grew to several hundred, and so a welfare association, in which the "graduates" helped the new arrivals, was organized. This Christian tribesman has not only earned the respect of his own people, but also the admiration and gratitude of the Australian government.[30]

---

[28] Wonderly, "Indian Work..." op. cit., p. 199.

[29] For a discussion of Friendship Centers see Melling, op. cit., pp. 92-103. A similar recommendation has been made for the Maori of New Zealand, see Ausubel, op. cit., pp. 137-159.

[30] Wesley J. Culshaw in a lecture delivered at Mindolo Ecumenical Centre in Kitwe, Zambia, January, 1967.

Healing

Through Communication

Confession, Catharsis, and Healing

THE shaman, Angutingmarik, a very sick woman named Nanoraq, and all the members of their Eskimo band are gathered at a curing session. The shaman has been walking back and forth slowly, breathing deeply, and at times groaning heavily. Finally he speaks:

Shaman: "It is you, you are Aksharquarnilik, I ask you, my helping spirit, whence comes the sickness this person is suffering? Is it due to something I have eaten in defiance of taboo, lately or long since? Or is it due to the one who is wont to lie beside me, to my wife? Or is it brought about by the sick woman herself? Is she herself the cause of the disease?"

Patient: "The sickness is due to my own fault. I have but ill fulfilled my duties. My thoughts have been bad and my actions evil."

S. (interrupting her): "It looks like peat, and yet it is not really peat. It is that which is behind the ear, something that looks like the cartilage of the ear. There is something that gleams white. Is it the edge of a pipe, or what can it be?"

Listeners (crying all at once): "She has smoked a pipe that she ought not to have smoked. But never mind. We will not take any notice of that. Let her be forgiven, tauva!"

S: "That is not all. There are yet further offenses which have brought about this disease. Is it due to me, or to the sick person herself?"

P: "It is due to myself alone. There is something the matter with my abdomen, with my inside."

(speeches omitted)

S: "Now this evil is removed, but in its place there appears something else; hair combings and sinew thread."

P: "Oh, I did comb my hair once when after giving birth to a child I ought not to have combed my hair; and I hid away the combings that none might see."

L: "Let her be released from that. Oh, such a trifling thing; let her be released, tauva!"

(speeches omitted)

S: "There is more to come. There are yet cases of work, of occupations which were forbidden, something that happened in the spring, after we moved over to this place."

P: "Oh, I gave my daughter a waist belt made of skin that had been used for my husband's quiver."

287

L: "Let this be taken away. Let her be released from it, tauva!"

S: "It is not yet taken away. She is not released from it as yet. Perhaps it has something to do with caribou. Perhaps she has prepared caribou skins when she ought not to have touched them."

L: "She has prepared caribou skins. She helped to stretch out the skins at the time when she was living in the same house with a woman who had her menses. Let her be released from that tauva!"

S: "She is not freed from her guilt even yet. It seems now as if the earth beneath our feet were beginning to move."

P: "I have picked moss at a time when I ought not to have touched the earth at all, moss to melt the lead for my husband's rifle bullets."

S: "There is more yet, more forbidden work that has been done. The patient has not only melted lead for her husband when it was taboo, but she did it while still wearing clothes of old caribou skin, she did it before she had yet put on the garments made from the new autumn skins."

L: "Oh these are such little things. A woman must not be suffered to die for these. Do let her be released."

S: "She is not released. It may perhaps prove impossible to release her from these burdens. What is it that I begin to see now? It must be blood, unless

it is human filth. But it is outside of the house, on the ground. It looks like blood. It is frozen, and covered with loose snow. Someone has tried to hid it."

P: "Yes, that was in the autumn. I had a miscarriage and tried to conceal it. I tried to keep it secret to avoid the taboo."

L: "This is certainly a great and serious offense. But let her be released nevertheless. Let her be released, tauva!"

(speeches omitted)

S: "She is not yet released. The sickness is yet in her body. I see snow whereon something has been spilt; and I hear something being poured out on it. What is it, what is it?"

P: "We were out after the salmon, and I happened to spill something from the cooking pot on the snow floor." [Salmon are not to be spilt.]

S: "There are more sins yet. There is more to come. She grows cleaner with every confession, but there is more to come. There is yet something which I have been gazing at for a long time, something I have had in view..."

(speeches omitted)

L: "Let it pass. Let her be released from that. Let her get well."

S: "Return to life. I see you now returning in good health among the living, and you, being yourself a shaman, have your helping spirits in attendance. Name but one more instance of forbidden food, all the men you have lain with though you were unclean, all the food you have swallowed, old and new offenses, forbidden occupations exercised, or was it a lamp that you borrowed?"

P: "Alas yes, I did borrow the lamp of a dead one. I have used a lamp that belonged to a dead person."

L: "Even though it be so, let it be removed. Let all her evils be driven far away, that she may get well."[1]

The preceding greatly abbreviated account of a curing session indicates what a central place confession plays in the treatment of disease in Eskimo culture. The interaction between the patient, the members of the community, the shaman, and the latter's helping spirit is designed to make it easier for the patient to confess her wrongdoings and broken taboos, which, in the view of the Eskimo, are the causes of her illness. The shaman and the audience pose leading questions and draw upon their knowledge of the patient's overt and covert acts, and make educated guesses about possible broken taboos. Each confession is thought to purge at least a part of the woman's illness. In the case quoted above, the con-

fession sessions were repeated three times a day for several days.

Confession of this nature, while by no means universal, has been found to have important cathartic and healing functions in many of the world's cultures. This paper proposes to highlight some of the major ethnographic findings concerning the function of confession. This résumé is to serve as a background for a discussion of confession in the indigenous church.

Motivating Confession

Confession, motivated by a desire to prepare for worship, has been found among peoples as diverse as the Incas of the Andean Highlands, the Aztecs of pre-conquest Mexico, and the Hebrews of ancient Palestine, but actually such "worship" motivation among tribal cultures is relatively rare.[2] Usually the motivations for confession are much more mundane—people confess only when illness, misfortune, calamity, or some natural disaster threatens their well-being. At other times the fear that such calamities might come as punishment for their unconfessed wrongs, is suf-

---

1 Knud Rasmussen, "An Eskimo Shaman Purifies a Sick Person," in William A. Lessa and Evon Z. Vogt, editors, Reader in Comparative Religion. An Anthropological Approach. Second edition. (New York: Harper and Row Publishers, 1695), pp. 410-414.

2 Christianity places a lot of emphasis on confession too. The Scriptures, both Old and New Testaments, frequently call for confession in relationship with worship (Psalms 32 and 51 and Matthew 5:23-24). I Cor. 11:27-32 definitely speaks of self-analysis and confession as a prerequisite to participation in Holy Communion. The Roman Catholic Church makes periodic confession obligatory for all the faithful, and most liturgically oriented Protestant Churches speak a prepared confession in unison as part of their regular worship services. But however valuable liturgical, prescribed, generalized or periodic confession may be, it can easily become a conscience-easing substitute for genuine personal confession.

ficient to produce confession. The fear motivation is often nurtured or augmented by gossip which makes the whole community aware of the transgression and serves to build up feelings of social isolation in the culprit. As the gossip circulates, it is usually reinforced by testimonials of calamities that have descended upon unrepentant sinners engaged in similar activities on previous occasions.

Illness and misfortune. In the case of the sick Eskimo woman described in the beginning of this paper, illness was considered to be the result of her own transgressions. In fact, it wasn't one major transgression, but rather a long list of broken taboos, stealing, and other minor misdemeanors. Such confession of one's own sin as a prerequisite for personal healing is widespread. It has been reported for native groups in the Americas, Africa, Asia, and the islands of the Pacific.

Speaking of the Canadian Ojibwa, A. Irving Hallowell says: "Any serious illness is believed to be a penalty for wrongdoing. The individual is encouraged to confess anything wrong he may have done in the past in order to facilitate recovery."[3] This also seems to be true of their neighbors: "Now one of the distinctive features of the Salteaux belief system is this: if one who is ill because of 'bad conduct' *confesses* his transgression, the medicine will then do its work and the patient will recover."[4]

An unmarried Nyansongo woman is having difficulty at the birth of a child which she conceived when she was "taken by stealth" by a classificatory father during a festival. The old women in attendance, becoming aware of the complications, have been busily recounting catastrophes that have resulted (at other deliveries) from unconfessed sex transgressions. Firmly believing that the current difficulties are due to unconfessed sex offenses, they press the young woman in labor for confession. The girl finally names twelve young men with whom she has been intimate, but the difficulty continues. Finally in desperation she confesses the incestuous relationship with her classificatory father. When shortly thereafter the difficulties are overcome and the baby is born normally, all the attendants opine that the relationship with her classificatory father has been the real cause of her labor problems, and that her confession has saved her life.[5]

The woman Alupwai, a Manus Islander, is lying near death's door. Her abdomen is grotesquely distended. She is continually groaning with pain and is in coma more than she is conscious. The seer has just diagnosed that her condition is definitely due to personal sin and has told her in no uncertain words that unless she confesses today, she will surely die today or tomorrow.[6]

---

[3] A. Irving Hallowell, *Culture and Experience.* (Philadelphia: University of Pennsylvania Press, 1955), p. 110.

[4] *Ibid.,* p. 272.

[5] Robert A. and Barbara B. LeVine, "Nyansongo: A Gusii Community in Kenya" in Beatrice B. Whiting, editor, *Six Cultures. Studies of Child Rearing.* (New York: John Wiley and Sons, Inc.), 1963, p. 103.

[6] F.R. Fortune, *Manus Religion. An Ethnological Study of the Manus Natives of the*

Often, however, it seems as if the illness need not be a result of only the patient's own shortcomings, but rather it can be caused by the sins of his kin, or even unrelated fellow tribesmen. In such cases, too, the actual culprits must be brought to confess if the sick person is to be restored.

A child among the Yurok of California is ill. Alice, the female seer, goes into a trance to discover the cause of the illness: "I see an old woman sitting on the Bald Hills and wishing something bad to another woman. That is why this child is sick." No sooner has the seer finished speaking, than the grandmother of the child confesses that on a certain day she was sitting on the Bald Hills attempting to practice sorcery on another woman.[7]

Even in the example mentioned earlier of Alupwai, who was said to be dying because of her own sin, the effects of her transgression were not considered only personal, for, when Alupwai finally confessed her lewd encounter with the deceased Pwanau, the whole village was up in arms—had she only confessed while Pwanau lay ill and had the proper expiation been made, Pwanau would today probably still be alive.[8]

In another example from the Manus Islands Popwitch is lying moribund. At once several kinsmen of Noan

and the dying Popwitch corner the former who is suspected of having seduced a "sister," and try to make him confess. They remind him that Popwitch's life is in his hands: "Confess now. Come, tell it all. Or do you want to murder?" Should the patient die, Noan's failure to confess will be held responsible for Popwitch's death.[9]

Among the Incas the non-private nature of wrongdoing was firmly believed. Thus community catastrophes were usually considered to be the result of accumulated unconfessed individual sin. Even the illness of the Inca himself was usually considered to be due to the sins committed by his subjects. Announcements of his illness quickly blanketed the empire, and the whole nation was called to confess their sins so that their ruler could be restored to health.[10]

Natural calamities. In an earlier paper the experience of a young, Bolivian Quechua murderer was cited. He had killed a fellow Quechua, but obstinately refused to confess and to make restitution to the aggrieved family. When a severe drought afflicted the region, the people at once linked the natural calamity to the unconfessed and unatoned transgression.[11]

Admiralty Islands. (Lincoln: University of Nebraska Press, Bison Books edition, no date), p. 322.

7 Erik H. Erikson, *Childhood and Society*, Second edition. (New York: W. W. Norton and Company Inc., 1963), p. 174.

8 Fortune, *op. cit.*, p. 220.

9 *Ibid.*, p. 156.

10 John Howeland Rowe, "Inca Culture at the Time of the Spanish Conquest," In Julian H. Steward, editor, *Handbook of South American Indians.* (Washington: United States Government Printing Office. (Smithsonian Institution. Bureau of American Ethnology Bulletin 143), Vol. 2, p. 305.

11 Jacob A. Loewen, "Socialization and Social Control: A Resume of Processes," PA Vol. 15, No. 4 (July-Aug. 1968), pp. 145-156.

In a similar vein, when two Manus Islanders were surprised by a sudden storm at sea and perished, a seer was called to find out whose unconfessed sin had occasioned the tragic death.[12]

However, not only so called primitives connect calamities with unconfessed sin. When a severe earthquake rocked Lima, Peru in October of 1966, people of all social strata were observed kneeling in the streets confessing their sins. One young woman excitedly affirmed: "I was so afraid, I confessed all the sins that I have ever committed."

The concept of connection between sin, illness, and misfortune is not alien even to the Scriptures. The disciples, seeing the man blind from birth, asked: "Who sinned, this man or his parents?" (John 9:2). Genesis 6 recounts how the wickedness of men caused the Lord to send the deluge to wipe out all the people except Noah and his family off the face of the earth. Again, in the case of David's sin of pride, a three-day plague decimated the nation of Israel (II Sam. 24).

Nor is modern Western Christianity free from feelings of relationship between unconfessed sin and calamity. When death or misfortune strikes, even we are prone to ask: "What have I done now that God would treat me thus?" Or when an unfriendly world power suffers a defeat, we are quick to assume that "God let them have their due."

Group Pressures for Confession

The mechanisms of group pressure have already been described in the paper on socialization and social control.[13] Gossip and the resulting isolation of the offending individual is the most usual pressure that is brought to bear on a person to make him confess wrong behavior. R.F. Fortune, describing the Manus religion, cites situation after situation in which pressure to confess was applied by the group on the individual who was suspected of having committed an offense. For example, when someone leaked out word that Noan had committed incest with his "sister" Lavian, the parents and relatives—indeed the whole Manus community—descended upon the pair with pressures to confess. When the two resisted, they were warned that sickness and death would descend upon them and upon their kin. In fact, what began as subtle social pressure developed into overtly spoken threats.

Thus when shortly thereafter, Popwitch a relative of the suspected pair, fell into a coma with blood gushing from his mouth—"a ghost has invisibly cut his neck"—the community reacted in panic. A new attempt was made by the relatives to force Noan to confess; however, no pressure on him availed. Frustrated, they hurried off to Lavian who for fear had stayed away from the house of the sick man. "Noan has already confessed to having seduced you. It is all out. Come, confess quickly and save Popwitch from death. We have come to let you have some of the credit in the confession also." Through this bluff the

12 Fortune, *op. cit.,* p. 204.

13 Loewen, "Socialization...," *op. cit.,* pp. 145, 156.

girl was cowed into making the necessary confession.[14]

The brainwashing techniques used by the Chinese Communists on American prisoners during the Korean War also capitalized on strong social pressures for producing confessions. As some individual buckled under pressure, he was forced to make his confession in public. The confessor was rewarded with the approval of the indoctrinators, and thus an attempt was made to generate social pressure on the rest of the group to confess their "war crimes."[15]

In the Manus situation we have already pointed out that social pressure can develop into overt threats. In some societies, however, it even goes as far as overt aggression. Among the Chipayas of Bolivia gossip and public accusation are usually the first steps to produce confession. But when these fail, the Chipaya often resort to physical violence — usually merciless beating.[16]

Plains Indians have been known to go even farther: where husbands suspected their wives of infidelity, they often mutilated the "sinners" in order to extract confession.[17]

[14] Fortune, *op. cit.*, pp. 145-146.

[15] Edgar H. Schein, "Interpersonal Communication, Group Solidarity and Social Influence," in Warren G. Bennis, Kenneth D. Benne and Robert Chin, editors, *The Planning of Change.* (New York: Holt, Rinehart and Winston, 1964), pp. 520-527.

[16] From a personal communication from Ronald Olsen of the Summer Institute of Linguistics, Bolivia.

[17] E. Adamson Hoebel, "Law-ways of the Commanche Indians," in Paul Bohannan editor, *Law and Warfare.* (Garden City, New York: The Natural History Press, 1967), pp. 201-202.

"Supernatural" Motivation for Confession

Frequently, confession of sin and broken taboo anticipates the actual illness or catastrophe, and thus the motivation for confession, as suggested earlier, is not the actual disaster, but the fear of impending misfortune. Here the active agent, at least in the ultimate sense, is the fear of the supernatural — be this God as in Christianity, the gods, fate, or the ghosts of the departed ancestors as in the case of the Manus Islanders. Because the supernatural is seen as having power and purpose to avenge moral and social infractions, men make their confessions to it as a means of forestalling its punishment.

In such cases as the Inca, where confession was a prerequisite for worship, and the animistic Tupinamba of Brazil, the very fear of the supernatural was usually great enough to produce confession. In general, however, it seems correct to say that usually the calamity itself or some prophet announcing the advent of the calamity is necessary to bring about confession. Jonah and the city of Nineveh can be cited as an example of the latter. In fact, it has been reported for the Congo that confession motivated by fear rather than by actual illness is viewed as a kind of character weakness.[18]

Since such "supernatural" intervention is viewed as predictable, societies often establish a specialized role — that of seer, shaman, prophet, medium, etc.—to foretell its advent. The means

[18] From a personal communication from Henry Brucks, former missionary to the Belgian Congo.

of "knowing" usually involves visions, oracles, auguries, divinations, etc. In the case of oracles, conversation is often established with the very venging spirit forces themselves. This is clearly demonstrated by the Manus approach, in which the supernatural, through the Sir ghost, carries on a running conversation with the medium. Of course, to motivate the confession from either the patient or the gathered relatives, the medium uses what Fortune calls the "third degree." During such conversations the ghosts of the departed make veiled pronouncements about community events. Such statements are sufficiently general to protect the oracle, but usually specific enough to give the "sinner" the feeling of detection. If the initial pronouncement fails to produce the desired response, the medium and the spirit control add more detail and more ramifications to increase the pressure. Greater detail could be used either to produce the confession or to increase its flow. Note, for example, the case of the curing of a small child from the Yurok in California. The medium, having gone into a trance by means of tobacco smoke, begins to detail her vision: "I see a man and a woman doing business (having sexual intercourse)." At once the father or an uncle of the sick child confesses his misdeeds. [19]

This phenomenon of increasing pressure is also seen in the Eskimo curing seance described earlier. The shaman, Angutingmarik, through the mediation of his helping spirit Aksharquarnilik, faintly "sees" objects that either the patient or the audience interpret in terms of broken taboos and other misdemeanors.

In the Inca practice of confession, auguries were used to determine the completeness of the confession made. If the auguries showed it to be partial, the penitent was called upon in no uncertain terms to confess all of his sins. [20]

Besides oracles of local origin, Manus Islanders also use "imported" seers from neighboring tribes. Such seers usually go to sleep while their souls proceed into the past or into some other geographical area to discover the causes of the illness or misfortune. At other times the seer becomes "possessed" and his familiar spirits speak through him revealing the cause of the calamity. As the seer makes his charges, the assembled relatives may again substantiate his accusations, thinking they have been discovered.

The Eskimos have another rather unusual method for applying "supernatural" pressure to obtain confession in times of major calamity. The shaman sends his soul on a journey to the bottom of the sea to the spirit or goddess of the sea called Sedna to discover what sins or broken taboos are causing their current lack of food, fuel, and skins. On arrival at the goddess' residence, the shaman gently strokes her hair, and thus the pacified deity is moved to reveal to him the crimes that have been committed. When his soul returns and reports, mass confession follows. [21]

[19] Erikson, *op. cit.*, p. 174.

[20] Rowe, *op. cit.*, p. 305.
[21] Knud Rasmussen, "A Shaman's Journey to the Sea Spirit," in William A. Lessa and

Resistance to Confession

It may be somewhat surprising to point out that even though confession is viewed as cleansing and healing in effect, and even though it appears if the society is supporting the individual in making his confession, there often is great resistance to it. Even in the case of the Eskimo woman where the whole community, as it were, was cooperating with the shaman and the patient to make considerable resistance on the part of the patient.

S: "Ha, if the patient remains obstinate and will not confess her own misdeeds, then the sickness will gain the upper hand and she will not get well. The sickness is yet in her body and the offenses still plague her. Let her speak for herself. Let her speak out. It is her own fault."

P: "I happened to touch a dead body without afterwards observing the taboo prescribed for those who touch dead bodies, but I kept it secret."

S: "She is not yet released. The sickness is yet in her body. I see snow whereupon something has been spilt. I hear something being poured out. What is it? What is it?"[22]

Such reticence to make confession is, of course, more understandable in the Manus situation where it entails

propitiatory payments which the relatives, willingly or unwillingly, have to make. However, even for the one confessing, there will be a severe loss of face Thus when moribund Alupwai confessed her lewd encounter with Pwanau, the village exploded with excitement and the drums beat out the story in gruesome detail.[23] What she had carefully hidden for decades, was now proclaimed loudly and publicly, and Alupwai cringed. Even when a young person among the Manus admits to his peers that he has committed a sexual misdemeanor, his very closest friends will endlessly repeat his sin publicly and with disdain, comparing it to "the copulation of dogs." No matter how penitent the confessor is, public ostracism will cause him to shun the people and to slink around the village like a cowed animal.[24]

In the case of a married Manus woman, the very hint of adultery would cause her to be flogged by her husband. Should she try and run away to her family, they would, of course, debar her, because if they received her they would have to make the expiatory payment on her behalf. One husband cruelly branded his unfaithful wife with a red-hot iron. In another case a brother cleaved his betrothed sister's skull with a piece of firewood when she confessed fornication.[25] In the light of these events we can appreciate a little bit more sympathetically Alupwai's tenacious resistance described by Fortune:

Evon Z. Vogt. editors. *Reader in Comparative Religion. An Anthropological Approach.* Second edition. (New York: Harper and Row Publishers, 1965), p. 460.

22 Rasmussen, "An Eskimo Shaman...," *op. cit.*, p. 413.

23 Fortune, *op. cit.*, p. 220.

24 *Ibid.*, p. 149.

25 *Ibid.*, pp. 43 and 131 respectively.

"First Alupwai resists the oracles of Paliau's titular mother. The relatives confess, but Alupwai remains silent. Later when a seer from a neighboring tribe is hired to discover the cause of her illness, all his allusions to transgressions are met in stony silence by the patient. Only after her brother Sali goes into coma and her own pains reach what seemed fatal proportions, does she weaken. But even then it isn't until after another medium has pointed out explicitly that not the sins of others, but that her very own sins are causing her suffering and prospective death; and still another medium definitely links her problem to Pwanau. Then "with clenched teeth in extreme agony she confesses her encounter with naked Pwanau many years back."[26]

The Goals of Confession

For the Incas,[27] Aztec,[28] and the Iroquois[29] confession seems to have been a means of restoring a proper relationship to the supernatural. This was also the motivation of the Hebrew day of atonement, when the sins of the people were confessed over the heads of two rams—one to be sacrificed and the other to be driven into the desert (Lev. 16). Likewise in Christianity, the confession of sin leads to divine forgiveness and to the restoration of fellowship between God and man.

More frequently, however, the object of such confession of sin and broken taboo is, of course, to restore social and moral equilibrium. In the example of the Bolivian Quechua murderer, confession was viewed as the necessary means to end the drought and to restore supernatural favor upon the community.

A.P. Elkin reports that among the nomadic Australian aborigines periodic public airings of problems were necessary to restore social well-being. As the bands wandered around gathering food, they were often separated from each other over long periods of time. Especially in times of scarcity, disputes, suspicions and feuds tended to arise. For this reason the annual ritual gathering provided an occasion during which all the complaints could be aired and settled. Those having whereof to accuse others, did so. The accused could countercharge. Even though blood would sometimes be drawn, ultimately confessions were made and the social balance and community unity restored. Once social peace had been restored, the community could again enter the sacred rituals in peace and harmony.[30]

A rather similar sequence has been reported for the Lengua in Paraguay. Annually during the dry season when the fish in the drying lagoons and the algorrobo pods around them provided the main food resource, bands met to celebrate puberty ceremonies.

---

[26] *Ibid.*, pp. 183-187 and 200.

[27] Rowe, *op. cit.*, p. 304.

[28] George Peter Murdock, *Our Primitive Contemporaries*. (New York: The MacMillan Company, 1934), p. 378.

[29] *Ibid.*, p. 317.

[30] A.P. Elkin, *The Australian Aborigines*. (New York: Doubleday and Company Inc., Anchor Books edition), p. 177.

During the periods of drinking, eating and dancing the proper atmosphere was established in which "innermosts" gradually relaxed enough to bring out hurts and to settle them.[31]

The Acawaio of Guyana even today use confession, especially the admission of guilt in response to a shaman-medium's oracular utterances, as a way of solving social tensions. Audrey Butt describes how shaman Francis in a trance was able to overhear the soul *(akwalu)* of an absent Acawaio, who was feuding with the patient, confess that its owner had blown magic upon the sick man. This public pronouncement of the shaman crystalized community attitude that something should be done. While the accused at first tried to insist on his innocence, the ultimate result was that the feud between the two men was ended.[32]

Sometimes confession is also used to stop certain evil events that have been set in motion through sorcery or witchcraft   Thus when a Navaho discovered himself becoming ill or suspected that the had been bewitched, he could call for a diagnostic session. If the medium could identify the witch, and if the latter confessed the curse or spell, the course of the evil could be stopped and the individual started on his way to recovery.[33]   Usually,

however, such confessions had to be accompanied by some type of ritual annulment of the spell or some counter magic.[34]

However, by far the most common goal of confession (already highlighted under motivation) was to restore health, whether mental or physical. In all the examples cited earlier— Manus, Eskimo, Inca, Tupinamba, etc.—the restoration of physical health was the predominant motivation. John Gillin provides us with an interesting example of the use of confession in the curing of magical fright—*espanto* or *susto* as it is known throughout Central and South America.   Such fright usually deals largely with emotional disturbances, which of course may be accompanied by physical symptoms. Alicia, the patient, has been afflicted with magical fright for the seventh time. She is taken to Don Manuel, the local curer, for healing. We describe only the second phase of the session which might be called the "confession." The healer has asked the patient to report freely the events connected with her illness. However, he has encountered considerable resistance. To overcome this, he looks her directly in the eyes and announces in a calm authoritative manner that she has been *espantado* 'frightened' near a certain river her husband foolishly lost money to a

31 Jacob A. Loewen, "Lengua Festivals and Functional Substitutes," *PA*, Vol. 14, No. 1 (Jan.-Feb. 1967), pp. 15-36.

32 Audrey Butt, "The Shaman's Legal Role," *Revista Do Museu Paulista*. Nova Série, Vol. XVI, 1965/66, pp. 154-158.

33 Paul Bohannan, *Social Anthropology*. (New York: Holt, Rinehart and Winston, Inc., 1963), p. 353.

34 Chaco Indians, like Lengua, Chulupi and Toba seemingly feel that confession is not able to reverse the effect of a curse. Thus one mother, attempting to eliminate an enemy, bewitched a piece of watermelon which her own child accidently ate.   The mother confessed and pleaded for help to stop the curse, but without avail; the child died. Their explanation was that once set in motion, a curse cannot be stopped.

loose woman. (This fact is known to the curer.) He now urges her "to tell her whole story." While he continues to look directly at her, she fidgets for several minutes and then breaks down, and in a flood of words tells of her frustrations and anxieties. During the recital of her whole story Don Manuel nods noncommitally but permissively, always keeping his eyes fixed directly on her face. When sufficient past history has been reviewed, he presses home: "But what frightened you this time?" She then continues to tell of her recent attack which developed when she and her husband were passing near the spot where the latter had been deceived by the loose woman. Manuel stops her and asks her to specify the spot in detail and to recount the events accurately. She had upraided her husband and the latter had seized a rock and struck her. This had precipitated her present *susto*.

The curer then informs the patient that he is confident that her present condition can be cured following her complete confession. He proceeds to make certain prescriptions and to set a date for another confession session a week later.[35]

Confession and the Indigenous Church

The fact that so wide a variety of societies across the world have found it necessary to establish and useful to maintain the practice of confession as a means of healing physical, mental, social and spiritual ills seems extremely significant. Since the members of the indigenous church, over and above the ordinary problems of life, are often involved in extensive culture change, and will frequently be exposed to severe pressures from the "pagan" society to backslide into the "old" way of life, one would assume that confession would be more or less imperative if believers are to successfully resolve their accumulating guilt and tension. If, to its significance in traditional practices, we add the important role that confession plays in the religious life described both in the Old and New Testaments, one would be tempted to conclude that an adequate practice of confession would be a prominent concern of missionaries and national church leaders. But is this really the case? Do mission-based or indigenous churches have adequate confession practices? What happens to confession in a society that practised it traditionally when such a society becomes Christian? How do the churches contribute to or work toward the cure of physical, social, mental or spiritual problems encountered by their members?

These and other questions form the concern of a sequel to this paper under the title "Confession in the Indigenous Church."

---

35 John Gillin, "Magical Fright," in William A. Lessa and Evon Z. Vogt, editors, *Reader in Comparative Religion. An Anthropological Approach*. Second edition. (New York: Harper and Row Publishers, 1965), pp. 402-410.

Confession in the Indigenous Church

THE El Mamey congregation of the Choco church in Panama was torn with dissension over the government supported school and its controversial teacher. Gossip, quarrels, and threats of violence had created severe inter-family tensions. Over and above the central school issues were personal problems of crops damaged by neighbors' animals, unpaid loans and wages, marital infidelities (or at least accusation of attempted seductions), and accusations of sorcery. When overt conflict and permanent damage to the community unity seemed imminent, Pastor Aureliano[1] called a church and community meeting. When the people arrived, they found that the benches in the chapel had been placed not in rows as usual for worship service, but in a circle around the perimeter of the chapel. The people came in small groups and entered the chapel with obvious discomfort—there was estrangement in the air. But the pastor welcomed them all, opened the meeting with some singing, and then told the assembled group that the time had come to confess offenses, to forgive each other, and establish peace in the church and in the community. For this part of the service he asked all the people to kneel by their benches facing the outside wall of the bulding. Then, setting the exam-

ple, he personally confessed his anger aganst the cantankerous school teacher and admitted that he too had maligned several of the men in the community. Then, after having apologized to the offended persons individually and to the people in general, he asked God's forgiveness in prayer. This catalytic self-exposure precipitated an extended session of confession and clarification of difficulties and led to mutual forgiveness and the reestablishment of fellowship. The young church had overcome a crisis that had threatened its very survival.

This experience not only illustrates the fact that the indigenous church needs the cleansing experience of confession, but it also demonstrates that in its own way such a church, of and by itself, is able to develop the necessary patterns for catharsis and reconciliation. In fact, a remarkably high percentage of tribal and folk societies have made indigenous use of confession — in its various shapes and forms — in their pre-Christian days to provide release from guilt and to facilitate personal and community healing.[2] However, when one compares mission-modelled tribal churches with tribal societes in general, one is almost alarmed to note that only a minority now have functional confession practices. Have

---

[1] Jacob A. Loewen and F. Glenn Prunty, "Aureliano: Profile of a Prophet," *PA*, Vol. 13, No. 4 (July-August, 1966), pp. 97-114.

[2] Jacob A, Loewen, "Confession, Catearsis and Healing, Aa, vol. 16, No. 2 (Merch-April 1969), PP.

expatriates discouraged or stifled native transparency? Has the imported model of service not been amenable to the development of therapeutic confession? If the tribe in pre-Christian times practised confession, what has happened to this practice under the influence of Christianity? This paper cannot even attempt to answer these questions, but it will attempt to strengthen missionary awareness in this area by highlighting the widespread felt need for confession and by describing some thought-provoking examples of confession and healing in the national churches.

The Need for Confession

There is no question but that the members of the indigenous church need the benefits of confession, not only in the general sense that all believers must confess their wrongs and shortcomings,[3] but also because they have some unique (or at least accentuated) problems. These special tensions result from (1) the influence of their pre-Christian socialization, (2) the conflicts precipitated by the encounter of their culture with the gospel, and (3) the imbalances produced by the cycle of change resulting from contact with other cultures and or conversion.

Pre-Christian tribal culture. In societies like the Dobu of Melanesia, the Chimane of Bolivia, etc., where hostility toward others was not overtly expressed but rather repressed and then surreptitiously vented by means of sorcery, even a dramatic conversion

experience often fails to effect a complete break with such past social patterns and the temptation to avenge hurts magically remains strong even for Christian converts. This can be seen in the confidential confession of a professed believer in such a society: Being a Christian is wonderful because if you have any enemies you can dispose of them through prayer and blowing. You just kneel behind the person you dislike in a prayer meeting, and while everybody is praying aloud, you mutter a curse, blow on him, and he will just die." If people from such a cultural background are to find release from the pull of sorcery, channels for releasing hostility without having to engage in such secret acts of aggression must be established.

Observations in various parts of the world confirm that group gatherings, formal or informal, usually afford some of the best settings for the release of repressed anger. The presence of the members of the community and the oratorical demands of a public indictment usually serve as safeguards against personal, violent confrontation between the protagonists. The actual nature of the gatherings vary greatly. In Africa it may be a formal court with judges and officers to assure proper. behaviour.[4] Among the Manus,[5] Aca-

---

[3] That our own North American Christendom is desperately searching for confession and forgiveness is highlighted in *Concern*: A pamphlet Series for Questions on Christian Renewal, No. 14 (Feb., 1967), p. 28.

[4] Paul Bohannan, *Law Warfare: Studies in the Anthropology of Conflict* (Garden City: The Natural History Press, 1967), pp. 3-291.

[5] R.F. Fortune, *Manus Religion: An Ethnological Study of the Manus Natives of the Admiralty Islands* (Lincoln: University of Nebraska press, Bison Books edition, original 1935), pp. 28, 156, etc.

waios,[6] etc., it may be the curing seance in which the medium helps elicit covert tensions and effects both their release and atonement. Among the Lengua festive gatherings with communal eating and drinking gener-arally provided the most appropriate settings. Under the relaxed conditions of eating and drinking repressed problems were brought into the open and solved.[7]

In fact, often the formal public expression of one's repressed hurt or anger functions as a prelude to owning one's own share in the culpable behavior. A dramatic group example of this phenomenon comes from the Chulupi of the Paraguayan Chaco, who spent two hours pouring out their anger and bitterness over the cruel acts perpetuated by their white neighbors, but who then went on to spend two and a half hours confessing their own aggressive behavior toward the whites. The Chulupi climaxed the occasion by calling on God for his forgiveness.[8]

Traditional behavior and the gospel. The Shiriana, a hunting tribe living in the jungles of Brazil and Venezuela, use chest beating and head clubbing as mechanisms to release tensions,[9] Even apart from the fact that these mechanisms are inadequate, it is hardly imaginable that such a manner of tension solving could be adopted by an indigenous church. The advent of the gospel would thus make imperative that substitute mechanisms be developed to solve the tensions and problems that are bound to arise even between Christians.

However, not all tension - solving behavior will be so glaringly contrary to Christian ideals. In fact, such practices as social control by means of gossip will probably remain unchallenged and unchanged, especially in an indigenous church which comes into being by means of group conversion. Someone may raise the question: Is it lawful for an indigenous church to use gossip for social control purposes? There is, of course, no universal answer for this question, but right or wrong, most indigenous churches will use gossip to hold their members in check. What is even more interesting is the fact that most societies, using gossip mechanisms for social control, also have ritual means of resolving the tension and thereby terminating the gossip about the trouble. For example, among the Manus gossip provides the oracles with the grounds for their accusations of sin in the event of illness. But once such sins have been confessed by the guilty party and the expiatory payments have been made, continued gossip itself becomes a sin and the object of Sir ghost vengeance. In fact even the oracles themselves will hesitate to revive confessed and expiated sin as an explanation for subsequent illnesses. Therefore, even more important than the question

---

[6] Audrey Butt, "The Shaman's Legal Role," *Revista do Museu Paulista*, Nova Série, Vol. 16, (1965-66), pp. 151-186.

[7] Jacob A. Loewen, "Lengua Indians and their Innermost," PA, Vol. 13, No. 6 (Nov.-Dec., 1966), pp. 252-272.

[8] Jacob A. Loewen, "The Way to First Class: Revolution or Conversation?" PA, Vol. 12, No, 5 (Sept-Oct,, 1965), pp. 193-209.

[9] Jacob A. Loewen, "Religion, Drives, and the Place where it Itches," PA, Vol. 14, No. 2 (Mar.-Apr., 1967), pp. 57-61.

of whether or not gossip is a legitimate social control mechanism, is the need to provide a way of resolving the indictments growing out of gossip, and thereby also terminating the very gossip itself, If gossip is not formally terminated, it can soon lose its beneficial effects in social control and become a damaging and cancerous social evil.

It is interesting to note that among the Salteaux, a North American Indian group, confession not only terminated the gossip about the evil act, it also provided release from any evil consequences for other participants;

> From the standpoint of the Salteaux society as a whole, confession is also a means by means of which the knowledge of confessed transgressions is put into social circulation. Confession among the Salteaux is not equivalent to confession to a priest, a friend or a psychoanalyst in Western culture. In our society, it is assumed that what is exposed will be held in absolute confidence, but among these Indians the notion is held that the very secrecy of the transgressions is one of the things that makes them particularly bad. This explains why it is that when one person confesses a sexual transgression in which he or she has participated with a second person, the latter will not become ill subsequently or have to confess. Once the transgression has been publicized, it is washed away or, as the Salteaux phrase it, "bad conduct

will not follow you anymore."[10]

From the culture of the Manus cited above, we can identify another problem. Illness and misfortune are always considered to be a direct result of personal or kin transgression. This spells double trouble for the indigenous church. In the first place, the church will need to provide some substitute way to work toward the healing of its infirm members. Otherwise the gospel becomes a partial message that is valid only for times of health, and calamities would demand backsliding into the old religion which provided mechanisms to deal with illness and trouble. In the second place, it must also deal with the world view that all illness is due to specific acts of sin. Here it is crucial to recognize that the mere substitution of a "physical" (naturalistic) germ theory of illness is not an adequate solution. Such an explanation of disease fails to deal with the psychomatic aspects of the illness and leaves the door wide open for the convert to seek cure of the "spiritual" aspects of his illness with an "unconverted" cure.[11]

In the paper on the Lengua innermost mention was made of the pattern

10 A. Irving Hallowel, *Culture and Experience*, (Philadelphia : University of Pennsylvania Press), 1955, p. 273.

11 J. W. C. Dougall, "African Separatist Churches, "*The International Review of Missions*, Vol. 4, No, 7, (July, 1956) p. 261, also A.P. Elkin, *The Australian Aborigines* (Garden City, N.Y.: Doubleday and Company, Inc., 1964), pp. 210-213. For a psychologist's discussion of this issue in Western culture see: Sidney M. Jourard, *The Transparent Self, Self-Disclosure and Well-Being*. (Princeton, N.J.: D. Van Nostrand Company, Inc., 1964), pp. 79-99.

of absenting oneself from the community when one's innermost developed too much tension. Today, with the Lengua having changed to sedentary agricultural subsistence, such mobility is no longer feasible. A man cannot leave his farm for six months at a time. Thus, Lengua believers have developed a new pattern of "confessing" in public those sins of other people that are upsetting their innermost. From the ideal Christian point of view one might question the "rightness" of such public accusation of others. However, as already mentioned earlier, public venting of grievances in the Lengua situation usually precipitates not only confessions by the accused, but generally also produces apologies for personal infractions on the part of the accuser. It seems to have become an important substitute for the earlier practice of leaving the community.[12]

Culture change. First of all, we must consider the problems that will result from contact with other cultures. Consider the effect of the establishment of a palm oil extraction industry in the heart of the Congo jungle. Such an industry was usually built up and operated by some foreign "boss" who drew both his labor and his raw materials from a number of tribes in the vicinity. Since the establishment was foreign and since a number of tribes were involved in its operation, the immediate grounds of the industry usually became a sort of no-man's-land in terms of social control. First of all, the mixture of people from the various cultures prevented the application of their

individual tribal norms to all; next, the new conditions produced by the presence of the industry were often not covered by tribal precedents; and finally, the boss usually also felt it necessary to establish his own imported standards which most of the people did not fully understand. The tragic results have been amply decried by tribespeople, missionaries and social anthropologists.

The above example, should also be an important mirror for missions, for the mission station often had a somewhat similar effect. The patients, students, and converts often came from a number of tribal backgrounds, each with its own patterns of behavioral standards and methods of social control. At the mission, however, tribal differences, especially for converts, were considered as part of the "old" life, since the "new man in Christ knows no tribal or cultural distinctions." The mission also often operated on a pattern of social control that was foreign and at best only partially understood. This meant that the people, isolated from their tribal controls, found themselves in a kind of social vacuum in which they were tempted to experiment with many types of previously forbidden behavior. Must of this new behavior, however, produced personal guilt and social alienation. Again, the absence of habitual control led to serious infringements upon the rights of others in sex, property sharing, etc., so that a fertile soil for hostility and aggression resulted. Even in the event that a person did want to solve or atone for some particular grievance or offense, what

---

[12] Loewen, "Lengua Indians...," *op. cit.*

was the proper way? His traditional pattern was not operative here. The new he did not understand or trust — if indeed it did provide any avenue for releasing the tension. It seems correct to assume that the church, whether intra-or intertribal in structure, should provide the social context within which confession, restitution, and atonement could be achieved. And indeed, it often has.

One missionary reports that after a meaningful confession experience at a multitribal mission setting, a young man, who had found release from his accumulated guilt, was so deeply moved he walked to his home village eighty miles away to confess the sins that he had brought with him when he left his home community. When the young man made his confession in his home community and told the village elders of the wonderful experience he had had, the elders accompanied the young man to the mission in order to learn more about the "God who looks deep down into man's stomach where the sore is." They too had "sores in their stomachs" and they wanted to know more about the God who could heal them. This experience of confession quite unintentionally became an evangelistic occasion.[13]

Further detribalization, which often results from culture mixture and the resulting culture breakdown, usually involves a shift from group based self-definition to more individual self-definition. This not only brings insecurity — it usually also increases

the person's sensitivity to hurt. Anthropologists have often pointed out that Christial evangelism with its appeal for personal conversion brings tremendous psychological conflict to sensitive souls who by virtue of their background have not been trained to stand alone. Such hurts can soon undermine the peace of heart of the convert as well as his determination to continue in the Christian way. Sad to say, if he tries to go back to his pre-Christian past, he will discover that he no longer fits there either.

Where culture change actually leads to the absorption of a tribal group into the national culture and the national church,[14] the conflicts and frustrations of the individual trying to become acculturated are often extremely severe. Canadian Indians who shared their feelings at the conference on church and culture in Winnipeg[15] left no doubt about the tremendous need Indians in urban areas of Canada felt to unburden themselves of their hurts and frustrations — in a way more acceptable than the oblivion of hard liquor. It would seem that the church would be eager to lend a listening ear and to create an atmosphere where such repressed tensions could be relieved and the guilt that has been accumulated, absolved.

Culture change following conversion. Equally serious difficulties are bound

---

13 Personal communication from the Reverend Henry Brucks, missionary to the former Belgian Congo.

14 Jacob A. Loewen, "From Tribal Society to National Church," PA, Vol. 15, No. 3 (May-June, 1968) pp. 97-111.

15 The Interchurch Conference on Christian Mission and Culture Change (held in Winnipeg, Manitoba, June 10-22, 1967).

to arise from the new imbalances that will result from the changes of behavior that conversion initiates. Missionaries report that living in a divided world — Christian and non-Christian — presented a tremendous problem for the earliest Lengua converts. Again and again when the community celebrated special occasions that led to drunkenness and sexual liberties, the new converts were drawn into participation. After one of the orgies a group of believers including a woman asked for a meeting with a missionary at which they could "tell it all." They wanted to clean their innermosts. A moving scene of confession followed and the resulting fellowship finally helped the converts to develop enough of an ingroup feeling so that they were able to support each other against the pull of undesirable social involvements. Missionaries cite this experience as the actual breakthrough in the establishment of the Lengua church in the area.

The Chulupi problem of converted husbands returning to cohabit with their wives rather than living with the unmarried during the period their wives were "building soul" in their infants, has been detailed elsewhere.[16] Our concern here revolves around the responsibility of the church to provide an avenue to air the resulting tensions, to promote forgiveness, and to restore personal and marital peace. A recent visit to the area showed several encouraging developments. First of all the former pattern of excommunication for husband-

and-wife quarrels has been discontinued. Next, the missionaries, having become aware of the actual cause of the marital troubles, are now opening their doors to all couples who want to come and unburden themselves (and a seemingly endless stream do come). Finally, the church is beginning to accept this area of tension as a legitimate concern for public discussion and planning.[17] The problem has not been solved, but the several avenues of confession are at least providing ways to discharge the tension without husband and wife having to engage in verbal and physical violence.

The Church as a Healing Community

A recent issue of *Concern*[18] was focused on the role of the church in helping its membership achieve release from sin. In the North American context it seems as if the church has to a certain extent abdicated its "loosing and forgiving" ministry to secular counselling agencies: social workers, psychiatrists, counselling columnists like Abigail Van Buren, etc.[19] The tremendous clientele of these agencies, however, points out how great the need for confession in times of rapid social change actually is.

That the need for confession is

---

16 Loewen, "The Way to First Class...," *op. cit.*, p.p. 195-197.

17 Help from another source seems to be in prospect with the appointment of a medical officer who will also study the issue of family planning.

18 Virgil Vogt, editor, *Concern* No. 14 (Feb., 1967). The whole issue is devoted to the church as a healing community.

19 Secular "forgiving agencies" are to be treated more fully in a separate paper under the title "Four Kinds of Forgiveness: Religious, Secular, Social and Personal."

even more acute in cultures that are changing from group-oriented to individual self-definition, is readily apparent. In fact, one could say that the church is really God's design for making those "who were no people to become a people" — a healing community in which men can freely admit their faults and find concerned people to pray with and for them (James 5:16, J.B. Phillips). That this is indeed happening, is demonstrated by examples such as the Choco church scene described earlier.

Motivating Confession

The cultural mechanisms for motivating confession have been described in detail in the paper "Confession, Catharsis and Healing."[20] For practical purposes we can say that these same mechanisms (fear of supernatural retribution, social disapproval, and group pressure) are also operative within the church. We only need to add that the Christian convert, in addition to his social environment, now has the Holy Spirit who activates his conscience to provide added motivation for confession.

This sensitivity on the part of tribal Christians to the Spirit of God has often been somewhat startling for westerners who are not used to such frankness. In one meeting where the tribal church leadership met to share honestly some of their defeats and victories of the past year, some visiting expatriates were invited to participate. When one of them admitted that the past year had been one of "much difference of opinion" in the institution where he worked, Indian Christians were struck by the shallowness of the confession, and one of them later inquired concerning the date of the expatriate confessor's conversion. When he learned that the person was a Christian of long standing, the tribal believer expressed amazement: "If he has been a Christian for many years, why is he so afraid to call his sin by name then?"

A.L. Kroeber has pointed out that it seems like a paradox that the Protestant Reformation, which so greatly sharpened man's guilt consciousness, should fail to provide adequate social mechanisms by which the accumulated guilt could be discharged through confession.[21] All too often an actual fear of confession, or maybe even better a fear of losing the esteem of others, is now being exported to the indigenous church, and missionary reticence to be transparent becomes a damper on the native transparency of face-to-face societies. That nationals are aware of missionary reticence to be transparent was effectively illustrated when the African, Festo Kivengere, at the Intervarsity Missionary Convention in 1961 said: "How can I open my 'box' when the missionary's 'box' is not only closed, but has a lock on it?"[22]

The Practice of Confession

In this section we want to look

---

20 Loewen, "Confession, Catharsis...," o.p. cit.

21 A. L. Kroeber, *Anthropology*. Revised edition. (New York: Harcourt, Brace and Company, 1948), p. 599.

22 Festo Kivengere, "Personal Revival," in Eric S. Fife and Arthur F. Glasser, *Commission, Conflict, Commitment* (Chicago: Intervarsity Press, 1962), pp. 27-46.

at a number of indigenous churches in action and describe examples of confession that take place in their fellowship. Obviously this section can only be illustrative, and its examples are limited largely to tribal churches which the author has been able to observe.

The Chulupi and the Northern Lengua have seemingly seized upon the Mennonite model of examining baptismal candidates with questions about their growth in faith and have extended this into a period of complete soul baring. First of all, the candidate of his own accord recounts the deeds of his old life and passes judgment upon them. However, once he has finished, members of the church community will ask questions and thus often elicit additional explanations and confessions. One could almost say that the veiled allusions of the shaman have been replaced by the leading questions posed by members of the church who have heard the community gossip and who are thus able to make educated guesses about the candidate's further involvements. However painful or cruel it may seem to the outsider, for the convert it is an opportunity to make a clean slate of it all.

An example of such a confession under church member questioning transpired at the recent baptism of Chief Manuel, who led the rebellion against the Mennonite colonists in 1962.[23] About a year ago Chief Manuel made a decision to stop his nomadic wandering and to become a Christian. Shortly thereafter he

---

23 Loewen, "The Way to First Class...," op. cit., p. 201;

asked for baptism. When he recently came before the congregation to be examined for baptism, Manuel spoke about his past life with extreme explicitness. His testimony and confession was an extended one. Among other things he highlighted especially two negative aspects of his old life: first of all, that his heart had been full of many evil purposes, "Because I was a man of strong purpose, I always proceeded to execute these purposes regardless of what the outcome might be. It did not make any difference to me whether people got hurt or killed; once I had made up my mind to do something, I just went ahead and did it." This certainly was the case when he became angry against the Mennonites and led the Indians in an uprising against them. The second item he mentioned was that in his old life he had always tried to gain the favor of the women: "I always sought to have as many women as possible on my side; for this reason I spoke praisingly to them and tried to do them favors and to give them gifts." While he did not explicitly point out that these favors had often led to sexual involvements, he was later called upon to clarify this during the question period that followed his testimony. In fact, several of the questions related to specific involvements and he was asked whether he intended to continue these or whether his manner of living would now be different. Manuel then detailed these and other of his affairs in utter transparency and told the church that he was now determined to abandon all his old ways and tha the would respect other people's wives and daughters.

In fact, it seems as if for the Chulupi, not the conversion but the baptismal ritual and its prerequisite confession is the most important event in their Christian experience, for some 1,300 people gathered for the service at which Manuel was baptized. Many of them came almost a week earlier so that they would be present not only at the ceremony itself, but would be able to listen to the testimonies of the candidates before the baptism as well. Observers report that not only believers seek to attend such confession sessions, for unbelievers also come. Even though the latter do not enter the church building, they stand at the open windows and listen to the confessions that are made by the people inside. The missionaries reported that the feelings among the unconverted ran so high that following this baptismal service a whole series of them came — several in tears of contrition — saying that having seen the baptism and having heard how people had cleansed their hearts, they, too, felt a deep desire to come and wondered how soon it would be possible for them to undergo the cleansing experience of baptism.

Four patterns of confession. During the survey of the practice of confession in the churches in one tribal area served by several missions and a larger number of missionaries, four patterns became apparent.

In one area there seemed to be little emphasis upon confession. True, when gossip highlighted the involvement of certain people in acts considered reprehensible by the church and the community, church leaders or relatives often spoke to the culprits, but the exhortation was more or less a kind of harangue to leave the evil deeds that they had been doing, rather than encouragement to confess the wrong done. Even in the event that the person admitted his guilt, no formal confession and communal forgiveness resulted.

In a second situation there was considerable emphasis on confession, but it was always made to the missionary who served as "father confessor" and also gave the "absolution." This missionary insisted that public confession was wrong and he forbade all such confession in the church. He also felt that since the tribal leadership participated in the village gossip, they thereby showed that they were not mature enough to hear and to deal with the confession of sins; and for this reason he had to exercise this role himself.

In another setting confession was usually made to a church leader or sometimes to several leaders conjointly. Even if the confession was made to one individual, he usually consulted some other leading persons concerning the case. The group of "elders" would then agree upon a punishment or penance which would then be communicated to the person making the confession. In checking the identity of these leading personalities, it was found that almost exclusively they were the first converts who had been baptized by the missionary himself. In fact, several of these people felt that later converts who had been baptized by Indian pastors probably did not possess the same spiritual prerogatives. In this setting too, public confession was not encouraged.

In a fourth setting there was a highly developed pattern of public confession similar to the one described for the Chulupi and Lengua at the beginning of this section. All problems were aired in public and in utmost detail. Frequently, of course, the confession began by the culprit going to one of the ministers or leaders and sharing his burden with them. However, the confessor was then encouraged to come before the church to make it right before all the people. When such a person got up before the church, he described his transgression in full detail. Should certain particulars be covered up, frequently questions were asked to elicit the missing details. In the case of sex transgressions the person would confess not only his part, but actually also give the names of all the other people who were involved. Should such individuals be present, of course, it frequently became a cycle of confession where each of these people also asked for personal forgiveness.

It may be instructive to make several interpretive comments about these different patterns of confession.

In the first place, in each case the missionary or his church practice seemed to be one of the major factors in the development of the existing pattern relating to confession.

Secondly, in the first setting where personal confession seemed to be rather undeveloped, some of the church services did include a pre-pared public confession as part of the service liturgy.

Next, in the first three settings both missionaries and nationals expressed concern about the unending gossip. The reason, of course, was that while gossip was being unconsciously used to stimulate confession, the absence of a formal public way to dispose of the problem left the people without a way of terminating the flow of gossip. Especially in those cases where confession was in private, the very public ignorance of what took place behind closed doors seemed to increase rather than to end the gossip cycle.

Finally, in all four settings gossip was the potent vehicle of social censure for reprehensible deeds, and basically it was also the positive medium that stimulated confession on the part of the culprits; and indeed, where the avenues were developed, it was the stimulus par excellence to completely settle problems. This was corroborated effectively by one missionary who said: "Sure, there is plenty of gossip; in fact, I can depend on it to provoke confession. I can be sure that within a few days of hearing some gossip, the culprit will come to me or the national leaders to confess."

This feeling about the positive power of gossip is well illustrated in a recent experience among the Chulupi. A youth, a recent graduate from school, was seduced by a teenage girl. She came to his sleeping quarters repeatedly to tempt him. A number of times he resisted and told her to go away, but in the end he succumbed. However, being aware that the liaison had been observed and that gossip would result, his feeling of guilt was so great that he came to the missionary and to the pastor of the church almost immediately to confess his wrong. While the church was dealing with his problem, of course, gossip concerning the girl's part was circulating freely.

The church decided just to forgive and not to discipline the youth because he had come of his own accord and quickly. Meanwhile the gossip about the girl increased in virulence until about four weeks later she finally came and confessed her part also. However, when she confessed before the church and recounted the events, she failed to state that she had "stolen" the youth. This was taken as a rather serious omission on her part by the congregation, because the Chulupi make a big difference between "stealing" i.e. taking the initiative, and "being stolen." However, when the church decided to suspend her from communion services for a disciplinary period, the crucial element was the fact that she had not come to own her guilt as soon as she heard that the young man's confession had indicted her [24]

Intervention to produce confession. In the previous paper discussing confession in the healing rituals of tribal societies, it was pointed out that frequently the shaman or the spirit medium applies considerable pressure to extract confession. Such pressure, of course, is based on gossip which is the actual source of the information for the medium; however,

the community does not rely only on voluntary response, it often fosters an institutionalized form of pressure to elicit confession. To many Western Christians this practice, or even that of public interrogation of candidates at baptism, seems rather repulsive. Hovever, if we recognize that many societies had patterns of pressure before they became Christians, and that therefore such practices may actually be cultural substitutes, our judgments may be tempered.

In addition one can point out that there is Biblical teaching enjoining personal intervention (Matthew 18: 15 - 18; James 5 : 19 - 20, etc.). Nevertheless, it is only honest to admit that unless there is widespread social approval either from the existing culture or as a result of strong Christian conviction, this responsibility is very frequently neglected. It certainly is being neglected among North American Christians today.

An instructive example of personal intervention has been reported from the Quechua in the Andean Highlands. An elder of one of the churches was reported to be secretly living with his dead brother's widow. Even though it was gossiped persistently, the elder denied it when formally confronted with the accusation. The church seemed impotent to do anything about it. Finally the godparents of his and the woman's marrige met to discuss the problem. They decided to apply pressure on the woman and were thus able to extract a confession from her. Then they went to speak to the accused elder. At first he not only denied everything, but actually

---

[24] Personal communication by Gerhard Hein, missionary to the Chulupi.

threatened to launch a defamation suit against the godparents of his marriage. When the latter, however, faced him with the woman's confession, he broke down and admitted his involvement.

Frequently personal intervention can be greatly strengthened by self-exposure. Some months ago the author was privileged to witness a session at which Pastor Aureliano dealt with some church problems. For some time community gossip had linked the teacher's name with that of a local wife. This Sunday morning the suspected wife came to the pastor telling her story. Some weeks ago, while her husband had been absent, the teacher had approached her with a proposition. Even though she had repulsed him, she knew that sooner or later gossip would bring this to her husband's ears, she herself told him as soon as he returned. The husband, however, did not believe in his wife's innocence and so began beating her. It was this beating that actually prompted the woman to come to the pastor. Since the author was talking to the teacher at the time, he unwittingly became a participant observer of the following scene. First Pastor Aureliano asked the teacher to make his statement to see whether his words would corroborate the woman's story. They did. Then the teacher apologized to the man for having attempted to seduce his wife. After the men had settled their problem, the pastor turned to the husband and asked whether he would not apologize to his wife for having beaten her when she was innocent. The husband, of course, found this to be very painful and at first he resisted energetically. Then Aureliano told him of a recent occasion on which he had wronged his own wife and how he as a Christian had gone to her to apologize. He justified such confession to one's wife as follows: "It is true, when we were not children of God, we never apologized to our wives for beating them. But now that we are children of God, our hearts are tender toward them and we apologize also to them when we wrong them. Is that not right, brother?" The result was that the man embraced his wife and apologized to her.

Genuine versus "True" Confession

There is no question but that confession has a sound Biblical basis. Nor is there any doubt that it can have beneficial effects, both socially and physically. However, it can be misused, and to prevent any misinterpretation as to the intent of this paper, we also include some cautions regarding the practise of confession.

In the first place, it is important to distinguish between cultures, for this will to a large extent determine what ought to be confessed and whether it ought to be done privately or publicly. Thus in a face-to-face society where everybody tends to know everything about everybody else, items of much greater intimacy will be public knowledge and therefore will also tend to demand public confession and forgiveness. In our own Western urban society, where lives and behavior are much more personal, confession will also tend to be on a more personal level.

Again we will need to distinguish genuine confession in search for forgiveness and with the intention of change from the more or less morbid "glorying in dirty linens" such as is peddled by secular magazines of the "True Confession" kind, as well as its religious counterpart in which the evangelist or some "famous" convert lovingly lingers over lurid details of a sordid past while giving his personal testimony. There is no doubt that this latter kind of confession also has some public appeal, for it permits people to "participate" vicariously in the forbidden without incurring technical guilt. This church form of "glorying in sin" has turned many more serious Christians away from all public confession. While one does not want to blame them, it is necessary, however, to point out that by going to the extreme of having no confession, many North American church people have been "condemned"

to a life of guilt-bearing without any hope of release or forgiveness. Readers interested in some practical "guidelines for self-exposure" may want to read an article under that same title which appeared in *His* some time ago.[25]

In conclusion we want to underscore that the poorly developed channels of confession seem to represent one of the major areas of weakness which North American churches are exporting to mission fields via their missionary ambassadors. This "foreign" model also seems to constitute one of the major handicaps for the development of wholesome national church life in many areas,[26]

[25] Jacob A. Loewen, "Guidelines for Self-exposure," *His*, January, 1967, pp. 30-32.

[26] For an analysis of a mission situation in which the introduction of confession and "cheap" forgiveness had very painful social and moral effects see John C. Messenger "The Christian Concept of Forgiveness and Anang Morality." PA, Vol. 6, No 3, (May-June, 1959), pp. 97-103.

The Social Context of Guilt and Forgiveness

A NUER youth has been badly wounded in the shoulder by a spear during a quarrel with a man from a neighboring village. The people of the two villages are really on friendly terms with each other and the spearer had no intention of killing the young man; for this reason his kinsmen at once send the spear with which the wound was inflicted to the youth's home with expressions of regret and best wishes for his speedy recovery. The elders of the wounded lad's village take the spear, bend its point, and then place it downward in a pot of cold water in order to "lessen the pain" and "to prevent inflammation".

Next morning a delegation from the wounder's village arrives leading a goat ready for sacrifice. This is a further indication that they regret the incident and are willing to pay compensation at once should the young man die. They do not want a blood feud and are hoping that the sacrifice of the goat will prevent any further complications, or as the Nuer put it, "that the wound will be finished with the goat." The visiting delegation now dedicates the sacrificial goat by rubbing its back with ashes and then ties it to a stake in front of the hut of the wounded youth's maternal grandmother. As this point one of the visitors delivers an invocation calling for a peaceful settlement of the dispute. His speech, addressed both to God (here called *kwoth* 'spirit') and the people, is really a detailed confession of how the incident occurred. It is concluded with a prayer for the wounded youth's speedy recovery.

Following this speech, the people from the wounded young man's village bring out a wether and also dedicate it with ashes. They pour a libation of water over the tethering peg and once more repeat the events of the conflict: "Ah God! We call on you about this wound. There is no enmity between us [the party of the injured youth and the party of the spearer]. This wound came of itself [they do not attribute it to the spearer because it was an accident and also because the youth will not die, and so there will be no *thung*, debt of homicide]. Throw the badness away with this ox [they call a sheep or a goat an "ox" or "cow" in ritual contexts]. Let the wound heal. Ah, God, it is only a headache [it is not a sickness of any importance — they speak of the most ghastly wounds in this way], let it be finished, let it go right on [heal without complications]. Let it be removed from the man's body. Let us be at peace."

Another man from the home village steps forward and makes an invocation: "Friend *(maath)*, God who is in this village, as you are very great we tell you about this wound, for you are God of our home in very truth. We tell you about the fight of this lad. Let the wound heal. Let it be ransomed [with sheep]..."

After a further word by the visitors both of the animals are sacrificed, and a part of the meat is prepared and then eaten in a ceremonial meal shared by the two groups. The offense has been confessed, atoned, and forgiven; so the people return home in peace.[1]

This Nuer experience of settling an offense illustrates several of the important social aspects of guilt and forgiveness: (1) the development and expression of guilt, (2) the three essential steps in the process of forgiveness (confession, expiation, and release), and (3) two of the most universal dimensions of forgiveness – the religious and the social. This paper proposes to highlight each of the mentioned aspects, in an effort the help missionaries make their cross-cultural ministry of forgiveness more adequate; because, in order to be truly effective, the emissary of reconciliation must be able to distinguish between those features which are universal, i.e. which are part and parcel of the human psyche, and those which are conditioned by the local culture.

The Nature of Guilt

Guilt is a universal phenomenon because men everywhere fail to live up to their moral ideals or else in selfishness infringe upon the rights of their fellows. However, not all guilt feelings can be labelled *true* guilt.

True and false guilt. There seem to be several separate usages of the true-false distinction in guilt. Psychologists and psychiatrists tend to label as *true* guilt those feelings of self-indictment that accompany the violation of norms which the individual has internalized as right. False guilt, on the other hand, is externally imposed guilt; such as when a community develops a pattern of contempt against a person or a group of persons, and the victim or victims may in time become conditioned to see themselves as inferior and guilty.[2] This has often been visibly demonstrated in the experience of known illegitimate children. As their peers were warned by their parents to avoid "these products of sin," the latter developed an acute sense of guilt about their origin.[3]

R.D. Laing uses the label *true or authentic* guilt for the recognition of not having been genuine or of not having "been oneself." Like Freud he considers all other guilt reactions as unauthentic or false, because they are the product of the person's cul-

---

[1] John Middleton, editor, *Myth and Cosmos: Readings in Mythology and Symbolism* (Garden City, New York: The Natural History Press, 1967), p. 117.

[2] Harry C. Bredemeier and Richard. M. Stephenson, *The Analysis of Social Systems* (New York: Holt, Rinehart and Winston, Inc., 1962), pp. 77-78, 522-523.

[3] Paul Tournier, *Guilt and Grace* (New York: Harper and Row, Publishers, 1962), p. 18.

tural upbringing.[4]

Paul Tournier in his book *Guilt and Grace* (French: *Vrai et fausse culpabilité*; German: *Echetes und falsches Schuldgefühl*) also makes a true-false distinction. However, he defines true guilt as estrangement from God (and therefore also from one's fellows) while false guilt is the feeling of condemnation that arises out of violation of cultural mores.[5]

Guilt and shame. Another important distinction must be made between guilt and shame. Anthropologists have usually defined guilt as self-condemnation resulting from the violation of internalized convictions of right and wrong. (This includes false guilt, for in the case of the latter, the person has internalized the society's negative evaluation of his own worth.) Shame, on the other hand, is the response to disapproval by one's own peers.[6] This definition correlates with David Riesman's distinction between the inner-directed person who experiences guilt and the other-directed person who experiences shame.[7] Both anthropologists and psychologists have pointed

out that American culture is rapidly shifting from its earlier guilt sanction to shame sanction.[8]

Face to face societies generally depend on gossip-triggered shame sanction to enforce obedience to socially accepted norms[9] However, one frequently finds that even in face-to-face societies these norms have been internalized to such a degree that many adult individuals experience independent guilt. This guilt is most evident in matters relating to broken taboos which are seen as supernaturally enforced. Any adverse circumstance following a violation will be interpreted as supernatural intervention, and will result in guilt.

The diversity in guilt reactions. There are, first of all, differences as to the nature of the behavior that will produce guilt. This will vary from individual to individual within a given society, but even more, from one society to another. Novelist Emile Zola highlights the individual variability in guilt reaction in the behavior of one of his characters who has committed a lust murder but feels no guilt about it. When the religious and legal communities press him to admit his guilt, he shamefacedly confesses that he once lustfully kissed the stocking of a woman.[10]

The cross-cultural differences of guilt reaction can be illustrated by

[4]R. D. Laing, *The Divided Self: An Existential Study of Sanity and Madness* (London: Penguin Books, 1965), pp. 129-133; Erik H. Erikson, *Childhood and Society* (New York: W. W. Norton and Company, Inc., 1950, 2nd edition published 1963), p. 90.

[5]Tournier, *op. cit.*, p. 67; *The Adventure of Living* (New York: Harper and Row, Publishers, 1965), p. 129.

[6]Margaret Mead, editor, *Cooperation and Competition among Primitive Peoples* (New York: Mc-Graw-Hill Book Co., Inc, 1937), pp. 307 and 343.

[7]David Riesman, *The Lonely Crowd* (New Haven: Yale University Press, 1966), pp. 14-22.

[8]Felix M. Keesing, *Cultural Anthropology* (New York: Rinehart and Co., Inc., 1958), p. 305.

[9]Mead, *op. cit.*, pp. 206 and 342.

[10]Theodor Reik, *Listening with the Third Ear* (New York: Pyramid Publications, Inc., 1965), p. 35.

the difference of reaction between a North American Christian and a Paraguayan Chulupi Indian both of whom believe that a husband should be faithful to his wife. Traditionally the Chulupi male would feel no guilt about sleeping with the unmarried girls during the time his wife was nursing their baby, but he would feel terribly guilty if he should sleep with his wife during lactation. Again, a Chulupi woman felt little or no compunction about strangling an infant at birth if the husband indicated that he did not accept the role of sociological father, but she would be unable to hide her intense guilt should she eat meat during her menstruation.

There are further personal and cross-cultural differences in the degree of guilt that a given violation produces. In our own society a man accidentally stumbling upon a naked woman would probably feel embarrassed, but certainly not guilty; while to a Manus Islander, looking upon the nakeness of a woman, even accidentally, would constitute a serious crime which unconfessed could mean that either he or his kin would become ill and die.[11]

Guilt and public knowledge. It is also important to realize that guilt is seldom entirely intrinsic. In face-to-face societies and in the so-called other-directed societies guilt is often dependent upon or at least increased by public knowledge of the infraction. This is illustrated dramatically in the following example from the North American Comanche: An old man had a very handsome grandson of whom he was very proud and of whom he liked to boast in public. One day the young man was sitting outside of his teepee in the presence of a large number of people. The grandfather, squatting beside the young man, saw a good-looking woman pass by. He at once nudged his grandson and slyly whispered: "That looks like the woman you had last night." The young man told his grandfather to go away. But the old man did not move; however he was obviously hurt when he said: "I didn't say anything wrong. I just said it looked like her." The grandson ignored the old man's words, but the latter kept on repeating them. The woman's husband was also there. Pretty soon he spoke up and said: "Yes, she's the one." When the group broke up, the offended husband went and shot both the old man's favorite horse and the young man's pony. He had been aware of the affair but was letting it ride, Once the grandfather made it public, however, there was an infraction to avenge.[12]

Bronislav Malinowski has reported a rather similar guilt-reaction among the Trobriand Islanders. People violated the incest taboo without any apparent feeling of guilt or public censure. However, if the partner in the violation ever admitted it publicly, the offender usually committed sui-

[11]R. F. Fortune, *Manus Religion* (Lincoln: University of Nebraska Press, Bison Books, 1934), p. 150ff.

[12]Paul Bohannan, editor, *Law and Warfare* (Garden City, New York: The Natural History Press, 1967), p. 189.

cide.[13]

Manifestations of guilt. There also are major differences in the manifestation of guilt. Psychiatrists point out that for the average North American blushing, turning pale, perspiring, etc., are often automatic reactions indicating that some infraction is or has been committed.[14] By far the most universal reaction to guilt however, is increased social distance. This involves not only the offender and any offended individual, but also the offender and the society at large. Guilt isolates and alienates. The Lengua demonstrate this alienation by leaving their home community as soon as their guilt is discovered. It is interesting to note that there is a growing awareness in social psychology and psychiatry that much of mental illness, especially neurosis, is the direct result of guilt. In fact, Hobart O. Mowrer has called neurosis "a medical euphemism for a state of sin."[15] He says:

> My own personal and professional experience and that of a small but growing number of other psychologists, psychiatrists and social workers shows that the so-called psychoneuroses and functional psychoses can be understood only

(sola!) in terms of palpable misconduct which has neither been confessed nor expiated.[16]

Paul Tournier says something rather similar conserning somatic illness:

> I speak from my own experience as a doctor... Many functional disturbances, and, in the long run, many organic lesions as well, are the direct consequence of unresolved remorse. That this is so is shown by the fact of their abrupt disappearance or reduction after confession. One has seen, for instance, cases where long-standing insomnia, palpitations, headaches, disorder of the digestive organs or of the liver have disappeared overnight after the confession of a lie or of an illicit love-affair.[17]

He cites examples of eczema,[18] blood deficiency,[19] and general poor health[20] that were based entirely on repressed guilt. He then goes on to quote a physician who found at least sixty percent of his arthritic patients had developed their problems in response to some inner moral conflict.[21]

---

[13]Charles P. Loomis, *Social Systems* (Princeton, New Jersey: D. Van Nostrand Company, Inc., 1960), p. 26.

[14]Reik, *op. cit.*, p. 143.

[15]O. Hobart Mowrer, *The New Group Therapy* (Princeton, New Jersey: D. Van Nostrand Company, Inc., 1964), p. 6. [Readers should be alerted to the fact that Mowrer does not always represent the mainstream of American psychiatric thinking, but his concerns in the area of guilt and forgiveness are worth serious consideration.]

[16]*Ibid.*, p. 20.

[17]Paul Tournier, *A Doctor's Casebook* (New York: Harper and Row, Publishers, 1954), p. 209.

[18]Paul Tournier, *The Strong and the Weak* (Philadelphia: The Westminister Press. 1963). p. 126.

[19]Tournier, *A Doctor's...op cit.*, p. 150.

[20]*Ibid.*, p. 211.

[21]Paul Tournier, *The Healing of Persons* (New York: Harper and Row, Publishers, 1965), p. 27.

Nor is the somatic response to guilt an exclusively Western phenomenon. A. I. Hallowell has pointed out that for the Saulteaux interpersonal guilt almost always finds expression in serious illness.[22]

Guilt and culture change. Finally we should underscore some of the problems of guilt conflict that arise when a culture is undergoing rapid and extensive culture change. In some cases there will be confusion as to when and about what to feel guilty; in others the guilt may be compounded, for the culprit will feel himself indicted under both the old and the new standards. Notice the conflict of standards in the following episode:

An unmarried Chulupi girl, a member of the church, was seeking a husband. Under the old standard she had to take the initiative and give herself sexually to a series of young men until one of them became her husband. According to popular belief she avoided becoming pregnant by sleeping with a different male each night. Once a young man sought her out for repeated visits, he was actually declaring that he wanted her for his wife and that he would also assume the responsibility of sociological father should she be with child. Now, however, with the new Christian standards the possibility of sexual contacts has been greatly diminished and a girl often becomes pregnant before she has found a husband. Once her pregnancy becomes visible, she usually stays away from

22A. Irving Hallowell, *Culture and Experience* (Pittsburgh: University of Pennsylvania Press, 1955), p. 110.

church services until she has given birth to her child in some hospital removed from the mission station. Let us now look at the experience of a specific girl. On the day following the delivery, her sister called for her and the baby, but on the way home from the hospital the new mother strangled her baby and buried it beside the trail. It was not until the hospital called to confirm the news of the baby's death that the missionary became aware of what had actually happened. He called on the girl, but she denied all guilt, saying the baby had not liked her milk; it had cried all night and then in the morning it had died. However, the date of the death was the day of her discharge from the hospital. The missionary spoke to the Chulupi church leadership asking them to investigate the facts and impressing them with the seriousness of the crime of killing one's own baby. The church elders followed his instructions and reported that the girl herself had indeed killed her child and that the council had now decided to kill her — they were just waiting for the missionary's permission. The missionary, of course, refused to permit such drastic action, and a public discussion resulted. At this meeting the girl told the whole truth, but justified her action by saying that the child had no (sociological) father. The girl's father, an older Chulupi, supported her, saying: "Her older sister already has two children without fathers and I am very deeply ashamed. I could not bear to have another bastard in the family." However, the church leadership, operating on the new standards, decided to punish the girl by making an announcement that nobody should marry her until she honestly repented for the murder of her child.[23]

The preceding example illustrates the conflicts between systems of standards in a changing society. Not only the young people are torn between two sets of ideals; the very tribal leadership is divided as to what values are primary (the father's counsel flatly contradicts the proposals of the church leaders) and how these values are to be enforced (if strangling) an infant – which was standard pre-Christian procedure – is really as serious a crime as the missionary says, then they as leaders are responsible for applying the maximum penalty).

Mechanisms for disowning guilt. Even though guilt is a universal social phenomenon, few people can readily "own" the fact that they have violated some of their internalized or at least professed standards or norms. The admission of guilt is not without price in terms of cost to the person's self-image, and certainly often has rather severe repercussions in terms of social opinion. R. F. Fortune describes this social cost among the Manus as follows:

> Confession will make all but the patient's close friends talk of the penitent's sin as if it were the copulation of dogs. The girl penitent, whenever for months after she has to appear in a public place, will slink through the village with

all the aspect and the air of a cowed dog. The penitent will avoid all public meetings as much as possible.[24]

Because of this cost man had developed a whole series of sociopsychological mechanisms to control or to reduce the pressures urging the admission of his guilt. Among the most common of these mechanisms are rationalization, repression, projection, and guilt-spreading [25]

Pseudo-release mechanisms. Release, as we have already suggested, is the final step in the process of forgiveness. However, often when the individual is unable to own his guilt and to find true forgiveness, he will attempt to rid himself of his guilt feeling by means of several pseudo-release mechanisms. One of these is annulling the bad deed by good works; thus a husband may bring flowers to his wife instead of apologizing to her for a wrong action, or a mother may read an extra story to her children to atone for her earlier outburst of temper. Keith Miller gives us a first person example of this mechanism when he says:

> For years when things went wrong around our house I would try to 'make things right' by bringing Mary Allen a present. But even if the surprise were a good one, it never seemed to strike a really deep chord of response. I sensed that she was somehow disappointed,

---

[23]Personal Communication from Gerhard Hein, missionary to the Chulupi.

[24]Fortune, *op. cit.*, p. 149.

[25]These mechanisms have been discussed in some detail in Jacob A. Loewen, ''Our Closed Doors and How we Keep them Closed,'' to be published in HIS Magazine.

though she managed to hide it well.[26]

There is a growing feeling that the reason funeral directors are able to sell such expensive funerals is that the surviving relatives are engaged in expiating unatoned guilt which they feel toward the deceased.[27]

Mowrer states categorically that hiding our sins by portraying our good deeds is the best road to destruction. Instead he calls for men to confess their sins and to hide their good works. This will give them credit and self-esteem.[28]

Another mechanism in this category is often associated with repression. After a person has deeply repressed his guilt, he develops an atoning behavior pattern which psychologists call reaction formation.[29] Thus, for example, a daughter represses her rancor against her mother into subconsciousness and then compensates for her hatred with anguished devotion.[30]

A further mechanism could be called "letting of steam." This can itself take several forms. Among the Shiriana it involves chest-beating or head-clubbing between individuals in tension. In some societies it can involve the confession of a socially acceptable sin while hiding the more serious guilt; e.g. a person may admit problems of temper but hide his marital infidelities. At other times it can involve an apology in general: "I am sorry I didn't behave as I should have;" or it can involve the use of a more socially accepted label for the transgression: "I wasn't quite honest," instead of saying: "I lied." At still other times it may involve confessing only a part of the guilt so as to relieve at least some of the pressure without really coming clean.[31] Even more common is an "accusative" confession, e g. "I just wanted to check if any of you were hurt by my behavior yesterday; I would like to have a clear record.' The "accusative" confession really tries to "pin" the onus on the other party.

Into this same category belongs "passing on the tension;" e. g. the employee who is angry with his employer, but vents his anger on the members of his own family, or Paul's mother (described by Bruno Bettelheim) who, driven by her own guilt, and illusions, perpetually berates her maladjusted son as stupid, lazy, etc.[32]

The Process of Forgiveness

As suggested earlier, a truly adequate process of forgiveness must include at least three steps: confession, expiation, and release. These three aspects of forgiveness are quite obvious in the case of the violated Kaka virgin reported by William D.

---

[26]Keith Miller, *The Taste of New Wine* (Waco, Texas: Word Books, 1965), p. 90.

[27]Jessica Mitford, *The American Way of Death* (New York: Crest Books, Fawcett Publications, Inc., 1963).

[28]O. Hobart Mowrer, *The Crisis in Psychiatry and Religion* (Princeton, New Jersey: D. Van Nostrand Company, Inc., 1961), p. 199.

[29]Bredemeier and Stephenson, *op. cit.*, p. 38.

[30]Tournier, *The Strong . . . op. cit.*, p. 27.

[31]Loewen, *op. cit.*

[32]Bruno Bettelheim, *Paul and Mary: Two Case Histories from Truants from Life* (Garden City, New York: Doubleday and Company, Inc., 1961), p. 67.

Reyburn. Some Kaka tribesmen living half a day's journey away have come to make a settlement in connection with a violated virgin. During the confession stage the events are examined and re-examined with microscopic realism. Shortly after dark the confession has been completed and an agreement has been reached as to the amount of the expiatory payment. The money and goods are now turned over to the plaintiff as payment for the infraction. However, before the transaction is complete, the past must be "swallowed" and peace must be established. Thus as soon as the settlement has been agreed upon, the women appear in the club house bringing the cooked leg of a sheep. The now-forgiven culprit and his adversaries wash their hands in a special bowl of water and then they pull apart the meat, exchange pieces, and eat the ritual *sataka* meal.[33]

The same three steps to forgiveness are vividly demonstrated in the Hebrew forgiveness ritual on the Day of Atonement. First, public confession of sin was made over the heads of two goats. Then one of the goats was slain in atonement and was burnt upon the altar as a sacrifice; and finally the other goat was led into the wilderness to show that the guilt had been removed, never to be found again.

We shall now look at each of these three aspects a little more closely.

Confession. The process of confession has been treated at length

in two separate papers;[34] however, several supplementary observation are in place.

1. The necessity of confession is not only based on the need for the righting of social wrong, it is also required by the guilty person's self-image. All to often he is deeply aware that he has been obtaining social belonging and respect under false pretenses; however, if he can find at least one member of the human race who will listen to him sympathetically and who, while knowing the the worst, will still love and respect him, the culprit finds that his own self-respect can also restored. On the basis of this one person's acceptance he can reasonably hope for the acceptance and respect of the society at large. There is no doubt that for most people the internal conflict between self-respect and social responsibility triggered by the transgression can only be terminated by some form of honest confession.[35]

2. Confession must be honest, open, and specific. Tournier has well pointed out that the incomplete release from guilt which plagues so many people derives from the fact that their confessions have not been open and specific enough.[36]

3. Mowrer adds that the confession must also be complete. He warns that very few people will be able to

33William D. Reyburn, "Christianity in Ritual Communication," PA Vol. 10, No. 4 (July-August 1963), p. 145.

34Jacob A. Loewen, "Confession, Catharsis and Healing," PA Vol. 16, No. 2 March-April 1969), pp. 63-74; and "Confession in the Indigenous Church," PA Vol. 16, No. 3 (May-June 1969), pp. 114-127.

35Mowrer, *The Crisis ... op. cit.*, p. 202 after Alfred Wilson, C. P., *Pardon and Peace* (New York: Sheed and Ward, 1954), p. 5.

36Tournier, *A Doctor's ... op. cit.*, p. 10.

make a complete confession in one sitting. He strongly criticises ministers who think that they have done their duty after they have listened to a person for two or three hours. He insists that there must be a series of sessions in which the guilty person is allowed to "free associate," i.e. to confess anything and everything of which he is consciously aware at the moment, but that further opportunities will be necessary so that additional ramifications of the guilt can be brought to the light. Because inhibitions and repressions often slow up this process, it is extremely important that an adequate amount of time be allowed to achieve a full and complete confession.[37]

4. Mowrer continues that the confession must be public. He indicts Reformation leaders who rightfully abrogated the evils of the medieval confessional, but who in turn removed even the "one human being" who could provide a social link in forgiveness, by introducing silent prayer and secret confession to God alone. He says that Reformation leaders were so impressed with the divine aspect of forgiveness that they forgot completely the aspect of social reconciliation. They developed powerful institutions, but in many cases have failed miserably in helping the vast majority of their adherents to achieve a satisfactory release from guilt.[38]

5. Mowrer also feels that such public confession should come at periodic intervals. He feels that not only would such confession be healing in nature, but it would also function as a preventative against becoming involved in guilt-producing behavior. He cites a Chicago bank that gives its employees a periodic lie-detector test because "it helps them to stay honest," or as Mowrer puts it "it increases their will-power."[39] Lest some feel that the Catholic confessional would meet Mowrer's requirement, he specifically says that it does not, for it removes the sinner too far from the essential social contact. The privacy of the confession, the distance of the priest from ordinary life, and the average perfunctory performance totally undermine its potential positive functions.[40]

6. To the above aspects we need to add the Christian premise that forgiveness through confession is possible only if there is genuine repentance and the intent to abandon the evil.

Some cautions. There is another side to confession, however, and we want to stress this by adding several cautions concerning its use:

1. Confession is not an immediate cure to all problems. If the internal pressures that were built up in order to produce the confession were very great, then the verbal catharsis may still be followed by a period of intense distress. Psychiatrist Anton Boisen has already illustrated this in the experience of the man who con-

[37]Mowrer, *The New Group . . . op. cit.*, p. 97.
[38]*Loc cit.*
[39]Mowrer *The Crisis . . . op. cit.*, p. 216.
[40]*Ibid.*, pp. 194-196.

fessed his infidelities to his wife, but who then went into such a severe emotional crisis that he had to be institutionalized for several months. Boisen points out that because his repression had been so severe, the emotional forces required to produce the confession had to be built up to such an intensity that once they broke through the defenses and produced the confession, it took several months before they had worked themselves out, and the individual could recover his emotional equilibrium.[41]

2. Confession can be easily abused and any misuse can be harmful. This is true both for the confessor as well as for the person hearing the confession. For the confessor the experience may merely be a compulsive form of exhibitionism rather than a genuine experience of catharsis; for the listener, in turn, the experience may just be a morbid kind of voyeurism. For the American public which is not used to public confession, certain guidelines may be advisable.[42] (a) The audience receiving the confession should include only those who are mature enough to cope with its content. For example, a child in an African society might be much better equipped by its cultural experience to cope with confessions in

matters of sex than an American child of similar age. (b) The audience, at least in non-face-to-face settings, should not be indiscriminate or casual as at a Sunday morning worship service. (c) The goal of the confession must be clearly focused on the quest of receiving forgiveness and not on developing the lurid details of the infraction.

3. A special type of misuse of confessions and forgiveness often grows out of social insecurity. In his quest for the assurance of acceptance by others, the insecure individual may may be tempted to confess wrongs he did not actually commit. Such confession is self-defeating, for the confessor is in actual fact alienating himself rather than establishing belonging because he himself knows that he is trying to gain acceptance under false pretenses.

Expiation. When the Comanche grandfather and his favorite grandson lost their best horses at the hands of the aggrieved husband, they experienced revenge rather than expiation. Expiation is a voluntary or at least an expected cost which actually or ritually atones for the transgression. Speaking of expiation Mowrer says that sin always impairs "the ease and the zest" with which man participates in social institutions, and it undermines interpersonal "confidence and security." For this reason repayment in the sense of sacrifice, suffering, and restitution (meaning replacement, restoration, putting something back) has long been widely

---

[41]Anton T. Boisen, "Religious Experience and Psychological Conflict," *American Psychologist*, Vol. 13, 1958, pp. 568-570 quoted in *Ibid.*, pp. 104-105.

[42]See Jacob A. Loewen, "Guidelines for Self-exposure," HIS Magazine, January 1967, pp. 30-32.

recognized as the basic expression of human justice and the means of again making oneself acceptable after having violated some established code of conduct or some social contract.[43] As already suggested in the preceding statement, expiation may take a wide variety of forms.

1. Restitution. The most obvious form of repayment is, of course, restitution by means of which the culprit repays the damages he has inflicted. Thus when a Chulupi woman sold another woman's burros and spent the money, she had to call upon her relatives to help her assemble the full price of the animals before she could be released from her guilt. Even the violation of the Kaka virgin mentioned earlier was viewed largely as a property infraction and therefore as requiring economic restitution.

2. Expiatory payments. In cases like that of the Manus Islanders, all infractions bring about Sir Ghost vengeance and only after full expiatory payments have been made to the living relatives of the offended ghosts, can the culprit be assured release from spirit vengeance. With the Manus Islanders such expiatory payments carry both a social and supernatural component. Consider the following scenes described by R. F. Fortune:

> On Friday morning Pope took propitiatory payment, kano, to Kemwai, to expiate the offense between Noan and Pwentshiam in Kemwai's house, and another propitiatory payment to Pwiseu's house to expiate Noan's having seen Puiseu's wife naked. Standing in his canoe before Kemwai's housefront Pope addressed the talipolalau calling them by name and saying: "Here is your payment, you ghostly ones, to expiate the evil done under your roof." The payment, a cedar wood box with its lock and key and a European axe, he had first placed on the house platform. Kemwai did not appear. But after Pope had gone away Kemwai, as the mortal ward of the talipolalau, took the offering made to them unto himself.[44]

In similar vein Fortune continues: "Next day at dawn Paliau offered up payment to pwanau and to other Sir Ghosts, the relatives of pwanau, and divided up the payment among the wards of the Sir Ghosts.[45]

It is important to recognize, however, that such expiatory payments often are almost entirely ritualistic or at least have greatly decreased economic utility. This can be seen in the case of the Nuer reconciliation cited in the introduction. The goat was called an ox; often even a cucumber can be called an ox in ritual contexts. This ritual aspect of expiation can also be seen in the following Colorado example. A shaman was

---

[43]Mowrer, The New Group... op. cit., p. 91.

[44]Fortune, op. cit., p. 151.
[45]Ibid., p. 223.

carrying on an illicit affair with a community girl. His wife, the girl's parents, and the community at large were deeply upset and came to the missionary for help. Upon his counsel, the people decided to send a delegation to speak with the offending individual. After his public confrontation, the shaman at once broke off the affair. Within a few days he killed one of his choice pigs and then sent pieces to all the relatives of the girl and other leading community individuals. To the missionary he sent the head.[46] This example also raises the question of whether the missionary received a piece because he was functioning as the representative of the supernatural. If this is the case, then we again see the social and the supernatural elements linked in the forgiveness process.

Such expiatory payment, however, need not necessarily be made to the offended individuals. In fact, Mowrer (facetiously or maybe even maliciously) says that most patients of psychiatrists consider the high fees they have to pay to their counsellors as part of the "sacrifice" or "expiatory payment" necessary for them to receive forgiveness and release from their guilt.[47]

3. Sacrifice. Sacrifice certainly involves a cost to the one seeking release, but it usually carries very strong overtones of supernatural atonement. That it is not the actual cost but rather the sacrificial ritual which is important becomes apparent in such practice as the Nuer substitution of a cucumber for an ox; or the poor Inca's substitution of a guinea pig for a llama. It is also seen in the Hebrew sacrificial code which permitted the poor individual to substitute a pigeon for a ram. The Hebrew atonement process in addition to its expiatory functions also had allusions to substitution, i.e. the animal which died, was dying in place of the culprit. In fact, even the criminal who paid for his crime by his own death had to recite a special ritual formula so that his sacrifice would indeed provide release for him and for the society: "May my death be an expiation for all my wickedness."[48] It is probably the element of equal substitution that caused the human victim to be rated as the utmost in sacrifice. For example, the Tahitians resorted to human sacrifice only in times of direst national calamity and then only after all other efforts had failed. The king then exhorted the people: "Let us offer a man as a sacrifice to atone for our unintentional offences and to regain God's favor in this our great

---

[46]A personal communication from Bruce Moore, missionary to the Colorado with the Summer Institute of Linguistics.

[47]Mowrer, *The New Group... op, cit.*, pp. 91-94.

[48]George Foot Moore, *Judaism in the First Centuries of the Christian Era* (Cambridge: Harvard University Press, 2 Vols., 7th printing, 1954), Vol. 1, p. 547.

distress."[49]

Sacrifice as a means of atonement has a more or less world-wide distribution. It is, of course, most prevalent in societies with a pastoral economy, but even such highly agricultural societies as the Iroquois sacrificed white dogs in atonement for tribal offences.[50]

4. Penance. Most major religions have placed strong emphasis upon penance. This usually involves some kind of bodily mortification. A Hindu *sadu* may sleep on a bed with projecting nails. A Roman Catholic penitent may be required to recite a certain number of Ave Marias or to abstain from certain comforts or pleasures. Again, many Protestant groups will exclude the disciplined individual from holy communion for a period of months even after full confession has been made. However, penance is not unique to the major Western religions. It was also found among the Maya, Aztecs, and Incas even before the advent of the Spanish Conquerors.[51] In the case of the Incas the penance prescribed by the priest often involved a night-long vigil in the cold beside the river in which the culprit washed away his sins.[52] The Crow of the Plains spent extended periods in solitary vigils, fasting, and hanging themselves up by thongs pulled through their chest and shoulder muscles.[53]

While Western religions have often ideally viewed penance as an attempt to impress the culprit with the seriousness of his infraction, the overtones of payment cannot be denied. A further dimension of penance – to evoke divine pity – seems to have played a rather prominent part in the religions of the Middle East. The ancient Hebrews operated on the principle that true penance always moved God to pity and that it was an ideal means of preventing divine punishment.[54] Hebrew prophets again and again called their people to "sackcloth and ashes" to prevent the wrath of God from destroying them. Even the Gentiles of the city of Nineveh escaped divine destruction when "the great and the small" heeded Jonah's warning of impending destruction and sought forgiveness in universal penance.

Among the Plains Indians of North America bodily torture such as extended vigils and fasts, and the pulling of thongs through chest muscles and

[49]Paul Radin, *Primitive Religion* (New York: Dover Publications, Inc., 1967), p. 180.

[50]George Peter Murdock, *Our Primitive Contemporaries* (New York: The MacMillan Company, 1934), p. 317.

[51]William L. Wonderly, "The Indigenous Background of Religion in Latin America," PA, Vol. 14, No. 6 (November-December 1967), p. 247.

[52]Julian H. Steward, editor, *Handbook of South American Indians*. Bureau of American Ethnology Bulletin 143 (Washington: Smithsonian Institution, United States Government Printing Office, 1946), Vol. 5, p. 580.

[53]Melville J. Herskovits, *Man and His Works* (New York: Aflred A. Knopf, 1966), p. 178.

[54]Moore, *op. cit.*, Vol. 2, p. 67.

shoulder muscles which then had to be ripped open, were probably more an attempt to buy supernatural favor than to atone for guilt, because such tortures often were essential requisites to a spirit encounter. However, E.H. Erikson interprets the Sioux sun dance in which young braves tore their back and chest muscles as a form of atonement for guilt accumulated during the process of growing up.[55]

5. Social sanction. Especially in medieval Europe and the Middle East penance also involved overt social sanction. The culprit was visibly marked so as to be exposed to social scorn and ostracism. Examples of this would be the famous Sünderhemd 'sinner's robe' which penitents were required to were publicly, the shorn head of the "fallen girl," and the branded "scarlet letter." Also to be included in this category are exile both in its literal and its figurative forms, such as prohibition to participate in certain church functions for shorter periods. In the case of the Lengua of Paraguay, exile was usually self-imposed and was probably not as much the result of a penitent attitude but rather was caused by an upset innermost.

Release. Once confession and expiation have been made, release is to follow. One might say that primarily this release involves the assurance that the culprit will no longer be subject to supernatural retribution. Note the expected release from the avenging Sir Ghosts in the following Manus quotation:

> ... *pwanau!* E! expiatory payment to you this. You struck them down. That was well. But they did not flee from their place. They all remained here. Later on you struck them down (again) and this time they fled.... You restore the soul stuff that you have! Send it to *topwal* who will send it to *poketa!* ... The real person, the real soul stuff is in your possession. Send this person to health. E! Expiation has come and has gone to all the ghosts who are great. All may grant your request. You made war. Expiation has come to you.[56]

However, there is also a social dimension to release. As said earlier sin and guilt produce estrangement, and confession and expiation are basically designed to re-establish fellowship. This was in evidence in both the Nuer and the Kaka examples cited earlier. The importance of such social release is very apparent in the following Lengua reconciliation scene.

A married student in the Bible school became a rather proficient singer and song director, but in characteristic Lengua fashion he shared none of his feelings or his learnings with his wife. She became so outraged, partly from the slight and possibly even more because of

---

[55]Erikson, *op. cit.*, p. 149.

[56]Fortune, *op. cit.*, p. 151

the earlier matrilineal dominance that was now being violated, that she burned his best clothes, his song books, and even his Scripture portions. When the young husband realized what she had done, he disappeared for a day. But twenty-four hours later he showed up in the Bible school quite ready to own his lack of communication with his wife, which, according to his own words, had triggered her violent reaction. In the meanwhile Lengua church leaders had called a public meeting for the evening. There the young man again repeated his guilt of non-communication. In the course of a lengthy discussion the wife also owned her anger. After all the participants had each said their piece and the husband and wife had agreed to amend their ways, the leader summarized the consensus and proclaimed that evil had now been removed. Then he pointedly asked the men: "Will you now stop talking about this?" When they answered in the affirmative, he called on the women, then the young people, and finally on the children. As evidence of the full release, the young man was back in church singing and directing the singing at the next evening's meeting.[57]

However, the release must also be personal, i.e. the person himself must be able to accept forgiveness.

[57]Personal communication from Gerhard Giesbrecht, missionary to the Lengua.

In other words, he must be able to forgive himself. This personal release restores the inner equilibrium and peace and there by sets in motion the process of physical and psychic healing. Mowrer underscores the aspect of personal release when he says:

But what is here generally overlooked, it seems, is that the recovery (constructive change, redemption) is most assuredly attained, not by helping a person reject and rise above his sins, but by helping him *accept them*. This is the paradox which we have not at all understood and which is the very crux of the problem. Just so long as a person lives under the shadow of real, unacknowledged, and unexpiated guilt, he *cannot* (if he has any character at all) "accept himself;" and all *our* efforts to reassure and accept him will avail nothing. He will continue to hate himself and to suffer the inevitable consequences of self-hatred. But the moment he (with or without "assistance") begins to accept his guilt and his sinfulness, the possibility of radical reformation opens up; and with this, the individual may legitimately, though not without pain and effort, pass from deep, perva-

sive self-rejection and self-
torture to a new freedom, of
self respect and peace.[58]

---

[58]Mowrer, *The Crisis ... op. cit.*, p. 54.

These three dimensions of forgiveness: the supernatural, the social
and the personal will be further
detailed in a separated paper under
the title "Four Kinds of Forgeveness.

Four Kinds of Forgiveness

The four kinds of forgiveness are: supernatural (divine), religious, social, and self-forgiveness. These are closely interrelated, and all are necessary for a full experience of forgiveness. The author investigates the dynamics and mechanisms of these four kinds of forgiveness, making use of insights from anthropology, psychology, and psychiatry.

I

A CARIBOU Eskimo community is suffering intense hunger – all the game has disappeared. The members of the tribe meet with their shaman leader in order to ascertain the cause of their troubles. The shaman goes into a trance and "sees" that the terrible sea goddess *Takanakapsaluk* has been offended by the many broken taboos and evil thoughts of the people: and in punishment she is now withholding their food supply. Acutely aware of their guilt, the people – adults and children – confess broken taboos, sins, and their countless wicked thoughts, but their condition continues to grow worse. There is only one remedy left – they must send the shaman "in person" to propitiate the angered deity. This involves a most difficult trip to the "bottom of the sea" where the goddess lives. It is a journey fraught with extreme difficulty and terror: falling stones, fierce mythological animals, and malignant spirits lurk everywhere to destroy any

human who might dare to embark upon this way. Only the most courageous shaman would so much as dare to try; for even if he should survive and arrive at the destination, he still has to confront the angry goddess who, with hair dishevelled and covered with filth (the product of human transgression) is seething with anger, because she is suffocating in the foul emanations of men's sins. She has to be cleansed and pacified if the people are to receive release from their punishment. On arriving, the shaman gently begins to wipe away the filth and to stroke and to comb the hair of the fuming goddess. Bit by bit her fury subsides until finally, when she is fully pacified, he is able to turn her face to see all the animals she has been hoarding. Her wrath placated, the goddess now releases men from their punishment and returns their food supply.[1]

[1] K. Rasmussen, *The Intellectual Culture of the Caribou Eskimo*, pp. 124-217, quoted from Paul Radin, *Primitive Religion: Its Nature and Origin* (New York: Dover Publications, 1957), p. 165.

II

Looking out of the window one day, a missionary to the Chulupi of Paraguay saw two women in a violent fight beside the village well. They had grabbed each other by the hair and were hitting each other with "no holds barred." He hurried out to separate them, but succeeded only after one of the deacons from the Chulupi church came to lend him aid. On being separated, one of the women, a believer, then took her waterpot, put it on her head and went home. However, when shortly thereafter the other woman, an unbeliever, passed her house, she again attacked her with renewed fury. Once again the deacon • separated them. Next day the two accidentally met in front of the store of a nearby village and fought another round. By this time, the believing woman was feeling very guilty and so she and her husband came to the missionary to make confession and to ask for help. Here is her story:

A donkey buyer, offering fancy prices for burros, came to our village, and the unbelieving woman cashed in on the bonanza. However, she sold not only her own animal, but also two belonging to me. Furthermore, she not only sold them without my permission, she spent all the money before I even found out what she had done. This made me so angry that I started to fight at the well.

However, the confession to the missionary was only a prelude, for the Chulupi church leadership was also moving to settle the quarrel. All the people who had sold donkeys, the relatives of the offended and the offending women, the missionary and other leading people of the village were called together to discuss the matter. At the meeting the fighting women, their relatives, and many others present spoke their opinions. Finally the leader called upon several who hadn't spoken yet; so they too spoke. When all had aired their feelings, he called for a settlement. The relatives of the offending woman helped her raise the money necessary to pay the aggrieved woman. The latter accepted the money and promised to "let go of her anger." The leader then called on the missionary to "seal the matter" in prayer. The guilt had been aired, restitution had been made, and social forgiveness had been achieved. Finally this social transaction had been divinely validated by the missionary's prayer.[2]

III

A very devout college senior had already on several occasions confessed her guilt: During the last two years in high school she had yielded at least in part to the approaches of one of her married teachers. The affair was terminated before it reached serious proportions; nevertheless severe guilt had been accumulated. She had asked God for forgiveness

[2] A personal communication from Gerhard Hein, missionary to the Chulupi.

earnestly and with tears on many occasions. In fact, she had already confessed her guilt to one of her closest friends, but she still could not find release. Finally, in a conversation with a sympathetic female relative, she realized her problem — she needed to forgive herself. She needed to admit that she — the good girl — had fallen far short of her own Christian ideals. She also had to accept the fact that no confession could undo her deed; that could only be forgiven. After struggling for several more days she at last was able to "own" these facts about herself, and with this honest admission she achieved a sense of peace and release — she had finally been able to forgive herself.

IV

Dear Ann:

I am 19, a sophomore in a midwestern university and considered good-looking and reasonably bright by my peers. I've been dating since I was 15 and, without boasting, I can truthfully say I've had more than my share of male attention.

During this summer, I met my ideal. We dated several times and I found myself saying "No" to others in the hope he would call. I loved being with him. On August 2 he was leaving for his vacation. We both hated to part and sat in the park for two hours saying good night. For some mys-

terious reason all my will power and good intentions vanished and I gave in. I told myself "This is love. Why should I deny him a true expression of my feelings?"

He sent a few postcards along the way but did not telephone me as I had hoped he would. Last night he returned — a changed man. He took me to supper and informed me that it would probably be our last date. These are his words: "You are not the girl I had hoped you were. Our last night together was a nightmare. You made me ashamed of myself. I could never marry you after that. I would always wonder if there had been others. This has been the greatest disappointment of my life."

So there's my story, Ann. I am trying to keep my chin up, but it isn't easy. I tell myself no decent man would treat a girl this way, but deep down I know it was my decision, not his — and all the rationalization in the world doesn't make it right.

Yesterday's Fool

The counseling columnist's answer to this confession in summary was: We will publish your letter as a warning to others, but in the meanwhile keep your chin up. You've just learned the hard way. Remember, even when a fellow asks the "big question" it doesn't really mean he is not the hero that you have been waiting for. Even heroes ask. If the girl says yes, however, he may well decide that she is not the heroine he has been waiting for.[3]

This college sophomore's guilt has been confessed publicly, though anonymously. It has been "atoned" by exposure and by the salutary warning it provides for others. However neither the divine nor the social aspects of forgiveness are in focus. The college sophomore, using one of the modern, non-religious channels, is trying to achieve secular forgiveness.

The preceding four accounts illustrate four kinds of forgiveness — supernatural, social, self, and secular — which form the concern of this paper. We want to discuss and further illustrate each of these four types of forgiveness in order to show:

1. That the first three types of forgiveness (divine, social, and self) are three essential aspects of a fully adequate process of guilt resolution. In a given setting and with different kinds of infractions, their relative, overt preeminence may vary, but the conspicuous absence of any one of them will leave the penitent with serious spiritual, social, psychic, and often even physical problems.

2. That the current popularity of secular forgiveness is in large part due to the failure of the church as a divinely ordained social institution to help man to deal adequately with his guilt.

[3]From Ann Landers's column entitled "The Big Question," *The Miami Herald*, Section C, Thursday, October 10, 1968.

Supernatural (Divine) Forgiveness

The supernatural, to which man appeals for release from, or which he tries to propitiate because of, his failures, assumes a variety of forms. In the Eskimo curing ceremony described in an earlier paper on confession,[4] the appeal for the release from guilt by the penitent and the supporting community was directed impersonally to the supernatural forces that avenge broken taboos by sending illness to man.

In the account of the Nuer reconciliation following the wounding of the young man described in an earlier paper on forgiveness,[5] the supernatural which was invoked as a witness to the social transaction was addressed as *kwoth* 'spirit.'

Among the Manus Islanders the supernatural is represented visually in the form of the bleached skulls which personify the souls of their deceased ancestors called Sir Ghosts. These supernatural forces stand in a direct kinship relationship to living persons.[6]

Traditional Hinduism provides its

[4]Jacob A. Loewen, "Confession, Catharsis and Healing", *Practical Anthropology* Vol. 16, No. 2 (March-April 1969), pp. 63-65. Quoted from William A. Lessa and Evon Z. Vogt, *Reader in Comparative Religion* (New York: Harper and Row Publishers, 1965), pp. 410-414.

[5]Jacob A. Loewen, "The Social Context of Guilt and Forgiveness," *Practical Anthropology* Vol. 17, No. 2 (March-April, 1970), pp. 80-96; quoted from John Middleton, editor, *Myth and Cosmos: Readings in Mythology and Symbolism* (Garden City, New York: The Natural History Press, for American Sourcebooks in Anthropology, 1967), p. 117.

[6]R.F. Fortune, *Manus Religion* (Lincoln: University of Nebraska Press, 1934) p. 3ff.

adherents with a pantheon of personalized deities which is so vast that it has been said to outnumber the actual population.

The ancient Hebrews addressed their appeal for forgiveness to Yahwe, whom they considered as their own exclusive God, for it was he who had chosen Israel to be his special people and had made an eternal covenant with them.[7] In Christianity, which is essentially based on this Hebrew tradition, God has already been universalized so as to make him the God of all nations (Acts 10:34-35).

The quest for supernatural forgiveness. The quest for supernatural forgiveness almost always involves either penance (Inca, Tupinamba, medieval Catholics, etc.), expiation (North American Plains Indians, Manus Islanders, Hindu sadus, etc.), or sacrifice (animal: Nuer, ancient Hebrews, etc.; human: Maya, Aztec, Hindu, etc.). Of these ritual accompaniments, sacrifices are the most conspicuous in that they imply a substitute in life and blood to atone for the guilt and to purchase the release of the culprit. Sacrifices can be personal or communal, and in their ultimate degree they require a human victim to atone for human guilt. The following two examples are merely illustrations of a wide range of sacrificial practices.

The monsoon rains had just finished destroying most of the crops when Hari Singh, a Ghaziabad street sweeper, returning from work found that his two pigs had wandered away

from home and had been locked up in the city pound. Since he had neither money nor prospect of getting any to redeem them, he was sure that this calamity was divine punishment for his wicked life. He was convinced that he must seek atonement, but he did not know how. That night the goddess *Kali*[8] appeared to him in a dream and told him what he must do. The next day he did it.

While his wife and children were at work rescuing the remains of their damaged crops, he took their four-year-old son Bihram, and screaming *Kali mai ki jai* 'Hail, Mother Kali,' cut his throat. He sprinkled some of the blood on the back of the black image and the rest he smeared on its forehead. Then he sat down under a tree waiting for the goddess to demonstrate her forgiveness by freeing his pigs.[9]

The preceding is an example of spontaneous non-ritual sacrifice. It stands in bold contrast to the highly ritualized human sacrifices of the Aztecs or even the following example of African animal sacrifice.

The Botswana of South Africa seek supernatural release from guilt in the following sacrificial ritual. While the priests kill two animals (a black one to atone for the evil deeds and a white one to purify the culprit), the penitent kneels and makes a full

---

[7]For the original covenant relationship see Genesis 12ff; for a prayer of forgiveness on the basis of the covenant relationship see Psalm 51.

[8]Kali is also called The Dark Mother. She is the wife of Siva, the great god of the Hindu pantheon. She is black and terrible, for death and destruction are her domain. Her tongue protrudes from her ugly mouth. Her eyes and the palms of her four hands are red. Her earrings are corpses and she wears a necklace of human skulls.

[9]*Time*, October 6, 1958.

public confession of his misdeeds. On completing his confession he drinks some of the warm blood of the sacrificed animals. Then the priest places some of the fatty entrails on the penitent's head and calls on the angered deity to accept this sacrifice of reconciliation and to release the penitent from guilt and retribution.[10]

Religious Forgiveness

Both of the preceding examples illustrate the fact that supernatural forgiveness almost always involves some kind of social dimension. In the Hindu example we see it in the human sacrificial victim. In the Tswana sacrifice we have the officiating priests and the observing public. In fact, these two dimensions are so inseparably intertwined with each other that it is often difficult to separate them.[11] This supernatural-social linkage (which we are here calling religious forgiveness) stands

[10]Radin, op. cit., p. 179.

[11]We can see this divine-social linkage in most of the examples of forgiveness we have cited. In the case of the Nuer youth the appeal for forgiveness was directed by the fellow villagers of the offending individual to both the fellow villagers of the wounded lad and the "spirit." In the Eskimo example cited in the introduction, the shaman, acting on behalf of the society which has individually and collectively confessed its sin, placates the angry goddess. In the Hebrew atonement ritual the priests and Levites function as representatives of both the divine and the society as they listen to the confession and perform the sacrifice. In the case of the college senior we have both confession to God and to people; however, it is probably correct to say that in a given transaction usually one or other of these dimensions predominates.

out boldly in the following account of reconciliation and forgiveness among the Chulupi.

Two profligate teenage girls insulted several older church women with some very vulgar sexual language. (This is the epitome of insult and evil, since the Chulupi avoid all direct reference to sex even between husband and wife.) The women became angry and a fight resulted. As time went on more and more women on both sides became involved in the dispute, until finally even a number of men were drawn in. Before long, however, several church people began to feel guilty and asked the missionary to help them arrange for a reconciliation meeting. The first part of the meeting was largely accusation and counter accusation, but gradually as more and more of the participants had spoken their mind, consensus in regard to the primary guilt of the two girls (of course, there was also clear recognition of secondary guilt of many other people) seemed to be emerging. The men therefore called for mutual apology and reconcilation; since the two girls, however, were not ready to own their guilt, they flared up in anger and stormed out of the meeting. The gathering dissolved with the matter unresolved.

Two weeks later was communion Sunday. When the group gathered, several of the men pointed out that before they could legitimately participate in holy communion, they would first have to settle the community problem. Obviously they could not deal with the offending girls, who, not being church members, were absent from the communion service. The leader began by exhorting all the believers to get rid of their bad feelings. After some discussion one of the men broke down and cried, admitting he had done wrong in joining the fight. Other men followed his example and confessed their part in the quarrel. After the men had set the pattern, the women followed suit and they too were reconciled. Then the Indian leaders called on the missionary to deliver a message from God's Word. The latter responded with a sermon on confession and forgiveness. When he finished, several of the Chulupi men rose to reinforce his words by pointing out that only as people forgive each other can they in turn receive divine forgiveness. Then having been reconciled publicly, the group celebrated their release in holy communion.[12]

The theology of forgiveness. This is not the place for a full-scale discussion of the theology of forgiveness. However, we must highlight some of the theological premises for the rituals and agencies of forgiveness which the Christian church purports to provide. The Christian practice of forgiveness, as we have suggested earlier, finds its origin in the earlier Hebrew rituals which demanded that the sinner confess his transgressions to Yahwe in the presence of the priests and the people (Leviticus 5:5). With his hands placed on the head of the sacrificial animal, which represented his personal substitute in the expiation for the sin committed,

the penitent made his confession. Then the priest as the human agent of the supernatural carried out the atonement ritual and pronounced the forgiveness. Even more dramatic was the great Day of Atonement in which the sins of the entire nation were confessed over the heads of two rams — one to be slain in sacrifice and atonement and the other to be led into the wilderness as a symbol of the removal of the guilt (Leviticus 16).

The ministry of John the Baptist, as recorded in the Gospels, consisted of a call to confession and repentance (Mark 1:4); and on the public confession of their sins the people were baptized. Jesus went even farther and stressed the mutual responsibility of the members of the believing community by assigning to them the functions of face-to-face soul nurture (Matthew 18:15-20) and "binding and loosing" of erring members of the church (Matthew 16:18-19; John 20:19-23). Some of the Epistles carry a similar appeal, as when James (5:13-20) calls for believers to confess their sins to one another and to pray for each other so that they may be healed. The Anabaptist wing of the Protestant church has tried to put this commission into practise and affirms that every believer can hear the confession of his fellows and can help them obtain divine forgiveness. They call this ministry the *priesthood of believers* since it delegates a share in the priestly function to every believer.[13]

---

[12]A personal communication from Gerhard Hein, missionary to the Chulupi.

[13]The name "priesthood of believers" is drawn from I Peter 2:9 where the believers are spoken of as a "royal priesthood" and the support or the practice of this priesthood is found in such passages as Matthew 18:15-20, Matthew 16:18-19, and John 20:19-23.

Retreat of the church from the priesthood of believers. If we look at the history of the Christian church we find that long before the Middle Ages the earlier practice of the priesthood of believers had largely given way to a professional priesthood with a monopoly on dispensing religious forgiveness. Theologians have raised the question whether this shift was not already well under way even in apostolic times, as signaled in the shift from the *homologeo* 'to confess, to admit or declare publicly' of John the Baptist's preaching to *metanoeo* 'to feel remorse, to change one's mind, to repent, to be converted' which predominates in the Pauline Epistles. But whatever the cause, there is no question that the original voluntary public confession had been largely replaced by compulsory, private confession in which a professional priest assigned penance and gave absolution. In fact, in the medieval church forgiveness had become a semi-commercial enterprise, since one could purchase indulgences, i.e. buy advanced "forgiveness" for sins one intended to commit and thus be free from incurring guilt and penalty when the forbidden act was actually committed.

The Protestant Reformation proposed to sweep away these and other abuses, but it did not in actual fact reinstate the priesthood of believers as a general practice; for with the Reformation emphasis on silent prayer and confession to God alone, even the one tenuous social link – the priest – was removed from the forgiveness process. In retrospect we have to admit that Luther's famous

Reformation slogan "the just shall live by faith" worked only as long as men lived in relatively closed communities with more or less permanent face-to-face relationships. With the advent of rapid urbanization, widespread mobility, and increasing social distance, more and more people have found that this "cheap grace" (as Mowrer calls the practice of confession to God alone) was no longer able to resolve their guilt. But the church, instead of realistically facing the declining relevance of its practice and developing the necessary socioreligious contexts for meaningful forgiveness, quietly retreated from the field and relinquished its Christ-given commission to minister to sin-sick souls and unprotestingly accepted the emphasis of 19th century psychiatry that these problems were based on constitutional and biochemical factors rather than on genuine guilt.[14] Even there where the post-reformation church did continue to involve itself in forgiveness, it largely slipped back into the medieval pattern of the minister operating as a professional rather than a "brother." However, as professionals concerned with souls ministers often left something to be desired. Many clergymen thought they had done their duty when they had listened to a man for an hour or two, at least if they had done so on several occasions. When a man came back too often they were prone to say: "He's a sick man who makes mountains out of molehills." They did not understand nor sympathize

---

14O. Hobart Mowrer, *The Crisis in Psychiatry and Religion* (Princeton, N.J.: D. Van Nostrand Co., Inc., 1961), p. 82.

with the deeper human problems that underlie the things such "sick" people say. Tournier points out that it was Freud who manifested "real love for the souls of men" for he had the patience to listen to them sympathetically for hundreds and thousands of hours.[15]

Mowrer goes even a step farther and accuses ministers of "preaching beyond their experience." He asserts that many clergymen have actually lost confidence in religion as an effective forgiving agency, for when they themselves have serious guilt problems, they almost invariably seek support and direction from a secular therapist rather than within their ranks.[16]

Having castigated ministers, Mowrer then proceeds to indict the whole congregation, which he calls "a pious fellowship that preaches salvation" but which can no longer tolerate the acknowledged sinner in its midst. In the church setting people have to conceal their sin from themselves and from the members of their fellowship, because most Christians would be horrified if a *real* sinner should suddenly be discovered among the "righteous." Mowrer concludes: "So we remain alone in our sin, living in lies and hypocrisy. The fact is that we all are sinners."[17]

---

[15]Paul Tournier *Secrets* (Richmond, Virginia: John Knox Press, 1965), p. 39.

[16]Mowrer, *op. cit.*, p. 157.

[17]*Ibid.*, p. 191, quoting Dietrich Bonhoeffer, *Life Together* (New York: Harper and Brothers, 1954), p. 110; see also Paul Tournier, *The Whole Person in a Broken World* (New York: Harper and Row, Publishers, 1964), p. 78.

Social Forgiveness

Like supernatural forgiveness, "pure" social forgiveness (except in relatively superficial social-etiquette-type infractions) is relatively rare, for in major reconciliations the supernatural element, where not overtly visible, is at least implicit in the social transaction. In an earlier essay we reported a Colorado reconciliation episode in which a shaman, involved extramaritally with a girl, broke off the affair in response to community action; and then killed a pig, and sent portions to members of the aggrieved family and leading individuals of the community including the missionary. Obviously the pig was serving as an expiatory payment, and the portions sent to the relatives and the community leaders were related to the social aspect of the atonement; however, the head sent to the missionary gives all the appearance of having supernatural implications.[18]

The social dimension. The importance of the social dimension in the forgiveness ritual has often not been fully appreciated by religious leaders, especially those within the mainstream of the Protestant tradition. On the other hand, Pentecostals in Latin America not only permit, they often encourage public confession and the accompanying social forgiveness. And it is this social dimension of the forgiveness which they offer that seems to account in large part for

---

[18]For more detail on this incident see Jacob A. Loewen, "The Social Context of Guilt and Forgiveness," *op. cit.*, p. 92.

their appeal to people of Catholic background who have found the secret confessional inadequate for achieving full assurance of forgiveness.[19]

Even in those societies in which a shaman applies pressure to extract confession from a patient in the process of magical healing, the social dimension is present in at least two aspects. First of all, the shaman's intervention is based on the common faith of the community, and so he functions as a representative of the community as a whole. Secondly, the members of the community are often present in person providing social support by singing, dancing,[20] and various types of antiphonal response.

Similarly, the Hebrew priest at the sacrifice and the Roman Catholic priest in the confessional are representatives of both the deity and the society from which man needs release. When the confessional becomes secret, however, the social dimension is severely weakened. It is precisely the social dimension that often makes confession to a fellow Christian so helpful, for in the involvement of this one person the whole church society is symbolically represented. We can thus generalize and say that when a priest or a minister serves as confessor by peer group consensus rather than by profession or by bureaucratic placement, he too can function as a representative of the group

as a whole. However, if he is separated from the community by ecclesiastical investiture, by professional expertise, or even more by celibate withdrawal from ordinary life, he compromises his function as social peer and weakens the social link in the forgiveness process.

The importance of the social dimension is obviously related to the way in which sin and guilt function. Sin, as Dietrich Bonhoeffer in his book *Life Together* points out, always withdraws the culprit from his community, and the more isolated the person becomes, the more destructive the power of sin over him. If we add to this the Reformation emphasis on the "with God only" transaction of forgiveness (which seldom suffices to legitimately integrate the culprit into the community) and compound this with the social distance that accompanies secularization and urbanization (which have left men floundering with very weak or broken interpersonal relationships), we begin to understand why the social dimension of forgiveness is so essential.

In other words, man needs a social context in which he can openly admit how far he is falling short of his ideals, but in which he will be accepted and loved in spite of his shortcomings, and in which he will be supported in every genuine effort to develop the kind of group approved behavior he really desires. Mowrer feels that our dependence upon society goes far beyond mere support. He suggests that even the desire to do right is dependent upon the social context.

---

[19] Julian H. Steward, editor, *Contemporary Change in Traditional Societies, Vol. 3: Mexican and Peruvian Communities* (Urbana: University of Illinois Press, 1967), p. 98.

[20] Lessa and Vogt, *op. cit.*, p. 400.

I am increasingly persuaded that will power or self-control is not nearly so much an individual matter as we sometimes think. Instead, is it not basically a *social* phenomenon? Here, in society, is where the norms and values reside, and the person whose life is open to social interaction and influence, has the benefit of social supports and sanctions. But the individual who embarks upon a policy of covertness and secrecy does not have this source of strength and soon finds himself the victim of uncontrollable temptation, and, as he is likely to experience it, a "weak will." Superficially, the difficulty lies in the area of his sexual drives and practices; but more fundamentally the problem is one of social integration or the lack of it.[21]

Group support. The fellowship that forgives and heals, the community that considers the sinner worth saving, and the social context that provides the penitent with the necessary support for learning new behavior represent the true priesthood of believers. Mowrer sees this function at its best not in the church of today, but in such organizations as the Salvation Army and Alcoholics Anonymous. He says:

> ...the most radically redemptive enterprises which we today know, notably the Salvation Army and Alcoholics Anonymous, are *lay* movements with "leaders" coming, not from our universities and seminaries, but from the ranks of their own converted and transformed personnel. Here the Priesthood of All Believers is more than a highsounding Reformation slogan; it is a living reality.[22]

Mowrer's thesis can be summarized as follows: The person overwhelmed by guilt is living in a self-created prison of duplicity and is denying his true identity. If he can be helped to overcome his unrealistic, moral fears and to repudiate his old strategy of secrecy and withdrawal, and instead be encouraged to "return to the community," he can be healed. He describes such a healing community in a therapy context. A woman whom he calls Marjorie had become so isolated by her guilt that she had to be institutionalized. But in the process of group therapy she was finally able to own her problem publicly. Mowrer describes how one day she burst out: "This morning Dr. Mowrer said I was not a very good mother," and before either the other patients or the psychiatrist could recover from their surprise she added: "And I am not." Then she described the specific incident which had precipitated her hospitalization. The relief she experienced from this confession was so dramatic that she was soon discharged from the hospital.[23] Analyzing this situation,

---

[21] Mowrer, *op. cit.*, p. 215.

[22] *Ibid.*, p. 150.

[23] O. Hobart Mowrer, *The New Group Therapy* (Princeton, New Jersey: D. Van Nostrand and Company, Inc., 1964), p. 109.

Mowrer points out that because Marjorie received so much approval and support from the other patients when she made her confession, she was able to appropriate social forgiveness. Nor did the benefit stop here --- Marjorie's courageous example was an inspiration to other patients, many of whom followed her example of transparency and likewise received help.

In his book *The Second Touch* Keith Miller describes in a first-person account such a fellowship setting in which social forgiveness can take place. Just before he left home to lead a men's retreat, Miller and his wife had a clash. In fact, it wasn't just an isolated spat; it was part of a vicious cycle of mutual harassment which they had not been able to overcome. But here he was with the responsibility of giving leadership to a group of church men, while he felt himself to be thoroughly unfit and dishonest.

> I realized that I really needed their prayers, and that I was just protecting myself and my reputation as a Christian by my silence, since many of them had been honest about the pressing issues in their lives. So I told the group what I have just told you. After a couple of minutes of silence, the man sitting next to me quietly confessed that he had had a remarkably similar weekend. Two other men then related almost identical experiences.... After we had talked awhile, my whole situation was in some way different.[24]

Because people are so ready to respond to transparency, Mowrer asserts that social forgiveness is really available at no monetary costs to everyone, if not in a church, then in somebody else's living room or in any other assembly of close friends. However, he goes on to point out that confession for social forgiveness does not mean that a person just furtively admits his sin to someone else; no, he must confess in the sense of honestly talking with his wife or with some close friends in order to become truly known. On the other hand, this does not mean that the erstwhile sinner has to "tell everyone," for everyone is not that interested in him. But if he really wants peace of mind, he must carry openness to the point that he does not care who knows about him. And if by sharing his life story with a stranger, he can help that person, he should be willing to do so.[25]

In the light of the above it is important here to point out that when a tribal society loses its social cohesiveness, and its traditional self-definition, social forgiveness will become increasingly more difficult to achieve. Canadian Indians are today deeply concerned about the fact that there is so much dissension on the reservation. They complain that their people are so "split up" that they cannot get together to do things cooperatively anymore. Nor is it only

---

[24] Keith Miller, *A Second Touch* (Waco, Texas: Word Books, 1967), p. 19.

[25] Mowrer. *The New Group Therapy, op. cit.*, pp. 18-19, 86.

a Canadian Indian problem; it is a matter of universal concern. For this reason societies undergoing rapid social change are in special need of a church community in which the inevitable tensions can be released and helped.

Forgiving Oneself

We have already pointed to the fact that self is to a large extent defined in the social context, and when a person does not live up to his ideals, his guilt tends to alienate him from his fellows. The alienation, of course, grows out of the fact that the person feels guilty not only for his original misdeed, but also because in his social interaction with others he projects "a role" by which he implicitly or explicitly makes certain claims about himself, and in turn demands certain things from his fellows. Since the person harboring the guilt knows that he is not the person he claims to be, he must of necessity hate himself for his dishonesty.[26] Mowrer says that when people affirm "I don't care what people think of me," they are really confessing that they are tormented by a guilty conscience and that they cannot honestly accept themselves. They are therefore projecting their non-acceptance upon others and are then rationalizing to cover up their ego deflation.

This leads us to the basic premise of this section. In order for a person to receive full forgiveness, he must be able to "own" his sin and to "forgive" himself. All too often, how-

ever, we attempt to help people to "rise above" their sins rather than to help them to admit their failures; but this is not the way to salvation. As long as a person lives under the shadow of real, unacknowledged and unexpiated guilt, he cannot, if he has any character at all, "accept himself," and all our efforts to reassure him will avail nothing. He will continue to hate himself and will suffer the inevitable consequences of this self-hatred. But the moment he begins to accept his guilt, the possibility of radical reformation opens up and the person may legitimately pass from pervasive self-rejection and self-torture to a new freedom of forgiveness and self-respect.[27] This was clearly shown in the case of the college senior in the introduction.

When a person is unable to own his guilt, he often becomes involved in a vicious cycle. Aware of not having been reconciled, he represses his own guilt and projects his unforgiveness on his fellows, but this only alienates him all the more and so he is further weakened to accumulate more guilt. Again, the guiltier the person feels, the less likely he also is to forgive the failures of his fellows. When this happens, he becomes guilty of the same lack of forgiveness he is projecting on others. The tragic result of this vicious cycle is that the man ultimately must lose touch even with his real self. Jourard says:

> We conceal and camouflage our true being before others to foster a sense of safety, to

---

[26] Erving Goffman, *The Presentation of Self in Everyday Life* (Garden City, New York: Doubleday and Company, Inc., 1959), p. 13.

[27] Mowrer, *The Crisis ... op. cit.*, p. 54.

protect ourselves against unwanted but expected criticism, hurt, or rejection. This protection is purchased at a steep price. When we are not truly known by the other people in our lives, we are misunderstood. When we are not known, even by family and friends, we join the all too numerous "lonely crowd." Worse, when we succeed too well in hiding our being from others, we tend to lose touch with our real selves.[28]

Secular Forgiveness

The label "secular forgiveness," as we have intimated earlier, is not on a par with the other three kinds of forgiveness. In a sense it stands as a polar opposite to supernatural forgiveness, for it represents an attempt at guilt resolution without even so much as an implicit supernatural validation. It differs from religious forgiveness in the fact that an overt social dimension is more or less obligatory, while in the latter the social element, at least in part, appears to be optional (because it is theoretically possible for man to make his transaction with God alone). This social element may, of course, be reduced to one person as in the case of the psychiatrist, and at other times it may occur even without an actual face-to-face confrontation as in the case of the counseling columnist. In psychiatric group therapy and in Alcoholics Anonymous it, of course, involves a more extensive social context.

It is no secret that in America and Europe the clientele of secular forgiveness is growing at a phenomenal rate.[29] In fact, the number and the kinds of agencies themselves are rapidly growing. Some of the more obvious "secular forgivers" are doctors, psychiatrists, psychologists, guidance counselors, social workers, astrologers, counseling columnists like Abigail Van Buren and Ann Landers, etc.

The origin of secular forgiveness When we look for the bases of the secularization of forgiveness, we find a number of interacting factors such as (1) the general secularization of life and the universe that has accompanied advancing scientific education, (2) increased specialization, specifically the development of specialists in the area of man's psychic life, (3) rapid urbanization with its accompanying increase in social distance and the growing sense of isolation of the individual from the social group, (4) the Protestant emphasis on dealing personally and only with God, (5) the general retreat of the church from the priesthood of all believers and its soul-healing functions, and (6) the fact that the practices of secular counseling are often more realistically geared to human psychic needs for achieving forgiveness. Several of these factors warrant additional comment.

Increased scientific specialization has not only produced more kinds of specialists, it has also been accom-

[28] Sydney M. Jourard, *The Transparent Self* (Princeton, New Jersey: D. Van Nostrand Company, Inc., 1964), p. iii.

[29] Eugene A. Nida, *Religion Across Cultures* (New York: Harper and Row Publishers, 1968) pp. 25, 43, 46, etc; and Kurt E. Koch, *Christian Counselling and Occultism* (Grand Rapids, Michigan: Kregel Publications, 1965).

panied, at least in the Western world, with a kind of "awe of expertise." The doctor, the psychologist, the psychiatrist, etc., all seem to know so much more about the human psyche than the minister that the people have more confidence in them. A recent publication gives the following reasons why the "doctor" figure is replacing the "priest" and the "brother" in man's quest for forgiveness: (1) The doctor deals with the penitent in terms of a doctor-and-patient role rather than in a person-to-person relationship, and when the sessions are finished, there need be no further personal or social involvement between them. (2) The doctor's involvement labels the problem as illness rather than as guilt or blame, so the person feels less indicted by seeking help there. (3) The penitent need not fear rejection because it is the doctor's role to accept people. (4) The doctor solves the patient's problems through his technical competence and not because he has any personal commitment to him. (5) The doctor serves the patient for payment, and once he has received his due, he has no further claim on the patient. (6) The doctor's code of ethics demands that he keep the problems confessed in strict confidence.[30]

It is probably correct to assert that secular counseling is often more realistic in its approach to helping people in distress. As we have earlier stated, ministers have often been taught to believe in the once-and-for-all tran-

saction of confession and forgiveness, and as a result they have often lacked the patience to help the guilty person make a complete confession, to find full release, and to develop a new behavior pattern. Psychiatry, with its emphasis on self-disclosure and authentic being, on the other hand, meets both the long-range need for support in role rehearsal by its repeated sessions, but it also prevents the counselee from overexposing himself by rigidly limiting the amount of time allotted for each individual session.

The problems of secular forgiveness. However, as has been pointed out by Mowrer and others, secular forgiveness, including psychotherapy, is not without its problems. Like the priest in the confessional, the professional counselor often does not meet the peer requirements of the guilty person for adequate social forgiveness. The counselor's acceptance is inadequate as a symbol of peer group acceptance, and while the guilt symptoms may be temporarily reduced, the person actually remains bound and unforgiven in his interaction with his peers.

In counseling college students as a "brother" and with considerable self-exposure, I was made painfully aware of the fact that my acceptance of a student, while helpful in the beginning stages, often fell short of the long-range need of social acceptance. For complete forgiveness the student had to be helped to face his problems transparently with accepting peers. Jourard underscores this fact in his comment on patients' statements like: "You are the first

[30] Virgil Vogt, editor, *Concern: A Pamphlet Series for Questions of Christian Renewal,* No. 14, February 1967, p. 25.

person I have even been completely honest with." This statement, he says, always makes him uncomfortable because it reveals the fact that this person is unable to talk with his spouse, family, or friends in a helpful way, and professional psychotherapy is but a very inadequate substitute for this.[31]

A further problem, especially for psychotherapy, rests in the area of payment. As already indicated, many patients unconsciously consider the high fees as a kind of expiatory payment. But such payment is false expiation; and the very discovery of this fact can be harmful to the patient.

Next, Freudian psychiatry, with its assumption that guilt is basically false because it proceeds either from an abusing superego for which the person himself is not responsible, or it is future guilt, i.e. guilt about actions the person is afraid to perform, often works only on the reduction of the guilt *symptoms*, and leaves the actual guilt unresolved.

Again, impersonal agencies like counseling columnists offer the penitent only such tenuous social links that one is left with serious questions as to their actual healing and forgiving value.

On the other hand, astrology and related agencies are not truly secular agencies, for while they may not appeal to a personal supernatural, their supposed source of power is the occult which, too, is supernatural. However, since the occult is usually considered negative in orientation, the very fear of "having sold oneself to the devil" may often make the cure worse than the original disease.

Finally, whether our science-minded generation approves of it or not, man everywhere seems to find full release from his guilt only when the process of forgiveness includes also a transcendent dimension. Since psychotherapy in general operates on a purely human plane, it denies, in spite of all its values the penitent one of the essential aspects of adequate forgiveness.

Conclusion

Even though this paper employs many examples of guilt resolution drawn from tribal cultures and indigenous churches, it is, in actual fact, a critique of the forgiveness practices of the organized church in Western Christendom and in Western culture in general. Since the missionary is a product of this Western guilt-resolving milieu, there is danger that he foist his inherited and often woefully inadequate practices upon the developing indigenous church. Even where he does not actively "push" an inadequate pattern, he may unconsciously or even consciously discourage or stifle patterns which the indigenous church would normally develop on the basis of its cultural background. It is hoped that this frank look at the problem will not only help to prevent harmful involvements for missionaries, but that it will actually encourage them to actively help the indigenous church to develop and to practice adequate guilt resolution.

[31] Jourard, *op. cit.*, p. iv.

Missionary

Method and Role

Field, Term, and Timing in Missionary Method

RECENTLY I was reflecting on the difference between our first term as missionaries to the Choco Indians in Colombia and the work as it is presently being carried on in Panama.[1] In the process I made what seemed to me a very startling discovery. The absence of a mission field for the Mennonite Brethren had ruled out the regular missionary term for the workers, and the combined absence of the two factors led to some very radical changes in the approach to the mission.

The Mennonite Brethren Mission field in Colombia included the southern part of the Department of Choco and a portion of the Department of Valle just south of the former.

When my wife and I volunteered for missionary service and were assigned to Colombia, we expected to invest our life in the work on the Mennonite Brethren Mission field in this country. The life of service was

to be cut into terms, the first of which was to be five years and the succeeding to be seven years each. These terms would be separated by periods of furlough of two and one half months per year of service. The objective of this life time of missionary work was to evangelize the lost and to establish the church on the Mennonite Brethren field in Colombia. Our personal assignment — that of evangelizing the Choco Indians, a task which first required reducing the Waunana language to writing and translating the Scriptures into it — was only a fraction of the total program; and as such it had to be coordinated with and subordinated to the demands of the entire field.

In the course of our first term we were given administrative responsibilities, were made responsible for a number of large building projects, and were placed in charge of several different stations. Assignments to vacancies in administrative and building responsibilities were especially easy because the task of reducing a language to writing did not involve a fixed schedule of public meetings and so it permitted greater flexibility than that of the stations which had established medical and educational institutions and a regular schedule of meetings. Thus only during the last year of our five-year term (which we

---

1 Jacob A. Loewen, "The Church Among the Choco of Panama," PA, Vol. 10, No. 3 (May-June 1963), pp. 97-108.

Jacob A. Loewen has recently accepted a position as Translations Consultant for the American Bible Society in South America. He was formerly Professor of Modern Languages, Anthropology, and Missions at Tabor College, Hillsboro, Kansas. This article is one of a series currently running in PA.

voluntarily extended by six months) were we actually able to dedicate ourselves to our Indian language assignment. At the end of that year we were able to give the Indians the first gospel message. The account of the experience is found in "Good News for the Waunana."[2]

Before we left our mission field at the end of our first term, in January 1953, the Colombian government signed a new twenty-five year concordat with the Vatican, in which large portions of Colombia (including the territory inhabited by the Choco Indians) were assigned to the state church as mission fields. This removed the legal basis for mission work by other churches. Even before we left the field for our first furlough, the Colombian missionary council had recommended to the Board of Missions that the Choco Indian work be transferred to Panama, because the concordat would not permit its continuation in Colombia.[3] However, since the complete impact of the concordat had not yet made itself felt and no clear direction was apparent at the time, the Board of Missions tabled this proposal.

After two years of furlough, during which we did graduate work in the United States, we returned to the Colombian field. But this time (partly because of the concordat and partly because of a new specific assignment)

we were not attached to the field council. We were given two years during which we were to study the five dialects (which later actually turned out to be ten) that made up the Choco language family. The goal was to measure the mutual intelligibility between the dialects in order to ascertain the number of translations that would be necessary to make the Bible intelligible to all the Choco Indians. Because we did not belong to the missionary council of the field, we were not transferable and thus were able to dedicate ourselves exclusively to the objectives that had been outlined in our new assignment.

As a part of this assignment, during April and May of 1956, the author studied the Sambu dialect, the only one of the current Choco languages native to Panama. F. Glenn Prunty of the New Tribes Mission and Vinton Johnson of the Foursquare Church Mission accompanied the researcher to the Sambu area. Both missions had expressed interest in accepting responsibility for evangelizing the Choco of Panama; and after some negotiations, the workers of these two missions divided the field among themselves.

In 1957 when the full impact of the concordat had become apparent and even the language research was no longer feasible, the Board of Missions recalled the author and his family and considered the Indian field in Colombia as closed. The proposal of transfer to Panama was now reconsidered; but since this field was already occupied by two other missions, this door also seemed to be closed.

[2] Jacob A. Loewen, "Good News for the Waunana," PA, Vol. 8, No. 6 (Nov.-Dec. 1961), pp. 275-278.

[3] "Report on the Work among Indians" (May 1953), an unpublished report to the Board of Foreign Missions of the Mennonite Brethren Church.

Absence of Field
and Term in Panama

With the closing of the field in Colombia and the prior occupation of the field in Panama by other mission societies, the Board of Missions saw no alternative but reassignment to another country. The missionaries concerned, however, felt that their ministry to the Choco people was unfinished. They had done a large portion of the linguistic and cultural research. They had finally reached a point where they could deliver the gospel message to the Indians. Upon the missionaries' request the Board of Missions made an attempt to negotiate a "share" in the field with the other two missions. For this purpose a meeting was called in Panama City in 1958 with the representatives from the three missions concerned. However, the agreement did not materialize. This meant that the Mennonite Brethren Mission had no field in Panama. Thus no missionaries could be sent there for a regular term of service. This led to new attempts at reassignment to other countries. The second refusal of reassignment necessitated the acceptance of self-employment in the United States.

Both families (Wirsche and Loewen) continued to have deep concern for the Choco people. They requested the Board of Foreign Missions to permit them to negotiate with the missions working in Panama for special assignments among the Choco Indians there. Behind this request was the feeling that possibly the Choco Indians themselves would reach across the border to bring the gospel to their fellow tribesmen in Colombia. The time for this work was now limited — first, by the time that was available to the self-employed (in teaching) workers during their school vacation in summer, and secondly, by the tolerance of the missions who had assumed responsibility for the field in Panama.

Change in Method

As already stated, the absence of a field for the Mennonite Brethren dictated that no regular term missionaries could be sent. Thus a regular Mennonite Brethren Mission program was also impossible. The ministry was no longer on a field but to a people and could be carried on only with the permission or by invitation of the missionaries who controlled the field. This automatically eliminated such items as stations, property, and denominational institutions. In fact, it ruled out a strictly denominational church. In terms of actual work, it permitted only such specific work assignments as would be feasible for a twelve-week summer period and which would be in the interest of the Indian people, of the national government, and of the missions who controlled the territory.

The first summer program in 1959 was a testing program for literacy materials, in which newly prepared primers in the Epera language were tried in the New Tribes Mission area served by F. Glenn Prunty, who actually became the sponsor of the first summer program.[4] (Since 1961 Mr.

---

[4] Jacob A. Loewen, "Sponsorship: The Difference Between Good News and Propaganda," PA, Vol. 11, No. 5 (Sept.-Oct. 1964), pp. 193-203.

and Mrs. Prunty have been working as independent missionaries with support from several Baptist churches in the United States.) This first summer program in turn sparked the visit to the U.S. by one of the best Indian readers enrolled in the testing program.[5] All succeeding missionary visits were made upon invitations from both the government[6] and Indian believers.[7]

Clear Short-term Objectives

In order to receive approval both from the missions controlling the field and the board that was to finance the summer program, it was necessary to define some clear-cut, short-term objectives — not necessarily short in effect, but short in the period of thrust. The duration of the program was limited by the amount of time available during the vacation of the teachers concerned. Several such short-term programs were realized: testing of new primers, a literacy campaign at El Mamey, literacy among the immigrant Waunana, and instruction in simplified Spanish. There was a certain amount of fear on the part of the sending mission board that such short-term work might necessitate almost complete repetition each

summer. To preclude such repetition the missionaries were forced to plan programs that would meet an immediate need in the Indian setting. Such programs had to produce results visible enough to be able to provide impetus for Indian people to continue to develop them. Within each period of thrust there had to be provision for training those who were to perpetuate the work among the other Indian people. In short, the work had to be self-sustaining as soon as it was initiated.[8]

Not only was it obligatory that the objectives be clearly defined before going to the field, but the missionaries also found it necessary to keep a detailed account of what actually transpired. First of all, the Board of Missions needed to see clear evidence that the short-term work was accomplishing its purposes. Where the short-term objectives proved to be unrealistic and different programs had to be initiated, the reasons for the new approach had to be given. All setbacks, deviations, and changes in the work had to be explained and documented. To be sure the objectives were being reached; or, if they were not being reached, to assure an early awareness of the situation, the missionaries found it necessary to have frequent periods of evaluation. Often weekly, or at least bi-weekly, a period of time was set apart in which through meditation and prayer, the work was reviewed up to the present point and new partial goals were set. These periods of on-the-field evaluation for

---

[5] Jacob A. Loewen, "A Choco Indian in Hillsboro, Kansas," PA, Vol. 9, No. 3 (May-June, 1962), pp. 129-144.

[6] Nicasio A. Vargas and Jacob A. Loewen, "Experiencia de Alfabetización con los Indios Chocoes," América Indígena, Vol. 23, pp. 121-125.

[7] Jacob A. Loewen, "Reciprocity in Identification," PA, Vol. 11, No. 4 (July-Aug. 1964), pp. 145-160.

[8] Jacob A. Loewen, "The Church: Indigenous and Ecumenical," PA, Vol. 11, No. 5 (Nov.-Dec. 1964), pp. 241-258.

intermediate goals proved to be a real boon in the work. False thrusts could thus be more readily identified, and the early awareness of them permitted correction. It also pin-pointed some very early danger spots where the missionary can easily become a hindrance to the development of an indigenous church.

A good example of an abrupt change in approach took place during the 1961 campaign when David Wirsche left for a second village to begin another reading campaign, only to discover that the first church that had just been organized on the previous day was already sending its first missionary to this same village. An on-the-spot rethinking of the situation convinced the foreign missionary that he must at once leave the area and permit the national missionary to assume the responsibility. So Wirsche retreated to a different place, and the national worker took over. The result was a second Choco group won to the Lord, trained and organized into a church before the missionaries returned for the next summer's visit.

Wirsche also reported that at the height of his enthusiasm of being able to quickly lead an Indian who had never previously been exposed to the written page, to become a reader of the word, he was most vulnerable to the temptation to personally teach many people to read. He constantly had to stop and remind himself that his job was not to teach all the Indians to read or even many Indians to read, but to teach Indians to teach other Indians to read. The analysis of the statistics of the number of teaching literates over against just readers at

the intermediate periods of evaluation provided a constant checkpoint in this respect.

Again, the nine-month absences from the work also permitted a more objective evaluation of the situation from a distance. Many events and situations could thus be rethought in depth. Some were seen in a very different light after they were considered from the vantage point of the American scene. Other things turned out to be entirely changed when the missionaries returned to the field nine months later.

Missionary No Longer the Source of Authority

One of the first differences from the earlier approaches that became apparent was the fact that the missionary could no longer assume the responsibility of "the smeller of breath" or "the policer of morals."[9] The very brevity of the missionary's stay and the much longer period of his absence made this quite unrealistic. The local group of believers must be held responsible for the church from the very beginning. The authority in the church had to remain unchanged by either missionary absence or presence. On the one hand, it intensified the missionaries' awareness that the national Christians must and can at once depend on the guidance of the Holy Spirit.[10] On the other hand, it highlighted the missionary's

---

9 These satirical terms come from James A. Michener, Hawaii (New York: Bantam Books, Inc., 1961).

10 Jacob A. Loewen, "The Choco and Their Spirit World," PA, Vol. 11, No. 3 (May-June 1964), pp. 97-104.

responsibility to encourage implicit obedience to the voice of God as coming through the word of God, rather than obedience to himself or even to the church that sent him. The Scriptures could no longer be taught as a book of doctrine, but rather as the voice of God speaking to the daily problems of people born into the new life of children of God. The brevity of the summer term did not permit the missionary to "catechize" the people in his interpretations of the Scriptures and of necessity demanded that much emphasis be placed on the natives' own reading of the Bible and on their own listening for the guidance of the Holy Spirit in the interpretation and the application of this word to daily Christian living. Similarly, the immediate thrust to train leaders both in literacy and in conducting fellowship meetings was imperative. But that even these few weeks were not too brief for temptations to train nationals for followership rather than leadership[11] can be seen in the experience of the family altar services mentioned earlier. Such items as the selection of those ready for baptism, the standards for church membership, and the discipline of the disobedient had to be approached as the responsibility of the national church, because it was obvious that most of such problems would be faced during the nine-month period of the missionaries' absence rather than during the three months of their presence. From visit to visit it became

---

[11] Eugene A. Nida, "The National's Relationship to Missions," *Commission, Conflict, Commitment* (Urbana: Intervarsity Press, 1961), p. 154.

apparent that (1) the believers were maintaining a much closer talking relationship to the world than had generally been the case in the station-centered work; and (2) the separation between the church and the world rested not on the absence or presence of cooperation with each other but on the change that had taken place in the attitudes of the believers towards evil spirits and towards their responsibility to God and their fellow men.

Probably one of the most moving examples of indigenous maturity was observed by David Wirsche when he inquired why the people were not in the services and whether they were no longer interested in the services. The leader informed him, "Oh yes, they're interested in the services. But we feel that it is more important just now to watch our rice fields. You see, according to our former local law we killed all pigs that invaded our rice fields when the rice was ready to harvest. But now, since we have become Christians, we do not do this. Now our neighbors are trying to take advantage of us and are turning all their pigs loose. For this reason all the families that have rice nearly ready to harvest are staying by their fields to watch that the neighbor's pigs do not destroy the rice; for we do not want to kill the neighbors' pigs any more. If we want to talk to our neighbors about God's way, we must be kind to them first. Then they will listen."

The Missionary as Brother and Priest

Since now the missionary was not the source of authority, his position in terms of church discipline and his manner of dealing with problems within the group of believers was also changed. Proceeding on the basis of the priesthood of believers, the missionaries now employed self-exposure rather than authority when dealing with discipline problems. They revealed some of the incompleteness in their own lives in order to point out that there must be continual growth even after many years of experience in the Lord and that confessing sins of commission and omission is an important facet of receiving forgiveness from God.

Probably one of the most interesting lessons in the short-term visits was the fact that the missionary could not even act as the temporary "ball carrier" in the missionary program. He could really function only as a catalyst. For this reason, the missionaries found that it was of utmost importance not to deviate from the "teaching others to teach others" policy at any time. The reading specialist found it necessary to begin at once to train the first reader to become a teacher for others wanting to learn to read. But in the very process he also found himself training a person who was called upon to act as a witness concerning the Scripture, because as soon as the new student progressed to the reading of the word of God he began to ask questions about it. This immediately cast the literacy teacher into the role of witness for God.

Even in terms of the form of the message that could be presented the missionaries realized that they now needed an "instant" message, one which was ready for consumption by the Indians without much previous experience and which they in turn could share with others without very much further preparation. This led to the extensive use of narrative as message form.[12] After the telling of the story, both the content and the application could be highlighted through questions. These questions and answers in turn opened the way for a maximum amount of dialogue.

One of the unexpected blessings from the extended periods of missionary absence was the natural death of false thrusts in the missionary approach. On returning to the field after nine months, the missionaries were surprised again and again to see some of their pet projects having atrophied, while others, which had been definitely marginal to the thrust of the previous visit, had actually taken root and had grown. This, of course, meant that the proposed program, which had often been based on the premise of the previous year's activity, now had to be modified to be able to capitalize on the areas that had actually grown and developed.

A second benefit that the repeated and extended separation from the work and the field, both by time and distance, provided was the fact that it permitted the missionaries to do much more analytic and evaluative thinking on the program. The current series of papers on the Choco mission running in PRACTICAL ANTHROPOLOGY is one of the direct results of these periods of evaluation.

---

12 Jacob A. Loewen, "Bible Stories: Message and Matrix," PA, Vol. 11, No. 2 (Mar.-Apr. 1964), pp. 49-55.

The Problem of Time

When the summer programs of the mission to the Choco of Panama were first proposed, one of the concerns of the sending Board of Missions involved the fear that a summer program of only twelve weeks of thrust was too short to establish an indigenous church program.[13] A concomitant concern was that the nine-month interval between programs would be too long for even a successfully initiated program to operate independently on "indigenous steam." Underlying these two fears was an even more basic apprehension that if a summer program should be succesful and if the nine-month period of entropy should prove to be too long for native initiative, this very entropy could lead to a serious disillusionment of the tribe. If such a disillusionment should take place, it might require more than merely repeating the work of the previous summer program — it could actually preclude the possibility of further fruitful work in the area.

It is only honest to admit that we, the workers, were not immune to these concerns. While this certainly was not the first occasion that we had been concerned about time and timing in our missionary career, it certainly was one of the most critical situations that we had experenced. Looking back now we can see how our own questions concerning the pros and cons of

a summer program and a nine-month interim, and the valid concerns expressed by the Board of Missions worked together to become a stimulus of sufficent strength and priority to cause us to schedule weekly, or at the longest, bi-weekly periods of evaluation throughout the duration of the first summer program.

These periodic evaluations proved to be invaluable and they have provided insight into and appreciation for a whole series of time and timing problems that face every missionary outreach. They can be loosely summarized in the following slogan statements: (1) too little and too late; (2) too much and too soon; (3) too much and/or too little for too long; and (4) a "fullness of time" for every step taken in accordance with the purposes of God.

Application of the Time Slogans

My earliest recollections of "too little and too late" are in connection with missionary reporting. Returning missionaries frequently repeated this slogan as an indictment against the churches in the homeland. They stressed that the churches were sending too few workers and this, generally, at too late a time. To compound the error, they were equipping these workers with too little in terms of tools and financial support. This meant that even the few that had been sent were able to wage only very limited battle against the expanding non-Christian masses of the mission fields. The missionaries were able to document this indictment with reports on how after years of sacrificial work, the missionary program

---

[13] For the outright assertion that short-term service cannot do a lasting job see: Lois Sorenson, "Practical Problems: A People in Transition," PA, Vol. 5, Nos. 5 and 6 (Sept.-Dec. 1958), pp. 222-227.

was experiencing retreat from area after area long before a strong indigenous church had been established there. Their proving of the too little and too late indictment against the church was at least in some measure instrumental in causing me to volunteer for missionary service. It symbolized my willingness to go and to do what little I could regardless of home support and final outcome.

While I do not want to deny that the church in Western Christendom has often failed to meet its responsibility, I, as one of those who at least tried to do his duty, must today say that the short-term experience in Panama has reversed in a large measure the application of this indictment from the church and has focused it on my own and on my fellow missionaries' service.

The most serious application to missionaries that this slogan, "too little and too late," finds, in my estimation, lies in the area of placing confidence in the national church and in its national leadership. In this respect, I feel, we have fallen behind not only in the amount and in the quality of the confidence that we have extended, but also in terms of the lateness of the time when we extended it. Thus as independence movements forced the missionaries out, nationals, who had been trained only for followership and who were not ready to assume the leadership that the work demanded, became the pilots under whose hand the ship of the national church had to try to navigate the restless sea of national independence or self-determination. The reason for the latter condition, of course, was that the missionaries themselves had done too much for too long. This type of time error is indulged in, especially in the areas of pastoring national churches, exercising church discipline, organizing programs, and in the general exercising of leadership. Foreign missionaries had frequently become the indispensable "big wheels" without which the mission machine could not operate. This in turn was really the root of so much and such strong anti-missionary feeling in the younger churches, and also the cause in the latters' alignment with so many of the extreme kinds of nationalistic movements directed against the mother church and against the country from which the missionary came.

Among the Choco of Panama who live in a folk society which, like so many other societies of this type, maintains itself largely by resisting outside influences, the "too much and/or too little for too long" slogan found another application. If the missionary message comes to such people in a continuous and sustained barrage without intervening periods for internal discussion and diffusion during which the pros and cons and the advantages and demands of the "new way" are weighed in group discussion, the most natural response of such a society is to react against the bombarding message; to treat it as an enemy attack and to reject it once and for all. Folk societies especially will need ample time for the message to diffuse and for the group to arrive at collective readiness to accept it.

The opposite in time, "too much

too soon," is another live danger. This is especially true in connection with the beginning of preaching, the calling of men to commitment, the structuring of the program, and the organization of the national church. It is so easy for even a very good and well-intentioned missionary to be trapped into becoming little more than a fiercely vocal propagandist in his preaching, or a modern spiritual scalp hunter in his call to commitment. There will be times of strong temptation to be an over-eager harvester who plucks the fruit while it is still green, or a high-pressure evangelist who engineers commitment on an undigested and unassimilated message. This is a special danger for the Western trained missionary, who has learned to convince men by reasoning with them concerning the truth. Where such an approach is used by a missionary with superior education who also is a representative of a more technologically advanced society, the recipient, a so-called primitive, may not be aware of any other polite alternative than to accept what his "superior" is recommending. And so he may make a premature commitment.

I believe we can say that all such time errors are counter to the purpose and the example of God. For me, the issue of doing too much too soon has become a very crucial one, especially since I have realized how long Almighty God prepared before delivering his message of redemption through his Son. I believe there is general agreement that God intended to redeem men from the very first moment of sin. And we will do well to consider that God did not only take many

years, but actually many generations, to develop both the ceremonial-action object lessons of the Hebrew religion and life and the words and ideological concepts in the Greek philosophical system before he felt it opportune to unveil his redemption through the Son: "But when the fulness of time was come, God sent forth his Son."[14]

On the other hand, in the matter of doing "too much for too long," I have been simply amazed at how long I personally have overlooked the significant precedent in the life and ministry of Christ. For thirty long years Christ learned to live and feel with men. This left him only a little more than three years of actual ministry to teach and to prepare those who were to be the witnesses of the redemption he was to effect. The confidence that Christ manifested in these twelve men is downright staggering when compared to any confidence that I have ever manifested in a fellow-worker, be he missionary or national.

Time for Preaching

I believe the question, "What is the missionary's chief aim and responsibility?" will be almost universally answered with, "To preach the gospel of Jesus Christ." In fact, it seems to me that for many Western Christians (missionaries included) the word "preaching" has actually come to be quite synonymous with their ideal of proclaiming the good news. I and many other missionaries have frequently bemoaned the fact that other duties — administrative, professional, and otherwise — kept us from fulfilling what we considered our first and

14 Galatians 4: 4.

major task: that of preaching the gospel.

While definitely unsettling, it was also exceedingly enlightening for me to listen to Luis Chicaisa, an Ecuadorean national evangelist of Quechua extraction, who in very frank terms told me what he had observed about the missionary program of the several missions in Ecuador that he knew. His basic complaint was that missionaries got off the plane and immediately began preaching. "In fact," he said, "I have known missionaries who have preached for many years and have never yet stopped to listen and to see whether anyone was understanding or even paying attention to their message." When I asked him for a remedy to this problem, he was quick to answer: "The remedy is in listening. A missionary should never attempt to explain the gospel to a Quechua Indian until he is able to converse with the man in terms of the man's own idiom." He said, "When you meet a Quechua Indian and want to witness to him, you should enter into a conversation with him. You should learn to appreciate his vocabulary. You should see whether you can find out what his concerns and problems are. And after you have talked with him for a while, you should be able to talk to him in terms of his own needs, his own worries, and in his own idiom." In other words, he was saying that much missionary witnessing is premature, before "the fullness of time."

Eugene A. Nida points out how a missionary in Africa effectively used the above learning approach in a tribal society. Whenever this mission-

ary entered a village, he would join the men around the campfire and for several days (weeks, if necessary) he would inquire of the elders concerning their local beliefs in God. Invariably the time would come when the elders would ask him, "And what about your God?"[15] This was "the fullness of time" for the delivery of the missionary's message.

The same kind of working toward the fullness of time can be seen in the approach of the missionary in Ecuador who taught the state church catechism to the people of the community (because they were not interested in the evangelical message) until several weeks later the elders asked him, "If you know so much about our religion, how come you are an evangelical then?"[16]

Mr. Chicaisa was very convinced that one of the big impediments of mission work in Ecuador was the heavy dependence on the scheduled preaching services. He felt that too many North American missionaries viewed the organized preaching service as the first and basic vehicle of missionary evangelism. And he, as an Ecuadorean, felt that scheduled preaching was something that should happen only much later in the contact with the gospel. For him the idea of renting buildings in many out-stations and villages for the purpose of using them as preaching points was definitely preaching prematurely — before the people were ready to receive the

---

15 Eugene A. Nida, "The Indigenous Churches of Latin America," PA, Vol. 8, No. 3 (May-June 1958), p. 118.

16 Ibid.

message that the missionary was proclaiming.

Of course, we need to underscore that an individual's witness can also be premature, even if it is a private person-to-person witness. It was very instructive for David Wirsche to observe that even the young Choco church was aware of the need for timing its witness to unbelieving neighbors. They discontinued their church services to watch their rice crops rather than kill the offending animals as was their former practice. This is working towards the fullness of time for witnessing.

In regard to the witness in non-scheduled meetings, Nida gives an interesting account concerning the Otomi Indians of the Mesquital region of Mexico:

> This group has no formal system of instruction for teaching the people. Rather they invite any new convert to come and live in the community for six months to a year, during which time he learns what it means to be a Christian. He participates in almost daily religious services, learns to pray by praying, learns to trust God through joint devotions and trials in the community, and is finally sent back to his own town or to another, where he becomes a member of one of more than twenty or so congregations meeting in various chapels throughout the region.[17]

Time for Diffusion

One of the important factors that David Wirsche and I feel we have learned through our experience of conducting only summer programs among the Choco of Panama is the

---

17 Ibid., p. 114.

fact that the nine-month absence during the year actually provided a time for the diffusion of the message. This diffusion time was very essential because it permitted the society to discuss the message informally in their homes, in the fields, and at social gatherings. They had time to discuss what a commitment would cost them and what kind of things would have to change in their culture and their personal lives.

Nida stresses the urgency of recognizing the need of time for diffusion in face-to-face societies. He rightly intimates that the average missionary, both by experience and by training, has come to believe in high-pressure evangelistic methods which will yield dramatic results overnight. For many the altar call has become almost synonymous with effective evangelism. Because of this background and conditioning the missionary will need to exert extra caution not to violate his welcome in the group-oriented society. Members of such traditionalist societies view themselves as one large family under whose umbrella there is security for all. The group maintains itself largely by resisting all the invasions that come from the outside world. These people cannot be pushed into making a quick decision. They need time to make up the "group mind." When confronted by a crash program, such societies will by reflex be inclined to reject it totally and at once. Should the evangelist become overanxious and urge even one or more of the more receptive individuals to step out for Christ, he may by that very encouragement precipitate the rejection of the message by the group as a whole. Any gap in the ranks of tribal solidarity immediately raises group fear, and by instinct the group will tend to close its ranks to resist the disintegrative element. "Allowing sufficient time for making decisions is the indispensable third principle in communicating with face-to-face societies."[18]

A second feature associated with time for diffusion that we feel we have learned in Choco evangelism is related to the amount of new material that is introduced at any given time. Because of the brevity of a ten- or twelve-week summer program, only a limited amount of material could be given in each area. While we bemoaned this fact at first, it actually turned out to be one of the important foundations for the success of the program. The time for diffusion sifted out those truths which were actually pertinent to the people; and when we returned nine months later, we found that these apposite truths had been rather generally accepted and were appreciated by the bulk of the society. Other truths that had been very meaningful to us, but which were not as relevant in their society, had just fallen by the wayside and had been forgotten. We concluded that the tendency to introduce a total doctrinal system very early in a national Christian's experience may not be the ideal.

There were at least three observations that led us to this conclusion. We noticed first of all that the early New Testament church did not have the full code of New Testament doctrine at its disposal on the day of

Pentecost or even at the founding of the Gentile churches, but rather the New Testament was written to meet specific problems as these arose in the churches; secondly, that the new Christian is often overwhelmed by the extensive list of do's and don'ts with which he is confronted; and thirdly, preliterate societies are not used to emphasizing the letter (the exact wording) of the law, because they are used to law spread by word of mouth, which (because it is oral) has a far greater emphasis on the spirit or principle of the law. Thus oral law is seldom codified. The wise men of the society deal with aberrations on the basis of the general precepts that are group accepted rather than a specifically worded law.

In a meeting that took place in Panama between the executive official of the mission and the leaders of the Choco church, it was very interesting to note that when the mission official inquired of them what they were going to do about Christian living, the Choco leaders informed him that they knew that they were not perfect. They knew there were many things in God's message that still had not been translated into their language, but they felt that it was not necessary that they should know it all now. They would first need to learn to obey at least those demands of the word which they already knew before receiving a complete catalogue of rules.

Another interesting observation was associated with the matter of learning to read. While the people accepted the message that came to them in face-to-face discussion and in the witness of the Choco believers and the mis-

18 Eugene A. Nida, *Message and Mission* (New York: Harper and Bros., 1960), p. 113.

sionaries, once they learned to read, this "obeying readiness" was greatly increased; and the common expression was, "Now I don't have to listen to what the other people are saying any more. Now I can know the message directly from God."

A further contribution of time for diffusion was the way in which it worked to help produce national leadership. Anthropologists have long pointed out that leaders of face-to-face societies will never move far ahead of the people's movement they are leading. Leaders can align themselves with a new thrust, but must then permit a period of diffusion during which the bulk of the people can also come to accept the new ideals. Once this general acceptance takes place, a leader is strengthened in his position and can take another step in the direction of the change in progress.

Time for Commitment

To return to the earlier mentioned discussion with Luis Chicaisa, the Ecuadorean evangelist, I would like to add his concern about the time for decision: "Even the mere fact of attending an evangelical service is a very serious decision for many an Ecuadorean Indian to make." He felt that the missionary practice of renting rooms and arranging for services in the communities and then inviting the people can spell a very serious problem for the average Quechua Indian. Many of them are interested in knowing more about the gospel, but they are not ready to be seen entering an evangelical meeting place. If they go to a meeting prematurely (on pressure from the missionary and not on the basis of inward readiness) and then their friends make fun of them or persecute them, they very often turn against the missionary's message.

When I countered with the suggestion that maybe it would be better not to rent the rooms for meeting places but rather to have the meetings in a believer's or a sympathizer's home, he contended that this created even a more serious problem. In fact, he claimed that he knew of people who had decided against the gospel because their casual missionary friends had encouraged them too early to open their homes for meetings. If a Quechua did open his home for an evangelical service and his friends and relatives began to brand him an evangelical before he was ready to bear such a reproach, he would then have to try to disassociate himself from the missionary and his message. Such disassociation often becomes a serious obstacle for these people to further listen to the gospel.

Mr. Chicaisa's suggestion was that if a missionary or an evangelist wanted to have services in such a person's home, he ought to sow the seeds of the idea that God might speak to this man and might ask him to open his home. He used the Spanish expression, *"si Dios quiere"* (if God wills). He felt that if a person opened his home under the conviction that such was the will of God or of "fate," this individual would not make any attempt to defend himself against the ridicule of the people but would be ready to identify himself with the gospel because it was "so willed by God."

I believe, especially in regard to conversion, the matter of a personal commitment to become a Christian, extreme caution needs to be exercised. Earlier we cited the danger of yielding to the temptation of urging some more receptive individual to lead the way by stepping out alone, but we must not close our ears to the warning expressed by Nida that missionaries must exercise utmost care to avoid "over-urging and high-pressuring" of even the genuinely interested person within the folk society. He points out that face-to-face societies are not as easily misled by overt decision for Christ as is the foreigner. Members of such a society will know full well whether the individual is making his decision as the result of careful and full personal deliberation, or whether the sympathizer is merely a culturally marginal gold-digger who, for personal gain, is willing to become another "spiritual scalp" scored by an insensitive evangelist. We certainly cannot hope to predict the way in which the Holy Spirit will work, neither with the individual nor with the group; but we must remind ourselves that the members of the folk society will be the first to know whether or not the man's decision is genuine. Encouragement of the insincere one will not only harm the sympathizer concerned, but will also become a serious obstacle to block the decision of others.[19]

Some years ago in Colombia I observed a missionary of a very zealous evangelistic nature, who came to a Negro area on the Pacific coast and began a very high pressure evangelistic program. Frequently, he would report by the mail of twenty, thirty, and more decisions for Christ that had been registered in the meetings of the week. But this only lasted for about three months. Then one day he brokenly confessed that his church was completely empty now. No one attended the meetings any more. Many of the people, who had responded to the missionary's altar call out of sheer politeness, had been seriously embarrassed by the premature commitment they had made or that the missionary thought they had made. Now their embarrassment prevented them from returning to the chapel.

Group Approach

If it is necessary to exercise caution against urging an individual, we need to consider that it may be wise to double and treble this caution when we face a whole folk society with a decision. Donald A. McGavran points to the fact that many Protestant come from "gathered church convictions." They are people who believe in an individual conversion and in the separated church. But he makes the point that the gathered church has been effective only in areas that were already nominally Christianized.[20] For this reason he urges caution in employing this approach for general missionary work in face-to-face societies. Missionaries of this background will tend to appeal to individuals in their witness to the nationals. They

19 Ibid., p. 114.

20 Donald Anderson McGavran, *How Churches Grow* (London: World Dominion Press, 1959), p. 20.

will examine all comers carefully to make sure that they exhibit the marks of true disciples. Many will be refused by the missionary, for he does not believe as much in numbers as in the purity of the church.[21] By this approach the new believers will automatically be withdrawn from the life of their society and from participation in most of the activities of the community. McGavran asserts, however, that he believes that most of the world's undiscipled peoples will become Christians through group conversions and people's movements. "When the conditions are right, groups of people accept Christianity. They will accept Christ along with their families and their kinship groups."[22] This, he insists, was the method of the New Testament church:

> There we see the passion of Pentecost, which rejoiced in three thousand baptized in a single day and hastened to baptize more and more till, a short time later, there were five thousand men (perhaps twenty thousand persons) in the church. The Lord was adding daily to their number. Multitudes were believing, and a great company of priests became disciples of Christ. After this, Paul and others continued to gather further multitudes from the synagogue communities around the Mediterranean Sea.[23]

To penetrate such a culture and to spark a people's movement will require that ample time be allowed for diffusion. It will also require a real sensitivity on the part of the messenger to ascertain the moment when both the individuals and the society as a whole are ripe for decision. This fullness of time for decision in the life of a face-to-face society is of extreme importance. Nida has pointed out what he calls the "curve of a people's movement." When a face-to-face society, whose culture is in a relatively steady state, is confronted by a new message and another culture, change begins. Such a change may be quite imperceptible at first, but very soon the group as a whole faces the question, "Do we want to continue to change, or do we want to return to the old?" Should the group decide to continue to change, it will enter a people's movement which can lead to group conversion. But should the missionary — who most likely comes from a gathered church background — not be able to accept the idea of group decision, the tribe as a whole may feel rejected. In reaction to such a rejection the whole group may become closed to further evangelism. At this crisis point the reaction to the new message can also take the form of a violent nativistic movement which, if defeated, will generally leave the culture in a state of disillusionment. This disillusionment can extend (and for many American Indian tribes has extended) over several generations before revitalization and reintegration will begin.[24]

But discipling is not the end; for the "Holy Spirit, through Paul and the other apostles, put such stress on personal responsibility, individual appropriation of the riches of God in

---

21 Ibid., p. 22.

22 Ibid., pp. 23-24.

23 Ibid., p. 24.

24 Nida, *Message and Mission*, op. cit., p. 145.

Christ Jesus, search for the things which are above, crucifying the flesh, renouncing Satan and all his works, and putting on the whole armor of God, that discipled companies became full individuals who were mature in Christ."[25]

McGavran sees discipling as the prerequisite stage for the "graduate school" of the gathered church; and unless we enroll many millions of "children in Christ" in the elementary school of people's movements, there will be few takers for the graduate program of the gathered church.[26]

Nida supports this and asserts that we who do not know the meaning of clan living do not really know what such a person faces. The individual who derives his personal and social security from his family unit, instinctively gives' it his complete and unthinking support. Even as an adult, such a person would find it extremely difficult to decide against or even apart from his family unit.[27] This is illustrated with an equivalent from our culture:

> It is as though we invited a neighbor child to go to the beach for a day with our family without consulting his parents. And generally his first response will be, "I'll go and ask my mother." In fact, if we handled an invitation rightly, we would ask his mother for him so that she would recognize the conditions as well as the genuineness of the invitation.[28]

25 McGavran, op. cit., pp. 24-25.

26 Ibid., p. 24.

27 Nida, *Message and Mission,* op. cit., p. 114.

28 Ibid., p. 114.

Time for Organization

Frequently, missionaries trained in North America bring to the field the ready-made pattern for organizing the indigenous church — a pattern which they learned in their Bible school, college, or seminary.[29] The plea of this article is to permit even the organization to grow out of the need of the national church when and as it becomes ready for it under the direction of the Holy Spirit.

Regardless of what society we may come to, we must remind ourselves that these people have functioned as a social group prior to our arrival as missionaries. They have been able to handle all the social affairs of their society in the past. If now we can learn to understand and adapt their ways, or better still, if we can stimulate them to develop the forms and service patterns congenial to their indigenous ideals, we have helped to launch a truly indigenous church. The latter alternative, of course, will be even more ideal where group conversion or a people's movement forms the backbone of the early acceptance of the gospel.

At least three separate aspects of the time-organization relationship need to be underscored here: (1) the time for organizing a group of believers into a church, (2) the timing of the assumption of responsibility and authority by the national believers in the organizational structure, and

29 Another frequent mold is the organization of the sending body. See William A. Smalley, "Cultural Implications of the Indigenous Church," PA, Vol. 5, No. 2 (Mar.-Apr. 1958), pp. 60-61.

(3) the readiness of the local church to function as a part of a conference of churches both in a regional and in an ecumenical scope.

It is not uncommon in America for churches to keep misions or mission churches dependent on the authority of the mother church over a period of many years. This phenomenon is not unknown on mission fields either. There are areas with no organized churches that have been under a missionary program for ten and twenty years. These areas contain many fine believers who have been baptized. But seemingly the right moment to organize them into a church (at least from the missionary's point of view) has never come. They never seem to arrive at full readiness to accept the responsibility for their own church and its program. There are several such experiences in my own missionary background. There were groups of converts, but the church organization was always delayed. Was the program out of the reach of the people? Wasn't God providing this group with necessary gifts? Or was someone doing too much for too long? Obviously in such situations native initiative has already been largely stifled, and the people have learned that they are not considered responsible and trustworthy. Somehow they do not feel themselves directly responsible to God, as if they were only second or third class sons of God.

Time for Relinquishing Authority

Of course, the moment we organize a church, that church assumes its place and prerogatives under God.[30]

As such it is vested with authority and responsibility for such matters as church standards, readiness for church membership, choice of leaders of the various kinds, development of the service times and forms, discipline and purity of the church, and outreach extending from the local "Jerusalem" to the uttermost parts of the earth.

Early believers among the Choco in the Jaque area had been baptized by F. Glenn Prunty, but no attempt had been made to organize these believers in a church. Thus in the summer of 1961 questions had to be asked such as: Who of the baptized should belong to the church? What should the standard of admission be? What would qualify new converts for baptism? Since the missionaries were only going to be there temporarily, it was apparent that all such decisions must immediately become the responsibility of the church under organization. Because the missionaries operated on the assumption that the Indian brethren were responsible, the latter never questioned their obligation. Several of the older men conferred with Aureliano and told the author which names to write on the church roll. They also assumed the prerogative to investigate the candidates that were to be baptized during the afternoon of the dedication Sunday, and those approved were baptized by Aureliano.

It was very instructive for me to have Luis Chicaisa complain to me

---

30 The authority of the church under the Holy Spirit is effectively stressed by Lesslie Newbigin, "Bringing our Missionary Methods under the Word of God," *Occasional Bulletin* (Missionary Research Library, Vol. 13, Nov. 1962), p. 7.

(after hearing the story of the Choco church) that he felt that one of the reasons the church in Ecuador was not growing was because the missionaries were withholding the power to baptize and to ordain. In these discussions I learned how keenly he and other national men felt about this so-called "withheld power" on the part of the missionary and his church organization.

This reminded me of conversations with some of the missionaries evacuated from the Belgian Congo after independence. They had expressed both amusement and surprise at the fact that many of the Congolese had tried to stop them from leaving and shouted at them to leave the African souls behind. Upon closer investigation, it turned out that these native people had restructured the meaning of the missionaries' hesitation to turn over authority and responsibility to the nationals. They reasoned that missionaries were really disguised agents of modern slavery. Formerly, black physical power was used in slavery; but now the process had been refined, and missionaries by baptizing and writing people's names into books were capturing African "soul power" with which to operate the American economy and keep white men rich.

That some kind of leadership must be established as soon as the church is organized is very obvious. But how much? Here again, we need to be careful that we do not encourage overly cumbersome organizational machinery. The structure must find its roots in the indigenous authority patterns and must grow under the prompting of the Spirit of God.

In order to test the situation among the Choco, the missionaries attending the dedication service at El Mamey decided to precipitate a problem. So they put too much money into the offering taken to raise funds to pay for some lumber that had been used in the church building. When the church saw itself with more than enough money, a discussion immediately ensued as to what to do with it. Should the pastor keep it? They asked the missionaries about the practice in the American churches. When these said that pastors took care of the preaching and that a treasurer or business manager usually took care of the finances, they decided to select a "keeper of the money." However, the man chosen by common consent did not have a suitcase with a lock. This problem was solved when a nearby mestizo merchant offered the use of his strong box to the treasurer-elect.

As already stated in the story of the Choco church,[31] there was a second potential leader in the congregation and the missionaries were concerned about what the conflict would do to the stability of the church. They had so far found only temporary solutions; but during the afternoon of the dedication day, in response to an appeal by the pastor for a missionary volunteer, this "extra" leader volun-

---

[31] That the development of indigenous service patterns will take time and experimentation is seen in: "The natives themselves can work out the consequent changes or cultural and social adjustments. They alone can do this, and it takes time, experience and experiment." A. P. Elkins, *Social Anthropology in Melanesia* (London: Oxford University Press, 1953), p. 148.

teered to become the first missionary. So on its organization day the Choco church had acquired three categories of leaders. All were highly functional, and seemingly no one questioned their readiness to do the tasks assigned.

Since this was the first actual attempt made to establish services by the Indians for the Indians, the missionaries tried to demonstrate to them all types of prayer, Bible study, and other meeting styles. It was interesting to note that the Indian brethren chose those styles that allowed a maximum amount of bi-directional communication: Question and answers, prayers for each other in answer to spoken requests, testimony meetings, Bible discussions, etc.[32] At no time was it necessary for a missionary to lead the services. He performed only assigned parts, while the Indian hosts always assumed the leadership.

Discipline and Church Standards

This responsibility must also extend to discipline and church standards. One of the men at Lucas, appointed by the chief to be a teacher of reading, turned out to be a very able leader and so was being groomed by the church for leadership. However, he balked at the meagerness of the recognition given him, thereby precipitating a church crisis. The church then appealed to the missionary for intervention. The missionaries, how-

ever, referred the problem back to the church, saying that the church had selected the leader and that they were also responsible to discipline him. The church decided to separate this man from any active leadership function for six months. Later when he repented, the church again permitted him to serve in leadership capacity.

As already indicated above in the paragraph on leadership, the time for the Choco church to assume the responsibility for outreach was immediately on organizing. We often expect a church to wait years and years before it is thought to be strong enough to assume a program of witness. I am raising the question for myself, "Are we thereby depriving the church of a large portion of its potential vitality?" The Choco church not only sent their missionary the day after organizing, but also on the very dedication Sunday, the group took inventory of the relatives they had on other rivers who could serve as bridges in their outreach to other areas.

Personally, I believe the most vivid lesson of my need to be sensitive to timing in the transfer of leadership came to me when I stayed at El Mamey after dedication Sunday to teach a kind of family worship service in the homes of the various believers. The style had been developed in the pastor's home and provided simple but meaningful fellowship. It seemed just the thing to do, and so I did. It also worked beyond expectation. The new reader in the next home read a Bible story and asked the questions. These were answered and discussed by the group. There was meaningful

---

[32] The development of the Choco services is described in Jacob A. Loewen, "The Church Among the Choco of Panama," PA, Vol. 10, No. 3 (May-June 1963), pp. 97-108, and "The Church: Indigenous and Ecumenical," PA, Vol. 11, No. 6 (Nov.-Dec. 1964), pp. 241-258.

circle prayer for each other's needs. I was deeply moved and happy when the Indians took me back to my hammock by canoe. I looked into the sky and just breathed a "thank you" to God. "Is there anything else, God, that I can do that will make this even better?" Then with sledge-hammer force something spoke within me: "You are out of the will of God." I spent a good part of that night in meditation, and by morning I knew I was usurping the pastor's duty. When I apologized for this next morning, instead of our polite Western, "Oh no, you were not doing anything wrong," there were grave nods of the head by the older men who said, "Now God is talking to him."

Through our observation of the outreach of the national church we have learned something interesting in regard to time for the transfer of authority from the mission group to the local church. When the Jaque group was invited to the Yavisa area by another mission, five Indian brethren followed the call and taught some forty-five people to read and baptized twenty-three individuals. Leader Aureliano reported that for the last several days he had not been teaching reading any more because he had found a good man who could serve as leader. He had spent these days teaching this man how to lead the services, to baptize and to administer communion. His reason was, "I didn't think we could come back very soon and I felt it was very important that they be able to do all the things a church should do, so they can grow like our church."

From its very inception when missionaries and mestizo believers from several denominations shared in the church dedication, the Choco church has exhibited some rather interesting ecumenical aspects. These are detailed in another paper.[33] Also since several missions have been involved in the Choco work in Panama, a certain amount of inter-church cooperation, like the evangelistic trip to Yavisa area cited above, has been possible. While I believe wholeheartedly that this cooperation and ecumenicity should be increased, I feel keenly that it should develop from a fellowship relationship rather than as a paper organization between mission societies or American churches, in which the indigenous people concerned have little or no say-so and for which they have no feeling of need.

I believe I can generalize that most missionaries, like myself, are really quite time conscious. But it is time consciousness connected with a schedule of activities and associated with "an exaggerated emphasis on the virtue of punctually."[34] The great lesson I have had to learn during the short-term assignments is that the time consciousness which I really needed was that of timing readiness, of the fullness of time. Here I must confess that my experience is still very limited. I feel I have only learned the first steps in the kind of sensitivity to the Spirit of God that the work of God requires.

---

33 Ibid.

34 Nida, *Message and Mission,* op. cit., p. 170

Bible Stories:
Message and Matrix

How can the missionary begin a relevant witness before he has an under-standing of the local culture? What kind of framework can be built, what kind of matrix, in which new Biblical information will be relevant, per-tinent, and understandable? The author feels that the answer to both of these questions is a carefully constructed, telescoped chronological series of Bible narratives.

THE purpose of this paper is to focus attention on the value of Biblical narrative in the early witness of a missionary to face-to-face societies: (1) As a form of the message that can be handled rather early in the missionary's experience and which can also be of immediate use in the witness of the new convert. (2) As an expansible matrix or framework within which the individual truths of the message can be anchored contextually.

Must the missionary to a new culture wait with the delivery of his message until he has completely grasped the ways of the culture? On the basis of the first thesis of this paper we would like to propose that the answer is a qualified *no*.

This thesis is that narrative, because of its extensive use in so many (if not all) cultures, its flexibility for emphasis, drama-tization, and personal style, and because

of its holding power over even a very heterogeneous audience, is a form par excellence for a beginning witness of the Good News.

We hasten to underscore that this is not the first recognition of the importance of narrative in missions. Moravian mission-aries[1] under Zinzendorf's tutelage and Dutch missionaries to the East Indies have been known for their heavy depend-ence on Bible stories in their missionary outreach. Joh. Warneck, the Dutch mis-sionary to the Bataks of Sumatra, states his case for Bible stories very succinctly when he says:

> The missionary today can go no otherwise to work; he goes among the heathen as a herald and proclaims to them the things God has done, is do-ing, and will do. He waits on the result. At first he is compelled by his defective knowledge of the language and of the mental life of the people to adopt a simple method of story telling. He is forced to confine him-self to telling Bible stories from the Old and New Testaments, waiting

Jacob A. Loewen is Professor of Modern Languages, Anthropology, and Missions at Tabor College, Hillsboro, Kansas. Previous articles in PA include "A Choco Indian in Hillsboro, Kansas," Vol. 9, No. 3 (May-June 1962), and "The Church Among the Choco of Panama," Vol. 10, No. 3 (May-June 1963).

[1] Rev. Jacob Limkemann of the American Bible Society makes this observation in a letter dated August 29, 1961.

perhaps impatiently for the time when he will be able to vanquish heathenism by an exposition of the deep thoughts of the Christian religion. The language of a primitive people presents fewest difficulties to the narrative form of address; a very simple man can understand a story. And, lo, the teller of Bible stories discovers that a new religious world is dawning upon the heathen through the simple narration of what God has done for men; that these stories are better fitted than any well thought-out address for making blinded idolaters acquainted with the living God; that the simple telling of what God has done in the course of human history makes his image plastic to them and himself, no longer a bloodless idea, but an acting, thinking, feeling person. The stories of the Bible are everywhere listened to with pleasure. The heathen are keenly interested in them, and get from them a clear conception of what the new religion desires and gives. It is the Bible stories that transform the religious thought of the Animist.[2]

Elsewhere in the same book he then shows that as this simply narrated message permeates the culture we must be prepared for not the individual conversion, so highly idealized in our European heritage, but for group response:

Insight into the psychology of these heathen people whose religious thought is not individualistic but communistic sets the much abused methods of medieval missions in a better light than that in which they are usually placed. As today among animistic people, the medieval missionary was forced to aim at the decision from whole tribes and nations, and it was only after these had decided as a whole to accept the new religion that the educative work of the church began. Protestant missions have been unwilling to enter on this path, having an honest aversion towards it.[3]

Examples of Group Conversion

Interestingly enough, this conclusion can be supported with a number of documented examples. G. F. Vicedom says that in New Guinea the repertoire of Bible stories learned by the students in mission schools became a crucial factor in penetrating Papuan resistance to the gospel and led to the ultimate group conversion of the tribe.[4] Analyzing the development of the Meo church, G. Linwood Barney lists Nai Kheng's message form — simple stories of episodes from Christ's life coupled with his personal testimony — as the second of three main factors responsible for the rapid tribal acceptance of the Christian faith.[5] Our own experience with the Waunana provides us with another example:

However, the surprise was to come. ... One day, weeks later, five Indians from the Siguirusua River came to the missionaries' house ... and here they delivered their news: "Chief Enrique sends you word that all the Indians on his river have decided to give God the hand and to walk on God's road. ... After you left we waited three days till the chief returned from his trip. We told him

---

[2] Joh. Warneck, *The Living Christ and Dying Heathenism* (Grand Rapids: Baker Book House, 1954).

[3] Ibid., p. 146.

[4] G. F. Vicedom, "An Example of Group Conversion," PRACTICAL ANTHROPOLOGY, Vol. 9, No. 3 (May-June 1962), pp. 123-128.

[5] G. Linwood Barney, "The Meo — an Incipient Church," PA, Supplement 1960, pp. 41-52. Reprinted from PA, Vol. 4, No. 2 (March-April 1957), pp. 31-50.

exactly what you told us, and he said that this was exactly what his people needed. Then he took us to the house nearest to the headwaters of the river, and had them tell the story. Thus we went from house to house till all the people knew. And now all the people have decided to give God the hand and to walk on God's road."[6]

If the impact of Biblical narrative appears to be overemphasized in these examples, we may do well to recall the record of Acts[7] where, under the direction of the newly out-poured Holy Spirit, the simple historical narrative of God's dealings with Israel and local application became the catalyst that precipitated not only the acceptance of the "new way" by three thousand men, but also a chain reaction of witness and additions to the church that by our present-day standards looks like nearly impossible mathematical multiplication.[8]

If the effect of the gospel message in the Acts account is to be considered normal even for our day, we must ruefully admit that in many areas of our mission endeavor we have experienced only very attenuated manifestations of the Holy Spirit's power and work. Ours is a record of seemingly shallow conversions with little newness of life, of an ephemeral church that appears to depend on outsiders for survival and which has shown little spontaneous local witness. In some areas —even after decades of missionary activity — the gospel message is still considered "foreign propaganda." If converts have

actually received a "full and complete" gospel, they seem to have accepted or assimilated only certain parts of it. In fact, even those parts that have been accepted sometimes appear to have been restructured so extensively that if the Good News value of the message has not been completely destroyed, it has at least been grossly compromised. This is especially true of the first or the very early message given to the people. Maybe a personal experience can best illustrate this point.

Message of Doom

While working on the survey of Choco dialects, we came to a small village where a Chinese merchant had a light plant. A traveling companion had with him a tape recorder and the recordings of several isolated Bible stories and messages that had been produced by providing a bilingual Spanish-Choco Indian with a Spanish version of a story. He had translated this text sentence by sentence. His sentence-by-sentence translation had been recorded as a continuous narrative. There was no introduction to the first story and no transition except a "minute" of silence between selections. This tape was played to the Choco Indians on three successive evenings. By this time the whole area had become deeply troubled. The garbled message of stories had been restructured as a continuous whole. The sound effects of animals and people crying and the realistic noise of the storm had so frightened them that all were expecting the imminent catastrophic end of the world! The already constant fear of the demons was now compounded by a dreadful fear of God. In this case an "unpegged" message that was meant to be "good news" became the thunder of impending doom. When the Indians, as a result, refused to

6 J. A. Loewen, "Good News for the Waunana," PA, Vol. 8, No. 6 (Nov.-Dec. 1961), p. 278.

7 Acts 2:1-42; 4: 4; 5:14; 6: 7.

8 C. H. Dodd, The Apostolic Preaching and its Developments (New York and London: Harper and Bros., 1936).

fulfill their banana contracts, the local merchants banded together to rid the community of the devastating message.

Equally dramatic are the examples of restructuring cited by Reyburn where Lolo polygamists reinterpreted church membership of first wives as eternal security for husbands; or the Kaka church members who restructured communion as magic to circumvent the punishment by mission laws in analogy to their own *sataka* ceremony.[9]

If we now take a second look at the earlier cited examples of the effective use of narrative from the point of view of the effect on the people's conduct, we notice that in each case the convinced hearers were willing to make some rather fundamental changes in both world-view and behavior patterns. It was not just the acceptance of an isolated truth here and there as demonstrated in the examples of restructuring. We believe that all will agree that such fundamental changes can only and should only take place within the framework of a fuller understanding of the program of God and not on the basis of a few isolated truths. In the light of this conviction, we would like to assert that over and above form, point of contact, emphasis, or even the meeting of felt need, the individual parts of the message need a matrix, a setting, which will meaningfully relate them to a whole and which will provide somewhat of a barrier against negative restructuring. This need, we feel, can in a large part be met by the second thesis of this paper: A core of Bible stories can early provide the essential matrix to make even such far-reaching changes.

However, before we procede to the accounts of the experiments with such a matrix of Bible stories, we would like to share both the experiences that led to the experiments and the ideals that underlie such a matrix.

Experiments and Ideals

Early in our missionary experience we found ourselves frustrated for want of a suitable medium to give the message to Spanish-speaking Negroes in South America. Preaching was out of the question and with more than ninety per cent being illiterate we could not read and discuss. So we began to tell Bible stories. We soon realized that sequence was as important as were the truths contained in the stories. So we began to tell the Old and New Testament stories in a chronological sequence over a period lasting many months. It was a very acceptable procedure for the faithful regulars, but was found seriously wanting for new additions or the erratic attenders. The latter two groups were not getting the basic framework within which to appreciate the individual stories or truths. When we were permitted to begin work among the Choco Indians several years later, we were already considering a telescoped version of the Bible narrative. Two more experiences — the negative experience with the recording of isolated stories, and the dramatic positive response of the Indians on the Siguirusua River told in "Good News for the Waunana"[10] — clinched the decision to prepare a series of Bible stories that could be told as a sequence in which major gaps would be bridged by such statements as "after a long time," "much later," and the like.

---

9 William D. Reyburn, "Meaning and Restructuring: A Cultural Process," PA, Vol. 5, No. 2 (March-April 1958), pp. 79-82.

10 J. A. Loewen, op. cit., p. 275.

The complete list of stories is as follows:

1. The origin of Satan, in order to distinguish the devil of the Scriptures from the many types of evil spirits with which native mythology is concerned.

2. The creation, first of all of the world and then of man. This provided an excellent point of contact.

3. The entrance of sin, the story of Genesis 3.

4. Cain and Abel, showing the sin and its effect in the life of the descendants of Adam and Eve.

5. The story of the deluge, which had a close counterpart in Choco mythology.

6. The Ten Commandments, as a basis for the sin concepts.

7. Prophecies concerning Jesus, which actually became the bridge between the Old and New Testaments.

8. John the Baptist and the preaching of repentance.

9. The birth of Christ, as God's act of redeeming concern.

10. The baptism of Jesus.

11. The ministry of Jesus, to illustrate that the mind of the minister must be the mind of a servant.

12. The calling of the disciples, as an example of call to service.

13. The feeding of the five thousand, as an example of a miracle in nature.

14. The rich man and Lazarus, illustrating the concept of life after death and of retribution.

15. The story of blind Bartimeus as an example of restoring of sight.

16. The resurrection of the young man of Nain.

17. Zaccheus, the example of a man whose life was changed by meeting Jesus.

18. The Prodigal Son, a message by Jesus showing how man is lost and how he can be found.

19. The announcements concerning Jesus' death: sort of a pre-program for some of the philosophies that had to do with the redemption of man.

20. The Last Supper, to show communion, fellowship, and self-examination.

21. Judas betrays Jesus, to show that even friends can betray him.

22. Jesus before Pilate, to show how often we do not do right because of the circumstances or the people around us.

23. The story of the crucifixion of Jesus with the two thieves, illustrating decision for and rejection of Christ.

24. The burial of Jesus, showing that there are also secret friends.

25. The resurrection of Jesus, to show that redemption was complete.

26. The ascension of Jesus and the promise of his return for his own, an attempt to highlight the blessed hope.

And how were the individual stories chosen? What criteria determined their inclusion?[11] In the first place, the narrative was to give the Indians a kind of overview of the Biblical message, a bird's eye view of the span of Biblical history. Second, the stories, especially those concerning origins, were chosen in order to qualify some of the local mythological ideas which showed both striking similarities to and fundamental differences from Biblical narrative. The similarities served as kinds of starting points and meaningful anchors. In areas where the Biblical mes-

---

[11] Harold Fehderau (who works in the Republic of Congo) in a letter dated April 22, 1963, suggests that certain guidelines for the choice of stories for such a matrix could come from a list of questions designed to bring to light the basic world outlook and philosophy of a people. He feels that such a published list of questions could help others apply a similar method in different parts of the world. What questions do some of the readers suggest? Why not send some to the editor of PA?

sage differed, the narrative became the occasion to point to the written records of the Word of God as the authentic record of origins. A third premise was the matter of introducing concepts such as sin, fellowship, prophecy, preaching, baptism, call of God, eternity, retribution, conversion, life after death, decision for and against the gospel, communion, failure of even those who call themselves children of God. The greatest emphasis, of course, was placed on the New Testament narrative of the life of the Lord Jesus Christ. In the fourth place, the choice of stories from the life of Jesus was to sample the life and ministry of Christ with special emphasis on his birth, death, and resurrection. From his ministry there were chosen such stories as his baptism, the calling of helpers, one miracle in nature, a healing, the resurrection of one who had died, a conversion story, and one parable. The events connected with the crucifixion were then given in greater detail. Conspicuous was the absence of mention of the Holy Spirit, because we were too uncertain about a name at that point in the work.[12]

Testing of the Series

The first use of the series was by F. Glenn Prunty, then a missionary with New Tribes Mission in Panama. Because of his own limitations in the Choco language, he used the translation of the story series suggested for the Panama area. One hearing of this "story" convinced an extended family group at Lucas of the relevance of the message, and on a succeeding visit Mr. Prunty found them ready "to give God the hand and to begin walking on God's road."[13]

In 1959 the series passed a second interesting test. The booklet of Bible stories was the final reader of a literacy program. At Chepo, Panama, a Choco Indian who had never previously heard the gospel accidently met the missionaries and entered literacy instruction. His progress was overwhelmingly rapid. In two and a half days he finished the seven-primer course. He was handed a Bible story book and a book of Choco mythology without explanation. When the missionary returned three hours later, the Indian was more than half through the Bible story book. His comment, "This is not a 'kuriwa story' (the Choco equivalent to our 'fox' stories or fables), is it? I never knew that God had said all these things. Things are really going to have to change at our house."

In 1961 the missionaries used the story series as a unit to give a gospel matrix for the Choco church at El Mamey. Individually the stories were then used to teach Biblical truth. These stories became popular very quickly, and the missionaries observed how easily the Indians used them in their church witness, as devotional reading within their homes, and for discussion with casual visitors. Since June 1961, with this series as their "message," the El Mamey church has been instrumental in starting four other church nuclei.[14]

We feel that the use of narrative has been a major factor in the success of the

---

[12] From Jacob A. and Anne Loewen, "Report on the Choco Language Research accompanied by a Test Translation of Bible Stories in the Epera Dialects," an unpublished report to the Mennonite Brethren Board of Missions, August 15, 1957.

[13] From a personal communication by Glenn Prunty to the author written January 10, 1958.

[14] A fuller description of this witness is found in Jacob A. Loewen, "The Church Among the Choco of Panama," PA, Vol. 10, No. 3 (May-June 1963), pp. 97-108.

witness to the Choco, and conclude this paper with the following summary of specific contributions:

1. It permitted us to give a relatively "whole" message very early in our language experience, long before such problems as the name for the Holy Spirit were solved.

2. The narrative form permitted us to meet the demand of cultural relevance in both form and content, while at the same time permitting us to avoid a number of theological problems that would have hindered comprehension for the novice.

3. It provided the expansible framework which permitted us to "anchor" the message of the Gospel of Mark as an expansion of the known message of God.

4. It has apparently prevented serious and harmful restructuring of the "new" message even though during most of the year the new churches were without the counsel of a resident missionary.

5. The "feedback" in the retellings, dramatizations, and local applications of the stories provided answers to serious translation problems.

6. The narrative simplicity offered new literates a personal encounter with a challenging and already culturally accepted, relevant message.

7. It provided the new Choco Christians with a form of the message that so closely paralleled their own folk tales that everyone could immediately begin retelling and sharing the Good News with others.

Literacy: Bridge in Choco Evangelism

ONE of the unsettling shocks I received very early in my missionary experience was the haunting awareness that I did not know how to make a congenial approach to the people to whom I had been sent to minister. Because I was not prepared to establish a transparent person-to-person relationship, I found myself taking refuge in formal preaching at scheduled meetings.[1] With time this mushroomed into an impressive roster of weekly meetings. At the station each week there were Sunday morning Sunday school, Sunday evening service, Tuesday evening Bible study, Thursday evening prayer meeting. In addition there were cottage prayer meetings in several private homes in the village, and finally there were the periodic weeks of special meetings with daily services.

Even though some variation occurred in the patterns, all the meetings were essentially sermon-centered. My wife and I grew unhappy about this situation, but we didn't know anything else to do. We hesitated to talk to our co-workers about it,

feeling that the problem probably lay in some kind of spiritual inadequacy in us which we could outgrow with discipline. But I do remember cautiously looking over my co-workers' activities and then coming to the realization — at first comforting but later frightening — that they must be facing similar frustrations. In fact, I found myself feeling even more uncomfortable about some of the solutions that I observed in the work of others around me. These included renting buildings[2] in the neighboring village outstations and scheduling a monthly itinerary of preaching services at these points to reach the whole area with the gospel, conducting street meetings in new areas of the city at which the message was broadcast over public address systems,[3] and organ-

---

[1] Walter R. Hearn, "To Whom Are We Talking?," PA, Vol. 8, No. 3 (May-June, 1961), p. 134, points out that this problem is not only a mission field problem. Many Christians of years' standing do not know how to relate themselves to non-Christians in our own culture and to give an effective personal witness concerning their faith.

[2] In 1962 a national pastor in Ecuador shared his deep concern with the author about such a practice. He felt that such meeting places, paid for by foreign money, would of necessity be regarded as propaganda stations. He pleaded instead for face-to-face contact. See Jacob A. Loewen, "Field, Term, and Timing in Missionary Methods," PA, Vol. 12, No. 1 (Jan.-Feb. 1965), pp. 1-22.

[3] Eugene A. Nida, in his book Message and Mission (New York: Harper and Brothers, 1960), p. 172, has shown what negative effects such impersonal means can have: "The use of loudspeakers tends to destroy the sanctity of religion, and the offense of booming the message into one's home, especially when it is not wanted, seems the height of inconsiderateness, if not insolence."

377

izing community-wide house-to-house distributions of free tracts and Gospels.[4]

There is a considerable tendency for missionaries to "barge ahead" irrespective of the local situation. One way in which this is done is through the free distribution of Scriptures and other Christian literature. Such materials seem to be so cheap and the people seem to be so ready to accept whatever is offered free that missionaries are deceived to the ultimate effectiveness of their endeavors. In the first place, a high percentage of such literature is never read and not infrequently the people react to the gospel as being nothing more than cheap propaganda. What is even worse, the distributor loses the priceless opportunity to communicate to the people in a context which they can fully understand, namely the necessity of the bookseller to convince the people of the desirability of his product in the process of selling.

A look beyond the boundaries of our mission led me to believe this was a rather widespread problem for American-trained missionaries. But, what could be even worse, it seemed that the missionaries were passing this problem on in the Bible institutes to the national workers whom they were training. For, when I looked at the national workers, I observed that their frustration was at least as great if not more acute than that of the missionaries. One young pastor, a graduate from a leading Bible school,

serving his first parish, confided to me that he was deeply frustrated. "I have only been in this pastorate for three months, but I have already visited all the communities in my parish. I have tried to organize meetings in all of the villages. I have tried to distribute tracts in every home. I have tried to arrange meetings in the homes of sympathizers. But everywhere I go people are just not interested in the gospel. I don't know anything more to do. Maybe I should quit."

Solutions to Frustration

I concluded that four of the most common solutions to this frustration were (1) to take refuge in formal meetings as I had done, (2) to develop extensive institutional programs, such as medicine, education, etc., (3) to go into impersonal campaigns of free tract and gospel distribution, and (4) to become frustrated to the point of emotional breakdown that led some to retreat from the service of the church.

The purpose of this paper is to suggest that the effective Christian witness involves the establishment of a communications bridge,[5] and to propose that in pre-literate societies the teaching of reading can serve as a perpetuable communications bridge of inestimable value. I want to define the bridge not merely as a point of contact, but also as the development of a relationship between two individ-

---

[4] Ibid., p. 178. Also see Eugene A. Nida, "The Relationship of the Social Structure to the Problem of Evangelism in Latin America," PA, Vol. 5, No. 3 (May-June, 1958), p. 119.

[5] Donald A. McGavran, in *Bridges of God* (London: World Dominion Press, 1955), refers to the social structure of pre-literate societies as a potential bridge for group evangelism. The usage of "bridge" in this paper is quite distinct, but the author nonetheless is indebted to McGavran for the inspiration.

uals which permits and even fosters two-way traffic in the form of meaningful friendly conversation and exchange of ideas. It can begin as a meaningful point of contact — a preliterate anxious to learn to read meets someone willing to teach him. But as the literacy teacher, lesson by lesson, continues to work in the interest of the learner, a confidence relationship gradually develops between them. Thus once the learner is able to extract meaning and truth from the printed page, he naturally turns to his new trusted mentor for counsel about, guidance in, and explanation of the new world of ideas that he finds there. By calling the bridge perpetuable, I want to say that many new literates with proper training can immediately turn around and establish a similar bridge between themselves and the next learners.

Varieties of Bridges

The idea of a bridge is not new. Medical work, disaster relief, education, agriculture, animal husbandry, and the like have been accompanying missionary programs ever since Jesus healed the sick and fed the multitudes while he was on earth. For Paul the Jewish synagogue and the messianic hope of the Old Testament were important points of contact for witnessing about Jesus Christ in a relevant setting to interested people. At Athens Paul used the Greek interest in new philosophy as a point of contact for his witness concerning the faith in Jesus Christ.

I believe that in most missionary enterprises medical service, education, agriculture, etc., were begun as means

to an end — they were usually not considered as an end in themselves, even though they met specific needs in the society.[6] To a large extent, they were instruments designed to help win the confidence of the people to whom the missionary wanted to proclaim the gospel. The confidence relationship that was thus established was to make the people more receptive for the missionary's message. Even though the very service that was being rendered was a part of the testimony of Christian love to the recipient, the real purpose of such service was that of establishing a bridge of confidence that would permit meaningful and effective communication between missionary and communicant.

It is readily apparent that there is no *one* universally applicable bridge; many differing items can function as an initial point of contact and maybe even develop into useful bridges in given situations.

At the simplest level, we find the approach as a *learner,* a person who is anxious to be instructed in local ways. A missionary in West Africa made this a regular practice during his itinerant evangelism. He would stop in villages for several days and especially in the evenings around campfire inquire of the elders concerning their belief. He never tried to explain his own faith until he was asked to do so by the elders. After

6 Eugene A. Nida, in a personal letter to the author, points out that literacy and colportage work are much more closely linked to evangelism than medical and educational institutions. He also rightly underscores that we must not feel that medical, educational, agricultural programs, etc. are not valid expressions of Christian concern in their own right.

he had spent long hours in learning from them, the village elders invariably asked him to reciprocate and to explain his beliefs to them. Nor was the missionary's purpose just to listen out of curiosity; he was convinced that in order to tell the people about God in a really relevant way, he must first learn what they thought about God. Only then would he be able to tell about the God of the Bible in terms of their thought premises.[7]

Luis Chicaiza, an Ecuadorean national evangelist, was emphasizing this same concern when he confided to the author the following evaluation of the several missions of his acquaintance.

1. Missionaries have too great an urgency to preach and to hand out tracts. All this is done even before they have listened and learned how to relate themselves meaningfully to the people.

2. The social services in agriculture, medicine, etc. are good; but they should grow out of the church program rather than function independently as is the practice all too often. This obviously points to the fact that these services have lost their "communications bridge" function and are becoming ends in themselves.

3. Unsolicited sermons, testimonies, tracts, and Bibles almost always lead to "mocking" the message, especially if the recipient's friends insinuate that he is being too friendly to the gospel. Such mocking is usually an attempt to convince one's unbelieving friends of one's loyalty to the old ways.

─────────

[7] Eugene A. Nida, "The Relation of Social Structure . . . ," op. cit., p. 118.

Learner Attitude and Approach

Chicaiza's suggestions about a good approach to a Quechua home definitely emphasize the learner attitude and approach.

1. Workers, national or missionary, should not be distinctive in their clothes. They should blend into the environment.

2. They should approach the home with the humility of a learner. A missionary might buy some native artifact after having inquired in detail about it. A national might pick up a plant or some object and elicit conversation from the host about it.

3. There is a point of contact in that all Quechua believe in God. The possibility of developing a bridge in this area should be carefully explored. During the entire conversation the worker should note language, idiom, ideals, and problems of the person; so that he can soon talk in the terms of the person's own idioms and world view.

Once the learner has found a meaningful point of contact in some concern of the new contact, help in the meeting of this concern can lead to growing confidence and to an ultimate useful communications bridge.

As an example of this, a Protestant missionary working in an Indian community in Ecuador used the community's loyalty to Christo-paganism to build a bridge by which to bring them the gospel message. Instead of decrying the paganism of their religion, he accepted the statement that their greatest need was for someone to teach their children the religion they had and so he began to teach the official church catechism to the community's children. After he had done this for several weeks, the elders of the village asked him in private, "If you know so much about our religion, how come you are an evangelical then?" This led to a solicited witness that could be meaningful and effective.[8]

Such a felt need may be physical or economical, as in the case of a missionary in Korea, an experienced agriculturalist, who combined instruction in the control of apple-borers that were destroying local orchards with his Bible conferences.[9]

This need can often be ascertained beforehand. Often charges can be made for the actual service. The author recently observed a lay preacher in Ecuador who had learned to vaccinate pigs and chickens against pests that struck these animals in the area, and who was now going from community to community vaccinating the animals and using this service as an occasion to speak to the people their spiritual needs. Even though he made a minimal charge for his services, his witness had the effect of John the Baptist's ministry in preparing the people to receive the more formal witness of the missionary.

Possibly one of the most universally applicable and yet often seriously neglected points of contact is Bible and literature colportage. Selling Bibles and other Christian literature has been successfully used by the Bible societies and by many pioneer missionaries. It is an excellent point of contact. Be-cause of the very nature of salesmanship, people expect the distributor to try to convince them of the desirability of the product he is selling. And, whether the person buys or not, the bookseller has a chance to witness to the truth and to the effectiveness of the good news. He also has a chance to challenge the customer who does buy to study this good news for himself and to obey it, if he finds it to be the truth.[10]

A more complicated bridge, both by the prerequisites in specialization and in its multiple applications, is the approach of the Summer Institute of Linguistics. This organization makes agreements with national governments to make linguistic and anthropological studies of the aboriginal peoples in the respective countries. It pledges itself to teach the tribes people to read and to provide for them the most wholesome literature, the Bible. This service is in the interest both of the government (since it brings the pre-literate society more into the orbit of the nation) and, at the same time, is an effective means of exposing the people to the gospel message in their own language.

The preceding is not intended as saying that medical work, agriculture, education, etc., do not have a valuable function today. But, as the earlier controversy over the so-called social gospel indicated, all too often what was intended as and even begun as a means to gain confidence, be it medical or educational, became an end in itself. It became an institution, a routine, a professional service that tied its personnel to one place. Many of our

8 Ibid.

9 T. S. Soltau, *Missions at the Crossroads* (Grand Rapids: Baker Book House, 1955), p. 31.

10 Nida, op cit., p. 119.

mission fields render poignant testimony to the large financial investments and the heavy involvements of missionary staff in institutions which were once started as a service of love to gain the confidence of the people. An additional problem that these services are facing today is the rapid rise in cultural standards in many of the so-called mission field countries of the world. This is demanding that the hospitals, medical specialists, school buildings, educators, etc., be of such a quality that they are almost forced to become ends in themselves. These institutions have been a source of embarrassment, of concern, and of frustration not only for many missionaries, who felt that they were being diverted from their main goal in missionary service, but also for the sending mission boards. And certainly they have often become a source of frustration to the national church, which (in the current flurry of indigenization) has found it very difficult to assume the administrative and financial burden involved in carrying on the institutional program that was established by the mission.

Literacy

Since the summer of 1959, David Wirsche and the author have been associated with a literacy program among the Choco Indians in the Darien of Panama near the Colombian border.[11] Here was a group of aborigines surrounded by Spanish-speaking mestizos and mulattoes. Many of

these Indians had attended Spanish schools in the mestizo villages but had never been able to really master reading. The typical community attitude toward them was, "Indians are unable to learn to read. They are just too stupid." The Choco themselves had come to accept this attitude as fact.

In the summer of 1959 the two men performed an experiment with ten Indians to see whether they could bypass this psychological block by teaching the Indians to read their own language, which had been transcribed as much as possible with Spanish orthography. The experiment proved overwhelmingly successful. The Indians not only learned to read their own language quickly, but they were also able to read Spanish as a by-product. This experiment became a point of real interest to the Panamanian ministry of education, which then encouraged the men to return to Panama to continue the experiment. In the summers of 1961 and 1962 the workers continued in this literacy program, which has not only led to a literacy for many people, but has also become a tool through which churches have been started — not singularly through missionary effort but rather as a result of the efforts of the Choco Christians themselves.[12]

This literacy approach permitted the missionary to enter a Choco community and to visit with the leaders there. In the course of the conversations reading and literacy were introduced. This invariably sparked

---

[11] Nicasio A. Vargas y Jacob A. Loewen, "Un Experimento de Alfabetización entre los Chocoes," *América Indígena*, 23: 121-125, 1963.

[12] For a more detailed report see Jacob A. Loewen, "The Church Among the Choco of Panama," PA, Vol. 10, No. 3 (May-June, 1963), pp. 97-108.

enthusiastic response. Yes, they wanted to learn. Here was something that was definitely in the interest of the community, for especially the leaders were concerned about being able to compete with the encroaching Spanish-speaking people around them. The chief and his advisers not only provided housing, food, and moral support but also often helped in the selection of those people who were most ready to learn and most apt to teach others.

A typical scene of the beginning of the teaching began with the literacy specialist producing a primer. Immediately a group of people gathered around the literacy expert, who would page through the reader pointing out the pictures and the words. The bright individuals who caught on rather quickly were thus identified by their prompt responses. The instructor would then take one of the best of these and begin working with this individual alone, teaching him to read the first primer, which was quite simple. After this individual had mastered Primer One, the missionary would call another of the promising individuals located earlier and place him alongside the first reader. He would then encourage this first individual to teach reading to the second. Generally, the first reader hesitated because he felt himself incapable; but under the prompting and with the help of the instructor he was able to work through the primer. Of course, assuming the role of teacher for another person exerted heavy pressure on the first reader to do his very best in reading.

As soon as the teaching of book one to the second individual was well under way, the visiting teacher taught Primer Two to the first student-teacher. Once the student finished all the seven primers he received his first reading book. This was a book of simple Bible stories designed to provide the reader with a synopsis of the scriptural truth.[13] Reading this "news" from God soon led to many questions and before long the teacher had departed from the reading lesson and found himself busily explaining the meaning of the items that had attracted the new reader's attention.

A case in point would be the chief's son whom David Wirsche accidentally met while visiting the river port. In the course of the greeting the Indian suddenly realized that this must be the man who taught people to read "in two days" (these were actual words of the Indian). The Indian was thrilled at the encounter. Would the missionary teach him to read? He had enough food for himself and his wife for three days. Wirsche knew that three days were really too little, but still he hated to turn down a man who came from such a remote river. Yes, he would teach him.

The Indian turned out to be exceptionally bright and really determined to master reading. For this reason Wirsche let him push ahead from primer to primer, even though he was still making more mistakes than was generally accepted. Only when he got stuck did the teacher make him go back to review and drill the point of the problem. As a result, the Indian

---

13 Jacob A. Loewen, "Message and Matrix: Bible Stories," PA, Vol. 11, No. 2 (Mar.-Apr., 1964), pp. 49-54.

had covered all of the seven primers just when the call for lunch was sounded at noon on the third day of his studies. Before the teacher left his pupil he gave him *God's Little Word,* the book of Bible stories described above, and said, "That will be our next reading book." When Wirsche returned two and a half hours later, he found the man reading aloud in the middle of the book. So he reprimanded him saying, "You should always begin reading a book at the beginning, not in the middle." To his surprise the Indian said, "That's just what I did. I started at the beginning and I haven't stopped reading since you left. I never knew God had said all these things." Then followed several hours in which the Indian asked his teacher for further explanation on some of "God's sayings" that puzzled him.

Literacy-Evangelistic Approach

In the introduction we said that this bridge is perpetuable — it can be built again by the newly literate convert who is interested in reaching his fellows. An excellent example of the use of this approach by the Choco themselves occurred early in 1963 when a team of five believers from the older (three years old) churches was invited to a new area for a literacy-evangelistic campaign. In the course of a two-week campaign they taught some forty people to read, led more than two dozen to accept "the way," baptized twenty-three of them, trained a leader, and left them as an organized functioning church. But let us look at how all this happened.

On their arrival in the new area the Indians went to visit the relatives of one of the members of the team. Of course, the arrival of the visitors attracted a lot of attention and many neighbors came to greet them. The group went through the usual ritual of greetings and then settled back to exchange news. It did not take long before the visitors had shared the "big news that people on their river were reading God's message in their own language and in Spanish. This was electrifying news. Would those teachers come to them also? At this point the leader produced a copy of Primer One and began to demonstrate to the excited group the method described above. As soon as the alert learners were identified, the team members each took one of them and began to give him individual instruction. As soon as the first person finished the course he was introduced to *God's Little Word.* The new ideas presented by this book again led to questions which the teacher answered delivering the good news. Private conversations grew into group discussions and so the evenings actually became informal evangelistic services. After the group broke up, individuals and family groups continued talking. Gradually some family groups were convinced and made a profession of faith. The adults were baptized upon making a public confession of their faith. Of this specific campaign the leader later reported that he had not even taught reading till the end, for he had suddenly realized that this group would need a leader and "power," if it were to survive. So he found an older man among the baptized who was willing to receive instruction on the matters of teaching, baptism, communion, etc. In fact this leader already baptized the last group of converts before the team left the area.

In this way more than two hundred and fifty Choco became literate in 1961 and 1963; and yet more than two-thirds of the people became literate not through missionary evangelism and instruction, but were taught to read by their own people.

In conclusion, let us summarize the contributions that literacy made to Choco evangelism.

1. It was in the interest of the national government and has led to continuing invitations from the country to return — not only to continue the experiment but also to help set up similar programs for other tribes of the country.

2. It provided us with a congenial means of establishing contact with new people. We could offer them something which they were convinced was in their interest.

3. It helped identify those who were interested in learning something new. People who were interested in learning to read generally also turned out to be open to the message of the new way.

4. It helped identify those who were capable of transmitting new ideas, because they became teachers in the literacy program; and so, even without our intending it to be so, they were asked to explain the message of the biblical reading material.

5. It disseminated in the form of simple reading material the real message that the missionary wanted to convey.

6. Especially for those who were or became Christians and who now learned to read, the "each one teach one" approach provided a convenient means of sharing the good news with their neighbors.

7. All this involved only a minimum of equipment, outlay, and preparation, for it was possible even for those who had never been in school formally to learn how to teach reading and to witness effectively to others concerning the good news.

Mission to Smaller Tribes:
Challenge, Problems, and Responsibility

Dear Brethren in Christ:

> *We have recently heard that there are tribes in area X which still have had little or no gospel witness. The Lord has called us to tribal work, and we would very much appreciate it if you could tell us a little more about the location, the condition, and the customs of these tribes. We are especially interested in a tribe that has never yet had a gospel witness. Any help you can give us will be deeply appreciated.*

> *Yours in Christ,*
>
> *(signed)*

SUCH letters as the above reflect the dedication of a large segment of Christendom to evangelize the unreached tribes in this generation. The challenge of tribes who have never heard the gospel has been stated in books like *Two Thousand Tongues to Go*[1] and *God Planted Five Seeds*.[2] The zeal to reach them is reflected in such organizational names as Unevangelized Fields Mission, Unevangelized Tribes Mission, New Tribes Mission, Regions Beyond Mission, South American Indian Mission, Bolivian Indian Mission, United Andean Indian Mission, etc. Many of the denominations — from Mennonites to Episcopalians — have also taken up the challenge.

[1] Ethel E. Wallis and Mary A. Bennet, *Two Thousand Tongues To Go* (New York: Harper and Bros., 1950).

[2] Jean D. Johnson, *God Planted Five Seeds* (New York: Harper and Row Publishers, 1966).

Favorable circumstances

Nor have circumstances been unfavorable to evangelizing these tribes. In Latin America, national governments have frequently encouraged mission organizations to work with tribes in hopes of "civilizing" them and eventually incorporating them into the national society. A number of countries have signed concordats with the state church turning over tribal groups to religious orders for "civilizing and Christianizing them." Paraguay, through its Department of Indian Affairs has turned over several tribes to evangelical missions for the same purpose. The Summer Institute of Linguistics/Wycliffe Bible Translators has contracts with a number of Latin American countries to reduce tribal languages to writing, to teach people to read, and to produce wholesome literature for them.

Modern technology has provided solutions to many problems that formerly made tribal work extremely difficult. The two-way radio permits missionaries working in the most isolated places to have immediate contact with the civilized world. Aviation has made it possible to bridge the difficult terrain between some urban centers and the most remote tribal society in a matter of hours. With modern advances in medicine, the white man can move with relative safety into areas that formerly were considered to be his grave.

Professionally, missionaries have never been better prepared. Not only can they acquire the necessary Biblical knowledge, but colleges and universities offer them training in a variety of useful disciplines such as linguistics for reducing aboriginal languages to writing, and anthropology for understanding the overt practices and the covert world view of even the most exotic cultures. There are Church Growth Institutes, Translators Institutes, Language Learning Institutes, etc.

For the missionary candidate himself there is an aura of romance and adventure connected with the thought of reaching a tribe that "has never heard."

The potential of small tribes

Quite apart from the external circumstances and romantic enticements, however, tribal societies do offer an exceedingly challenging opportunity to missionary witness. Most of them are face-to-face societies whose animistic religion offers no organized resistance to the systematized teachings of Christianity. Whoever is willing to be their friend will be received as a friend, be he trader, anthropologist, or missionary. Their "primitive" living conditions make even the simplest item of the missionary's culture fascinating; and not having learned that there are many dishonest people in this world, tribespeople tend to accept that which is told them more trustfully than those of us who have been sophisticated by "civilization."

In fact, for most tribal people, anything that is printed must of necessity be true. During the course of our first literacy campaign with the Chocó of Panama we decided to make some changes in the orthography in order to conform Chocó writing more closely to Spanish orthography. So we began making the necessary changes in the primers. However, when one of the Indian students saw us making changes in the books, he was aghast: "Who in the world are you to change that book? That was written!"

Psychologically, many tribes represent a "prepared and fertile" field for missionary witness. In the first place, if they have had little contact with the outside world, they haven't learned that they are "inferior," and therefore, when they accept Christianity they have no inhibitions about witnessing to their fellows and neighbors. Very frequently there exist circumstances within their own setting that will encourage them to accept a new religious faith. Many tribes of New Guinea who for centuries had been engaging in intertribal warfare were glad for the arrival of the gospel and its message of not killing because, they said, "We are just tired of killing."[3]

Occasionally epidemics or natural catastrophies have already shaken the tribe so severely that the missionary finds highly developed messianic expectations, which represent a wide open door for his message. Just before we presented the gospel to the Waunana for the first time, the tribe had been rocked by accounts of visions and dreams announcing the imminence of another deluge. When the first message was given to them during the time they were "calling on *Ewandama* 'God'" to prevent the flood, they eagerly accepted the good news.[4]

A missionary to the Motilones in Colombia reported that at first there had been very little response to missionary preaching, especially since the missionary did not take part in the "son of corn" festival which was the annual fertility rite preceding the planting of corn, their major staple. When the missionary assured them that he prayed to God and that the latter would protect his crop, they were amazed but incredulous. That year a freak hailstorm destroyed the tribe's communal corn field, while the missionary's patch remained unscathed. The result was a wholesale turning to the gospel because it offered so much more protection to their corn crop than their own ritual.[5]

[3] Wesley Culshaw, in a lecture on mission work in New Guinea, delivered at the Translators Institute at Kitwe, Zambia, January, 1967.

[4] Jacob A. Loewen, "Good News for the Waunana," PA, Vol. 8, No. 6 (Nov.-Dec., 1961), pp. 275-278.

[5] Personal communication from Ernest Fowler of Latin American Mission in Colombia.

(This is not to suggest that it was an ideal motivation for becoming Christians, but it is an example of what sometimes happens.)

On the other hand, there are tribes who have already had a little contact with civilization and have experienced some of its disintegrating effects on their way of life. Having come to realize the inadequacy of their own spiritual resources for coping with the problems growing out of contact, they eagerly grasp for new spiritual values. The Chulupi Indians of southern Paraguay found employment in the cane fields of Argentina, only to discover that prostitution and commercial liquor were ravaging many of their major tribal values. They became so disturbed because of these pernicious influences that they decided to migrate north to the Mennonite colonies where there was "no liquor and no prostitution." When a mission to them was opened, many accepted the gospel with alacrity.

Last, but by no means least, is the exciting potential of total impact. First of all, if the group is not scattered over too wide a geographic area, the reduced number of the small tribes makes it possible to influence the whole group relatively simultaneously. Next, the face-to-face structure of such societies almost always makes it easy to develop group consensus and group turning to the gospel. (Usually, of course, some key people make the first decision and their decision then becomes generally accepted by all.) Also, changes of culture that need to be made can be immediate and total without reservoirs of people still continuing in the old way. Finally, progress in "Christianization," once started, seems to proceed rapidly when proper guidance is available.[6]

However, we should not be led to believe that all tribes are actually waiting to welcome the missionary. Even a psychologically "ready" tribe may in actual fact reject the message because of problems resulting from the nature of the contact or the method of evangelism. The paragraphs that follow will highlight some of the areas where mistakes are most frequently made.

Establishing contact

Looking at first contacts with a new tribe from the missionary's point of view, we have to admit that even the fact of contact sometimes demands ultimate sacrifice. It cost the lives of five missionaries to make contact with a group of less than two hundred Aucas in Ecuador.

When a "wild" tribe harrassed oil company workers in one of the southern republics, the company tried hard to make friendly contacts with these people, but all their efforts failed. Finally a priest volunteered his services to the company. A small plane was put at his disposal. This plane was painted bright red so that it could be easily identified when it flew over the areas where the Indian villages were located.

As the plane buzzed over the villages, trade goods of all kinds were

dropped as gifts. All of the gifts were wrapped in red, or at least tied with a bright red ribbon. After about a month of drop-contact, the priest proceeded to leave gifts on the trail in a kind of silent barter which is often used between hostile tribal groups.

When these gifts also were consistently removed and tribal artifacts and meat left in exchange, the priest decided that the conditions for a face-to-face encounter had been established. He instructed the mining company personnel that they should not expect him back before thirty days. When two weeks passed and nothing had been heard from him, the oil company people became uneasy and a search party was sent out. The party found him just a few yards beyond the point where the barter goods had been placed on the trail. He was lying face down with a long arrow in his back and a red ribbon tied to the arrow. The tribe had no objection to trade, but they did not want personal contact.

Recently several missionaries were trying to establish contact with a tribal group. They had to leave their advance base camp unexpectedly for a few days, and when they returned, everything they had left had been destroyed. The canned goods had been opened and poured out, the air mattresses had been slashed, and bedding torn to shreds.

Occasionally a tribe is divided in its readiness for contact. Some may want contact, others may be against it. Such an internal conflict seems to have been part of the motivation

---

[6] Just as there can be total group acceptance of the message, face-to-face groups can by the same token reject the gospel en masse.

in the killing of the five missionaries in Ecuador.

In 1963 I was personally able to visit the "wild" Ayoreos who were trying to establish contact with the settlers in the Paraguayan Chaco. When they were rejected some of them wanted to continue trying, but others did not. The result was serious intra-tribal struggle in which many lives were lost. The day before our visit to their camp, five men had been killed. They had become tired of trying to relate to the whites and had decided to go back to the bush. As soon as they left, others, who wanted to continue contact, pursued and killed them.

And what is such contact like? Recently a mission publication described the first contact of some missionaries with such a new tribe:

We had been seeing evidence of the presence of the Indians for several days already, but we never saw anyone. Then one afternoon we suddenly met some of them on the trail. We called out friendly greetings and several of them came to meet us. They were very friendly so we gave them some food and some gifts. Later others joined us and we spent the rest of the three days we remained with them mainly in trading. I was finally down to my last shirt, having traded all the extra clothes I had with me.

From the tribe's point of view we need to underscore that the sudden arrival of strange white people is not without problem. In some of the jungles of South America small groups have lived by themselves for decades without ever meeting other people. Missionaries to a Brazilian tribe reported that many individuals who were thirty years of age had not had contact with more than two hundred people during their lifetime. Bands of the same tribe who lived only several weeks' journey from each other had never had contact. When such people are suddenly confronted with a white man, they are faced with a real dilemma: Is this a bona fide human being, or is this a dangerous spirit being?

Most of the tribes have well-developed beliefs about spirit beings and of soul wanderings in regions beyond this world, so the spirit origin of the white man is often the easiest "rational" answer for them. This is especially true if the white man arrives by plane, as is so often the case in mission survey teams; the very means of locomotion is one usually ascribed to the spirit beings of their mythological and demonological pantheon. And, of course, the daily conversations by two-way radio don't help to dispel the impression of the "other world" origin of the intruders!

A group of missionaries to a Brazilian tribe recently reported they were convinced that after several years of contact, the majority of the tribes people still did not fully believe that they were human beings. Other missionaries have told how tribesmen have pinched them and have felt them to make sure they were really human beings with flesh and bones. In fact, in one case in which a missionary lost his life on making contact with a tribe, this seems to have been the motivation—an Indian felt the missionary and finally took his spear and pushed it into his groin to see whether he was mortal He was !

The endless train of supplies the plane brings to the resident missionary becomes another supporting element to the notion of supernatural origin; only supernatural beings have unlimited resources. Whatever is needed — medicine, food, tools — the missionary just speaks into the little box, and the next morning the "flying canoe" brings it.

Problems of missionary residence

If trade goods play an important part in establishing initial contact, they usually play an even more prominent part once the missionary establishes residence. The advent of the missionary's family usually involves the building of a home, an airstrip, and a garden. Often the mission program requires auxiliary buildings such as dispensaries, schools, churches, etc. In all this construction the missionary is dependent on local labor. Since money is of little or no value in such isolated areas, payment for services usually involves trade goods—knives, guns, shells, shot, cloth, clothing, etc. In fact, the European settlers in the Paraguayan Chaco report that during their earliest contacts with the Lengua Indians the latter were quite content to work if they were supplied with food. Thus, if a person wanted to clear some land, he just planted a large patch of watermelons. When the watermelons were ready to eat, he invited the tribe to eat and work. As long as the watermelons lasted, the Lengua would work at clearing the land. Such trade-goods-as-payment, however, spells a number of problems for missionary-tribal relations.

In the first place, while the missionary's need for labor will decrease once the airstrip and residence have been built, the tribal appetite for trade goods is just beginning to develop. This can be the beginning of rather serious problems. At the beginning the missionary encourages everybody who is able to work to do so, but when the station has been established and only maintenance is required, he can provide employment for just a few people at a time, and even for them work is available only intermittently.

Next, most tribespeople will consider whatever is given in exchange for work as a gift rather than as payment. When only a few people are permitted to work and get "gifts," feelings of favoritism are almost inevitable. I remember an anthropologist who used bush knives and axes as payments for his informants when he first visited a Colombian tribe. However, the principle of paying for service was not understood The Indians interpreted his selective giving as a sign of favoritism, and strong jealousies arose. His three-week visit culminated in three revenge deaths.

A further problem arises when the missionary becomes aware that the tribal appetite for trade goods is outdistancing the missionary's need for service. When this happens, he usually tries to develop ways and means of producing tribal capital to pay for the desired trade goods. This often involves selling hides, artifacts, or garden products. But the market may be far away, and probably the only means of transportation is by air. In my travels as a translation consultant I frequently find myself returning from a tribal visit with a load of high-smelling hides of tigers, snakes, and wild pigs One missionary reported that vegetable squash was one of the few things which the people in his area could raise in abundance and which they brought to his house for trade. He was unable—because of his conscience—to send them away empty handed, so he traded for squash; then, so as not to let all of it spoil, his family had to eat squash daily—baked, fried, "in puddings and out of puddings."

A fourth kind of problem arises especially in those areas where the tribe has already been exposed to the serf-patron relationship so common in Latin America. By employing people for building his residence or an airstrip, the missionary engages in patron behavior and consequently is assigned a patron role. If after the initial months his need for labor diminishes, and the tribespeople can no longer acquire the goods they want in exchange for work, they very often accuse the missionary of being a poor master. Thus, he who would be the bearer of the Good News has now become a "bad employer."

This employer-employee relationship is even more fraught with danger once there are believers. I have to confess to my own shame that during our early mission work in Colombia we always tended to favor believers with employment. In a way it was natural We appreciated their interest in the Lord's work, we knew that they needed the income which employment with us could provide, and therefore we gave them preference. This course of action is a "natural" for linking Christianity and material goods in the minds of the people.

If we add to this the size of the missionary's outfit and his apparent wealth—at least in comparison with the tribe's poverty—we can see how these things give rise to the belief in the minds of the tribespeople that he is rich because he is a Christian. So they, too, accept Christianity in order to become wealthy. But now the missionary is unwilling to "let them have their share." Thus, by the time the missionary has learned the language and is ready to begin his witness, he has already compromised his effectiveness to a large extent through the dissatisfactions that have arisen because of the trade goods and employment practices.

Closely related is the matter of limited sharing. The missionary has been trained to believe in personal property, and therefore he views the food supplies for which he has actually paid twice—once to buy and again to send in by air—as his very own property. Most tribal societies will hardly agree with this view. Food supplies are to be shared, and to be shared by all alike. The limited sharing of the missionary is interpreted as unwillingness to share, and non-sharing is the behavior of enemies. Actually, most missionaries do try to share a good portion of their supplies, but usually the tribe is far too big and the missionary resources are much too small for them to be able to share in depth with the whole tribe. They can only share very minimally with the whole group; if they should try to feed all the people for even one day, their whole salary for the month would be consumed.

Likewise, few tribes will understand the "saving for a rainy day" philosophy which characterizes the Western Christian ethic. Therefore, the missionary practice of storing several months' supplies behind lock and key seldom receives positive interpretation, even by the most friendly tribespeople.

Another real problem that arises out of missionary residence in the tribe involves the privacy which the missionary family needs in order to function normally. Those who have tried living "native" in a tribal setting know what a trying experience this is. There is never a minute of privacy during daylight hours. Even if you have your own hut it will be filled with people from dawn till the wee hours of the night. You can close the doors if you like, but people will be looking through the windows or cracks. The Western concern for privacy in most face-to-face societies is nothing less than a proclamation of psychological distance. It stands as a blatant contradiction to the missionary's overt words and deeds of friendship.

Misinterpretation

A further source of difficulty are the foibles of the missionary's customs — things that in themselves are utterly unimportant but which are part of his way of life. For example, two single lady missionaries in a tribal situation found their lime-juice-and-sugarwater substitute for orange juice was interpreted as a contraceptive device. For years their work was largely unsuccessful because instead of listening to the message, the people were busy trying to figure out when and how they consorted with men. The people knew that tribal women drank lime juice once in a while when they had been unfaithful to their husbands, but these women drank it daily.

In another case the informant whom a missionary brought to the city kissed his wife, children, and all his relatives before boarding the plane for his first flight. The missionary was greatly amused because kissing was not a part of tribal culture, but his amusement disappeared when he realized that his kissing had been interpreted as a type of pre-boarding magic. When the informant was asked whether he had been afraid to fly in the plane, he said, "Oh no, I wasn't afraid because I made the same kind of magic which the missionary always makes before he enters the plane; I also 'mouth-sucked' my wife and children."

On the opposite side of this coin are the tribal taboos which the missionary is bound to violate. Very frequently such taboos are violated unconsciously. The missionary is just not aware of the meaning of what he has done. There was, for instance, a menstruating lady missionary who ate meat from the tribal pot and thereby threw the whole tribe into a terrible panic. They "knew" that if a menstruating female ate meat the hunters would no longer be able to kill animals; in fact, all the animals; would become sterile and die, and famine would kill the whole tribe.

Missionaries are especially bound to give offense where the taboos involve the supernatural. Some missionaries have felt it necessary to prove that the fetishes feared by the people are really powerless. Westerners have often assumed that a demonstration that nothing happens to the person who violates the taboo will convince tribal people that their fears are unfounded. Actually, such behavior seldom undermines their belief in the taboos. If nothing happens to the missionary at the moment, the people may rationalize that the missionary—being a spirit-being himself—just has stronger "medecine" than was contained in the fetish. More usually, however, they will fear that the taboo violated by the missionary will venge itself upon the people who didn't prevent the desecration from taking place. Therefore, when some calamity later befalls the tribe, it is frequently interpreted as being the result of the missionary's infraction.

Turrado Moreno tells about the priest, Santos de Abelgas, in Paraguay who violated a taboo in order to show the Guarani Indians that there was nothing to their superstition of "magic darts." When this missionary died of cancer seven years later, the people immediately pointed out that the taboo killed him.[7]

Residence in the tribe will bring the expatriate missionary into a ringside seat of cultural events, many of which he will consider objectionable: infanticide, killing of the aged, bodily mutilation, etc. There is real danger that not only with the believers, but even long before there are any believers in the tribe, the missionary will drift into the policeman's role to prevent child killing, to regulate sex behavior, and to stop objectionable festivities.

Inter-tribal warfare has been an especially knotty problem. Missionaries have very frequently introduced guns to provide meat for their own larder and also to make living easier for the tribal society. In fact, where the appetite for trade goods has outgrown the bow and arrow capacity, guns are a necessity to get enough hides to provide the Indian with the capital to acquire trade goods. However, if these "hunting" guns are misused for killing, the missionary is in double trouble—he preaches against killing but has now provided the tools for murder.

Recently a situation of this nature developed in a Brazilian tribe. The Indians from the mission station killed six people from a neighboring band to settle an old score. The missionary was horrified and confiscated the twenty or so guns before the government should hear about the event and indict him as an accomplice who

[7] Fray Angel Turrado Moreno, *Etnología de los Indios Guaraúno* (Caracas: Tercera Conferencia Interamericana de Agricultura, 1945).

made possible the killings. The tribespeople, however, were greatly angered. They knew that their enemies would come and seek revenge, but now the missionary had left them completely unarmed In their anger they called him a thief, claiming that he had stolen rifles from them which they had legitimately acquired through trade.

The missionary as administrator

Even though a missionary may succeed in staying out of the policeman's role, he generally will fall into the role of chief or governor because in some way or other he manipulates the affairs around his station. An administrator is seldom able to be the counsellor, spiritual confidante, and pastor of his subordinates, and this will be doubly true for the expatriate. His administrative decisions will frequently vitiate his capacity to function as a soul winner.

Another very frequent role problem[8] for the resident missionary arises from his trade goods association. First of all, as indicated earlier, he wants to help the tribespeople develop capital for acquiring trade goods, and so he tries to build up some type of gainful employment for them. Secondly, he is often upset so severely by the outrageous "daylight robbery" of the Indians by itinerant traders[9]

8 For a fuller discussion of the role problem in missionary work, see Jacob A. and Anne Loewen, "Role, Self-Image, and Missionary Communication," PA, Vol. 14, No. 4 (July-Aug. 1967), pp. 145-160.

9 For a fuller discussion of the problem of tribal and national societies, see Jacob A. Leowen, "Tribal Societies and National Church," to appear in PA.

—usually nationals of the country— that he opens a mission store to stock the trade goods most wanted by the people. He sells the goods at cost, of course, since he isn't in business to gain money. But now he is actually functioning as a cutthroat competitor to the national traders.

In fact, more than one missionary has ruined, or at least seriously compromised, his missionary service through such trading involvements. One missionary, incensed that traders were paying the Indians only one third of the actual value for their produce, decided to teach both the Indians and the traders a lesson. He bought the Indians' entire crop one year just below the actual market value. (The slight margin was to help pay for the storing and later marketing of the produce.) He reasoned that the Indians now knew the real price and that the traders would have to pay a better price the next year.

The next year he did not buy any produce, but the traders didn't either. They, too, decided to teach the Indians a lesson for dealing with the missionary. That year the Indians lost their entire crop. Why wasn't the missionary buying, now that he had established the merchant role? Gossip suggested that he had made enough in the one year so that he didn't need to buy any more. When he then had to leave the field for furlough, the gossip was confirmed. And the Indians? They got a quarter of the fair price for their produce once the traders resumed buying again.

Another problem that is often associated with missionary residence in the tribe is a premature appeal for individual conversion. Once a minimum friendship basis has been established with tribespeople, they find it very hard to be calloused and unresponsive to the appeal of a friend. In their desire to please, individuals and groups may make commitments before they are ready. Such premature "conversions" on the part of individuals can sometimes alienate the whole tribe and cause the whole group to turn against the gospel. Where such a commitment comes at a group level, it often results in a very shallow experience. The missionary, sensing this shallowness, becomes desperate in his attempts to deepen it. But instead of sharing his personal experience as a model for growth, he often resorts to abstract teaching of the gospel and to strong-arm methods to suppress some of the most offensive behavioral evils.

One of the consequences of missionary residence that is often overlooked is the effect of the Westerner's presence on tribal health. We generally think of the missionary as the kind dispenser of medicines for diseases for which tribal people know no cure. This is true only in part, for we also have to admit that often the missionary is the channel for the introduction of various types of diseases that were previously unknown to the tribe. These range from common colds through so-called contagious diseases — whooping cough, measles, smallpox, diphtheria—to tuberculosis.

Traders, rubber hunters, and miners have often brought syphilis to tribal societies; but interestingly enough, because of the extensive spread of yaws, a non-venerial disease caused by a spyrochete that is almost identical to the agent which causes syphilis, many South American tribes have at least partial immunity to syphilis. However, they possess no immunity whatsoever to the so-called childhood diseases of our Western society. One missionary reported recently that a tribe which ten years ago when the mission first contacted it numbered three thousand, has less than a thousand survivors today after whooping cough, measles, and smallpox has decimated it.

I saw one community where a missionary child, returning from missionary children's school to spend the vacation with his parents, brought a mild case of whooping cough with him. The child, of course, had been vaccinated and his infection was not severe; but twenty Indian children died in the community. A non-Christian anthropologist once bitterly complained that "the people the parents are trying to save are going to be killed by the missionary children."

The cycle of change that conversion initiates

The gospel's impact upon a society very frequently changes the total way of life of a people. In Paraguayan Lengua society the discontinuation of infanticide under missionary pressure resulted in a tremendous population increase. This population increase made it impossible for the Lengua to continue nomadic existence because they were no longer able to find an adequate food supply by hunting and gathering. This, in turn, meant that the Lengua had to shift their pattern of livelihood from nomadic hunting and gathering to sedentary living and agriculture—a most painful experience.

For most nomadic or semi-nomadic people, sedentary living brings serious health problems. First of all, their unsanitary living habits tend to contaminate the area rather quickly. Such parasites as hookworm become a real menace when these people live too long in one place. Then, too, permanent buildings in themselves are a health hazard for people who formerly eliminated much of the opportunity for infection to spread by burning all houses when someone died.

Statistics show that eighty percent of the "generation of contact" of a tribe will die through communicable diseases which are introduced by white men—whooping cough, diphtheria, smallpox, measles, tuberculosis. If the remnant is less than one hundred people, the tribe will not survive contact. The sad fact is that this is no abstract assertion. Missionary upon missionary can render testimony to decimating epidemics of these diseases. The tribe which three years ago numbered three hundred people, today has less than a hundred survivors, and unless the situation rapidly changes, there will be no survivors in another three years.

The area in which the missionary most frequently feels compelled to introduce change after conversion is that of sex and family living. But sometimes these "Christian" solutions to pagan problems create untold hurt. In an earlier paper we reported how a Shiriana believer was led to kill in order to replace the wife which he had lost under missionary instruction.[10]

The area that Christianity wants to change most fundamentally, of course, is the area of world view and values. But it is here that we have often been the least successful. Very often, rather than fundamentally changing the values of a people, we have merely produced surface changes in behavior and introduced deep-seated frustrations.

Earlier we mentioned the linkage of Christianity to material welfare in the eyes of many people. Rebellions such as the one which the former Belgian Congo experienced after independence find their origin to a large extent in the frustration that results when the hope for material wealth is not realized. In Oceania many cargo cults are dramatic examples of the tremendous frustrations that Christianity has brought into tribal societies.[11] The Christian message was only partially understood, but this was enough to introduce doubts concerning the traditional way and to raise aspirations for the future. When circumstances did not improve materially, however, the resulting frustrations were expressed in such violence as the Mau-Mau movement in Africa.[12]

10 Jacob A. Loewen, "Religion, Drives, and the Place Where It Itches," PA, Vol. 14, No. 2 (Mar.-Apr., 1967), pp. 49-72.

11 For a discussion of messianic and rebellious movements resulting from severe cultural and religious frustrations, see Vittorio Lanternari, *The Religions of the Oppressed: A Study of Modern Messianic Cults* (New York: Alfred A. Knopf, Inc., 1963). Also in paperback Mentor Books, 1965.

12 Jomo Kenyatta, *Facing Mount Kenya: The Tribal Life of the Gikuyu* (London: Secker and Warburg, 1959).

Conclusion

There is probably no missionary experience that is more spiritually exhilarating than bringing the Good News to a tribe that has never heard the message before; and few groups are likely to be more responsive to such a message than face-to-face tribal societies. But their very openness spells a tremendous responsibility for the missionary. This responsibility is not discharged merely with the delivery of a relevant message—indeed, the missionary messenger must also assume responsibility for the direction which the cycle of change, that his presence and the tribal conversion experience will set into motion, will eventually take.

On the other hand, the statistics of epidemics resulting from contacts with Westerners are sobering, if not frightening. Some may even argue that the missionary has no business to go to the tribes with the gospel. Here we need to underscore the fact that no tribe will be able to maintain its isolation in our modern expanding world. In fact, the availability of vaccines for almost all of the killing contagious diseases actually impresses upon the missionary the responsibility to go quickly so as to be able to save both the tribal body and the tribal soul.

And when he goes, the missionary will have to reconcile himself to the fact that he will make mistakes—in contact, with trade goods, because of his residence, or even in employment. However, if he can approach his task with a degree of awareness of the potential problems, he is bound to be more cautious and more sensitive, and therefore less apt to precipitate difficulties that will result in long-range hurt to the tribe.

Being forewarned of the problems of long-term residence, he will be ready to consider other approaches. Short-term visits are a possibility which may offer certain advantages. For example, short-term visits will prevent the missionary from developing a policeman's or governor's role; they will permit the message which he brings to diffuse in the tribe so that group decision can be possible; they will prevent the missionary from calling out individual converts prematurely; they will let the leadership and service patterns of the indigenous church develop without undue outside interference; and they will be a means of teaching converts to depend on the Holy Spirit rather than on the missionary for guidance in solving problems.

Short-term visits will also mean that the missionary will be more dependent on the tribe for his livelihood during the period of his stay. At the same time, he will have an opportunity of reciprocating in depth with those individuals who will come to spend some time in his home at his base of operations. This sharing in depth with a few will go a long way to eliminate the feelings that the missionary is unwilling to share his material benefits with tribal people.

To avoid being viewed as an "other-world creature" he will need to keep his technological gadgetry at a minimum; and, if he is not resident in the tribe, this will be even more necessary. Furthermore, he must be very "human" in his relationships with the people. If God found it necessary to become "flesh" and to live among men, surely the missionary must be willing to share his humanity and his culture in honest self-exposure. If the missionary has as great a willingness to be known as he has an interest to know, many of the misconceptions about him and his way of life will be eliminated and the stage set for effective bi-directional communication. Such communication channels will not only be adequate for communicating the Good News, but for helping the tribal church to develop indigenously, and for building the necessary bridges between the tribal society and the national church within whose orbit of influence the tribal church exists.[13]

13 This theme will be developed in Loewen, "Tribal Societies . . .," op. cit.

A Message For Missionaries From Mopass

A. RICHARD King concludes his evaluative study of Canadian Indian education *The School at Mopass: A Problem of Identity*[1] with a critique of church-operated education, and in the process indicts the whole missionary program as often being an obstacle rather than a help in the Indians' quest of becoming well-integrated Canadians. Obviously King is not a friend of missions, but some of his criticisms ring so true that at least this missionary found himself wincing repeatedly as he read them – they cut awfully close to the marrow. There are critical observations on missions interspersed throughout most of the book, but they are most heavily concentrated in the conclusion, from which we present some excerpted paragraphs. King's major indictments, which have been summarized as paragraph headings in the appended commentary, can be grouped into three categories: (1) concerning the missionary and his personality, (2) the missionary's message, and (3) the mission school (station) setting.

For the children, the residential school constitutes a social enclave almost totally insulated from the community within which it functions; yet Mopass School

reflects in a microcosmic, but dismayingly faithful manner the social processes of the larger society. Two distinct domains of social interaction exist independently: Whiteman society and Indian society. Where these domains overlap, they do so with common purposes shared at the highest level of abstraction – but with minimal congruence of purposes, values and perceptions, at the operating levels of interaction. The Whiteman maintains his social order according to his own perceptions of reality. The Indian bears the burden of adaptation to a social order that he may perceive more realistically – and surely he perceives it with a different ordering of reality – than does the Whiteman. From his perceptions, the Indian finds it impossible to accept the social order and, at the same time, impossible to reject it completely. He therefore creates an artificial self to cope with the unique interactive situations...

To maintain in an equilibrium within their own peer group and in their relations with the impersonal adult society, the Indian children adopt the mechanism of creating a school self that functions only within the school

A. Richard King, *The School at Mopass: A Problem of Identity* (New York: Holt, Rinehart and Winston, Inc., 1967), 96 pp.

boundaries. If this artificial self is not consciously developed, it is at least partially recognized and consciously controlled. The children sustain themselves with the conviction that their "real self" is not this person in the school at all.

Thus, long before the end of experiences at the residential school, the fundamental barriers between Whiteman and Indian are firmly developed, not so much by a conscious rejection on the part of the Whiteman as by a conscious rejection on the part of the Indian child. The sterile shallowness of the adult model presented by the school Whitemen serves only to enhance – and probably to romanticize – memories of attachments in the child's primary family group, and to affirm a conviction prevalent among the present adult Indian generation that Indians must strive to maintain an identity separate from Whitemen...

An inevitable conclusion is that the organized purveyors of Christianity bear the brunt of responsibility for the nonfunctional adaptation of Indians in today's Yukon society. This conclusion is not an indictment of any church, or of the good and conscientious people who have made contributions by way of church responsibilities. It is, rather an assertion that Canadian society has forced upon the churches collectively, both by default and by actual direction, a function that the churches are

incapable of performing. In a sense the Christian churches have been the Whiteman's scapegoat – the buffer instruments with which he hoped to assuage his collective guilt and polish his tarnished conscience.

Christianty was "given" to the Indian by means of the churches and church schools, as a primary acculturative pathway. In all of the contact period and down to the present times, churches were the chosen instruments for "dealing with" Indians. To Indians, church people were the Whitemen most genuinely interested in them; and church people appeared to have a status in Whiteman society that guaranteed acceptance in that society if one identified with the Whiteman's church. Yukon Indians accepted Christianity so wholeheartedly that, within two generations, they had abandoned basic cultural patterns in a matter [*sic: probably* manner] seldom before known to anthropological science. Language, technology, and custom became archaic overnight. Their very name identities and attendant patterns of ceremony and tradition were totally abandoned in favor of Christian identification.

Unfortunately, their newly acquired morality concepts proved to be unrelated to political and economic power in the Whiteman's society; or, at least, related in a manner not clear to Indians. Christian morality is not a set of precepts by which White busi-

ness men do business or White
workingmen labor or White social leaders accumulate prestige
and wealth. Christian morality
is the Whiteman's symbolization
of a set of ideals which *he* recognizes as unattainable, but which
he supports by means of an institutionalized social appendix
called a church because this set
of ideals acts as a source of forgiveness which compensates for
the complexity of his individual
rationalizations of self-interest
and his acquisitive motivations.
The subtle complexities of guilt
-sin-forgiveness-salvation which
have been developing among
Whitemen for nearly two thousand years have not been easily
transferable to Indians within
only a few generations.

The Whiteman was – and is –
willing to give his idealized
moral order to the Indian. Indeed,
he is quite insistent about it!
He was not – and he is not –
willing to give political and economic power to *anyone* if he can
keep it for himself. To the Indian,
whose indigenous individualistic
morality was very similar to that
of the Whiteman's – minus the
superimposed Christian ideals –
the new morality introduced by
the Whiteman seemed a wonderful protective device for the
stabilization of society, represen-
ting a great advancement for man.
But the disillusion of finding
that the "new morality" was only
verbalization and not a set of
functioning precepts for living,
has proved bewildering and disin-

tegrative. Indian attitudes have
shifted from eagerness to be a
part of that society to eagerness
to get what one can *from* that
society.

Such an attitude is reinforced
by the would-be martyrs who come
with a missionary zeal. Whereas
the true missionary is seldom
concerned with a direct-self-
gratification, the deviant, mis-
placed "missionaries" feel themselves to be self-sacrificing bearers
of truth and light to a shadowed
place of sinful error. This becomes
an essential motivation and a
broad justification for such inadequate individuals, perverting the
intent of their institution and
their society. These individuals
are incapable of recognizing any
validity in another belief system,
With these people controlling
the school, there is no possibility
of consulting with Indian adults
or of treating Indians as equals
in the planning of educational
experiences for the children.
They seldom demonstrate a truly
internalized set of values or guid-
ing concepts. Such people often
originate in culturally deprived
segments of their own society
and bear scars from compensating
for their own origin. Understanding neither themselves nor
their own purposes, much less
the institutional purposes of their
church, government, or society,
the core of the residential school
operating personnel can fall back
upon only the pecking order –
mechanisms of very primitive
social organizations. Inherent

in their closed belief systems are perceptions of hostility everywhere, a universe in which one must fight for the slightest recognition, a population with base and sinful motivations, and the capacity to achieve ultimate personal gratification only by the means of identifying one's self with the highest possible authority.[2]

The Missionary

The missionary is often a culturally marginal person in his one society. We have been conditioned to think of missionary volunteers as being the "cream of the crop," as people who have achieved a high degree of spiritual maturity and dedication. King, however, insists that many, if not most missionaries are basically marginals even to their own culture. Before we reject his assertion outright, we need to recognize that missionaries in actual fact often do have some social problems. A recent, though somewhat limited, study of missionary candidates showed that those who were rated highest by mission boards as "dedicated," "surrenderd," or "spiritual" manifested the greatest social distance – both in degree and in scope. They were alienated not only from the mainstream of their home society but from human beings in general. Even where such isolation is not too apparent when the missionary first goes to the mission field, it usually stands out in bold relief by the time he comes home on furlough, for returned missionaries are notorious for their pessimistic

pronouncements on the home scene which they characterize as "definitely slipping, if not going to the dogs." Statements of this nature, of course, merely underline the fact that the returned missionary feels himself marginal not only to the mainstream of his society, but also to his home church constituency.

Often the very act of volunteering as a missionary is motivated by a kind of otherworldliness that has become a part of the role expectations for truly evangelical missionaries.[3] Such people turn their backs on the major concerns of their contemporaries in their own society, they step out of their social setting and ordinary living to engage in "winning souls" for a heavenly kingdom. In a society that ordinarily gauges the worth of a person in terms of measurable production, missionaries stand out as unique do-gooders whose work is to produce only unmeasurable "spiritual" returns. It is no wonder, therefore, that returning missionaries frequently feel themselves out of place or at least out of step with the home society. I remember hearing of a group of missionaries at a missions conference who were invited to a deacon's home which had a TV set in every room. When this "successful" homeland Christian expounded his philosophy of life, several of the missionaries immediately abandoned his place in disgust – they found the atmosphere of this-worldliness in the deacon's home too stifling.

Sometimes even volunteers who

2*Ibid.* pp. 86-90.

3Jacob A. Loewen and Anne Loewen, "The Missionary Role," *PA*, Vol. 14, No. 5 (September—October, 1967), pp. 193–208.

were not marginal to their own society when they first entered missionary service, become so, due to the pressures of the missionary role. In fact, the missionary's remoteness from his own culture seems to grow with each successive term on the field. Many older missionaries feel decidedly uncomfortable on home leave, and can relax only once they get back to the field. Often it is this alienation from their own society rather than their close identification with the native society that motivates them to retire on the mission field.

This lack of integration in the home mainstream, King asserts, leads to great personal insecurity and defensiveness on the part of the mission staff. Toward each other this is expressed in mutual mistrust and in jockeying for positions of authority; toward Indian children it is expressed in social and psychological distance. In spite of the highest ideals taught in class, the staff reacts in strictly institutionalized role behavior toward the student, i.e. all communication remains on a station-to-station level because the insecure staffer cannot risk person-to-person involvement.[4]

King also asserts that the missionary often comes from the culturally deprived segment of his society, and instead of making a sacrifice for the Lord, the mission job is actually the best he could manage with his qualifications. Here I felt personally indicted. As a recent immigrant to Canada and a member of a minority

---

4Jacob A. and Anne Loewen, "Role Self-image and Missionary Communication," PA, Vol. 14 No. 4 (July—August, 1967), pp. 145—160.

church, growing up in extreme poverty, I was deprived of a high school education and had to settle for Bible institute instead. On graduation I volunteered for missionary service because it seemed the best way to serve the Lord and to be able to earn a living at the same time. My education up to that point didn't qualify me for much in the homeland, and that for which I did qualify, I had no desire to take up. I don't think I was dishonest in dedicating myself to God as a missionary; but looking back today I see how my deprivation played a major part in the decision.

On the other side of this coin, observers have pointed out that when missionaries do get advanced university degrees, especially doctorates, a high percentage of them then gravitate away from the missionary role into the mainstream at home. This is not to say that they lose either their faith or their vision, for many of them continue to make significant contributions to church and community life. King would, of course, insist that they stepped out of the missionary role because their advanced education overcame the alienation gap between them and their society, and their wider horizon made them uncomfortable in the traditional missionary role.

The Missionary is atoning. Those who have entered deeply into the personal lives of missionary personnel have often been surprised at the many individuals who are basically atoning for something in their past by serving on the mission field. However, King's indictment is not concerned so much with this type of personal atonement;

he wants to suggest that the whole missionary role and motivation in American society grows out of collective guilt. The high standard of Western living, the conspicuous self-interest motivation, and the tragic history of White-native relationships form the basis of a deep-seated and universal guilt complex. The missionary functions as a scapegoat or a sacrificial atonement for this collective guilt. Churchmen themselves have pointed out that the average church member considers the missionary to be a kind of substitute for him in service, suffering, and sacrifice. Since the "ordinary" church member supports the missionary by prayer and money, he also vicariously participates in the latter's self-abnegation and thus atones, at least in part, for his own selfish life.

Missionaries tend to have a sacrifice complex. Anthropologists and sociologists have long pointed out that life is made up of a vast inventory of role relationships into which people unconsciously maneuver each other. King seems to say that home church people have succeeded by their words and deeds in making missionaries believe that they *really are sacrificing saints.* And he may be more right than we are willing to admit. Recently in a women's meeting (made up of missionary women, U.S. AID personnel, government employees, and businessmen's wives) a Christian woman, whose husband is in business abroad, reprimanded several missionary women who were talking volubly about the great sacrifices that missionaries in the jungle make. Her reproof in essence was:

"I get somewhat tired of hearing about missionary sacrifices. I was a missionary for a term myself, and when my husband and I decided that we could be of more help by establishing an implement business abroad, we did not forsake sacrificing for selfish living, for financially we are actually struggling more now than we were as missionaries." Another non-missionary wife added: "It is not sacrifice nor the lack of it that brings us abroad, it is what we believe to be God's will for us. Let's be realistic. Each of us *chooses* what he wants to do with his life, and self-fulfillment is not sacrifice, it is satisfaction."

Obviously not all missionaries feel their "sacrifice," but King would say that those who do are expressing their misplacement and alienation from their home society with it. The psychologist would probably add that the degree of sacrifice felt would indicate how deeply the person was repressing his desire to be part of the home mainstream.

Missionaries can build their egos at the expense of the parish. Regardless of how remote the missionary may feel toward the setting of his origin, it is there that he desires to get recognition. If he is dependent upon personally collecting his support, his efficiency in enacting the expected missionary role, especially while on furlough, will to a large extent determine his capacity to raise funds to support himself and his program. In one of the South American countries nationals were complaining about being the "stocks and bonds" of missionary support — missionaries needed their poverty and depravity to have something tear-jerking to report. After several nationals had spoken with deep emotion on this subject, the author as chairman of the meeting tried to summarize their impassioned speeches in the following question, "Do you mean that missionaries *use you and your problems* to earn self-esteem from their people back home?" When the nationals present broke into a standing ovation, all of us missionaries were somewhat shocked by the intensity of their spontaneous reaction; we hadn't realized how deeply the nationals felt that they were being used.

The Missionary represents an inoperative model. The mission was the White man's chosen way to help the Indian acculturate to White society, and the missionary was the immediate White model for the Indian to emulate. This has spelled double trouble. In the first place, the functions of missionaries in a mission setting represented only a very small segment of the possible roles in White man's society; and secondly, and even worse, none of the mission roles, however well the Indian might emulate them, would fit him to operate successfully in White society, for the Indian could hardly expect to be accepted as teacher, a doctor, a preacher, etc. in the White community. On the other hand, roles which the Indian could fulfill do not usually form part of the missionary role inventory. King states that Indians firmly believed that since missionaries had status and respect in their society, they too would be accorded equal or at least similar status and respect

if they accepted the Christian religion which the missionary taught. But this expectation turned out to be false. Regardless of how "Christian" Indians became, they were not accepted as equals by the mainstream of White society. Nor was this true only when missions to the Indians first began – it is still a fact today in Indian boarding schools, on mission stations, and in White society at large.

King's description of the Indian child who actually tries to copy the missionary model and then gets "mortally" hurt, is deeply moving. Once the rejection by White society sinks in, the child retreats in shame realizing that he has been labelled as a person without worth. Since the child cannot flee literally it defends its ego by developing an artificial school self and a deeply negative attitude toward Whites. These school experiences immunize the child, as it were, against any attempt that may later be made to help him to function meaningfully as a member of White society.

Missionaries may present a warped conception of the universe. Because missionaries have rejected the major portion of their society's life and values as evil, King asserts they have therefore developed a biased or warped worldview. They see the universe around them as inherently evil and hostile, and they react defensively against everything that that is different from themselves. In spite of the fact that they are kind and overtly accepting of the Indian, they actually reject people who are different in culture or belief. Thus, Indians are seen as objects of paternalistic attention, and Whites who differ from them are seen as "enemies of the cross." This limited view is especially marked in regard to their values and their conceptions of right and wrong. They generally represent a rather limited, rigid and absolutist system of ethics which treats everything outside of itself as suspect, if not evil. As a result they are narrow and defensive. This covert negative attitude toward the Indian is frequently amplified through the fact that their mission work does not show the hoped-for success. Since they find it hard to accept any personal responsibility for this failure, they unconsciously project it on the Indian and covertly hate him for making them fall short of their ideals. This attitude precludes any possibility of them talking openly and as equals with the parents of their Indian students and thereby arriving at a more relevant solution to the children's school problems.

King's strong words reminded me of a missionary who on the request of the nationals had to be repatriated when the country of his mission achieved independence. His deep-seated rejection of the nationals and their culture erupted during a missionary report in which he described the aborigines as so filthy, irresponsible, and corrupted by satanic practices that he had difficulty seeing them as human beings.

The Message

Utopian and unrelated to life. Author King has some equally strong words about the missionary's message. White man's society, he says, pays lip service to the idealistic morality which the Christian church preaches, but operates according to a completely different system in daily life. In fact, for White society as a whole the church is a pious appendage which is scrupulously separated from weekday living. King states that when the Indian was first faced with Western values, he discovered that his own individualistic values were basically quite compatible with the White man's code of ethics. He saw in Christian teaching a superior way of protecting and stabilizing the best in society. The Indian thus went all out to accept it. Within two generations he abandoned his own codes and values and tried to become part of the White man's system, but he was hurt twice in the process. First, because the code he learned at the mission was not really the one by which White society operated in daily life (and if it was applicable, the Indian could not make the necessary adaptations). The newly accepted code of morality thus became a hindering encumbrance rather than an operational framework. Secondly, he was hurt because the mainstream of White society did not actually intend to share its political and economic power with the Indian. The kind, paternalistic missionary who was supposed to be the way to acculturation was in actual fact himself not integrated into the mainstream of White society which was really using its emissary as a buffer to keep from having to interact with the Indian. Even though King doesn't say it overtly, he is here referring to the phenomenon of the culture broker which of late has been receiving considerable anthropological attention.[5] The principle is this: whenever two societies come into contact with each other, they tend to develop brokers. These brokers can function in one of two ways: (1) to help the two different parties who have something to offer each other to meet and transact for mutual benefit, e.g. a buyer meeting a seller; (2) to serve as a go between for two parties who do not really care to interact in person. Both of them interact only with the broker and thus do not have to face each other in person. Missionaries, according to King, are brokers of the second type whose basic function is to serve as buffers to make it unnecessary for the White man in general to have to face the Indian

Verbalized but not lived. King asserts that Christian morality is a symbol of the White man's highest ideals – ideals which he verbalizes but which he, by and large, considers unattainable. In actual fact, for the mainstream of White society they are not a "set of functioning precepts by which White businessmen do business or White working men labor or White social leaders accumulate prestige and wealth," but this "inoperative" code, according to King, is the very heart of the missionary

message. Obviously King is here speaking of the discrepancy between the real and the ideal in Christian living. This double standard – which returning missionaries themselves have often decried – is a source of severe frustration for the Indian who sees the hypocrisy of it all more plainly than the White man himself. This frustration is especially acute because though in most mission fields the aborigine is exposed only to the missionary and not to the mainstream of the missionary's society, the Canadian Indian observes, meets, and makes business transactions with typical Canadians. He thus becomes deeply aware both of the double standard in the life of the average Canadian and of the discrepancy between his actual operational code and missionary teaching.

This experience of seeing the daily life, not only the Sunday ideal, has become quite a problem for Lengua and Chulupi Christians in the Paraguayan Chaco, for they too meet not only the missionaries, but also have to work for and live with the average White European colonists who support the mission.

King suggests that the Indian has recognized the blatant hypocrisy which this double standard represents, and that this recognition has inoculated him against trying or even wanting to become part of the White system. He is now merely seeing what he can get *from* White society.

However, this double standard, King asserts, operates not only in the larger White society, it is also

5 Robert Hunt, "Agentes Culturales Mestizos: Estabilidad y Cambio en Oaxaca," *América Indígena*, Vol. 28, No. 3 (July 1968), pp. 596–609.

part and parcel of the daily life of the staff in the mission-operated school. The staff teaches Christian ideals in class, but outside of it they used mainstream methods of jockeying with each other for prestige and authority.

Sin-guilt-forgiveness-salvation. Being at least partially aware of this double standard and his falling short of the ideal, the White man has accumulated considerable guilt. To deal with the latter, King says, he has developed an elaborate religious system by which his guilt can be forgiven and he can be saved. However, this sin-guilt-forgiveness-salvation message which was developed over a long period of the White man's experience is largely irrelevant to the Indian who comes from an entirely different worldview and a different cultural past. The missionary continues preaching, but, says King, his message doesn't scratch where it itches.

The Missionary Setting

The mission as primary acculturative pathway. White society has relegated to the mission the impossible (at least under the established circumstances) task of helping the Indian to become a functioning part of White man's society. According to King, White society selected the missionary or rather "created" the missionary role because it operated outside of the mainstream of the White economic and power structure. Such a marginal missionary was the logical choice to become the buffer between White society and the Indian with whom the former did not intend

to share political and economic power. According to King, the missionary's basic assignment was to keep the Indian in his place. (This is an expression that is frequently also heard about the Negroes in North America). The mainstream of White society never really intended the missionary to be the vehicle of integration. The missionary's assignment was to Christianize the Indian so that the latter like the missionary himself would be useful, but remain marginal. Once the Indian was converted, the missionary was to control him so that he would not disturb the White man's routine nor his conscience. King also underscores what Black Power people are saying very emphatically in North America today: the White man will never relinquish economic and political power willingly; he yields only to superior force or under the threat of economic loss.

The indictment that the missionary is a buffer and a salve for the White's conscience is not without foundation. As a young man the author worked with a children's mission which was basically designed as an approach into non-Christian homes via the children. When the number of converts and baptismal candidates from various types of marginal groups increased, the sending churches became embarrassed and decided to discontinue this type of ministry in the immediate environs and sent their workers into the more remote northern parts of the province. The basic motivation, of course, was that local marginal converts were too difficult to integrate, and since it was not ready to accept them as equals, the local church insulated itself against the need for further interaction with such people by relocating the mission at a distance.

In most mission fields this brokerage problem is compounded by a related factor, namely that the missionary is not even a marginal member of the mainstream national society into which the tribal society eventually must be integrated. In fact, it is not uncommon for the missionary to a tribal society to be both geographically isolated and totally alienated from the national society. In a number of cases the missionary has thus become an obstacle rather than an acculturative bridge for the tribal convert.[6]

Reading King's indictment reminded me of my early missionary experience in South America. I must confess that I cringed inwardly as I recalled how intensely I had disliked the Negro majority (90 percent) which was brazenly abusing the Indian minority (5 percent) with whom I had identified deeply. My "righteous" efforts to help the underdog certainly built no bridges; instead they increased the distance between the two groups. Nor was I unique, for my more recent observations in South America have shown that my attitude was merely average.

School/mission as microcosm. According to King the social distance, the discrimination, etc. that was maintained between the White school staff and the Indian students was actually a duplicate in miniature of

6 Jacob A. Loewen, "From Tribal Society to National Church," PA, Vol. 15, No. 3 (May-June, 1968), pp. 97–111.

the situation in the society at large. In fact, he would consider the boarding school to be the practice arena in which the Indian child rehearsed the roles that it would later play as an adjunct to White society. The child was exposed to some of the benefits of White society, but it was taught that it could not share them. The vast gulf between the two societies was subtly revealed in the attitude of the missionary teachers who considered themselves as making sacrifices while teaching Indians. The inevitable result was that the Indian child developed a split view of itself. In school and in interaction with White society in general it portrayed an artificial, false self of irresponsibility and lethargic responses; the real self was identified with the ideal Indian back home. For the adult the real was the "good old Indian way" which could never be a reality again. But King alludes to winds of change. Organizations like the Canadian Indian Youth Council (like its American counterpart – the Negro Black Power movement) have now by and large recognized that the Indian needs a new self-respecting self-image, and definite efforts are being made to overcome the false identity in relationship to White society. Slogans such as "black is beautiful" are an attempt to create an ideal apart from that of the Whites by which members of the minority group can develop self-respect. What is really frightening for missions in all this is that these new avenues for building self-respect are completely divorced from the church and its message. Does this mean that the Biblical "good news" about all tribes, languages and races becoming equal children in God's family is not applicable to Canadian Indian living in a White-dominated society?

Kings's analysis obviously speaks only of one side of the mission story — the seamy side, but it is a side that missions and missionaries will do well to face honestly. It goes without saying that not all missionaries are guilty of all the indictments he makes, but it is very doubtful that many will be able to excuse themselves from all of them.

Jacob A. Loewen and Anne Loewen

Role, Self-Image and Missionary Communication

SOMEWHAT over a year ago my wife and I underwent a new and, for us, somewhat shaking experience. We added a new role relationship to our pattern of married life.

As newlyweds we had gone to college together, sharing many classes. During ten years of missionary service we had cooperated closely in the responsibilities and problems of our work. In fact, we considered ourselves a rather successful "team." When circumstances forced us to leave the mission field I joined the faculty of Tabor College, and my wife, Anne, began to teach foreign languages in secondary school. Although there was some overlap in our fields of interest, we developed rather separate teaching careers. While we enjoyed our separate assignments, we often looked back somewhat nostalgically at the cooperate teamwork in the past.

During the course of this college teaching I became active in research and writing and began to employ secretarial help. Then, after seven years of working on our "separate" careers, a change in my employment opened the possibility for renewed team effort. Therefore Anne resigned from her teaching position and became my secretarial assistant. Both of us looked forward with enthusiasm toward a rich, meaningful, cooperative experience, and were rudely surprised when our first efforts at cooperative work produced tension.

I had dictated my correspondence, as was my practice, and Anne's first task was to transcribe a series of letters. Having typed the first letter, she asked for the address; and without really interrupting my work I pointed to the address file, operating, I suppose, on the premise that the secretary's time was less valuable than my own. Though I saw them only in retrospect, a series of similar incidents occurred in rapid succession. After another of these I became aware that Anne's typing was becoming slower and slower; finally she stopped, turned around, and asked, "Why are you so different here in the office from the way you are at home? Will it always be like this? Aren't you going to be polite anymore?"

It took several similar exchanges before we realized that we were facing something more than mere sensitivity on Anne's part. Once we did, we stopped and tried to face the problem squarely. After an honest exchange of ideas and feelings we decided that we needed to add another complement of roles to our relationship.

But this was much easier said than done; we had no sooner decided to also be boss and secretary than I noticed that Anne was struggling

412

even harder than before. We stopped again and found Anne was competing against some very ill-defined images of my former secretaries. I had had some very efficient ones, but also some very poor ones. When I had been either very happy or very frustrated, I had spilled over at home, and out of these disconnected outbursts Anne formed her impressions. On the one hand she feared she would not be able to match the best, and on the other she was afraid that since she had been "hurt" by my "boss" behavior, I would now be extra polite and not let her know when I was dissatisfied with her work.

Actually on the second count her fear was unfounded, for I slipped out of the "boss" role again and again and expressed my disappointment in very "un-office-like" terms. The adjustment has taken time, effort, and mutual patience, but in the process both of us feel that we have learned something of the deep significance of roles and self-image in our lives. In fact, this experience began to throw light on all sorts of problems we had encountered during our missionary service, and so we have decided to share some of the lessons we have learned. We present them in two separate essays.

Roles in human interaction

At the very heart of missionary assignment lies the relevant communication of the gospel. Even though this is most frequently thought of as more or less synonymous with oral proclamation, most of us will readily admit that the messenger's actions and his personal character will also play important parts. However, few missionaries and friends of missions have stopped to realize that the actions and character of the messenger are largely determined by the person's status, role, and self-image, for communication can only take place within a social context.

Roles define relationships

Each member of a given society occupies a series of statuses in relationships to other individuals of this society; and each status carries with it certain roles which are the behavioral expectations of that society.[1] We could thus distinguish between status and role by saying that status defines a person's positional relationship within the social hierarchy, while role describes the dynamic behavioral aspect of this person acting out the expectations associated with a given position. The structure of the society and the number of individuals with whom a person interacts will determine the number and kind of statuses and accompanying roles he will have.

Roles usually come in reciprocal pairs—a parent is unthinkable without a child; likewise there can be no teacher without a student. Such pairs

---

[1] An earlier draft of this paper was written without the dimensions of status. Kenneth A. Olenik, now professor of sociology at Aurora College, read this draft and suggested that the positional dimension of status ought to be distinguished from the behavioral aspect of role throughout the paper; however, the authors have decided to introduce it only where accuracy of definition or clarity of function make it necessary. Otherwise the term "role" has been used loosely to cover both the static and the dynamic aspects. This usage follows Paul Bohannan, *Social Anthropology* (New York: Holt, Rinehart and Winston, Inc., 1963).

complement each other in terms of the mutual behavioral expectations. Paul Bohannan calls them complementary role pairs or poles. He distinguishes them from interrelated or linked pairs which he labels a role syndrome.[2] The roles of wife and mother represent such a syndrome in our society, and it is expected that these roles be played by one person.

A further function of status and role is to provide the individual with standardized forms of behavior which meet the expectations of society. At the same time the behavior of the role participants provides him with feed-back on the quality of his performance. When the expected complements of behavior appear, the participants have a sense of social security. Many of the so-called preliterate cultures have developed rather elaborate patterns of avoidance between individuals who (because of their respective statuses or positions in their culture) may not establish sexual relationships. Again, with others who are potential sexual intimates, the so-called joking relationships permit all types of familiarity. This standardization of expectation in terms of role behavior can also be seen in our own culture in such admonitions as, "That is no way to act toward your mother," (or your teacher, etc.)

The function of both the positional relationship in the social organization and the behavioral role patterns have been well summarized by Joyce O. Hertzler:

Thus statuses and roles are the

basis of both the structural adjustment and the functional coordination of the individual and the groups of a society to each other, by means of which they know where they stand and how they are related in the structural whole, and what is required, permitted, and forbidden in the functional whole.[3]

Such patterns of "standardized" behavior also provide a kind of positional protection for the actor in new or in otherwise precarious situations. For example, a non-leader by personality may find himself pushed into the position of chairman of a committee. If he carefully follows the accepted behavior – *Robert's, Rules of Order* –he can mask his "weakness" and be a "successful" chairman.

Often these different social positions are accompanied by visible symbols such as uniforms, caste marks, or special positions within a gathering of people. Thus, during the day on a hunting expedition the tribal shaman functions as an "average" Indian; but when he puts on his shaman's headdress at night to perform magic to make the hunt successful, both his behavior and the reactions of his fellow Indians towards him change. Such external signs as special dress, badges, and positional locations at social functions serve as useful signals for change of status and role both for the role player and for the rest of the "participants of the cast."

While most anthropologists and

---

[2] Ibid., pp. 28-29.

[3] Joyce O. Hertzler, *Society in Action: A Study of Basic Social Processes* (New York: The Dryden Press, 1954), pp. 167-168.

sociologists clearly distinguish between the positional aspect of status and the functional aspect of role, this paper will use the word "role" in a loose sense to cover both of these aspects, except in instances where ambiguity or misinterpretation could result.[4]

The multiplicity of roles

Not only do all of us as members of a society play roles, but everyone of us plays a multiplicity of roles. The same individual may have a husband role, a boss role, a club member role, etc. All of us shift into different roles in different settings in the course of our daily experience. In our own complex Western societies where we enter into relationships with a vast number of individuals, a person will have an extensive inventory of role relationships.

This multiplicity of roles does not function only on the synchronic plane with different people, it is also operative diachronically. In the course of his life the individual will have an extensive sequence of roles. In many of the so-called primitive societies such age-linked status-role transitions are marked by rites of passage.[5] These rites function as overt signals to the initiate and to the society of their new mutual relationship. Because such rites of passage are not consistently observed in our own culture, anthropologists have been led

to speculate that possibly many of the problems of teenage rebellion against society find their roots in the confusion over the actual time of transition from childhood to adulthood. For purposes of the driver's license maturity comes at the age of sixteen, in terms of certain other activities at the age of eighteen, still others at the age of twenty-one, and in terms of auto insurance it comes only at twenty-five.

Not only with different persons in different settings do we function in different role relationships, however; we actually have different role relationships with the same individuals in different settings. When the role participants are not aware of these role changes, difficulties, misinterpretations, and tensions are bound to arise from the resulting changes in behavior and expected response.

We are well aware that a mother, who is also the teacher of her children in a classroom, will need to impress them with the difference in their mutual role relationship in these two social settings. Or consider the situation of the neighbor and friend who is also the traffic judge and must deal with his friends in his capacity of judge when they commit traffic violations.

Role consistencies

Because we play such a multiplicity of roles—often several roles with the same individual—it is important

---

[4] Bohannan, op. cit, p. 26ff; also see Felix Keesing, *Cultural Anthropology, the Science of Custom* (New York: Rinehard and Company, Inc., 1958), pp. 244-245; and Ralph Linton, *The Study of Man* (New York: Appleton-Century-Crofts, Inc., 1936), chapter 8.

[5] Arnold Van Gennep, *The Rites of Passage.* Translated from the French by Monica B. Vizdom and Gabrielle L. Caffee. (Chicago: University of Chicago Press, 1960).

to recognize that the roles of a mature person will cluster around a common core. They will reflect one "real self." Paul Bohannan has already pointed out that we need to make a distinction between the social personality and the individual personality. He defines the former as the "role-playing aspect of self" and the latter as the "real self."[6] This is a very important distinction because it highlights the fact that the standardization of behavior is relative. Every woman who is a mother plays the role of mother in her "own way." This personal modification of the role, usually called style,[7] permits the actor's real self to "shine through" in all his roles. In other words, even though an individual is related to other persons in a number of different roles, the participants will always be aware that they are dealing with the same individual because his action is anchored in one "self."

In my earlier church life I experienced some rather serious difficulties with a certain church executive. We were on friendly terms as a whole, but on several occasions we developed very severe misunderstandings. It was only after a series of these difficulties that I realized the source of our problem. We were related to each other in a number of role pairs. First, he was my friend and confidante with whom I could freely discuss all of my concerns; next, he was an executive of a major church board with which I was employed; and third, he was a senior officer in the hierarchy of the

church to which I also belong. On several occasions we had reached certain conclusions in private discussions and I had acted upon them, only to find that later in public this person took a very different position. At first I assumed that he was dishonest, but I had to learn that our difficulties actually resulted from the differences of premises and values on which he operated in these different roles. It became exceedingly important for me to be aware of the "hat he was wearing" at the time of our conversation. If he sat behind his desk he was probably functioning in the executive role; if he came to sit beside me in front of the desk, he most likely was in the role of my friend and confidante; if I wanted to have "executive" support, I needed to be sure that he was functioning in his executive role at the time of reaching the agreement.

Role sincerity

Having made a distinction between the "real" personality and the social personality, we would like to develop the fact that this separation also makes it possible to distort the reflection of one's self, if not to hide it entirely. Where the true self is honestly reflected in role playing, we could speak of role sincerity, but where there is marked discrepancy we could speak of role insincerity. Role insincerity, therefore, is possible because the standardized patterns of role behavior can also be used as masks or disguises of actual character or intent. Role insincerity is further abetted by the presentation of the external status markers which raise

6 Bohannan, op. cit., p. 28.

7 Loc. cit.

the expectation that the concomitant patterns of standardized behavior will follow.

For example, a person intending to murder someone may don the uniform of a Western Union messenger and get past the guard of the hotel into the victim's room without raising the suspicion of either. On accomplishing his mission he discards the "borrowed" status marker to prevent his identification. Again, the role of Red Cross or Salvation Army solicitor is so accepted in the average American community that malevolent individuals can extract voluntary donations from unsuspecting householders with surprising ease.

During my early mission experience in Columbia I had an opportunity to observe a case of role insincerity in the field work of a continental anthropologist who had come to study the Chocó culture. When he first visited the Indians he had with him several boxes of axes and knives. He had planned to use these as gifts for informants, but he found that the Indians were very eager to buy them from him. Selling the goods also prevented the jealousy which seemed to accompany giving. He became so impressed with the possibility of the role of an ambulent merchant that he decided to do his research in this guise. Since he was not actually a merchant, however, and was inexperienced in this role, he had been cheated and almost all of the beads had water soluble color. When he sold them to the Indians, they felt that the merchant was intentionally cheating them and so they pressed for redress. Having invested all his capital in the beads, he was unable to give refunds to the Indians. Even though he now tried to explain his true purpose to the Indians, they were deeply angered by his role insincerity. As a result, his communication with them broke down completely and he had to retreat in disgrace with field work unfinished.

The above, of course, is a drastic example of intentional deceit. Not many of us have ever engaged in such blatantly fraudulent role behavior. However, I suspect that on occasion most of us find ourselves "tempted" to project a "better than actual" or at least a "different than real" image of ourselves by means of accepted role behavior. Maybe it would ring truer if we described this phenomenon in the reverse, saying that on occasion our real self retreats behind standardized forms of role behavior which function as a mask to hide our actual emotions. Nor is this behavior unilateral; often it is indulged in by all the participants in a role nexus. Consider the following example from missionary experience—for neither the most dedicated westerner nor the most humble national are immune to role insincerity.

A certain missionary wife whom we knew very well had a lot of difficulty overcoming her ethnocentrism and accepting nationals as persons. Consequently she found it very difficult to entertain them in her home. She always felt that they were dirty or disease-bearing and would endanger the health of her family. When her friends finally helped her become aware of the psychological distance between her and the nationals, she was shocked. But instead of trying to deal with her attitude, she began "playing the role" of a friendly hostess who frequently invited nationals to her home for tea. Many of us—her missionary friends—thought she was overcoming the difficulty, until one day a group of nationals visiting in our home began discussing the situation. One of them mentioned that nationals were not allowed to enter the home of this missionary. Anne corrected this person, saying, "But look weren't you at her house the other day?" The national retorted, "Right, we were at her *house*, but she would never let a native come into her *home*." The negative paramessage of the missionary's actual feelings toward the natives was clearly being read by the latter. They knew that she was just "playing the role" in order to mask her true intent and feeling. She fooled only herself and her countrymen—never the nationals. But the nationals, by visiting and responding in a similar polite way, were actually partners in the missionary's duplicity. We need to face the naked truth. When we cannot enter into the role genuinely and only "play the role," the way we play it generally gives us away.

Roles and communication

In his book *The Meaning of Person* Paul Tournier has pointed out the importance of the distinction between the social and the real personality for interpersonal communication. Truly meaningful communication can only take place between real personalities.

The whole difference between an individual and a person is that the individual associates whereas the person communicates. There is the same difference between the meaning of personage and the person. The personage is an external appearance which touches the personage of others from outside. The person communicates inwardly with the second person, the "thou."[8]

What Tournier calls personage-to-personage we want to label the station-to-station approach in communication. The distinction between station-to-station[9] and person-to-person communication can be illustrated with the following example.

A student pastor in rural North America was hurrying through the pine woods one afternoon when he unexpectedly met a disconsolate young stranger at the river bank. They began to chat casually without introductions. The boy was completely natural and uninhibited since he took the new arrival to be just an "ordinary person." In utter openness he acted his real, ordinary self. Later that day the two met again in a formal situation, and the young boy turned deep red in embarrassment. "I'm sorry, sir," he blurted out. "If I had known who you were, I would never have talked to you like that." But the "damage" was done—the person-to-person contact had been established—and a helpful

---

8 Paul Tournier, *The Meaning of Person* (New York: Harper and Row, 1957), p. 129.

9 Personal communication from Miss Ellen Ross working with the Comisión de Alfabetización y Literatura Aymara in La Paz, Bolivia.

and friendly communication developed between the two in spite of the station discovery. Had the pastor carried his "role marker," or had the youth sensed the minister's "station," he would also have responded by "station"— as a good-for-nothing, rebellious young rake.

In contrast to the above, consider the following scene which was described to Paul Tournier by a patient:

He explains to me that he has just come from the house of a friend who represents his country in the United Nations organization. A brilliant reception was in progress there and the house was thronging with all the important international figures of Geneva. He gives me a vivid, penetrating description of it. Behind the bowing and the smiles, behind the friendly words and the witticisms, the empty phrases, and even their silences and their aloofness—all were playing a cautious game. Each sought to dissemble his own real thoughts— his secret intentions—while trying to unmask those of his neighbor.[10]

While we may be ready to admit that the station-to-station type of communication is characteristic of the diplomatic world, we would hardly expect to find it in a missionary setting; but it also has its missionary manifestation. Festo Kivengere, the African evangelist, shook the audience at the Intervarsity Missionary Conference in 1960 when he related the account of the missionary who

was urging two African nationals to confess their spiritual problems to him without any reciprocal openness on his part. When the latter kept on insisting, one of the Africans finally burst out, "How can I open up my 'box' when yours is not only closed, but locked?"[11]

The above example illustrates an attempt by a missionary to remain "station" while trying to establish communication with a "person." We all readily reject the station-to-station approach, but we have to admit that the station-to-person approach is even more damaging, for the "receptor person" cannot help but read the "source station" approach as a negative paramessage which speaks a far more potent language than any words the "station" may utter. Let us remember that even God in the person of the Word became a "person" so that he could truly communicate with men person-to-person.

Roles and language

Recent studies of English and other languages have pointed out the fact that in languages there are not only regional and social class differences, but situational levels of language as well.[12] For English Dr. William L. Wonderly lists four situational variants: formal, regular, casual, and intimate. He suggests that these four variants could be analogous to the following clothing styles: black

---

[10] Tournier, op. cit., p. 28.

[11] Festo Kivengere, "Personal Revival," *Commission, Conflict, Commitment* (Chicago: Intervarsity Press, 1962), pp. 27-47, pp. 192-193.

[12] John S. Kenyon, "Cultural Levels and Functional Varieties of English," *College English*, Vol. 10 (1948), pp. 31-36.

tie and tails, business suit, sport clothes, and dressing gown respectively.[13] This would mean that an "intimate" role would need to be matched by a similar intimacy of language style. If situation and language style are incongruent, communication is frustrated. Consider the account of a very popular young man who began to court a college "wall flower" with great ardor, but who all the while kept his conversation with the young lady at a regular level. When after a month of very intense courtship he proposed marriage, the young woman collapsed emotionally. She was completely shattered psychologically, because the ardent courtship and the proposal of marriage had not been matched with the proper level of language.

William L. Wonderly has observed that there are very few missionaries in Latin America who can actually establish intimate roles with nationals. While their cultural identification with the people may be such as to make possible a familiar role, as exemplified in the use of *tu* in address, they do not have a comparable control of the casual language forms in the Spanish language. Even when they do attempt to establish such a *tu* role by using the familiar pronoun in their speech, the Spanish national is often mis-cued by the incongruity of the language style which usually remains at a regular level.[14]

13 William L. Wonderly, *Bible Translation into Common Language*. Prepublication draft, p. 17.

14 William L. Wonderly, "At Home in a Second Language," PA Vol. 13, No. 3 (May-June 1966), pp. 97-102.

Roles and self-image

Our personal experience with the boss-secretary role pair recounted earlier showed another dimension of role playing. Even when Anne was ready to play the secretarial role, she found that her "ideal secretary" image was creating problems for her.

Each person not only has a general self-image of himself, but he also develops idealized conceptions of himself in each of the roles he plays in life. This idealized conception includes both the valuation of his own status worth, and the ideal form of himself which he would like to portray with his role playing. Frequently this idealized conception of oneself stands in conflict with the position which society has accorded the individual. When he senses that others' valuation of his person is less than his own idealized conception, he generally tries to do something about it. The two most familiar ways of handling this valuation discrepancy are the so-called "inferiority" and "superiority" complexes. To deal with valuation discrepancy, the person with the inferiority complex retreats behind defenses that are designed to keep his role participants from "proving" the inferiority that they attribute to him. He will try to avoid all situations which could demand a downward revision of his self-valuation. For example, a person may volunteer to be secretary of a committee when he really wants to be the chairman and feels that he could do a far better job than the chairman elect; but he is afraid to volunteer for the top position lest it provide the occasion through which the others' lesser valuation be proven correct.

Consider the following encounter with a college student who often came to our house to drink coffee. During his first year in college the student in question earned rather poor grades. One day he was talking with my wife, who was encouraging him to do better work. He promised her, "Next year I'm going to buckle down and study harder. I'm going to cut out the girls to whom I've been dedicating a major portion of my time during this year." Sometime during the course of the next school year he was again drinking coffee in our home. When my wife reminded him of his resolution and asked him how his grades were coming, he somewhat self-consciously admitted, "About the same as last year—C's and an occasional B."

"I thought you were going to work for B's and A's this year."

"Yes," he admitted, "I was really intending to do that, but you know how it is. I'm living in the dorm this year, and with all the bull sessions, there just isn't enough time to really buckle down and study. And, after all, the classroom isn't the only place to get an education!"

I had been listening to this conversation in silence. Since I knew the student rather well I asked him whether he would permit me to make an alternate analysis of the reason why he was not studying any harder this year than the previous year. He readily agreed, and so I suggested: "You are one of the younger members of your family. You have several brilliant older brothers and sisters.

At home you were always considered to be 'less capable.' The bright ones were held up as ideals which you should emulate. You resented this very much. In revenge you became the biggest rascal in high school. This provided you with several benefits. First, your orneriness gave you an excuse for not studying; and second, you got a lot of attention--you were constantly being called into the principal's office.

"When you left home for college, you had really decided to turn over a new leaf and buckle down to study. But as you took up studies in your new environment, you realized that same old, gnawing fear had come along with you: 'What if my parents should be right and I really am not as smart as my brothers and sisters!' So you began to devise new ways of avoiding being put to the test. During the first year you used girls as an excuse; this year you are using bull sessions as an excuse; next year you will have still another excuse. But could the real reason be that your self-valuation is not quite realistic? In your heart you say that if you should study, you could do as well as your brothers and sisters. But you are really afraid to put this to the test for fear that your parents' valuation, and not your own, will be proven correct. Therefore, you are unconsciously using all types of subterfuge to protect your idealized valuation of yourself."

The superiority complex is likewise a reaction to a situation in which the individual faces a social setting in which he is accorded less worth than he ascribes to his ideal self. This approach to the problem leads the person to compensate. He tries to add the "missing" portion to the other person's valuation through bragging, bravado, humor, antics, etc. Sometimes such behavior actually serves not only to prevent the role participants from giving expression to their lesser valuation, but it also serves as a decoy to detract the observer's attention from reading the unwanted para-message. In each case—inferiority or superiority complex—the person plays his roles in a manner which is not a true expression of himself. His unrealistic self-image prevents him from playing even his legitimate roles in a genuine manner.[15]

Cross-Cultural differences in roles

Roles are universally recognized "blueprints for behavior" suitable for a given social position. But just as there are great differences of culture, so there is an equally great diversity in roles which a culture "recognizes." These differences in role behavior can in a large measure be summarized under the following categories: (1) differences in the role inventory or role network, (2) differences in role content and function, (3) differences in role valuation, (4) differences in role preparation.

Differences in role inventory

When one steps out of the Western world and its network of roles, one must be prepared for the fact that many of the familiar roles will be absent, and in their place there may

be a variety of new ones. For example, most westerners who serve as missionaries have never had any previous experience with the role of the shaman who communicates with the spirit world, nor have most of them had any experience with the role of a second or third wife in a polygamous household.

Differences in role inventory can be subdivided into a least two categories: the overall number of role relationships recognized in a culture, and the number of roles any given individual will play. The first can be called the role network of the culture, and the latter we will call the person's role set.[16] Both role network and role set, however, are determined by the overall organization of the culture. One would expect marked differences between the role sets of a matriarchal society and those of a patriarchal society. A society with a rigid caste system must of necessity develop a number of role relationships which are not found in an egalitarian society. A society in transition that is developing various types of specialists will also develop new role relationships to govern intercourse between the society members and the developing specialists. In fact, we can generalize and say that all distinctive features of social organization will be matched by covering role relationships. Some of these roles – such as harem eunuch, Aztec sacrificial victim and male transvestite – may shock the newcomer by their strangeness. Usually, how-

---

15 Paul Tournier, *The Strong and the Weak* (Philadelphia: The Westminster Press, 1963).

16 Harry C. Bredemeier and Richard M. Stephenson, *The Analysis of Social Systems* (New York: Holt, Rinehart and Winston, Inc., 1962), p. 117.

ever, these "strange" roles are not the ones with which the missionary will most likely have conflict. There is far more danger for him in the possibility of misinterpreting roles which have an apparent similarity to those of his own culture.

Difference in role content and function

We are often in danger of assuming that since male and female, sex and marriage, and parents and children are universal, therefore their respective roles will also be similar, if not identical. Nothing could be further from the truth. It is absolutely naive to assume that even a seemingly identical kinship term will trigger identical role behavior. Each kinship term is a linguistic tag for a series of role relationships, but we must be prepared for unlimited diversity in content and function when we cross cultural boundaries.

William D. Reyburn, describing certain aspects of Kaka kinship, points out how vastly different the area of meaning of Kaka and Western kinship labels are. For the Kaka, "mother" includes not only the biological mother, but all her sisters and the wives of all the men whom a person calls "father." This includes all the husbands of both father's sisters and mother's sisters. Again, the word *nyari* wife includes not only ego's wife (or wives), but also his wife's younger sisters, his older brothers' wives, and the wives of mothers' brothers, for all of these are legitimate sex partners for him.[17]

_____
17 William D. Reyburn, "Kaka, Kinship, Sex and Adultery," PA Vol. 5, No. 1 (January-February 1958), pp. 1-21.

We may consider it natural for the mother who has given birth to a child to go to bed, but in many societies where the couvade is practiced, it is not the mother, but the father, who goes to bed. In these societies the matter of physical birth is considered less important than the transmission of the soul which comes from the father. Since the soul of the child is not considered to be firmly rooted until the navel cord has healed, the father must remain in bed until that time, lest physical effort on his part cause the child's soul to leave the body.

Many non-Western cultures separate the role of father into two distinct functions: biological fatherhood and sociological fatherhood. On the basis of our experience we are prone to assume that the biological father of the child will also play the role of sociological father and therefore be responsible for the child's discipline. In a school situation in Africa a missionary complained about the fact that it was almost impossible to get fathers to discipline their children. The reason was that the role of sociological father belonged not to the biological father, whom the missionary held responsible, but to the maternal uncle, who also left his property to his nephew when he died.

Another obvious area of role distinction we find in the great differences in division of labor between sexes. In the New World coiled pottery is almost always made by women; in the Old World wheel-made pottery is almost exclusively made by men. Ralph Linton notes that Arapesh women regularly carry the heavier loads because "their heads are considered harder and stronger," while in the Marquesas wives spend most of their time primping, and husbands not only do all the hard physical work but also most of the housekeeping, child tending, and even cooking.[18]

It has been interesting to observe a number of North American-South American marriages. There is a marked difference in the role expectations of husband and wife between these two areas. Latin American women marrying North American men are usually quite happy to play the North American role, but the opposite combination seems to involve more problems. Seldom have we seen a North American woman willing to assume completely the South American female role. Usually the husband must make the greater role adjustment, and either the couple moves entirely into the North American role pattern, or the husband renounces most of his Latin American status and role prerogatives and permits the North American wife to dominate the marriage relationship.

Differences in role valuation

There are at least two kinds of differences in role valuation: first, the distinct role hierarchies of individual cultures; and second, the difference of emotive reaction that given roles evoke in the participants.

We can illustrate the hierarchical arrangement of roles from our own culture. Wives of missionaries ask

18 Ralph Linton, "The Nature of Status and Role," in Walter Goldschmidt, *Exploring the Ways of Mankind* (New York: Holt, Rinehart and Winston, Inc., 1960), p. 326.

again and again: What is my first obligation—missionary, wife, or mother? In fact, every wife will have to decide whether she is wife first or mother first. Most Christians would affirm that they are Christians first and citizens second; in practice, however, it often is reversed—people are citizens first and Christians second. The same is true of denominations and Christianity at large. Here, however, there seems to be movement toward a shift in relative value and ecumenism is trying to place universal Christianity above individual denominational loyalty.

On the cross-cultural level this difference in role valuation will be most obvious in terms of the positional or status aspect associated with role behavior. In a pastoral society the sheep or cattle herder may be ranked very highly; in a predatory hunting-and-gathering society, however, the role of warrior is highly prized while the role of shepherd is viewed as "something for women and children."

There is another dimension to role hierarchy which is worthy of note. This involves role syndromes or linked roles. Thus in the Toda society of India the dairying husband also functions as priest. In this culture the dairyman-priest syndrome by far outranks the dairyman-husband combination.

The difference of emotive reaction to given roles can be easily illustrated by means of the role of father. It is "normal" for the missionary to speak about God as our Father because this is scriptural usage; and since in many societies the father also functions as benefactor to his children, this analogy usually conveys warm emotional overtones. However, in many Latin American lower class homes, the word father does not evoke the same kind of warm emotion. The home is built around the woman and mother. She may be one of several common-law wives, and the children's experience with the father will be sporadic and often negative. They may see him only when he comes into the home drunk in search of sex.[19] For people who have grown up fearing the man called father, the emotional value attached to the fatherhood role will be entirely different from what it will be for those who have experienced a father's love, warmth, and protection. For this reason Latin American Catholicism has "tempered" or "balanced" the Father image of God with the "mother" figure of the Virgin.[20]

Differences in role preparation

Certain roles (actually statuses and accompanying roles) are assigned to the individual automatically; e.g., male and female roles. This is also true of caste, nobility, or slave positions in the social hierarchy of a culture. For other roles the individual must work or prepare. Statuses requiring preparation are often referred to as achieved statuses. For our society achieved status includes the president of the country, the doctor, the

basketball center, etc. For tribal cultures it could include the role of chief or shaman, except where these positions are hereditary.

Even relatively automatic changes of status and role, such as the transition from childhood to puberty, are still marked by a definite ritual in many societies. These transition-marking events are collectively referred to as rites of passage. The Lengua of the Paraguayan Chaco recognize at least seven stages in a man's life, each marked by ritual transition. Such Christian practices as baptism and confirmation are usually viewed as rites of passage by anthropologists.

These rites usually have both clarificatory and preparatory function. By clarificatory we mean that they define the person's new role obligation, and also "inform" all role participants of their respective new role reactions. By preparatory we mean that such rites usually include a period of instruction, apprenticeship, or trial by means of which the person acquires efficiency in the performance of the role. Thus classes for candidates for baptism or confirmation are an example of role preparation.

Role rehearsal is often a very important preparatory feature. Children are usually encouraged to "play" their future adult roles in childhood games. The people with whom the child interacts serve as models for emulation. Speaking of sexual roles in life, J.L. Hampson refers to daydreams, fantasies, erotic imagery, and games of pretend and mimicry as a part of our

19 Oscar Lewis, *Five Families. Mexican Case Studies in the Culture of Poverty* (New York: Basic Books, Inc., 1959).

20 Eugene A. Nida, "Mariology in Latin America," PA Vol. 4, No. 3 (May-June 1957), pp. 69-74.

role rehearsal.[21] Bredemeir and Stephenson call premarital sex another example of role rehearsal.[22]

In societies which do not have preparatory or transitional rites, role rehearsal usually is provided for by a period of permissiveness during which the role partners gain efficiency in the performance of their respective roles. Such labels as newlywed, freshman, greenhorn, novice, and apprentice mark the special status of persons learning a new role.

Roles for the newcomer

Earlier we pointed out that in many of the so-called primitive societies intercourse between people is highly structured. Such structured "expectations" are usually reflected in extensive networks of consanguinal, affinal, or even fictitious kinship labels. When a newcomer enters such a society, its members will not know how to act toward him until he has been duly incorporated into this network of relationships. This is why early North American explorers and traders often found it necessary to become blood brothers to individual tribesmen. Once such a nexus has been established, the whole group knows how to behave toward the person.

Even where status-role classifications are not as formally marked as in the case of blood brothers, the society will have ways of relating

even an outsider to the group. In fact, since such informal "classification" may happen "covertly" as far as the newcomer is concerned, he may actually remain unaware of the position assigned to him and of the accompanying role expectations. In a society's attempt to deal with such a foreigner, they may assign to him a position and roles which are entirely incongruous with his basic purpose. Phillip L. Newman provides us with an excellent example of this in the description of his field work with the Gururumba.[23]

When anthropologist Newman arrived in Gururumba country and asked for permission to put up his tent beside one of their villages, the tribesmen just stood and watched without any kind of overt response. It took several days before this apparent aloofness was resolved. Finally a group of men came to him and welcomed him to the community, saying that they were glad that now their tribe would also have a "red man" just like the other tribes around them. It was only months later when the anthropologist had become more conversant in their language that he found out who these "red men" were. They were ranchers or miners who were a source of income-through-employment for the tribe. Most of them did not exhibit behavior worthy of emulation. Many of them were exploiting the people shamelessly. But until the Gururumba were able to categorize the anthropologist, they did not know

[21] John L. Hampson, "Determinants of Psychosexual Orientation," in Frank A. Beach, ed., *Sex and Behavior* (New York: John Wiley and Sons, Inc., 1965), pp. 119-123.

[22] Bredemeir and Stephenson, op, cit., p. 117.

[23] Phillip L. Newman, *Knowing the Gururumba* (New York, Holt, Rinehart and Winston, 1965), pp. 8-13.

how to react to him or what behavior to expect from him. Once they ascribed the status of "red man" to him, however, they were ready to welcome him. Needless to say, it was a most unwanted role for the anthropologist, but the experience points out the society's "covert obligation" to classify newcomers in order to know how to act toward them.

As in the case of anthropologist Newman, the newcomer may not recognize the role assigned to him. He may even be entirely unaware of the fact that a place in the society has been assigned to him. However, he can be sure that no people will react until some classification has been made. The problem with unawareness of such assignments is the frustration which the newcomer will create because of his ignorance. He will leave undone the expected and do the unexpected. Nor will his "aberrant" behavior be judged neutrally; it will be judged in the light of the role expectations. This may make the newcomer liable to very serious indictments. Jesus can serve as a case in point. The Jews crucified him because he did not meet their expectations as Messiah.

As already indicated earlier, most societies allow for a period of trial and error in role rehearsal. This period of grace can be the newcomer's salvation. If, however, he persists in his unpredictable behavior beyond the limit allowed, he will be judged unreliable, if not false. Should a missionary find it difficult to establish rapport after months of contact, we would suggest a careful investigation of any possible conflict in role expectations.

A related problem arises from "roles" which the new missionary, or newcomer in general, appropriates. He behaves in a given way and in the society this behavior "belongs" to a given role. Since the newcomer engages in this behavior, the culture "assumes" that he is functioning in that role. The problem comes when the person fulfills only a part of the expected behavior. Thus many missionaries, in their effort to help people economically, have in tribal eyes assumed the role of patrón or feudal master. When they then refuse to fulfill certain other patrón behavior, people are confused, frustrated, and even angered. They question the person's sincerity and honesty.

In conclusion, we need to remind ourselves that none of us can escape role playing – neither in our own culture nor in any foreign culture we enter. How well we function in any context will be largely determined by the quality of our role behavior.[24]

---

24 The implications of this article will be further spelled out in the next issue of PA in an article by the same authors, entitled, "The 'Missionary' Role."

Jacob A. Loewen and Anne Loewen

The "Missionary" Role

I CAN still recall the day.[1] I was seventeen and studying in Bible school. I had reached an important decision during the day and when I came home after classes I eagerly shared it with my mother: "Mother, I have decided to volunteer for missionary service."

I expected my mother to be glad that I had chosen such a noble profession, but instead she burst into tears. Somewhat embarrassed I began to apologize for hurting her, but she stopped me and said, "I am not crying because I'm sad; I'm crying because I'm glad." Then she proceeded to tell me the following story:

> You were a problem baby. Your father died of typhus when you were three months old. From six months to five years your body was covered with eczema. I was a penniless young widow. There were no decent medical facilities in our area in Russia, so we tried various folk remedies. But your condition steadily became worse. Finally your whole body was covered with scabs, and when I lifted you out of the cradle in the morning your hair was dried to the pillow and part of your scalp would pull off. I was desperate. Neighbors and "friends" who dropped in and saw the scabby, vile-smelling child piously intoned, "Oh, that God would take him." This cut into my heart like a knife. Finally, after one such experience, I dropped to my knees beside your cradle and said, "God, if you cannot heal the child, take him now. If you will heal him, dedicate him to you as a missionary."

Then mother threw her arms around me and exclaimed, "Son, I'm crying because I'm so happy. God has heard my prayers. My son will be a missionary." Mother was proud because her son had chosen the highest and best.

I think I am correct in generalizing and saying that my mother's reaction—my son has chosen the highest and best—is a typical, "good" Christian attitude. Things have changed somewhat in the last decade, but I believe it is still true that the role of missionary is the challenging ideal of the dedicated Christian at his best.

A missionary – the ideal

Professionally, missionary service is usually classified as ministerial, but it outranks the minister in the home church in "sacrifice and dedication." The missionaries represent the spiritual elite of the church. James Scherer's description of missionary status can probably be considered

<hr>

[1] This paper is a continuation of Jacob A. Loewen and Anne Loewen, "Roles, Self-Image, and Missionary Communication" PA, Vol. 14, No. 4 (July-August 1967), pp. 145-160.

characteristic of Western Christendom:

Pietism reintroduced the double standard into Protestantism after the Reformation had abolished it. It placed the missionary on a pedestal higher than the average Christian. He now became that selfless, consecrated servant of Christ who gloried in sacrifice and personal privation. He was the inspirational hero of countless novels and romances, shedding light in dark places through his personal incandescence. His sacrifices and goodness enabled him to be placed on a pedestal, for he represented a seemingly higher standard of Christian obedience. Yet the disparity between the missionary and ordinary Christians had its compensations: the average layman could vicariously share in the work of his hero through prayers and gifts, visits and correspondence. It is safe to say that this became the dominant missionary image of the 19th century in many Christian congregations. It continues to exercise its influence today.[2]

While actual poverty is not necessarily a prerequisite, the missionary is generally visualized as being a recipient—a person whom good-hearted church people ought to support. This became very apparent to us during our own missionary experience. People in the home churches which we visited would frequently take one

aside and say, "Now I have a suit which I have outgrown and which might fit you. If you are interested, I would be glad to give it to you." Special occasions in the life of "average" Christians can be celebrated "spiritually" by sending some gift to the missionary.

However, the "sacrifices" connected with his role also entitle the returned missionary to a certain amount of recognition. There will be many appearances on the church platform. He will be the recognized guest at church conventions. Local newspapers will feature descriptions of his mission field and service. Even civic clubs will readily accept the missionary as an authority in foreign affairs.

The ideal – a problem to the missionary

This idealized role, however, may also create several kinds of problems for the missionary himself.

In the first place, being on the receiving end continually may be difficult for his own self-image, and there is the danger that he will compensate for this compromise of his dignity by being the "giver" to the nationals when he reaches the foreign society. In other words, he has to swallow his pride in the home situation, but he rescues his compromised self-image in the non-Western setting by being highly paternalistic.

Then, the deference with which he is treated in his home society can easily become a way of life—it is his due reward. He may even expect it when he reaches foreign shores. It is not at all uncommon to find seriously disillusioned missionaries.

---

2 James A. Scherer, *Missionary Go Home! A Reappraisal of the Christian World Mission* (Englewood Cliffs: Prentice Hall, 1964), p. 63.

They arrived in the foreign land believing that they would be respected ambassadors bringing good news to a people who were waiting to hear it; but instead of politeness they met rudeness, exploitation, and insulting epithets. Even in the absence of such dramatic rejection, most missionaries leaving their home society and proceeding to a foreign culture experience a certain amount of insecurity. Since it is human to try and find security, it is extremely important that the missionary be aware of the idealized aspects of his role so that he may recognize symptoms of insecurity and proceed to meet them before he harms his communicative ministry.

Another problem is that the "near-perfect-saint" status with which the home congregation stereotypes the missionary may seriously hamper his counselling. All of his "holy" exterior may make sinful people afraid to reveal their unholy weaknesses to him. Or, bedazzled by his own artificial halo, the missionary may easily confuse his counsel with absolute truth. One psychologist who was visiting with missionaries expressed grave concern over the hostility with which they reacted when anyone questioned the infallibility of their counsel.

In the fourth place, one of the expected aspects of a missionary's spiritual role is a strong sense of urgency to "save souls." While Bible schools, especially, have been very effective in impressing missionaries with this sense of urgency, they apparently have not been as successful in equipping them to play this role effectively. Thus when missionaries fail to win many converts, they develop severe feelings of frustration, guilt, and failure. To cover up this "failure" they often engage in a compulsive whirl of activities with little reflection as to immediate or long-range evangelistic goals.

Finally, it needs to be underscored that because the missionary has been raised in an environment that holds such an idealized conception of his role, he must recognize that there will be moments of truth in which he will come face to face with the fact that he still is far from living up to the ideal which he and his senders hold. As this awareness that his daily life does not measure up to the ideal increases, there is serious danger that instead of admitting and dealing with this discrepancy, the missionary will become more and more pious in his overt behavior. He may repress rather than solve the problems, and try to rationalize any obvious failures. Continued repression will automatically increase subconscious pressure. He is thus exposed to the danger of attempting to compensate for his repression by projecting his guilt on his fellows, and he then proceeds to take his tension out on them. This has been cited by several observers as the basis of much inter-missionary friction.

Interestingly enough, such hostility is most frequently directed at the co-workers from his homeland, possibly so as not to endanger his relationship with the national constituency. When the missionary does slip and reveal his incompleteness before a national, his "ideal" consciousness may lead him to try to "atone" for the failure by extra kindness rather than by forthrightly confessing his failure. For example, the missionary may actually lose his temper with a national, but because this action is beneath his spiritual dignity and definitely does not fit his missionary role, he rationalizes that the national probably didn't realize that he was angry; and at the next meeting, instead of an apology, there is an overly warm and brotherly reception.

One missionary in Africa made the startling discovery that while overtly she did not really manifest the temper that she felt inside, her houseboy, recounting his daily experiences around the campfire in the evening, was telling the people that his "mamma" gets mad "like the devil." He was actually wondering whether she was a Christian because he did not see how a person who was a real Christian could become that angry. In this case the paramessage of the missionary's covert feelings had not been disguised in the least by the pious role she played. Her real self was being read very clearly by the nationals who were associating with her.

Paul's missionary role

Much has been written about the missionary methods of Paul and the necessity of applying them today. While I seriously question that we can duplicate Paul's situation because we are living in a very different day, it is valuable to look at the roles Paul used in his ministry. There is certainly little evidence that Paul's role resembled that of the twentieth-century missionary. I have personally been quite intrigued to find that in each place Paul went he first visited the Jewish synagogue. In the Jewish setting Paul played the role of the ambulent teacher-preacher. This role was well known and widely accepted among the Jews, for by means of it the Jewish leadership maintained the faith among their scattered people in the diaspora.

However, when Paul went to the Gentiles, he assumed the role of philosopher-teacher according to the Greek pattern. In Ephesus we find him moving from the Jewish synagogue to one of the private Greek lecture halls. Here he gathered a group of disciples or followers around him just like other Greek philosopher-teachers. These disciples then became the nucleus of the local church among the Gentiles.

The missionary role in non-western culture

To most American Christians the very word "missionary" implies crossing cultural boundaries. To question the universal validity of this role approximates the sacriligious; only the unregenerate and the apostate would have the gall to do it. But is the "missionary" role legitimate across cultural boundaries? We must face this question squarely. If my missionary status and its role behavior are transported bodily into a non-Western culture, what will those behavior patterns mean in the new environment? How will my role fit into the target culture? Will it be necessary for me to play different roles so that rapport and communication with the people can be established? Are there new or different roles that would be more appropriate in the culture in question?

There is ample evidence that the missionary role as it comes from the West has not been understood; in fact, it has often been seriously misinterpreted. In 1962 a local resident missionary and two visiting Americans participated in a special service with the Chocó church in Panama. Using the two American visitors as models, the speaker challenged the Chocó congregation to emulate their example and to become witnesses for their Lord. "These men have left their homes and their families. They have given up opportunities to earn money. Why? They did this in order to be able to come here and to tell their friends, the Chocó, the message of Jesus Christ. We must learn from them, for we, too, must leave our work and our families to share this message with our people on other rivers."

After this service was over the two visitors took the speaker aside and pointed out to him, "You mentioned the two of us in the message this afternoon, but why didn't you mention the resident missionary? Don't you think he will feel hurt? After all, he gives his full time to this work and we only gave up our vacations."

To this the leader replied, "But I cannot use him as an example. He isn't making any sacrifice. He doesn't work for a living like you and I do. In fact, there are people in your country who are paying him to live here!"

Not only has the missionary role been misinterpreted—it has actually hurt the church. James A. Scherer has already pointed out that missionaries, for all their personal zeal and dedication for witnessing and soul-winning, have singularly failed to pass on this burden to their converts. Could it be that the role of a foreigner "paid to live here and to preach" short-circuited the Holy Spirit's efforts to lead the new converts to witness? It seems to us that there is evidence that this is so.[3]

In one of the South American capitals a mission program was begun some fifteen years ago. Since this was in a city with many fine Catholic cathedrals, a beautiful church was built with foreign funds: "We need to provide an attractive place for the people to worship." For the first twelve years the pulpit was filled with "good" American preachers with excellent command of the national language. Then came the flurry of indigenization. A young national was sent to seminary for three years. On his return he was duly installed as "national pastor of an indigenous church." But after six weeks the church threw out the national pastor and asked for the missionary. While flattered at their confidence in his preaching, the missionary nevertheless realized that all was not well. So he decided to take a different road to indigenization. He launched an "every member a witness" campaign. The church seemed enthusiastic. Literature was printed, training classes were instituted, and the whole congregation was mobilized. There was one last meeting before launching the campaign in a selected suburb. The

---

3 Ibid., pp. 72-73.

missionary leading the meeting asked, "Are there any questions?" To his painful surprise a leading figure asked what the wages would be for those who participated in the campaign. "Wages? Why, no one is getting paid! We all do this as a Christian responsibility...."

Before he could finish, others interrupted him, "That is not true that nobody is going to be paid! You are being paid!"

From this incident, at least two facts stand out. First, the foreign missionary's role was no model for believers to emulate. Secondly, the missionary's basic motivation had been obscured because of his foreign support. Many of us do not think of our allowance as salary—it is "just a little to keep us among the living." But the nationals have often given this "little" a completely different interpretation.

Recently I lectured at a mission on the problem of models for the indigenous church. At the end of my lecture a missionary timidly said, "Recently we sent out a group of Indian graduates from our Bible school. Each went to a village of his tribe (several tribes were represented in the group) and began preaching. Before long they began sending word, 'I have had the people cut the timbers for building a church. They have also cleared a garden plot for me and planted things so that I will have food. Send me the trade goods so that I can pay the people.'" The missionary then asked, "Do you think they have used us as a model?" Quite obviously they had, for this was exactly the pattern of operations at the Bible school.

Misunderstanding the missionary motive

In an earlier essay we have pointed out the fact that the Congolese blamed the missionaries for having written down their names in the church records, thereby tying up their soul power.[4] The people in general, and the rebel *Jeunesse* in particular, had interpreted the missionaries' interest in their soul, baptism, and church membership as a new kind of soul slavery. African soul power was being stolen to operate Western factories, leaving the Congo without power and progress. James A. Bertsche, in his report on the rebellion, points out how methodically the *Jeunesse* tried to destroy all foreign items: money, watches, glasses, shoes, etc. They only wanted one thing – their *mavu* – their native earth. They wanted to free their country from "foreign oppression" so it could become great.[5]

Frequently merchants and traders have preceded the missionary in an area. Their role and profit motive have been well understood. Even though the missionary disclaims any profit motive and does not engage in "business," there are few settings where the missionary image has not been made "guilty by association" with the profit motive. Either his approach was interpreted as so well camouflaged that people just had not

4 Jacob A. Loewen, "The Way to First Class: Revolution or Conversion," PA, Vol. 12, No. 5 (Sept.-Oct. 1965), p. 206.

5 James E. Bertsche, "Congo Rebellion," PA, Vol. 12, No. 5 (Sept.-Oct. 1965), p. 216 ff.

yet understood how he made his profit, or he was viewed as being in cahoots secretly with the merchant world.

"The missionary came first," says the African. "Then followed the trader. Last came the soldiers with guns to kill, conquer, divide, and rule. Missionaries were the means by which the white people lulled Africans to sleep while they took away our land and freedom. . ."[6]

Of course, missionaries cannot claim complete innocence. Few mission programs have been launched without exerting influence on the local economy. No amount of disclaiming can hide the fact that money is involved in constructing buildings, making airstrips, and working on agricultural projects.

A missionary to the Toba church of the Argentine Chaco recently reported how every mission effort which became involved in missionary-Toba finances has come to a bitter end because Indians always misinterpreted the motives and roles of the foreigners involved.[7] Toba could understand white man's profit motive and they understood their own total sharing pattern. No sooner had a missionary disclaimed the profit motive and given a "little finger" to the sharing pattern than he was in trouble. Why? Because the Toba found his partial sharing completely incomprehensible and wrong. They viewed it as blatant hypocrisy.

Several years ago Samuel U. Moffet wrote a rather indicting essay on the role and image of the twentieth-century missionary:

Perhaps our trouble is that most of the world no longer identifies us with Christ. To most of the world the symbol of a missionary is not even the saver of souls or the builder of the Kingdom. It may be unjust, but to most of the world the symbol of the Christian missionary is a soft, white, rich westerner. And why should the people follow that? They look at the communist—whatever else you may say about the communist, you must credit him with this—and see that he is ready to sacrifice, to suffer and die. Then people look at us who have lost the marks of our suffering Lord.[8]

Many missionaries and other dedicated Christians have felt that this loss of identification with Christ was largely due to the "machine age approach to missions," with planes, boats, two-way radios, and endless electronic gadgetry forming such a prominent part of the missionary's outfit. There is no question that the super-abundance of material equipment has added to the problem, but to our mind several deepseated "psychological gadgets" in the missionary's role paraphernalia are the actual culprits.

The first of these is the lack of reciprocity.[9] It is not the quality nor

---

[6] George Wayland Carpenter, *The Way in Africa* (New York: Friendship Press, 1959) p. 148.

[7] Personal communication from Albert Buckwalter, Mennonite missionary to the Toba.

[8] Samuel U. Moffet, "The Christian Mission," *His* (June 1958), pp. 6-9.

[9] For more detail see Jacob A. Loewen, "Reciprocity in Identification," PA, Vol. 11, No. 4 (July-August 1964), pp. 145-160.

the amount of equipment a missionary has; it is his attitude toward these items that counts. Is the missionary's guest room "exchangeable" with the national's branches-and-grass shelter? If so, there is no problem. If car (even a Cadilac) and canoe are exchangeable, their difference in purchase price is of little import. Likewise, if missionary and national "personal worth" are exchangeable, then the years of education or the lack of them are no barrier to brotherhood.

The second "gadget" may be even more crucial. It involves the question of the context from which the missionary expects support in building up his self-image. Missionaries are in real danger of "using" their missionary role and the mission field as a means of building and "feeding" their self-image. The question is: With which church—home or national—is the missionary identified? Into which church is he psychologically integrated for purposes of achieving esteem? We all need recognition—which counts more: that of national Christians or that of the North American supporting group? For faith missionaries whose support depends on form-letter solicited contributions, there is even more danger that the nationals become the "stocks and bonds" of the missionary's economic security, rather than this equals in God's sight.

I recently had a rather embarrassing experience. I drew the above problem to the attention of a conference of nationals and missionaries; and to my chagrin the nationals cheered, clapped their hands, and ex-

claimed, "Right, that's the problem! That's the *big* problem!"

The missionary arrives in a new culture

As stated earlier[10] when a newcomer arrives on a tribal scene he must somehow be related to the existing social structure so that people will know how to act toward him, and how to expect him to act toward them. Usually the missionary is not the first outsider who arrives on the tribal scene, and for this reason he may not be able to start off with a "clean slate" in developing his role set. But whether he is the first or not, he will be given a position or positions in the social hierarchy and will be expected to behave accordingly. Thus missionaries to a Brazilian tribal society found themselves classified as *hekura* 'evil spirits.' The reasons, of course, were complex. Their arrival by plane was a close equivalent to the way *hekura* travel. Their daily two-way radio contacts—speaking with the "other world"—provided additional clues. Then their skin color, their "non-human" behavior, and their endless resources arriving by plane all added to the conviction. The basic reaction toward *hekura* is fear. Only a few specialists can control them, and that never fully. It is little wonder that the missionaries found it almost impossible to penetrate deeply into tribal confidence. How could they trust the missionary if the latter's basic humanity was in doubt?

In another contact with a new tribe a missionary was speared by a tribes-

10 Loewen, "Roles, Self-Image, and Missionary Communication," op. cit.

man. The group seemed friendly. They looked at and touched everything the missionary group had. They pinched and felt the missionary's white skin. Finally one Indian took his spear and pressed it into the white man's side. It almost seems as if he were performing a test to see whether or not the missionary was a mortal.

In most South American societies which we have been able to observe, the white man is not unknown. But the white men of their past experience have consistently filled a narrow range of roles–usually that of *patrón* 'feudal master', or colonial police officer. It is most normal, therefore, to also classify the missionary in one or the other or both of these categories. In fact, it is our feeling that most missionaries to tribal societies in South America have been stereotyped by the people into these categories, and this usually not entirely without reason.

Let us look at the *patrón* role. Isn't employment usually one of the first results of the arrival of the missionary? There is a house to build, an airstrip to make, a garden to plant, etc. Frequently the tribe is actually functioning in a *patrón*-serf role set already, and so the missionary merely offers to be a better *patrón*. (This was also the experience of the Cornell University group working with the people at Vicos.)[11] In fact, there are many examples of missionaries who have almost "purposely" stepped into the *patrón* role. They saw the

[11] See "The Vicos Case: Peasant Society in Transition," *The American Behavioral Scientist*, Vol. 8, No. 7 (March 1965), pp. 1-33.

injustice of the *patrón* exploiting the Indian, their sense of social justice was outraged, and so they set out to help the Indian. This help has ranged all the way from buying up the accounts (which the *peón* owed his *patrón*) to helping the Indian get an honest price for his products. At any rate, many missionaries find themselves in what for most of them is the really unwanted role of *patrón*.

The other "popular" role for missionaries is that of policeman. Most tribal societies have had their "brushes" with national law. The police commissioner for many of them is an unpleasant figure–a person before whom one must play dumb, for he tries to enforce some strange foreign justice, usually identified as tribal injustice. Then comes the missionary. He, too, is very concerned about stopping them from doing what they have always been doing. Even though the missionary's concern usually is to keep converts from getting involved in immoral drinking orgies, witchcraft, and the like, for all practical purposes he functions as a policeman for the whole tribe.

Anne and I still recall with deep embarrassment our own involvements in policing Chocoano morals. Four hundred years of slavery and largely non-family living had produced a pattern of morality which was far removed from our Christian ideal. Again and again, as believers whom we were favoring with employment (and thereby providing means with which to acquire another mistress) got involved with other women, I followed them and urged them to confess and ask forgiveness. They knew that if they didn't confess or if they went back after confessing, we would fire them. As a result, our mission became one big cops-and-robbers game. Employees helped each other to keep information from our ears. Instead of accomplishing our purposes we actually only helped people out of some unwanted liaisons. This freed them to seek other, greener pastures.

Recently I had occasion to visit a non-Protestant mission in which the missionaries were really "majoring" in the policeman's role. Indians were stealing so much that each missionary carried a giant ring of keys to unlock and lock every door he used. Premarital sex was another major concern, and to prevent it all the unattached girls above seven years of age were nightly locked into an enclosure with a twelve-foot wall. The irony of the situation was that the missionaries had not realized that it was the female who chose the sex partner in that culture, and so when they put the braces of the wall on the inside of the enclosure, they provided an excellent ladder for the girls to climb out and rendezvous with the fellows. Watching the girls climb out of the "pen" was a major source of evening entertainment for adults and children who gathered around to watch. Then the rest of the evening was spent recounting the most interesting escapades of the past and laughing at the missionaries.

Protestant legalism has often pushed missionaries into perpetrating "monstrosities" of justice, such as the excommunication laws used in one African church: the first illegiti-mate child – no communion for three months; the second child–no communion for six months; and the third–no communion for nine months.[12] Colonial governments, too, have their record of similar comic justice, such as the French law making adultery a civil offence and punishable with a fine. It provided Kaka society with a monetary yardstick for regulating their co-husband pattern. Each new co-husband brought so much money into the man's treasury.[13] But beyond the travesty this role has made of justice, lies the sad fact that the missionary has sold his birthright of redemptive burden-bearer for a mess of policing pottage.

Another very frequent role is that of governor-chief-colonial officer rolled into one. This is especially true of very small societies or mission stations which dominate an entire village. In such cases the missionary easily becomes law-giver, law-enforc-er, and judge all in one. In one such society the missionary "settled down" a group of nomadic hunter gatherers. The whole group accepted Christianity, so education and church made residence in one place imperative. But the game reserves were fast being depleted with the introduction of fire-arms. In order to prevent the premature extermination of game (and, therefore, the end of this station also) the missionary limited the shot which a person could buy at the mission store. To enforce this ration he had the chief forbid the people to

12 Carpenter, op. cit., p. 60.

13 William D. Reyburn, "Polygamy, Economy and Christianity in Eastern Cameroun," PA, Vol. 6, No. 1 (Jan.-Feb. 1959), p. 11.

wander to civilization where they could buy all the shot they wanted.

The above illustrations by no means exhaust the inventory of locally assigned roles for the missionary, but they are examples in the light of which each missionary can evaluate his own role situation.

Missionary role sincerity

We now come to the matter of the way in which missionaries fulfill the expectations of their role participants. At least two areas need to be explored: the fulfillment of the role relationships which the missionary himself tries to project, and the fulfillment of roles assigned by the society with or without the awareness of the missionary.

When we first entered the Waunana tribe in Colombia, we explained to the Indians that we had come to learn their language in order to teach them to read and write. However, since the work with the Indians was only part of the organization's missionary program in Colombia, and since we had mastered the official Spanish language, it was very easy for the mission to use us in various and sundry capacities outside of the Indian work. The result was that several years passed and still we had made no headway beyond what had been accomplished during the first weeks of Indian language study. Finally, four years had elapsed. One day a delegation of Indians came to us and said, "Jaco, you are a liar. Years ago you came and said you wanted to learn our language so that you could teach us to read. But you are a liar. You have not learned our language. You

speak less of our language now than you did the first days when you came here." I believe this precipitated possibly one of the more serious crises in our lives. It was only too true. We had not fulfilled the role which we had projected. Our failure to fulfill the role now caused the Waunana to question both the honesty of our character and the validity of our message.

However, far more damaging for our witness is the unfulfillment of roles assigned to us by the culture. Consider the case of the missionary who reacts against the injustice of the *patrón* system and acts to remedy the situation. He buys up the accounts of the Indians to free them from an abusive *patrón*, he helps them market their produce in a distant market where they get a just price, or he tries to help the Indians develop some new way of making a living apart from the *patrón*-serf relationship. What happens? As far as the tribal people are concerned he has assumed the role of *patrón*. They now come to him and ask him for credit or for the purchase of guns, saws, etc. He refuses: "I do not float loans."

As a result the tribesman is confused. "He says he wants to be good to us—a good *patrón*. He freed us from that other exploiter, so why doesn't he want to finance us? Even the 'exploiter' did that for us."

Or, as actually happened in one area, after the serfs had been freed by the missionary, they came to him for work. Of course, he wasn't interested in employing them. He told them to work on their own. The Indians became angry. They called the missionary a deceiver. The missionary was deeply hurt by the ingratitude of the people he had freed from virtual slavery. Both were frustrated because the missionary was willing to fulfill only a few selected aspects of the *patrón* role which the Indians had assigned him. But this partial fulfillment was unintelligible to the Indians. They interpreted it as role insincerity — the missionary was a very dishonest and irresponsible *patrón*.

In many areas the missionary's partial assumption of the *patrón* role has actually seriously hurt the Indians. In one setting a priest broke the hold of the landholders, only to find that he could not manage the "cantankerous" Indians once they were free. As a result the priest retreated and the landlords punished the Indians for following the "imposter."

A second kind of hurt resulting from the upset in the *patrón-peon* role set comes from the rapid decrease in productivity. Frequently when *patrón* pressure is removed, the Indian stops working and resorts to begging. This has caused more than one missionary to give up the people as hopelessly lazy.

The missionary needs to honestly assess what roles he has assumed or which have been assigned to him by the people. Even at best his behavior will miscue the people. During my Chocó dialect survey I assumed the role of the "young man getting to know the world." It was a very relevant role and was well understood by the Indians. However, there was a miscue in my behavior. I carried two boxes — one a watertight aluminum container for my camera, recording equipment, and papers, and the other a case for my hammock, a change of clothes, and a few supplies. These boxes were always interpreted as containing merchandise, and visitors at first glance took me for a traveling merchant. While the Indians usually did not speak to me about it, they asked my host what I was selling. The host would then clarify my role, saying that I was not a merchant — I was just "getting to know the world." The usual retort was, "Well, if he's getting to know the world, why is he carrying so much stuff?" Miscues of even more serious nature are bound to abound in a missionary's behavior; for this reason we need to take very seriously the matter of role sincerity. Wherever possible, we must avoid jeopardizing our testimony through lack of fulfillment of expected behavior.

We have a feeling that the problem between the Toba and missionaries in the realm of money lies at the level of role insincerity. Toba know total sharing and they know profit. When the missionary begins partial sharing, he enters the orbit of the sharing complex. When he stops short at any point, the Toba interpret his hesitation as unwillingness to fulfill his role. For them it is insincerity, dishonesty, and hypocrisy at their worst.

Unfulfilled role expectations are also probably the basis of the findings of the psychologist friend of ours who spent some time in India on a special educational assignment. He reported that both Christians and non-Christians complained about a basic lack of integrity in missionaries. To put it bluntly—they felt that most missionaries were liars.

Missionary role insecurities

Like other persons crossing culture boundaries, missionaries are subject to culture shock. Kalervo Oberg describes this phenomenon as follows:

> Culture shock is precipitated by the anxiety that results from losing all our familiar signs and symbols of social intercourse. These signs or cues include the thousand and one ways in which we orient ourselves to the situations of daily life: when to shake hands and what to say when we meet people, when and how to give tips, how to give orders to servants, how to make purchases, when to accept and when to refuse invitations, when to take statements seriously and when not. Now these cues which may be words, gestures, facial expressions, customs, or norms are acquired by all of us in the course of growing up and are as much a part of our culture as the language we speak or the beliefs we accept. All of us depend for our peace of mind and our efficiency on hundreds of these cues, most of which we do not carry on the level of conscious awareness.

> Now when an individual enters a strange culture, all or most of these familiar cues are removed. He or she is like a fish out of water. No matter how broadminded or full of good will you may be, a series of props have been knocked from under you, followed by a feeling of frustration and anxiety.[14]

When we look at the details of what Oberg calls culture shock we recognize at once that the experience involves the absence of many familiar landmarks in role behavior. Because roles come in pairs, proper role performance always is dependent on feedback between the participants. Thus when our role behavior no longer elicits the expected response, we begin to feel uncertain and frustrated. But this may be mutual, for if the tribal participants have assigned us a "niche" in their social structure, and if we consistently do not come through with the expected behavior, they too will be perplexed and frustrated.

I am reminded of a recent encounter with the Peruvian traffic police. I was unable to determine whether or not a given street was closed, but after driving a few blocks we found cars returning, so decided to retreat. We could not return the way we had come because it was a one-way street. When we worked our way through another narrow street, we met a policeman who, instead of helping us, stopped us and told us in rather offensive language that he was going to teach us foreigners to respect the traffic laws of the country. Even after years of living in Latin America I had another attack of culture shock. My expectations of the role of a traffic officer were upset and my whole system rebelled at the "injustice."

It is obvious that the role behavior of the "foreigner" will seldom be

[14] Kalervo Oberg, "Cultural Shock: Adjustment to New Cultural Environments." PA, Vol. 7, No. 4 (July-August 1960), p. 177.

able to meet the expectations of a different culture one hundred percent. We always hope, however, that in time it will more and more approximate that goal. If it doesn't, our chances of adequate communication are greatly decreased, for our unfulfilled role behavior and our unexpected incongruent actions will be "speaking louder than our words." Few persons can live under such uncertain conditions without extreme reaction. The responses can be of two kinds: reactionary or compensatory.[15]

Reactionary behavior begins with strong feelings against the society which is making us insecure. We reject their ways as pagan, sinful, and uncivilized. We refuse to conform to local standards. While in many cases such non-conformity may be entirely legitimate and part of the basic missionary purpose, we need to distinguish between the behavior resulting from what will be in the best missionary interest in the long run and what is merely a reaction to our lack of role communication.

The protective aspect of this host culture rejection causes us to regress and to seek to protect ourselves. We avoid the offenders and close ourselves off in the privacy of the missionary residence alone or with fellow missionaries. At this point there is great danger that we also retreat to our home church to bolster our self-image through eliciting sympathetic letters.

The compensatory response usually involves pulling on more snuggly our

___
15 Loc. cit.

missionary halo: the way of God's prophets is lonely and rugged. Once having separated our self-image from the people as a whole, we can direct ourselves in outgoing paternalism to those few who do show some of the response we are expecting to our missionary role. By being kind in the face of "rejection" we rationalize ourselves into believing that we are fulfilling our role responsibilities with the self-denial of good followers of Christ.

At this point there can arise a danger that the missionary's self-image may become linked to the success or failure of the responsive individuals. In his effort to help them succeed, the missionary becomes so involved with running their lives for them that he cannot permit them to become free responsible agents.

After I had been involved in counselling with college students and had demonstrated great patience with their problems, Anne one day asked me, "Why is it that you do not have the same amount of patience with our own children that you seem to have with people with whom you counsel outside of our home?" This led to some serious self-analysis on my part; and I had to conclude that, at least in my situation, I was able to play the role of an "objective" counsellor to the people outside my home because my self-image was in no way involved in their ups and downs. But when it came to my own children, I felt that my own self-image was deeply involved; I, myself, would be judged by the quality of my children's behavior. Because of this personal involvement, it was very difficult for me to be the objective counsellor the children needed. This danger also exists for the missionary in his relationship with his spiritual children. The missionary may feel that he cannot baptize or he cannot give positions of leadership to his converts because "they aren't ready yet." But isn't this really an admission that our attitudes toward the converts are wrong? Could it be that we feel so deeply involved with the success of the people that we cannot trust the Spirit of God to lead them independently?

Missionary role-consciousness

It was the purpose of these two essays to make missionaries conscious of role-playing and the problems it entails. It is possible for us, however, to become excessively conscious of our roles and our self-image (whether it is what I think I should be or what I think I am). This can be as unhealthy as perpetual preoccupation with one's health or one's looks. Continual self-primping, self-pulse taking, and self-personality probing may in themselves become marks of immaturity and can lead to insecurity and paralysis of initiative. Hyper-role-consciousness is a disease which makes transparent communication difficult, if not impossible. It may make it difficult for us to be our "real" selves. We see ourselves as merely "players" on a giant stage.

In our effort to fulfill a role properly, we may become enslaved in a series of do's and don'ts — the dictates of "society's expectations" which prevent us from being relaxed, normal human beings. Or, we may try to be part of the audience, craning our necks to see our performance as others see it. Such a situation would certainly inhibit all spontaneity and would of necessity degenerate into downright insincerity and hypocrisy.

In its ultimate degree, role-consciousness could lead to either of two extremes: smugness or despair. One of the critics of a preliminary draft of this paper provided illustrations of these two extremes:

> Some years ago, observing busy executives "executing" in a large city, I was reminded irresistibly of Little Jack Horner in the Mother Goose rhyme. Like Little Jack, they stuck in their thumb and pulled out their plum and said, "What a good boy am I." The role player can become completely wrapped up in his role and so sees himself as the wonderful "plum puller."

At the other extreme there is Little Miss Muffet who could not cope with the big, fuzzy spider and so in despair ran away from reality.

Mental hospitals offer abundant examples of people who have despaired in trying to live by the expectations of their fellows.

While excessive role-consciousness can become a hindrance, it is probably also correct to admit that there is just as much danger that missionaries will be involved in role playing of all kinds without being aware of the fact.

There is no escape from role playing as long as we are members of human culture and have to associate with other people. But there needs to be an honest attempt to understand both the roles that we play in our own culture and also the roles that we will need to play in the target culture. For the effective proclamation of the good news,[16] there will need to be a willingness to deny ourselves — to lay aside any roles which will hinder the communication of the gospel; and, again, a willingness to assume any new roles—to become all things to all men in order to save some. Let us not forget the example of Jesus Christ, who laid aside his divine status, accepted the role of a servant and was obedient even unto death[17] so that he could not only *communicate* God's message, but that, indeed he could *be* God's message to men.

16 Several useful roles for the missionary in an era of intense national consciousness have already been highlighted or at least alluded to in essays that have appeared in PA. In the interest of economy of space we will not detail these roles at this time, but only list them and supply a few references.

Learner: Eugene A. Nida, "The Relationship of Social Structure to the Problem of Evangelism in Latin America," PA, Vol. 5, No. 3 (May-June 1958), p. 118; Jacob A. Loewen, "Reciprocity in Identification," PA, Vol. 11, No. 4 (July-August 1964), pp. 148-149.

Mirror: John Beekman, "Minimizing Religious Syncretism Among the Chols," PA, Vol. 6, No. 6 (Nov.-Dec. 1959), pp. 241-250. Regarding mirror for self-recognition, see Jacob A. Loewen, Albert Buckwalter, and James Kratz, "Shamanism, Illness and Power in Toba Church Life," PA, Vol. 12, No. 6 (Nov.-Dec. 1965), pp. 250-280 [especially p. 280]; Jacob A. Loewen, "Missionaries and Anthropologist Cooperate in Research," PA, Vol. 12, No. 4 (July-August 1965), p. 168. Regarding the need-clarifying mirror, see Jacob A. Loewen, "The Way to First Class: Revolution or Conversion?" PA, Vol. 12, No. 5 (Sept.-Oct. 1965), pp. 205-208; and "Missionaries and Anthropologist...," op. cit., pp. 170-171. Regarding image-sorting mirror for evaluating alternatives, see Jacob A. Loewen,

"The Church: Indigenous and Ecumenical," PA, Vol. 11, No. 6 (Nov.-Dec. 1964), pp. 246-247; "Missionaries and Anthropologist...," op. cit., pp. 170-173.

Source of alternatives: Ibid. pp. 171-172; "The Church: Indigenous...," op. cit., pp. 246-247.

Catalyst: Ibid., pp. 247-248; "The Way to First Class...," op. cit., pp. 203-205; "Shamanism, Illness and Power...," op. cit., p. 279; Jacob A. Loewen, "The Church Among the Chocó of Panama," PA, Vol. 10, No. 3 (May-June 1963), p. 107; Jacob A. Loewen, "Self-Exposure: Bridge to Fellowship," PA, Vol. 12, No. 2 (March-April 1965), p. 62.

Stimulus for indigenous experimentation: A. P. Elkin, *Social Anthropology in Melanesia* (London: Oxford University Press, 1953), p. 148; "The Church: Indigenous...," op. cit., pp. 249-254; Jacob A. Loewen, "Field, Term, and Timing in Missionary Method," PA. Vol. 12, No. 1 (Jan.-Feb. 1965), pp. 20-21.

Friend of court: See Eugene A. Nida, *Message and Mission* (New York: Harper and Brothers, 1960), p. 110; "The Church; Indigenous...," op. cit., pp. 248-249; Jacob A. Loewen, "Aureliano: Profile of a Prophet," PA, Vol. 13, No. 4 (July-August, 1966), pp. 112-113.

17 Philippians 2: 5-8.

Other Books by the William Carey Library

General

Church Growth and Group Conversion by Donald A. McGavran $2.45p

The Evangelical Response to Bangkok edited by Ralph D. Winter $1.95p

Growth and Life in the Local Church by H. Boone Porter $2.95p

Message and Mission: the Communication of the Christian Faith by Eugene Nida $3.95p

Reaching the Unreached: A Preliminary Strategy for World Evangelization by Edward Pentecost $5.95p

Verdict Theology in Mission Theory by Alan Tippett $4.95p

Area and Case Studies

Aspects of Pacific Ethnohistory by Alan R. Tippett $3.95p

The Baha'i Faith: Its History and Teachings by William Miller $8.95p

A Century of Growth: the Kachin Baptist Church of Burma by Herman Tegenfeldt $9.95c

Church Growth in Japan by Tetsunao Yamamori $4.95p

A New Day in Madras by Amirtharaj Nelson $7.95p

People Movements in the Punjab by Margaret and Frederick Stock $8.95p

The Protestant Movement in Italy by Roger Hedlund $3.95p

Protestants in Modern Spain: the Struggle for Religious Pluralism by Dale G. Vought $3.45p

The Religious Dimension in Hispanic Los Angeles: A Protestant Case Study by Clifton Holland $9.95p

Taiwan: Mainline Versus Independent Church Growth by Allen J. Swanson $3.95p

Understanding Latin Americans by Eugene Nida $3.95p

Theological Education by Extension

Designing a Theological Education by Extension Program by Leslie D. Hill $2.95p

An Extension Seminary Primer by Ralph Covell and Peter Wagner $2.45p

The World Directory of Theological Education by Extension by Wayne Weld $5.95p

Textbooks and Practical Helps

Becoming Bilingual: A Guide to Language Learning by Donald Larson and William A. Smalley $5.95xp

God's Word in Man's Language by Eugene Nida $2.95p

An Inductive Study to the Book of Jeremiah by F.R. Kinsler $4.95p

Bibliography for Cross-Cultural Workers by Tippett $3.95p $5.95c

Principles of Church Growth by Weld and McGavran $4.95xp

Manual of Articulatory Phonetics by William A. Smalley $4.95xp

The Means of World Evangelization: Missiological Education at the Fuller School of World Mission edited by Alvin Martin $9.95p

Readings in Missionary Anthropology edited by William Smalley $4.95xp